The UX Book
Agile UX Design for a Quality User Experience

The UX Book

Agile UX Design for a Quality User Experience

Second Edition

REX HARTSON

PARDHA PYLA

MORGAN KAUFMANN PUBLISHERS

AN IMPRINT OF ELSEVIER

Morgan Kaufmann is an imprint of Elsevier
50 Hampshire Street, 5th Floor, Cambridge, MA 02139, United States

Library of Congress Cataloging-in-Publication Data
A catalog record for this book is available from the Library of Congress

British Library Cataloguing-in-Publication Data
A catalogue record for this book is available from the British Library

ISBN: 978-0-12-805342-3

For information on all Morgan Kaufmann publications
visit our website at https://www.elsevier.com/books-and-journals

Working together
to grow libraries in
developing countries

www.elsevier.com • www.bookaid.org

Publisher: Katey Birtcher
Sr. Acquisitions Editor: Steve Merken
Sr. Content Development Specialist: Nate McFadden
Production Project Manager: Stalin Viswanathan
Sr. Designer: Miles Hitchen
Cover design by Christina Janczak, UX Designer, Cloudistics, Inc.

Typeset by SPi Global, India

Last digit is the print number: 9 8 7 6 5 4 3

"Don't panic!"[1]

---

[1]Douglas Adams, *The Hitchhiker's Guide to the Galaxy*

Contents

Part 2: Usage Research

Part 3: UX Design

Part 4: Prototype Candidate Designs

Part 5: UX Evaluation

Preface

Welcome to *The UX Book*, the second edition. We thought we'd better begin by making sure everyone knows that "UX" is short for user experience. In simple terms, the user experience is the phenomenon felt by users before, during, and after usage—usually a combination of usability, usefulness, emotional impact, and meaningfulness.

GOALS FOR THIS BOOK

Imbue an understanding of what a good user experience is and how to achieve it. Our main goal for this book is simple: to help readers learn to recognize, understand, and design for a quality user experience (UX). Sometimes, a quality user experience is like an electric light: when it works, nobody notices. Sometimes, a user experience is really good and is noticed and even appreciated, and it leaves pleasant memories. Or sometimes, the effects of a bad user experience persist in the user's mind. So, early in the book, we talk about what constitutes a positive user experience.

Emphasize design. What is less obvious than understanding a quality user experience is how to design for it. Perhaps the most significant change in this edition is that we stress design—a kind of design that highlights the designer's creative skills and insights and embodies a synthesis of technology with aesthetics and meaningfulness to the user. In Part 3, we show you a variety of design methods to help you get just the right approach for your project.

Give a how-to approach. We have designed much of the book as a how-to-do-it handbook and field guide, as a textbook for students aspiring to be UX professionals and for professionals aspiring to be better. The approach is practical, not formal or theoretical. Some references are made to the related science, but they are usually to provide context for the practice and are not necessarily elaborated.

Other goals for the reader. Beyond our main goal of helping readers learn about UX and UX design, other goals for the reader experience include ensuring that:

- You get excited about UX design.
- The material is easy to learn.
- The material is easy to apply.
- The material is useful to students and professionals.
- For you, the reader, the experience is at least a little bit fun.

Provide broad coverage. Our goals for scope of coverage include:

- Depth of understanding—detailed information about different aspects of the UX process (like having an expert accompanying the reader)
- Breadth of understanding—as comprehensive as space permits
- Broad range of application—the process and the design infrastructure and vocabulary, including guidelines, are not just for GUIs and the web, but for all kinds of interaction styles and devices, including ATMs, refrigerators, road signs, ubiquitous computing, embedded computing, and everyday things.

USABILITY IS STILL IMPORTANT

The study of usability, a key component of a quality user experience, is still an essential part of the broad and multidisciplinary field of human-computer interaction. It is about getting our users past the technology and focusing on getting things done. In other words, it is about designing the technology as an extension of human capabilities to accomplish something, and to be as transparent as possible in the process.

BUT USER EXPERIENCE IS MORE THAN USABILITY

As our discipline has evolved and matured, more and more technology companies are embracing the principles of usability engineering, investing in sophisticated usability labs and personnel to "do usability." As these efforts are becoming effective at ensuring a certain level of usability in the products (thereby, leveling the field on that front), new factors have emerged to distinguish competing product designs.

We will see that, in addition to traditional usability attributes, user experience entails social and cultural, value-sensitive design, and emotional impact—how the interaction experience includes "joy of use," fun, aesthetics, and meaningfulness in the lives of users.

The focus is still on designing for the human rather than on technology, so, "user-centered design" is still a good description. But it is now extended to knowing users in newer and broader dimensions.

A PRACTICAL APPROACH

This book takes a practical, applied, hands-on approach, based on the application of established and emerging best practices, principles, and proven methods to ensure a quality user experience. Our approach is about practice, drawing on the creative concepts of design exploration and visioning to make designs that appeal to the emotions of users, while moving toward processes that are lightweight, rapid, and agile—to make things as good as resources permit, and not waste time and other resources in the process.

PRACTICAL UX METHODS

In the first edition, we described mostly rigorous methods and techniques for each UX lifecycle activity, mentioning more rapid methods here and there. UX designers who need rigorous methods to develop large-scale systems in complex domains will still find what they need in this book. But this edition reflects the fact that agile methods have taken on a much bigger role in UX practice. We have adopted a practical stance with respect to rigor and formality, and our processes, methods, and techniques are a practical compromise between rigor and speed that will suit a very large percentage of all projects.

FROM AN ENGINEERING ORIENTATION TO A DESIGN ORIENTATION

For a long time, the focus in HCI practice was on engineering, taking its cues from usability engineering and human factors engineering. Our first edition mostly reflected this approach. In this new edition, we are moving away somewhat from an engineering focus to more of a design focus. In an engineering-centric view, we started with constraints and tried to design something to fit those constraints. Now, in a design-centric view, we envision an ideal experience and then try to push the technology limits to make it happen and realize the vision.

AUDIENCES

Anyone involved in, or wishing to learn more about, creating products that engender a quality user experience will benefit from this book. One important audience is *students and the instructors* who teach them. Another important intended audience includes UX practitioners: *UX professionals* or others who take on the role of a UX professional in project environments. The perspective of professionals is very similar to that of students; both have the goal of learning, only in slightly different settings and perhaps with different motivations and expectations.

Our readership comprises all kinds of UX professionals, including UX designers, content strategists, information architects, graphic designers, web designers, usability engineers, mobile device app designers, usability analysts, human factors engineers, cognitive psychologists, cosmic psychics, trainers, technical writers, documentation specialists, marketing personnel, and project managers. Readers in any of these areas will find the hands-on approach of this book valuable and can focus mainly on the how-to-do-it parts.

Software people who work with UX professionals—including software engineers, programmers, systems analysts, software quality-assurance specialists—can also benefit from this book. Software engineers who find themselves called upon to do some UX design will find this book easy to read and apply because UX design lifecycle concepts are similar to those in software engineering.

WHAT'S CHANGED SINCE THE FIRST EDITION?

Sometimes, when you set out to write a second edition, you end up essentially writing a new book. That is the case with this edition. So much has changed since the first edition, including our own understanding of, and experience with, the process. Porter put it this way, long ago: "The present work on the Health, Pleasures, Advantages, and Practice of Cycling is based largely on the author's previous writings on the same subjects, and principally on a volume bearing the same name which he published in 1890. But the changes that have taken place since the other work was written have been so great that no mere revision, but a complete rewriting proved necessary, in order to eliminate portions that were out of date, and to add very much that was new and important." (Porter, 1895).

NEW CONTENT AND EMPHASIS

Here are some of the new topics or approaches to material you will find in this edition:

- Increased focus on design. Many of the process-oriented chapters are infused with a new emphasis on design, design thinking, and generative design. We even changed the subtitle of the book slightly to reflect this emphasis (to *Agile UX Design for a Quality User Experience*).
- New approach to processes, methods, and techniques. The early chapters establish process-related terminology and concepts as context for discussion in later chapters.
- The entire book is oriented toward an agile UX lifecycle process as a better match to the now *de facto* standard agile approach to software engineering. We have also introduced a model (the funnel model of agile UX) to explain the role of UX in various different development environments.
- Commercial product perspective and enterprise system perspective. These two quite different kinds of UX design settings are now explicitly recognized and treated separately.

TIGHTENED UP THE VERBOSE TEXT

We got feedback on the first edition from people who want us to tighten up the writing. To make the second edition easier to read, we tried to make it concise by eliminating repetition and verbosity. We hope you will agree that we did our best at addressing this.

A MORE RELAXED APPROACH TO GRAMMAR AND WRITING STYLE

To enhance readability, we have adopted some changes in the mechanics of writing. We moved toward a more informal, and hopefully more readable, style by relaxing some grammatical rules. Good grammar is important. However, some of the old grammatical constraints make the writing and reading awkward. For example, many people now feel that split infinitives are often easier on the ear (to more casually communicate) than the more formal alternative.

Most of those rules were never real, anyway. And, in case you are a stickler about these "rules," they may not be what you think. It's not that the language has evolved through modern usage to make the breaking of these rules the new norm. It's more that these so-called rules never were real (O'Conner & Kellerman, 2013, p. 24). And, beyond that, (for the *real* sticklers) there is nothing to split in an infinitive, because the word "to" is technically not part of the infinitive. Famous authors such as Shakespeare, Donne, and Wordsworth have been "splitting infinitives" since the 1200s. So, we hope we won't be faulted for easing up on some grammatical rules that some have thought to be ironclad, but which are really optional. See also Pinker's book, The Sense of Style (Pinker, 2014).

How we are relaxing the grammar. We may occasionally allow a sentence to start with a conjunction. And that's perfectly good when it's needed. We sometimes find a preposition a good thing to end a sentence with. We're also now in the habit of using contractions. By some standards, they are verboten in published writing, but, you have to agree, informal speech flows nicely with contractions, and we see no reason you can't experience that same pleasant cadence in your reading.

Another example of something you're not supposed to do is have a one-sentence paragraph, but sometimes it's a nice way to highlight a point.

In addition, we use personal pronouns, a practice not usually admired in formal writing but, well, we're trying to be less formal. So, instead of saying, "the reader will notice...," we'll use the less formal and friendlier, "you will notice..." Similarly, we'll use "we" or "us" to refer to ourselves, the authors. Sometimes, we'll say "I" or "me," and you might have to guess which of us that means.

Another area where we will be relaxed is anthropomorphic wording, which might cause some grammarians to roll over in their ivory towers, but sometimes, it's just easier, and readers will always know what we mean. For example, we might say, "Figure X shows such and such," when, of course, we mean, "in Figure X, we show such and such." I'll bet that, if we hadn't mentioned that one here, most readers wouldn't have even noticed.

Gender-specific pronouns. We have observed that literary acrobatics to avoid the use of gender-specific pronouns can lead to considerable stiffness in writing. We are saddled with a language that has built-in gender traps that are difficult and awkward to avoid. Sometimes, you can just use the plural—for example, instead of "the user must type Ctrl-Shift-Alt-Delete often, and he will find that difficult," you can say, "users must type Ctrl-Shift-Alt-Delete often, and they will find that difficult." At least that is better than the dreadful mix of number in "the user must type Ctrl-Shift-Alt-Delete very often, and they will find that difficult." Other approaches to de-gendering can result in graceless, lashed-together combinations such as he/she or s/he or the ungainly and mysterious "one," as in "When one takes on the role of UX professional, then one must be very brave."

We solve this gender trap by hitting it head on. We use "he" or "she" when useful and will try to stay out of political trouble by using each gender equally often. Can you tell if we are counting?

Relaxing about references. Most of the references cited will be in a standard academic-style. But sometimes, a less formal source is sufficient and practical. In particular, occasionally we'll use a reference to Wikipedia for a "definition" of a commonly-used term. Yes, sometimes Wikipedia and other similar sources can be flawed, but we will do our best to avoid anything questionable.

Also this. And we shall struggle to never use the word "plethora."

WHAT WE DON'T COVER

To begin with, this book is not a survey of the HCI field, nor is it a survey about user experience. It is also not about human-computer interaction research. Although this book is large and comprehensive, we could not hope to include everything about HCI or UX. We apologize if your favorite topic is excluded, but we had to draw the line somewhere. Further, many of these additional topics are so broad in themselves that they could (and most do) fill a book of their own.

Among the specific topics not included are:

- Accessibility, special needs, and the American Disabilities Act (ADA)
- Internationalization and cultural differences
- Standards
- Ergonomic health issues, such as repetitive stress injury
- Specific HCI application areas, such as societal challenges, healthcare systems, help systems, training, and designing for elders or other special user populations
- Special areas of interaction such as virtual environments or 3D interaction
- Computer-Supported Collaborative Work (CSCW)
- Social media
- Personal information management (PIM)
- Sustainability (we had originally planned to include this, but space ran out)
- Summative UX evaluation studies

ABOUT THE EXERCISES

A hypothetical system called the Ticket Kiosk System is used as a UX design example to illustrate the material in throughout the process chapters. In this running example, we describe activities that you can imitate to build your own designs. The exercises are an integral part of the learning from this book. In its use of hands-on exercises based on the Ticket Kiosk System, the book is somewhat like a workbook. After each main topic, you get to apply the new material immediately, learning the practical techniques by active engagement in their application. The book is organized and written to support active learning (learning by doing), and should be used that way.

The exercises require medium-level engagement, somewhere in between the in-text examples and full project assignments.

Take them in order. Each process chapter builds on the previous ones and adds a new piece to the overall puzzle. Each exercise builds on what you learned and accomplished in the previous stages—just as in a real-world project.

Do the exercises as a team if you can. Good UX design is almost always a collaborative effort. Working through the exercises with at least one other interested person will enhance your understanding and learning of the materials greatly. In fact, many of the exercises are written for small teams (for example, three to five people) because they involve multiple roles.

The teamwork will help you understand the kinds of communication, interaction, and negotiation that take place in creating and refining a UX design. If you can season the experience by including a software developer with responsibility for software architecture and implementation (at least for a working prototype), many important communication needs will become apparent.

Students should do the exercises as team in the classroom. If you are a student in a course, the best way to do the exercises is as team-based in-class exercises. The exercises are adapted easily for classroom use as an ongoing, semester-long interactive set of in-class activities to understand needs, design solutions, prototype candidate designs, and evaluate the UX. The instructor can observe and comment on your progress, and you can share your "lessons learned" with other teams.

UX professionals should get buy-in to do the exercises at work. If you are a UX professional, or you aspire to learn on-the-job to be a UX professional, trying to learn this material in the context of your regular work, the best way of all is an intensive short course with team exercises and projects. We used to teach just such a short course.

Alternatively, if you have a small UX team in your work group (perhaps a team that expects to work together on a real project), and your work environment allows, set aside some time (say, two hours every Friday afternoon) for the team exercises. To justify the extra overhead to pull this off, you might have to convince your project manager of the value added.

Individuals can still do the exercises. Do not let the lack of a team stop you from doing the exercises. Try to find at least one other person with whom you can work, or, if necessary, get what you can from the exercises on your own. Although it would be easy to let yourself skip the exercises, we urge you to do as much on each of them as your time permits.

TEAM PROJECTS

Students. In addition to the small-scale series of in-class activities in conjunction with the book exercises, we offer fully detailed and more involved team projects. We consider this semester-long sequence of team projects an essential part of learning by doing in a course based on this book. These team projects have always been the most demanding, but also the most rewarding, learning activity in the course.

For this semester-long team project, we use real clients from the community—a local company, store, or organization that needs some kind of interactive software application designed. The client stands to get some free consulting and even (sometimes) a system prototype in exchange for serving as the project client. A sample set of team project assignments is available in the Instructor's Guide, available to instructors from the publisher.

UX professionals. As a way of getting started in applying this material to your real work environment, you and your coworkers can select a low-risk, but real, project. Your team may already be familiar and even experienced with some of the activities we describe and may even already be doing some of them in your development environment. By making them part of a more complete and informed development lifecycle, you can integrate what you know with new concepts presented in the book.

ABOUT THE AUTHORS

Rex Hartson is a pioneer researcher, teacher, practitioner, and consultant in HCI and UX. He is the founding faculty member of HCI (in 1979) in the Department of Computer Science at Virginia Tech. With Deborah Hix, he was co-author of one of the first books to emphasize the usability engineering process, *Developing User Interfaces: Ensuring Usability Through Product & Process.* Hartson has been principal investigator (PI) or co-PI at Virginia Tech on a large number of research grants and has published many journal articles, conference papers, and book chapters. He has presented many tutorials, invited lectures, workshops, seminars, and international talks. He was editor or co-editor for *Advances in*

Human-Computer Interaction, Volumes 1–4, Ablex Publishing Co., Norwood, New Jersey. His HCI practice is grounded in over 30 years of consulting and UX Design training for dozens of clients in business, industry, government, and the military.

Pardha S. Pyla is an award-winning designer and strategist with deep expertise in envisioning and delivering industry-leading products. He is a seasoned leader with a record of establishing exemplary user experience and product development practices. He is a pioneering researcher in the area of coordinating software engineering and UX lifecycle processes and the author of several peer-reviewed research publications in human-computer interaction and software engineering. He has received numerous awards in recognition of his work in design, research, teaching, leadership, and service.

Acknowledgments

I (RH) must begin with a note of gratitude to my wife, Rieky Keeris, who provided me with a happy environment and encouragement while writing this book.

I (PP) owe a debt of gratitude to my parents, my brother, Hari, and my sister-in-law, Devaki, for all their love and encouragement. They put up with my long periods of absence from family events as I worked on this book. I must also thank my brother for being my best friend and a constant source of support all my life.

We are happy to express our appreciation to Debby Hix for a career-long span of collegial interaction. We are also grateful for the long-term professional associations and friendships at Virginia Tech with Roger Ehrich, Bob and Bev Williges, Manuel A. Pérez-Quiñones, Ed Fox, John Kelso, Sean Arthur, Mary Beth Rosson, and Joe Gabbard.

We are indebted to Brad Myers of Carnegie Mellon University for his support of this book from the start.

Special thanks to Akshay Sharma in the Virginia Tech Department of Industrial Design for giving us access to photograph the ideation studio and working environment there, including students at work and the sketches and prototypes they produced. And finally, our thanks for the many photographs and sketches provided by Akshay to include as figures in design chapters.

It is with pleasure we acknowledge the positive influence of Jim Foley, Dennis Wixon, and Ben Shneiderman, with whom our friendship goes back decades and transcends professional relationships.

We are grateful for the diligence and professionalism of the reviewers and editors for their valuable suggestions that have helped make the book much better.

I'll (RH) always be grateful for the warm welcome I received from Phil Gray and the people in the Department of Computing Science at the University of Glasgow who hosted my wonderful sabbatical in 1989. Special thanks to Steve Draper, Department of Psychology, University of Glasgow, for providing a comfortable and congenial place there to live.

Many thanks to Kim Gausepohl, who helped as a sounding board for ideas about integrating UX into real-world agile software environments. And we extend our appreciation to our long-time friend Mathew Mathai and others in the Network Infrastructure and Services group in the IT organization at Virginia Tech. Mathew was instrumental in giving access to a real-world agile development environment and the invaluable learning experience that went with it.

Special thanks to Ame Wongsa for the many insightful conversations over the years about the nature of design, information architecture, and UX practice, and for providing us with the wireframes for the camping application example. We also thank Christina Janczak for providing us with the mood boards and other visual designs for this example, as well as the design for the book cover.

Finally, we are grateful for all the support from Nate McFadden and all the others at Morgan Kaufmann. It has been a pleasure to work with this organization.

Guiding Principles for the UX Practitioner

Be goal-directed.

If it ain't broke, you can still fix it and make it fantastic.

Don't be dogmatic; use your common sense.

Envision usage in context.

The answer to most questions is "it depends."

It's about the people.

Everything should be evaluated in its own way.

Improvise, adapt, and overcome.

But first, plan, prepare, and anticipate.

Keep calm and carry on.

Failure is a good option. Only we call it succeeding by learning early about what doesn't work.

The answer is 42.

Introduction

Part 1 contains introductory information that will prepare you for the process chapters in several parts that follow. Chapter 1 is mainly about concepts, terminology, and definitions. It will ground you in what UX, UX design, and the user experience are, including the components of UX.

While Chapter 2 introduces the idea of UX lifecycle processes, methods, and techniques, Chapter 3 is about important concepts of UX design and development that we will use throughout the rest of the process chapters: scope and rigor, and how rigor trades off with speed, cost, and risk avoidance in a project.

Chapter 4 is about the funnel model of agile UX, which is a way to envision an agile process for UX design that can fit within an agile software engineering process. Chapter 5 sets the stage for you to get into the process chapters. It includes the concepts of a UX studio and how a project gets started, and introduces a running example for all the process chapters.

What Are UX and UX Design?

Fine art and pizza delivery, what we do falls neatly in between.

– David Letterman

Highlights

- Definition and scope of UX.
- UX design.
- The components of user experience:
    - Usability.
    - Usefulness.
    - Emotional impact.
    - Meaningfulness.
- What UX is not.
- Kinds of interaction and UX.
- A business case for user experience.

1.1 THE EXPANDING CONCEPT OF INTERACTION

In the first edition of this book, interaction was just starting to be more than how people used computers. The notion of interaction in the context of UX has continued to evolve, from a human and computer working together to accomplish a goal to being, as in Fig. 1-1, *a very broad term referring to a wide variety of communication and collaboration between a human and an artifact in an ecology.*
Interaction artifact. So, what is an *interaction artifact?* It's a *system, device, service, instrument, mechanism, object, or environment that can communicate with a human, in either or both directions.* Artifacts, then, may include the building or room you are in, the chair you may be sitting in, kitchens, an ATM, an elevator, appliances like refrigerators, cars and other vehicles, most kinds of signage, homes, the workflow of the DMV, and voting machines.

Ecology

In the setting of UX design, the ecology is the entire set of surrounding parts of the world, including networks, other users, devices, and information structures, with which a user, product, or system interacts. Section 16.2.1.

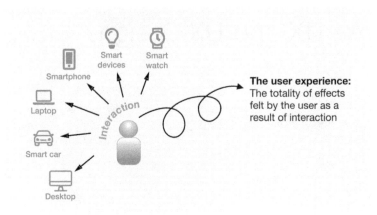

Fig. 1-1

Human-artifact interaction and the resulting experience.

Expanding concept of interaction. It is not just the variations of devices (artifacts) that have changed but the nature of interaction itself. For example, 25 years ago, interaction primarily happened on desktops which were either at home or work. The nature of interaction was primarily with a keyboard, mouse, and a monitor. Then, interaction extended to handheld devices like mobile phones and pagers. The former made it possible to do rudimentary tasks using highly modal interaction. The latter made it possible for an interrupt-driven interaction when someone was paged. That then evolved to using a stylus with the advent of PDAs. The interaction required learning a new input format with the PDA glyph language or using an on-screen tiny keyboard that could be touched with the stylus. Then came touch smartphones and tablets which made the stylus redundant. Now, there is a smart watch that changes the nature of interaction to a combination of touch and scroll wheel. Then there are smart glasses, VR (virtual reality goggles), and smart living environments that let users interact using yet other modalities.

Because interaction is so broad and pervasive in our world, good UX design will necessarily have a substantial positive impact on our lives.

1.2 DEFINITION OF UX

1.2.1 Distinction From "UI"

In times past, people talked about "UI," referring to the user interface and usually referring to the user interface software. This idea of the UI is, in broad terms, the software medium underlying interaction and not of much interest in our context. UX design includes the design of the interaction and much more (e.g., the conceptual design, the ecology, etc.), but not of the UI software.

We have read some literature referring to UI design as visual design and UX design as more about interaction design. Perhaps you could say that UI is one of the portals through which users interact, and that designing it involves various subdisciplines. In the literature, the look, feel, and emotional aspects of a given UI are often seen as the responsibility of a visual designer. The structure of tasks on the UI and how those are supported in relation to the other tasks supported by the UIs of other devices in the ecology is the responsibility of an interaction designer. And the software of implementing those specifications is the responsibility of software engineers. In other words, UIs are various portals in the ecology.

In the general public, however, the terms UI, HCI, and UX are used somewhat interchangeably.

1.2.2 Distinction from "HCI"

Along these lines, there is also the term "HCI," which stands for "human-computer interaction" and refers to the whole field of study. This term is mostly used now in reference to the academic side, including research and development, whereas "UX" is the more popular term for the practice of HCI in the field.

1.2.3 What Does "UX" Mean?

Because it's clear that this whole book is about UX, we need to get right to the point about what UX is. As we said in the Preface, the two letters "UX" are a popular acronym that stands for "user experience." Those two letters stand for the whole practice, all the work that is done in this field, and the final user experience that comes out of that work.

In September 2010, an international group met at the Schloss Dagstuhl (*Demarcating User eXperience Seminar*) to tease out the nature of user experience and to help define it limits. In their follow-up report (Roto, Law, Vermeeren, & Hoonhout, 2011), they point out that the multidisciplinary character of UX has led to multiple definitions from multiple perspectives, including UX as theory, UX as a phenomenon, UX as a field of study, and UX as a practice. In this book, we take the latter point of view, the perspective of UX design in practice.

1.2.4 The Rise of UX

Early large mainframe computers of the preconsumer era were used to run large enterprise software systems, and users were trained to use a system for specific business purposes. "Interaction" was via punch cards, paper tape, and paper printouts, so there really were no system-development considerations of usability or UX.

Enterprise System

A large information system used within an organization, typical of those developed and used within IT departments in organizations (Sections 3.2.2.4 and 3.4.2).

Then the personal computer put computing on a business user's desk, and the consumer movement put computing in people's houses. Customer service and support was the first to discover that expanding the marketplace to "mere mortals" without an adequate understanding of how the product was being used had a major impact on support costs.

Smart devices and the Internet put computing in everyone's hands and made it possible for business to interface directly with the consumer. The paradigm shifted from users needing training to use a system to requiring the system to fit user expectations and, thus, the path to usability, HCI, and UX was inevitable. Digital natives now think of computing as something that is there—it is transparent to them that there is a design behind the product. They simply expect it will work.

For more background on the history and roots of UX, see Section 6.2. Also see Section 6.3, on shifting paradigms in HCI and UX.

1.2.5 What Is User Experience?

User experience, of course, is a kind of experience and "experience is a very dynamic, complex, and subjective phenomenon" (Buchenau & Suri, 2000), depending heavily on context of the associated activity.

User experience is the totality of the effects felt by the user before, during, and after interaction with a product or system in an ecology.

Our job, as UX designers, is to design that interaction to create a user experience that is productive, fulfilling, satisfying, and even joyful.

Key characteristics of a user experience reflected in the definition above are:

1. It is a result of interaction, whether direct or indirect.
2. It is about the totality of the effects.
3. It is felt internally by a user.
4. It includes usage context and ecology.

1.2.5.1 Interaction, direct or indirect

Interaction between a human and a designed artifact can be direct (e.g., operating on a device and getting feedback) or indirect (e.g., feeling the effect of seeing and thinking about an artifact).

1.2.5.2 Totality of effects

Following up on the second characteristic of a user experience, as the Dagstuhl report (Demarcating User eXperience Seminar, 2010) says, the effects of interaction include the user's entire "stream of perceptions, interpretations of those perceptions, and resulting emotions during an encounter with a system."

That totality of effects of interaction includes:

- The influence of usability, usefulness, and emotional impact during physical interaction.
- The full unfolding of effects over time.

As an example of effects felt over time, consider a potential user researching a product or system, seeing advertising and reviews, and anticipating ownership. Once the product is bought, the effects include product packaging and the "out of the box" experience; seeing, touching, and thinking about the product; admiring the product, using it, and retaining and savoring (or not) the pleasure of usage.

Finally, the user experience can include the individual's feeling about the company that produced the product or system and its reputation and branding, as well as the pride of ownership and how the product has acquired meaning in the user's lifestyle, extending into a broad cultural and personal experience.

1.2.5.3 User experience is felt internally by the user

Clearly, it is the user who has the experience. Therefore, user experiences from interaction under the same conditions can vary across individual users.

1.2.5.4 Context and ecology are crucial to user experience

An ecology is the complete usage context including all parts of the world the user comes in contact with related to the interaction. The user can be part of multiple ecologies (e.g., work versus home). Within an ecology, there could be multiple specific usage contexts (e.g., stressful work conditions or pleasurable play conditions). And each such context affects the user experience.

1.3 UX DESIGN

1.3.1 Can a User Experience Be Designed?

The perceptive reader may have already spotted a small inconsistency. We have used phrases "UX design" and others talk about "designing a user experience." But you can't design something that occurs internally in a user. So, phrases like "UX design" really don't quite make sense, but we trust you will understand that this means designing *for* the user experience.

1.3.2 Importance of UX Design

The importance of UX is becoming more widely recognized and UX design has taken center stage. As a senior VP of IBM said, "There's no longer any real distinction between business strategy and the design of the user experience" (Kolko, 2015a, p. 70). Knemeyer (2015, p. 66) agrees, by saying, "user experience

(UX) has become a mission-critical consideration for companies in every industry, and of every shape and size."

One way to highlight the importance of good UX design is by examples of the high cost of bad UX design. As an example, poor UX design in the architecture of buildings and living spaces can impose costs that persist for a long time. "Too often, the people who design and construct buildings and parks don't worry about whether they will work properly or what will they cost to run. Once the project is complete, they can move on to the next job. But the public has to live with badly built, poorly designed buildings and spaces; and taxpayers often have to foot the bill for putting them right again."[1]

Bad UI/UX design costs an enormous amount of money and more importantly, lives. Distractions due to bad UX designs for operating cars can lead to traffic accidents, injuries, and even death.

The same caution applies to UX design for operating aircraft and ships at sea. For example, the crash of EgyptAir Flight 990 in 1999 (Section 32.6.3.3) was determined to be caused by poor usability in the design of cockpit controls. And the collision of the USS McCain[2] is said to be the result of bad UX design of the navigation console.

In the medical domain, the need for good UX design is perhaps even more compelling with respect to the effects of safety in everyday operation. As Nielsen[3] reports, "A field study identified 22 ways that automated hospital systems can result in the wrong medication being dispensed to patients. Most of these flaws are classic usability problems that have been understood for decades."

1.4 THE COMPONENTS OF UX

As illustrated in Fig. 1-2, user experience is a combination that includes these factors:

1. Usability.
2. Usefulness.
3. Emotional impact.
4. Meaningfulness.

---

[1]John Sorrell, 2006. The cost of bad design, *Report of the Commission for Architecture and the Built Environment,* http://webarchive.nationalarchives.gov.uk/20110118134605/http://www.cabe.org.uk/files/the-cost-of-bad-design.pdf.
[2]https://arstechnica.com/information-technology/2017/11/uss-mccain-collision-ultimately-caused-by-ui-confusion/
[3]Jakob Nielsen, April 11, 2005, *Medical Usability: How to Kill Patients Through Bad Design,* https://www.nngroup.com/articles/medical-usability/

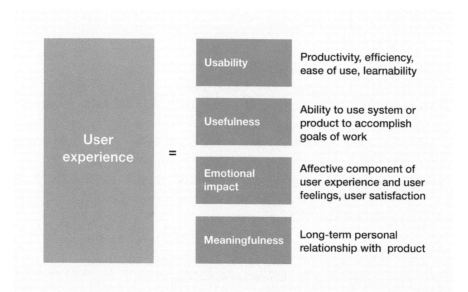

Fig. 1-2
The components of UX.

1.4.1 An Analogy With Fine Dining

To illustrate the possible components of user experience, we borrow from the domain of fine dining. The usefulness of a meal can be reckoned in terms of nutritional effectiveness, perhaps felt in terms of health values.

Usability in a dining experience can also be reckoned, to some extent, by practical considerations. For example, if the food served is tough and difficult to cut or chew, or it takes too long to prepare and serve, that will certainly impact the usability component of the dining experience. Lack of the necessary eating utensils will also count against dining usability.

For many of us, though, eating is a largely emotional experience. Perhaps it starts with the pleasure of anticipation. The diners will also experience a perception of, and emotional response to, the dining ambiance, lighting, background music, and décor, as well as the quality of service, aesthetics of food presentation, friendliness of the staff, and how good the food tasted.

1.4.2 Usability

Long ago, the field of Human-Computer Interaction (HCI), the umbrella academic discipline for UX, was pretty much just about usability, which includes (ISO 9241-11, 1997):

- Ease of use.
- User performance and productivity.

- Efficiency.
- Error avoidance.
- Learnability.
- Retainability (ease of remembering).

Affordance

A feature in a user's environment, for example, in a UX design, that helps the user do something (Section 30.1.2).

Even now, usability is still a very important part of UX. As the field has focused on more glamorous parts of the user experience, sometimes the foundational component, usability, has been forgotten. For example, the so-called flat design style popular these days looks and feels visually attractive but lacks an important affordance that reveals which elements on the screen are clickable and which are not. Without good usability, it is rare that the other components of the user experience will even be considered.

1.4.3 Usefulness

The second component is usefulness, perhaps the forgotten stepchild of the user experience. Usefulness is utility. Usefulness is about the power and functionality of the backend software that gives you the ability to get work (or play) done. It's the real underlying reason for a product or system.

Hassenzahl and Roto (2007) characterize usability and usefulness as serving a user's *do* goals, such as checking one's email or posting a comment on Facebook.

1.4.4 Emotional Impact

The third component is emotional impact, an affective part of user experience. As the term implies, emotional impact embraces how users feel emotionally about an interaction (Norman, 2004), including user satisfaction.

Although there were earlier academic papers about emotion in the user experience, Norman (2002) was one of the first to bring the topic to light on a broad scale, relating it to his theme of everyday things. Now there are conferences dedicated specifically to the topic, including the biennial Conference on Design & Emotion,[4] the goal of which is to foster a cross-disciplinary approach to design and emotion.

While technically all of the user experience is emotional because it is all experienced internally by the user, there are some user experience factors that are more purely emotional, factors that are felt up close and personal during the usage of technology (whether high technology or low), factors that take

---

[4]http://www.designandemotion.org/en/conferences/

the user beyond simple satisfaction to fun, enjoyment, and self-expression, with sometimes strong emotional consequences.

Emotional impact can be experienced in many ways, including:

- Joy of usage.
- Pleasure.
- Excitement.
- Fun.
- Curiosity.
- Aesthetics.
- Novelty.
- Surprise.
- Delight.
- Play.
- Exploration.
- Coolness.
- Appeal.
- A sense of identity.
- Happiness.
- Enthusiasm.
- Enticement.
- Engagement.
- Pride of ownership.
- Affinity, attractiveness, identifying with a product.
- "Wow" in UX design.

For a discussion of fun interaction at work, see Section 6.4.

1.4.4.1 Why include emotional impact?

Hassenzahl, Beu, and Burmester (2001, p. 71) and Shih and Liu (2007) put it this way: users are no longer satisfied with just the efficiency and effectiveness of usability; they are also looking for emotional satisfaction. Norman (2004) uses more practical terms: "attractive things make people feel good." Users now seek pleasure in product use and aesthetics (Hassenzahl, 2012; Norman, 2002; Zhang, 2009) in product design, and the products we own and use can arouse strong feelings of importance and social status, especially if it is a high-tech, esoteric product.

Emotional impact in interaction can have positive impact on economics and job performance; beneficial emotions can lead to better job satisfaction, decision making, and other behavior (Zhang & Li, 2005). As Norman (2004) shows us, positive emotions can have great impact on learning, curiosity, and creative thought.

1.4.4.2 Deeper emotions

While most of the emotional impact factors are about pleasure, they can be about other kinds of feelings, too, including affective qualities such as love, hate, fear, mourning, and reminiscing over shared memories. Applications in which emotional impact is important include social interaction (Dubberly & Pangaro, 2009; Rhee & Lee, 2009; Winchester III, 2009) and interaction for cultural problem solving (Ann, 2009; Costabile, Ardito, & Lanzilotti, 2010; Jones, Winegarden, & Rogers, 2009; Radoll, 2009; Savio, 2010).

Social and cultural interactions entail emotional aspects such as trustworthiness (especially important in e-commerce) and credibility (believability). Design for emotional impact can also be about supporting human compassion—for example, in sites like CaringBridge[5] and CarePages.[6]

1.4.4.3 Joy, excitement, and fun

The most basic reason for considering joy of use is the humanistic view that enjoyment is fundamental to life.

(Hassenzahl et al., 2001)

We have adapted an example from Bill Buxton's book on sketching user experiences (Buxton, 2007b) that illustrates the difference when emotional impact is a factor. In Fig. 1-3, we have a picture (like that of Buxton's Fig. 32) of a mountain bike (Buxton, 2007b, pp. 98–99).

This bike is standing there ready for you to hop on and ride away on great adventure. But this image doesn't show the adventure, and that adventure is the user experience.

Now contrast that with the next picture in Fig. 1-4 (like Buxton's Fig. 33) that doesn't even show the whole user (rider) or even the whole bike (Buxton, 2007b, pp. 100–101).

What it does do, though, is capture the excitement of the user experience. The dynamic spray of water conveys the fun and excitement (and maybe a little danger). The blood and adrenaline are pumping as you career over the bumpy

---

[5]https://www.caringbridge.org
[6]https://www.carepages.com

Fig. 1-3

A beautiful mountain bike just waiting for you to ride it.

Fig. 1-4

The true mountain bike experience.

rocks, and the scenery rushes by madly in a blur of motion. That is what you are buying—the breathtaking thrill of the experience of using the bike.

1.4.4.4 Attractive designs somehow work better

For many users, an attractive design just seems to work better and make people feel good (Norman, 2002, 2004). It's kind of like when you get your new car washed and cleaned up—it seems to run better.

1.4.4.5 Engagement and enticement

Churchill (2010) characterizes engagement in terms of flow, fascination, attention held, and being "lost in time." The psychological concept of flow entails full involvement, energized focus, and exclusion of all but the central activity (Churchill, 2010, p. 82). Engagement can span usage episodes to the point it contributes to long-term meaningfulness. Enticement, a quality that draws the user in, is closely related (Churchill, 2010; Siegel, 2012).

1.4.4.6 Coolness and "wow" in UX design

These days, consumers are used to, and even expect, products that are really cool (Holtzblatt, 2011). Coolness and "wow" in the design are becoming "required" elements of emotional impact in the user experience (Hudson & Viswanadha, 2009).

Meaningfulness

A personal relationship that develops and endures over time between human users and a product that has become a part of the user's lifestyle (Section 1.4.5).

Example: A Convincing Anecdote About the Importance of Emotional Impact

David Pogue makes a convincing case for the role of emotional impact in user experience using the example of the iPad. In his *New York Times* story (Pogue, 2011), he explains why the iPad turned the personal devices industry upside down and created a whole new class of devices. But when the iPad came out, the critics dubbed it "underwhelming," "a disappointment," and "a failure." Why would anyone want or need it?

Pogue admits that the critics were right from a utilitarian or rational standpoint: "The iPad was superfluous. It filled no obvious need. If you already had a touch screen phone and a laptop, why on earth would you need an iPad? It did seem like just a big iPod Touch." Yet as Pogue claimed, the iPad at that time was the most successful personal electronic device ever, selling 15 million in the first months. Why? It has little to do with rational, functional, and utility appeal and has everything to do with emotional allure. It is about the personal experience of holding it in your hand and manipulating finely crafted objects on the screen. Once you have one, you find ways to make it useful.

1.4.4.7 Role of branding, marketing, and corporate culture

In some cases, the user experience transcends the effects felt due to usability, usefulness, and joy of use. Users can get wrapped up in the whole milieu of what the manufacturer stands for, their political affiliations, how the product is marketed, and so on. What image does the brand of a product stand for? Is it a brand that uses environmentally sustainable manufacturing practices? Do they recycle? Consequently, what does the fact that someone is using a product of that particular brand say about them? These factors are difficult to define in the abstract and more difficult to identify in the concrete.

Consider the case of Apple in the late 2000s and early 2010s. The culture of designing for user experience was so deeply engrained in their corporate culture that everything they produced had a stamp of tasteful elegance and spectacular design. This kind of fanatic emphasis on quality user experience at Apple extended beyond the products they produced and even seeped into other areas of their company. When they made an employment offer to a new employee, for example, the package came in a meticulously designed envelope that set the stage for what the company stood for (Slivka, 2009).

And that aura also pervaded Apple retail stores. A *New York Times* article (Hafner, 2007) extoled the enchanting aura of Apple stores: "Not only has the company made many of its stores feel like gathering places, but the bright lights and equally bright acoustics create a buzz that makes customers feel more like they are at an event than a retail store." The goal of one new store in Manhattan was to make it "the most personal store ever created." This carefully designed user experience has been very successful in generating sales, return visits, and even tourist pilgrimages.

Example: Branding and Passion for the Pontiac Car

There is an interesting story from General Motors about valuing (or not) branding and product passion. In October 2010, the board of directors quietly discontinued the Pontiac car from the GM line of brands. Of course, the direct cause was the transition through bankruptcy, but the beginning of the end for Pontiac started 26 years earlier.

Before that, Pontiac had its own separate facilities for design and production. Owners (and wannabe owners) were passionate about Pontiac cars, and Pontiac employees had been devoted to the brand. The brand had its own identity, personality, and cachet, not to mention the notoriety from custom muscle cars such as the GTO and the Firebird TransAm, as seen in the movie, *Smokey and the Bandit*.

In 1984, however, in its great corporate wisdom, GM lumped the Pontiac works in with its other GM facilities. The economically based decision to merge facilities meant no separate ideas for Pontiac design and no special attention to production. After that, there was really nothing special to be devoted to, and the passion was lost. Many believe that decision led to the decline and eventual demise of the brand.

1.4.5 Meaningfulness

While usability, and often even emotional impact, is usually about a single usage occurrence, meaningfulness is, as it says in Fig. 1-2, about how a product or artifact becomes meaningful in the life of a user. *Meaningfulness comes out of a personal relationship of the product with its human user that endures over time.* It is epitomized by the feelings of companionship many have for their smartphones, to the point that some users become physically uncomfortable if they become separated from their phones. Meaningfulness is exemplified by the feeling of comfort and safety felt by a hiker in response to a hand held GPS.

Meaningfulness is closely related to the more academic concept of phenomenology.

1.5 WHAT UX IS NOT

While UX is becoming more and more an established part of the technology world, some misconceptions and mischaracterizations still linger.

1.5.1 Not Dummy Proofing or User Friendliness

Usability and UX are not dummy proofing or idiot proofing. While it might have been mildly cute the first time people who didn't know much about usability used these terms; they are insulting and demeaning to users and designers alike.

Similarly, usability and UX are not about being "user-friendly." This is a misdirected term that trivializes UX design. Users are not looking for amiability; they need an efficient, effective, safe, and maybe aesthetic and fun tool that helps them reach their goals.

1.5.2 Not Just About Dressing Things Up in a Pretty Skin

Another prevalent misconception about the early usability and human factors people was that they were the ones you send the design to at the end to dress it up and "make it pretty." As Steve Jobs has put it, "In most people's vocabularies, design means veneer. It's interior decorating. It's the fabric of the curtains and the sofa. But to me, nothing could be further from the meaning of design. Design is the fundamental soul of a man-made creation that ends up expressing itself in successive outer layers of the product or service (Steve, 2000)," as cited by Dubberly (2012). Kolko agrees: "Design doesn't just make things beautiful, it makes them work" (Kolko, 2015a, p. 70).

Human Factors

An engineering discipline dedicated to bringing science and technology together with human behavior and biological characteristics for design and maintenance of products and systems for safe, effective, and satisfying use (Section 6.2.4).

Adding UX design as a "spread-on" layer at the end is what we call the "peanut butter theory"[7] of UX, because it seems to be based on the premise that, after the product is developed, you can spread this nice thin layer of UX all over the top of it. You don't have to know much about UX or software these days to know that can't work.

1.5.3 Not Just a Diagnostic View

In the early days of usability, many companies had large software engineering teams, along with a small pool of human factors experts, who would get loaned out briefly to a project team, usually at the end of the project, at which time they were expected to perform "usability testing." This led many to think of "doing usability" as equivalent to usability testing, a view we call the "priest in a parachute"[8] approach.

After the team had pretty much committed to the design, the human factors people were to drop down into the project, give it their blessing, and go away! There's no time left to fix noncosmetic problems found at this stage. There are no resources left to invest in the product before it must be shipped.

Example: The Black & Decker Snakelight and How Evaluation Can't Do It All

Fig. 1-5 shows a Black & Decker Snakelight in the context of usage. It's very flexible and even looks a little bit like a snake.

You can change its shape so it stands by itself on a workbench or anywhere you need, such as under the kitchen sink. To come up with this concept, Black & Decker did usage research before doing any design. They observed large numbers of flashlight users to see what they used flashlights for and how they used them.

They quickly discovered that people who use the flashlight to see better while they were doing tasks usually needed their hands free to do the task. If they had instead taken a purely diagnostic view, they would have looked at a typical flashlight and they would've fixed all of the problems they could find with that design, but they never would've thought of something totally new like the Snakelight.

---

[7]Thanks to Clayton Lewis for this metaphor.
[8]This one is also due to Clayton Lewis, if we recall correctly.

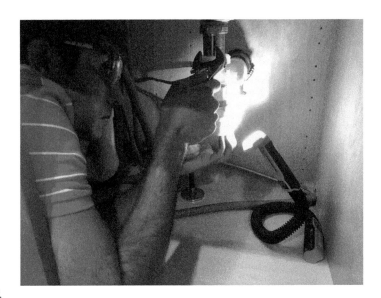

Fig. 1-5
A Black & Decker Snakelight.

1.6 KINDS OF INTERACTION AND UX

Not all interaction is for a particular task between a user and a GUI for something like adding an item to a calendar. Some interactions continue through lots of different states in time and space and through different environments. Instead of just a one-off exchange, an interaction can be about a transaction that spans a system and expands into a series of exchanges and encounters over a long span of time.

We have identified a few different kinds of interaction that we can correlate with different kinds of user experiences.

1. Localized interaction.
2. Activity-based interaction.
3. System-spanning interaction.

1.6.1 Localized Interaction

Localized interaction is localized with respect to both time and system. It is simple interaction with a single "product," one device in the user's ecology (the world of devices, systems, communications, etc.) surrounding the user. It's task-oriented, bounded, and limited, and it occurs in a very short time within one interaction environment and with one single goal, such as using your laptop to check your email or using an ATM to make a withdrawal of cash. Therefore, design is focused on interaction.

1.6.2 Activity-Based Interaction

Norman introduced activity-based design (Norman, 2005) as a way to describe interactions that go beyond simple tasks. An activity is one or more task thread(s), a set of (or possibly sequences of) multiple, overlapping, and related tasks. It can involve:

- Interaction with one device to do a set of related tasks.
- Interaction across devices in the user's ecology.

Interaction with one device to do a set of related tasks. As an example, suppose you are searching for a compact digital camera online. You might follow links to reviews, decide on one, and put it in the "cart" and then follow links to other, similar products. You can also follow other links to accessories you might want (e.g., SD memory card, camera case, wrist strap, USB cable for downloading), and so on. Even though this involves multiple different tasks, users think of it as doing one activity.

Norman (2005) describes "mobile phones that combine appointment books, diaries, and calendars, note-taking facilities, text messaging, and cameras" as devices to support communication activities. "This one single device integrates several tasks: looking up numbers, dialing, talking, note taking, checking one's diary or calendar, and exchanging photographs, text messages, and emails." The many tasks can then be combined together in usage within one overall activity.

Example: iTunes Ecology

As an example, consider how people use iTunes. Although this example involves multiple devices and tasks, to the user, it is about managing personal music. iTunes is designed to have its own surrounding ecology to support several related activities. For example, I might use iTunes to update my iPod. Suppose I want to remove some music and one audio book and then create some playlists. Then, I want to buy some new music and add it to my mobile devices. When iTunes opens, I see that there is a newer version of iOS for my iPod, so I download and install that, and restart the iPod. Then, I buy and download the music into my iTunes library and synchronize the iPod with iTunes to get the new music set up. The best UX design (not really what you get with iTunes as it is today) will be one that seamlessly supports moving from one of these tasks to another.

Activity-Based Interaction
Interaction in the context of one or more task thread(s), a set of, or possibly sequences of, multiple, overlapping, and related tasks, often involving more than one device in an ecology. Sections 1.6.2 and 14.2.6.4.

1.6.3 System-Spanning Interaction

Interaction across devices in the user's ecology. System-spanning interaction is a kind of activity-based interaction, often involving multiple parties in multiple work/play roles, multiple devices, and multiple locations.

Example: Power Lines Are Down

Here is an example of a transaction with a relatively simple goal of getting electric power service restored to a user who finds the power is out in his house. This example and our Fig. 1-6 are borrowed and adapted from Muller, Wildman, and White (1993a).

The activity begins by our user calling his neighbor (Fig. 1-6). The neighbor says his power is out, too, and he thinks a power line is down in the neighborhood. Our hero then calls the power company customer service and asks if it can be

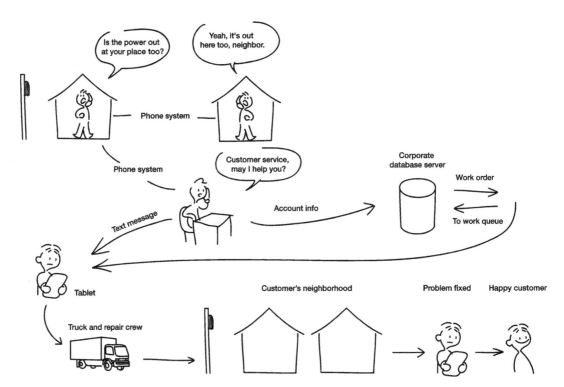

Fig. 1-6

System-spanning activity to fix downed power lines (adapted from Muller et al. (1993a)).

fixed. The customer service person posts a work order in a queue in a central database, with account number, customer name, phone number, address.

Customer service also sends a text message to a technician in the field, who checks the queue on his portable tablet and picks up the work order, hops in his truck, and drives to that neighborhood. He and his crew fix the power lines, and he reports the job done on his portable tablet. The customer is happy.

From this one simple example, you can see an ecology involved in one user activity that includes the user as customer, the power company, its customer service, customer accounts, the power company's central database, a work order queue, a work order, power company field technicians, and the power lines. The ecology of this activity also includes the telephone system, the neighbor on his phone, a text message, the technician's portable tablet, the technician's crew, and a fleet of power company trucks.

The user's workflow is a continuum across the ecology, and information pervasiveness, or shareability and accessibility across the whole ecology, is the glue that ties the different subsystems within the ecology. We talk about how to design for system-spanning interaction in Section 16.2.4, on designing the ecology.

1.6.4 The Dagstuhl Framework of Interaction and UX

Participants in the Dagstuhl seminar (Roto et al., 2011, p. 8) have modeled the kinds of UX (and kinds of interaction) in terms of the scope of time. Starting with the earliest, they feature:

- Before usage: Anticipated UX.
- During usage: Momentary UX, one-off encounters.
- After usage: Episodic UX, now and then periods of usage interspersed with nonusage.
- Over time: Cumulative UX, views of a system as a whole after having used it for a while.

These different kinds of UX, depending on time spans, overlap and confirm our definition of the totality of effects (Section 1.2.5.2). Anticipated UX includes feelings engendered by researching a product, reading reviews, and so on. Their momentary, episodic, and cumulative UX intersect in various ways with our localized, activity-based, system-spanning, and long-term interaction. Their cumulative UX placed importance on user opinions of systems that they use frequently, such as a laptop, desktop PC, an operating system, or a word processor. Our long-term interaction overlaps and extends beyond their cumulative UX. If the cumulative UX is positive, we call it meaningfulness (Section 1.4.5).

Meaningfulness

A personal relationship that develops and endures over time between human users and a product that has become a part of the user's lifestyle (Section 1.4.5).

1.7 SERVICE EXPERIENCE

Service experience and service design are specialized applications of UX (Forlizzi, 2010). Forlizzi says service design is UX design for a user or customer experience within a "transactional journey" (Forlizzi, 2010, p. 60). Forlizzi makes an effort to distinguish the two, but to us, her definition just confirms that service design is UX design applied to a customer journey: it's "transactional" and helps, "a customer achieve a goal."

Service experience is about applying the principles we are talking about in this book toward a customer's experience of buying something or receiving some service. It's about customer touch points in their user experience journey.

It usually involves a storytelling narrative of a UX experience distributed over time and often distributed over different locations. For example, the service experience of a patient going to a hospital for elective surgery could involve their arrival experience, checking in and going through lines, getting processed, etc.

The customer journey is an abstraction of the main path. Users also experience deviations, edge cases, breakdowns, pinch points, and problems that crop up. Much of the usage research data (Chapter 7), analysis (Chapter 8), and modeling (Chapter 9) captures the mechanical steps of this journey. Hopefully it can also capture the emotional impact felt along the way.

Example: Presurgery Hospital Visits

Consider this description of how one health organization in our area organized the workflow of its service to surgery patients.

It started with the family physician, where symptoms were explored, and a tentative diagnosis was made. The doctor decided that further tests were needed to properly diagnose the problem.

Next stop was the local hospital, where they took X-rays and performed an MRI, yielding a final diagnosis that surgery was required.

Next, the patient went to the hospital in the nearest large city, where the surgery was to occur. To get there, the patient had to use driving directions received in email. Upon arrival, there were a rather complex set of parking directions and walking and entrance directions. The patient was then processed by a series of people who specialized in various preadmission and preparation activities. And on a later date, there was a preop appointment.

Surgery was easy for the patient, no instruction necessary. Postsurgical care, however, required a sequence of prescriptions and trips to the pharmacy to fill them, and phone calls to surgical staff at the hospital with questions about recovery. Several follow-up appointments were required with the surgeon, tapering off to follow-up appointments with family physician.

1.8 WHY SHOULD WE CARE? THE BUSINESS CASE FOR UX

Ingenious by design; hassle-free connectivity

– On a Toshiba satellite receiver box

If you don't have a convincing business case for UX, you really have to conclude that, although it might be interesting, at the end of the day, UX is just an academic exercise.

1.8.1 Is the Fuss Over Usability Real?

In the past, this might have been a question usability practitioners had to face. UX is now recognized as a key job role in product development and as a key part of the development process. We don't have to defend UX and usability anymore because UX has penetrated most corporate and organizational development groups and projects. The success of "design thinking" (Brown, 2008) in business (the mindset of getting organizations to think like designers, applying design principles and practice to businesses and business processes) is one reason, and the rise of Apple is another.

1.8.2 No One Is Complaining and It Is Selling Like Hotcakes

It is easy to mistake certain positive signs as indicators that a product has no UX design problems. Managers often say, "This system has to be good; it's selling big time," or, "I'm not hearing any complaints about the user interface." Here it can be more difficult to make the case for UX to managers because their usual indicators of trouble with the product are not working. On closer inspection, it appears that a system might be selling well because it is the only one of its kind or the strength of its marketing department or advertising obscures the problems. And, sometimes, regardless of poor user experience, some users simply will not complain.

Here are some indicators to watch for:

- Your help desk is getting too many calls.
- Your users are accessing only a small portion of the overall functionality your system offers.

- There are a significant number of technical support calls about how to use a particular feature in the product.
- There are requests for features that already exist in the product.
- Your competitor's products are selling better even though your product has more features.
- Your developers or marketing are saying, "It might not be easy to use right off, but with training and practice, it will be a very intuitive design."

This book can help you address these issues.

1.8.3 Cost Justification

In the early days of usability, many people didn't believe in it, especially people in management. Usability engineers felt obligated to justify their existence and prove the value of their work. They did it by cost justifying usability (Bias & Mayhew, 2005; Mantei & Teorey, 1988), which involved examples of how much money a design improvement could save, given the time it took to perform a transaction involving the old design and the new design and the frequency by which the transaction occurred. That kind of cost-benefit analysis was good, as far as it went, but realistically, other factors were more compelling; customers and users were becoming more computer-sophisticated and less tolerant of poor interaction designs. And marketing people were becoming more aware of the demand for good design and getting into the act by demanding good design from their own organizations.

So, these days, the idea of cost-justifying UX design work is out of date. No one asks for cost justification on the software engineering side and the same is starting to be true on the UX side, too. Managers are realizing that it pays off in many ways to focus on getting a product or system right the first time. The result will be less total time, less money, and less negative impact on customer goodwill.

Example: An Anecdote From Consulting About the Importance of Getting the UX Right the First Time

A real-world, web-based, B2B software product company in San Francisco had a well-established customer base for their large complex suite of tools. At some point, they made major revisions to the product design as part of normal growth of functionality and market focus. Operating under at least what they perceived as extreme pressure to get it to the market in "Internet time," they released the new version too fast.

The concept was sound, but the design was not well thought through and the resulting poor usability led to a very bad user experience. Because their customers had invested heavily in their original product, they had a somewhat captive market. By and large, users were resilient and grumbled but adapted. However, the company's reputation for user experience was changing for the worse, and new customer business was lagging, finally forcing the company to go back and completely change the design for improved user experience. The immediate reaction from established customers and users was one of betrayal. They had invested the time and energy in adapting to the bad design and now the company changed it on them—again.

Although the new design was better, existing users were mostly concerned at this point about having a new learning curve blocking their productivity once again. This was a defining case of taking longer to do it right versus taking less time to do it wrong and then taking even longer to fix it. By not using an effective UX process, the company had quickly managed to alienate both their existing and future customer bases. The lesson: if you work in Internet time, you can also crash and burn in Internet time!

The Wheel: UX Processes, Lifecycles, Methods, and Techniques

2

Highlights

- The need for process.
- Basic process components for UX:
    - The UX design lifecycle, the idea of the Wheel.
    - Lifecycle activities.
    - UX design lifecycle process.
    - Lifecycle subactivities.
    - UX design methods.
    - UX design techniques.
- The fundamental UX lifecycle activities:
    - Understand Needs.
    - Design Solutions.
    - Prototype Candidates.
    - Evaluate UX.
- UX design techniques as life skills.
- Choosing and appropriating UX processes, methods, and techniques.

2.1 INTRODUCTION

2.1.1 Where Are We Heading?

Now that you are getting into the process-oriented chapters, it is important to remember that this is all about UX design, not at all about software. What we produce is a UX design, usually represented as a prototype. These designs will be realized in software by developers, software engineers, and programmers, using a corresponding software engineering lifecycle (Section 29.3).

2.1.2 The Need for Process

Long ago, software engineering folks recognized that having a process is necessary for developing complex systems, and it's something they invest enormous resources (Paulk, Curtis, Chrissis, & Weber, 1993) into defining, verifying, and following. On the UX side, Wixon and Whiteside were ahead of their time while at Digital Equipment Corp in the 1980s and put it this way (Whiteside & Wixon, 1985), as quoted in Macleod, Bowden, Bevan, and Curson (1997):

> *Building usability into a system requires more than knowledge of what is good. It requires more than an empirical method for discovering problems and solutions. It requires more than support from upper management and an openness on the part of all system developers. It even requires more than money and time. Building usability into a product requires an explicit engineering process. That engineering process is not logically different than any other engineering process. It involves empirical definition, specification of levels to be achieved, appropriate methods, early delivery of a functional system, and the willingness to change that system. Together these principles convert usability from a "last minute add on" to an integral part of product development. Only when usability engineering is as much part of software development as scheduling can we expect to regularly produce products in which usability is more than an advertising claim.*

Without guidance from a UX design process, practitioners are forced to make it up as they go along. If you have seen this happen in your projects, you are not alone. An approach without a process will be idiosyncratic. What practitioners do will be dictated and limited by their own experience. They will emphasize their own favorite ways to do things while other important process activities fall through the cracks. Finally, as Holtzblatt (1999) puts it, following a process for product development is a useful hedge against "the relentless drive of an organization to ship 'something' by a given date."

2.1.3 What Do You Get by Having a Process?

Process is a guiding structure. A process is a guiding structure that helps both novices and experts deal with the complex details of a project. A process enforces a systematic approach, bringing order to what could be very chaotic, especially within a large and complex project.

Process acts as a framework to ensure novice designers are on track to a quality product and on the path to becoming experts. For experts, a process acts as a checklist to make sure they do not miss any important aspects of the problem in the heat of productivity. It helps designers answer questions such as "Where are we now?" and "What can/should we do next?"

Process offers reliability and consistency. A documented process offers a way to use basically the same approach from project to project and from one team member to another.

Process provides scaffolding for learning. Design is all about learning. A process provides a fabric on which you can build a knowledge base of what you have learned, applying organizational memory from similar previous efforts to incorporate lessons learned in the past. This fabric, in turn, helps train novice designers in the ways of UX at that organization or in the discipline at large.

Process provides a shared conception of what you are doing. A documented process lets everyone know how a product or system (software plus UX) is being developed. Process also helps your team coordinate and communicate by externalizing the state of development for observation, measurement, analysis, and control—otherwise, communication among the project roles about what they are doing is difficult because they don't have a shared concept of what they should be doing.

Reliability, UX Evaluation

Refers to the repeatability of a UX method or technique from one UX practitioner to another and from one time to another for the same practitioner. Section 21.2.5.2.

2.2 THE BASIC PROCESS COMPONENTS FOR UX

2.2.1 UX Design Lifecycle

A lifecycle is just what it says: *It's a cycle of the life of a UX design, from inception to deployment and beyond.*

2.2.2 UX Lifecycle Activities

Lifecycle activities are the high-level things you do during a lifecycle (Fig. 2-1):

- Understand Needs (of users).
- Design Solutions.
- Prototype Candidates (for promising designs).
- Evaluate UX.

In Section 2.3, we'll follow up on these fundamental lifecycle activities in more detail.

2.2.3 UX Design Lifecycle Process

A UX lifecycle process is a representation of how you put the lifecycle activities together in a sequence over time and how the lifecycle activities—the boxes of Fig. 2-1—are connected in the flow of the process, usually represented in the form of a flow

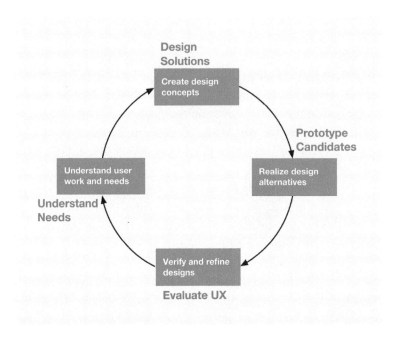

Fig. 2-1

The basic UX design lifecycle process in terms of elemental lifecycle activities.

chart diagram. Fine distinctions are unnecessary here, so we use the terms "process," "lifecycle," and "lifecycle process" more or less interchangeably.

2.2.4 The Wheel: A Model of the UX Lifecycle

If we expand this abstract cycle a bit to include feedback and iteration, we get a kind of UX lifecycle template of Fig. 2-2, which, as an analogy, we call "the Wheel." This is because it goes around in circles, and with each rotation it brings you closer to your destination.

This basic picture is the blueprint for the process common to almost any kind of design; it applies whether the design scope is just a small piece (chunk) of a product/system or the whole system.

2.2.5 Lifecycle Subactivities

Each lifecycle activity is substantial enough to be described in terms of its own set of subactivities. *Lifecycle subactivities are the things you do during a single lifecycle activity.*

Example subactivities for the Understand Needs (Section 2.3.1) lifecycle activity include:

- Data elicitation.
- Data analysis.

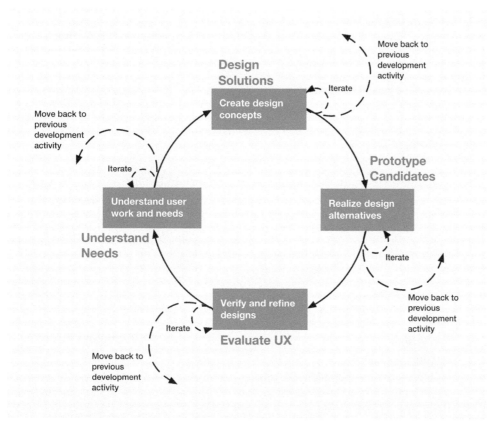

- Data modeling.
- Requirements extraction.

Fig. 2-2

The Wheel: A lifecycle template illustrating the process part of this book.

2.2.6 UX Methods

In our vocabulary, *a method is a way one can carry out the whole or part of a given lifecycle activity or subactivity.* An example of a method for the Understand Needs lifecycle activity is Usage Research (which we will describe in Part 2 of this book).

2.2.7 UX Techniques

Finally, in our usage, *a UX technique is a specific detailed practice you can use to perform a step within an activity, subactivity, or method.* A given UX design technique could be useful in a variety of different lifecycle activities and is not tied to a specific UX method. Examples of UX techniques for the data elicitation activity within the usage research UX method are:

- User interviews.
- Observation of users at work.

2.2.8 A Hierarchy of Terms

To distinguish the levels among descriptions of ways things can be done in UX design, we end up with a kind of hierarchy of terminology:

- Process, or UX lifecycle process.
- UX lifecycle activities and subactivities.
- UX methods.
- UX techniques.

These terms, despite their common appearance in the literature, are usually vague and ill-defined within the discipline. We have chosen to shade the definitions of these closely related terms to reflect the meanings we think are most commonly understood within this loose kind of hierarchical relationship, examples of which are shown in Table 2-1.

Waterfall Lifecycle Process

One of the earliest formal software engineering lifecycle processes; an ordered linear sequence of lifecycle activities, each of which flowed into the next like a set of cascading tiers of a waterfall. Section 4.2.

2.3 THE FUNDAMENTAL UX LIFECYCLE ACTIVITIES

In this section, we look more in depth at the individual UX design lifecycle activities and subactivities. Much of this book is about these topics.

The four basic UX lifecycle activities of Figs. 2-1 and 2-2 are:

- **Understand Needs**, to understand users, work practice, usage, the subject-matter domain, and, ultimately, needs for the design.
- **Design Solutions**, to create designs as solutions.
- **Prototype Candidates** (of promising solutions) to realize and envision promising design candidates.
- **Evaluate UX**, to verify and refine designs with respect to the user experience they afford.

Table 2-1

Informal hierarchy of process, methods, and techniques with simple examples

Lifecycle process	Traditional waterfall process (Section 4.2)
Lifecycle activity	Understand Needs (Part 2)
Subactivity	Elicit usage information (Chapter 7), analyze usage information (Chapter 8), model system or product usage (Chapter 9), codify needs (Chapter 10)
Method	Usage research, surveys, and competitive analyses (for elicit information subactivity); usage research analysis (for analyze information subactivity); flow, sequence, task models (for model usage subactivity); formal requirements (for codify needs subactivity)
Technique	Interviews, observations, affinity diagramming, etc.

For a given iteration, each box of the figure represents a method for carrying out the corresponding lifecycle activity. The choice of which method is to be used depends on the design situation (Section 2.5).

The depiction of UX lifecycle activities in distinct boxes is a convenient way to highlight each activity for discussion and for mapping to chapters in this book. In practice, however, these activities do not have such clear-cut boundaries; there can be significant intertwining and overlap (Section 5.2).

2.3.1 The Understand Needs UX Lifecycle Activity

The Understand Needs lifecycle activity is used to understand the business domain, users, work practice, usage, and the overall subject-matter domain. The most popular method is some variation of usage research and the most rigorous version includes these subactivities, each of which is detailed within its own chapter:

- Data elicitation (Chapter 7): Interview and observe users at work and gather data about work practice, users, usage, and needs.
- Data analysis (Chapter 8): Distill and organize usage research data.
- Data modeling (Chapter 9): Create representations of user characteristics, information flow, tasks, and work environments (for collaboration, sharing, archival, rehearsal, immersion).
- Requirements extraction (Chapter 10): Codify needs and requirements.

In Fig. 2-3, we illustrate the data elicitation subactivity as it is done with possible methods and techniques.

2.3.2 The Design Solutions UX Lifecycle Activity

Design Solutions is perhaps the most important lifecycle activity and the one with the broadest purview. Typical subactivities of this activity change dramatically over time as the project and the product evolve and mature through these basic "stages" (Fig. 2-4):

- **Generative design:** Ideation and sketching to create design ideas (Chapter 14), low-fidelity prototyping (Chapter 20), and critiquing for design exploration (Section 14.4).
- **Conceptual design:** Creating mental models, system models, storyboards, low fidelity prototypes of conceptual design candidates (Chapter 15).
- **Intermediate design:** Developing ecological, interaction, emotional design plans for most promising candidates (Chapters 16, 17, and 18), creating illustrated scenarios, wireframes, medium fidelity mockups of design forerunners, and identifying design tradeoffs to compare design candidates.

Usage Research

A method for performing the Understand Needs UX lifecycle activity in which users are interviewed and observed in their work context. Pertaining to gathering detailed descriptions of work domain knowledge and existing work practice for the purpose of understanding work activities and user needs to inform design to support the work practice. (Section 7.2).

Immersion

A form of deep thought and analysis of the problem at hand—to "live" within the context of a problem and to make connections among the different aspects of it (Section 2.4.7).

Storyboard

A visual scenario in the form of a series of sketches or graphical clips, often annotated, in cartoon-like frames, illustrating the interplay between a user and an envisioned ecology or device (Section 17.4.1).

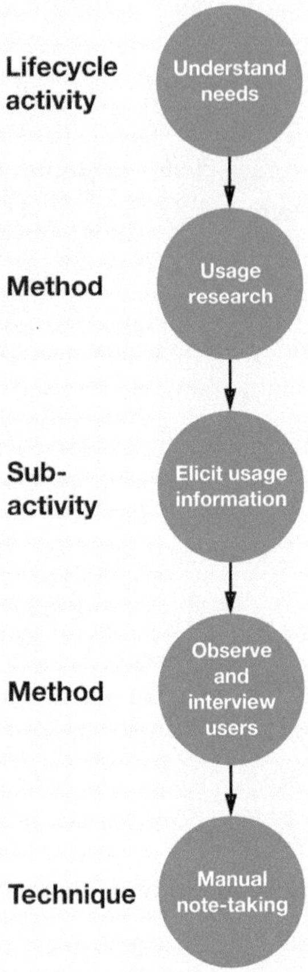

Fig. 2-3

The data elicitation subactivity of the Understand Needs lifecycle activity.

■ **Design production:** Specifying detailed design plans for implementation of the emerging design choice (Chapters 17 and 18).

The relative importance of each of these subactivities depends on the design situation, especially the kind of product or system being created.

2.3.2.1 Interpretation of "design": broad versus narrow

A point of potential confusion arises from ambiguity in the way the term "design" is used in UX and other fields. On one hand, the whole of Fig. 2-1 is called the UX design lifecycle. So, one might conclude that this whole diagram depicts the answer to: what is UX design?

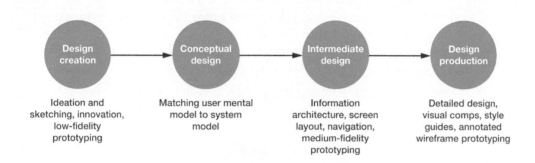

Fig. 2-4

Typical Design Solutions subactivities.

But the astute reader might note there is also a box at the top called Design Solutions within this lifecycle. Maybe that's what UX design is. In fact, both ways of using the term are useful, but we lack the vocabulary to distinguish them.

We sidestep the ambiguity trap by following the loose conventions of the field and using "design" with both meanings, hoping that context will provide clarity. If context doesn't disambiguate our meaning, we'll call out the specific meaning.

Broad interpretation. In the broad interpretation, "design" is the overall UX design lifecycle process. In simple terms, the UX process is a UX design process.

Narrow interpretation. In the narrow interpretation, "design" is just a single activity within the UX lifecycle and its subactivities are shown in Fig. 2-4. This narrower view also allows us to keep design separate from discussion of other lifecycle activities, such as Understand Needs or Evaluate UX. As a lifecycle activity on its own, design is important enough to have its own definitions, activities, theory, and practice.

The narrow view has led to misconceptions. The narrow view, considered alone, may have contributed to a long-held misunderstanding of the role of UX designers in projects. As Tim Brown (2008, p. 84) says, "Historically, design has been treated as a downstream step in the development process—the point where designers, who have played no earlier role in the substantive work of innovation, come along and put a beautiful wrapper around the idea. Not seeing design, especially UX design, in the broad view, project teams have been slow to invite designers into the whole process."

Different views of design have led to different views of prototyping. The different views at different levels of UX design offer a good way to distinguish the two kinds of prototyping and evaluation that Buxton (2007b) points out. Prototyping, evaluation, and iteration for getting the *right design* is part of the narrow view within the design creation subactivity. Getting the *design right* is the goal of prototyping, evaluation, and iteration within the broader overall UX lifecycle process. In the narrow context, prototyping is used within the design-creation subactivity as sketching and rapid low-fidelity prototypes, while higher-fidelity prototypes occur in the subactivity for the Prototype Candidates activity in the overall UX design lifecycle.

2.3.3 The Prototype Candidates UX Lifecycle Activity

Here, prototyping is a full-fledged lifecycle activity to realize and envision promising design candidates. The main subactivity is to create representations of design to required fidelity in the form of:

- Paper prototypes.
- Wireframes and wireflows.
- Click-through wireframe prototypes.
- Physical prototypes.

Like sketching, prototype building is usually done in parallel with, and in conjunction with, design; a prototype is an extension of the idea of a sketch. As designs evolve in designers' minds, they produce various kinds of prototypes as external design representations. Because prototypes are made for many different purposes, there are many kinds of prototypes, each with its own methods and techniques, as discussed in Chapter 20.

Prototypes are made at many different levels of fidelity, including low fidelity (especially paper prototypes such as printouts of static wireframes, for design exploration and early design reviews), medium fidelity (such as click-through wireframe prototypes), and high fidelity (programmed functional prototypes), and "visual comps" for pixel-perfect look and feel.

2.3.4 The Evaluate UX Lifecycle Activity

This activity is about verifying and refining the UX design to ensure we are getting the design right. Subactivities and possible alternative methods for the Evaluate UX activity to assess, verify, and refine designs might include:

- **Collect evaluation data**: Evaluate designs with empirical or analytic methods to simulate or understand actual usage and produce evaluation data.
- **Analyze evaluation data** (for identifying critical incidents, root causes).
- **Propose redesign solutions**.
- **Report results**.

Methods abound for doing the activities and subactivities of UX evaluation. From lightweight and rapid to thorough and laborious, from full empirical studies to quick and dirty inspections, depending on the design situation. Also, there are different methods and techniques for evaluating the different components of UX: usability, usefulness, emotional impact, and meaningfulness. These will be covered in detail in Part 5.

2.4 UX DESIGN TECHNIQUES AS LIFE SKILLS

In the context of this book, UX techniques are used in UX design situations. Because these techniques are also used for problem-solving in our everyday lives, we also think of them as *life skills*—basic generic skills for solving problems, helping designers and nondesigners thrive as human beings.

In addition, some techniques appearing in our process chapters are very specific to UX processes. Here are just a few examples:

- Card sorting (Section 8.6.1): A technique for organizing data collected, for example, in usage research or in UX evaluation so you can understand and make sense of them.
- Think-aloud: A data collection technique used within the lab-based evaluation method for the Evaluate UX lifecycle activity where participants are prompted to verbalize their thoughts and plans as they interact with a design prototype or system.
- Note taking: A technique for gathering raw user data in the *elicit information* subactivity (Chapter 7) of the Understand Needs lifecycle activity that includes variations such as audio recording, video recording, hand written notes, and notes typed on a laptop.

There are many UX design techniques out there and more are being described in the literature and used in practice over time (Martin & Hanington, 2012).

Here we describe the most important techniques, viewed as generic skills, according to our experience as researchers and practitioners in this field. Most should seem familiar because you will have encountered them or used them in other contexts. Here you can think of them as a kind of preview of things that will come up in later chapters.

2.4.1 Observation

Observation *is the practice of witnessing an ongoing activity with the objective of understanding underlying phenomenon.* Things to look for include exceptions, surprises, generalities, patterns, workflows, sequencing, what works and what doesn't, problems and barriers, and how people react to problems (or if they do). Observation provides the inputs for reasoning and deduction, but the ability to observe effectively can be elusive.

Inspection (UX)

An analytical evaluation method in which a UX expert evaluates an interaction design by looking at it or trying it out, sometimes in the context of a set of abstracted design guidelines. Expert evaluators are both participant surrogates and observers, asking themselves questions about what would cause users problems and giving an expert opinion predicting UX problems. Section 25.4.

It can take practice to develop the skill to observe. UX professionals have to train themselves to know when they are seeing something important and not let it slip away because it doesn't register. As George Perkins Marsh (1864, p. 10) said (and Sherlock Holmes persistently demonstrated), "Sight is a faculty; [but] seeing is an art."

Example: Observation of a Car Wash Workflow

Here is an example of the observation technique in a real-life setting, an example about observing a car wash workflow problem. On a recent trip to Buster's Auto Spa, our local car wash, I had to sit in line almost half an hour to get into the car wash. I guess most people would read the paper or listen to music to pass the time. But, being blessed/cursed with UX designer skills, I was curious about the cause of the delay.

In Fig. 2-5, we show a simplified sketch of the entrance to the car wash, pretty much like the entrance to any car wash. Note that this is a practical example of at least two other techniques, abstraction (next section) and sketching (Section 2.4.9).

Most of the time the car wash works well, but occasionally it has a work flow problem. When a customer wants the interior of the car cleaned, the attendants use a large vacuum cleaner mounted in a fixed location at the entrance.

Fig. 2-5

Entrance to Buster's Auto Spa.

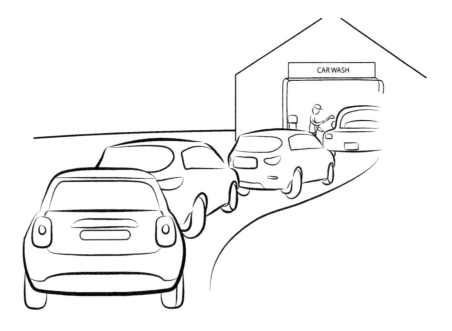

Vacuuming can take 10 minutes, during which time no cars are moving through the car wash—bad for the car wash company and bad for customers who have to wait in line behind the car being vacuumed. Customer waiting is especially bad because getting your car washed is something you usually do on the way to something else. Further, the narrow lane leading up to the entrance makes it almost impossible for customers to bail. Of course, I began to think about different designs of the facility that would solve the problem. What would you recommend?

Exercise 2.1: Make Some Deeper Observations

Your first exercise is here. Active learning means learning by doing. The best way to learn the processes described in this book is by doing the exercises. We have organized your participation in the process chapters at three levels: examples for you to follow in the text, a more or less parallel set of exercises to do with a group or on your own, and a set of extensively specified team project assignments (http://www.theuxbook.com/). We start you off here with an easy one.

Observe a customer service counter at Costco or similarly busy department store and prepare findings. Include descriptions of what is taking place, the flow, breakdowns, etc.

2.4.2 Abstraction

Abstraction is the practice of removing detail irrelevant to a given objective. "Abstraction is considered to be a key skill underlying most activities in computer science (CS) and software engineering (SE)" (Hazzan & Kramer, 2016). The result is a clearer picture of what is important without the distraction of extraneous matter. In other words, abstraction is the separation of the wheat from the chaff. Abstraction also entails the ability to generalize from an example. You have to be able to comprehend and extract the essence of a particular observed incident or phenomenon as an instance of a more general case or principle.

Consider the case of building a house where you as a designer (architect) are interviewing users (residents) of a house you are going to build. Different users mention different needs:

- User A: I would like to have a fan in the kitchen to clear any cooking smells.
- User B: I like to open my windows to the study and let in fresh air.
- User C: I do a lot of gluing in my workshop and need to have large windows and doors so the chemical smells don't overwhelm me.

All these specific instances can be abstracted under a generic idea of ventilation for the house that will lead to a design that solves all the individual problems in the list

2.4.3 Note Taking

Note taking is the practice of efficiently capturing descriptions of observations. It includes a set of techniques for qualitative data collection.

Techniques for note taking include making hand written notes, typing notes on a laptop, recording the essence on audio, or recording on video. However you do it, note taking should be done as an almost subconscious activity without distracting your cognitive processes from the observation activity. This usually means using the simplest means possible, like hand written notes or notes typed on a laptop. I recorded my notes about the car wash problem on a pocket digital audio recorder that I have with me always and transcribed them when I got home.

To be efficient, you must apply abstraction during note taking to capture the essential points while keeping the verbiage to a minimum. Notes can include sketches and/or models, analogies, or any other descriptive mechanism, bringing additional techniques into the mix.

2.4.4 Data/Idea Organization

Data organization is the practice of sorting data by category to make raw data understandable. Techniques for data organization include:

- Card sorting.
- Affinity diagrams.
- Mind-mapping: "A mind map is a diagram used to visually organize information. A mind map is often created around a single concept, drawn as an image in the center of a blank landscape page, to which associated representations of ideas such as images, words and parts of words are added. Major ideas are connected directly to the central concept, and other ideas branch out from those."[1]
- Concept mapping: "A concept map or conceptual diagram is a diagram that depicts suggested relationships between concepts. It is a graphical tool that instructional designers, engineers, technical writers, and others use to organize and structure knowledge."[2]

---

[1]https://en.wikipedia.org/wiki/Mind_map
[2]https://en.wikipedia.org/wiki/Concept_map

Card sorting is commonly used to organize menu structures in desktop applications. Designers list all the actions the system should support and each action is printed on a card. Users are then asked to organize them into groups. Affinity diagrams, hierarchical schemes for organizing larger sets of data, will be covered in detail in Chapter 8. Mind-mapping and concept-mapping are techniques used to externalize ideas and data that are loosely structured and connected.

2.4.5 Modeling

Modeling is the practice of representing complex and abstract phenomenon along particular dimensions to simplify and aid understanding. It is a way to explain or categorize aspects of the problem space.

Modeling is a specific kind of abstraction, usually to identify and represent objects, relationships, actions, operations, variables, and dependencies. Modeling is a way to organize and present information for deeper understanding. It's a way to draw generalizations and relationships from raw data.

As an example of modeling as a life skill, consider the personal research you do before buying a car. You will encounter all kinds of information about cars. In order to compare one car against another, you need to organize this information with some kind of model. Your model might include dimensions for consideration, which might be style, aesthetics, and technical specifications. Under styles, you might consider convertibles, SUVs, and sedans. Under aesthetics, you might consider body shapes, aerodynamic appearance, and colors available. Under technical specifications you might consider cost, MPG, horsepower, torque, and all-wheel drive versus front-wheel drive.

2.4.6 Storytelling

Storytelling is the practice of using narrative to explain aspects of a phenomenon or design with the objective of immersing the audience in the phenomenon.

Storytelling is a technique often used in the field of advertising. It can be more compelling to tell stories of people who use a product and who get pleasure and/or utility from it in their lives, than just to list advantages of the product.

Storytelling is also a good life skill that can be used in a wide variety of situations. A real estate agent telling the story of a house, when it was constructed, who lived there before, and who lives there now is more compelling than just talking about square footage and other features. The stories enable us to envision how we might live in this house and make our own memories there.

A more practical and useful example for the readers of this book comes from what we've noticed in our years of experience doing job interviews with aspiring UX designers and researchers. We noticed that job candidates who resorted to storytelling when they introduced themselves or when they did design portfolio walkthroughs were always more interesting and relatable. Storytelling helped these candidates communicate the context of a project, including the design brief, the challenge, the politics and the culture in a rich and engaging way. In contrast, candidates who did a "presentation" of their portfolio one design slide at a time were not as effective because there was no glue to put together the disconnected design snapshots in each slide into a narrative we could relate to.

2.4.7 Immersion

Immersion is a form of deep thought and analysis of the problem at hand—to "live" within the context of a problem and to make connections among the different aspects of it.

Immersion is about surrounding yourself in your UX work area (see UX design studio in Section 5.3) with the artifacts of creative design (posters, notes, sketches, photos, diagrams, quotations, goal statements) as in a war room. You close yourself off from outside distractions and everything you see acts as a kind of cognitive scaffolding and a catalyst that helps spawn design ideas.

The artifacts act as stimuli that trigger framings and bring to the surface connections and relationships. Everything you see acts as a kind of cognitive scaffolding and a catalyst that help spawn ideas.

Consider this example of immersion in a non-UX setting. When a police detective is trying to solve a difficult crime, she might isolate herself in a "war room" set apart from other distractions of the job or its surroundings. She will become steeped in the problem and surround herself with artifacts, such as photos and sketches of the crime scene, police and witness reports. She might also post a timeline on the wall (a kind of flow model of how things unfolded) along with sketches of the life stories of people involved. She studies the problem so intensely that she "becomes" the perpetrator.

Finally, although much of your immersion will necessarily occur in your UX studio, immersion on-site (where the system you are building will be used) can be an effective supplemental immersion space for analysis and design (Schleicher, Jones, & Kachur, 2010).

Framing

The practice of posing a problem within a particular perspective based on a pattern or theme that structures the problem and highlights the aspects you will explore (Section 2.4.10).

2.4.8 Brainstorming

Brainstorming *is the practice of interactive group discussion for exploring different ideas, problems, and solutions:*

- Must be done as a group activity. Each person's inputs and discussion stimulates, triggers thoughts, and inspires the others.
- Is a major skill in the Design Solutions lifecycle activity to highlight different perspectives and generate different framings of a phenomenon or a problem.
- Can be used in the Evaluate UX lifecycle activity to create solutions to identified UX problems.
- Can be used in any situation where the problem is open ended. For example, who are potential users of this system? Where can we find participants for evaluation?

More about brainstorming as part of ideation, sketching, and critiquing in UX design can be found in Chapter 14 on generative design.

2.4.9 Sketching and Drawing

Sketching *in UX is the practice of drawing simple pictures and diagrams depicting the essence of problems and solutions.*

It is a way to externalize analysis and exploration of objects, their relationships, and an emerging understanding of the problems and solutions. The most important point about sketching is that it is not about art or aesthetics. It's about communication of ideas. So, don't worry if your sketches are not perfectly proportioned and artistic. See Section 14.3.1.1 for a description of how sketching is used as an integral part of generative design.

A sketch is a kind of prototype. It uses an abstract representation, highlighting the salient features to aid visualization. Sketching actually helps your thinking by the embodiment of engaging the hand-eye connection to cognition in the brain (Graves, 2012). This can boost cognition in the creative act (Section 14.3.1.3). Sketching must always occur with ideation. As Buxton (2007b) says, "If you are doing design, you are sketching."

Sketching is a life skill with wide range of applications in everyday life. Reorganizing furniture in your home? First make a sketch of the envisioned configuration or layout. Substantiate it with a model of your workflows for that room and immerse yourself in the usage context of that room.

2.4.10 Framing and Reframing

Framing and reframing *comprise the practice of posing a problem within a particular perspective.*

Framing builds a perspective that structures the problem and highlights the aspects you will explore. A framing is a pattern or a particular theme from which we view everything as we are in the process of finding solutions. In the specific context of a framing we can ask "what if?" and "why don't we do this?" Framings are reusable and gain strength with reuse.

To create a framing, you must go back to the basic elements of the problem, the underlying abstract phenomenon, identify what is really going on, the essence of the problem, and ignore all the rest as noise. Because framing is a specific kind of brainstorming, it is best done as a team activity.

Nigel Cross (2001) describes a book by Kees Dorst (2015) as providing "a practical new approach to design-led innovation. His frame creation approach enables the addressing of difficult and wicked problems through the use of design thinking."

Here is a non-UX example of how different framings lead to different solutions in any kind of problem solving in almost any setting. For example, suppose you have occasional flooding of fields along the flood plains of a river near a town. If you frame it as a problem of too much water coming down the river, it will lead you to focus on design solutions in the form of dams or other ways to control the flow into the valley. Alternatively, if you frame it as a problem of the river overflowing its banks, you might turn to a system of dikes to keep the water within the banks. Or, if you frame it as a natural occurrence to work with instead of fighting against, you will require landowners to build homes only above the flood plain.

Coming back to the problem at Buster's Auto Spa, we can see it as a practical example of framing. Clearly, designers of the car wash had framed the design mainly in terms of the simplicity of only the normal ("happy path") flow. However, careful observation of the workflow in other car washes might have led them to a problem framing that included the case of vacuuming the interior and a design that accommodated that operation in a different space that didn't block the normal flow.

2.4.11 Reasoning and Deduction

Reasoning and deduction *is a long-standing practice of applying logic to process observed facts, fit them together, and arrive at a logical conclusion.*

The observations are the predicates of the logic and the conclusions are deductions. Reasoning and deduction are a way of synthesizing new facts through the use of logic as applied to existing facts.

In UX, reasoning and deduction are often used to arrive at user needs based on usage research, design features based on needs, tradeoffs and constraints based on insights from the work domain. We will see examples of this in Chapter 10 where we deduce system requirements from usage data.

2.4.12 Prototyping and Envisioning

Prototyping *is the practice of producing or building a model or mockup of a design that can be manipulated and used at some level to manifest or simulate a user experience, which can be evaluated.*

Prototyping extends the idea of sketching. As the main output of UX design, a prototype is a platform for envisioning and evaluating efficacy of a design as a problem solution. See Chapter 20 for much more about prototyping.

2.4.13 Critical Thinking

Critical thinking *is the practice of "objective analysis of facts to form a judgment. The subject is complex, and there are several different definitions which generally include the rational, skeptical, unbiased analysis or evaluation of factual evidence."*[3]

Critical thinking is the essential core of UX evaluation for testing, reviewing, diagnosing, verifying, or validating a candidate design solution. This kind of evaluation requires skills for observation, abstraction, data collection, note taking, and reasoning and deduction, plus the ability to make judgements, rankings, and ratings.

See Part 5 for much more about UX evaluation.

2.4.14 Iteration

Iteration *is the practice of repeating a cycle of analysis, design, prototyping, and evaluation to refine an understanding of a concept or to improve a design as a problem solution.*

A simple non-UX example of iteration is seen in the rereading and reediting of a paper or report that an author might do before submitting it.

2.4.15 UX Techniques Are Used in Combination

When used in UX design or as life skills, these techniques are usually combined within methods. For example, a police detective must combine skills to solve crimes, including observation, note taking, storytelling, immersion, brainstorming, sketching, framing, and reasoning and deduction.

---

[3]https://en.wikipedia.org/wiki/Critical_thinking

We will have more to say about these techniques wherever we use them in the later process chapters, especially in the ideation, sketching, and critiquing of Chapter 14.

2.5 CHOOSING UX PROCESSES, METHODS, AND TECHNIQUES

Within any given project, you have to choose UX processes, methods, and techniques for the UX lifecycle activities and subactivities.

2.5.1 The UX Lifecycle Process Choice

The UX lifecycle process choice is made at the highest level. The way things have worked out in the world has had a large influence on that choice. The software engineering (SE) world has adopted an agile lifecycle process almost universally and we, in UX, are making the same choice of an agile lifecycle process, to keep pace with our SE project partners. As in SE, an agile UX process is one in which you manage change during the process by delivering UX designs in small chunks.

While much of this book can apply to nonagile UX lifecycle processes, we intend this book to be about agile UX. But, as we will soon see, that can mean many things depending on multiple factors and where you are in the overall process. In Chapters 4 and 29, we will tell you the full story of what this means in practice.

2.5.2 The Idea of Appropriating Methods and Techniques

There is an abundance of UX design methods. "HCI is awash in methods and the theories that underlie them" (Harrison, Back, & Tatar, 2006). So, how can you make sense of what you need for your project?

The usual practice in a book like this, or in a course on UX design, is for the author or instructor to take a method-oriented approach to lay out his or her favorite UX methods and proceed to show why that is *the* way to do UX design. In this edition, we think it makes more sense to start with the idea of a design situation, especially the product or system being designed, and talk about how to match it by appropriating an approach that can achieve it, based on goals and expected outcomes.

This idea of appropriating design methods comes from Harrison and Tatar (2011) and it simply means that you take "standard" methods you have learned

---

Agile Lifecycle Process

A small-scope lifecycle process (UX or SE) in which all lifecycle activities are performed for one feature of the product or system, and then the lifecycle is repeated for the next feature. An agile process is driven by needs formulated as user stories of capabilities instead of abstract system requirements and is characterized by small and fast deliveries of releases to get early usage-based feedback. Section 4.3.

about and modify and adapt them to your specific design situations, making them your own methods (appropriating them).

The Harrison and Tatar "method of methods" idea is so simple on one level that it can easily get lost in the voluminous literature on UX design methods. But their method of methods idea is also powerful and important, especially for teaching design, both to new students and to experienced practitioners.

2.5.2.1 Design situations: Dependencies that govern lifecycle activity, method, and technique choices

Harrison and Tatar (2011) describe a **design situation** as *the circumstances under which a design method will be applied and appropriated.* "Design situation" is a good umbrella term because it includes the target product or system and the project and all of its context, including the type of product or system, the client, the users, the market, the subject-matter domain and its complexity plus the designer's familiarity with it, and the project team and their capabilities, skills, and experience.

2.5.2.2 Choosing methods and techniques

Whenever you need to design for a lifecycle activity, you will have a set of methods and techniques to choose from. For example, suppose you need to choose a method to carry out the Understand Needs lifecycle activity. As an example, one of the most popular of such methods is called usage research, a method for interviewing and observing real users to understand their work activity (Part 2 of this book).

Early method and technique choices constrain later ones. Earlier choices of methods and techniques can constrain later choices by suggesting, eliminating, or dictating appropriate methods and techniques for subsequent choices. For example, methods and techniques used for data analysis in a given situation will depend on what kind of data you have, and how the data were collected.

2.5.2.3 Mapping project parameters to lifecycle activity, method, and technique choices

To summarize, in Fig. 2-6 we show the mapping from project parameters to possible choices of UX methods. While there are some general guidelines for making these mapping choices, fine-tuning is the job of project teams, especially the project manager or product owner (the person responsible for success of the product and for pursuing business goals, Section 5.4.1.5). Much of it is intuitive and straightforward.

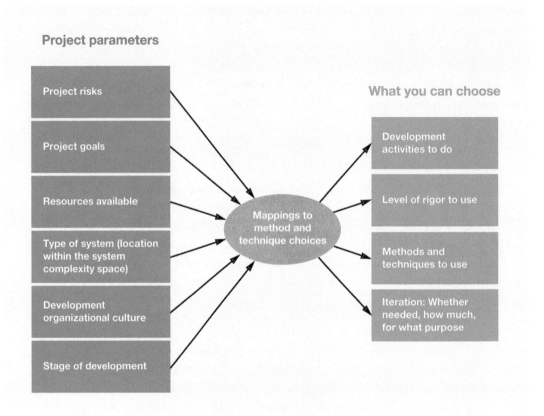

Fig. 2-6

Mapping project parameters to agile UX method choices.

Scope, Rigor, Complexity, and Project Perspectives

3

- The need for rigor in a project.
- Complexity and risk aversion as influences on the need for rigor.
- Scope of delivery.

3.1 INTRODUCTION

We are going to get into UX lifecycle activities soon, but first let's discuss a few parameters that define a design situation and the impact they have on lifecycle choices.

3.1.1 Rigor and Scope: Project Parameters that Determine Process Choices

In any design situation, you need to make choices. Even within an agile UX process, no one UX lifecycle activity or method is one size fits all. Your job is to adopt and adapt UX lifecycle activities, methods, and techniques to specific project conditions (Section 2.5.2). Most of the high-level process choices hinge on two major determiners, rigor and scope.

3.2 RIGOR IN A UX METHOD OR PROCESS

3.2.1 What Is Rigor?

The rigor of a UX design lifecycle activity, method, or technique is determined by the degree of formality, thoroughness, precision, and accuracy with which you perform all the steps. It is also about how meticulously you maintain and document completeness and purity of data—especially usage research and UX evaluation data—collected.

Completeness. Completeness entails thoroughness of methods, which means covering every step in full. Completeness also applies to the usage research and evaluation data. This attention to detail helps designers touch all the bases and fill in all the blanks so that no functions or features are forgotten.

Purity. Purity means being as accurate as possible in your data; in particular, it involves not allowing new spurious "data" to creep in. For example, for high data purity, designer insights or conjectures should be tagged with metadata, identifying and distinguishing them from actual user input.

We refer to the methods for maintaining this completeness and purity of data as rigorous methods.

Example: Building a House: A Possible Need for Rigor

Using an example of house building, imagine the designer (architect) capturing a data item during data elicitation in the predesign Understand Needs activity (Section 2.3.1). In this example, that translates to the architect talking with the potential homeowner, where he learns that the owner wants a whole-house backup generator next to the house.

Later, as the architect in his studio becomes immersed in the design situation to understand the requirements and constraints for the building, he realizes the need to check on possible constraints as to the location of the generator. On a visit to the county building inspector's office, he captures the necessary information regarding the minimum distance between a backup house generator and both the outer edge of the house and the gas main for the house.

In a low-rigor approach, this constraint would just be captured as a simple note or even just kept in the designer's head as "the generator needs to be at least four feet from the gas main and at least four feet from the outer wall of the house." In a rigorous approach, the same constraint would be captured with all the relevant metadata (e.g., identifying the applicable safety code or local building conventions) in a structure that makes it easy to query and trace back, if necessary. It could be something along the lines of:

> Type: External constraint
> Description: Any external device with an engine, such as a backup generator, shall be placed at least four feet from all structures attached to the foundation of the house, including decks, porches, awnings, and uncovered decks.
> Source: Middleburg County building code VT-1872, page 42.
> Verified by: Ms. Jane Designer
> Date noted: June 13, 2016

This kind of rigor due to specificity and completeness is not always necessary during the building of a small house, but it could be important (or maybe even required by law) in a commercial building project.

3.2.2 Complexity as an Influence on the Need for Rigor

3.2.2.1 The system complexity space

One big reason you can't define one set of methods for designing all systems is that there is a spectrum of system and product types with a broad range of risk versus needs for rigor in lifecycle activities and methods. In this and the next few sections, we look at some possibilities within this spectrum.

In Fig. 3-1, we show a system complexity space defined by the dimensions of interaction complexity and domain complexity (defined in the next two sections). While there undoubtedly are other ways to partition the space, this approach serves our purpose.

3.2.2.2 Interaction complexity

Interaction complexity, represented on the vertical axis, is about the intricacy or elaborateness of user actions, including the difficulty of cognitive actions, necessary to accomplish tasks with the system.

Low interaction complexity usually corresponds to systems that support smaller tasks that are generally easy to do, such as ordering flowers from a website. High interaction complexity is usually associated with larger and more difficult tasks, often requiring special skills or training, such as manipulating a color image with Adobe Photoshop (a high-functionality software application for managing and processing large collections of images and photographs).

3.2.2.3 Domain complexity

On the horizontal axis, we show work domain complexity, which is about the degree of intricacy and the technical, or possibly esoteric, nature of the corresponding field of work. Convoluted and elaborate mechanisms for how parts of the system work and communicate within the ecology of the system contribute to domain complexity.

User work in domain-complex systems is often mediated and collaborative, with numerous "hand offs" in a complicated workflow containing multiple dependencies and communication channels, along with compliance rules, regulations, and exceptions in the way work cases are handled. Examples of high work-domain complexity include systems for geological fault analysis for earthquake prediction, global weather forecasting, and complete healthcare systems.

Low work-domain complexity means that the way the system works within its ecology is relatively simple. Examples of low domain complexity include that

System complexity space

A two-dimensional space defined by the dimensions of interaction complexity and domain complexity, depicting a spectrum of system and product types with a broad range of risk versus needs for rigor in lifecycle activities and methods (Section 3.2.2.1).

Ecology

In the setting of UX design, the ecology is the entire set of surrounding parts of the world, including networks, other users, devices, and information structures, with which a user, product, or system interacts (Section 16.2.1).

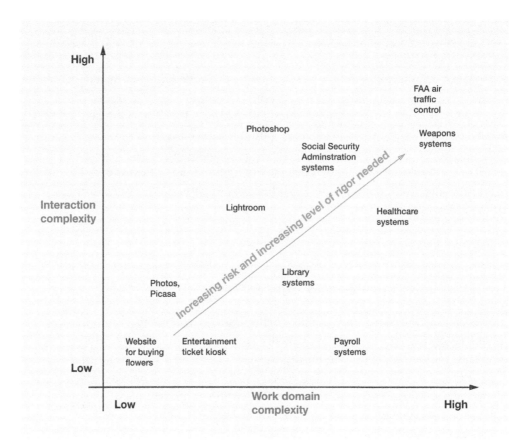

Fig. 3-1

The system complexity space: interaction complexity versus domain complexity.

same website for buying flowers and a simple personal calendar management application.

3.2.2.4 The system complexity space quadrants

Simple interaction, simple work domain. The simplest quadrant is in the lower left corner of Fig. 3-1, where both interaction and work domain are the least complex. This quadrant contains smaller websites, certain interactive applications, and many commercial products. Just because this is the simple-simple quadrant, however, does not mean that the products are overly simple; the products of this quadrant can still be sophisticated.

There is an abundance of relatively simple systems in the world. Some, but not all, commercial software products are domain-simple and interaction-simple, at least relative to large systems of other types. Again, the website for ordering flowers is a good example of this quadrant. Interaction is very simple; just one main task involving a few choices and the job is done. Work domain complexity is also relatively simple because it involves only one user at a time and the workflow is almost trivial. Many apps on mobile devices, a significant segment of the commercial product market, are simple-interaction and simple-domain.

Although emotional impact factors do not apply to every system or product in this quadrant, emotional impact can be very important here, especially with respect to factors such as aesthetics or fun or joy of use. The smartphone and the personal mp3 music player are good examples of commercial products in this quadrant that have emotional impact issues, including meaningfulness (emotional impact within long-term usage).

Because systems and commercial products in this quadrant have less complexity, they generally require less rigor.

Complex interaction, complex work domain. As you move all the way across the diagonal in Fig. 3-1, you reach the upper right quadrant where you find interaction-complex and domain-complex systems, which are usually large and complicated.

Serious systems. Serious systems live in the far upper right corner of the system complexity space. An example is an air traffic control system used to decide the landing orders for an incoming airliner. An air traffic control system has enormous domain and interaction complexity, with workflow and collaboration among a large number of work roles and user types. Another defining example for this quadrant is a large system for the Social Security Administration.

For large domain-complex systems, such as military weapons systems, you are most likely to encounter resistance to innovation. Radical designs are not always welcome; conformity can be thought more important. Users and operators, in some cases, commit operations to habit and perform tasks with learned behavior even if there are better ways. Work practice change must be approached with caution.

This sector of serious systems within the system complexity space usually has little, if anything, to do with emotional impact factors such as aesthetics, fun, or joy of use.

Enterprise systems. Among the kinds of systems one sees in the rest of this quadrant are the so-called enterprise systems, large information systems used within organizations that have typically been forgotten in discussions of usability and user experience. Gillham (2014) puts it this way: "Most big businesses globally are locked into some kind of enterprise technology. Unfortunately, such systems

Risk

The danger or possibility of things going wrong, of features or requirements being missed, or the result not meeting the needs of users; possibility of not accommodating legacy needs or not complying with legal or safety constraints (Section 3.2.4).

are not only fiendishly difficult to install and maintain, but often equally challenging for the workforce to use. When the stakes are so high, why is the user experience of enterprise systems so bad?"

The highest need for rigor. The domain-complex and interaction-complex quadrants are where you find the highest risks and, therefore, the highest need for rigor to manage risk. These project conditions include:

- When you have the greatest regulatory compliance requirements.
- When the importance of error avoidance in usage is highest (e.g., in mission-critical systems such as for air traffic control or for military weapons control).
- When you cannot risk getting these things wrong and the cost of failure is unacceptable.
- When you have a contractual obligation for high rigor.

Because of their sheer size and this need for rigorous processes, these systems are typically among the most difficult and expensive to design and develop.

Complex interaction, simple work domain. In the upper left quadrant of Fig. 3-1, one of the "in-between" quadrants, we see interaction-complex and domain-simple systems. It is typical of an interaction-complex system to have a large volume of functionality resulting in a large number and broad range of complex user tasks. The older-style digital watch (not a smart watch) is a lightweight but good example. Its interaction complexity often stems from a large variety of modal settings using overloaded and unlabeled push buttons. The domain, however, is still simple, being mainly about "what time is it?" Workflow is trivial; there is only one work role set within a simple system ecology.

Attention in this quadrant is needed for interaction design—myriad tasks, screen layouts, user actions, and even metaphors. Rigorous formative evaluation may be needed for the consistency and usability of the conceptual design and the detailed interaction design. The focus of modeling will be on tasks—task structure and task interaction models—and perhaps the artifact model, but not much attention will be given to work roles, workflow, or most of the other models of Chapter 9.

Artifact model

A representation showing how users employ, manipulate, and share key tangible objects (physical or electronic work practice artifacts) as part of the flow in their work practice (Section 9.8).

For simple work domains, regardless of interaction complexity, usage research rarely results in learning something new that can make a difference in informing design. So less rigor will suffice leading up to design creation. For design creation, however, complex interaction requires careful and systematic brainstorming, ideation, and sketching, plus iterative evaluation and refinement as well as attention to emotional impact factors.

Simple interaction, complex work domain. In the lower right quadrant of Fig. 3-1, the other "in-between" quadrant, we see interaction-simple and domain-complex systems. In this quadrant, user tasks are relatively simple and easy to understand, so less attention to task descriptions is needed. The key effort for users in this quadrant is understanding the domain and its often esoteric work practice. Designers need rigorous usage research to focus on conceptual design and easy-to-understand user models of how the system works. Once that is understood, the interaction is relatively straightforward for users. Tax preparation software for average households is a good example because the underlying domain is complex but the data entry into forms can be simplified to a step-by-step process.

Sometimes systems for managing libraries, shown in the middle of the work domain complexity scale near the bottom of Fig. 3-1 fall into the simple-interaction, complex-work-domain quadrant. Typical library systems have low interaction complexity because the range of tasks and activities for any one user is fairly circumscribed and straightforward and the complexity of any one user task is low. Therefore, for a library system, for example, you do not need to exercise much rigor in the modeling of tasks.

However, a full library system has considerable domain complexity. The work practice of library systems can be esoteric and most UX designers will not be knowledgeable in this work domain. For example, special training is needed to handle the surprisingly important and highly controlled small details in cataloging procedures. Therefore, a rigorous approach to usage research may be warranted.

Gradations within the system complexity space. Some systems or products clearly fall into one quadrant or the other, but other projects can have fuzzy quadrant boundaries. Websites, for example, can belong to multiple quadrants, depending on whether they are for an intranet system for a large organization, a very large e-commerce site, or just a small site for sharing photographs. Products such as a printer or a camera are low in domain complexity but can have medium interaction complexity.

Healthcare systems typically cross system complexity space quadrants. Some parts internal to a small doctor's office might be relatively simple. But large healthcare systems that integrate medical instrumentation, health record databases, and patient accounting have complex work domains. Similarly, machines in a patient's hospital room can have a fairly broad range of technical tasks and activities, giving them relatively high interaction complexity.

The healthcare domain is also saddled with more than its share of regulation, paperwork, and compliance issues, plus legal and ethical requirements—all of which lead to high work domain complexity and a high need for rigor in UX lifecycle activities and methods.

3.2.3 Domain Familiarity as an Influence on the Need for Rigor

Even if a domain is not complex in absolute terms, if it is unfamiliar to the UX designer, it will seem complex, at least at first. Familiarity with the target domain is part of the designer's cognitive scaffolding for understanding the design problem. The way to achieve this domain familiarity is by initially using UX methods with high rigor.

Our example of house building (Section 3.2.1) is in a domain that is at least somewhat familiar to us all. Now, consider a domain that is more specialized and esoteric, the domain of financial portfolio analytics and management. If the designer is not very familiar with this domain, there is a greater need for capturing as much detail from users and usage as possible so they can go back and refer to it for clarification or education.

In my (Pardha) practice in this domain, I often encountered unfamiliar terminology. Or, sometimes users from different portfolio management firms described different practices and philosophies on investment in different ways, making it more difficult for me to maintain a unified understanding of the domain. During usage research data collection sessions with clients, users, and subject matter experts (SMEs), in order to maintain rigor, it was often important to capture metadata such as who said what and where they worked because that detail was important for later analyses to contextualize what was said.

3.2.4 Risk Aversion Influences the Need for Rigor

Risk is the danger or possibility of things going wrong, of features or requirements being missed, or the result not meeting the needs of users; possibility of not accommodating legacy needs or not complying with legal or safety constraints.

As we hinted in Section 3.2.2.4, an important goal-related factor in choosing the level of rigor in the UX design lifecycle activities and methods is aversion to risk. There are cases where not getting the UX design right creates high risks, often because of requirements for things such as legacy accommodation, legal constraints, or safety concerns. *A legacy system is an old method, technology, computer system, or application program, of, relating to, or being a previous or outdated computer system with maintenance problems that date back possibly many years.*[1]

---

[1]https://en.wikipedia.org/wiki/Legacy_system

The less the tolerance for risks the more the need for rigor in the lifecycle activities, methods, and techniques. But of course, high rigor throughout the lifecycle process will add cost and time to complete.

3.2.4.1 The risk of data loss

The most significant data loss in the UX design process is a loss of completeness. For reasons of speed and economy, the data get condensed, summarized, and otherwise abbreviated. You can avoid data loss by recording (audio or video) every detail of user interviews and observations. But it is tedious and costly to transcribe the recordings and the result is a ton of text to wade through to separate the important stuff from all the noise and unimportant verbiage; it's almost never worth it.

So usage researchers often just take notes to summarize the main points to themselves. Although this technically introduces a loss of completeness, it doesn't necessarily reduce the quality or usefulness of the data. Raw data usually need a step of abstraction, anyway, to remove irrelevant detail and to highlight what is important. But you can take this abstraction too far. By being lazy or careless or not taking enough time, you start to lose data that could be important later in the overall process.

3.2.4.2 Risks associated with legal, safety, and compliance constraints

Systems such as air traffic control systems, healthcare and medical records systems, and financial systems have legal requirements with respect to public safety risks that must be taken very seriously. Designing a product for the financial industry requires a process that accounts for compliance to complex federal regulations built into the business process involved in using the product. Your lifecycle activities and methods need to incorporate sufficient rigor to ensure (and possibly even prove) that the system meets all those compliance checks.

3.2.5 The Stage of Development within Your Project as an Influence on the Need for Rigor

The stage of development within your project is another determiner of the need for rigor. All projects go through different "stages" over time. Regardless of method choices based on other project parameters, the appropriateness of a level of rigor and corresponding choices of UX methods and techniques for lifecycle activities will change as a project evolves through these stages of development. For example, early stages might demand a strong focus on rigorous usage research to obtain the most user, usage, and domain knowledge upfront.

Abstraction

The process of removing extraneous details of something and focusing on its irreducible constructs to identify what is really going on, ignoring everything else (Section 14.2.8.2).

But there might be very little emphasis on rigorous evaluation in early stages. Spending large resources on early evaluation could be a waste because the design is still fluctuating. So for early stages, it might be better to use lightweight, rapid, and frequent evaluation methods. As an example, to evaluate an early conceptual design you might choose a quick design review.

In later stages of evaluation, to refine a now-stable design, you might move to UX inspection of a low-fidelity prototype and eventually to the more rigorous lab-based testing using a higher-fidelity prototype, increasing the amount and quality of data you need to retain in each step. It takes more rigor to keep track of this extra data.

3.2.6 Project Resources: Budgets, Schedules, and/or Personnel Capabilities are Determiners of Rigor

High rigor costs money and takes time. Slim budgets and short schedules are practical realities that can constrain your lifecycle activity and method choices and restrict the level of rigor you are able to provide.

Another important kind of resource is person power. How many people do you have, what project team roles can they fill, and what UX skills, experience, and training do they bring to the project?

UX professionals with extensive experience and maturity are likely to need less of the formal aspects of rigorous methods, such as thorough usage research or detailed UX evaluation goals and targets. For these experienced UX professionals, following the process in detail does not add much to what they can accomplish using their already internalized knowledge and honed intuition.

3.2.7 Being Rapid in Lifecycle Activities, Methods, and Techniques

While some methods are inherently more rigorous than others (e.g., lab-based evaluation compared to inspection methods), it is important to note that any method can be performed across a range of rigor. Applying an evaluation method (or any method) with more rigor can achieve more complete and more accurate results, but will take more time and is more costly. Similarly, by taking shortcuts you can usually increase speed and reduce costs of almost any UX evaluation method, but at the price of reduced rigor.

3.2.7.1 Not every project needs rigorous UX methods

For many projects, certainly in the commercial product perspective and often in the enterprise system perspective, high rigor isn't necessary, isn't worth the cost, or simply isn't possible given limited project resources.

In response, less rigorous UX methods and techniques have evolved in the literature and practice that are faster and less expensive but still allow you to get good results from your effort and resources.

3.2.7.2 Rapid methods are a natural result

When higher rigor is not required, the point of working at a lower level of rigor is to reduce lifecycle cost and time. Most of the time you can be less rigorous by abbreviating the "standard" rigorous methods and techniques, which means taking shortcuts, skipping unnecessary steps, and maintaining only the most important data. Or you can use rapid alternative methods that are inherently less rigorous.

3.2.7.3 Over time our need for rigor has diminished

As another factor, UX practice has matured and we have gotten better at our craft. As a result, we don't need to be as rigorous and thorough in most common UX situations. The plodding and burdensome fully rigorous process has been abandoned as an outlier. A rare project that requires full rigor will come with specifications about what to do and how to achieve it. Now the "standard" method for each lifecycle activity is just a "regular" process, which is a combination of a practical middle-of-the road rigor and some obvious ways to be efficient.

3.2.7.4 Rapidness principle: Work as rapidly as you can

Regardless of other factors, you should always seek the fastest way to do things. The principle underlying all choices of lifecycle activities, methods, and techniques is: *Go as fast as you can, subject to constraints imposed by project goals and the need for rigor.* Ries (Adler, 2011) says it is a misconception that if you work slowly and deliberately, you will produce a better product and you'll be able to fix problems as you go. The agile approach to both UX and SE (software engineering) has proven this misconception wrong.

Being economical and lightweight is now a way of life for a designer and is part of the foundation of agile processes (see next section). Even when you need a rigorous approach, you should be just doing what comes naturally in making smart choices and not wasting time or resources needed to do things that won't really contribute to your final design. For example, an otherwise rigorous approach could be done without one or more of the types of models (Chapter 9) if they are not essential to the project.

3.3 SCOPE OF DELIVERY

Our use of the term "scope" refers to how the target system or product is "chunked" in each iteration or sprint for delivery for agile implementation. UX roles deliver their designs to the SE people in chunks of a given size and the SE role consumes the chunks of UX design as specifications for code, which it then implements and delivers as chunks of possibly some other size of functional software to clients and users.

In a large scope, chunks are composed of multiple features or even large portions of the system. In a small scope, synonymous with agility, chunks are usually comprised of one feature at a time. Even large and complex enterprise systems are being developed with small-scope approaches in agile software development these days. We, the UX designers, will always end up delivering our designs in chunks of a small scope within an agile UX process.

However, some early UX design work (for example, to establish the conceptual design) may require a larger scope. And, of course, a large scope does offer a nice structure for describing the UX lifecycle activities in this book.

Example: Large and Small Scope in Building a House

Here we return to that familiar setting, that of designing and building a house, to illustrate the trade offs between large and small scope in simple terms. By the time the full house is completed and delivered, a custom house designer should have addressed a range of user needs and issues, including:

- User lifestyle to be supported.
- User preferences, specifications, and requirements.
- Work flows of occupants.
- Zoning laws and other external constraints.
- Ecology of the house (the setting, the neighborhood).
- User/owner values (efficiency, greenness, footprint).
- Style (modern, colonial, Spanish).

Here's how scope plays out in terms of how you approach designing and building a house:

- Large scope: Design the whole house first and build it all before delivering it to the client.
- Small scope: Design one room (for example, the kitchen) first, build it, and deliver it to the client, and follow up with another room, say the living room, and so on, in a series of "increments" until the whole house is completed.

Large scope. Normally, in a large-scope approach, much of the construction is done in an "assembly line" manner for reasons of cost. The foundation people start and then the framing people do their thing. Then you bring in the electrician and he wires the whole house. Then you bring in the plumber and she installs plumbing in the whole house. Then you bring in the drywall person and he puts up all the interior walls, and so forth.

Small scope. For practical reasons, a small-scope approach is not used in house construction, but let's explore that possibility to see what the trade offs might be.

Suppose this house is being designed and built for an eccentric (and wealthy) software engineer and he wants to do an experiment to see if a small scope can work for house building, too. As in the case of software, there would have to be some infrastructure built first to support the incremental features to come. In software, this might be essential parts of the operating system and other software services that each feature would call on. In house building, this would be laying the foundation, framing in the skeleton, and establishment of infrastructure shared among rooms (e.g., main breaker box for electrical service). That's always done first, anyway.

Then the client (the adventuresome software engineer) would ask for "delivery" of a feature (for example, the kitchen) in two weeks. The electrical work, plumbing, drywall installation, woodwork, painting, and so on would be done for just the kitchen. The client would show up and possibly even use the kitchen to cook something and then give feedback, and you would certainly learn things that could be used on subsequent rooms.

Then you have to get all these people back to do their thing for the next room, increasing the cost and time delays substantially. It would also drive the contractor crazy. So, if you wanted to do this as an experiment, you would have to pay significantly more. Therefore, while a small-scope approach is effective and efficient in UX and software engineering, it is not an efficient way to build a house.

3.4 THE COMMERCIAL PRODUCT PERSPECTIVE AND THE ENTERPRISE SYSTEM PERSPECTIVE

Most of this chapter has been about process parameters such as rigor, scope, and complexity. Another factor that influences your UX design approach is whether it comes from a commercial product perspective or an enterprise system perspective. Obviously, it isn't appropriate to use the same method to design a smartphone as you would, say, an enormous corporate resource management system.

3.4.1 The Commercial Product Perspective

We use the term "commercial product perspective" (or "product perspective" for short) to describe situations in which the target of our designs is a personal object (a consumer product), such as a device or software app, that a user buys for private use. The product perspective is a consumer perspective.

A product still can involve multiple users (e.g., people sharing music) and multiple activities (e.g., buying music, organizing music, etc.). These cases can be thought of as small systems within the product perspective; for example, a network of educational and entertainment devices connected to the cloud.

3.4.1.1 Single-user products

The usage context of a single-user product design perspective is usually quite narrow and simple. Examples include games designed to be played by one person, personal calendar applications, portable music players, and smartphones.

However, a single-user product does not necessarily have to be a single application used in isolation, but it can be set in a network of communicating applications supporting activity-based usage. An example is the coordinated use of a calendar, a contacts list, and email.

3.4.1.2 Multiuser collaborative products

Multiuser products are somewhat similar to systems in the enterprise system perspective in that usage involves multiple users and actors spanning multiple activities and there could be a flow of information or even usage artifacts. But the setting is different. Unlike the enterprise system perspective setting of an organization and the organizational goals, the multiuser product perspective setting is more like a user community with its own goals, which could be cooperative or competitive. Examples include families sharing music on a set of smartphones and family interactions with living room devices such as Amazon Echo.

3.4.2 The Enterprise System Perspective

We use the term "enterprise system perspective" to refer to situations where the work practice involves multiple users and actors spanning multiple activities, usually in an organizational setting. The goal of work practice in this perspective is to further the business goals of that organization. Organizations contain numerous and often widely different system usage roles, each contributing to a part of the overall work that gets accomplished. These types of products are typically not owned by a single user and are not as tangible or self-contained in their manifestation to the user. They can be somewhat abstract and disembodied from the people who use them.

Of course, some projects will have design targets that fall somewhere in between the two perspectives.

Now that we have discussed the issues of scope, rigor, complexity, and their impacts on process choices, we are now ready to talk about what it takes for the UX lifecycle to work in an agile context. For this we introduce the funnel model of UX design in the next chapter.

Agile Lifecycle Processes and the Funnel Model of Agile UX

Highlights

- Challenges in building systems.
- Change happens.
- Change creates a gap between the reality of requirements and the designer's understanding of the same.
- Success relies on being able to close that gap and respond to change.
- The old waterfall process.
- Embracing an agile lifecycle process.
- Scope and chunking are the most important characteristics.
- Agility is an outcome of chunking.
- Agile UX.
- Agile software engineering (SE).
- Looking at change in terms of divergence between understanding and reality.
- The funnel model of agile UX.
- Late funnel activities: Syncing with the SE sprints.
- Early funnel activities: Upfront analysis and design.

4.1 CHALLENGES IN BUILDING SYSTEMS

4.1.1 Change Happens During a Project

4.1.1.1 Evolution of project requirements and parameters

These days, much of the discussion about lifecycle processes is about how well they can respond to change. Why is the ability to respond to change so important? First of all, perhaps the biggest single lesson learned in the history of software engineering (and UX design) is: *change is inevitable.* Over the course of a project, most project parameters change, including:

- Requirements (statement of system needs).
- Product concept, vision.
- System architecture.
- Design ideas.
- Available technology.

For simplicity, we will refer to this set of project parameters as the "requirements." Here are some things we know:

- Technology is constantly changing; technology evolves to be better and faster and there are technological paradigm shifts (new products, new uses of old products).
- Because change occurs over time, the longer the time to deliver a release that can be evaluated, the more change can occur between original requirements and evaluation feedback.
- Because a larger scope means a larger time to delivery, to mitigate the impact of change, the scope needs to be small.

Stating this as a prerequisite for success:

Prerequisite 1: In a successful project, the scope needs to be small, so the time it takes to deliver a release is limited.

4.1.1.2 External changes

Things in the world at large also can change during a project, such as:

- Technology available at the time.
- Client's directions and focus (possibly due to shifting organizational goals or market factors).

Because these changes are external to the process, we have little control over them but we have to be responsive.

4.1.2 Two Views of These Changes
4.1.2.1 Reality

The "reality" view of change reflects true changes and reveals "real requirements" as they evolve within the project.

4.1.2.2 Designer's understanding of these changes

For simplicity in this context, we will use the term "designer" to denote the UX designer and the whole team, including relevant SE roles. The designer's view of change reflects the designer's understanding, awareness, or perception of the changes and is the result of evaluation feedback.

4.1.3 The Gap Between Views

There is a gap between the reality of requirements and the designer's perception of requirements. The designer's view of requirements usually lags reality in time and falls short of reality in content, but a successful project needs this gap to remain small.

Putting it as another prerequisite:

Prerequisite 2: In a successful project, the gap between reality (true requirements) and the designer's understanding of the same needs to remain small.

Prerequisite 2 interacts with Prerequisite 1 in that a larger scope of the delivery results in a greater time it takes to deliver. The greater time it takes, the more the evolution of needs and the larger the gap.

Also, because initial requirements were based only on perceived needs, there is a gap to begin with, compounding the problem.

4.1.4 Responding to Change

The ability of the designer and the whole team to react to changes during the project depends on closing the gap between reality and the designer's view of reality—that is, how well the designer's understanding tracks the real requirements. This is all about the choice of lifecycle processes, an important subject of this book.

4.1.5 Closing the Gap

Closing the gap between real requirements and the designer's understanding of real requirements entails updating the designer's understanding as change occurs (i.e., as project parameters evolve). Updating the designer's awareness happens through learning afforded by feedback in the process (next section).

4.1.6 True Usage is the Only Ascertainer of Requirements

Perceived requirements are described by envisioning usage. In contrast, the ability to track changes and thereby know real requirements depends on learning from real usage feedback. Framing this as another prerequisite:

Prerequisite 3: Feedback from actual usage is the only way to know real requirements.

We can't know the real needs until after using the system. But of course, there is a dilemma: You can't build the system to try it out without knowing the requirements.

This dilemma must be addressed by a lifecycle process that can handle constant change. No, that isn't strong enough. Your lifecycle process doesn't just have to handle change; it must incorporate change as an operational feature of the process, and it must embrace constant change as a necessary mechanism for learning throughout the process (Dubberly & Evenson, 2011).

This means you need a lifecycle process that gives feedback on requirements before the whole system is built as well as feedback at every step from real usage, which is the key to learning about how conditions are changing.

4.1.7 Communicating Feedback About Requirements

Even when all the prerequisites so far are met, there can still be barriers to a successful project due to faulty feedback communication, gaps in the transfer of what is on the user's mind to what is on the designer's mind.

4.1.7.1 Communication problems on the user's side

Depending on users to tell you what is wrong with a system is not always reliable because users:

- Are not necessarily knowledgeable about technology and the overall system.
- Might have trouble formulating problems in their own minds (e.g., inability to abstract from problem instance details).
- Might lack the ability to articulate feedback about requirements.
- Might give feedback based on what they *think* they want.
- Have biases about certain aspects of the system.

And, even if users understand and articulate good requirements, it is possible that the designer misunderstands, a normal problem in written and verbal communication.

We can sum this up as another prerequisite:

Prerequisite 4: In a successful project, feedback about requirements must be communicated effectively.

4.2 THE OLD WATERFALL SE LIFECYCLE PROCESS

The original waterfall process was developed in the preconsumer era when most systems were large enterprise systems and users were trained to use a system for specific business purposes. There really were no system-development considerations of usability or UX.

4.2.1 The Waterfall Process was an Early SE Attempt to Get Organized

The waterfall process (originally called the waterfall model (Royce, 1970)) was among the earliest of formal software engineering lifecycle processes. The waterfall process is one of the simplest (in form, at least) ways to put lifecycle activities together to make an SE lifecycle process. The process was so named because it was described as an ordered, essentially linear sequence of phases (lifecycle activities), each of which flowed into the next like the set of cascading tiers of a waterfall (Fig. 4-1).

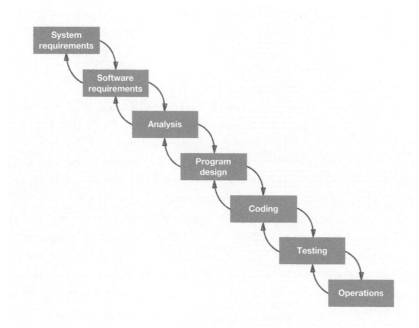

Fig. 4-1

Cascades from phase to phase in the waterfall model (adapted from Royce, 1970).

The objective of the waterfall process was to deliver the full system at once. Because this process was an attempt to overcome the previous "Wild West" approach to software, it was methodical and tended to be rigorous. It also helps to know that the systems being built at that time were mostly large enterprise or government systems. But, because it operated with large scope in the extreme, the waterfall process was also slow, cumbersome, unmanageable, and not very responsive to change.

For more about how the waterfall model got started see Section 6.5.

4.2.2 The Waterfall Process Did Have Some Feedback, But Not the Right Kind

4.2.2.1 Verification and validation of phase work products

The waterfall process did not entirely lack feedback before the whole system was delivered. To introduce a formal evaluation component, software people added evaluation in the form of verification and validation (V and V) (Lewis, 1992) at the end of each phase. Verification was to show that the software met specifications and validation was to ensure that it fulfilled its purpose. V and V helped a bit by periodically checking with users to see if the needs were still "valid" and on track.

4.2.2.2 But this wasn't enough

While V and V was a way to incorporate some client feedback after each phase, the ability to track the reality of changes was limited because feedback:

- Was at a large level of scope.
- Occurred only at the end of each large phase.
- Was based on analytic reality checking, not real empirical usage data (because there was no system yet to use until the entire system was delivered at the end of the lifecycle).

These bullet items imply that the waterfall process failed to meet Prerequisite 3 (need feedback based on real usage) because it was a whole scope process, and could not get to real usage until the very end.

To make it worse, the waterfall process also failed to meet Prerequisite 1 (need to limit the time to delivery) and Prerequisite 2 (the gap between reality and the designer's understanding must be small) because whole scope systems take a long time to build and, so, a significant amount of change happens before any feedback can occur, causing the gap from reality to grow very large.

4.2.2.3 Change discovered was too expensive to address

When problems were inevitably discovered at the end of each phase, it was expensive to go back and fix the whole system at that point. New requirements discovered during later stages kicked off expensive rework because they invalidated the previous phases' deliverables. Studies done at the time showed how a problem detected during implementation was many times more expensive to fix than if it was detected during requirements. Although the phase deliverables were not the real system, a heavy commitment of resources was made to correcting those because that was the only thing they could adjust. Even if everything was corrected with the new insights, the waterfall process still failed to meet Prerequisite 3 (feedback must be based on real usage).

4.2.2.4 Feedback was not communicated well with respect to user needs

And, with respect to the feedback they did get in the waterfall process, it often failed to meet Prerequisite 4 (communicating user feedback accurately) because at that time the emphasis was on the system and not the user. V and V addressed communication issues to an extent by giving users the opportunity to review the emerging system design, but SE people took a system perspective and focused on "under the hood" issues. And often these emerging system design artifacts were too technical and abstract and not relevant for users to understand.

4.2.2.5 The bottom line

The outcome was that, because the waterfall lifecycle process represented the ultimate in batching with very large scope rather than incremental results, it didn't produce enough feedback along the way to handle change very well. Because of the large scope, users and clients saw little of the actual product or system until the project had passed through all the lifecycle stages. By that time, many things had changed but there had been no opportunities within the waterfall model lifecycle to learn about these changes and respond along the way. That meant UX and SE people had to work very hard and rigorously in each lifecycle activity to minimize the problems and errors that crept in, making it a slow and laborious process.

The culture of this era was that of a very long product or system shelf life because change was too difficult. All this was no problem for the team, though, because they were getting ready to disband and go off to other assignments. But of course, for the client and users it was a different (and sadder) story: goals were missed, some requirements were wrong, other requirements were not met, the system had severe usability problems, and the final deliverable didn't satisfy its intended purpose.

For more about silos, walls, and boundaries and the disadvantages of the waterfall model lifecycle process, see Section 6.6.

4.3 EMBRACING AN AGILE LIFECYCLE PROCESS

An agile lifecycle process (UX or SE) is small-scope approach in which all lifecycle activities are performed for one feature of the product or system and then the lifecycle is repeated for the next feature. An agile process is driven by needs formulated as user stories of capabilities instead of abstract system requirements and is characterized by small and fast deliveries of releases to get early usage-based feedback.

Because of the problems with the waterfall process discussed in the previous section, a search for alternative SE processes led to the idea of agile SE. In the waterfall process, you do each lifecycle activity for the entire product or system. In an agile lifecycle process, you do all the lifecycle activities for one feature of the product or system and then repeat the lifecycle for the next feature.

Agile processes are generally fast, very iterative, and responsive to change. This makes sense because the word "agile" means nimble or responsive to change.

Agile processes address:

■ Prerequisite 1 (*In a successful project, the scope needs to be small so the time it takes to deliver a release is limited*) by delivering the first chunk relatively quickly because it takes less time to implement.

■ Prerequisite 2 (*In a successful project, the gap between reality (true requirements) and the designer's understanding of the same needs to remain small*) and Prerequisite 3 (*Feedback from actual usage is the only way to know real requirements*) by delivering a small chunk that customers can use, thereby bridging the gap between perceived needs and real needs.

■ Prerequisite 4 (*In a successful project, feedback about requirements must be communicated effectively*) by:

  ■ Formulating the needs as user stories of capabilities instead of abstract system requirements.

  ■ Making the stories about small manageable features instead of the whole system.

Also, by the time agile processes came along, the world of system development was embracing smaller and less complex systems. While there is some development of the large enterprise or government systems of the waterfall days, development is leaning toward smaller and less complex consumer applications. This is a trend that worked in favor of agile processes.

4.3.1 Scope and Chunking are Key to Real Usage Feedback

Chunking is the breaking up of requirements for a product or system into small groups, each corresponding to a release, usually based on features, entailing a set of tasks related to a feature.

In the software engineering transition from the waterfall process, the chunking of features into a small scope for each iteration of the process was the key to getting the feedback necessary to track changes in understanding that occurred with real usage.

Fig. 4-2, adapted from Kent Beck's Extreme Programming book (Beck, 1999), gives us a visual idea of how truly small the scope is in an agile approach. As the figure shows, the waterfall process makes one big pass through the lifecycle activities for the whole system at a time. An iterative approach takes a step toward smaller, but still fairly large, chunks and results in multiple passes. But it isn't until we get to large numbers of frequent iterations for very small chunks that we see the true essence of an agile approach—agility.

Eric Ries, in his book on lean startups (Ries, 2011), declares that *agility is perhaps the single most important thing in successful product development*. It's not so much about brilliant ideas, technology, far-seeing vision, good timing, or even luck. Instead, *you should have a "process for adapting to situations as they reveal themselves."* Lean UX is one variation of agile UX that focuses on producing a minimum viable product (MVP) in each sprint.

In an agile software engineering process, a sprint is a relatively short (not more than a month and usually less) period within an agile SE schedule in which "a usable and potentially releasable product increment is created."[1] "Each sprint has a goal of what is to be built, a design and flexible plan that will guide building it, the work, and the resultant product increment." A sprint is the basic unit of work being done in an agile SE environment. In short, it is an iteration associated with a release (to the client and/or users).

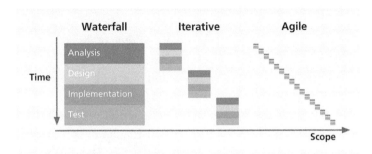

Fig. 4-2

Scope and size of deliverables in the waterfall, iterative, and agile process (adapted with permission from Beck (1999)).

---

[1]https://www.scrum.org/resources/what-is-a-sprint-in-scrum.

Agile SE processes do this by delivering to the client and/or users meaningful small-scope product or system chunks of capabilities and working software features with every iteration. That way, we never go too far down an unproductive path before we can make a course correction. This constant minimizing of the gap between perceived needs and real needs is how agile processes meet Prerequisite 2.

4.3.2 On the UX Side, We've Always Had a Measure of Agility Without Chunking

Frequent iteration, feedback, learning, and responsiveness to change have always been important goals in UX, too. In fact, the discipline of UX design was built on these as foundational principles. In UX, we didn't need to do chunking to achieve them.

To meet Prerequisite 1, we use fast prototypes to reduce the time it takes from conception to feedback time.

There have been many ways of keeping the gap between user and designer small to meet Prerequisite 2. We run all our models and work products by the client. We have users participate in ideation and sketching for design. We do early and frequent evaluations using low-fidelity prototypes. In other words, we can simulate the experience for the user at a large-scope level and learn from it without building the real system. And, in UX, user feedback is not usually sought a feature at a time. A quality user experience is better achieved and evaluated more holistically, using a top-down approach with a large scope.

UX processes met Prerequisite 3 by simulating real usage via prototypes.

Finally we met Prerequisite 4 (communication of requirements feedback) by using participatory design. In addition, all our artifacts are about usage and user concerns, not system ones.

Participatory Design

A democratic process for UX design actively involving all stakeholders (e.g., employees, partners, customers, citizens, users) to help ensure that the result meets their needs and is usable. Based on the argument that users should be involved in designs they will be using, and that all stakeholders, including and especially users, have equal input into UX design (Section 11.3.4).

4.3.3 But SE Hasn't Had the Luxury of Making User-Facing Prototypes

In a way, this has been easier for the UX people. On the SE side of things, most of the concerns are about system aspects. Therefore, their artifacts are about representations of the inner workings of the system and they tend to be abstract and technical.

On the UX side of things, we are dealing with what the user sees and feels. Therefore, it is easy for us to give the user a flavor of a particular design concept by mocking up these user-facing aspects using prototypes. The SE people couldn't make meaningful low-fidelity mockups. To show something to users in preagile days, they had to build the whole working system.

To be fair, the SE side did experiment with rapid prototyping (Wasserman & Shewmake, 1982a, 1982b), but it was never really part of their classical process models.

4.3.4 And SE Wasn't That Interested in Users, Anyway

Before agile processes, the SE people were not known for talking with users about envisioned behavior with just a sketch or mockup. They didn't have touchpoints with users that focused on the product side of things to situate the users in the design solution domain.

Rather, the SE people historically focused on the process side of things and in technical issues such as code structure, code understanding, and code reusability. If anything, they looked for ways to make it better for the programmer, not the end user.

Their "aha" moment arrived when they figured out that they could flip their approach to delivering chunks that people can use and give product-oriented feedback. In the software engineering (SE) development world agile[2] approaches have quickly become the de facto standard.

4.3.5 So Why Have we in UX Followed SE into an Agile Approach?

There is a practical reason why UX designs still might have to be chunked for delivery to the SE people: to keep pace with sprints on the agile SE side. The SE people are the system builders. Even if we provide designs of the full system at once, they will build it in chunks. So, as a discipline, agile UX has evolved to fit that model of development. We now deliver our UX design chunks to the client, users, product owners, and other stakeholders for direct feedback and we deliver our UX designs in chunks to the SE people for implementation.

See Chapter 29 on connecting agile UX with agile SE for more about the characteristics of agile processes.

4.4 THE FUNNEL MODEL OF AGILE UX

Because of the confusion about how the UX designer needs to work in collaboration with an agile SE process, we created what we call *the funnel model of agile UX, a way of envisioning UX design activities before syncing with agile SE sprints (for*

---

[2]In the SE world, the term "Agile" has been granted a capital "A," giving it special meaning. Because we don't want to make fine distinctions that don't matter in our context, we won't deify the concept but will stick with the lower case "a."

overall conceptual design in the early funnel) and after syncing with SE (for individual feature design in the late funnel). When we say "agile UX" in this book, we mean agile UX as set within this model, the basis throughout all the process chapters.

4.4.1 Why a New Model Was Needed

Agile UX became the way to bring design for the user experience to agile SE. But there were problems with the way agile UX was approached initially:

- Being agile was interpreted as going fast.
- Following agile SE flow in sprints suffers from a fundamental mismatch with UX concerns.

4.4.1.1 Speed kills: Rapidness and agility are not the same

Sometimes people confuse being agile with being fast. *While an agile process will often be rapid, agility isn't defined by rapidity.* Being rapid just means working faster; being agile is about chunking for design and delivery so we can react to new lessons learned through usage.

Arnowitz (2013, p. 76) cautions us that, while agile processes are almost always associated with speed, a single-minded focus on speed is almost guaranteed to be detrimental to the quality of the resulting user experience. Putting speed above everything else is a reckless response to pressure for rapid turnaround and is "proven to create Frankenstein UIs within a mere two to three iterations. That's speed" (Arnowitz, 2013, p. 76). As an analogy, when you're driving a car and starting to get lost, driving faster won't help.

4.4.1.2 The single biggest problem: UX was expected to follow the agile SE flow completely

The SE world has turned essentially all agile and the UX world has struggled to follow suit. Many people thought agile UX workflow should mirror agile SE flow exactly in order to keep in sync with agile SE development. So the UX teams started churning out chunks of UX design. But a good UX design is holistic, cohesive, and self-consistent and these new agile UX practitioners hadn't done the upfront work necessary to establish a coherent overview. And, by the time they got into sync with the SE sprints, the "design" became fragmented.

Arnowitz (2013, p. 78) says that the way agile processes are usually practiced, they are design-hostile environments. And design is what we do in UX. Embodying the opposite of a holistic view, agile practice can easily promote fragmentation.

What was missing was a way for UX to do some kind of initial large-scope usage research and conceptual design before getting into a small-scope rhythm with SE. There was some literature about this problem, but it was mostly discussed as an exception or special case. In the "funnel model of agile UX" of the next section, we show how to include some upfront usage research and design in a mainstream view of agile UX.

4.4.2 Introducing the Funnel Model of Agile UX
The funnel model of agile UX, shown in Fig. 4-3, has two major parts: the early funnel on the left and the late funnel on the right.

4.4.2.1 Scope in the funnel model
The vertical dimension of the diagram is scope. A larger funnel diameter (taller in the vertical dimension of Fig. 4-3) at any point on the funnel represents a larger scope there. And a small diameter means smaller scope at that point. Fig. 4-3 shows a typical case where the scope of the early funnel is larger than the scope of the late funnel.

4.4.2.2 Speed and rigor in the funnel model
The horizontal dimension of the diagram is time, representing how long activities in the funnel take to play out. The stripes or segments depicted on the funnel visually represent iterations or sprints and the length of a segment represents the duration in time of that sprint and, by implication, the speed of methods and

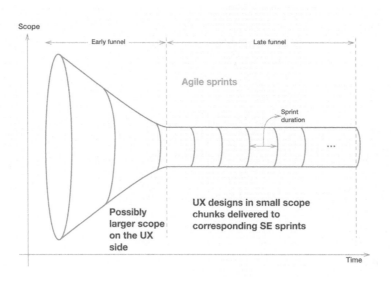

Fig. 4-3

The funnel model of agile UX.

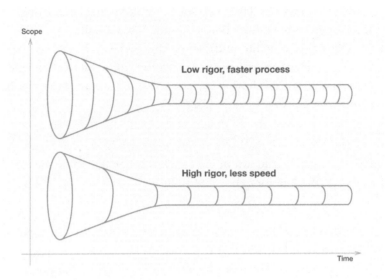

Fig. 4-4

Low rigor and high speed versus high rigor and slow speed in the funnel model.

techniques that have to be used in a given iteration. Longer sprints usually correspond with higher rigor, which will need methods and techniques that are more thorough and meticulous for that iteration (Fig. 4-4).

4.4.3 Late Funnel Activities

The late funnel, or the "spout" on the right side of Fig. 4-3, is where the agile UX and agile SE processes are working in synchronism. Here, the goal of both the UX and SE sides is typically described in terms of small chunks within a small scope (represented by the small diameter of the funnel spout) delivered within a relatively small time increment (narrow sprint duration stripe).

In theory at least, each delivered software chunk is tested until it works and then integrated with the rest. The result of that is regression (looking back) tested until it all works. The idea is to be able to start and end each iteration with something that works (Constantine, 2002, p. 3). Constant and close (but informal) communication produces continuous feedback.

4.4.3.1 Syncing agile UX with agile SE sprints

The UX team provides a design chunk, which the SE team implements along with its design of the corresponding functionality in a sequence of sprints (Fig. 4-5).

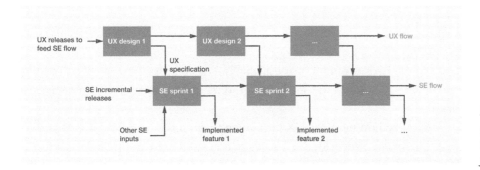

Fig. 4-5
Syncing agile UX with agile SE sprints in the late funnel flow.

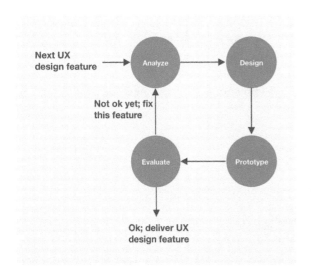

Fig. 4-6
Mini agile UX lifecycle process within a sprint.

Once agile SE gets into the rhythm of going through sprints to produce implementations of chunk as features, the idea of agile UX is to sync with agile SE by providing UX design for each feature in turn, as shown in Fig. 4-5.

Each UX design box contains a mini UX lifecycle such as the one shown in Fig. 4-6.

We'll talk much more about how the agile UX and agile SE processes are coordinated in Chapter 29.

4.4.4 Early Funnel Activities

Before we can do the small-scope incremental releases in the synchronized late-funnel flow of Fig. 4-3, we have to start with a full-scope analysis and design up front in the early funnel. UX must start the design for a new system with a top-down view to understand the ecology and needs and to establish a conceptual design.

This is a requirement for UX because of the nature of UX design. Unlike code that is invisible to the user, UX design is not. Code is malleable in that it can be structured and refactored in every release. Redoing the design of the UI like that will drive the users crazy.

This upfront UX activity, the solution to the second problem described in Section 4.4.1.2, which is sometimes called "sprint 0" because it precedes the first sprint in the late funnel, is to establish:

- An overview, a skeleton on which to put the features.
- A solid coherent conceptual design to guide the design for the features.
- An initial top-down design.

This will entail as much of these upfront activities as necessary to understand needs and workflow:

- Usage research.
- Analysis.
- Modeling.

This early funnel work is what puts "UX strategic design decisions up front, where they belong" (Arnowitz, 2013, p. 78).

In the next section, we look at some examples of large-scope early funnel cases.

4.4.4.1 The need to establish a conceptual design

A conceptual design is a high-level model or theme of how the system works. It acts as a framework to aid users in acquiring their own mental model of how the system behaves. In any project charged with designing and building a brand new system or a new version of a confusing existing system, you will need to establish a clear conceptual design upfront as scaffolding for a coherent overall UX design. Conceptual design is, by its nature, a large-scope notion. Small scope at this point is likely to lead to a fragmented conceptual design.

After the conceptual design is established, the UX team can move to a small scope in the late funnel to deliver the detailed UX designs of individual features to the SE side in increments.

Example: Developing a New Smartphone Design From Scratch

Suppose your project is to create a brand new smartphone to compete with the current market leaders. It has been decided that this entails an entirely new and innovative conceptual design—a design that is better, and more exciting to consumers, than existing options offered in the market.

This case might require a significant large-scope effort in the early funnel to create a full conceptual design, to set the overall ecology of the smartphone, and to create a cohesive design upfront. It's just not possible to design a phone operating system or a brand new consumer-facing application without beginning with a large-scope design on the UX side. Beyond the point where you have established a consistent conceptual design, the project can then adopt the usual small scope in the late funnel to deliver the UX design.

As an interesting note in this case, even after the UX and SE roles end up in lockstep in the late funnel as they release chunks of the smartphone operating system, end users may not see those chunks. This is a case where the learn-through-frequent-customer-releases method doesn't necessarily work because you cannot release a new smartphone to end users in chunks.

4.4.4.2 Small systems with low complexity

Small systems with low complexity are an example of using a large scope, but for a different reason—because the system has low complexity and can be handled in a single shot.

Small systems with low complexity don't usually benefit much from a small-scope approach on the UX side. So, in fact, you can use a large scope through the whole funnel (picture the whole funnel being almost as wide as a wide mouth). If the system isn't large, there may not be enough of a "pipeline" or breadth of system features or complexity for the UX team to chunk the designs into small-scope increments. In other words, the size and complexity of the system can easily be handled with a large scope in the whole funnel and delivered to the SE side in large scope, leaving them to decompose it into features for their own small-scope implementation, if necessary.

4.4.4.3 SE needs a funnel model, too

The people on the SE side also need to do some upfront analysis and design, at least to establish the system architecture. So, maybe there are really two overlapping funnels.

4.4.4.4 The nexus of early and late parts of the funnel

The transition to the late funnel is a crucial point in a project; it's the beginning of "crunch time," where you get in gear and sync with the agile SE people. Now is the time that user stories drive your design iterations, but the deep understanding (in total) that you developed in usage research and modeling informs the design.

Prelude to the Process Chapters

5

Highlights

- How UX processes, methods, and techniques intertwine over time.
- The UX design studio.
- Project commission: How does a project start?
- Key UX roles.
- The Middleburg University Ticket Transaction Service and the new Ticket Kiosk System: Our running examples for the process chapters.
- The product concept statement:
  - How to write a clear and concise product concept statement.

5.1 INTRODUCTION

This minichapter is an introduction to the UX process chapters. It contains a mix of a few topics prefatory to the process chapters.

5.2 INTERTWINING OF PROCESSES, METHODS, AND TECHNIQUES

Although we present the UX lifecycle activities in separate chapters to focus on learning about each one at a time, the reality of UX practice is that the UX process is a fabric of interwoven lifecycle activities, methods, and techniques. UX design activities are not performed in a nice orderly sequence but are intertwined within the process, even occurring simultaneously.

Lifecycle activity

The high-level things you do during a UX lifecycle, including understanding user needs, designing UX solutions, prototyping candidate designs, and evaluating those designs (Section 2.2.2).

Examples of Intertwining

As an example of intertwining, consider the important UX design activity of prototyping. For starters, prototyping is featured as a major lifecycle activity in a chapter of its own. But prototyping is also an indispensable UX technique that appears in many different guises in many different places. A prototype is a tangible manifestation of any idea that needs to be evaluated. Prototyping in some form can appear in almost any method for performing almost any activity.

In addition to being used as the platform for UX evaluation (Part 5), multiple low-fidelity rapid prototypes, called sketches in this context, are used to explore competing design ideas in ideation (a kind of brainstorming, Chapter 14).

As a concrete example, a wireframe is an important kind of prototype. Quick and dirty wireframes are used as sketches for exploring design ideas as part of early design. Finished and detailed wireframes are used to convey design ideas to stakeholders and for implementation in Chapters 17 and 18 on designing the interaction and designing for emotional impact.

Wireframe

A visual template of a screen or webpage design in the interaction perspective, comprised of lines and outlines (hence the name "wire frame"). A skeletal representation of the layout of interaction objects such as tabs, menus, buttons, dialogue boxes, displays, and navigational elements (Section 17.5).

5.2.1 Activity Timing

Another area where practice strays from the "pure" activity description is the timing of how things happen. For example, in our usage research data elicitation discussion (observation and interviewing of users, Chapter 7), it might seem that all user visits happen in one contiguous time period. But in practice that is rarely the case. The data elicitation activity can occur on and off over a period of time because of a variety of project constraints, including scheduling, user availability, and concurrent and unrelated projects happening simultaneously. In our experience, we have never been able to do all data elicitation in one go even if we had a large team of researchers and designers. We could never schedule them like that. So we would start with the first user, gather usage data, and start early modeling and synthesis and even some design while we wait for the next user visit. After that next visit, we would update the models and the design ideas with the new data as necessary.

To a lesser extent but still not uncommon are situations where we would even have some early designs and prototypes done that we would take to users that were scheduled further out on the calendar. If we tried to account for that in the elicitation discussion, we would have had to cover the material on early modeling, design ideation, sketching, and early wireframing in multiple and overlapping discussions. It would have resulted in a mashup that was difficult to sort out by you, the reader.

The practice of UX evaluation presents another example of how timing can vary. For example, we present design production in isolation as a chapter in the book part on design. UX evaluation comes in later chapters, but in fact by the time design production is done, most formative evaluation (evaluation for the purpose of refining the design) is usually done, too. And before wireframing is done, most other kinds of prototyping (building a preliminary version, Chapter 20) are also done. A true-to-life description of this would bring much of the evaluation and prototyping discussion upfront before design production is complete. Here is a typical sequence of activities we have seen in practice:

- Data elicitation with few early users.
- Analysis and modeling of data collected.
- Ideation and sketching for generative design based on analysis and emerging models.
- Early wireframes or prototypes of emerging designs.
- Data elicitation from more users:
  - Show users emerging design ideas and wireframes at the end of elicitation sessions for feedback.
- Update usage data models and designs with new insights.
- Increase fidelity of wireframe details as confidence on emerging designs grows.
- Evaluate with more users using more rigorous methods (e.g., in a UX lab).
- Update usage data models and designs with evaluation findings.
- Design production and hand off to the software engineering team.

5.2.2 Can We Describe It that Way in a Book?

If we try to account for these parallel and concurrent streams of activities in a stream-of-occurrence style in this book, we run the risk of repetition. Even if we could pull that off, the result would be a little of this and a little of that, with no complete description of anything in one place. That makes a confusing jumble for the reader who is trying to understand each part of the process.

As an analogy for the reader, it would be like someone trying to learn the process by observing a UX professional—you see the process unfold in overlapping bits. You have to deduce how to piece it together. If something changes, you have to update your understanding until you eventually have the big picture that extensive experience brings.

To resolve this in favor of clarity for the reader, our process chapters are organized mainly by UX design activity. But we also try to indicate how these activities actually happen in the field. To this end, we also use some incremental disclosure. For example, in Chapter 7 on data elicitation for usage research, we have a section on early data modeling where we reveal just enough to get started on modeling in parallel with data elicitation. But we don't say everything about modeling here because that would be a distraction from data elicitation.

Wireframe

A visual template of a screen or webpage design in the interaction perspective, comprised of lines and outlines (hence the name "wire frame"). A skeletal representation of the layout of interaction objects such as tabs, menus, buttons, dialogue boxes, displays, and navigational elements (Section 17.5).

Formative evaluation

A family of diagnostic UX evaluation methods using mostly qualitative data collection with the objective to form a design, that is, for finding and fixing UX problems and thereby refining the design (Section 21.1.5).

Similarly, we introduce some early wireframing in the chapter on generative design (UX design creation, Chapter 14) but reserve the full treatment of wireframing for the prototyping chapter (Chapter 20). We also have a little bit about early informal evaluation to show how we critique these early wireframes.

5.2.3 Readers Need a "Pure" Description of Each Lifecycle Activity

For clarity, we feel the reader must start with a more or less "pure" description of each major UX design lifecycle activity separately, without the distraction of how they are interleaved. That doesn't follow the UX principle of giving information to the user/reader just as needed, but it is the only approach that:

- Facilitates immersion by focusing the reader on a single topic at a time.
- Limits repetition in the narrative by covering a topic only once.
- Effectively helps readers use this book as a reference while doing a particular UX activity.

Once armed with these modules of knowledge, we hope the student or practitioner can adopt, adapt, and interleave the appropriate choices and combinations of methods and techniques as needed in any particular design situation or project.

5.3 A DEDICATED UX DESIGN STUDIO, AN ESSENTIAL TOOL FOR TEAMWORK

Before we get started with usage research data elicitation, this is a good time to talk about an indispensable tool for every UX group: *the UX design studio.*

5.3.1 Why You Need a UX Design Studio

A UX design studio is:

Immersion

A form of deep thought and analysis of the problem at hand—to "live" within the context of a problem and to make connections among the different aspects of it (Section 2.4.7).

- A home for your team.
- A place for immersion.
- A shared workspace for colocation and constant collaboration.
- A place for externalizing the state of the design by posting all your work for discussion and brainstorming.

As Bødker and Buur (2002) urge, every UX group needs to set aside a physical work space, a design studio, as a home base for the team to meet and do ideation, individual work, design collaboration, and other group work.

The UX studio is where you immerse your team in the artifacts of analysis and design. When you walk in the room and close the door, you are in the world of the design and the rest of the world and its distractions disappear. This means you need your whole team colocated enough so you can all meet in the UX studio at almost any time (Brown, 2008, p. 87).

5.3.2 What You Need in Your UX Design Studio

A good design studio will have:

- Comfortable seating.
- A conference table.
- Work tables to lay out prototypes and other design artifacts.
- White boards for group sketching.
- Ample wall space for hanging posters, drawings, diagrams, and design sketches.
- A door that can be closed.
- Shared displays on which team members can show work artifacts from their laptops.

5.3.3 Dedicated Space

Your UX design studio space needs to be a place that:

- Is constantly available without the need for reservations.
- Allows all artifacts to remain displayed from one work session to another.
- Meets the unpredictable need for frequent and immediate communication.

5.3.4 The Virginia Tech Industrial Designs Studio: The Kiva

In Fig. 5-1, we show an example of a collaborative ideation and design studio, called the Kiva, in the Virginia Tech Department of Industrial Design. The Kiva was originally designed and developed by Maya Design in Pittsburgh, and is used at Virginia Tech with their permission.

The Kiva is a cylindrical space in which designers can brainstorm and sketch in isolation from outside distractions. The space inside is large enough for seating and work tables. The inner surface is a painted metallic skin that serves as an enveloping whiteboard and can also hold magnetic "push pins." The large-screen display on the outside can be used for announcements, including group scheduling for the work space.

In Fig. 5-2, we show immersion and collaboration within individual and group workspaces for colocation of designers, just outside the Kiva.

Fig. 5-1

The Virginia Tech ideation and design studio, the "Kiva" (photo courtesy of Akshay Sharma of the Virginia Tech Department of Industrial Design).

Fig. 5-2

Individual and group designer workspaces (photos courtesy of Akshay Sharma of the Virginia Tech Department of Industrial Design).

5.4 THE PROJECT COMMISSION: HOW DOES A PROJECT START?

All projects have some kind of starting point. Projects are spawned by any of a number of forces, including marketing strategy, management edict, a product sponsor, a system client, inventive ideas, perceived needs to improve an existing product or system, and so on.

The commission to undertake a system-oriented project rarely comes from within the UX design or software engineering (SE) group, but instead as a mandate from upper management. The notion of a new product can hatch in the form of a business brief, often from marketing within an established product-oriented organization.

For the project team, things begin with some kind of project commission document or statement that is a proposal for creating the project. Depending on the organizational situation, the project commission document can include boiler plate items such as project duration, budget, management plan, personnel roles, etc.

A project commission document is likely to be very high level and possibly ill defined. It becomes the first responsibility of the UX design team, especially the product owner (just below in Section 5.4.1.5), to fill in the gaps during the product definition stage and firm up the vision in the product concept statement.

5.4.1 Key UX Team Roles from the Start

5.4.1.1 Usage researcher

This is a person who does usage research activities such as data elicitation, data analysis and modeling, and UX requirements specifications.

5.4.1.2 UX designer

This is a person on the UX team who does UX design, such as design creation, conceptual design, and/or design production for user interaction.

5.4.1.3 Graphic or visual designer

A graphic designer is responsible for visual communication, branding, and style, eventually in pixel-perfect visual "comps."

5.4.1.4 UX analyst

This is a person on the UX team who does UX evaluation. Often, in small teams, the same person may perform the duties of usage researcher and UX analyst.

5.4.1.5 Product owner

Some UX teams have either a product owner, a product manager, or both. The definitions of the roles of product owner and product manager can vary between project teams. The product owner is more likely to be associated with the UX team. Many companies don't even have a product manager, whose role is mainly about setting up meetings and scheduling.

Typically, the product owner:

- Is close to users.
- Knows the product context within the client's domain, business strategy, and competition.

> **Product concept statement**
>
> Concise mission statement for the project team, a vision statement or a mandate, an explanation of the product to stakeholders and outsiders. Internally, it is a yardstick to help set focus and scope for development. The audience is very broad, including high-level management, marketing, stockholders, and even the general public (Section 5.6).

- Is responsible for the success of the product and for pursuing business goals.
- Keeps the product on track with the overall vision.
- Is in charge of writing/creating:
  - The product concept statement.
  - User stories.
  - User personas.
- Works with SE in planning implementation sprints and managing prioritized backlog of agile user stories (Chapter 29).

5.5 THE MIDDLEBURG UNIVERSITY TICKET TRANSACTION SERVICE AND THE NEW TICKET KIOSK SYSTEM

As a running example to illustrate the ideas in the text, we introduce the Middleburg University Ticket Transaction Service (MUTTS), a hypothetical public ticket sales system for selling tickets for entertainment and other events. This information about MUTTS is the kind of thing you discover in data elicitation, the subject of Chapter 7. This project is a good example of a combined product perspective and enterprise system perspective—it's a system but it's used much like a product by the general public.

5.5.1 The Existing System: The Middleburg University Ticket Transaction Service (MUTTS)

Middleburg, a small town in middle America, is home to Middleburg University, a state university that operates a service called the Middleburg University Ticket Transaction Service (MUTTS). MUTTS has operated successfully for several years as a central campus ticket office where people buy tickets for entertainment events, including concerts, plays, and special presentations by public speakers. Through this office, MUTTS makes arrangements with event sponsors and sells tickets to various customers. There is considerable interest in improving and expanding MUTTS.

The current business process suffers from numerous drawbacks:

- Until recently, all customers had to go to one location to buy tickets in person.
- MUTTS has now partnered with Tickets4ever.com as a national online ticket distribution platform. However, Tickets4ever.com suffers from low reliability and has a reputation for a poor user experience.

- Current operation of MUTTS involves multiple systems that do not work together very well.
- The ability to rapidly hire temporary ticket sellers to meet periodic high demand is hampered by university and state hiring policies.

5.5.1.1 Organizational context of the existing system

The desire to expand the business coincides with a number of other dynamics currently affecting MUTTS and Middleburg University.

- The supervisor of MUTTS wishes to expand revenue-generating activities.
- There is a general consensus that the new system should provide a much improved user experience in several areas.
- To leverage their increasing national academic and athletic prominence, the university is seeking a comprehensive customized solution that includes the integration of tickets for athletic events. Currently, tickets to athletic events are managed by an entirely different department.
- By including tickets for athletic events that generate significant revenue, MUTTS will have access to resources to support other aspects of their expansion.
- The university is undergoing a strategic initiative for unified branding across all its departments and activities. The university administration is receptive to creative design solutions for MUTTS to support this branding effort.

5.5.2 The Proposed New System: The Ticket Kiosk System

The working name for the new system is the Ticket Kiosk System, which was commissioned in a business brief by the university administration and MUTTS management. A high-level decision has been made to mandate a ticket kiosk as the core of this project. As designers, we need to keep an open mind and be prepared to steer the project toward a better solution, if one arises upon immersion in the problem space.

Early on, the scope of the project must be addressed in the business brief as a road map for all that is to follow. For example, does the design cover kiosk maintenance, payment arrangements, arrangement of agreements for purchase of tickets to outside organizations, and so on? These issues reflect other work roles in the ecology of the system, each of which, if included in the project, will have its own set of tasks to be designed for, especially in the interaction design.

Ecology

In the setting of UX design, the ecology is the entire set of surrounding parts of the world, including networks, other users, devices, and information structures, with which a user, product, or system interacts (Section 16.2.1).

5.5.3 Rationale

MUTTS wants to expand its scope and add more locations, but it is expensive to rent space in business buildings around town and the kind of small space it needs is rarely available. Therefore, the administrators of MUTTS and the Middleburg University administration have decided to switch the business from a ticket window to kiosks, which can be placed in many more locations across campus and around town.

Middleburg has a reliable and well-used public transportation system operated by Middleburg Transit, Inc. There are several bus stops, including at the library and the shopping mall, where buses come and go every few minutes with good-sized crowds getting on and off. Most such locations have space for a kiosk at a reasonable leasing fee.

Management expects an increase in sales due to the increased availability (kiosks in many places) and increased accessibility (open continuously). Also, there will be cost savings in that a kiosk requires no personnel at the sales outlets.

5.6 THE PRODUCT CONCEPT STATEMENT

It's the job of the product owner and the UX team to crystallize the product concept in a clear mission statement addressed to all stakeholders (Note: depending on the whether you are designing a commercial product or an enterprise system, you will have a product concept statement or a system concept statement. For simplicity, we use the term "product concept statement" as a more general term).

Stephenie Landry, vice president of Amazon Prime Now, starts a project by writing the product concept statement as a press release, working backward from there to deduce high-level needs and requirements and design. In the product concept statement for Amazon Prime Now, she promised a user experience that would be "magical" (Landry, 2016).

Tony Fadell, creator of the Apple iPod (Moore, 2017), who says product design and marketing are closely related, also creates a press release as one of the first steps in designing a new product.

The nature of a product concept statement. A product concept statement is:

  ▪ Concise, typically 100–150 words in length.
  ▪ A mission statement for the project team, a vision statement, or a mandate.
  ▪ A way to explain the product to stakeholders and outsiders.
  ▪ A yardstick to help set focus and scope for development internally.
  ▪ Not easy to write (especially a good one).

Because of the need for the statement to be short and concise, every word is important. A concept statement is not just written; it is iterated and refined to make it as clear and specific as possible.

- The audience for the product concept statement is very broad, including high-level management, marketing, the board of directors, stockholders, and even the general public.
- Refine and update as necessary as you proceed through the lifecycle activities.
- Post your product concept statement in your design studio as soon as possible. It will guide all UX design activities.

5.6.1 What's in a Product Concept Statement?

An effective product concept statement answers at least the following questions:

- What is the product or system name?
- Who are the users?
- How will they use it?
- System: What problem(s) will the system solve (broadly including business objectives)?
- Product: What are the major attractions to, or distinguishing features of, this product?
- What is the design vision and what are the emotional impact goals? In other words, what experience will the product or system provide to the user?

Example: Product Concept Statement for the Ticket Kiosk System

The TKS will replace MUTTS, the old ticket retail system, by providing distributed kiosk service to the general public. This service includes access to comprehensive event information and the capability to rapidly purchase tickets for local events such as concerts, movies, and the performing arts.

The new system includes a significant expansion of scope to include ticket distribution for the entire MU athletic program. Transportation tickets will also be available, along with directions and parking information for specific venues. Compared to conventional ticket outlets, the Ticket Kiosk System will offer increased (24/7) access, reducing waiting time, and far more extensive information about events. A focus on innovative design will enhance the MU public profile while fostering the spirit of the MU community and offering customers a quality experience. (128 words)

Iteration and refinement. Your product concept statement will evolve as you proceed with the project. For example, "far more extensive information about events" can be made more specific by saying "extensive information including images, movie trailers, and reviews of events." Also, we did not mention security and privacy, but these important concerns are later pointed out by potential users. Similarly, the point about "focus on innovative design" can be made more specific by saying "the goal of innovative design is to reinvent the experience of interacting with a kiosk by providing an engaging and enjoyable transaction experience."

Concept statements for large systems. For very large systems, you might need a system concept statement for each major subsystem, if each subsystem has its own goals and mission statement.

5.6.2 Introduction to Process-Related Exercises

How to approach these exercises: The exercises are for learning, not for producing a product, so you don't have to complete every detail if you think you have gotten what you need out of it. You should be able to learn most of what you can get from most exercises in an hour or so. In the case of a team within a classroom setting, this means that you can do the exercises as in-class activities, breaking out into teams and working in parallel, and possibly finishing the exercise as homework before the next class. This has the advantages of working next to other teams with similar goals and problems and of having an instructor present who can move among teams as a consultant and mentor. We recommend that student team deliverables be prepared in summary form for presentation to the rest of the class, if you have time, so that each team can learn from the others.

Choosing a product or system for these exercises: Choosing a product or system for these exercises should take some thought because you'll be using the same choice for most of the exercises throughout the process chapters.

Your choice of a target application system for the exercises should be gauged toward the goal of learning. That means choosing something the right size. Avoid applications that are too large or complex; choose something for which the semantics and functionality are relatively easy to understand. However, avoid systems that are too small or too simple because they may not support the process activities very well.

The criterion for selection here is that you will need to identify at least a half-dozen somewhat different kinds of user tasks. Look for something with an interesting ecology. You should also choose a system that has more than one class of user. For example, an e-commerce website for ordering merchandise will have users from the public doing the ordering and employee users processing the orders.

For practitioner teams in a real development organization, we recommend against using a real development project for these exercises. There is no sense in introducing the pressure to produce a real design and the risk of failure into this learning process.

Exercise 5.1: Product Concept Statement for a Product or System of Your Choice

Goal: Get practice in writing a concise product concept statement.

Activities: Write a product concept statement for a product or system of your choice. Iterate and polish it. The 150 or fewer words you write here will be among the most important words in the whole project, so write thoughtfully.

Deliverables: Your product concept statement.

Schedule: Given the simplicity of the domain, we expect you can get what you need from this exercise in about 30 minutes.

5.7 WELCOME TO THE PROCESS CHAPTERS

After the next chapter, the background chapter for Part 1, we move into Part 2 of the book, where we do usage research to understand needs and requirements. Part 3 is all about design, followed by Part 4, which is about prototyping. The process chapters are completed in Part 5, about UX evaluation.

Background: Introduction

6

Highlights

- Brief history and roots of HCI and UX.
- Shifting paradigms in HCI and UX.
- Fun interaction at work.
- Other topics related to phenomenology.
- Who introduced the waterfall model?
- Silos, walls, and boundaries.

6.1 THIS IS A REFERENCE CHAPTER

This chapter contains reference material relevant to the other chapters of Part 1. This chapter is not intended to be read through as a regular chapter, but each section is supposed to be read when a reference to it in the main chapters is encountered.

6.2 BRIEF HISTORY AND ROOTS OF HCI AND UX

This is a terse capsule of the history and roots of HCI and UX. The coverage is by no means a survey of the vast contributions in this large field.

It is a matter of debate exactly when computer usability was born. We know that it was a topic of interest to some by the late 1970s, and by the early 1980s, conferences about the topic were being established. Although work was being done on "human factors in computers" in the 1970s and earlier, HCI was emerging at various universities in the late 1970s and 1980s and had been going on at IBM (Branscomb, 1981), the National Bureau of Standards (now the National Institute of Standards and Technology), and other scattered locations before that.

Many believe that HCI did not coalesce into a fledgling discipline until the first CHI conference (Conference on Human Factors in Computer Systems) in Boston in 1983. But it probably began at least a couple of years before with the "unofficial first CHI conferences" (Borman & Janda, 1986) at the May 1981 ACM/SIGSOC conference, called the Conference on Easier and More Productive Use of Computer Systems, in Ann Arbor, Michigan, and the March 1982 Conference on Human Factors in Computer Systems in Gaithersburg, Maryland.

Human-computer interaction in general and usability and UX in particular owe much of their origin and development to influences from many other related fields.

6.2.1 Frederick Winslow Taylor: Scientific Management

On a timeline, our story begins very early, more than a century ago, with the advent of a concept called scientific management. Sometimes called "Taylorism," this method was created by Frederick Winslow Taylor, a mechanical engineer. He is also known for helping formulate a national (in this case, the United States) imperative for increased industrial efficiency. Taylor sought to define "best practices" of the time to reform our inefficient and wasteful, even lazy, ways of operating private and government enterprises and factories (Taylor, 1911).

Taylor came up with two tenets to increase the productivity of our workforce, tenets that remained popular for the next 40–50 years:

- Rather than trying to find the right person for a task (i.e., someone who already has the knowledge and skills for the job), we must train the person to fit the task.
- The system rather than the person must come first.

With more than 100 years of hindsight, we can now see that he pretty much got it backwards but, at the time, it was an important idea for engineering the workplace.

6.2.2 Early Industrial and Human Factors Engineering

WWI: Designing the human to fit the machine. By the time we were involved in World War I from roughly 1914–18, Taylor's ideas for industrial engineering were in full stride. Training was used to fit the human to work with the machine. Engineers built aircraft with all their controls and displays and then brought in potential pilots and trained them to fit the designs.

WWII: Birth of human factors and ergonomics. By the time we were engaged in World War II, the notion that you can train any human to fit any design was showing some cracks, which became substantial enough to start a new discipline, called human factors and ergonomics.

Col. Fitts and Cpt. Jones. The early heroes in this new field included Col. Paul Fitts and Capt. Richard Jones. US Air Force officials were concerned about airplane crashes suffered by experienced World War II pilots. Very fit, highly trained, and highly motivated people were making significant errors in task performance in the field. No matter how extensive the training or flying experience, pilots were making dangerous mistakes while operating the controls in the cockpit. Well-trained pilots were failing to detect the enemy on radars and were making "pilot errors" in airplane cockpits. Fitts and Jones (1947) concluded that the cause could not be flaws in training.

So, they studied critical incidents that may have led to airplane crashes. To better understand what was going on, they started interviewing pilots to see what problems they had, a practice that lives on today.

BT-13 airplane. In some of these interviews, Fitts and Jones talked with pilots of the BT-13 aircraft, who described unsettling scenarios they encountered during take off. As the plane was rolling down the runway, the pilot wanted to adjust the pitch of the prop to give more thrust but instead "accidentally" adjusted the fuel mixture, causing a loss in power and the need to abort the takeoff.

Instead of pulling the prop pitch lever, the pilot was pulling the fuel mixture lever. Why? The two levers were right next to each other and looked exactly like one another. Therefore, it was easy to make a slip and grab the wrong lever, an act they came to understand could not be avoided by any amount of training.

B-17 airplane. In similar interviews, pilots of the B-17 bomber related comparable stories about landing the plane. In one such story heard frequently, as they came in for a landing the pilot asked the copilot to turn on the landing lights. But somehow the copilot "accidentally" hit the flaps switch. The plane nosed into the runway and suffered serious damage. Fortunately, the pilot and copilot survived and, therefore, could report the incident.

The reports of Fitts and Jones are among the very earliest that recognized the causal connection between design flaws, rather than human errors, and mishaps in user performance.

Lt. Alphonse Chapanis. The third hero of this era was Lt. Alphonse Chapanis, a human factors researcher called in to investigate another peculiar behavior: pilots of B-17s, B-25s, and P-47s would retract the landing gear after landing! Why were these people doing such a foolish thing? And why was that happening with just these aircraft and not others? Through observations and pilot interviews, they discovered that the controls for retracting the landing gear and the controls for adjusting the flaps after landing were, you guessed it, similar in appearance and located right next to each other.

Chapanis realized that he couldn't change the design of the layout of controls in these mass-produced aircraft, so he came up with a clever in-the-field fix. He put two different kinds of knobs on these controls—one was a circular object much like the wheel from a rolling chair and the other was a wedge-shaped solid object. Then, through tactile feedback without even looking, a pilot can feel the circular, wheel-like object and know that's for the wheels. When the pilot felt the wedge-shaped handle, he knew that's for the flaps.

This must have been one of the very earliest examples of redesign to meet user needs, adding cognitive affordances through an understanding of how users were using a design in a way that was different from the designers' original intent.

6.2.3 Dreyfuss, after WW II

In the mid-1950s, in his seminal book *Designing for People,* Henry Dreyfuss, an American industrial designer, wrote that difficulties in interaction with a product are not necessarily the fault of the human user, but often it is because the designer has failed.

6.2.4 Human Factors Meets HCI

Human factors is about making things work better for people. For example, think about building a bridge: You use theory, good design practice, and engineering principles, but you can't really know if it will work. So you build it, but who's going to be the first one to test it? Well, that's one of the reasons we have graduate students.

– Phyllis Reisner

Human factors is an engineering discipline dedicated to bringing science and technology together with human behavior and biological characteristics for design and maintenance of products and systems for safe, effective, and satisfying use. It's not surprising that, when human factors entered the computer age, it made a good fit with the emerging field of human-computer interaction and usability.

In fact, many ideas and concepts from human factors laid the basis for HCI techniques later on. For example, the idea of task analysis was first used by human factors specialists in analyzing factory workers' actions on an assembly line. For many working in human factors engineering, the move to focus on HCI was a natural and easy transition.

Psychology and cognitive science. Much of the foundation for HCI has also been closely related to theory in psychology, derived from adaptations of psychological theory and models of human information processing (HIP) (Barnard, 1993; Hammond, Gardiner, & Christie, 1987). Concepts such as user modeling and user performance metrics were adopted into HCI from cognitive and behavioral psychology and psychometrics.

Perhaps the most important application of psychology to HCI has been in the area of modeling users as human information processors (Moran, 1981b; Williges, 1982), which offered the first theory within HCI. Most human performance prediction models stem from Card, Moran, and Newell (1983), including the keystroke level model (Card, Moran, & Newell, 1980), the command language grammar (Moran, 1981a), the Goals, Operators, Methods, and Selections (GOMS) family of models (Card et al., 1983), the cognitive complexity theory of Kieras and Polson (1985), and programmable user models (Young, Green, & Simon, 1989).

HCI was also influenced by the empirical aspects of psychology. For example, Fitts law (relating cursor travel time to distance and size of target) (Fitts, 1954; MacKenzie, 1992) is clearly connected to kinesthetics and human performance.

Like human factors engineering, cognitive psychology has many connections to design for human performance, including cognition, memory, perception, attention, sense and decision making, and human behavioral characteristics and limitations, elements that clearly have much to do with user experience.

Human Information Processing (HIP)

An approach to HCI based on the cognitive science metaphor of "mind and computer as symmetrically coupled information processors" (Harrison, Tatar, & Sengers, 2007) (Section 6.4.2).

6.2.5 Computer Science: Hardware and Software Foundations of Human-Computer Interaction

In the 1960s, more people with less technical training were getting into contact with computers. Up until this time, all user interaction was keyboard based—until the very first experimental pointing device, the first mouse (Fig. 6-1), invented by Douglas Engelbart.[1]

At this time, interaction devices were not standardized; you couldn't take an input device from one computer and use it on the next. So a new focus in computer science emerged in creating devices, interaction styles, and supporting software for interoperability and for human ergonomics. Soon (c.1960), we were in an era of research and development on keyboards, CRT terminals, text editors, and training manuals. At this point, the main participants in HCI from computer science were software people and much of the work was about input/output devices and user interface programming.

Software engineering. The closest kin of human-computer interaction and usability engineering on the computer science side is the more mature discipline of software engineering. Despite very different philosophical underpinnings, the

[1]https://en.wikipedia.org/wiki/Computer_mouse.

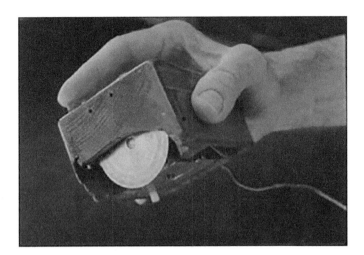

Fig. 6-1

The first computer mouse (from SRI International).

two fields have development lifecycles with similar and complementary structures, including activities such as requirement gathering, design, and evaluation.

In an ideal world, one would expect close connections between these two lifecycles as they operate in parallel during the development of a unified interactive system. However, in the past, these two roles typically have not communicated with one another much until the very end when actual implementation starts. This was often too late, especially when interaction design concerns have serious software architectural implications. One of the reasons for this apparent lack of connection between the two lifecycles is because of how these two disciplines grew, without either one strongly influencing the other. In fact, barring a few exceptions, the software engineering and usability engineering researchers and practitioners have mostly ignored one another over the years. Fortunately, this is changing in today's agile approaches.

Interactive graphics, devices, and interaction techniques. A new thread began appearing in the literature and practice on the computer science side of the HCI equation. This work on interactive graphics, interaction styles, software tools, dialogue management systems, programming language translation, and interface "widgets" was essential in opening the way to practical programming techniques for bringing interaction designs to life on computers.

The origin of computer graphics is frequently attributed to pioneers such as Ivan Sutherland (1963, 1964) and solidified by masters such as Foley and colleagues (Foley & Van Dam, 1982; Foley, Van Dam, Feiner, & Hughes, 1990; Foley & Wallace, 1974) and Newman (1968). For an insightful account of the relationship of graphics to HCI, see Grudin (2006).

The 1980s and 1990s saw a burgeoning of hardware and software development to support the now familiar point-and-click style of interaction, including the Xerox Star (Smith, Irby, Kimball, Verplank, & Harslem, 1989) and the Lisa and Macintosh by Apple. Personal computing brought with it a kind of democratization of computing—computing for everyone, not just the elite geeks.

In the context of an interaction technique (Foley et al., 1990), an interaction object and its supporting software were often referred to as a "widget." Programmers developed libraries of widget software to support programming of graphical user interfaces. Early graphics packages took interaction beyond text to direct manipulation of graphical objects, eventually leading to new concepts in displays and cursor tracking. No longer tied to just a keyboard or even just a keyboard and mouse, many unusual (then, and some still now) interaction techniques arose (Buxton, 1986; Hinckley, Pausch, Goble, & Kassell, 1994; Jacob, 1993). Myers led the field in user interface software tools of all kinds (Myers, 1989, 1992, 1993, 1995; Myers, Hudson, & Pausch, 2000), and Olsen is known for his work in user interface software (Olsen, 1983).

So many people contributed to the work on User Interface Management Systems (UIMS) that it is impossible to even begin to recognize them all. Buxton, Lamb, Sherman, and Smith (1983) were among the earliest thinkers in this area. Others we remember are Brad Myers, Dan Olsen, Mark Green, Jim Foley's group at GWU, and our researchers at Virginia Tech. Much of this kind of work was, and still is, reported in the ACM Symposium on User Interface Software and Technology (UIST), a conference specifically for user-interface software.

The commercial world followed suit and we worked through quite a number of proposed "standard" interaction styles, such as OSF Motif (The Open Group). Developers had to choose from those available mainly because the interaction styles were not interoperable. Each approach was tied closely to its own software tools for generating the programming code for interaction designs using the devices and interaction styles of these approaches. Standardization led to today's GUI platforms and corresponding styles.

This growth of graphics and devices made possible one of the major breakthroughs in interaction styles—direct manipulation (Hutchins, Hollan, & Norman, 1986; Shneiderman, 1983), changing the basic paradigm of interaction with computers. Direct manipulation allows opportunistic and incremental task planning. Users can try something and see what happens, exploring many avenues for interactive problem solving.

6.2.6 Changing Concepts of Computing and Interaction

For a long time, interaction was about screens full of data fields displayed on dumb terminals connected to mainframes. When PCs first came along, their screens pretty much looked the same—full of panels containing data fields.

Paradigm

A model, pattern, template, or intellectual perception or view guiding a way of thinking and doing. Historically, with respect to a field of thought and work, it is thought of as coming in waves over time (Section 6.4).

Interaction (in UX)

A broad term referring to a wide variety of communication and collaboration between a human and a device, product, or system in an ecology (Section 1.1).

Then along came GUIs, the Internet, and the web. And now it is going well beyond that to all kinds of personal, handheld, and mobile devices as well as devices embedded in appliances, homes, and cars—and beyond.

Sitting in front of a desktop or laptop usually conveys a feeling of "doing computing" to users. But, when we drive a car we don't think of ourselves as "doing computing," yet we are using the car's built-in computer and maybe even a GPS. As Mark Weiser (1991) said, "the world is not a desktop."

6.2.6.1 Disappearing technology

Interaction, however, is doing more than just reappearing in different devices such as we see in web access via mobile phone. Weiser (1991) said "… the most profound technologies are those that disappear." Russell, Streitz, and Winograd (2005) also talk about the disappearing computer—not computers that are ceasing to exist, but disappearing in the sense of becoming unobtrusive and unremarkable. They use the example of electric motors, which are part of many machines we use daily yet we almost never think about electric motors per se. They talk about "making computers disappear into the walls and interstices of our living and working spaces." The next two sections are about kinds of interaction that can occur in this disappearing technology.

6.2.6.2 Embedded, ubiquitous, and ambient interaction

Embedded interaction, ubiquitous interaction, and ambient interaction are somewhat related concepts having to do with the relationship of devices and systems as well as their interaction with their environments. The terms are very similar and there is much overlap.

Embedded interaction. An embedded system is a computational system (a computer-like device) set within another device or system—for example, a control unit embedded within a home appliance. We can walk around with wearable computing devices embedded in our clothing or within a shoe. In a project at MIT, volunteer soldiers were instrumented with sensors that could be worn as part of their clothing to monitor heart rate, body temperature, and other parameters to detect the onset of hypothermia (Zieniewicz, Johnson, Wong, & Flatt, 2002).

Practical applications in business already reveal the almost unlimited potential for commercial applications. Gershman and Fano (2005) cite an example of a smart railcar that can keep track of and report on its own location, state of repair, whether it is loaded or empty, and its routing, billing, and security status (including aspects affecting homeland security). Imagine the promise this shows for improved efficiency and cost savings over the mostly manual and error-prone methods currently used to keep track of railroad cars.

In fact, you can embed radio frequency identification (RFID) chips and even GPS capabilities into almost any physical object and connect it wirelessly to the Internet. Such an object can be queried about what it is, where it is, and what it is doing. You can ask your lost possessions where they are (Churchill, 2009; Gellersen, 2005). There are obvious applications to products on store or warehouse shelves and inventory management. More intelligence can be built into these objects, giving them capabilities beyond self-identification to sensing their own environmental conditions.

Ubiquitous interaction. As the term "ubiquitous" implies, ubiquitous interaction technology—often called ubiquitous computing (Weiser, 1991) in the literature—can exist almost anywhere. Interaction technology can reside in appliances, homes, offices, stereos and entertainment systems, vehicles, roads, and objects we carry (briefcases, purses, wallets, wrist watches). This interaction in everyday contexts is taking place without keyboards, mice, or monitors. As Cooper, Reimann, and Dubberly (2003) say, you do not need a traditional user interface to have interaction.

Kuniavsky (2003) concludes that ubiquitous computing requires extra careful attention to design for the user experience. He believes ubiquitous computing devices should be narrow and specifically targeted rather than multipurpose or general-purpose devices looking more like underpowered laptops. And he emphasizes the ecological perspective: We need to design complete systems and infrastructures rather than just devices.

An example of distributing the "system" into the environment is the "Amazon Dash" order buttons. These are buttons you have around the house that, when pressed, will place a preconfigured order. So an Amazon Dash button next to a washing machine in the laundry room can be pressed to order detergent when you are running low. That is the only capability of the button. These buttons also leverage tangible and embodied interaction advantages because of the physicality of pressing the button to order a product.

Ambient interaction. As the term "ambient" implies, ambient interaction technology is "environmental" in that it is in everyday surroundings and, as such, it can also be thought of as embedded and ubiquitous.

Your house, its walls, and its furniture can surround you with interactive technology. An ambient system can extract or sense inputs from the environment and take the initiative to communicate with humans and with other objects and devices (Tungare et al., 2006) without a deliberate or conscious action by a user. The simplest example is a thermostat that senses the ambient temperature and adjusts the heat or cooling accordingly. As a more sophisticated example, a "smart wall" can proactively extract inputs it needs by sensing a user's presence and identifying the user with something like RFID technology. It is still user-system interaction, only the system is controlling the interaction and the human "user" may not always be aware, or need to be aware, of the interaction.

This kind of interaction is sometimes called "ambient intelligence," the goal of considerable research and development aimed at the home living environment. In the HomeLab of Philips Research in the Netherlands (Markopoulos, Ruyter, Privender, & Breemen, 2005), researchers believe "that ambient intelligence technology will mediate, permeate, and become an inseparable common (element) of our everyday social interactions at work or at leisure."

Everyday objects such as milk and groceries can be tagged with inexpensive machine-readable identifiers, allowing changes in those artifacts to be detected automatically. This means your mobile phone can keep in touch with your refrigerator to track items you need (Ye & Qiu, 2003). And, as you approach the grocery store, you get a reminder to stop and pick up some milk.

More and more applications that were in research labs are now moving into commercial adoption. For example, robots in more specialized applications than just housecleaning or babysitting are gaining in numbers (Scholtz, 2005). There are robotic applications for healthcare rehabilitation, including systems to encourage severely disabled children to interact with their environment (Lathan, Brisben, & Safos, 2005); robotic products to assist the elderly (Forlizzi, 2005); robots as laboratory hosts and museum docents (Sidner & Lee, 2005); robot devices for urban search and rescue (Murphy, 2005); and, of course, robotic rover vehicles for unmanned space missions (Hamner, Lotter, Nourbakhsh, & Shelly, 2005).

6.2.6.3 Situated, embodied, and tangible interaction

Situated interaction. While embedded, ubiquitous, and ambient technologies take something of an outside-in ecocentric perspective, as in how the environment relates to the user, situated, embodied, and tangible interactions take a somewhat user-centric inside-out perspective, as in how the user relates to the environment.

Situated awareness refers to technology that is aware of its context. As an example, this includes awareness of the presence of human users in an activity space. In a social interaction setting, this can help find specific people, help optimize deployment of a team, or help cultivate a feeling of community and belonging (Sellen, Eardley, Izadi, & Harper, 2006).

Being situated is all about a sense of "place," the place of interaction within the broader usage context. An example of situated awareness (credit not ours) is a cell phone that "knows" it is in a movie theater or that the owner is in a nonphone conversation; that is, the device or product encompasses knowledge of the rules of human social politeness.

Embodied and tangible interaction. Complementing situated awareness, *embodied interaction refers to the ability to involve one's physical body in interaction with technology in a natural way, such as by gestures.* Antle (2009) defines embodiment as, "how the nature of a living entity's cognition is shaped by the form of its physical manifestation in the world." As she points out, in contrast to the human as information processor view of cognition, humans are primarily active agents, not just "disembodied symbol processors." This implies bringing interaction into the human's physical world to involve the human's own physical being.

Embodied interaction, first identified by Malcolm McCullough in *Digital Ground* (McCullough, 2004) and further developed by Paul Dourish in *Where the Action is* (Dourish, 2001), is central to the changing nature of interaction. Dourish says, "how we understand the world, ourselves, and interaction comes from our location in a physical and social world of embodied factors." Embodied interaction is action situated in the world.

To make it a bit less abstract, think of a person who has just purchased something with "some assembly required." To sit with the instruction manual and just think about it pales in comparison to physically doing the assembly—holding the pieces and moving them around, trying to fit them this way and that, seeing and feeling the spatial relations and associations among the pieces, seeing the assembly take form, and feeling how each new piece fits. This is exactly the reason that physical sketching gives such a boost to invention and ideation. The involvement of the physical body, the motor movements, the visual connections, and the potentiation of hand-eye-mind collaboration lead to an embodied cognition far more effective than just sitting and thinking.

Although tangible interaction seems to have a following of its own (Ishii & Ullmer, 1997), it is very closely related to embodied interaction. You could say that they complement each other. *Tangible interaction involves physical actions between human users and physical objects.* Industrial designers have been dealing with it for years, designing objects and products to be held, felt, and manipulated by humans. The difference now is that the object involves some kind of computation. And there is a strong emphasis on physicality, form, and tactile interaction (Baskinger & Gross, 2010).

More than ever before, tangible and embodied interaction calls for physical prototypes as three-dimensional sketches to inspire the ideation and design process.

Ideation

An active, creative, exploratory, highly iterative, fast-moving, and usually collaborative, brainstorming process for forming ideas for design (Section 14.2).

Sketching

The rapid creation of free-hand drawings expressing preliminary design ideas, focusing on concepts rather than details. Is an essential part of ideation. A sketch is a conversation between the sketcher or designer and the artifact (Section 14.3).

6.2.7 Evolving Importance of UX
6.2.7.1 Emerging desire for usability

Initial tolerance of a poor user experience. In the distant past, computer usage was esoteric, conducted mostly by a core of technically oriented users who were not only willing to accept the challenge of overcoming poor usability, but who sometimes welcomed it as a barrier to protect the craft from uninitiated "outsiders." Poor usability was good for the mystique, not to mention job security. And for other users, being new to this incomprehensible technology meant acceptance of the learning and frustration ahead.

Dancing bear software. Sometimes, even more recently, we have what Cooper (2004, p. 26) calls "dancing bear" software. It is where an amazing idea triumphs over poor design. It is about having features just so good users cannot do without it, even if it has a terrible interaction design. Just having a bear that can dance leads one to overlook the fact that it cannot dance very well. Success despite poor interaction design can be used as a justification for resisting change and keeping the bad design ideas: "We have been doing it that way, our product is selling phenomenally, and our users love it." Think of how much better it could be with a good design.

6.2.7.2 The rise of usability engineering

Roughly in the 1990s, the focus moved to usability engineering, which focused heavily on elaborate usability evaluation methods. It has been more than two decades since the first usability engineering "process" books, such as Nielsen (1993), Hix and Hartson (1993), and Mayhew (1999), emerged from this period. This era encompassed early human-computer interaction (HCI) concepts, but still had a bit of a software flavor (e.g., in the software tools for user interface implementation) as well as "standards" for look and feel. This era of the discipline did much to improve usability of software everywhere and to raise awareness of the need to do so.

6.2.7.3 The rise of user experience

Up until about 1990, the focus had been mostly on methods—how can we come up with a prescriptive process that teams can use to realize some level of usability in the final product, usually in a business or professional setting?

But computers, especially personal computers, were becoming more affordable to individuals and it was more important for the average person to attain a good overall user experience in their use. Sometime about 2000, voices like that of Don Norman moved the focus from the narrow concept of usability to a broader idea of the user experience (UX), embracing more of the total usage phenomenon and including emotional impact. And that's where we are with this book!

6.3 SHIFTING PARADIGMS IN HCI AND UX

A paradigm is a model, pattern, template, or intellectual perception or view guiding a way of thinking and doing. Historically, with respect to a field of thought and work, thought of as coming in waves over time.

Harrison et al. (2007) tell us that designers approach design problems with a particular worldview, embracing specific practices, expectations, and values. They call these worldview paradigms, models of thinking that come as waves of thought in time.

Some of the history of HCI and UX can be seen as "waves" of these paradigms, shifting over time. About the same time, Susanne Bødker introduced her own concept of a third wave of HCI in her keynote address at NordCHI 2006 (Bødker, 2015).

Harrison et al. (2007) distinguish three major intellectual waves that have formed the field of HCI:

- Engineering—human factors engineering and usability engineering: To optimize the match between human and machine. The metaphor of interaction is about a match of human and machine.
- Human information-processing model and cognitive science: This wave emphasized models of the relationship of the human mind to computers and theories of what is happening in the human mind during and with respect to interaction. The metaphor of interaction is "human minds are like information processors."
- Phenomenology: This wave focuses on the experiential quality of interaction. The metaphor of interaction is about making meaning (more on this when we talk about phenomenology) and how users experience meaning within an artifact and its use.

Human Factors

An engineering discipline dedicated to bringing science and technology together with human behavior and biological characteristics for design and maintenance of products and systems for safe, effective, and satisfying use (Section 6.3.4).

The driving force of their third paradigm was the fact that the essence of social and situated actions was at odds with both the usability-oriented engineering paradigm and the cognitive logic of the human information processor approach. Given the initial reluctance of HCI as a field to embrace the phenomenological paradigm, the Harrison et al. paper was an evangelical wake-up call to pay attention and include the phenomenological paradigm in mainstream HCI.

6.3.1 Engineering Paradigm

With its roots in software and human factors engineering, the engineering paradigm in HCI prescribed starting with an inventory of the functionality envisioned for a new system and proceeding to build those items with the best quality possible given available resources. The engineering focus is on functionality, reliability, user performance, and avoiding errors. Recognizing that user interaction deserved attention on its own, usability engineering emerged as a practical approach to usability with a focus on improving user performance, mainly through evaluation and iteration.

The engineering paradigm also had strong roots in human factors, where "work" was studied, deconstructed, and modeled. An example is the study of an assembly line where each action required to do work was carefully described. It was a purely utilitarian and requirements-driven approach. Alternative methods and designs were compared and success was measured by how much the user could accomplish.

6.3.2 Human Information Processing (HIP) Paradigm

The HIP approach to HCI is based on the cognitive science metaphor of "mind and computer as symmetrically coupled information processors." This paradigm at its base is about models of how information is sensed, accessed, and transformed in the human mind and, in turn, how those models reflect requirements for the computer side of the information processing. It was defined by Card et al. (1983) and well explained by Williges (1982).

6.3.3 Phenomenological Paradigm

Harrison, Tatar, and Sengers called their third HCI design paradigm the "phenomenological matrix" (Harrison et al., 2007).

Phenomenological aspects of interaction are part of what was called the "hedonic phase" (the rise of interest in emotional impact), about how we embrace artifacts, devices, and products and take them into our personal world. The phenomenological paradigm is about social and cultural aspects of interaction, interaction involving our whole bodies and spirits.

6.3.3.1 Making meaning

The metaphor of interaction within the phenomenological paradigm is a form of meaning making (Harrison et al., 2007) in which an artifact (device, product, or system) and its context are mutually defining and subject to multiple interpretations by designers, analysts, users, and other stakeholders.

Use, usage, usability, usefulness, and functional descriptions all refer to what you can do with a product. Phenomenology is about what the product means to the user.

Meaning and meaning construction are central to the phenomenological view of interaction. Meaning is constructed on the fly, often collaboratively, in context and situations. "Interaction is an essential element in meaning construction" (Harrison et al., 2007). Information is interpreted through viewpoints, interactions, histories, and local resources. Meaning and knowledge are very much local to (strongly situated in) the person who is the user and the interaction. Because knowledge and meaning are "situated" or "embodied," both are influenced, even defined or constructed, by where you are and what you are doing, especially socially. This is why there are many contexts and, therefore, many perspectives and many interpretations versus one correct understanding and one correct set of metrics.

6.3.4 All three paradigms have a place in design and development

Consider, as an example, the design of an automobile.

Engineering view. Emphasis in the engineering view is on functionality, features, and reliability. Importance is given to performance (speed and acceleration) as well as fuel economy.

Also in the engineering view, human factors and ergonomics are paramount. For example, steering wheel thickness must fit an average human's hand size and strength. Same for seat height, the fit of the curve on the seat to the human lower back, and safety restraints.

Human-information processing view. The presentation of critical information needed for driving must meet the limits of human signal detection. Information displays and interaction devices must support cognitive and decision making actions.

Phenomenological view. In contrast, the phenomenological view of car design is about how a car can become an integral part of the owner's lifestyle. It's about appeal and coolness of the ride, the joy of driving, possibly the thrill of speed, and pride of ownership.

6.4 FUN INTERACTION AT WORK

6.4.1 What about Fun at Work

Emotional impact factors such as fun, aesthetics, and joy of use are obviously desirable in personal use of commercial products, but what about in task-oriented work situations? Here usability and usefulness aspects of user experience are obvious, but the need for emotional impact is not so clear.

6.4.2 Fun Can Make Some Work More Interesting

However, there is evidence that fun can also help at work to break monotony and to increase interest and attention span, especially for repetitive and possibly boring work such as that performed in call centers. Fun can enhance the appeal of less inherently challenging work, for example, clerical work or data entry, which can increase performance and satisfaction (Hassenzahl, Beu, & Burmester, 2001). It is easy to see how fun can lead to job satisfaction and enjoyment of some kinds of work.

Emotional and rational behaviors play complementary roles in our own lives such that emotional aspects of interaction are not necessarily detrimental to our reasoning processes for doing work. For example, software for learning, which can otherwise be dull and boring, can be made more interesting with a dose of novelty, surprise, and spontaneity.

6.4.3 But Fun Can Trade Off with Usability

However, fun and usability can conflict in work situations. Too simple can mean loss of attention, and consistency can translate as boring. But less boring means less predictable and less predictable usually goes against traditional usability attributes, such as consistency and ease of learning (Carroll & Thomas, 1988). Fun requires a balance: not too simple or boring, but not too challenging or frustrating.

6.4.4 Fun Is Not Compatible with Some Work Situations

Some work roles and jobs are simply not amenable to fun as part of the work practice. Consider a job that is inherently challenging and that requires full attention to the task, such as air traffic control. It is essential for air traffic controllers to have no-nonsense software tools that are efficient and effective. Any distraction due to novelty or even slight barriers to performance due to clever and "interesting" design features will be hated and could even be dangerous. For this kind of work, users often want less mental effort, more predictable interaction paths, and more consistent behavior. They especially do not want a system or software tool adding to the complexity.

Certainly the addition of a game-like feature is welcome in an application designed primarily for fun or recreation, but imagine an air traffic controller having to solve a fun little puzzle before the system gives access to the controls so that the air traffic controller can help guide a plane heading for a mountain in the fog.

Waterfall Lifecycle Process

One of the earliest formal software engineering lifecycle processes; an ordered linear sequence of lifecycle activities, each of which flowed into the next like a set of cascading tiers of a waterfall (Section 4.2).

6.5 WHO INTRODUCED THE WATERFALL MODEL?

It's unclear who gets the credit (or blame) for first expounding on the waterfall model for software development. Royce (1970) is the most frequently cited source and probably the first formal description of the process. By association with that publication, Royce is credited with "inventing" or introducing the process. But this is a misconception as the method had already been in use for some time and, it seems, the Royce paper was intended as a critique of the method as one that didn't work. And, by the way, it wasn't called the "waterfall model" until 1976 (Bell & Thayer, 1976).

And the Royce paper was, in fact, preceded (by some 14 years) by a presentation by Benington (1956) that described it as a method used to develop software for the SAGE[2] project. This paper was later republished (Benington, 1983) in a historical perspective, and Bennington added a foreword stating that the process wasn't intended to be used in a strict top-down way and that it depended on a prototype stage. In 1985, the Department of Defense decided to make the waterfall approach a software development standard (Department of Defense, 1998) for their software development contractors.

Because the waterfall process was so organized and systematic compared with any previous approach, you might have called it the Frederick Taylor (Section 6.3.1) movement of software engineering.

6.6 SILOS, WALLS, AND BOUNDARIES

The boxes of the waterfall model (Fig. 4-1) were sometimes called "silos" because they strongly compartmentalized the lifecycle activities, a compartmentalization that was usually reflected in the developer or contractor's organization. One group or department had sole responsibility for requirement specifications and nothing else. A different department did design while a completely separate department was tasked with implementation.

6.6.1 Working in Silos

Each group working within its own box was typically organized under hierarchical administrative authority. These departmental organizations were referred to as "silos" because of their vertical organizational structure and their isolation from the other departmental groups. Requests for major decisions bubbled up to the top of each silo and the decisions filtered back down to the troops on the ground.

Rather than being inclined to collaborate in decision making, groups were more likely to be motivated to compete against each other. Worse, they couldn't

---

[2]The Semi-Automatic Ground Environment, a 1950s system of large computers and the associated NORAD cold war computer network that coordinated data from many radar sites and processed it to produce a single unified image of the airspace over a wide area (https://en.wikipedia.org/wiki/Semi-Automatic_Ground_Environment).

collaborate if they wanted to because silos make it impossible to have a shared understanding of the big picture.

It's not that a silo-based approach implies a lack of competence. Each group does its thing really well. Inside a silo you can find well-sharpened skills and even close communication. But that communication cannot easily penetrate silo walls. When these organizations started forming multidisciplinary cross-disciplinary teams, with members representing each silo, it turned out to be nearly impossible to make timely decisions about important issues. The representatives had to take each major issue back to their respective groups, then up and down the silo to get a decision, and finally return to the composite team.

And each silo group will find any desire to be innovative overcome by a motivation to protect itself against risks and fear of being blamed for failure. Fear of failure is justified because there is so much going on in the other silos that designers have no control over. It is only natural to say "no" to any suggestions to be innovative and stray from run of the mill, almost guaranteeing the real risk of a mediocre overall design at best.

Silo-oriented organizations encourage people to rally around project and administrative boundaries rather than rallying around the products or systems they are supposed to be developing. They also hide behind platform boundaries. For example, because mobile apps require different talents for analysis, design, implementation, and even marketing, it's easy for separate business, product, and engineering silos to emerge for your mobile development. This will, of course, lead to a chasm of disconnect between the mobile, desktop, and web versions of your app.

Can you expect high morale in such an environment? No. Instead of engagement, excitement, and energy, you will usually see finger pointing, disputes about ownership, poor communication, blocked collaboration, and duplication of effort on some things while other things fall through the cracks. You will usually see people "just doing their jobs" in their own specializations. If you add in any geographic distribution of the team, even in different buildings, you have completely killed any chance of being able to respond to change as it occurs during the process.

6.6.2 Throwing it Over the Wall

Work in any box of the lifecycle couldn't begin until they received the output documents from the previous box. So, for example, nothing could happen in the design group until the requirements group completed their work and "threw the documentation over the wall" from their silo to the next.

And when is it time to throw it over the wall to the group doing the next phase? It's easy: just look at the calendar. When the scheduled end date for the current phase arrives, you are done. All unresolved problems are also given to the next silo and the former owners of these problems are quite happy they will never see them again. The walls or boundaries are the hand-off points for both documentation and responsibility. This putting off of harder problems can continue until, at some point, it is painfully obvious that something is badly wrong. You have something critical that needed to be fixed a long time ago. Now it's time to see what the project manager is made of.

6.6.3 Many Projects Collapsed Under the Weight

In the software engineering (SE) world, the waterfall model has proven to be difficult in practice, at least for larger and more complex systems. Because this kind of top-down lifecycle process is very thorough and features a full system overview upfront, it was said that these systems were designed holistically and that sounds like a good thing. But, in fact, this long and drawn-out lifecycle has proven to be unsustainable in practice, resulting in projects that are over budget, behind schedule, can't manage change, or just plain failed.

6.6.4 UX Design Suffers

A marketing manager might understand the needs that get expressed as requirements and a business analyst might own the resulting features, but neither has anything to do with creating the design. Today, a UX specialist might create the interaction design, but in this kind of development environment, a software engineer or programmer or web developer will change that design as needed to put it together in the software, undermining the UX design and creating the real, but not always satisfying, user experience.

Usage Research

2

Part 2 addresses the lifecycle activity of understanding user needs. To understand user needs, the UX professional must understand the work and work practice, including work roles, challenges in current practice, breakdowns and workarounds, inefficiencies, constraints, regulations, culture, so on. The primary method described for obtaining this broad range of understanding is usage research. Other approaches are variations and abbreviations of the usage research method.

The foundation of our material on usage research goes back to the work of Karen Holtzblatt and others on contextual inquiry and contextual design (Beyer & Holtzblatt, 1997; Holtzblatt, Wendell, & Wood, 2004). Another influence was Constantine and Lockwood (1999).

This lifecycle activity of understanding user needs begins with usage research data elicitation, usually accomplished through observing and interviewing people in user work roles. Data elicitation is best done in the real work environment.

Next is usage research analysis, which involves distilling the essence of usage research data into elemental work activity notes, extracting work activity notes that are inputs to user stories, requirements, and usage research data models.

The remaining work activity notes can be organized via a work activity affinity diagram, a bottom-up technique for organizing lots of disparate pieces of usage research data into a hierarchical structure.

The UX practitioner brings it all together to synthesize a full understanding of user work practice, the work domain, and user needs.

Usage Research Data Elicitation

7

Highlights

- The concepts of work, work practice, and work domain.
- Data elicitation goals and our approach.
- Before the visit:
  - How to prepare for undertaking usage research activities.
  - How to get ready to conduct usage research by meeting with customers and potential users to gather usage research data.
- During the visit: How to collect data during the usage research field visit.
- Kinds of information to look for.
- Writing good raw data notes.

7.1 INTRODUCTION

7.1.1 You Are Here

We begin each process chapter with a "you are here" picture of the chapter topic in the context of The Wheel, the overall UX design lifecycle template (Fig. 7-1). Within the Understand Needs lifecycle activity, this chapter is about the data elicitation subactivity, in which you observe and interview the client and users to meet the goal of understanding user needs by acquiring a thorough knowledge of user work practice (or play practice) using an existing product or system.

A work activity is a set of jobs or tasks comprised of sensory, cognitive, and physical actions made by users to meet a goal in the course of carrying out the work practice. Data elicitation is an *empirical* process to gather real user work activity data. Data analysis in Chapter 8 is an *inductive* (bottom-up) process to organize, consolidate, and interpret the user work activity data. Chapter 9 is about the *synthesis* of various design-informing models (e.g., task descriptions, scenarios, user personas) and Chapter 10 is about a *deductive* analytic process for organizing and representing user stories, needs, and requirements.

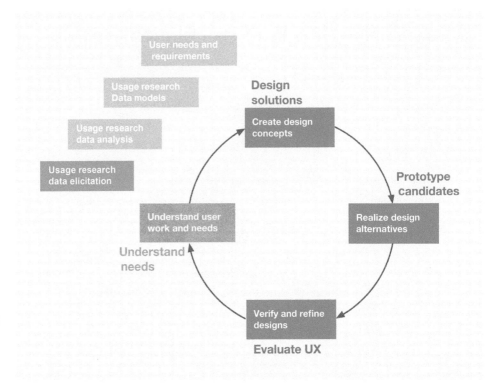

Fig. 7-1

You are here in the usage research data elicitation subactivity chapter within the Understand Needs lifecycle activity, in the context of the Wheel, the overall lifecycle process.

7.1.2 Usage Research Isn't about Asking Users What They Want

There has been some criticism of usage research, saying it is a flawed way to drive design because users often don't know what they want or need. Users are not designers.

This criticism is not just unfair; it's wrong. It's based on the incorrect perception of what usage research is. Usage research is not about asking users what they want in the design. Rather, usage research is about understanding user work practice and work activities in that context. It's your job as a UX team member to deduce their design needs.

For an anecdote about encountering usage data in the wild, in this case involving an elderly woman in a voting booth, see Section 11.2.

As we said in Section 2.5.2, each process chapter provides a variety of methods and techniques to match the needs of your project. Your job is to sort out the parts most applicable for your project based on perspective, scope, and the need for rigor.

For information about the history and roots of contextual inquiry and usage research, see Section 11.3.

7.2 SOME BASIC CONCEPTS OF USAGE RESEARCH DATA ELICITATION

7.2.1 The Concepts of Work, Work Practice, and Work Domain

User work. We use the term "work" (or "play") to refer to what needs to be done, or user goals within a given "problem" domain. In most cases, the term "work" will be obvious. An example is using a CAD/CAM application to design an automobile.

User work practice. "Work practice" is *how* people do their work. Work practice includes all activities, procedures, traditions, customs, and protocols associated with doing the work, usually as a result of the organizational goals, user skills, knowledge, and social interaction on the job.

If we are talking about the context of using a consumer product, such as a personal device or software product, then the work practice includes all user activities involved in using that product. If the product is, say, a word processor, it is easy to see its usage to compose, share, and edit a document as part of the work practice.

Work domain. The *work domain* is the complete context of the work practice, including the usage context of an associated system or product. In practice, we use "work domain" to include an entire industry (e.g., healthcare, cloud technology, or finance). In other words, a work domain is the broader context of an industry and includes multiple organizations (each a different work context) where the work is performed.

If the work context spans an organization such as a business, the project has an enterprise system perspective. If the work context is that of a product, such as a mobile mp3 music player, the problem domain is the work/play milieu of that product and the project has a commercial product perspective.

7.2.2 Understanding Other People's Work Practice

■ *A prerequisite to understanding needs.* Understanding user work practice is a necessary means on the path to understanding their needs.

Scope (of delivery)

Describes how the target system or product is "chunked" (broken into what size pieces) in each iteration or sprint for delivery to the client and users for feedback and to the software engineering team for agile implementation (Section 3.3).

Enterprise system perspective

A design viewpoint in which the design target is a large organizational information system (Section 3.4.1).

Product perspective

A design viewpoint in which the design target is a personal object (a consumer product), such as a device or software app, that a user buys for private use. The product perspective is a consumer perspective (Section 3.4.1).

▪ *A prelude for requirements.* This is not about requirements yet, but it's about understanding how users do their work. This will lead to insights about what it would take in a system design to support and improve the effectiveness of that work.

▪ *UX designers should make the effort.* Designers might think they know what is needed in a design to fit user needs. In a typical project without usage research, though, designers often waste time in arguments, discussions, and opinions.

▪ *It takes determination to learn about other people's work.* Often, details that drive the work are hidden beneath the surface: the intentions, strategies, motivations, and policies. People creatively solve and work around their problems, making their barriers and problems less visible to them and to outsiders studying the work.

7.2.3 Protecting Your Sources

Except for unusual circumstances, it is essential in your entire usage research process to maintain participant confidentiality and anonymity. This is especially important in cases where you have observed, synthesized, deduced, or were given insights that were about problems and breakdowns arising due to social and political issues in the work practice.

Talking about situations involving breakdowns due to bad management or flawed work practices (modeled in social models) is especially dangerous for your participants if there is a chance the sources will be revealed. Make this your unbreakable rule: *When you take data and models back to anyone, users or management, everything must be anonymous.* Otherwise, participants will be reticent about coming forward with valuable insights.

Participant

A participant, or user participant, is a user, potential, or user surrogate who helps evaluate UX designs for usability and user experience. These are the people who perform tasks and give feedback while we observe and measure. Because we wish to invite these volunteers to join our team and help us evaluate designs (i.e., we want them to participate), we use the term "participant" instead of "subject" (Section 21.1.3).

7.2.4 Not the Same as Task Analysis or a Marketing Survey

Your client might say, "We already do that. We do task analysis and marketing surveys." How should you respond to that? The simple answer is that they are not the same.

Task analysis is a systematic human factors technique of examining user tasks by studying the structure of tasks and task steps. This doesn't give enough insight into situations where tasks are interwoven or where users need to move seamlessly from one task to another within the work context.

Similarly, you cannot substitute market research for usage research. Marketing data are about sales and can identify the kinds of products and even features customers want, but do not lead to enough understanding about how people work or how to design for them. They are just two different kinds of analysis and you may need both.

7.2.5 Are We Studying an Existing Product/System or a New One?

At the end of the day, the answer might be "both." Analysts, designers, and users can be strongly biased toward thinking ahead to the new system, but almost everything we do in usage research *starts* with the existing system and work practice.

And for almost any new product or system, there is almost always *some* kind of existing practice. As an example, consider the Apple iPod (below).

Example: Innovative iPod Still Follows an "Existing" System

Many people considered the iPod to be a unique innovation at its conception. But, thinking about its usage context, it is basically a personal music-playing device (and much more) that still follows a history of existing products, going back to before we had electronic music players.

Looking at work activities and not devices, we see that people have been playing music for a long time. The iPod is another in a series of progressively sophisticated devices for doing that "work" activity, starting with the phonograph invented by Thomas Edison, or even possibly earlier ways to reproduce "recorded" sound.

If no one had ever recorded sound in any way prior to the first phonograph, then maybe you could say there was no "existing system" on which to conduct user research inquiry. But this kind of invention is extremely rare, a pure innovative moment. And you still might learn something about how people listen to live music. In any case, anything that happens in sound reproduction after that can be considered follow-on development and its use can be studied in user research inquiry.

7.3 DATA ELICITATION GOALS AND OUR APPROACH

Overarching goal: *Understand the work practice through the lens of existing users by visiting their work context and learning about them, how they do work, and what their work practice entails, including the challenges or hurdles they face and any workarounds they employ.*

7.3.1 Eliciting Data to Synthesize a Broad Overall Picture

Each such investigation (of a user) provides a different perspective into the work practice. This is like the perspective each blind person has while feeling an elephant (Section 8.9) in that famous parable where each blind person "sees" the elephant as something different. It is up to the usage researchers to gather the different perspectives and put them together to synthesize the elephant in the room.

7.3.2 It Requires Real Detective Work

In the field, researchers need to play Sherlock Holmes and do real detective work to tease out clues about the work practice with the goal of later constructing this complete picture of the work. The real story of how users actually do the work is often not in the surface observables. It may be easier to perceive how they are supposed to do it or even how they say they do it. If you ask users to describe how they do something, they tend to describe a sanitized or "canonical" flow and omit important details and workarounds outside the idealized or prescribed practice. This is because, with practice, such details about work get incorporated and internalized into routines. This is further aggravated by the fact that humans have a tendency to selectively recall and sometimes distort aspects of events after the fact.

Example: Discovering the Whole Area of Inventory by Following Leads

As an example of following leads, this is a real story told by a team doing a project for one of our classes. The client was in retail sales and the conversation part of the interview had centered on that concept, including serving their customers, making the sale transaction, and recording it.

However, during this conversation, the word "inventory" was mentioned once, in the context of point-of-sale data capture. No one had asked about inventory, so no one had mentioned it until now.

Our good ethnographic detectives, recognizing a clue revealing another area of work activities, pounced on that word and pursued a new train of thought. What about inventory? What role does it play in your point-of-sale data capture? Where does it go from there? How is it used and for what? How do you use inventory data to keep from running out of stock on items in demand? Who orders new stock and how? Once an order is sent, how do you keep track of it so it does not fall through the cracks? What happens when the new stock is delivered? How do you know when it arrives? Who works in receiving and what do they do? How do you handle partial shipments? How do you handle returns?

7.3.3 Tactical Goals

Understanding the work practice ecology: It is important to understand the broader connections among the work practice that are perhaps not the focus of the design team. Examples include outside systems that users of the target system rely on to get their job done. For example, do they use external news sources, data feeds from other services, third-party payroll systems? How do those systems interface with their immediate system in getting work done?

Understanding the information hierarchies and work flows: This has to do with mapping out key work flows in current work practice. For the enterprise system perspective, ask for screenshots of key screens and samples of reports or other work artifacts (ask to print them while on the visit and take notes on those artifacts). Ask to show how they would do such and such activity, including infrequent ones.

Understanding market forces and trends: In order to be truly innovative, the UX team must understand the client's market perspective, what the broader trends are, who the leading players are, where their domain is going, and the client's thoughts on the competition. What they like, what is better in their system, how they are different. For example, if the design brief is to design an automobile, it is important to understand broader trends such as self-driving cars and the shift away from fossil fuels. Users provide a unique perspective compared to other sources of marketing data because they live in this and know of friends or have experiences from previous jobs.

Here is a preview of the steps of data elicitation:

- Prepare for field visits.
- Conduct field visits to the customer and to where people will use the product or system:
  - Observe and interview people while they use the existing product or system (or a similar one, if the target product or system doesn't exist).
  - As you encounter usage research data points, write raw usage research data notes.
  - Gather any artifacts associated with the work practice.
  - As time permits, make sketches, diagrams, and/or photos of the product or system usage in its physical environment.

7.3.3.1 Using usage research data rather than opinion

Most of the time these days, early funnel UX work goes smoothly. But sometimes when you get into the late funnel and a larger team is involved, design ideas can be challenged. This is when you need usage research data in hand as a neutral arbiter of design disputes. This can be especially useful when you are being perceived as getting off course with your "innovation" and it's a battle against changing the status quo.

Sometimes we need a way to be sure design discussions/arguments don't come down to just a difference of two equal opinions but, rather, having the weight of usage research data on your side. "Yes, that is how we have done it in the past, but users say it's not the best way."

Artifact

An artifact (work artifact) is an object, usually tangible, that plays a role in the work flow of a system or enterprise—for example, a printed receipt in a restaurant (Section 9.8).

Early funnel

The part of the funnel (agile UX model) for large-scope activity, usually for conceptual design, before syncing with software engineering (Section 4.4.4).

7.4 BEFORE THE VISIT: PREPARE FOR DATA ELICITATION

Goal: *Learn everything you can about the client, the company, the business, the domain, and the product or system to be prepared and productive during the field visits.*

7.4.1 Learn about the Subject Domain

Do your homework. Start by learning everything you can about the subject domain of the product or system. While designing for complex and esoteric domains, working first with the client and subject matter experts helps shorten usage research data elicitation by giving you a deeper understanding of the domain. Data elicitation can now include validating this understanding with users.

- Learn about the culture of the work domain in general—for example, the precise and conservative financial domain versus the laid-back art domain.
- Know and understand the vocabulary, technical terms, acronyms, or slang of the product or system work domain.

Going on a field visit without first having a basic understanding of the domain can be supremely unproductive. This point is most important in esoteric domains where the jargon and concepts encode a great deal of meaning and nuance. When the users realize you don't know the basics about the domain, they will spend most of their time explaining the general concepts and giving you an off-the-cuff "tutorial" on the domain instead of discussing how they navigate its nuances. It will be an inefficient use of your time and of theirs.

7.4.2 Learn about the Client Company/Organization

- Identify client business goals.
- Get a feel for the customer's organizational policies and ethos by looking at their online presence (e.g., their website and their participation in social networks, user group sites, and related blogs).
- Learn about the competition.
- Learn the related best practices in this domain, this industry, and this company.
- Learn about any existing legacy systems.

7.4.3 Learn about the Proposed Product or System

- Check the initial product or system conceptualization documents (Section 5.6) for early statements about system functionality and structure and even the system architecture.

Legacy system

An old process, technology, computer system, or application program, of, relating to, or being a previous or outdated computer system with maintenance problems that date back possibly many years (Section 3.2.4).

■ Look at the history of the company's existing and previous products. If they are software products or systems, download trial versions to get familiar with existing design themes and capabilities.

■ Seek third-party reviews of the existing product or system. Look for branding, reputation, and competition in this product market segment.

7.4.4 Decide on Your Data Sources

The first choice of a data source for understanding user work practice and needs is often users who actually use the current product or system in the field.

But, depending on your project and its needs, the need for rigor, the cost of observing and interviewing users, and the availability of users as participants, you can consider supplemental or alternative data sources, including:

■ Subject-matter expert (SME) interviews.
■ Focus groups.
■ User surveys.
■ Competitive analysis.
■ Domain expertise through education.
■ Be your own domain expert.

7.4.4.1 Interview subject-matter experts (SMEs)

A subject-matter expert (SME) is someone with a deep understanding of a specific work domain and the range of work practice within that domain. Interviewing SMEs instead of users is definitely a faster technique to consider. And, although users can probably give you the best usage data information (e.g., unpredictable problems that crop up in real usage), SMEs can give other important kinds of information, such as an inside view of how a system should work. They can also provide deeper insights into variations of the work practice across that domain. For example, what are the differences between trading on the "buy-side" and "sell-side" desks on Wall Street? Further, they can provide insights into how the same type of activity is practiced at different sites. For example, how are sell-side traders at investment bank A different from those at B? How is the supply chain at purely online retailers such as Amazon different from combination brick and mortar plus online ones such as Walmart? Further, how is Walmart's supply chain different from the supply chain at Target? The idea is that they have insights into the philosophies and strengths of different businesses and organizations in the domain. Although these issues aren't the same as the actual work practice details where the rubber hits the road, they can have a profound influence on work practice.

Even when you do plan to interview users, working with subject matter experts before you talk to users can help shorten the activity by giving you a deeper understanding of the domain from the start.

7.4.4.2 Use dual experts

Sometimes, you are fortunate enough to recruit what they call "dual experts," experts in UX and the work domain. An example is a designer of Adobe Lightroom (a high-functionality software application for managing and processing large collections of images and photographs) who is also deeply involved in photography as a personal hobby. Another example is a designer of a GPS who is a truck driver or who travels extensively in an RV.

7.4.4.3 Listen to focus groups

A focus group (Krueger & Casey, 2008) is a technique wherein a small group of representative users or stakeholders discuss responses to broad questions and themes introduced by a moderator. Focus groups can be useful in eliciting a revealing conversation about more complex issues. Focus groups are good at identifying broad themes and issues in a work practice. They help unearth contrasting opinions and rationale for those opinions. They are good for getting at emotional impact issues, such as what participants like, dislike, love, or hate about the work practice. They are *not* good at identifying how-to details because the focus group is usually located away from actual work and work artifacts. The usual cautions about group dynamics apply. For example, you need to watch for dominant participants drowning out quieter ones.

7.4.4.4 Employ user surveys

User surveys are great for prioritizing themes. You can list different aspects of the work domain and ask users to rank or comment on their importance. You can ask for open-ended feedback, too, but these questions usually suffer from poor or selective recall. They can also suffer from vocal minority biases: respondents may have an axe to grind because of a bad experience and a desire to vent. There may be other biases; for example, certain types of users may be more prone to take time to participate in surveys and they may not be representative of the user population.

7.4.4.5 Do competitive analysis

An analysis based on comparison with market competitors can expose strengths and weaknesses and can help identify capability gaps and shortcomings. However, competitive analysis does not provide insight into usage. Even if a product has many features, all those features may not be used by the user

---

Emotional impact

An affective component of user experience that influences user feelings. Includes such effects as enjoyment, pleasure, fun, satisfaction, aesthetics, coolness, engagement, and novelty and can involve deeper emotional factors such as self-expression, self-identity, a feeling of contribution to the world, and pride of ownership (Section 1.4.4).

Focus group (in UX practice)

A small discussion group of representative users or stakeholders aimed at identifying broad themes and issues in a work practice (Section 7.4.4.3).

population. This kind of analysis is more of a marketing tool for making feature matrix comparisons than it is for usage related data.

7.4.4.6 Acquire domain knowledge through education
Sometimes you can prepare for usage research by educating yourself, learning through classes and other training about the core concepts, technologies, business practices, and trends in the subject matter of the work domain.

7.4.4.7 Be your own domain expert
Sometimes, if you are in fact a user (especially of a product or device), you can rely on your own experience and insights to understand users and their needs. For example, Apple designers are also Apple device users. And that has sometimes been the sole basis for design at Apple. Generally, though, being your own expert as an exclusive approach to data elicitation is recommended only as a fallback in case talking with users or SMEs is not possible, feasible, or affordable.

7.4.5 Choose Visit Parameters
The data elicitation method we describe in the bulk of this chapter is a mix of some rigor and some obvious ways to be efficient. This is not a fully rigorous method but rigorous enough for 99% of the projects out there, especially in agile environments.

However, you still have choices among the parameters of how you do data elicitation. If you choose to do your data elicitation with users in the field, this is the time to choose parameters.

Depending on the nature of your project, whether it is in the commercial product perspective or the enterprise system perspective, the need for rigor versus speed, and so forth, you need to decide as a team on:

- How many visits you can or should make?
- How many users you can or should interview per visit?
- What kind of user roles and users to involve?

The answers are usually found in what it takes to meet your goals, subject to constraints of budget and schedule. For example, simply make as many visits as necessary to meet the goal of understanding work. Decide on the most effective length for each session based on what you need to take home from each session.
Less rigorous data elicitation. When budget and schedule constraints require you to be even more rapid in data elicitation, be economical in your parameter choices and take short cuts:

- Interview and observe fewer users:
  - Choose fewer numbers of more experienced users; you will learn to squeeze out a great deal of useful information from a small number of users.
- Use fewer observation and interview sessions per user:
  - Just one day's worth of talking to users about their work practice can make a big difference in your understanding of the work domain to inform the design.
- Be smart in capturing data; abstract your notes down to the clean and uncluttered essence (as you gain in experience, you will get very good at filtering inputs on the fly).

These shortcuts increase efficiency, usually without much of a downside from reduced thoroughness and loss of data accuracy.

More rigorous data elicitation. Very large enterprise systems, such as a new air traffic control system, are truly outliers and won't be seen by most UX professionals. In those projects, a high level of rigor may be mandated and, if so, steps to achieve it will be prescribed. In such extreme cases, you might have to use additional rigor in maintaining the traceability of each data item you collect during the elicitation phase. This often involves assigning unique IDs to each user and tagging each usage research data item with the source ID. This allows you to maintain a record of all subsequent insights derived from that source. We call this tagging your usage research data with metadata.

7.4.6 Data Elicitation Goals Based on Scope

In agile UX, you may end up doing usage research in both the large-scope early funnel (Section 4.4.4) and the small-scope late funnel (Section 4.4.3). These two passes at usage research will generally be two different kinds of usage research occurring in two different parts of the overall UX lifecycle process.

In the early funnel, you will conduct high-level usage research to obtain a general overview to establish an overview of system structure and build up inputs to the broad conceptual design. You will focus on high-level task structure and all the user stories, user needs, and requirements.

In the late funnel, you will focus on one (or a few) user stories to obtain detailed inputs to drive low-level interaction design for task sequencing and navigation. You'll be gathering supplementary information to refine your models, answer questions, and fill in gaps.

7.4.7 Organize Your Data Elicitation Team

Goal: *Pick a team with the skills appropriate for this client and domain to be effective in, and capable of, understanding this work practice.* For example, choose people with a background in that domain, possibly including subject matter experts (SMEs).

Scope (of delivery)

Describes how the target system or product is "chunked" (broken into what size pieces) in each iteration or sprint for delivery to the client and users for feedback and to the software engineering team for agile implementation (Section 3.3).

Early funnel

The part of the funnel (agile UX model) for large-scope activity, usually for conceptual design, before syncing with software engineering (Section 4.4.4).

Late funnel

The part of the funnel (agile UX model) for small-scope activity, for syncing with agile software engineering sprints (Section 4.4.3).

- Decide how many people to send on the visits and how many visits to make. Two or three is often enough, but this varies widely depending on the nature of the system. Set your own limits, depending on your budget and schedule.
- Decide on the kinds of people (i.e., their skills) who should go on each visit (e.g., user experience people, other team members, subject matter experts, and other people familiar with the product domain). A multidisciplinary mix is always best.
- Plan the interview and observation strategy and the team roles.

Tip from the field: Don't send an inexperienced UX person or someone without domain knowledge. We learned from experience one time when we were all busy and sent an intern who was trained but lacked experience. This can turn off your valuable resources and you can lose access to cooperative users.

7.4.8 Recruit Participants

If you decide on users as your data elicitation information source:

Rely on the client to help. Get help from your client in selecting and contacting a broad range of participants from the potential user population.

Recruit locally for users of consumer products. For lots of consumer products, such as shrinkwrap word processor software, users abound and you can recruit users to interview, for example, via:

- Email lists.
- Your website or the client's website.
- Social media.
- Client's customer base.
- Local advertising outlets, such as Craigslist.

Plan to see multiple users in the enterprise system perspective. Each user may have a different take on how the broader work domain functions. Include:

- All work roles in that work practice.
- Grand-customers (customers of the customer, if any) outside the user's organization.
- Indirect users who need direct users to interact for them (for example, ticket sellers at a cinema are direct users of the ticketing software where the moviegoers are the indirect users).
- Managers.

Make every effort to get access to important but "unavailable" people. For projects in some domains, you might be told that users are scarce and generally unavailable.

For example, management might resist giving access to key people because they are busy and "bothering" them would cost the organization time and money.

- Make the case for meeting at least some of these users to develop an understanding of their work activities and the potential cost of not including their work in the new design.
- Ask for just a couple of hours with key users. Persevere.

7.4.9 Identify Settings in Which to Study Usage

Usage context is essential. In the enterprise system perspective, the setting is the business organization that is using the system. In the commercial product perspective, the setting is wherever the product is used. For example, if the product is a camera, the work happens pretty much anywhere.

7.4.10 Establish Need to Observe Users in Their Work Context

Especially for the enterprise system perspective, the environment, the people, and the context of the interview should be as close a match as possible to the usual working location and working conditions. Don't be led to a conference room, for example, because "it is much quieter and less distracting there."

One approach to avoid users describing mandated policy instead of actual practice is to ask them to demonstrate what they did yesterday (after confirming yesterday was a typical day), then make it easy for them to walk through the steps (leveraging doing versus recalling).

For an example of how the Social Security Administration established an extensive ecological environment for doing usage research and evaluation, see Section 11.4.

7.4.11 Establish Management Understanding of Need to Keep Pressure Off Interviewees and Give Them Freedom to Comment Honestly

Make sure that the observations and interviews are conducted without undue political and managerial influences. Users must feel comfortable in telling the "real" story of the everyday work practice, with guaranteed anonymity.

7.4.12 Prepare Your Initial Questions

Just as football quarterbacks sometimes script their initial series of plays, we recommend that you script your initial interview questions to get you off to a good start. There is no real secret to the questions; you ask them to tell you and to show you how they do their work. What actions do they take, with whom do they interact, and with what do they interact? Ask them to demonstrate what they do and to narrate it with stories of what works, what does not work, how things can go wrong, and so on. For product perspective, for example a digital camera, the following questions can be starting points: What are the things users do when taking a photograph? With whom do they interact? What do they think about? What concerns and challenges do they have while taking pictures? Does it work well in low light situations?

7.5 DURING THE VISIT: COLLECT USAGE DATA

7.5.1 Set the Stage Upfront

- Get off to a good start by establishing rapport with the client.
- Explain the purpose of the visit, to learn about how people use, or will use, their product or system and that it's to inform design.
- Explain your approach.
- If necessary or appropriate, promise personal and corporate confidentiality.

7.5.2 Interviewing versus Observing: What They Say versus What They Do

Observation can be necessary. Observation (a basic UX technique, Section 2.4.1) can help you see work activity with an independent eye. It is not always easy for users to consciously describe what they do, especially in work that has been internalized. Humans are notoriously unreliable about this. Simonsen and Kensing (1997) explain why interviews as an exclusive data-elicitation technique are insufficient: "A major point in ethnographically inspired approaches is that work is a socially organized activity where the actual behavior differs from how it is described by those who do it."

Interviewing can be necessary. Narration by the user can augment your observations with information about motivation, feelings, and other "hidden" aspects. Get your participants to demonstrate all the ways they use the product or system and have them "think aloud."

Using observation alone, you can miss some important points. For example, an important problem or issue simply might not come up during any given period of observation (Dearden & Wright, 1997). For example, some payroll tasks happen only at the end of the month. Unless there is an opportunity to do a visit during that time, the only way is to ask them to walk though how a typical payroll task happens by pretending it's the end of the month now.

Think-aloud technique

A qualitative empirical data collection technique in which participants verbally express thoughts about the interaction experience, including their motives, rationale, and perceptions of UX problems, especially to identify UX problems (Section 24.2.3).

7.5.3 Hints for Successful Data Elicitation

Listen to what the user says is needed. Even though it is the job of your team to deduce needs and requirements from the usage research data, users will suggest things they would like to see in the system, too. Make raw data notes of any design suggestions and ask for reasons underlying those suggestions that come from users. In usage research analysis, these notes will be essential as inputs to user stories as requirements.

Partner with users. Help the participants understand that you have to deeply understand their usage. Get them to tell specific stories about their usage and how they feel about the product or system.

Be a good listener and a good detective. Let the users talk and probe with specific questions.

- Don't expect every user to have the same view of the work domain and the work; ask questions about the differences and find ways to combine their views to get the "truth."
- Capture the details as they occur; don't wait and try to remember it later.
- Be an effective data ferret or detective; follow leads and discover, deviate from the script, extract, "tease out," and collect "clues."
- Be ready to adapt, modify, explore, and branch out.

Avoid interjecting your own views. Don't offer your opinions about what users might need. Don't lead the user or introduce your own perspectives. Follow your leads with questions, not hypotheses for the user to confirm. For example, consider this user comment: "I want privacy when I am buying tickets." You might be tempted to say: "You mean, when you are looking for events and buying tickets, you do not want other people in line to know what you are doing?" To which the user might respond: "Yes, that is what I mean." A better way to handle the user's comment here would have been with a follow-up question, such as "Can you elaborate what you mean by wanting privacy?"

7.5.4 Kinds of Information to Look for
7.5.4.1 Specific Information to Look for

As you interview and observe to elicit data, you should keep an eye out for specific kinds of usage research data:

- User work roles (Section 9.3.1).
- User personas (Section 9.4).
- Inputs to user stories and requirements (Section 8.3.1).

User work role

Not a person but a work assignment, defined and distinguished by a corresponding job title or work responsibilities. A work role usually involves system usage, but some work roles can be external to the organization being studied (Section 7.5.4.1).

- Work practice artifacts (Section 9.8).
- Flow of information and artifacts (Section 9.5).
- User tasks (Sections 9.6 and 9.7).
- Physical work environment (Section 9.9).
- Information architecture (Section 9.10).
- Photo ops.

Each of these will be briefly explained in the subsections that follow.

User work roles. What work roles—the jobs users perform as defined by the set of tasks they are responsible for—do users assume as they use the system to do work? What are the characteristics of people in these roles? What do people in each role do? How do different people in those roles work together? Capture as a simple list of annotated work roles.

User persona information. A user persona is a UX design artifact to guide design to meet the needs of a variety of different kinds of users. User personas help designers focus on specific user characteristics rather than trying to design for all users or even for the "average" user. Data elicitation is a good time to seek out information for building user personas. While you may pick up bits and pieces of such information as you perform other kinds of data elicitation, you may have to conduct a brief interview to get all the details.

Example: How Lana and Cory View and Use Entertainment in Their Lives

Following is an edited excerpt from such an interview for creating a persona with respect to the design for the Ticket Kiosk System. It demonstrates a question and answer approach to data elicitation, with the specific learning objectives for building personas.

> Cory: We take time out a couple of times a week to do something different, to get away from our routine. That can range from going to see a movie, to visiting a museum, to going out with friends, to traveling in the immediate area.
> We have seasonal activities like hiking or swimming at the beach. So it would be great for us to have information on a kiosk about good places to go hiking, with information about nature for viewing and degrees of difficulty on various trails.
> One of our main interests is in keeping informed about events that are going on in town. We hear about many things through word of mouth and we always wonder how many other events are there that we don't hear about. Many of these events we do attend and we have fun in doing so, but we often have to seek that information out by asking our friends. It would be nice to have a resource that would give us that information reliably without having to seek it ourselves. If there was a kiosk at bus stops, for example, we would definitely see them and see what is going

on more currently. It's like the New York City taxi system; they have a computer in the back seat and you can peruse information about the weather, interesting news, and entertainment information.

Lana: I often use the bus and I usually have to wait for it at least a little while. In that time, it would be nice to have access to information about town activities, such as festivals, especially weekend activities, both local and in nearby areas.

Q: Would it bother you to have strangers looking over your shoulder and seeing what you are looking at?

Lana: No, that is not a concern. We do lots of other things, like using ATMs in public and that usually isn't a problem. If you bought tickets at the kiosk, you would want to be sure that the financial aspects were safe and secure.

Cory: Having multiple minikiosks would give everyone equal access and no one would have to look over anyone's shoulders.

At a bus stop, the people are all there for the same purpose, so there is a small amount of shared goals and a little bit of camaraderie while waiting for a bus to come. So there is a common bond but it is also nice for everyone to have their own personal space and, if you give them something to focus on, it could be the basis for common conversations and even discussion about events and entertainment-related issues. On one hand, it can be a social facilitator and an interesting diversion as you wait. Someone might ask if anyone has seen such-and-such a movie and some might respond with varying opinions of the movie, leading to a general discussion.

But in the end, we would get the most value out of a resource through which we can just passively receive event information.

Cory: Kiosks at bus stops and train stations would also be very valuable for out-of-town visitors.

Q: What kind of things would you want or expect in such a kiosk?

Both: There is one more thing we would like to see in a kiosk at a bus stop: public service announcements. Among those, we'd like to see reminders of "bus etiquette," covering such topics as loud boisterous behavior, imposing use of cellphones, etc. Good designers could package these announcements in an entertaining way, so they weren't just blown off by the bus riders.

Lana: I'm thinking also about the case where I see something on the kiosk that I think is interesting and I want to show it to Cory when I get home. Like maybe this weekend there is going to be a jazz festival at a certain sculpture garden and I want Cory to know about it. It would be nice to have a button to touch to cause some kind of link or download to my iPhone or iPod. But there could be problems with security, viruses, etc., if you opened up your personal devices to receive downloads from public machines. Maybe you could offer possibly free "subscriptions" to the kiosk system service so you can send yourself information safely. Another, perhaps safer, way to do this is to provide various "keywords" associated with each different screen. You could jot down the key-word for the screen you want to share and the other person could search on that keyword at another kiosk at a later time.

Another interesting option in a public kiosk for entertainment information is a feature to see movie reviews from popular sites like rottentomatoes.com and for anyone in the public to post reviews of the entertainment events. Suppose, for example, that I could leave a review of a movie I really didn't like, along the lines of the way people give reviews for items on amazon.com. That review would become part of the total information about that movie for all subsequent kiosk viewers. To keep a balance and offset "information vandals," people could also review or refute other reviews, as they often do on Amazon.

Lana: As a balance to the routine of our jobs, we both crave opportunities for learning and personal growth, so we seek entertainment that is more sophisticated and more interesting, entertainment that challenges us intellectually. So we would want the spectrum of entertainment events to include the symphony, the ballet, museums, modern dance performances, and operas.

At the other end of the spectrum, there are some days I know that my mind needs a rest and I seek something more like mindless entertainment, often something that will make me laugh.

Inputs to user stories. A user story is a short narrative describing a feature or capability needed by a user in a specific work role and a rationale for why it is needed. A user story is employed as an agile UX design "requirement." One of the most important things to look for in data elicitation is the basis for writing user stories. As you observe users and as users talk about their work practice, try to identify situations that will make good user stories that later can drive agile UX design. These include statements about what features are wanted or needed and information about things that need to be done by people in various user work roles. Look for very specific, low-level user wants or needs that reflect specific problems or opportunities, along with motivations and potential payoffs.

What capabilities do users want and why? You can even ask specific questions to draw out information specific to desired features or subfeatures. In practice, data elicitation for user story inputs has expanded to include most information about requirements and desired features, regardless of whether they came explicitly from a user's mouth. See Section 10.2.1 about the evolved role of user stories in design requirements.

Artifacts of the work practice and how they are used. What artifacts do users employ, manipulate, and share as part of their work practice? Artifacts gathered in usage research data elicitation provide a rich source of understanding of work practice and are essential to immersion by the team. These artifacts are also great conversational props within data elicitation as we interview the different roles that use them.

An artifact model shows how tangible elements (paper, other physical or electronic objects) are used and structured in the business process flow of doing the work. For example, guest checks, receipts, and menus are common artifacts associated with the work practice in a restaurant for ordering, preparing, delivering, and charging for food. They provide avenues for discussion given the fact that almost every restaurant uses these artifacts over and over again.

What are things that work with this kind of artifact for order taking? What are some breakdowns? How does a person's handwriting impact this part of the work activity? What is the interaction like between the wait staff and the restaurant's guests? And the interaction between the wait staff and the kitchen staff?

The usage research data elicitation team must pay close attention to, and take notes on, how work practice artifacts are created, communicated, and used. Ask questions to elicit information about the roles of artifacts. What are those notes scribbled on those forms? Why are some fields in this form left blank? Why is there a sticky note on this form? Perhaps a signature is required for approval on

Immersion

A form of deep thought and analysis of the problem at hand—to "live" within the context of a problem and to make connections among the different aspects of it. Section 2.4.7.

other kinds of documents. This model is one reason why observers and interviewers must collect as many artifacts as possible during their usage research data elicitation field visits to users.

In addition to physical artifacts, don't forget to ask about electronic objects that are part of the work practice flow. Think about printouts of emails, input forms in software, screenshots, and so on.

Flow of information and artifacts. In the context of usage research, an artifact is an object important to the work practice being studied. For example, it could be a receipt in a restaurant or a car key in an auto repair shop. How do information and artifacts flow through the system as work gets done? If you have time, it's helpful to capture flow data in a simple sketch (e.g., a flow diagram). If you have even more time (which we said you probably wouldn't), check your flow diagram with users to see if they agree.

User tasks. Capture data about task structure in a simple hierarchical (indented) list of tasks and subtasks. Capture data about how to do a given task as a list of a few ordered steps, possibly interspersed with system feedback.

Physical work environment. What is the physical layout of the workspace and how does it impact work practice?

Information architecture. What information do users access, manipulate, share, output, or archive as part of their work and how is it structured for storage, retrieval, display, and manipulation?

Photo ops. Where possible, take photos of the work practice in action to supplement your usage research data. Especially look for opportunities to take photos of the physical work environment and artifacts being used.

Information architecture

Design of information structures for organizing, storing, retrieving, displaying, manipulating, and sharing. Information architecture also includes designs for labeling, searching, and navigating information. Section 12.4.3.

7.5.4.2 General information to look for

Surprises—the interesting and the unusual, the good, the bad, and the ugly. In addition to the normal expected things, keep an eye out for the unusual—surprises, interesting episodes, excitement, and joy—things to emphasize in the design. By the same token, watch out for negative surprises, disappointments, and breakdowns—things to avoid or fix in the design.

Emotional and social aspects and meaningfulness in work/play practice. In the domain of commercial products, especially personal products such as a camera, mobile phone, or music player, emotional impact can play a central role in usage and design for the user experience. What evidence is there of joy, aesthetics, and fun in usage? What opportunities are there to design for more of the same?

You might have to dig deeper to see evidence of emotional impact in the enterprise system perspective. You may find that customers and users are less likely to mention emotional aspects of their work practice because they think that is about personal feelings. They might think that is inappropriate in the context of technology and functional requirements. So you must try harder to uncover an understanding about emotional and social aspects of work practice. For example, where and when are people having fun? What are they doing when they have fun? Where do people need to have fun when they are not?

In the enterprise system perspective, emotional impact and meaningfulness can also occur in a negative form. Look for ways to fight job boredom. Does anyone hint, even obliquely, that they would like their job to be less boring? What about the work is boring?

Where is there stress and pressure? Where can job stress be relived with aesthetics and fun? But also be aware of work situations where it would be distracting, dangerous, or otherwise inappropriate to try to inject fun or surprise.

Meaningfulness in the long term. Meaningfulness is a long-term phenomenon usually associated with the product perspective, but it can occur in the system perspective as well. What are the long-term emotional aspects of usage? What parts of usage are learned over longer times? Where is it appropriate for users to give the system or product "presence" in their lives?

Consider a product such as a digital camera, which is not something a user interacts with in the moment and then forgets. Personal products like this can develop into objects of emotional acceptance into one's life and lifestyle. The more people carry a camera with them everywhere they go, the stronger these emotional ties. This behavior is not something you can observe if you just visit once and ask some questions. That means you may have to look at long-term usage patterns, where people evolve new ways of usage over time (see section on shadowing below).

And meaningfulness goes beyond immediate usage. For example, what does a camera's *brand* mean to people who carry it? What does a personal product say about its owner? How about the style and form of the device and how it intersects with the user's personality? Does the user associate the camera with good times and vacations, being out taking photos with all his or her worries left behind?

Shadowing and the user journey. Data elicitation for meaningfulness can benefit from a special technique called shadowing. Shadowing is a technique for user observation in which the UX person follows a user around, taking notes about typical usage within the daily routine. Usually this technique is pure observation in which the observer does not ask questions or make comments or try to influence user behavior. If the different kinds of usage entail moving among multiple locations, the observer follows and documents what is sometimes called the "user journey."

Shadowing can be useful in the enterprise system perspective, too. As an example, a visit to the hospital can involve a user experience journey through a multitude of settings, starting with the drive to even find the hospital. Arrival can present an overload of signage and difficulty in finding a parking spot. Then finding the right entrance out of a dozen possibilities, finding the receptionist, and getting to the appropriate clinic. Checking in is followed by entertaining yourself while you wait and finally getting to see the physician. After that, you have to make a follow-up appointment, which means consulting your calendar, stopping at the pharmacy to pick up a prescription from the doctor, and getting back to find your car.

Example: The SnakeLight: Understanding Work Practice in a Customer Journey

The example we used in Section 1.5.3 also shows why it helps to understand how your users do their activities and how they use products and systems. This example of the effectiveness of in situ user research inquiry comes to us from the seemingly mundane arena of consumer flashlights. In the mid-1990s, Black and Decker was considering getting into handheld lighting devices, but did not want to join the crowded field of ordinary consumer flashlights.

So, to get new ideas, some designers followed real flashlight users around and documented their customer journey. They observed people using flashlights in real usage situations and discovered the need for a feature that was never mentioned during the usual brainstorming among engineers and designers or in focus groups of consumers. More than half the people they observed during actual usage under car hoods, under kitchen sinks, and in closets and attics said that some kind of hands-free usage would be desirable.

They made a flashlight that could be bent and formed and that can stand up by itself. Overnight, the "SnakeLight" was the product with the largest production volume in Black and Decker history, despite being larger, heavier, and more expensive than other flashlights on the market (Giesecke et al., 2018).

Activity-based interaction data and the broader ecology. An activity is a set of related task threads that work together to reach a higher-level goal. Usually, activities involve sequences of multiple overlapping tasks that go together in a broader ecology than just the context of a given task.

As we said in Section 1.6.2, Norman (2005) gives this as an example of an activity-based approach to smartphones: "Mobile phones that combine appointment books, diaries and calendars, note-taking facilities, text messaging, and cameras—can do a good job of supporting communication activities. This one single device integrates several tasks: looking up numbers, dialing, talking, note taking, checking one's diary or calendar, and exchanging photographs, text messages, and emails."

Find usage data that support activity-based interaction. And, where possible, try to organize usage research data in terms of activities rather than just individual tasks.

7.5.5 Capture the Data

"Stream of occurrence" notes. Clients and users are very busy, so you won't usually have much time with them. During the visit, especially if the work domain is unfamiliar, you usually won't have time for much except taking notes. We call it "stream of occurrence" note taking, because you take notes about whatever is occurring at the time it happens and just add it to the set of notes you have, without any time to try and interpret or organize them in the field.

If the domain is familiar and observations aren't going too fast, you might do some sketching to represent work flow and other important characteristics.

Handwritten note taking. In our experience, the most popular way to take notes is by long-hand writing in a notebook. Handwriting has the advantage of being the least distracting to the data elicitation process. Furthermore, it is the most flexible with respect to being able to do quick sketches and annotations to notes or any work artifacts.

Typing notes in a laptop. Some prefer typing in a laptop. This can work if you are good at typing and if having a laptop in the data elicitation environment can be inconspicuous. You must be able to type notes without:

- Being distracted from your focus.
- Seeming intrusive to users.
- Giving the impression that what users say will be captured "on the record."

With capturing data in a laptop comes the advantage of electronic sharing of notes.

Rarely make audio recordings. If you are unfamiliar with the domain and much of what is said in the field doesn't make much sense to you, you might consider making audio recordings of what they say. But:

- This is not efficient use of data elicitation.
- Don't forget that everything you record will also have to be transcribed.

So, in almost all cases, we do not recommend audio or video recording for data capture in the field. There usually isn't time for it, it's often too complicated, and you rarely get much in return.

7.5.6 For High Rigor, Maintain Connections to Data Sources

In cases requiring high rigor and traceability of usage research data and model components to original sources, you can tag raw data notes with "data source IDs," IDs of the people from whom the notes were elicited. To protect anonymity, use an ID number and not the person's name. Keep the list of names and IDs in a secure place.

Source IDs will allow you to go back to the original sources of the raw data if questions, disagreements, or interpretations of the data become an issue later in the process. Most projects do not require this kind of rigor.

Example: Tagging a Raw Data Note with Source ID

Below is an example of a raw data note that describes a barrier in the workflow model of the ticket buyer. It has been tagged with an "8," the ID of the person from whom the data was elicited:

> *It is too difficult to get enough information about events from a ticket seller at the ticket window. I would like to be able to find my own events and not depend on the ticket seller to do all the browsing and searching. [8]*

7.5.7 Writing Good Raw Data Notes

- Be concise:
  - Abstract out all but the salient points.
  - Avoid verbatim quotes.
  - Eliminate rambling narration.
- Make your raw data notes as modular as possible:
  - Paraphrase and synthesize.
  - Make each work activity note:

- A simple declarative point.
- Easily read.
- Understood at a glance.
- Containing just one concept, idea, or fact.

Exercise 7-1: Usage Research Data Elicitation for the Product or System of Your Choice

Goal: Get practice in performing usage research data elicitation

Activities: The best conditions for this exercise are to work as a team and have a real client.

If you are working with a team but do not have a real client, divide your team members into users and interviewers and do a role-playing exercise. If you are working alone, invite some friends over for one of your famous pizza-and-beer-and-usage-research parties and have them play a user role while you interview them. We have found that you get the best results if you follow this order: eat the pizza, do the exercise, drink the beer.

Do your best to suspend disbelief and pretend that you and your users are in a real situation within the context of your domain of investigation. Interviewers each take their own transcripts of raw data notes as you ask questions and listen to users talk about their work activities in this domain.

Deliverables: At least a few pages of raw usage research data notes, handwritten or typed. Include a few interesting examples (something unexpected or unique) from your notes to share.

Schedule: Assuming a relatively simple domain, we expect this exercise to take about 1–2 hours.

7.5.8 Getting the Most Out of Data Elicitation

In summary, getting the most value from the investment in usage research data elicitation (yours and the user's investment) involves being prepared by doing your homework upfront and by being a keen observer.

Unfamiliar domains. If you, the UX professional, don't know much about the work and problem domain, you may find data elicitation to not be as productive as you need. You are likely to get just a skin-deep tutorial on the domain and not learn much about the subtleties of the work practice. This is usually not a good way to use time in the field with participants.

In such situations, in practice, most of the conversation during an elicitation visit is focused on designers trying to understand everything that is thrown at them in the form of jargon, concepts, and terminology. The users don't have time to educate the designers because they are busy and their time is valuable. This is perhaps the main reason why elicitation visits under these conditions are not the most informative. Because you and the users can't get past the barriers of unfamiliar terminology and esoteric knowledge of the work practice to get at the understanding of user needs that you require, these sessions end up being education for the designers at a surface level.

Understanding the elephant. The goal of usage research is to piece together different perspectives into a cohesive picture. This is like the blind men feeling different parts of the elephant and coming away with a different understanding of what an elephant is (credit not ours; source unknown). So the researchers should be on constant lookout for variations, breakdowns, and workarounds. They need to seek out contradictions and opposing perspectives espoused by the users.

Usage Research Data Analysis

8

- Distill the essence from your usage research by synthesizing work activity notes from raw data notes.
- Make your work activity notes:
  - Elemental (about just one idea).
  - Brief and concise.
  - Complete.
  - Modular.
- Extract work activity notes that are inputs to user stories and requirements.
- Extract work activity notes that are inputs to usage research models.
- Organize the remaining work activity notes:
  - Simple methods for organizing small amounts of data.
  - Building WAADs for larger amounts of data.
- Large example.
- Synthesize the "elephant" that is user work practice, work domain, and user needs.

8.1 INTRODUCTION

8.1.1 You Are Here

We begin each process chapter with a "you are here" picture of the chapter topic in the context of The Wheel, the overall UX design lifecycle template (Fig. 8-1). Within the Understand Needs UX design lifecycle activity, this chapter is about the data analysis subactivity in which you analyze the usage research data you elicited in Chapter 7, furthering your goal of understanding the work context for the new system you will design.

8.1.2 Overview of Usage Research Analysis Subactivities

The overall goal of usage research analysis is to understand the user's work practice in the broader work domain of the product or system to be designed.

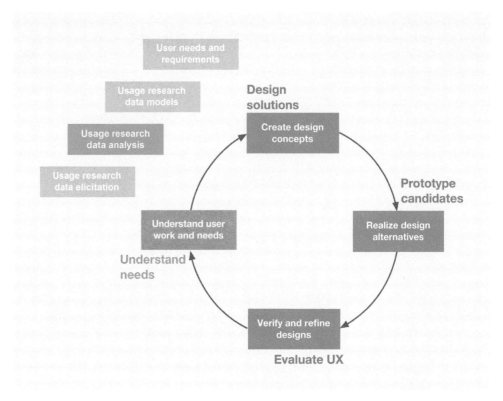

Fig. 8-1

You are here in the usage research data analysis chapter within the Understand Needs lifecycle activity, in the context of the Wheel, the overall lifecycle process.

If the system or product you are working on is large, unfamiliar, and/or domain complex, you can come away from usage research data elicitation feeling overwhelmed. This is when you can use the power of the UX process to distill and organize the usage research data.

A work activity note is brief, clear, concise, and elemental (relating to exactly one concept, idea, fact, or topic) statement used to document a single point about the work practice as synthesized from raw usage research data.

The subgoals of the main subactivities of usage research analysis (as illustrated in Fig. 8-2) are:

- Goal: *Distill the essence of what you discovered in usage research:*
  - Synthesize work activity notes from the raw data.

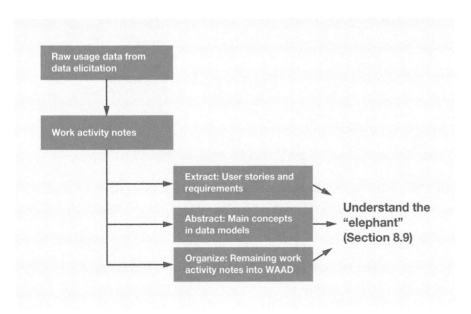

Fig. 8-2

A flow diagram of the usage research data analysis.

■ Goal: *Enumerate features and capabilities users will need in the system or product:*

  ■ Extract work activity notes that are inputs to user stories and requirements (Section 8.3).

■ Goal: *Capture and explain different aspects of work practice as sharable representations:*

  ■ Extract work activity notes that are inputs to data models (or integrate the notes directly into the data models) (Section 8.4).

■ Goal: *Capture other details of the work practice, lessons, or insights in discrete microsummaries:*

  ■ Put aside the remaining work activity notes as inputs to the work activity affinity diagram (Section 8.5).

■ Goal: *Create a representation of the overall understanding of the work practice, excluding things that are already in the models:*

  ■ Organize the remaining work activity notes into categories (Section 8.6), possibly within a work activity affinity diagram, or WAAD (Section 8.7).

■ Goal: *Understand the whole domain and work practice picture* (Sections 8.8 and 8.9):

  ■ Synthesize all the usage research data.

Domain complexity

The degree of intricacy and the technical, or possibly esoteric, nature of the corresponding field of work. Domain-complex systems are often characterized by convoluted and elaborate mechanisms for how parts of the system work and communicate, having complicated work flow containing multiple dependencies and communication channels. Examples include an air traffic control system and a system for analyzing seismic data for oil exploration (Section 3.2.2.3).

8.2 DISTILL THE ESSENCE FROM YOUR USAGE RESEARCH BY SYNTHESIZING WORK ACTIVITY NOTES

Break each raw data note into its work activity notes. Make each work activity note brief but complete, self-standing, and modular. With your team in your UX studio, collaborate on making sense of the raw data you have gathered:

Synthesis

The process of integrating diverse inputs, facts, insights, and observations of parts of a concept to make conclusions that characterize and aid understanding of the whole concept (Section 8.9).

1. Start with the set of raw usage research data notes that came from data elicitation in Chapter 7.
2. Look at each raw data note in turn.
3. For each raw data note, synthesize each work activity note in turn.

8.2.1 Work Activity Notes can be Handwritten or Typed into a Laptop

While the process can work if you write the work activity notes on scraps of paper or Post-it notes, you might also want to consider capturing the notes in computer-readable form, whether in a word processor, a spreadsheet, or directly into a database system. This facilitates sharing, manipulating, and printing as needed.

8.2.2 Make Each Work Activity Note Elemental

A work activity note is a data note that refers to or relates to exactly one concept, idea, fact, or topic. Elemental means that the note is a simple constituent, uncompounded, basic note. Make each note brief, clear, and concise.

Example: Synthesizing Work Activity Notes for the TKS

Consider this raw data note:

> *It is too difficult to get enough information about events from a ticket seller at the ticket window. I would like to be able to find my own events and not depend on the ticket seller to do all the browsing and searching.*

There are at least two elemental work activity notes that can be synthesized simply by breaking apart the two sentences:

> *It is too difficult to get enough information about events from a ticket seller at the ticket window.*
> *I would like to be able to find my own events and not depend on the ticket seller to do all the browsing and searching.*

The latter of which can perhaps be shortened to:

> *I want to be able to browse and search for my own tickets to events.*

Example: Synthesizing Work Activity Notes for the TKS

As another example of synthesizing elemental notes for the TKS, consider this raw data note:

> *I like to keep up to date with what is going on regarding entertainment in the community.*
> *I especially want to know about current and popular events.*

Again, there are at least two work activity notes that can be synthesized simply by breaking apart the two sentences:

> *I like to keep up to date with what is going on regarding entertainment in the community.*
> *I especially want to know about current and popular events.*

Example: Synthesizing Work Activity Notes

For this example, let's start with this user comment in the raw data:

> *It is difficult to get enough information about events from a ticket seller at the ticket window. I always get the feeling that there are other good events that I can choose from but I just do not know which ones are available. But the ticket seller usually is not willing or able to help much, especially when the ticket window is busy.*

A concise synthesized note:

> *I would like to be able to find my own events and not depend on the ticket seller to do all the browsing and searching.*

8.2.3 Make Each Work Activity Note Brief and Concise

- Filter out all noise, fluff, and irrelevant verbiage.
- Rephrase, condense, and distill—boil it down to the essence.
- Make each work activity note easily read and understood at a glance.
- Make a clear, specific, and focused point, conveying the substance of the issue in question.
- Retain the original meaning and remain true to the user's intentions.

Example: Brief and Concise Data Notes

Consider, again, this raw data note:

> *There are often long lines and the ticket sellers are usually too busy to give you much help in choosing events. And, when they do pay attention, it is usually difficult to get enough information about events from a ticket seller at the ticket window.*

It can be paraphrased and condensed into the following concise notes:

> *I don't like buying tickets at the central ticket office.*
> *The ticket office usually has long lines.*
> *The ticket sellers are usually too busy to help.*
> *I can't get enough information about events from ticket sellers.*

Example: Brief and Concise Data Notes

Consider this rather long raw data note:

> *I'd like to see a ticket kiosk in town here. I'd try it out and maybe I would use a kiosk to buy tickets for events around town. I'd also use it just to find information on what's going on. It would have to be close to where I live or work or shop.*

The first two sentences are mostly noise, just comments without much to say about design. They do not become work activity notes.

The third sentence can be interpreted as a general statement about using the kiosk as a community information source, a concise version of which is:

> *Use kiosks as a community information source.*

The last sentence can be synthesized and generalized as a note about kiosk location:

> *Locate kiosks near where people live, work, and shop.*

8.2.4 Make Each Work Activity Note Complete

Be specific; avoid vague terms. Resolve ambiguities and missing information as you synthesize the work activity notes (more on completeness in the next section).

8.2.5 Make Each Work Activity Note Modular by Retaining Context

Modular in this context means that each note is complete enough to stand on its own, a note that everyone can understand independently of all the others. Each note should be a single-topic piece that can be rearranged, replaced, combined, or moved around independently of the others. If notes are split to be elemental, this means preserving any context that each split-off piece gets from its companions.

8.2.5.1 Don't use an indefinite pronoun, such as "this," "it," "they," or "them" unless its referent has already been identified in the same note

As a corollary, make sure each work activity note does not contain unresolved indefinite references. State the work role that a person represents rather than using "he" or "she." Add words to disambiguate and explain references to pronouns or other context dependencies.

Example: Don't Lose Context When Splitting

Important to potential customer: A method such as the one just above is absolutely essential for getting to the needed information the fastest way, especially if you already know the name of the event.

This is an example of how NOT to do elemental notes. Note how the reference to *A method such as the one just above* became unresolved after this note was split off from the preceding part.

Example: Retaining Context When Splitting

But it (the ticket printer failing) could happen, no matter how careful you are, given the amount of traffic and usage. What then? Need a customer service phone (e.g., hardwired to the company representative).

Notice how the reference to "it" is resolved by adding a parenthetical explanation of the indefinite pronoun.

Example: Avoiding an Unresolved Indefinite Pronoun in a Data Note

Suppose when another note was split to make it more modular, one of the resulting notes is:

He didn't ask me if I wanted to see a movie.

At the time the original note was split, this part should be disambiguated to read:

The ticket seller didn't ask me if I wanted to see a movie.

Example: Not Using an Unresolved Indefinite Pronoun in a Data Note

From a system viewpoint, we can see that not printing tickets at the kiosk would be easier, but no one would want the tickets sent to their home. It's a big confidence issue about getting the tickets immediately.

If these two sentences get separated for modularity, you need to explain what "It's" means in the second one:

Printing tickets in the kiosk is a big confidence issue about getting the tickets immediately.

8.2.6 Additional Information to Accompany Work Activity Notes

If rationale information (why a user feels a certain way or does a certain thing) exists in the raw data, it should be considered to go along with the corresponding work activity note.

An example of a note that includes rationale is:

> *I do not ask for a printed confirmation of my ticket transaction because I am afraid someone else might find it and use my credit card number.*

This could be made more general to be a rationale for security about credit card information:

> *Extremely high priority requirement:*
>
> (1)   *Must protect user credit card information.*
> (2)   *Provide option of not printing confirmation of a transaction.*
> (3)   *Obfuscate sensitive payment information (e.g., credit card) on a transaction conformation.*

If there are two reasons in the rationale for the idea or concept in the note, split it into two notes (repeating the context), as those two notes might eventually end up in different places.

8.2.7 For High Rigor, Maintain Connections to Data Sources

In cases requiring high rigor and traceability of usage research data and model components to original sources, you can tag work activity notes with "data source IDs," which are IDs of the people from whom the related raw data note was elicited. The source ID tag is passed along to the work activity note from the tag on the related raw data note.

Source IDs will allow you to go back to the original sources of the raw data if questions, disagreements, or interpretations of the data become an issue later in the process. Most projects do not require this kind of rigor.

Example: Tagging a Work Activity Note with Source ID

In the example at the end of Section 7.5.6, we had a raw data note that described a barrier in the workflow model of the ticket buyer, tagged with a source ID of "8." This is the unique identifier of the individual we interviewed. The best practice is to maintain confidentiality by excluding real names and maintaining the name-ID mapping somewhere else. The corresponding work activity note, synthesized in analysis, will also retain that tag:

It is usually difficult to get enough information about events from a ticket seller at the ticket window. [8]

8.2.8 Preview of Sorting Work Activity Notes into Categories

The simplest way to describe this process and to practice it is to use each work activity note in just one "category" (used here as a convenient term for different representations of work and needs (e.g., models vs. user stories vs. the WAAD)). However, while we describe it this way for expediency, there might be times when a given work activity note is useful in more than one place to form different perspectives on the data. So, we urge you to use the usage research data in whatever way possible to create a full understanding of the "elephant" (a reference to the parable of the blind men who each "see" an elephant differently, Section 8.9) that is the work practice and work domain.

In this sorting of work activity notes, you are just sorting them out as *inputs* to the categories. You are not yet writing user stories or requirements or making models from these notes (the one exception is merging a note into an existing model if that is just as easy as sorting it into the modeling category).

In sum, you start with the full set of work activity notes you just extracted from the raw usage research data.

1. Extract work activity notes that are inputs to user stories or requirements and put them in a user stories and requirements pile.
2. Extract work activity notes that are inputs to data models and put them in a data models pile (or experienced UX professionals may find it convenient to merge them directly into existing models).
3. Treat the remaining work activity notes as inputs to the work activity affinity diagram (WAAD) and put them in their own pile.

8.3 EXTRACT WORK ACTIVITY NOTES THAT ARE INPUTS TO USER STORIES OR REQUIREMENTS

8.3.1 User Stories and Requirements

A requirement is a small-scope or large-scope statement, formal or informal, of a necessity that is essential to be included in a design. A user story is a small-scope requirement, written in a particular format.

A requirement, generally used in nonagile environments, is written as a statement within a requirements document (Section 10.3.5). A user story, the essence of agile requirements, is written as a short narrative description about a

Scope (of delivery)

Describes how the target system or product is "chunked" (broken into what size pieces) in each iteration or sprint for delivery to the client and users for feedback and to the software engineering team for agile implementation (Section 3.3).

Waterfall lifecycle process

One of the earliest formal software engineering lifecycle processes; an ordered linear sequence of lifecycle activities, each of which flowed into the next like a set of cascading tiers of a waterfall (Section 4.2).

capability, function, or feature that is wanted or needed in the product or system (Section 10.2.2).

During a time when the Waterfall process was prevalent, we used requirements to codify what was needed in the system in formal statements. Those requirements were targeted as features the system should support. There was a flavor of system-centeredness. In the agile world, the focus is on delivering meaningful capabilities to the user. So these days there is more emphasis on stating the needs using that perspective and user stories are one popular way of doing that.

8.3.2 Extracting Inputs to User Stories or Requirements

It is useful to keep related information with notes extracted as inputs to user stories or requirements. For example, keep information from these notes about related user work role(s) and the reason why the feature is desired.

Because we want this set of inputs to user stories or requirements to be as complete as possible, data analysis is the time to interpret any note mentioning a want or need for a feature, functionality, or design as a user story or requirements note, regardless of whether those wants or needs were actually expressed by a user.

See Chapter 10 for more about user stories and requirements.

Example: Extracting Inputs to User Stories for the TKS

Consider these work activity notes coming out of the example in Section 8.2.2:

> *I like to keep up to date with what is going on regarding entertainment in the community.*
> *I especially want to know about current and popular events.*

Both sentences can be interpreted as inputs to user stories representing slightly different perspectives.

Example: Extracting Inputs to User Stories for the TKS

Consider these two related work activity notes:

> *I want to see reviews and other feedback from people who have already seen the show.*
> *[Design idea] Consider including capability for people to add reviews and to rate reviews.*

The first is an obvious candidate as an input to a user story. The second is a design idea that might well be transformed into the form of a user story.

A larger example appears right after Section 8.7.

8.4 EXTRACT NOTES THAT ARE INPUTS TO USAGE RESEARCH MODELS

After dealing with raw data notes relating to user stories and requirements, the next kind of data to look for is the work activity notes relating to usage research data models. You can either extract them to use them as inputs to data modeling (making simplified data representations by abstracting out unimportant details, Chapter 9) or, if it is easy to do, integrate them directly into the corresponding models right now.

8.4.1 Modeling Started Back at the Project Beginning

Much of what goes into the models starts at the beginning before you ever go into the field for usage research. This is especially true for models such as user work roles and the task structure as well as the basics of the flow model.

Some information for the models might come from early project commission documents (e.g., business proposal, design briefs) and early discussions with the client while setting up the project. By the time you get to usage research, you should already know a bit of what is in some of the models.

In many projects, much of the modeling done after data elicitation will be to verify and refine the models and to fill gaps. This chapter is about extracting the model-related notes as inputs to modeling (or, in some cases, putting them directly into the models). The next chapter, Chapter 9, is where we tell you more about how to continue the modeling.

Example: Extracting Model-Related Data

Consider this work activity note from the end of Sections 8.2.3 and 8.2.7:

> *It is usually difficult to get enough information about events from a ticket seller at the ticket window.*

This can be represented as a barrier in the workflow model of the ticket buyer.

8.5 THE REMAINING WORK ACTIVITY NOTES BECOME INPUTS TO YOUR METHOD FOR ORGANIZING THE NOTES BY CATEGORY

You should have all the remaining work activity notes after notes that can be used as inputs to user stories or requirements and the models have been extracted. These "leftover" work activity notes are now treated as inputs for organizing the notes by category.

8.5.1 Print Work Activity Notes

Although you can use handwritten work activity notes, some prefer to print the notes. If you have captured your work activity notes in computer-readable form, it might now be convenient to print them out for use in making the work activity affinity diagram. You can print the notes on yellow Post-it note stock, such as the kind that has six peel-off Post-it labels per page.

Notes printed or handwritten on colored bond printer paper formatted, say, six to a page, also work fine. If your work activity notes come from a database, you can use the "mail-merge" feature of your word processor to format each note into the table cells for either plain paper or Post-it printing.

Affinity diagram

A bottom-up hierarchical technique for organizing and grouping large amounts of disparate qualitative data, such as the work activity notes from usage research data, to highlight the issues and insights in a visual display (Section 8.7.1).

Exercise 8-1: Work Activity Notes for Your Product or System

Goal: Get practice in synthesizing work activity notes from your usage research data.

Activities: If you are working alone, it is time for another pizza-and-beer-and-usage-research-analysis party with your friends.

- However you form your team, appoint a team leader and a person to act as note recorder.
- The team leader leads the group through raw data, synthesizing work activity notes on the fly.
- Be sure to filter out all unnecessary verbiage, fluff, and noise.
- As the work activity notes are called out, the recorder types them into a laptop.
- Everyone on the team should work together to make sure that the individual work activity notes are disambiguated from context dependencies (usually by adding explanatory text in italics).

Deliverables: At least a few dozen work activity notes synthesized from your raw usage research data. Highlight a few of your most interesting synthesized work activity notes for sharing.

Schedule: Based on our experience with these activities, we expect this to take you an hour or two.

8.6 ORGANIZE THE WORK ACTIVITY NOTES

Goal: *Organize your work activity notes to identify unifying and underlying themes about the work domain.*

In a small-to-medium size project, the size of your set of work activity notes will be tractable and can be organized with a modicum of time and effort. A large, complex project or a project with a high need for rigor can require more effort because you may have a large number of work activity notes to go into the work activity affinity diagram. Here is how to do it for almost any project:

- If the set of work activity notes is small and the project is simple, organize the work activity notes into a hierarchical bullet list.
- If the set of work activity notes is medium-size and not too complex, organize the work activity notes with the card sorting technique (next section).
- If the set of work activity notes is large, your project is complex, and/or there is a need for high rigor, organize the work activity notes in a work activity affinity diagram, or WAAD.

8.6.1 Card Sorting Is a Simple Technique for Data Organization

Card sorting is a participatory affinity identification technique used to organize sets of data items (e.g., ideas, concepts, features) into a hierarchy of categories, each grouped by a common theme (Martin & Hanington, 2012, p. 26). It is an easy, inexpensive, and effective method of organizing data into categories.

Ideas that need to be organized are printed or written one per card. Give a small group a stack of these cards. Ask the participants to group the cards into piles that seem to be about similar or closely related concepts, using any criteria they choose. Listening to the group discussion that occurs is helpful in understanding their mental processes that led to the categories. Each pile is given a representative category label. According to Kane (2003), "The approach can be used to identify the major content categories of a website or to organize system functions into a useful collection of menus." In some ways, card sorting is like a one- or two-level affinity diagram. If you need a bit more organizing power than this, you can create a WAAD (see next section).

8.7 FOR HIGHER RIGOR IN COMPLEX PROJECTS, CONSTRUCT A WAAD

8.7.1 Affinity Diagrams

Affinity diagrams are a bottom-up technique for organizing lots of disparate pieces of data, such as the work activity notes from your usage research data. Affinity diagramming came from Kawakita Jiro, a Japanese anthropologist, as a means to synthesize large amounts of data from the field (Kawakita, 1982). An affinity diagram is a hierarchical structure in which notes about similar ideas are grouped together (by affinities). We adapt affinity diagramming as a technique for building a work activity affinity diagram (WAAD) to organize and group the issues and insights across your usage research data and show it in a large visual display.

A WAAD is an affinity diagram, a hierarchical bottom-up technique for organizing disparate pieces of data, used to sort and organize work activity notes in usage research analysis, pulling together work activity notes with similarities and common themes to highlight common work patterns and shared strategies across all users.

An affinity diagram is used to:

- Organize the work activity notes you synthesized in the previous section.
- Provide a structure that yields sense.
- Afford visualization of the user's work.
- Suggest ideas for designs.
- Helps generalize from instances of individual user work activities to broader work themes.

Our description of WAAD building here is at a medium level of rigor. You should choose an approach that fits your needs for a tradeoff between rigor and efficiency. WAAD building in most real projects tends to be very informal.

8.7.2 Prepare Your Work Space and Your Team

- *Set up your work space.* Prepare a large posting and working space on the walls of your design studio or on the tops of work tables.
- *Work together.* This is highly collaborative work.
- *Democratic process.* None of the data is "owned" by any team member.

8.7.3 Compartmentalize the WAAD, Separating it by User Work Roles

Often, the set of tasks performed by one user work role is separate from those performed by others. For example, consider the Middleburg University Ticket Transaction Service (MUTTS) ticket seller and the MUTTS database administrator. Each performs different work with different concerns and needs.

This allows us to divide the task structure into separate structures at the highest level, one for each user work role. This separation is how we can use work roles to divide and conquer to control complexity. It becomes easier to do analysis and design for one work role at a time.

Following this approach in analysis, we divide the WAAD into multiple separate WAADs to simplify the WAAD-building process. Many (most) of your work activity notes will be associated with, or apply to, just one given user work role.

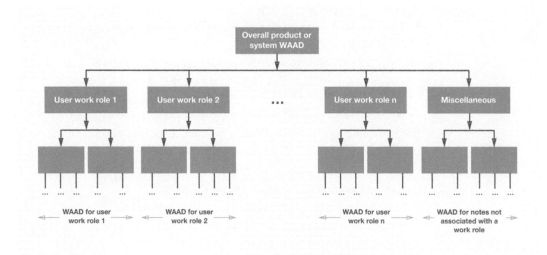

Fig. 8-3
Work activity affinity diagram compartmentalized by user work roles.

- Put sticky notes up along the top of your posting space with labels (we suggest a different color from that of the work activity notes) labeled by user work role, as in Fig. 8-3.

Of course, you will still have some work activity notes that aren't tied to a specific work role, which go into a WAAD for miscellaneous notes (also in Fig. 8-3). You may still also have to deal with an occasional work activity note that involves more than one work role, probably by splitting or duplicating the note.

8.7.4 The Bottom-Up Process of WAAD Building
8.7.4.1 Posting work activity notes

- Consider each work activity note in turn.
- Decide which user work role (or "Miscellaneous") sub-WAAD is the best fit.
- If there is no note yet posted in this sub-WAAD or if the note to be posted doesn't fit the theme of any existing group in the most appropriate sub-WAAD:
  - Start a new group by posting the work activity note somewhere under the sub-WAAD (this is how the WAAD grows in breadth).
  - Add a topic label to identify the theme of this new group (see next section on labeling).
- If the current work activity note fits the topic of an existing group already under this sub-WAAD:

- Add it to that group.
- Adjust the label as necessary to encompass the new note, adjusting the "meaning" of the group or expanding its scope.
- Continue in this fashion, growing and evolving groups of work activity notes.

8.7.4.2 Labels for groups of notes

- Decide on an initial label for the affinity theme of this group and write it (usually on a Post-it or note paper of a color different from that of the work activity notes):
  - A precise group label is important for capturing the essence, gestalt, or meaning of the group.
  - A group label denotes the exact scope of the group.
  - Avoid wordings with low descriptive power, such as "general."
  - A highly descriptive group label makes it so you don't have to look at the notes anymore to know what the group is about.
- Post the label above the work activity note, as the heading of the group.

As an example of the importance of precision in labels, a team in one of our sessions used the label "How we validate information" when they really needed the more precise label "How we validate input data forms." A subtle difference, but important to the intended affinity for that group.

8.7.4.3 Growing labels with growing groups

As a group grows by the addition of new work activity notes, the theme represented by the set of notes taken as a whole can expand and the label should be expanded accordingly.

Example: Growing Labels with Growing Groups

Look at the purple label in the middle of Fig. 8-4. This shows a label that has had terms added to it in the course of evolution within a group of work activity notes for the Ticket Kiosk System (TKS).

Note that we will be using real data from MUTTS from which the notes in this example are drawn. You may wish to see what these data look like in raw and work activity note form. See the book website (http://www.theuxbook.com/) for a representative listing of the MUTTS/TKS usage research data.

That group label started out as just "My concerns about security." Notes about privacy and trust got added to this group because those concepts have an affinity with security. The group label was expanded to track this expanding theme so it can be clearly understood without having to look at the notes in the group. Fig. 8-5 is a closeup of that topical label, showing how extra descriptive terms were added at different times to enlarge its scope during the process of building

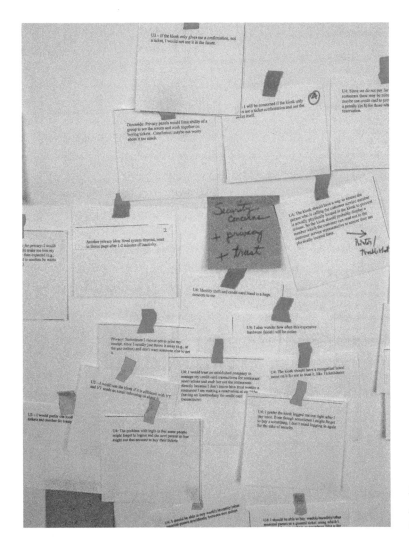

Fig. 8-4

A group with a growing topical label.

Fig. 8-5

A topical label that has grown in scope during affinity diagram building.

the affinity diagram, expanding its purview to include security, privacy, and trust concerns.

8.7.4.4 Splitting large groups

As groups grow from taking in more and more work activity notes, they can get too large and the topic too general to be useful in organizing the work activity notes. Split groups with more than about 10–12 work activity notes as follows:

- Find one or more subtopics within the group.
- Split the group into one or more subgroups based on affinities or commonalities with the subtopics.
- Add precise (and usually narrower scope) labels to each new subgroup.
- Add a "supertopic" label (see explanation below) above to represent this group of new subgroups (usually some variation of the group topic before splitting).
- The new subgroups are now hierarchical "children" of that supertopic label (this is how the WAAD grows in height).

Supergroup labels and subgroup labels. Keep paying attention to all the group and supergroup labels. When you split a group and create several new labels, including the one for the new supergroup, this is a time when labels can suffer in precision and effectiveness. Adjust labels to maintain their descriptive power and their power to discriminate between groups, without looking at the notes within the groups. Apply this test for coherence within a group: Does the label express what all the notes have in common?

Example: Group Splitting in the WAAD

At the top of Fig. 8-6, we see the updated group label, "My concerns about security, privacy, and trust," that resulted from the growth of the label in Fig. 8-5. As notes further built up in that group, it became too large and had to be split. It was tempting to split this one into the three subgroups already named in this label. However, before that the team decided that there were security-related issues in the organizational perspective that were somewhat different from those of the customer. So they first split the top label into "Our organizational perspective" and "My customer's perspective. As an aside, to be modular by retaining context, each of these should explain what those perspectives are about, namely security, privacy, and trust.

The team followed up with the obvious split of "My customer's perspective" into the three kinds of security-related concerns, as you can see in the three blue labels on the right side of the middle of the figure for: "My need for fraud protection," "My feelings about trust," and "My need for privacy."

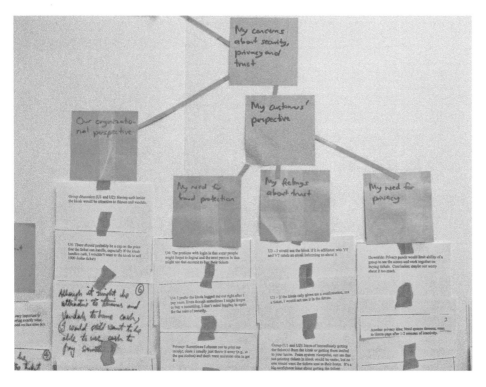

Fig. 8-6
Group affinity labels
(in blue).

8.7.4.5 As you work

Keep refining and reorganizing the groups and labels. The order and organization of the groups and their labels should be considered flexible and malleable.

- Split a group if its notes address more than one topic (i.e., if some work activity notes don't quite fit the group topic).
- Combine two groups if they are about the same topic.

Keep it moving. Don't get distracted with details and sidebar discussions.

- Highlight the more important notes.
- Don't get tangled up in premature discussions about design or implementation.

Topical labels for groups evolve. Groups will grow and morph as they mature into more clearly defined sets of notes, each related by affinity to a specific topic. This is what Cox and Greenberg (2000) call *emergence*, "… a characteristic of the process by which the group interprets and transforms … raw [data] fragments into rich final descriptions."

8.7.5 Use Technology to Support WAAD Building

A very large wall space works well for WAAD building (Fig. 8-7).

Fig. 8-7

Team working to build a WAAD.

For teams that do WAAD building frequently, there are higher-tech WAAD-building tools. In Fig. 8-8, we show a team at Virginia Tech using affinity diagram software on a high-resolution large-screen display as an alternative to paper-based work activity note shuffling (Judge, Pyla, McCrickard, & Harrison,

Fig. 8-8

Building a WAAD on a large touchscreen.

2008). Each analyst can select and manipulate work activity notes on a laptop or tablet before sending them to the wall for group consideration, where they can move them around by touching and dragging.

8.7.6 Continue Organizing Groups into a Hierarchy

In Fig. 8-9, showing part of the affinity diagram for MUTTS, you can see groups (blue labels) connected into supergroups (pink labels).

Similarly, you can group second-level groups to form a third level with yet another level of labels. As with group labels, wording of higher-level labels has to represent their groups and subgroups so well that you do not have to read the labels or notes below them in the hierarchy to know what the group is about.

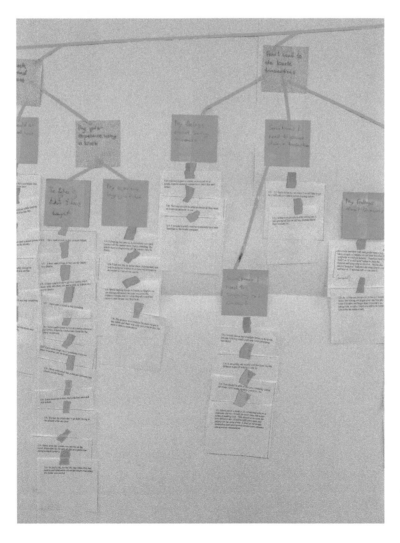

Fig. 8-9

Second-level superlabels for supergroups shown in pink.

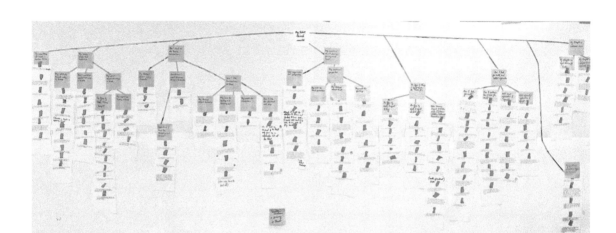

Fig. 8-10

The WAAD that we built for the MUTTS example.

In Fig. 8-10, you can see a photo of a large part of the overall WAAD we built for MUTTS.

Just as a further example of WAAD structure, Fig. 8-11 is a close-up photo of the MUTTS WAAD showing details for three groups having an overall label, "The type of things I expect to use the kiosk for."

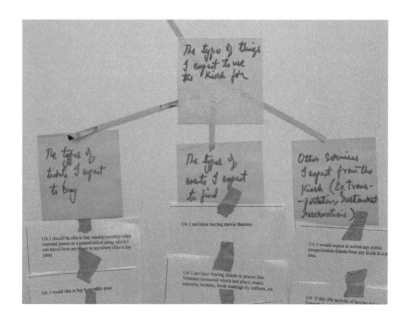

Fig. 8-11

A closeup of the MUTTS WAAD.

8.7.7 At the End, Create "Highlights"

Create a highlights display. Finally, as your team discusses the posted contextual data notes, it is useful to pull out the main and most interesting points and display them as highlights to focus on what's most important.

Example: Sorting Out TKS Work Activity Notes

As a summary of most of this chapter, the following is a large example of sorting out work activity notes obtained from TKS data. This example was based on about 120 selected data notes from the usage research for the TKS. We used the data sorting techniques described in Section 8.6.1 and put each note into these structures: requirements, models, and the WAAD.

Even though this example did turn out to be rather large, it is something many readers and instructors have asked for since the first edition came out. We wanted to include enough data notes to be realistic and to represent most of the important categories in the results but still not be too large for inclusion in this chapter.

The contents in this example are generic data notes, obtained before we had developed the concept of work activity notes. They are probably somewhere between raw data notes and work activity notes. Any flaws you spot in these notes make them like notes you might see in a real project, which is what they are.

Most of those under requirements could just as well be under user stories. Also, as we said earlier, each note could appear in more than one place in this organizing structure, but we choose just one for simplicity.

Here is how we did the analysis for a small selected sample of data notes.

23: The kiosk should remind people to take the ticket and credit card (at the end of the transaction).

Requirements > Interaction design > Transaction flow

Note to reader: These sequences of terms in italics are an attempt to show path names using node labels within a hierarchical organizing structure.

13: Need graphical display of seating arrangements (text description of types of seating not meaningful enough to decide).

Requirements > Interaction design > Features > Visual display of seating arrangements

11: Sort by categories (sports, movies, etc.), date/time, price, location. User drills down into hierarchical structure.

Requirements > Information architecture > Structure, organization by category

18: It will be very important to have a confirmation page showing exactly what I'm buying before I pay (as good online sites do).

Models > The flow model

106: I would like to be able to browse by different topics (type of event). For example, in big cities, even in music there will be different genres.

Models > Task models

70: I would use the kiosk if it is affiliated with Middleburg University and MU sends an email informing us about it.

Work activity affinity diagram > User ticket-shopping behavior > Likelihood of using a kiosk

02: Idea: Although marketing people might not think to put a kiosk next to the ticket window at the ticket office, it would be very helpful for people who get there and find the ticket office closed.

Work activity affinity diagram > Business issues > Kiosk locations

Example: Large Example of Sorting Out Work Activity Notes for the TKS Project

Requirements

Interaction design
  Transaction flow

18: It will be very important to have a confirmation page showing exactly what I'm buying before I pay (as good online sites do).

21: The kiosk should remind people where the ticket comes out.

22: Part of the ticket selection *process* is the option to view the map to the venue.

23: The kiosk should remind people to take the ticket and credit card (at the end of the transaction).

57: Need a "bread crumb" kind of trace of my progress through the kiosk system, showing what I've done in a step-by-step display at the top.
  Features
    Visual display of seating arrangements

10b: Look at seating options versus prices, will I find an option allowing several friends to sit together?

13: Need graphical display of seating arrangements (text description of types of seating not meaningful enough to decide).
    Access to "more information"

12: Alternative (*to seeing top events on first page*): have a button for current events and recommendations on first page. Make the button very obvious so no one can miss it. Have a "More" button to see more details and narrow down the choices. [Interpretive comment: This is a very specific design idea (at the level of saying it is a button). This happens frequently in this kind of usage research data and appears in several data notes in this example. You could change the words a bit to make it less design-centric. For example, you could change "button" to "option" or "capability."]

49: I need lots of information to make my choices. Need an "additional information" button for each event, sort of like Netflix, to give me a short synopsis (4–5 sentences in a paragraph), like the text of an online movie trailer.

Calendar-driven choices

51: High-priority need/want: Calendar on front page. Pick date and click "What's going on today?" or "What's going on for this date?"

55: Choosing date and time. Kiosk gives options for current day, this coming weekend, within the current week, etc. Future dates selected from an interactive calendar image.

Shopping cart concept

56: Kiosk needs a concept of a shopping cart, so a customer can buy tickets for more than one event without starting over. This should even work for two different sets of tickets (different seats and prices) for the same event.

128: A shopping cart model will facilitate buying different types of tickets in one go.

Information architecture

Content

Information about what's going on around town

05b: I'd also use it just to find information on what's going on around town.

143: For example, sometimes I want to see information about popular events that are showing downtown this week.

Event- or activity-related content

08: I'd want it (*the kiosk*) to include more than just movies and sports—for example, museums, concerts, special shows.

10a: Buying—for example, student tickets to Hokie basketball. Need to declare status (student vs. public).

116: I envision buying admission to local Friday night bars, local play houses, major concert halls, sporting events.

Structure, organization by category

11: Sort by categories (sports, movies, etc.), date/time, price, location. User drills down into hierarchical structure. [Again, this is a design idea. Sometimes certain work roles give very specific design ideas because of their experience. Even though it is the UX designer's job to interpret them, you should capture them as design ideas to consider.]

Information organization for display

06 Recommendation (top priority)—I'd want to see the most current events (top picks for today and tomorrow) on the first page, so I can avoid searching and browsing for those.

49B: An "additional information" button for each event would give me more details.

Information organization for storage and retrieval

52: High priority: Access event information by event title (directly) or by type (event category). For titles, could use alphabet to choose from at top (like some websites for, for example, the employee directory of a company).

53: Use "intelligent" mappings from a select letter of the alphabet. This will map to any event of any type that could conceivably be associated with that letter. For example, if user chooses "B," it would list Middleburg University basketball, Orioles baseball, the Blue Man Group. Similarly, an "S" would lead to sports and then a "B" would lead to basketball and baseball. [Again, this is full of specific design ideas.]

Functionality

Searching

83: I would like to be able to search for events by price, artist, venue, and/or date.

104: If I am looking for a specific band, I expect a Google style search where I type in the name of the band.

112: It would be really nice to be able to search for interesting events, say, within two blocks from where I am currently.

Browsing

74: I would like to be able to browse all events on the kiosk.

106: I would like to be able to browse by different topic (type of event). For example, in big cities, even in music there will be different genres.

107: I would like to be able to browse by locations.

Sorting

75: I would like to be able to sort the results I find using some criteria.

Personal privacy

15: Sometimes a kiosk has a time-out feature to help protect privacy (so the next person can't see what I was doing, if I forget to clear it when I leave).

47: Privacy: I don't want people in line behind me to see what I'm looking at and what I'm doing, so I need some kind of limited viewing angle for the screen or "privacy screen" at the side (like on old-style open phone booths).

48: Downside: Privacy panels would limit the ability of a group to see the screen and work together on buying tickets. Conclusion: maybe not worry about it too much.

Transportation tickets

100: I would expect to access any public transportation tickets from any kiosk in a particular area.

101: I would expect to be able to buy one-way passes, day passes, and monthly passes.

110: I would like to be able to specify source and destination and look for travel options even if I am not at either of those places.

Activity-based design

108: I think after buying tickets for an event, prompting "Would you like to get transportation tickets to get there?" would be good.

123: While using the kiosk to buy entertainment tickets, I would like to have the functionality to plan for an entire evening (transportation, event tickets, and dinner reservations).

Models

Note: The notes we list under each model below would actually be integrated into the corresponding models and not appear as notes, as they do here.

User work roles

No notes mentioned a user work role directly. Everyone involved already knew the main roles.

User personas

76: If I find a ticket for an event I would like to go to, I will call my friends before buying tickets.

04: If I'm in Middleburg, I'd probably just go to the venue; at home (Charlotte), I'd buy online.

70: I would use the kiosk if it is affiliated with Middleburg University and MU sends an email informing us about it.

88: In a big city, I will be spending more time commuting, so if there is a kiosk in the metro station I will be more likely to use it.

60: I have used a kiosk in grocery stores, retail stores with self-checkout and to pick up tickets at a movie theater.

136: Identity theft and credit card fraud are huge concerns to me.

The flow model

18: It will be very important to have a confirmation page showing exactly what I'm buying before I pay (as good online sites do).

21: The kiosk should remind people where the ticket comes out.

22: Part of the ticket selection *process* is the option to view the map to the venue.

23: The kiosk should remind people to take the ticket and credit card (at the end of the transaction).

24: Part of the ticket selection process is getting directions for how to get there.

Task models

14: I'd want to be able to use cash, credit card, or debit card to pay. I'd slide my credit card as I do at a gas station.

18: It will be very important to have a confirmation page showing exactly what I'm buying before I pay (as good online sites do).

21: The kiosk should remind people where the ticket comes out.

22: Part of the ticket selection *process* is the option to view the map to the venue.

51: High-priority need/want: Calendar on front page. Pick date and click "What's going on today?" or "What's going on for this date?"

74: I would like to be able to browse all events on the kiosk.

75: I would like to be able to sort the results I find using some criteria.

106: I would like to be able to browse by different topic (type of event). For example, in big cities, even in music there will be different genres.

107: I would like to be able to browse by locations.

113: It would be really nice to be able to filter down search results from a query by event type, etc.

114: I would like to specify a station name and say what events are within two blocks of that station.

Artifact model

37: From a system viewpoint, you can see that not printing tickets at the kiosk would be easier, but no one would want the tickets sent to their home. It's a big confidence issue about getting the tickets immediately.

38: Need an option to print out the *driving* directions.

Physical environment model

02: Idea: Although marketing people might not think to put a kiosk next to the ticket window at the ticket office, it would be very helpful for people who get there and find the ticket office closed.

41: *About needing a printer in the kiosk*: System view: huge maintenance and reliability problem! You absolutely cannot ever allow any kiosk to run out of paper or ink or to have the printer go down. Otherwise, the customer will be very upset and probably never use the kiosk again.

84: I would prefer the kiosk to have a touchscreen instead of a keypad.

105: I also wonder how often this expensive hardware (kiosk) will be stolen.

Information architecture model

11: Sort by categories (sports, movies, etc.), date/time, price, location. User drills down into hierarchical structure.

49: I need lots of information to make my choices. Need an "additional information" button for each event, sort of like Netflix, to give me a short synopsis (4–5 sentences in a paragraph), like the text of an online movie trailer.

52: High priority: Access event information by event title (directly) or by type (event category). For titles, could use alphabet to choose from at top (like some websites for, for example, the employee directory of a company).

53: Use "intelligent" mappings from a selected letter of the alphabet. This will map any event of any type that could conceivably be associated with that letter. For example, if user chooses "B," it would list Middleburg University basketball, Orioles baseball, the Blue Man Group. Similarly, an "S" would lead to sports and then a "B" would lead to basketball and baseball.

Work activity affinity diagram

User ticket-shopping behavior

Generally, how I might use a kiosk

01: Normally, I buy tickets at the venue of the event just before the event. For special events, I might buy online.

76: If I find a ticket for an event I would like to go to, I will call my friends before buying tickets.

79: I will only browse to find out about new events, not to buy immediately.

80: I might even go home and compare prices on other websites (compared to the kiosk).

Likelihood of using a kiosk

04: If I'm in Middleburg, I'd probably just go to the venue; at home (Charlotte), I'd buy online.

05a: I'd like to see a ticket kiosk in town here. I'd try it out and maybe would change to buying tickets at the kiosk for events.

70: I would use the kiosk if it is affiliated with Middleburg University and MU sends an email informing us about it.

72: If I had 30 minutes to spare at the metro station and there was a kiosk, I might browse it.

Familiarity with using kiosks

60: I have used a kiosk in grocery stores, retail stores with self-checkout and to pick up tickets at a movie theater.

61: I have used a kiosk to buy movie tickets at a theater.

62 I have used a kiosk to buy concert tickets.

63 I have used a kiosk to buy boarding tickets for the metro.

Trust issues

131: The kiosk should be located in a nice location for me to trust it. If it is in a shady location, I will not trust it.

135: I would trust an established company to manage my credit card transactions for restaurant reservations and such but not the restaurants directly because I don't know how trustworthy a restaurant I am making a reservation at could be (having an intermediary for credit card transactions).

136: Identity theft and credit card fraud are huge concerns to me.

Business issues, decisions
Branding and appearance

68: A kiosk has to be presented in a professional way; it needs to look official.

69: It (the kiosk) should not look cheap like a holder for free brochures.

Kiosk locations

02: Idea: Although marketing people might not think to put a kiosk next to the ticket window at the ticket office, it would be very helpful for people who get there and find the ticket office closed.

07: Proximity: It (*a kiosk*) would have to be close to where I live or work or shop.

64: A kiosk would be helpful in the theater for when there are long lines.

Kiosk hours

03: Most of my free time is outside normal business hours and after many businesses are closed.

Credit card usage

14: I'd want to be able to use cash, credit card, or debit card to pay. I'd slide my credit card as I do at a gas station.

Cash transactions

17: It's complicated to recognize bills (cash) and dispense change.

19: Having cash inside the kiosk would be attractive to thieves and vandals.

20: Regardless of the difficulties it might present to designers, I would still want to be able to use cash to pay sometimes.

Printing tickets

37: From a system viewpoint, you can see that not printing tickets at the kiosk would be easier, but no one would want the tickets sent to their home. It's a big confidence issue about getting the tickets immediately.

39: If ticket(s) I buy from the kiosk are going to be mailed to my home, I'd worry about getting them in time for the event.

40: If you buy tickets at the kiosk and they are mailed to your home, you need a receipt, so would have to have a printer in the kiosk, anyway.

41: *About needing a printer in the kiosk*: System view: huge maintenance and reliability problem! You absolutely cannot ever allow any kiosk to run out of paper or ink or to have the printer go down. Otherwise, customers will be very upset and probably never use the kiosk again.

42: But it (the ticket printer *will* go down) *could* happen, no matter how careful you are, given the amount of traffic and usage. What then? Need a customer service phone (e.g., hardwired to the company representative).

Keyboards versus touchscreens

44: Keyboard? Soft keyboard on touchscreen only; never a real keyboard on a public kiosk!

84: I would prefer the kiosk to have a touchscreen instead of a keypad.

Include video trailers?

50: Also, need video trailers. Downside: expensive to produce and take too long, holding up other people in line.

Include restaurant reservations?

125: Because we do not pay for a reservation at a restaurant, there may be misuse of the kiosk. So maybe use credit cards to prevent misuse and declare a penalty (in $) for those who do not show up at a reservation.

Vandalism and theft

105: I also wonder how often this expensive hardware (kiosk) will be stolen.

Include shopping suggestions?

71b: How about offering shopping suggestions like Amazon does: Others who have bought tickets for this event have also considered this other event?

Opting out

127: There should be an easy way to say no to suggestions after I buy a ticket or something (so people are not pressured to buy all this related stuff that are is based on purchases I made).

Design decisions

Privacy, security

Bail out of transaction

58a: To use at Metro station: Need a quick cancel to bail you out immediately and go to the home screen without leaving a trace of what you were doing (for privacy with respect to the next customer).

58b: To recover later, need a quick path to a specific item. Maybe use event ID#s to get there directly next time, like using a catalog or item number in search for online shopping.

Time out of transaction

16a: Need *a time-out feature for privacy*, to close out window after one customer leaves and before the next one arrives.

59: Another privacy idea: Need system timeout, reset to home page after 1–2 minutes of inactivity. But this could interfere with task performance (e.g., take a couple of minutes to call your friend on the cellphone to confirm tickets). Therefore, need a "hold" or "I'm still here" button to reset the timeout and keep your work alive. Maybe also need a "progress" indicator showing time to reset and beep at 15 seconds left, so can save it.

Downsides

16b: I would worry that timing out might make me lose my work if it takes me longer than expected (e.g., taking time to call a friend to confirm he wants tickets for the same event).

Help, customer support

132: The kiosk should have a 24/7 customer service number prominently displayed.

User accounts?

137: I do not expect to create an account on a kiosk. I prefer dummy transactions that I fire and forget.

138: The user should be able to choose if they want to create an account.

139: I wouldn't mind creating an account on a web interface to the kiosk company.

Necessity for logins

140: User acts require logins and some people might forget to logout and the next person in line might use that account to buy their tickets.

141: I prefer the kiosk logged me out right after I pay once. Even though sometimes I might forget to buy something, I don't mind logging in again for the sake of security.

8.7.8 Observations from This Example

The above exercise reflects how this process would happen in a realistic project:

- The data notes are not the best examples of properly synthesized work activity notes.
- Many categories in the results overlap, and many notes went into more than one category. These observations reflect the fact that each of these categories is just one way to view the overall picture of the project with its own perspective.
- Some of the category names could have been better. This reflects a realistic problem that occurs when people sort things into categories.
- Almost every note could have gone into the WAAD. That is because it's the nature of a WAAD to not exclude any topic. This also makes the WAAD a nice visual representation of the whole project. As we decided what to put in the WAAD, we used this heuristic: If the note was about a feature, it went into requirements or a user story. The WAAD got notes about general context and design issues. In the end, the requirements seemed to be the largest output of the process, but the WAAD also was substantial.

8.8 LEAD A WALKTHROUGH OF THE WAAD TO GET FEEDBACK

If feasible in your budget and schedule, bring in users and clients and other stakeholders to walk them through your WAAD to share your findings and to get feedback. The purpose of doing a walkthrough is communication, to explain your process briefly and share an appreciation of user work activities and associated issues with all stakeholders.

Guidelines for sharing your findings:

- For management, emphasize high-level issues, cost justification, data integrity, security, and such corporate goals.
- Highlight the most important points and issues discovered.
- Create interest with unexpected things learned.
- Show graphical representations; flow models can be the most effective, as they show your interpretation of the flow of information and materials within their business process.
- Sell your usage research process.

Get management and software developers engaged to show them the effectiveness of your process.

Exercise 8-2: WAAD Building for Your Product or System

Goal: Get practice in building a WAAD to organize you work activity notes by category.

Activities: If you are working alone, this will be the last time you have to buy pizza, at least in this chapter.

However you assemble your team, using the work activity notes created in the previous exercise, do your best to follow the procedure we have described in this chapter for WAAD building.

Take digital photographs of your work process and products, including the full WAAD, some medium-level details, and some closeups of interesting parts. Hang them on your fridge with magnets.

Deliverables: As much of the full WAAD for your system as you were able to produce. It is probably best to keep it rolled up into a bundle for safekeeping unless you have the luxury of being able to keep it taped to the wall. You should also have the digital photos you took of your WAAD. If you are working in a classroom environment, be prepared to share the photos in a narrated slide show and to discuss your WAAD and the process of building it with other teams in the class.

Schedule: This is one of the more time-consuming exercises; expect it to take 4–6 hours.

8.9 SYNTHESIZE THE "ELEPHANT" THAT IS USER WORK PRACTICE AND NEEDS

Synthesis is the process of putting together diverse inputs, facts, and observations of parts of a concept to make conclusions that characterize and aid understanding of the whole concept.

Each of the models we will discuss next provides a different perspective into the work domain. As we mentioned previously, it is like the blind men and the elephant (source unknown). The role of synthesis is to find connections among these models and put pieces together to form the whole elephant. Teasing out the connections through combination, fusion, and other ways of sifting through the data unearths hidden relationships and insights into the work domain. This is where immersion pays off.

The task structure model (Section 9.6) might reveal the elephant skeleton, and maybe the task sequence model (Section 9.7) reflects its skin. Perhaps the flow model (Section 9.5) shows how the elephant moves.

Sometimes you need to create hybrid models (Section 9.12) to integrate multiple views into the same frame and unearth different connections and flesh out the true nature of the elephant. For example, in the MUTTS effort we discovered in one of our information models (Section 9.10) for a student user class that each student at MU carries an ID card called the MU passport. This passport is a magnetic card (like a debit or credit card) and carries money that students can spend at all campus eateries. We had another information model for the payment options. During the synthesis exercise we discovered that allowing students to use their MU passport as a payment option would be a big user convenience factor.

Immersion

A form of deep thought and analysis of the problem at hand—to "live" within the context of a problem and to make connections among the different aspects of it (Section 2.4.7).

Usage Research Data Modeling

9.1 INTRODUCTION

9.1.1 You Are Here

We begin each process chapter with a "you are here" picture of the chapter topic in the context of The Wheel, the overall UX design lifecycle template (Fig. 9-1). Within the Understand Needs UX design lifecycle activity, this chapter is about the data modeling subactivity in which you represent the usage research data you elicited in Chapter 7 in simple models.

9.1.2 What Are Usage Research Data Models and How Are They Used

Modeling, a basic life skill (Section 2.4.5), is a way to organize some kinds of raw usage research data into representations to inform UX design. Each model provides a different perspective into the overall picture of work practice. Models use abstraction (another life skill) to boil things down to the essence and turn usage research data into actionable items for design.

Abstraction

The process of removing extraneous details of something and focusing on its irreducible constructs to identify what is really going on, ignoring everything else (Section 14.2.8.2).

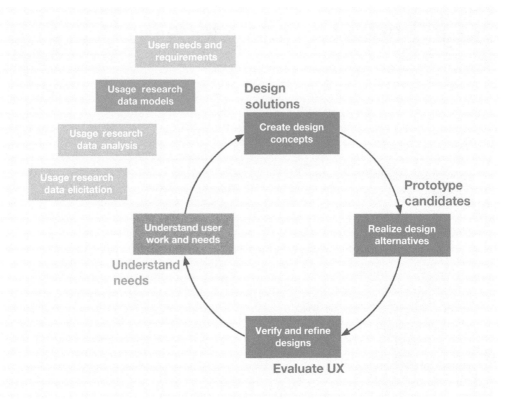

Fig. 9-1

You are here in the subactivity of constructing usage research data models within the Understand Needs lifecycle activity, in the context of The Wheel, the overall lifecycle process.

Usage research models also provide some boundaries and checklists of things that have to be included in the design. Most of all, the models offer an immersive mental framework of design parameters.

9.1.3 Kinds of Data Models

Not every data model is appropriate for every project. In this chapter, we present the models in an order that approximately represents importance and frequency of use:

- The most commonly needed models—in almost every project you should make these models: User work role model and flow model.

- If there is a broad range of user characteristics for any given user work role, consider making a user persona.
- If there are a large number of different user tasks, organize them with a task structure model, such as the hierarchical task inventory.
- If some user tasks are a bit complex, describe them with task sequence models.
- If the work practice is artifact-centric, describe them with an artifact model.
- If the work practice is influenced by physical layout, describe that with a physical work environment model.
- If the data and information users need to store, retrieve, display, and manipulate are complex, represent it with an information architecture model.
- The social mode is the least commonly used model, needed only when social and cultural interactions among the people involved in the work practice are complex and/or problematic.

Artifact model

A representation showing how users employ, manipulate, and share key tangible objects (physical or electronic work practice artifacts) as part of the flow in their work practice (Section 9.8).

9.1.4 Modeling Should Already be Well Established

Starting from the project commission (Section 5.4), basic model-related information is among the earliest things that you learn. The project proposal or business brief that kicks off the project and the early client meetings to define the project all provide basic inputs to at least:

- The user work role model.
- The flow model.
- Task models.

Early usage research, especially data elicitation and analysis, helps fill in gaps and refine concepts. Later usage research is for confirming points and answering questions about the models.

So, by the time you get here, some of your modeling should already be established. We describe it here to get all the modeling methods and techniques in one place rather than as it will occur in your project, interspersed throughout project commission, usage research data elicitation, analysis, and modeling.

9.2 SOME GENERAL "HOW TO" SUGGESTIONS FOR DATA MODELING

9.2.1 How Modeling Can Overlap with Usage Research Data Elicitation and Analysis

For simple things such as data about user work roles and information flow, you can already start sketching out some early models even as you are onsite, eliciting usage research data. This will allow you to pass these early models by users for confirmation (or not).

User work role

Not a person but a work assignment, defined and distinguished by a corresponding job title or work responsibilities. A work role usually involves system usage, but some work roles can be external to the organization being studied (Section 7.5.4.1).

Hierarchical task inventory (HTI)

A hierarchical structural representation of task and subtask relationships for cataloguing and representing the hierarchical relationships among tasks and subtasks that must be supported in a system design (Section 9.6).

In usage research analysis (Chapter 8), as you encountered an elemental data note that related to a data model, you either set it aside as an input to modeling or you merged it into that model (Section 8.4). So, for example, if you are now considering a note about a user work role, see if that work role is already fully represented in the user work role model. If not, merge in any new information (e.g., add a new user work role to the list). If the elemental data note mentions a new path of flow of an artifact or information, add an arc and maybe a new node to the flow model (a simple graphical representation of how information and artifacts flow through the system, Section 9.5). If the note mentions a new task for a given user work role, add it to the hierarchical task inventory for that user work role and start a task sequence model for it.

Elemental data note

A data note from either usage research or UX evaluation that is brief, clear, concise, and refers to or relates to exactly one concept, idea, fact, or topic (Section 8.2.2).

9.2.2 For High Rigor, Maintain Connections to Data Sources

You will not usually require high rigor and traceability of usage research data and model components to original sources. However, if rigor and traceability demands it, you can carry forward source IDs assigned to elemental data to maintain a connection from model components to data sources. This allows you to go back to the original sources of the raw data in question to resolve questions, disagreements, or interpretations of the data.

Example: Tagging Model with Source ID

In the example at the end of Sections 8.2.3 and 8.2.7, we had an elemental data note that described a barrier in the workflow model of the ticket buyer:

Barrier

In the context of usage research, a problem that interferes with normal operations of user work practice, impedes user activities or task performance, interrupts work flow or communications, or interferes with the work practice (Section 9.7.2.3).

> *It is usually difficult to get enough information about events from a ticket seller at the ticket window. [8]*

Where possible, the flow model will also be tagged with "[8]" here, to maintain this "chain of custody" of data source information.

Because most projects do not require maximum rigor of this kind, we do not pursue this source ID tagging in the rest of this chapter.

9.3 THE USER WORK ROLE MODEL

The work role model is one of the most important models and every project needs one. This model, at its base, is a simple representation of user work roles, subroles, and associated user class characteristics. It is essential to identify the operational user work (or play) roles as early in usage research as possible.

9.3.1 What is a User Work Role?

A user work role is not a person, but a work assignment defined by the duties, functions, and work activities of a person with a certain job title or job responsibility, such as "customer" or "database administrator." Job titles themselves, however, don't necessarily make good names for user work roles; you should use names that distinguish them by the kind of work they do.

For example, the MUTTS ticket seller who helps customers buy tickets does entirely different tasks with the system than, say, the event manager who, behind the scenes, enters entertainment event information into the system so that tickets can be offered, purchased, and printed.

Many people can play the same work role. For example, all cashiers at a bank might fall under the same work role, even though they are different people.

A work role can:

- Involve system usage or not.
- Be internal or external to the organization, as long as the job entails participation in the work practice of the organization.

As an example of what kind of raw data to look for in usage research data, any information about the "ticket buyer" in the Ticket Kiosk System should be merged into that user work role model.

Reminder: MUTTS is the old system, using a ticket window and the Ticket Kiosk System is the new system, using public kiosks.

> **MUTTS**
>
> MUTTS is the acronym for Middleburg University Ticket Transaction Service, our running example for most of the process chapters (Section 5.5).

Example: Work Role Identification for MUTTS

The two obvious work roles in MUTTS already mentioned are:

- Ticket buyer, who interacts with the ticket seller to learn about event information and to buy event tickets.
- Ticket seller, who serves ticket buyers and uses the system to find and buy tickets on behalf of ticket buyers.

Among the other roles we discovered early in usage research are:

- Event manager, who negotiates with event promoters about event information and tickets to be sold by the MUTTS ticket office.
- Advertising manager, who negotiates with outside advertisers to arrange for advertising to be featured via MUTTS—for example, ads printed on the back of tickets, posted on bulletin boards, and on the website.
- Financial administrator, who is responsible for accounting and credit card issues.

- Maintenance technician, who maintains the MUTTS ticket office computers, website, ticket printers, and network connections.
- Database administrator, who is responsible for the reliability and data integrity of the database.
- Administrative supervisor, who oversees the entire MU services department.
- Office manager, who is in charge of the daily MUTTS operation.
- Assistant office manager, who assists the office manager.

9.3.2 Subroles

For some work roles, it can be useful to distinguish subroles defined by different subsets of tasks the work role does. Examples of subroles for the ticket buyer role include student, general public, faculty/staff, and alumni ticket buyers.

9.3.3 Mediated Work Roles

Some "users" serve roles that do not use the system directly but still play a major part in the workflow and usage context. We call these users "mediated users" because their interaction with the system is mediated by direct users. Cooper (2004) calls them "served users" and they still have true work roles in the enterprise and are true stakeholders in the system.

Mediated roles are often customers and clients of the enterprise on whose behalf direct users such as clerks and agents conduct transactions with the computer system. They might be point-of-sale customers at a retail outlet or customers needing services at a bank or an insurance agency. The working relationship between the mediated users and the agent is critical to the resulting user experience. The ticket-buyer role for MUTTS is a prime example of a user role whose interaction with the computer system is mediated (by the ticket seller).

Exercise 9-1: Identifying User Work Roles for Your Product or System

Goal: Get a little practice at identifying work roles from your work activity notes.

Activities: By now you should be pretty certain about the work roles for your system. Using your user-related work activity notes, identify and list the major work roles for your product or system.

For each role, add explanatory notes describing the role and add a description of the major task set that people in that role would be expected to perform.

Work activity note

A brief, clear, concise, and elemental (relating to exactly one concept, idea, fact, or topic) statement used to document a single point about the work practice as synthesized from raw usage research data (Section 8.1.2).

Deliverables: A written list of work roles you identified for your system, each with an explanation of the role and a brief high-level description of the associated task set.

Schedule: A half hour should do it.

9.3.4 User Class Definitions

A user class for a work role or subrole is defined by a description of relevant characteristics of the potential user community that can perform that role. Every work role and subrole will have at least one user class.

User class definitions can be defined in terms of such characteristics as demographics, skills, knowledge, and special needs. Some specialized user classes, such as "soccer mom," "yuppie," "metrosexual," or "elderly citizen," may be dictated by marketing (Frank, 2006).

As an example of a user class, the set of people in the town-resident subrole of the ticket-buyer role in the new Ticket Kiosk System might be expected to include inexperienced (first-time) users from the general public. Another user class for this work role could be senior citizens with limited motor skills and some visual impairment.

The characteristics used to distinguish user classes can involve almost any credential or qualification that describes attributes needed to perform the corresponding work role.

9.3.4.1 Knowledge- and skills-based characteristics

User class characteristics related to knowledge and skills include:

- Background, experience, training, education, and/or skills expected in a user to perform a given work role. For example, a given class of users must be trained in retail marketing and must have five years of sales experience.
- Knowledge of computers—both in general and with respect to specific systems.
- Knowledge of the work domain—knowledge of and experience with the operations, procedures, and semantics of the various aspects of the application area the system being designed is trying to address.

For example, a medical doctor might be an expert in domain knowledge related to an MRI system, but may have only novice-to-intermittent knowledge in the area of related computer applications. In contrast, an administrator in the hospital may have little overall domain knowledge about MRI systems, but may have more complete knowledge regarding the day-to-day use of related computer applications.

Some knowledge- and skills-based characteristics of user class definitions can be mandated by organizational policies or even legal requirements, especially for work roles that affect public safety.

9.3.4.2 Physiological characteristics

User class characteristics related to physiological characteristics include:

- Impairments, limitations, and other ADA-related considerations.
- Age. If older adults are expected to take on a given work role, they may have known characteristics to be accommodated in design. For example, they can be susceptible to sensory and motor limitations that come naturally with age.

Physiological characteristics are certainly where accessibility issues can be found. Within work roles, you may also find subclasses of users based on special characteristics such as special needs and disabilities.

Example: User Class Definitions for MUTTS

Ticket seller. Minimum requirements might include point-and-click computer skills. Probably some simple additional domain-specific training is necessary. When we interviewed ticket sellers at MUTTS, we discovered that they did have a manual explaining the job responsibilities, but over time it had become outdated and eventually was lost.

Because ticket sellers are often hired as part-time employees, there can be considerable turnover. So, as a practical matter, much of the ticket seller training is picked up as on-the-job training or while "apprenticing" with someone more experienced, with some mistakes occurring along the way. This variability of competence in the work role, which is the main interface with the public, is not always the best for customer satisfaction, but there does not seem to be a way around it at MUTTS.

Exercise 9.2: User Class Definitions for Your Product or System

Goal: Get practice in defining user classes for work roles, similar to the example above.

Activities: Using your user-related usage research data notes, create a few user class definitions to go with the work roles you identified in the previous exercise. Describe the characteristics of each user class.

Deliverables: A few user class definitions to go with the work roles identified.

Schedule: About 30–45 minutes should be enough to get the most out of this assignment.

9.3.5 Post the Work Role Modeling Results

Post a visual representation of the updated and refined work roles, subroles, and user classes in a central location within the design studio, so everyone can refer to it during design.

9.4 USER PERSONAS

A persona, or user persona, is a narrative description of a specific design target of a UX design for a user in one work role. A persona is a hypothetical but specific "character" in a specific work role. As a technique for making users real to designers, a persona is a story and description of a realistic individual who has a name, a life, and a personality, allowing designers to limit design focus to something very specific.

User personas are a user model that is very closely tied to design. We don't make personas for users of the old, existing product or system because we use them to guide the design for the new system. However, they are introduced here with the user models because they are derived from usage research data about users.

9.4.1 What Are User Personas?

First of all, it's important to note that each persona we make applies to exactly one user work role. So you can make a persona for each user work role or just for the important ones.

You can't make a single design that is the best for everyone who might fill the corresponding work role. If you try, you will often end up with a design that is so general it doesn't work well for anyone. So it has been suggested that you create a persona as a specific design target.

A persona is not an actual user, nor necessarily a typical user, and certainly not an average of users. Rather, a persona is a pretend user or a "hypothetical archetype" (Cooper, 2004) person that must be served by the design. Each persona is a single "user" with very concrete characteristics, representing a specific person in a specific work role with specific user characteristics.

9.4.2 Extracting Data for Personas

During usage research analysis, as you look at each work activity note, if it is about a particular user as a person and says anything about their personality and habits and how that person uses the product or system, it is a good candidate for consideration as an input to a user persona model.

Here are a few example elemental data notes that are candidates for inputs to user personas in the TKS:

- I usually work long hours in the lab on the other side of campus.
- I like classical music concerts, especially from local artists.
- I love the sense of community in Middleburg.
- Sometimes I need to buy a set of tickets with adjacent seating because I like to sit with friends.
- I like to buy MU football game tickets in a group so I can sit with my friends.

The main discussion about constructing personas and using them to guide design is in Chapter 14 on generative design.

9.4.3 A Preview of How to Create Personas

For any given work role, personas are defined by user goals arising from their subroles and user classes. Different subroles and associated user classes have different goals, which will lead to different personas and different designs.

Starting with user research data, you first create multiple candidate personas for each user work role. Each persona is a description of a specific individual who is given a name, a life, a personality, and a profile as a person, especially with respect to how they use the new product or system. Making personas precise and specific is paramount. Specificity is important because that is what lets you exclude other cases when it comes to design.

Then the hard part is to choose one to design for. Through a process to be described in the design chapters (Part 3), you will choose one of those personas as the one primary persona, the single best design target, the persona to which the design will be made specific. The trick is to make the target design to be *just right* for your chosen persona and to *suffice* for the others. This part is deferred until the design chapters.

Example: Personas for the Ticket Kiosk System

An example of a persona for the student subrole in the Ticket Kiosk System could be that of Jane, a biology major who is a second-generation MU attendee and a serious MU sports fan with season tickets to MU football. Jane is a candidate to be the primary persona because she is representative of most MU students when it comes to MU "school spirit." Another persona, Jeff, who is a music major interested in the arts, is also an important one to consider to add breadth to the design.

Exercise 9.3: Early Sketch of a User Persona

Goal: Get some experience at writing a persona similar to the example above.
Activities: Select an important work role within your system. It is best if at least one user class for this work role is broad with the user population coming from a large and diverse group, such as the general public. Using your user-related usage research data, create a persona, give it a name, and get a photo to go with it. Write the text for the persona description.
Schedule: You should be able to do what you need to learn from this in about an hour.

9.5 THE FLOW MODEL

The flow model is one of the most important models and every project needs one.

9.5.1 What Is a Flow Model?

The flow model, at its base, is a simple graphical representation of how information and artifacts flow through the system as it is used. It's essential to identify the basic system flow as early in usage research as possible. A flow model gives you an overview of how information, artifacts, and work products flow among user work roles and parts of the product or system as the result of user actions. For example, how does a song or piece of music flow as it is purchased, downloaded from the Internet, and loaded or synchronized to a personal device?

A flow model is a bird's-eye picture of the work domain, its components, and interconnections among them. It's a high-level view of how users in each work role and other system entities interact and communicate to get work done. A flow model is especially about how work gets handed off between roles; the places where things are most likely to fall through the cracks. As Beyer and Holtzblatt (1997, p. 236) put it: "The system's job is to carry context between roles."

9.5.2 Central Importance of the Flow Model

Because the flow model is a unifying representation of how the system fits into the workflow of the enterprise, it is important to understand it and get it established as early as possible. Along with the user work role model, the flow model is the centerpiece of immersion in your UX design studio. Even though your early usage research data will be incomplete and not entirely accurate, you can refine it as a clear picture of the work domain, system, and users slowly emerges. If necessary, you should go back to your users and ask them to verify the accuracy and completeness of the flow model.

Immersion

A form of deep thought and analysis of the problem at hand—to "live" within the context of a problem and to make connections among the different aspects of it (Section 2.4.7).

9.5.3 How to Make a Flow Model

Starting very early in the UX lifecycle:

- Draw the evolving flow model diagram as a graph of nodes and arcs.
- Start by drawing people icons, labeled with the work roles, as nodes.
- Include roles external to the organization.
- Add nodes for other entities, such as a database into which and from which anything related to the work practice can flow.
- Draw directed arcs (arrows) representing flow, communication, and coordination necessary to do the work of the enterprise, between nodes.
- Label the arcs with what (e.g., artifact, information) is flowing and by what medium (e.g., email, phone calls, letters, memos, and meetings).
- In usage research analysis, as you encounter elemental notes that describe how work flows in the organization, set them aside as inputs to the flow model or merge them directly into the evolving flow model.

Flow model

A simple graphical diagram giving a big picture or overview of work by representing how information, artifacts, and work products flow among work roles and system components within the work practice of an organization (Section 9.5).

Flow models include non-UI software functionality, too, when it is part of the flow; for example, the payroll program must be run before printing and then issuing paychecks. If you make a flow model of how a website is used in work practice, do not use it as a flowchart of pages visited. However, it should represent how information and commands flow among the sites, pages, backend content, and users to carry out work activities.

Sometimes you have to make your flow model very detailed to get at important specifics of the flow and to unearth important questions regarding who does what in depth.

Post a large image of the flow model prominently in your UX design studio as a central part of immersion.

Example: Sketching the Flow Model for MUTTS

The simple early MUTTS flow model of Fig. 9-2 is centered on the ticket-buying activity between the ticket seller and ticket buyer roles, based on sketches made in data elicitation and related elemental data notes encountered in usage research analysis.

Interaction between the ticket buyer and ticket seller might begin with a question about what events are available. The ticket seller then sends a suitable request for this information to the event database and the information in a response flows back to the ticket seller, who then tells the ticket buyer. After one

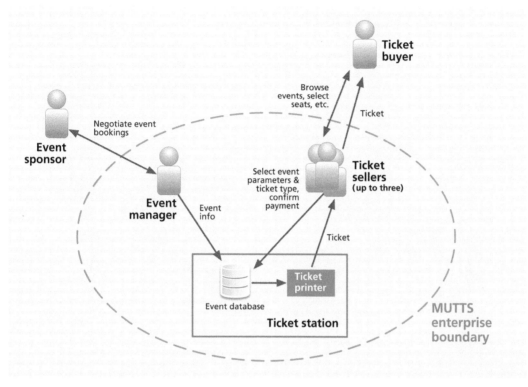

Fig. 9-2
Simple early flow model for the existing MUTTS.

or more such interactions to establish what tickets are available and which ones are desired by the ticket buyer, a ticket purchase request flows from ticket buyer to ticket seller and to the event database. The transaction is consummated with payment and the request then flows to the ticket printer. Printed physical tickets flow to the ticket seller and are then given to (flow to) the ticket buyer.

Example: Extending the MUTTS Flow Model

As more elemental data notes related to the flow of the ticket-buying process emerge in elemental data notes during usage research analysis, we can extend and refine the MUTTS flow model. For instance, in Fig. 9-3 we added an online ticket source, Tickets4ever.com, partnering with MUTTS.

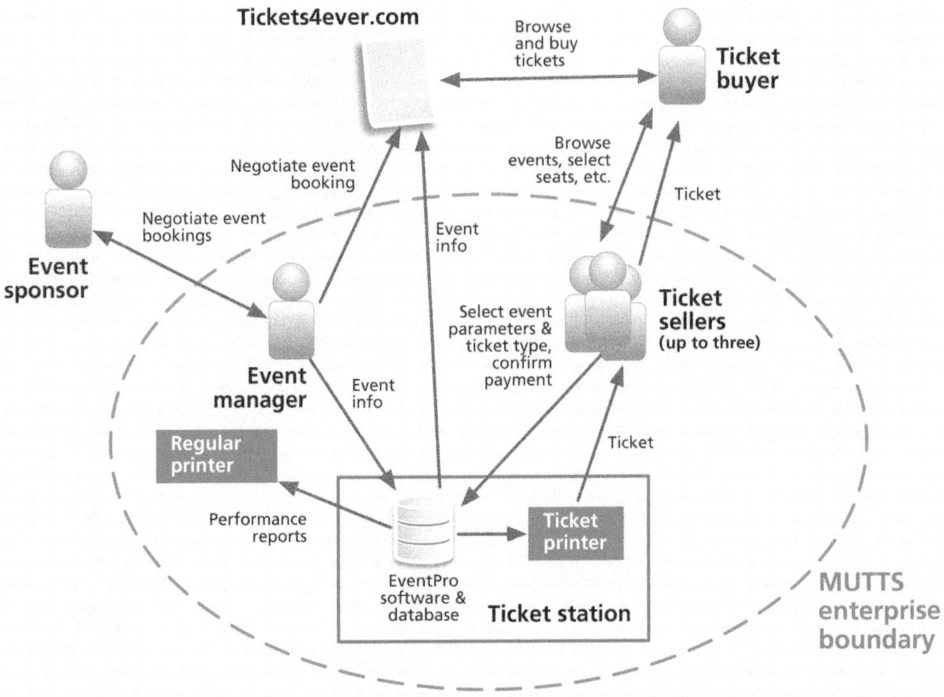

Fig. 9-3

A further step of the flow model sketch of the MUTTS system, showing Tickets4ever.com as a node.

Eventually, the flow model for MUTTS evolved into a rather full diagram, as shown in Fig. 9-4.

Note interactions among roles not involved directly in ticket buying or selling, such as friends and/or family of the ticket buyer in the upper right-hand corner of the diagram, standing there with the ticket buyer or on the cell phone, communicating about choices of events, dates, seats, and prices.

Exercise 9.4: Creating a Flow Model for Your Product or System

Goal: Get practice in making an initial flow model sketch for the work practice of an organization.

Activities: For your target system, sketch out a flow model diagram in the same style as our flow model sketch for MUTTS showing work roles, information flow,

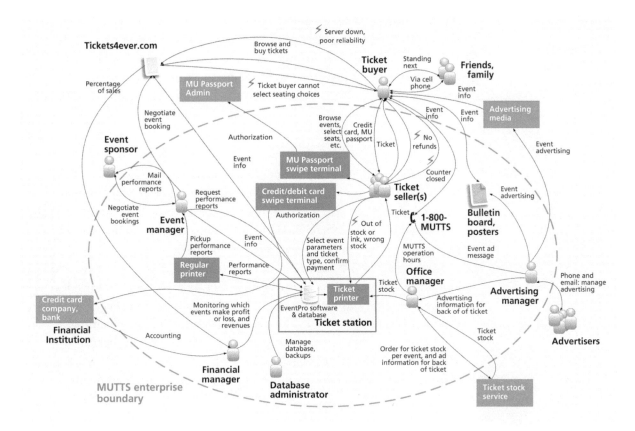

Fig. 9-4
Flow model of our version of MUTTS.

information repositories, transactions, etc. Draw on your raw usage research data and construct a representation of the flow of data, information, and work artifacts.

Start with representing your work roles as nodes, then add in any other nodes for databases and so on.

Label the arcs to show all flow, including all information flow and flow of physical artifacts:

- Show all communication, including direct conversations, email, phones, letters, memos, meetings, and so on.
- Show all coordination necessary to do the work of the enterprise. Include both flow internally within the enterprise and flow externally with the rest of the world.

If you do not have enough usage research data from your limited data elicitation exercise, look up other comparable similar business practices to make this work. **Deliverables:** A one-page diagram illustrating a high-level flow model for the existing work process of your target product or system.

Schedule: Given a relatively simple domain, we expect this exercise to take about an hour.

9.5.4 The Customer Journey Map, a Kind of Flow Model

In Section 7.5.4.2, we described collecting data about extended usage by "shadowing" users and documenting the customer journey, "the product of an interaction between an organization and a customer over the duration of their relationship."[1] Here in data modeling, this kind of data can be represented by what is sometimes called a customer journey map.

As a specific activity model of a different kind of flow in usage, a customer journey map is a "map" of how a customer or user experiences a product or service over time and through space. It is definitely an ecological view of user experience and can often involve pervasive information architecture.

The customer or user passes through and interacts with the ecology over time and through space. A customer journey map tells a story of usage to clients and helps UX designers understand their special work practice and needs.

9.6 TASK STRUCTURE MODELS—THE HIERARCHICAL TASK INVENTORY (HTI)

9.6.1 The Task Models

Task models (task structure and task sequence models) represent what users do or can do. The primary task structure model is the hierarchical task inventory.

The task models are essential for informing UX design. When the elemental data note you are considering in usage research analysis mentions a user task or feature, it is a good candidate to incorporate into a task model.

9.6.2 Benefits of a Task Structure Model

If your product or system has a large number of user tasks in many different categories for many different user work roles, a task structure model such as the hierarchical task inventory (HTI) is a good way to organize the tasks. Task structure models are used to catalog the tasks and subtasks that must be

Pervasive information architecture

A structure for organizing, storing, retrieving, displaying, manipulating, and sharing information that provides ever-present information availability spanning parts of a broad ecology (Sections 12.4.4 and 16.2.3).

Ecology

In the setting of UX design, the ecology is the entire set of surrounding parts of the world, including networks, other users, devices, and information structures, with which a user, product, or system interacts (Section 16.2.1).

---

[1]https://en.wikipedia.org/wiki/Customer_experience

supported in the system design. Like functional decompositions, task inventories capture hierarchical relationships among the tasks and subtasks.

Task structure models:

- Represent what user tasks and actions are possible in the work practice and work environment, using the system or not.
- Are essential for informing UX design, telling you what tasks (and functionality) you have to design for in the system.
- Serve as a checklist for completeness in the emerging design (Constantine & Lockwood, 1999, p. 99).

A hierarchical task inventory has other advantages, too, with respect to later organizing and managing user stories and as a guide for creating a complete set of user stories as requirements.

9.6.3 Tasks versus Functions

Informally, we may use the terms "task" and "function" more or less interchangeably when talking about the features of a system. But, when we wish to avoid confusion, we use the term "task" to refer to things a user does and the term "function" to things the system does.

When the point of view is uncertain, we sometimes see a reference to both. For example, if we talk about a situation where information is "displayed/viewed," the two terms represent two viewpoints on the same phenomenon. It is clear that "display" is something the system does and "view" is something the user does, as the user and system collaborate to perform the task/function. Within usage research analysis, of course, the user (or task) viewpoint is paramount.

9.6.4 Create an HTI Model

A simple task structure can be easily represented as a hierarchical (indented) list of tasks and subtasks. More complex task structures are best represented in an HTI diagram.

Hierarchical task inventories can be constructed top-down, bottom-up, or both. Large, more general tasks are decomposed into smaller, more specific, and more detailed tasks.

9.6.5 Hierarchical Relationships

Location within the diagram indicates a hierarchical relationship between tasks and subtasks. If task A is immediately above task B in an HTI diagram, as in Fig. 9-5, it means that task B is a subtask of task A and task A is a supertask of

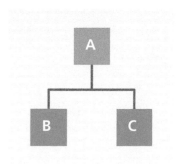

Fig. 9-5

Hierarchical relationship of task A, the supertask, and tasks B and C, subtasks.

task B. The litmus test for this relationship is: If you are doing task B, you are necessarily also doing task A, because task B is part of task A.

The best way to name tasks in this structure is as an <action> <object> pair, such as "add appointment" or "configure parameters," or in an <verb> <adjective> <noun> triple, such as "configure control parameters."

9.6.6 Avoid Temporal Implications

The hierarchical relationship does not show temporal ordering. In Fig. 9-6, we depict an incorrect attempt at a hierarchical relationship because selecting a gear is not part of starting the engine—that is, it fails the litmus test mentioned above.

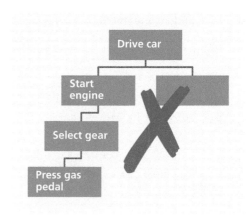

Fig. 9-6

An incorrect hierarchical relationship attempting to show temporal sequencing.

Example: A First-Level HTI Diagram for MUTTS

Starting at the very highest level of tasks for MUTTS, you have the major task sets performed by each of the work roles, such as the financial administrator, the database administrator, the event manager, the advertising manager, and the ticker buyer. Using an "action-object" approach to task naming, these major task sets might be called "manage finances," "manage database," and so on, as shown in Fig. 9-7.

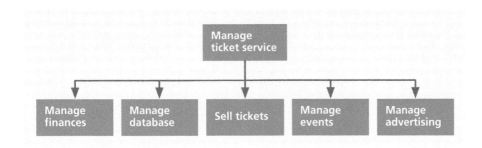

Fig. 9-7

Sketch of the top levels of a possible hierarchical task inventory diagram for MUTTS.

9.6.7 HTI Can Often be Decomposed by User Work Role

The full HTI for a nontrivial system can be enormous. Fortunately, there is a way to control this complexity. Usually you can partition the full HTI by user work roles because the set of tasks performed by one user work role is usually separate from those performed by others. The first level from the top is where this separation by user work roles is seen (Fig. 9-8), resulting essentially in a separate HTI diagram for each user work role.

The team can usually consider each user work role diagram more or less separately in analysis and design. Of course, there are system-spanning issues and parts of the design that involve multiple user work roles, but this imperfect compartmentalization helps a great deal by allowing UX designers to look at the whole system a piece at a time.

The HTI for just the ticket seller role in MUTTS is shown in Fig. 9-9. The "sell tickets" task encompasses all event searching and other subtasks that necessarily go into making a final ticket sale.

Exercise 9.5: HTI for Your Product or System

Goal: Get some practice creating an HTI diagram.

Activities: Using your task-related work activity notes and what you know about your product or system, make a simple HTI diagram for your system.

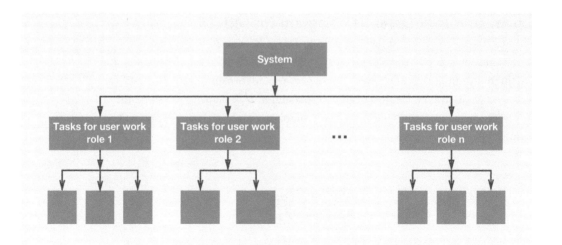

Fig. 9-8

Separation by user work roles at the top of a task hierarchy.

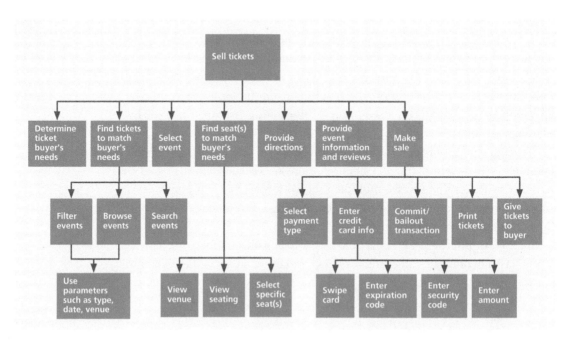

Fig. 9-9

Example HTI for the ticket seller role in MUTTS.

Deliverables: Simple HTI diagram(s) for the product or system of your choice.
Schedule: An hour should be enough to get what you need from this exercise.

9.7 TASK SEQUENCE MODELS

If you have elemental data notes that describe user tasks, you can represent them with a number of different task sequence models.

9.7.1 What Are Task Sequence Models?

Task sequence models are step-by-step descriptions of how users perform tasks with a product or system. User actions and system responses are often separated into dual (or multiple) "swim lanes." Task descriptions have certain "boilerplate" parameters, as described in the subsections below.

Other kinds of task sequence models are used to highlight user workflow. These include state diagrams, which are a kind of hybrid abstraction between a flow model and a task-sequence model that shows user navigation and how information and artifacts in the user workflow are passed among user work roles and other active agents (e.g., a database system).

*Scenario*s. A scenario is a description of specific people performing work activities in a specific work situation within a specific work context, told in a concrete narrative style as if it were a transcript of a real usage occurrence. Scenarios are deliberately informal, open ended, and fragmentary narrative depictions of key usage situations happening over time.

A *usage scenario* is a description of a way someone uses an existing product or system. A *design scenario* is a description of envisioned usage of a product or system being designed.

Example: Simplest Early Task Sequence Model—Usage Scenario for a Menu Planning Application

Sometimes the earliest effective task sequence model is a usage or design scenario, a narrative description of things users will do with a proposed system as captured during usage research data elicitation. Here is one such example.

This example is taken, with permission, from a graduate-level HCI class student project about a (food) menu management system. As these students said in their report: written at first at a high level, these scenarios were expanded to include more detail and were used to check the emerging design against requirements, identify system states, and to identify tasks and even early prototype interface features.

State diagram (in UX)

A directed graph in which nodes are states which correspond to screens (in the broadest sense), and arcs (or arrows) are transitions between states resulting from user actions or system events. Used in wireflow and wireframe prototypes to show navigation among screens (Sections 9.7.6 and 20.4.4.2).

Scenario 1: Lois's father, who is diabetic, will be moving in with her while her mother is in the hospital. Lois is not accustomed to cooking for someone who is diabetic. Because she is also on a diet, she also wants meals that are low fat. To make things easier, she turns to Menu-Bot, her computerized meal planner, to develop meal plans suitable for both her father and herself.

Lois first creates a new meal plan and sets it up to cover three days. For the first day's breakfast, she decides on a simple meal of coffee, juice, and toast. Because she and her father both work, she decides to prepare a simple seafood salad that they can take with them to work for lunch.

However, for dinner she wants a menu with a main dish, a soup, and two side dishes; a dessert would also be nice. Because she doesn't want to have to wade through all the recipes in Menu-Bot but only those low in sugar and fat, she requests that it provide her with only chicken dishes that are classified as low sugar (suitable for hyperglycemic individuals) and low fat. For the main course, she selects from the set that Menu-Bot recommends: low-fat and low-sugar dishes of asparagus and crab soup, lemon chicken, green beans, and herb-baked potatoes.

Later that evening, returning from work first, Lois's father decides to try his hand at cooking. Having seen Lois use Menu-Bot, he opens up the meal plan she has prepared and selects the evening menu. Not being very experienced at cooking, he lets Menu-Bot instruct him in the steps of food preparation and cooking.

Scenario 2: Bob likes to cook so many different types of food that his kitchen is cluttered with cookbooks. In the past, locating recipes that he is "in the mood for" was a gargantuan feat. Now, however, he has Menu-Bot to help. He is planning a dinner party for six guests and has already made up his mind to serve baked salmon with an almond sauce on wild rice, along with lemon butter squash. So he enters just those dishes directly into the system and gets some good recipes that will go well together. However, he still needs an appetizer and dinner wine, so he lets Menu-Bot recommend them and, seeing that they are good, he adds them to the dinner menu.

Exercise 9-6: Usage Scenarios as Simple Task-Sequence Models for Your Product or System

Goal: Get some practice in writing usage scenarios as early, simple task-sequence models.

Activities: Select one or two good representative task threads for one of your user work roles, for example, the customer.

■ Write a couple of detailed usage scenarios, referring to user roles, tasks, actions, objects, and work context.

▪ Work quickly; you can clean it up as you go.

Deliverables: A few usage scenarios to share and discuss.
Schedule: An hour should be enough time for this one.

9.7.2 Components of Task Sequence Models
9.7.2.1 Task and step goals

A task or step goal is the purpose, reason, or rationale for doing the task or taking the step. Called the user "intent" by Beyer and Holtzblatt (1998), the goal is a user intention, in the sense of being "what the user wants to accomplish" by doing the task.

9.7.2.2 Task triggers

A task trigger (Beyer & Holtzblatt, 1998) or step trigger is something that happens, an event or activation condition, that leads that user to initiate a given task or task step. For example, an incoming phone call leads to filling out an order form. If the user logs into a system, it is because a need arose, maybe the need to enter data from a form.

Triggers are easy to identify in your data notes in usage research analyses. New work arrives in the user's inbox, a new aircraft appears on the air traffic controller's screen, an email request arrives, or the calendar says a report is due soon.

9.7.2.3 Task barriers

Indications of task barriers in your usage research data include user problems and errors that get in the way of successful, easy, and satisfying task or step completion. Task barriers are "pain points" or "choke points" that frustrate users and block productivity or flow. To indicate barriers in our data models, we will use the Beyer and Holtzblatt symbol of a graphical red lightning bolt ($\nearrow$), which you should put at the beginning of an indented line explaining the barrier. If the user's reaction or response to a barrier is known through the usage research data, add a brief description of that right after the barrier description among the task steps.

Task barriers are of special interest in UX design because they point out where users have difficulties in the work practice, which in turn are key opportunities for improvement in the design.

9.7.2.4 Information and other needs in tasks

An important component of a task description is the identification of unmet user information and other needs at any step, one of the largest sources of barriers in task performance. The usage research data elicitation and analysis processes and modeling can help you identify these needs, which you can represent with specific annotations. Just before the step in which the need occurs, add an indented line beginning with a red block "N,"—N—followed by a description of the need.

9.7.3 How to Make a Step-by-Step Task Sequence Description

- In either usage research analysis or here in modeling, as you encounter elemental data notes that mention tasks, task steps, or subtasks, merge them into the appropriate evolving task sequence model.
- Sequential steps can be written as an ordered list without the need for flowchart-style arrows to show the flow:
  - Linear lines of text are less cluttered and easier to read.
- Start by showing the most common steps users would take:
  - This is sometimes called the "happy path" or the "go path."
  - This gives a quick and easy-to-understand idea of the basic task without clutter of special cases.

> **Task-sequence model**
>
> A step-by-step description of how a user might perform a task with a product or system, including task goals, intentions, triggers, and user actions (Section 9.7).

At the beginning, individual task interaction models will be mostly linear paths without branching. Later you can add the most important branching or looping (Section 9.7.4) to cover conditional and iterative cases.

So, for example, an initial task interaction model for an online purchase might not show a decision point where the user can pay with either a credit card or PayPal. It would just be a linear set of steps for the task of buying a ticket with, say, a credit card. Later, a separate linear path for the alternative of paying with PayPal is merged, introducing a decision-making point and branching.

Going from a user story to a related task sequence model to a wireframe design is a very natural path that works well in agile UX design. This is another example of how modeling can be distributed throughout the UX lifecycle.

Example: Rudimentary Task Sequence Model for MUTTS

Consider an extremely simple step-by-step task sequence representation for a MUTTS ticket transaction:

MUTTS Ticket Buyer	MUTTS Ticket Seller
1. Wait in line until turn.	2. Greet ticket buyer.
3. Describe event for which tickets are wanted.	4. Look up event in database. How many tickets will be needed?
5. State number of tickets.	6. Look up venue seating chart. Describe available options by seat location and price.
7. Select seats.	8. Calculate and state total cost. How would you like to pay?
9. Pay with credit card.	10. Give tickets, receipt, and card to ticket buyer.

You can see that this is a bare task sequence skeleton. You will add other steps and details as you learn about them.

Example: More Detailed Step-by-Step Task Interaction Model for MUTTS

Task name: Finding entertainment for a given date (performed by ticket seller on behalf of ticket buyer).

Task goal: Helping a ticket buyer choose and buy a ticket for entertainment for this coming Friday night.

Task trigger: Ticket buyer arrives at the MUTTS ticket window on the way home from work on a Thursday evening, thinking ahead to the weekend.

Note: It can help analysis and discussion to number the steps so you can refer to them, as we do in this example.

Ticket Buyer	Ticket Seller
1. Tell ticket seller about general goal of wanting to find an entertainment event for the next night (Friday night).	
2. Ask agent about available types of entertainment.	3. Tell ticket buyer that there are plays, concerts, movies, and sports.
4. Not enough information yet to decide on the category. Ask to see examples of different types.	

Step goal: Consider examples of entertainment events.

5. Ask what events are available for Friday night.

Barrier ⚡: Agent sees that the number of results is too large to sort through or tell the customer about.

Response to barrier:

	6. Ask customer how to filter results or narrow it down (e.g., "Tell me more about what you like").
7. Ask about something within reasonable walking distance downtown or near a Middleburg bus stop.	8. Tell about some possibilities.

Task continues:

9. Think about the list of possibilities.

✏: It is difficult to think about specific events while remembering all the others given orally on the list.

Response to barrier:

> 10. Make a few sketchy notes by hand.

Trigger: Movies seem attractive to ticket buyer.
Goal: Find a movie to see.

> 11. Tell agent about switching focus to just movies.
> 12. Tell agent to use the same criterion about being   13. Tell about within reasonable walking distance downtown or near a   possibilities.
> Middleburg bus stop.
> 14. Consider possibilities and finds a few he likes.
> 15. Write choices down on paper.

Trigger for interruption to embedded task: Thinks a friend might also like these movies.
N: Needs to know friend's opinion of the selections.
Goal: Contact a friend to help narrow these last few choices down and pick something together.

> 16. Ask agent to please wait.
> 17. Call friend on cellphone.
> 18. Make choice with friend.

Trigger: Choice made, ready to buy two tickets.
Goal: To buy tickets.

> 19. Tell agent to buy two tickets to   20. Set up transaction in computer.
> selected movie.
>
>   21. Ask: Cash or credit card?
> 22. Give agent credit card.   23. Swipe card.
> 24. Sign credit transaction.   25. Print tickets and receipt.
>   26. Give printed tickets and return credit card and receipt.

9.7.4 Beyond Linear Task Sequence Models

Branching and looping. Although step-by-step task sequence models are primarily for capturing linear sequences of representative task steps, sometimes you encounter a point in the work practice where there is a choice. You can generalize the task sequence representation by showing this choice using branching, as shown with arrows on the left side of Fig. 9-10.

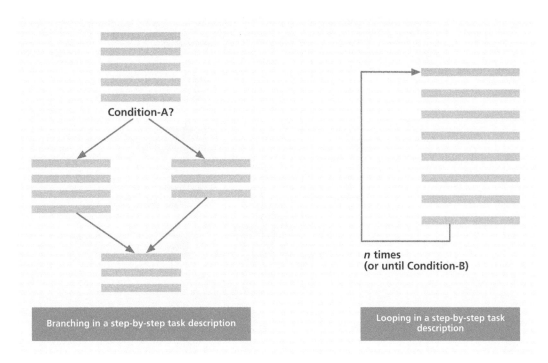

Fig. 9-10

Branching and looping structures within step-by-step task sequence models.

Similarly, if you observe iteration of a set of tasks or task steps, you can represent that as shown on the right side of Fig. 9-10. For sets of steps that are repeated or iterated, note the number of iterations or the condition for termination.

Example: Task Sequence Branching and Looping for MUTTS

In Fig. 9-11, we show a sketch of task sequence representation for selling tickets with MUTTS. Note several instances of looping to iterate parts of the task and, in the bottom box, branching to accommodate two different cases.

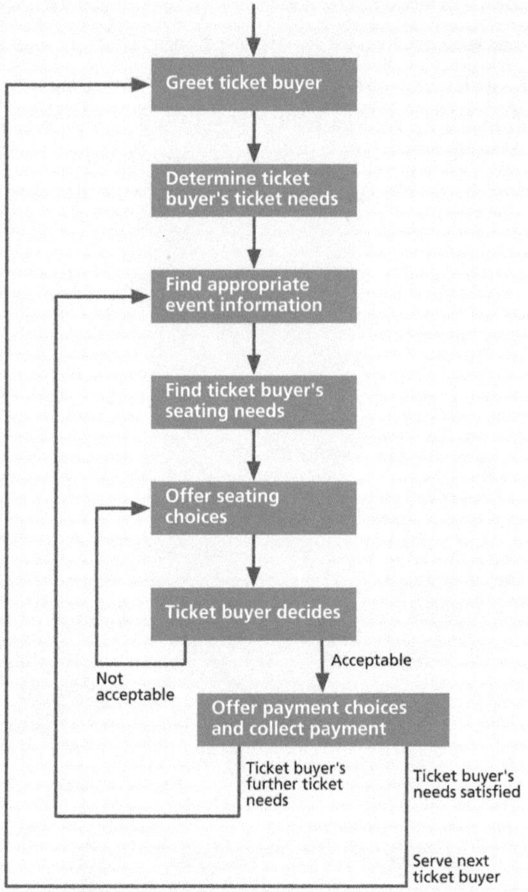

Fig. 9-11

Task sequence branching and looping for MUTTS.

9.7.5 Essential Use Case Task Sequence Models

By combining the best characteristics of step-by-step task descriptions and software use cases, Constantine and Lockwood (1999, p. 100) created essential use cases as an alternative task sequence modeling technique. An essential use case (Constantine & Lockwood, 2003):

- Is a structured narrative.
- Is expressed in the language of users in the work domain.
- Describes a task associated with a single user intention or goal.
- Is abstract.

Naming essential use cases. According to Constantine and Lockwood, each essential use case is named with a "continuing verb" to indicate an ongoing intention, plus a fully qualified object, for example, "buying a movie ticket." Essential use cases capture what users intend to do and why but not how. An example would be searching for a particular entertainment event but nothing about user actions, such as clicking a button.

An essential use case is abstract. The term "essential" refers to abstraction. An essential use case contains only steps that are the essence of the task. The representation is a further abstraction in that it represents only one possible task thread, usually the simplest thread without all the alternatives or special cases. Each description is expressed as a pure work-domain representation, independent of technology or how it looks in the UX design. As an abstraction, an essential use case is a skeleton on which a task description can be woven.

Essential use cases help structure the interaction design around core tasks. These are efficient representations, getting at the essence of what the user wants to do and the corresponding part played by the system.

To illustrate, in Constantine and Lockwood's (2003) ATM example, the user's first step is expressed as an abstract purpose, the "what" of the interaction: "identify self." They do not express it in terms of a "how"; for example, they do not say the first step is to "insert bank card." This is a deceptively simple example of a very important distinction.

> **Abstraction**
>
> The process of removing extraneous details of something and focusing on its irreducible constructs to identify what is really going on, ignoring everything else (Section 14.2.8.2).

Example: Essential Use Case for TKS

Table 9-1 contains an example, cast in the same fashion as Constantine and Lockwood (2003). Notice how these descriptions are abstract.

Table 9-1

Example essential use case: Paying for a ticket purchase transaction (with a credit or debit card)

Ticket Buyer Intention	Ticket Seller and System Responsibility
1. Express intention to make a transaction.	2. Request user to identify self.
3. Identify self.	4. Request to state desired transaction.
5. State desired transaction.	6. Initiate possible negotiation of transaction parameters.
7. Participate in possible transaction negotiations.	8. Summarize transaction and cost.
	9. Request transaction confirmation.
10. Submit confirmation.	11. Conclude transaction.

Note how the abstraction leaves room for design. For example, user identification could be accomplished via a credit card. Transaction confirmation could be submitted in the form of a signature and the transaction could be concluded with a receipt.

For a brief discussion of the roots of essential use cases in software use cases, see Section 11.5.

Exercise 9.7: Task Sequence Model for MUTTS Ticket Buying

Goal: Create your own more detailed essential use case model for the ticket-selling task done by the ticket agent in the MUTTS ticket office.

Activities: Select a key ticket-buying agent task and give it a name.

Break one possible task performance thread into steps, including all the steps involving interacting with the customer outside the system, and for each step where appropriate:

- Identify user intent.
- Task triggers.
- Note any possible breakdown points.

Write one out as a task sequence.

Deliverables: A task sequence, written out as an essential use case model.

Schedule: Should take about 30 minutes.

9.7.6 State Diagrams: The Next Step in Representing Task Sequencing and Navigation

A state diagram, a kind of hybrid between a flow model and a task sequence, is often useful for representing details of flow and navigation in the interaction view of design. A state diagram is a form of flow model, used to represent state changes (navigation among screens) in response to user input actions. This is an abstraction to show and understand the main workflow patterns and paths. See also Section 20.4.4.2.

While a state diagram can be used to represent any level of detail, initial state diagrams are most useful for establishing initial wireframes if you stick with the main navigational paths and leave out unnecessary detail, such as error checking, confirmation dialogue, etc. In a transactional system, the flow model can get very complex and edge cases can multiply. An abstract state diagram can help you find the essence of the flow to form the backbone of the simplest version of the wireflow design. When you get to designs of wireframes for system screens, you can think of each screen as being a state in the state diagram. You are designing for things that "live" in that state. To avoid repetition with the full description of state diagrams, we refer you to Section 20.4.4.2 for more about what state diagrams are and how to make and use them.

In early design, your state diagrams can easily be translated into the structure of a wireframe. More details and examples are given in Chapter 20.

9.8 ARTIFACT MODEL

Not all work practice is artifact-centric but, if it is, describe key objects with an artifact model. What artifacts do users employ, manipulate, and share as part of their work practice? Now is the time to take the artifacts (e.g., paperwork) involved in product or system usage that you collected in data elicitation and incorporate them into a simple artifact model. *An artifact (work artifact) is an object, usually tangible, that plays a role in the work flow of a system or enterprise—for example, a printed receipt in a restaurant.*

9.8.1 What's in an Artifact Model?

At this point, your artifact model is probably just a collection of labeled artifacts plus some notes about them. Examples of artifacts include:

- Work practice forms.
- Sketches.
- Props.
- Memos.
- Significant email messages.
- Correspondence templates.
- Product change orders.
- An order form.
- A receipt.
- Paper or electronic forms.
- Templates.
- Physical or electronic entities that users create, retrieve, use, or reference within a task and/or pass on to another person in the work domain.
- Photos (with permission) of the work place and work being performed.
- Other objects that play a role in work performed.

Work artifacts are one of the most important entities that gets passed from one work role to another within the flow model.

Example: Work Artifacts from a Local Restaurant

One of the project teams in our user experience class designed a system to support a more efficient workflow for taking and filling food orders in a local restaurant, which was part of a regional chain. As part of their data elicitation, they gathered a set of paper work artifacts, including manually created order forms, "guest checks," and a receipt, as shown in Fig. 9-12.

Wireflow

A prototype that illustrates navigational flow within an interaction design, representing flow as a directed graph in which nodes are wireframes and arcs are arrows representing navigational flow among the wireframes (Section 20.4.3.1).

Wireframe

A visual template of a screen or webpage design in the interaction perspective, comprised of lines and outlines (hence the name "wire frame"). A skeletal representation of the layout of interaction objects such as tabs, menus, buttons, dialogue boxes, displays, and navigational elements (Section 17.5).

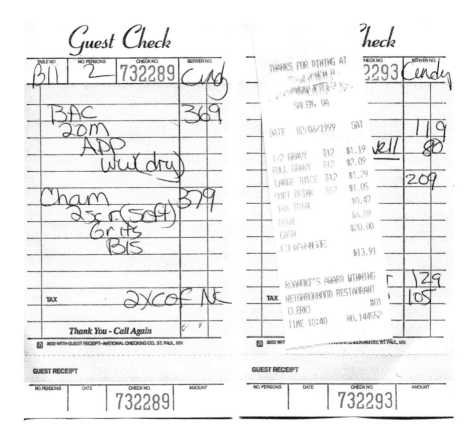

Fig. 9-12

Examples of work artifacts gathered from a local restaurant.

These artifacts are great conversational props as a team interviews those in the different roles that use them. They provide avenues for discussion because almost every restaurant uses these artifacts over and over again. What are things that work with this kind of artifact for order taking? What are some breakdowns? How does a person's handwriting impact this part of the work activity? What is the interaction like between the wait staff and the restaurant's guests? And the interaction between the wait staff and the kitchen staff?

9.8.2 Constructing the Artifact Model

How do you make the artifact model? Well, you now have a collection of artifacts that you gathered in usage research data elicitation, including sketches, copies of paperwork, photographs, and real instances of physical work practice artifacts.

As appropriate, make posters as exhibits ready for discussion and analysis. Attach samples of each artifact and photos of their use to poster paper (e.g., a blank flip chart page). From your data notes, add annotations to these exhibits to explain how each artifact is used in the work practice. Add stick-on notes associating them with tasks, user goals, and task barriers.

These posters are tangible and visual reminders of user work practice that everyone can walk around, think about, and talk about and, by themselves, are a centerpiece of immersion.

But the real importance of work practice artifacts is in how they tell a story within the overall flow. How seamlessly does a given artifact support the flow? Does it cause a breakdown? Is it a transition point between two systems or roles? In this regard, artifacts are an essential component of the flow model.

Example: Combining the Artifacts Into a Restaurant Flow Model

It is easy to think of artifacts associated with the flow model of a restaurant. The first artifact encountered by a person in the customer work role, delivered by the person in the wait-staff work role, is a menu, used by the customer work role to decide on something to order.

Other usual restaurant work artifacts include the order form on which the wait-staff person writes the original order and the guest check (Fig. 9-12 above), which can be the same artifact or a printed check if the order is entered into a system. Finally, there might be a regular receipt and, if a credit card is used, a credit card signature form and a credit card receipt. Artifacts in restaurants, as they do in most enterprises, are the basis for at least part of the flow model. In Fig. 9-13, you can see how restaurant artifacts help show the workflow from order to serving to concluding payment.

The artifacts, especially when arranged as part of a flow model, can help make a connection from usage research data to thinking ahead about design. For example, the waiting and boredom shown in the figure pose a "barrier" to the customer, represented by a red lightning bolt ($\nearrow$). But that waiting time is also a design opportunity. Providing music, news, or entertainment during the wait can alleviate the boredom and gain a competitive advantage in the market.

Example: Artifact Model of Car Keys and Repair Orders in an Auto Repair Shop

As a nonrestaurant example of artifacts in work flow, consider the keys to a customer's car as a central artifact in the work practice of an auto repair facility. First, they may be put in an envelope with the work order, so the mechanic has the keys when needed. If you are working for a project like this and are not able to

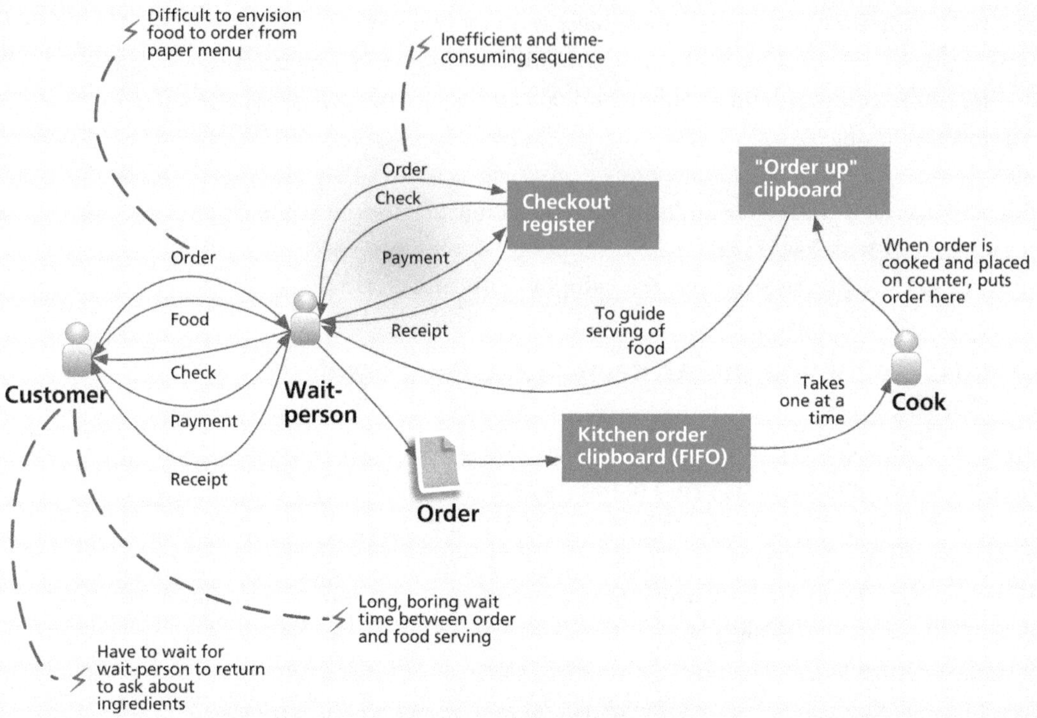

Fig. 9-13

Early sketch of a restaurant flow model with focus on work artifacts derived from the artifact model.

get access to actual keys, improvise. Get a set of old keys that no one needs anymore and use them as a stand-in for the real thing in the artifact model.

After repairs, the keys are hung on a peg board, separate from the repair order until the invoice is presented to the customer and the bill is paid. To support immersion, you should make yourself a mockup of the peg board and a repair order and add them to the growing collection of artifacts in the model.

9.9 PHYSICAL WORK ENVIRONMENT MODEL

Physical models are pictorial representations of the physical layout of work locations, personnel, equipment, hardware, physical parts of the ecology, communications, devices, and databases that are part of the work practice, especially important where the physical layout of entities in the flow matter in the outcome of the work. For example, the location of desks on a trading floor in a financial institution could be important because of the many exchanges of information that happen through sign language and other verbal communications between traders.

In usage research analysis, as you encounter elemental data notes related to physical workplace layout and how it impacts work practice, merge them into the evolving physical model. Also look for any photos you captured during your elicitation visits. Include sketches, diagrams, and photos of the working environment:

- Physical workspace layout.
- Floor plans (not necessary to scale).
- Where people and important objects stand and where they move to during interaction.
- Locations of:
    - Furniture.
    - Office equipment (telephones, computers, copy machines, fax machines, printers, scanners).
    - Communications connections.
    - Work stations.
    - Points of contact with customers and the public.

As an example, show in a restaurant where the customer tables are and where the wait staff go to submit and pickup orders. Make posters of the diagrams and photos, annotated with notes about the physical layout and any problems or barriers it imposes. Post them in your design studio.

Because a physical model shows the placement and paths of movement of people and objects within this workspace layout diagram, it can be used to assess the proximities of task-related equipment and artifacts and task barriers due to distances, awkward layouts, and physical interference among roles in a shared workspace.

Example: How a Friend Used a Physical Model to Help with a House

For example, in the design for her house, a friend worked out a model of workflow within a physical model and found that the traditional American proclivity for putting the clothes washer and dryer in the basement gave a very poor proximity-to-task-association ratio for the task of doing laundry. Enlarging the dressing room and putting the washer and dryer in there improved this ratio enormously.

Physical work environment model

Pictorial representation of the milieu in which work gets done, including the physical layout of work locations, personnel, equipment, hardware, physical parts of the ecology, communications, devices, and databases that are part of the work practice (Section 9.9).

Similarly, the flow of fresh vegetables from the car to the kitchen led to moving the garage from the basement level to the living floor level (aided by a steep grade). In both cases, the changes brought the physical model elements much closer to their location of use in the design.

Looking further at the veggie flow in the physical model led to an efficient design of a kitchen island as a shared food preparation and cooking area—cleaning at the veggie sink, flowing over to slicing and dicing, and then flowing to sautéing under a bright light and a vent hood.

9.9.1 Include Hardware Design, When Appropriate

In some projects, especially in the commercial product perspective, hardware devices can have enormous importance. For example, if you are designing a new smartphone, this is about considering industrial design, material, production issues, heating, and other physical issues such as interference with any wireless antennas in the device, temperature tolerances, and weather proofing. As another example, for the TKS, hardware concerns might include selecting kiosk locations, printers in kiosks, and susceptibility to vandalism and theft. The design of the kiosk itself will require industrial design skills.

9.9.2 Include Environmental Factors, When Appropriate

When creating physical models, also think of all the physical characteristics of a workplace that can affect work activities and add them as annotations. For example, a steel mill floor is about safety concerns, noise, dust, and hot temperatures—conditions where it is difficult to think or work. A system with a terminal on a factory floor means dirty conditions and no place to hold manuals or blueprints. This may result in designs where the use of audio could be a problem, needing more prominent visual design elements for warnings, such as blinking lights.

Example: Physical Model for MUTTS

In Fig. 9-14, we show the physical model for MUTTS. The center of workflow is the ticket counter, containing up to three active ticket seller terminals. On the back wall, relative to ticket sellers, are the credit card and MU Passport swiping stations. This central ticket-selling area is flanked with the manager's and assistant manager's administrative offices.

Barriers not shown in this figure include a barrier to the ticket buyer lines: At peak times, customers may have to wait in long lines outside the ticket window. The scanner in the manager's office, used to digitize graphical

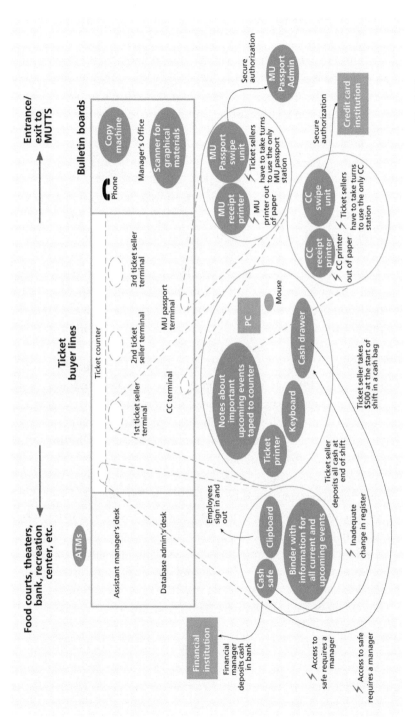

Fig. 9-14
A physical model
for MUTTS.

material such as posters or advertisements for website content, presents barriers to usage: It is very slow and is not in a convenient location for all to share.

The ticket printers can also introduce barriers to workflow. Because they are specialized printers for ticket stock, when one goes down or runs out of paper or ink, the employees cannot just substitute another printer. They have to wait until the technician can get it serviced or, worse, until it can be sent out for service.

9.10 INFORMATION ARCHITECTURE MODEL

If the data and information users need to access, store, display, and manipulate is complex, represent it with an information architecture model. What information do users use and interact with as part of their work and how is it structured?

Information architecture is usually fairly simple in the product perspective but could be quite complex in the enterprise system perspective. In projects where, for example, a database is central to work flow and/or data definitions and data relationships are crucial to understanding the work, information architecture can be intricate and essential to understand early.

In usage research analysis, as you encounter elemental data notes related to the structure of any system data or information involved in the work practice, merge them into the information architecture model.

An example is information about the fields and data types represented within personal contact information within a "contacts" application, such as for name, address, and phone number.

The TKS is a good example of a system centered on data objects such as events and tickets. Simple information structures can be represented as a list of information objects and their attributes, such as event name, event type, and event description.

The means for representing more complex structures such as a patient health record involve database schemas and entity-relationship diagrams. Database schemas, which can be huge, tie together usage and design, and are the basis for information displays and data field layouts in wireframes.

Also identify information that has to be "pervasive," that is, shared among users and devices over a larger ecology (Chapter 16). Pervasive information must have a consistent appearance and accessibility across multiple different work contexts.

Example: Information Architecture Modeling

Consider information about events in the MUTTS database. A general event record might have attributes like this:

- Event name.
- Event type.
- Event description.
- Range of dates event is occurring.
- Ticket costs:
    - Seat types and costs.
    - Reserved status.
- Venues:
    - Location.
    - Capacity.
- Directions to venues.
- Video trailers.
- Photos.
- Reviews.

Suppose you have to register each ticket buyer, especially if they pay by credit card. The ticket buyer might have attributes like these:

- Name.
- Address.
- Email address.
- Phone number.

There might also be a relationship between events and ticket buyers, including these attributes:

- Date of reservation.
- Seat number.
- Cost of ticket, as paid.

9.11 THE SOCIAL MODEL

Our social model is based on Beyer and Holtzblatt's (1988) cultural model. In practice, the social model is the least commonly used model, especially in agile environments. It is needed only when social and cultural interactions among the people involved in the work practice are complex and/or problematic.

The social model can be difficult to make because the information needed is seldom volunteered by users during data elicitation. A social model diagram can be difficult to understand because the arcs and labels of a graphical representation are too busy and too detailed; plus, all that structure isn't really necessary. It can be difficult to apply a social model to inform UX design because, technical design solutions for social problems can be elusive. We include this model mainly for completeness.

9.11.1 The Social Model Captures the Culture of the Shared Workplace

The social model captures the communal aspects of the users' organizational workplace as a social setting, and how they impact how things get done in the work environment, including:

Workers often have issues connected to:

- Work roles.
- Goals.
- How things get done in the work domain.
- Other workers.

9.11.2 Simplified Approach to the Social Model

In the first edition of this book, we spelled out a detailed and complicated way to make a social model as a graph with labeled nodes and arcs. Feedback from instructors and students revealed how difficult this model was to teach and learn. Feedback from UX professionals helped us realize that almost no one in this field would take the time and effort to make such a complicated model in a real project.

So, for those who want or need to make a social model, we have tried to reduce it to the most important aspects. It ended up being one case where a structured textual representation was simpler than a graphical one. See the example of a social model for MUTTS below.

9.11.3 Identify Active Entities

Active entities in a social model include all user work roles and can include any nonindividual agent or force that participates in, influences, or is impacted by the work practice, internal to or external to the immediate work environment.

In addition to the work roles and entities internal to the client organization, there are external roles that interact with work roles, including outside vendors, customers, regulatory agencies, "the government," "the market," or "the competition."

Example: List of social model entities for TKS

Our example of a social model for MUTTS starts with the roles. We identify the ticket seller and ticket buyer as the main ones, represented as list items at the highest level. You will almost always want to include the ambience and work domain as a nonhuman entity. The administrative supervisor, database administrator, and office manager are also shown in this list for TKS:

- Ticket seller.
- Ticket buyer.
- Ambience.
- Work domain.
- Administrative supervisor.
- Database administrator.
- Office manager.

9.11.4 Identify Kinds of Issues, Pressures, Worries, and Concerns

Categories of social model issues include matters such as:

- Concerns and worries.
- Influences exerted or felt.
- Job pressures.
- Issues affecting job performance.

More specific examples include:

- The overall flavor or feeling in the workplace.
- Organizational philosophy and culture.
- Workplace ambience and environmental factors.
- Professional and personal goals of workers.
- Political structure and realities.
- Thought processes, mindsets, policies, feelings, attitudes, and terminology that occur in the work environment.
- Legal requirements and regulations.
- Organizational policies.
- Subversive activities.

Personal and professional interrole influences. People in different work roles can influence people in other work roles on both a personal and a professional level. For example, the model may reflect plain old interpersonal or interrole frictions and animosities.

Power influences. There are many kinds of power within most organizations. Employees can "pull rank" based on official job titles. Also, people who proactively take on leadership roles can exert power. Influence also comes from the strength or authority a person exerts in a work role. In meetings, to whom does everyone listen the most? When the chips are down, who gets the job done, even it if means working outside the box?

Workplace ambience. The atmosphere of the workplace can have a psychological impact on users. For example, sometimes you might encounter a working environment that employees consider to be "toxic." If not addressed, this kind of social environment can lead to employee burnout, rebellion, and other counter-productive behavior.

Example: A Doctor's Office

It is possible to imagine a doctor's office as a stressful environment for employees. The general mood or work climate is rushed, chronically overbooked, and behind schedule. Emergencies and walk-ins add to the already high workload. The receptionist is under pressure to make appointments correctly, efficiently, and without errors. Everyone feels the constant background fear of mistakes and the potential of resulting lawsuits. Employees can't wait for the work day to end so they can escape to the relative peace of their homes (or the local pub).

Professional goals versus personal goals. Two different roles might view the same task from the perspective of different goals. For example, a manager might be concerned with capturing very complete documentation of each business transaction, whereas the person in the work role that has to compile the documentation may have as a goal to minimize the work involved. If we do not capture this secondary user goal in our analysis, we may miss an opportunity to streamline that task in design and the two goals may remain in conflict.

Subversion among the ranks. Be sure to include in your social model how people think and act negatively in response to dissatisfaction. Is the watercooler or the break room the center of subversive coordination? Is subversion or passive-aggressive behavior a common answer to power and authority? How strong is the "whistleblower" mentality? Does the organization thrive on a culture of guerilla activity?

9.11.5 Add Concerns and Influences to the Social Model List

In usage research analysis, as you encounter elemental data notes related to social concerns in the workplace, merge them into the evolving social model. Add the corresponding active entities to the list and, indented under each entity, add any related concerns and issues.

Example: A Social Model for MUTTS

Here is an excerpt of what a social model might look like for MUTTS:

- Ticket buyer:
  - Feels pressure:
    - From those in line to get done fast.
    - To get good seats for popular events.
  - Worries about:
    - The system completing the transactions correctly.
    - Losing the personal service I like so much if it's changed to a kiosk.
    - Losing my tickets or my money if the system has an error.
    - Losing money due to the no-refund policy.
  - Experiences barriers to work in the form of:
    - Noise and distraction of public location interfere with thinking and decision-making.
    - Can't see all the choices upfront.
- Ticket seller:
  - Feels pressure:
    - Pushback from users about the no-refund policy.
    - To please customers.
    - Peak periods mean fast pace and hard work.
  - Worries about:
    - Complaints about service that can ruin job reviews.
  - Is subject to external influences of:
    - The administrative supervisor, who shows up occasionally and causes stress.
    - The administrative supervisor, who is not familiar with daily operations and can impose unrealistic expectations.

- Administrative supervisor:
  - Worries about not generating enough revenue.
  - Would like to increase revenue with other merchandise sales, including over-the-counter commodities such as candy, gum, and aspirin plus merchandise souvenirs, T-shirts, hats, and banners.
- Database administrator:
  - Pressure to:
    - Maintain data integrity.
    - Keep system up and running continuously.
  - Experiences barriers to work in the form of:
    - Event manager's phone, the constant ringing of which makes it hard to concentrate, especially when something is going wrong.

Exercise 9.8: A Social Model for Your Product or System

Goal: Get a little practice in making a social model diagram.

Activities: Identify active entities, such as work roles, and represent as bullets in a list. Include:

- Groups and subgroups of roles and external roles that interact with work roles.
- System-related roles, such as a central database.
- Workplace ambience and its pressures and influences.

Next identify:

- Concerns and perspectives to be represented subbullets in the list.
- Social relationships, such as influences between entities, to be represented as subbullet items under appropriate entities.
- Barriers, or potential barriers, in relationships between entities to be represented as red bolts of lightning (⚡).

Deliverables: One social model diagram for your system with as much detail as feasible.

Schedule: This could take a couple of hours.

Exercise 9.9: A Social Model for Smartphone Usage

Sketch out an annotated social model for the use of an iPhone or similar smartphone by you and your friends. We're giving you lots of leeway here; make the most of it.

9.12 HYBRID MODELS

While we describe each usage research data model separately for clarity, in practice models are often combined for efficiency. For example, because the flow model includes at least the major user work roles, you don't necessarily need a separate user work role model. You can just label the user work role nodes of the flow model with the user work role names and annotate them with user class characteristics. Later, you can even label flow model nodes with the corresponding personas.

The goal of modeling is to represent a useful perspective or perspectives about the work domain for the design situation. Purity of each model is not the goal. Do what it takes to capture what you learn about the work domain. For example, if the work practice centers around a physical space, like a ticket office, combine the physical model and flow model into a hybrid model.

9.13 MODEL CONSOLIDATION

In a large project, if you construct your models with multiple subteams working in parallel, you will get multiple models of the same type. Now is the time to consolidate the model versions by merging them into one model. The key idea is to induce generalizations, that is, a bottom-up process to build a general model from the important pieces of specific data.

As an example, start with representations of single-user stories of task steps in the existing work practice. Merge the description of essentially the same task created with data from several users, and factor out the differences in details. The result is a more abstract or more general representation of the interaction, representing how most or all users do the task.

When flow modeling is done by different subteams, each model can be different. The same work role might get modeled in different ways, yielding different work role descriptions and work role names. Because these various versions of the flow model are about the same workflow, they can be consolidated essentially by merging them.

Example: Flow Model Consolidation for MUTTS

Figs. 9-15, 9-16, and 9-17 are partial flow models constructed by groups who observed and interviewed different people of the overall organization and work practice.

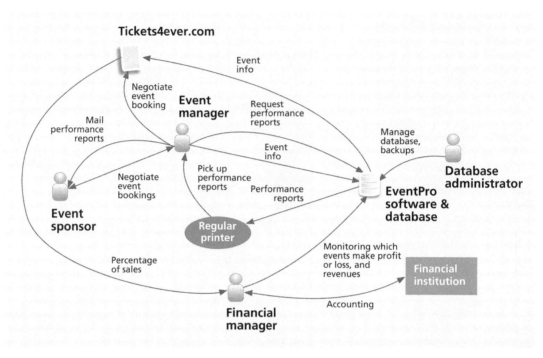

Fig. 9-15

*Flow model from a group
who observed and
interviewed the event
manager, event sponsors,
the financial manager, and
the database administrator.*

Look back at Fig. 9-4 to see how the three parts of the overall flow model came together in model consolidation.

9.14 WRAP UP

9.14.1 Barrier Summaries Across All Models

Many of the models tell partial stories from different perspectives, but no one model highlights all the barriers discovered in usage research data elicitation and analysis. Yet it is the barriers to work practice and user performance that most directly inform design ideas for the new system. So it can be helpful and informative to extract barrier-related information from the models and summarize the barriers in one place.

Barriers to usage are of special interest because they point out where users have difficulties in the work practice. Anything that impedes user activities,

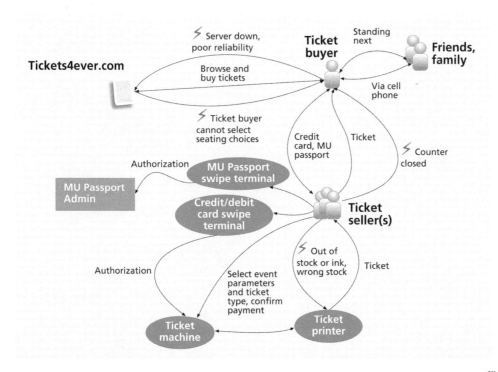

Fig. 9-16

Flow model from a group who mainly observed and interviewed ticket buyers and ticket sellers.

interrupts workflow or communications, or interferes with the performance of work responsibilities is a barrier to the work practice. Because these barriers also represent key opportunities for improvement in the design, it is useful to collect them all into a single summary of barriers.

9.14.2 Post Data Models in Your UX Design Studio

Make your models visual in sketches and posters prominently displayed as part of the immersion in your design studio. Assemble your artifacts into an organized display.

Considerations about posting in your UX design studio.

- In early stages, it might be best to draw your diagrams and figures on whiteboards, where it is easy to discuss and update them.

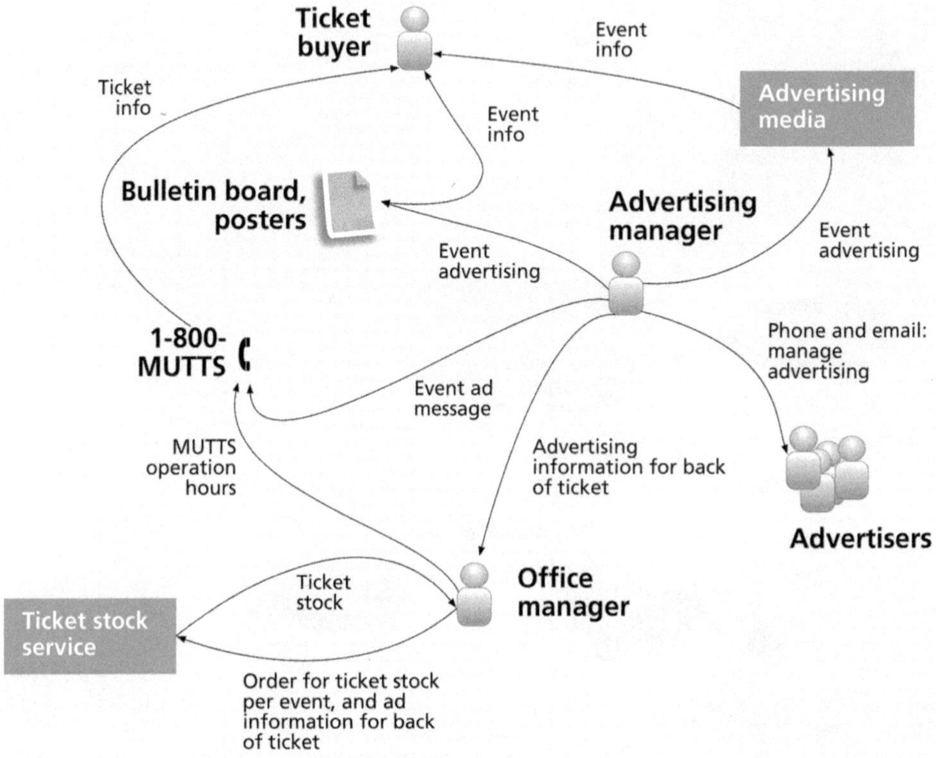

Fig. 9-17

Flow model from a group who observed and interviewed the office manager, the advertising manager, and external advertisers.

- Later, you can transfer the diagrams to nicely printed posters taped to the wall.
- Assemble your artifacts into an organized collection on a central work table.
- At some point in projects of any realistic size, you will end up with more materials to post than you have space for posting, so:
  - Be judicious; trim out the less important items.
  - Post artifacts and diagrams that will have importance throughout the entire project.
  - Diagrams, images, and sketches that you will use less frequently could be kept in your laptop and, when needed, shown via a projector.

- Beyond this, larger amounts of shared information can be kept in sharable files (e.g., in Dropbox or Google Drive).
- Retire postings for which the usefulness has diminished over time.
- Remember, anything posted carries the task of keeping it up to date.
- As you move to designs, almost all the early postings give way to annotated wireframe sketches, which become the language of communication.
- Posted wireframe sketches also support design walkthroughs with stakeholders.

UX Design Requirements: User Stories and Requirements

10

- The concept of requirements for UX design.
- User stories as the agile way to express UX design requirements.
- UX design requirements are needed in rare situations.
- Validate user stories and requirements with users and stakeholders.

10.1 INTRODUCTION

10.1.1 You are Here

We begin each process chapter with a "you are here" picture of the chapter topic in the context of The Wheel, the overall UX design lifecycle template (Fig. 10-1). Within the Understand Needs UX design lifecycle activity, this chapter is about the subactivity in which you codify as user stories and UX requirements, the UX design wants and needs you discovered in usage research.

10.1.2 User Stories and Requirements Are About Codifying UX Design Wants

The point of usage research (all of Part 2) is to discover and learn about the UX design wants and needs. The point of user stories and requirements (this chapter) is to codify those wants and needs as inputs to the design of the target product or system. There are several ways to express these design needs, including use cases, user stories, and requirements. In this chapter, we stress the latter two.

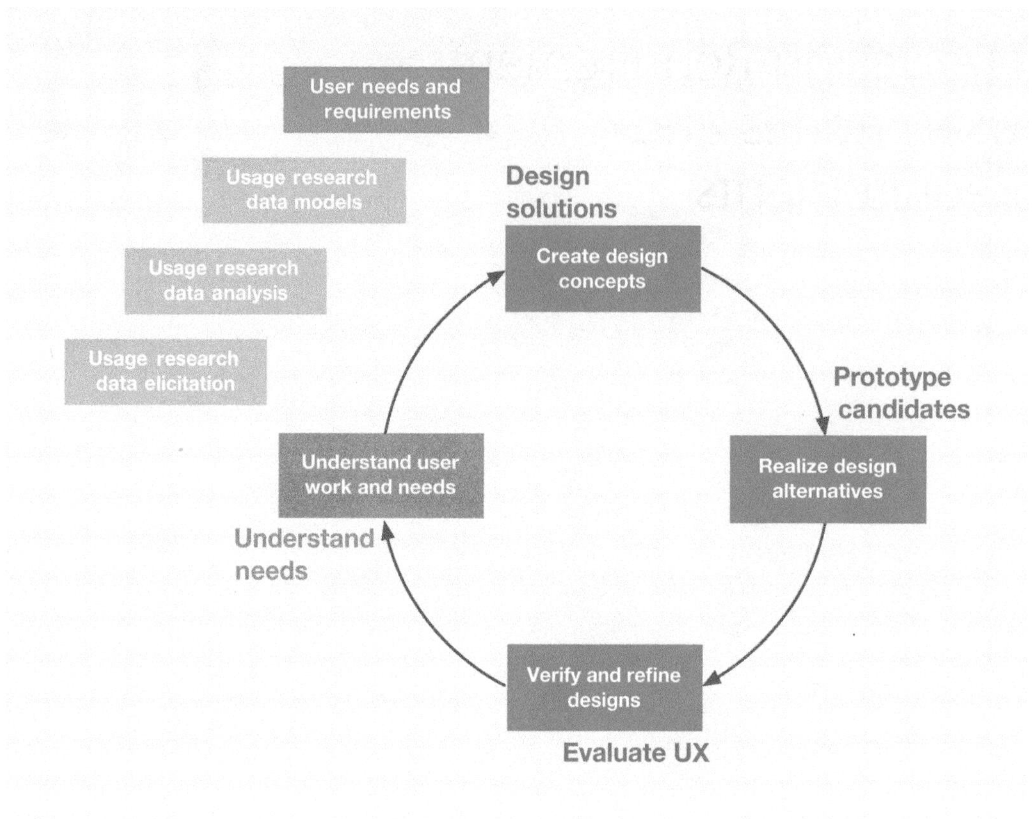

Fig. 10-1

You are here in the chapter on the user stories and UX requirements subactivity within the Understand Needs box, in the context of the overall Wheel UX lifecycle process.

10.1.3 Introduction to User Stories

User stories are an agile way of capturing what is to be designed. User stories:

- Involve user inputs.
- Are stated in the perspective of usage.
- Are stated from a customer perspective.
- Were made popular by agile proponents.
- Are now the de facto standard in industry.
- Are focused on delivering chunks of meaningful capabilities to users.

There are other means for stating design needs from these perspectives, but user stories are the popular way.

10.1.4 Introduction to Requirements

As we said in Section 4.2, back in the old days, when the Waterfall process was widespread, it was traditional to codify what is needed in the system in formal statements called requirements. Those requirements were targeted as features the system should support. There was a flavor of system-centeredness.

Today formal requirements are rarely used and, when they are, it is usually because of a focus on the software engineering (SE) side, where there is a huge subdiscipline dedicated to requirements.

10.1.5 Choose the Approach You Need

We have two major sections in this chapter: one on user stories and one on requirements. Choose one depending on your design situation. If you need to use a rigorous full-scope approach because you are working in the complex-interaction and complex-work-domain quadrant of the system complexity space or if you are contractually obligated to do so, adopt formal requirements. Otherwise, choose user stories, especially for an agile process.

10.1.6 Requirements in the UX World
10.1.6.1 Requirements as design goals, not constraints

In the old days, requirements were immutable and absolute. "You *shall* provide these features and functions and you *shall* do it in the way we say." This dictatorial view of requirements left no room for creativity in design solutions and no flexibility to adapt to change as it inevitably occurred.

But today's UX mentality is all about design (Kolko, 2015b); we value design over requirements. Rather than even thinking about requirements, we should think about how great products "require vision, perseverance, and the ability to do amazing things in the face of perceived impossibility" (Kolko, 2015b, p. 22).

In today's agile environments, we like to view requirements, especially UX design requirements, not as constraints but as design goals with the freedom to interpret *how* the design should achieve these goals (Kolko, 2015b).

Waterfall Lifecycle Process

One of the earliest formal software engineering lifecycle processes; an ordered linear sequence of lifecycle activities, each of which flowed into the next like a set of cascading tiers of a waterfall (Section 4.2).

System Complexity Space

A two-dimensional space defined by the dimensions of interaction complexity and domain complexity, depicting a spectrum of system and product types with a broad range of risk versus needs for rigor in lifecycle activities and methods (Section 3.2.2.1).

Scope (of Delivery)

Describes how the target system or product is "chunked" (broken into what size pieces) in each iteration or sprint for delivery to the client and users for feedback and to the software engineering team for agile implementation (Section 3.3).

10.1.6.2 UX requirements versus UX design prototypes as SE requirements

To some extent, UX and SE share requirements because both UX and SE participate in the ultimate outcome: the delivered system. But UX people also have their own design requirements (far left side of Fig. 10-2). The SE people, on the right side of the figure, are responsible for implementing everything, so they will have requirements for:

1. The UX parts.
2. The functional parts.

The SE people have evolved their own ways of understanding the functional or backend requirements from a user story about a given feature. These functional requirements are to support the tasks, navigation, etc., being designed on the UX side. As a practical matter, UX prototypes—usually wireframe prototypes—are the vehicle for conveying requirements for the UX parts to the implementers (center of Fig. 10-2).

Wireframe Prototype

A prototype composed of wireframes, which are line-drawing representations of UX designs, especially the interaction design of screens (Section 20.4).

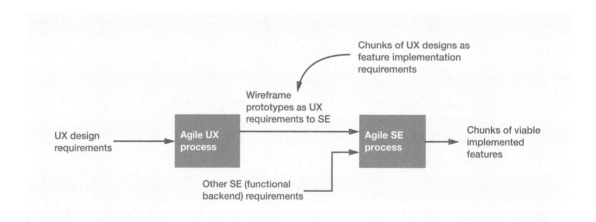

Fig. 10-2

The relationship between UX design requirements and UX prototypes as UX design representations for SE requirements.

10.1.6.3 Software and functional implications of UX design requirements

Because of the close relationship of requirements in UX and SE, this activity is a good time to coordinate among UX, SE, and your client. In fact, it is a good time to be proactive and make sure the SE team is aware of functional requirements on their side that are reflected by task requirements on your UX side.

10.1.7 Formal Requirements are Waning in Popularity

For decades, formal requirements and requirements engineering (Young, 2001) have been a staple component of software engineering and a formal written requirements document was *de rigueur.*

But now, even in the SE world, the importance of requirement specifications is fading, primarily because they don't really work (Beck & Andres, 2004). There is an increasing recognition that:

- Detailed formal requirements cannot ever be complete.
- Detailed formal requirements cannot ever be 100% correct.
- Detailed formal requirements cannot be prevented from changing throughout the lifecycle.

But in both UX and SE, we still need some kind of design requirements, and that is where user stories come in.

10.2 USER STORIES

In today's world, user stories are the de facto approach to both UX design and SE implementation requirements in late-funnel agile development. In usage research analysis, you gathered up a collection of all elemental data notes related to user stories and requirements (Section 8.4). Now is the time to convert them into real user stories and/or UX design requirements. Codifying UX design requirements can be considered the final step of the Understand Needs lifecycle activity.

10.2.1 The Truth About User Stories
10.2.1.1 Asking users what they wanted was originally discouraged

One of the more serious problems with user stories starts with the definition, which is billed as a statement by a user about something (a feature or capability) a user wants. But the original theory of contextual inquiry (usage research) (Beyer & Holtzblatt, 1998) is based on UX analysts determining what users *need* to support their work. The original pure contextual inquiry was not about users saying what they want because they are not trained UX designers and it's our job to determine user needs.

10.2.1.2 How can user stories make for complete requirements?

Even if we can get good UX requirements as user stories from users, it's unlikely that users would present us with a *complete* set of requirements. So we have to conclude that not all user stories will be coming from users. We get what we can from users, but the goal is not completeness. We, as UX research analysts, must write additional user stories to fill in the gaps.

10.2.1.3 Cleaning up the user stories

UX practitioners must edit existing user stories to make them effective in our process. This means we usually have to change what the user said to make it more accurate, more general, more complete, and more sensible—to the point where they usually end up not really being something a user said at all. So, as a practical matter, those in the field have resorted to writing user capability requirements as user stories as though users had expressed them, giving the whole collection a uniform format.

Irrespective of who wrote them, user stories capture a need, and they are effective at naturally dividing up requirements into items of small scope.

10.2.2 What is a User Story?

A user story is a short narrative describing a feature or capability needed by a user in a specific work role and a rationale for why it is needed, used as an agile UX design "requirement."

User stories arise out of usage research data and they can be based on problems users have with an existing product or system or they might reflect needs for new features in a new design. Now it's time to get your work activity notes related to user stories out again as inputs to writing the user stories.

As a practical matter, user stories describe existing everyday product or system usage or desired capabilities. A user story is a kind of small-scope requirement (Section 3.3). Gothelf and Seiden (2016) define a user story as a narrative in the user's voice describing, "the smallest unit of work expressed as a benefit to the end user" (minimum viable product or MVP).

As such, a user story describes a single capability needed for a specific user work role with a specific benefit. Following this definition, a user story tends to be small scope and atomic. Because of its small size and scope, some say a user story should fit on one $3'' \times 5''$ card.

10.2.3 Team Selection

Gather a multiperspective team to write user stories from elemental data note inputs. UX designers, of course, should be well represented, as should be the customer, client, and user perspectives.

10.2.4 Writing a User Story

In our terminology, this translates to a brief narrative statement of a single user need, stated in the voice of a given user work role and in this format:

As a <relevant user work role>
I want to <the desired small-scope capability in everyday product or system usage>
So that <the reason why, the added value this capability will deliver>.

Example: User Stories for TKS

Consider this raw data note:

> I think of sports events as social events, so I like to go with my friends. The problem is that we often have to sit in different places, so it is not as much fun. It would be better if we could sit together.

This is typical of raw data notes. It is a bit more rambling than concise, so you have to work at it a little to extract the essence of a corresponding user story:

As a student ticket buyer
I want an MU basketball ticket-buying option to get several seats together
So I can sit with my friends.

This is definitely about a desired small-scope capability. It refers to one choice in seat selection as a parameter of the ticket-buying task.

As a further example, consider this raw data note:

> I sometimes want to find events that have to do with my own personal interests. For example, I really like ice skating and want to see what kinds of entertainment events in the nearby areas feature skating of any kind.

This is pretty specific, but you can deduce a slightly more general version for your user story:

As a ticket buyer
I want to be able to search for events by event type or descriptive keyword
So I can find the kinds of entertainment that I like.

Here is another raw data note:

> I occasionally find it convenient to see recommendations for events that are similar to ones I like, like in the listing of what others who looked at this item got from Amazon.com.

This can become a user story for a specific feature:

> As a ticket buyer
> I want to be able to see recommendations for events similar to ones I find and like
> So I can find other events I like that I might otherwise miss.

This user story as a UX requirement has a built-in implied backend system requirement, namely that during a transaction session, the Ticket Kiosk System (TKS) functional software will have to keep track of the kinds of choices made by the ticket buyer along with the choices of other ticket buyers who bought this item. This similar capability at Amazon is a design model for this feature.

10.2.5 Extrapolation Requirements in User Stories: Generalization of Usage Research Data

User statements in raw data notes can be quite narrow and specific. Sometimes you will need to extrapolate from these statements to get a more useful and general case.

For example, suppose ticket buyers using MUTTS, in anticipation of a kiosk, expressed the need to search for events based on a predetermined criterion but said nothing about browsing events to see what is available. So you might write an extrapolation requirement to include the obvious need also to browse events as an extrapolation of the previous user story about being able to search for events by keywords.

> As a ticket buyer
> I want to be able to browse events with filters for category, description, location, time, rating, and price
> So I can find relevant events in context.

As another example, in a raw data note, a ticket buyer says:

> *I really would like to be able to post an MU football ticket for exchange with a ticket in another location in the stadium to be able to sit with my friends.*

In our extrapolated user story, we broadened this to:

> As a ticket buyer
> I want to be able to post, check status of, and exchange student tickets
> So I can change reserved tickets for seats where I can sit with my friends.

This user story implies a corresponding system requirement for customer accounts of some kind, presumably where they can log in using their MU Passport IDs.

Example: Inputs to User Stories as UX Design Requirements for the TKS

Here are some examples of elemental data notes for the ticket buyer work role in the TKS that are on the way to being user stories, along with their first- and second-level structural headings. Space limitations preclude listing the huge number of user stories written for the TKS, but you should get the idea.

Transaction Flow

Existence of feature

I want to be able to pause, save, and later resume a ticket-buying transaction.

System implications: Will require accounts, including logging in and out, etc.

Shopping Cart Issues

Accessibility of shopping cart

I want to be able to view and modify the shopping cart at all times.

Shopping cart versatility

I want to be able to add different kinds/types of items (example, different events, sets of tickets for the same event, etc.).

Note: This is important because it has implications on how to display shopping cart contents with dissimilar types of objects.

Transaction Flow

Timeouts

I want the system to have a timeout feature that removes my transaction from the screen if I haven't made any actions after a certain amount of time.

So it will protect my privacy.

Extrapolation: Ticket buyer shall be made aware of the existence and status of timeout, including progress indicator showing remaining time and audible beep near the end of the time-out period.

Extrapolation: User shall have control to reset the timeout and keep the transaction alive.

Extrapolation: User's need to keep transaction alive shall be supported by automation; any user activity triggers reset.

Immediate exit

I want to be able to make a quick exit and reset to the home screen.

So, if I have to leave (e.g., to catch a bus) suddenly, I can quit in the middle of a transaction.

Corollary to consider: User shall have a way to quickly return later to a specific item they were viewing just prior to an immediate exit.

Notes: Maybe user will use an event ID number for direct access next time. Or the system can remember state by using an account.

Revisiting previous steps (going back)

I want to be able to revisit a previous step easily.

So I don't have to go through multiple back actions.

Transaction progress awareness

I want to be able to track the progress of an entire transaction (what is done and what is left to do) using a "bread crumb trail."

So I don't have any confusion as to what I still have to do for a successful completion.

User reminders

I want to receive a reminder to take the ticket(s) and credit card at the end of each transaction.

So I don't forget and walk away, thinking I have completed the transaction.

Checkout

I want to see, before making a payment, a confirmation page showing exactly what is being purchased and the total cost.

So I can be confident in what I am purchasing.

10.2.6 Organize Sets of User Stories for Use in UX Design

Hierarchical Task Inventory (HTI)

A hierarchical structural representation of task and subtask relationships for cataloguing and representing the hierarchical relationships among tasks and subtasks that must be supported in a system design (Section 9.6).

In real-world projects, you may end up with a large number of diverse user stories. You need a way to organize them. We organize user stories by a kind of design affinity, grouping user stories by sets of related features or by related tasks. Because UX user stories are stories about user capabilities, they are closely related to user tasks and you can use structures similar to the hierarchical task inventory to organize them. This allows us to consider related features together. For example, we should look at the browse-by-event-type task at the same time we look at browsing by location or searching by event type.

Organizing around the HTI is also a way to manage the collection of user stories and helps us maintain completeness of the collection. This reliance on having an HTI is one big reason we need the early part of the funnel model.

Early Funnel

The part of the funnel (agile UX model) for large-scope activity, usually for conceptual design, before syncing with software engineering (Section 4.4.4).

Think about an HTI-like user story structure with the individual user stories at the lowest level. A group of user stories having the same parent node in the structure will be related by being about the same user task. User stories having the same grandparent node will be a larger group, related to a broader task, and so on. When you consider user stories for UX design, you usually will select the user stories related to the same parent or, in some cases for a large sprint, the same grandparent.

It is important to note, however, that this hierarchical task-oriented configuration of user stories is for organizing only, and is not a way to prioritize them for design and development. For that, see the next section, Section 10.2.7.

Example: Group of User Stories Related to Finding (Browsing and Searching for) Events

Consider the partial user story structure for the ticket buyer work role, as shown in Fig. 10-3.

The box at the lower left contains a group of user stories that are related to the user tasks of browsing and searching to find an event of interest for which to buy tickets. This box can also later hold links to wireframes representing the corresponding UX designs, as each box is prioritized and built.

Sprint

A relatively short (not more than a month) time period within an agile software engineering schedule in which a working and releasable product increment is implemented. It is a unit of work being done in an agile SE environment; an iteration associated with a release (to the client and/ or users) (Sections 3.3, 29.3.2, and 29.7.2).

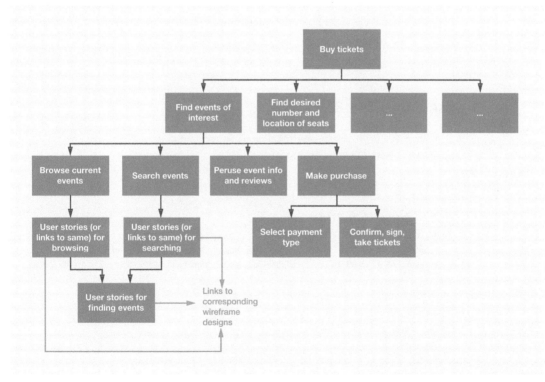

Fig. 10-3

A partial user story structure for the ticket buyer work role.

This box will contain, possibly among others, the user stories corresponding to the following example requirement notes taken from the example following Section 8.7.7.

Searching

83: I would like to be able to search for events by price, artist, venue, and/or date.

104: If I am looking for a specific band, I expect a Google-style search where I type in the name of the band.

112: It would be really nice to be able to search for interesting events say within two blocks from where I am currently.

Browsing

74: I would like to be able to browse all events on the kiosk.

106: I would like to be able to browse by different topics (type of event). For example, in big cities, even in music there will be different genres.

107: I would like to be able to browse by locations.

Sorting

75: I would like to be able to sort the results I find using some criteria.

The corresponding user stories are easy to visualize as:

Searching

User Story TKS 83:

As a ticket buyer
I would like to be able to search for events by price, artist, venue, and/or date
Because I want maximum flexibility in searching.

User Story TKS 104:

As a ticket buyer
I expect a Google-style search where I type in, for example, the name of a band
Because I don't want to be constrained by special formats in searches.

User Story TKS 112:

As a ticket buyer
I want to be able to search for events by proximity to a given location
Because I seek maximum power in searching.

Browsing

User Story TKS 74:

As a ticket buyer
I would like to be able to browse all events on the kiosk
Because sometimes direct searches don't reveal enough context.

User Story TKS 106:

As a ticket buyer
I would like to be able to browse by different event characteristics, such as music genre
So I can find events I like when I only know the types of events I'm looking for.

User Story TKS 107:

As a ticket buyer
I would like to be able to browse by locations
So I can find something nearby, not requiring transportation.

Sorting

User Story TKS 75:

As a ticket buyer
I would like to be able to sort the results I find using some criteria
Because sometimes searching produces too many results to go through without any ordering.

10.2.7 Prioritizing User Stories for Design and Development

In the previous section, we organized by related tasks to manage the collection of user stories. This is not the same as prioritizing for design and development. The task-oriented structure is just an organization scheme, but not necessarily an execution plan, meaning that we don't attempt to design and develop the complete user stories at once in one release.

Rather, this prioritization is guided by a business-oriented concept, namely of delivering minimum viable product (MVP) releases—that is, to produce something initially, however limited, that can be deployed immediately and evaluated to get feedback from actual use. For example, a system might get only a browse capability but no search function in the first version, or a first version might accept only credit cards but not other forms of payment such as the MU passport card. Such an MPV is how you get user feedback quickly, which is the whole idea of an agile process.

Early Funnel

The part of the funnel (agile UX model) for large-scope activity, usually for conceptual design, before syncing with software engineering (Section 4.4.4).

For this kind of prioritizing of user stories, Patton (2014) uses a construct he calls user story maps, which are well described in his book but are beyond our scope here.

At design time, even though the UX design team might deliver the designs of detailed tasks for each of these user stories separately, it is very likely that they will all be considered together as a group because they are so closely related. This is exactly the reason why UX cannot always do agile as well as SE. Hence the need for early funnel to organize the user stories by related tasks in a hierarchical structure such as the HTI before designing and implementing them in sprints. In a purely agile shop, though, UX may not have a choice and may be forced to do fragmented design.

This topic of prioritizing for design is not in the scope of this chapter. See Chapter 29 for more about how user stories are prioritized for design and implementation.

10.3 UX DESIGN REQUIREMENTS

Your user story structure will be an effective approach to UX needs for user capabilities. Do you even need more formal requirements? It's rare, but you might use formal requirements if:

- You have a need for them in your own process.
- If your customer or client must see a requirements document.
- A formal requirements document is a contractually required deliverable.

And, if you have to do formal requirements for UX design, this section tells you how.

System Complexity Space

A two-dimensional space defined by the dimensions of interaction complexity and domain complexity, depicting a spectrum of system and product types with a broad range of risk versus needs for rigor in lifecycle activities and methods (Section 3.2.2.1).

10.3.1 Degree of Formality Can Vary

The formality of requirement statements can vary depending on project needs. Formal design requirements can be necessary in some projects, including projects:

- In the high-rigor quadrants of the system complexity space.
- With constraints for compliance to certain standards.
- With a high need to avoid risk.

For projects not requiring maximum rigor, a simple structured list will suffice as an effective way to keep track of the system capabilities for which we will be designing.

10.3.2 Team Selection

For creating requirements, a broad team is best. Select a cross-disciplinary team, including UX designers, software people, and client representatives, plus possibly system architects and maybe managers.

10.3.3 The Requirements Structure Evolves

As you edit elemental data notes used as inputs to requirement statements, you will bring them together into a requirements structure, organized hierarchically by issues and features, much like the HTI. In addition, many of the categories in the WAAD will represent design needs. The hierarchical categories will evolve as needed to accommodate each new elemental data note.

Example: Initial TKS Requirements Structure

The following is just an example of what we might see emerging as an initial requirements structure for TKS:

Personal privacy and trust issues.

Items in the artifact model (e.g., printed tickets, credit cards).

Items in the physical environment model (e.g., physical aspects of kiosks and their locations).

Business issues, decisions:

Branding and appearance.

Kiosk locations.

Credit card usage.

Cash transactions.

Printing tickets.

Keyboards versus touchscreens.

Kinds of events supported (including restaurant reservations and transportation tickets).

Help, customer support.

Customer accounts and logins.

> **Artifact Model**
>
> A representation showing how users employ, manipulate, and share key tangible objects (physical or electronic work practice artifacts) as part of the flow in their work practice (Section 9.8).

10.3.4 Compose Requirements Statements

As you will see, most applicable elemental data notes from usage research will be easy to express as requirements. As you consider each note:

- Ask what user needs are reflected by the note.
- Write it as a requirement statement.
- Find where it fits into the evolving requirements structure.

10.3.5 The Requirement Statement and Requirements Document

A generic structure of a requirement statement that has worked for us is shown in Fig. 10-4. A requirements document is essentially a structured set of requirement statements organized on headings at two or more levels.

Name of major feature or category within structure

Name of second-level feature or category

Rationale (if useful): Rationale statement (the reason for the requirement)

Note (optional): Commentary about this requirement

Fig. 10-4

Generic structure of a requirement statement.

We show two levels of headings, but you should use as many levels as necessary for your requirements.

Not every point in a data note will generate a need or requirement. Sometimes one note can reflect more than one need. A single need can also lead to more than one requirement. Examples of data notes, user needs, and corresponding requirements are coming soon.

Example: Writing a TKS Elemental Data Note as a Requirement Statement

Consider this usage research data note from the TKS:

I am concerned about the security and privacy of my transactions.

Concern about security and privacy is a system-wide issue, so this note can directly imply a high-level design requirement statement:

Shall protect the security and privacy of ticket-buyer transactions.

Note that at this level, requirements can involve both UX and functional requirements.

Finally, it is easy to fit this into the requirements structure, assuming there is already a category for personal privacy and trust issues, as shown in Fig. 10-5.

```
Security

     Privacy of ticket-buyer transactions

     Shall protect security and privacy of ticket-buyer
     transactions.

     Note: In design, consider timeout feature to clear
     screen between customers.
```

Fig. 10-5
Example requirement
statement.

Example: Generalizing Data Notes to Express TKS Needs as Requirement Statements

If the elemental data note is very specific, you might have to abstract it to express a general need. Consider this data note:

> Normally, I buy tickets at the venue of the event just before the event. For special events, I might buy online. Then I usually have to buy Metro tickets to get there at a different kiosk in a totally different location. If I could buy all these different tickets at one kiosk, that would give me one-stop shopping for events.

This is about treating events as broad entertainment activities and having sufficiently broad coverage of tickets for "event content" so the kiosk can be a one-stop shopping location for entertainment events. This means extending "event content" to include, for example, restaurant reservations and transportation tickets in conjunction with events, as in Fig. 10-6.

```
Business issues, decisions

     Kinds of events and tickets supported

     Shall provide tickets and reservations for a broad
     range of needs associated with an entertainment
     activity.

     Note: This should include tickets for events and
     transportation and restaurant reservations.
```

Fig. 10-6
Example requirement
statement.

Example: A Possibly Unexpected TKS Requirement

Data note:

> Although marketing people might not think to put a kiosk next to the ticket office, it would be very helpful for people who get there and find the ticket office too busy or closed.

This data note, about locating a kiosk near a ticket office, might reveal an unexpected need because you might not think of it. A possible resulting requirement statement is shown in Fig. 10-7.

Fig. 10-7
Example requirement statement.

Business issues, decisions

Kiosk locations

Shall provide a kiosk located near the ticket office.

Note: This requirement serves users when the ticket office is too busy or is closed.

Emotional Impact

An affective component of user experience that influences user feelings. Includes such effects as enjoyment, pleasure, fun, satisfaction, aesthetics, coolness, engagement, and novelty and can involve deeper emotional factors such as self-expression, self-identity, a feeling of contribution to the world, and pride of ownership (Section 1.4.4).

Work Activity Note

A brief, clear, concise, and elemental (relating to exactly one concept, idea, fact, or topic) statement used to document a single point about the work practice as synthesized from raw usage research data (Section 8.1.2).

10.3.6 Things to Look for in Your Requirements Notes

10.3.6.1 Keep an eye out for emotional impact requirements and other ways to enhance the overall user experience

When writing requirements, don't forget that we are on a quest to design for a fabulous user experience and this is where you will find opportunities for that, too.

Work activity notes with user concerns, frustration, excitement, and likings offer opportunities to address emotional issues. Especially look out for work activity notes that make even an oblique reference to "fun" or "enjoyment" or to things such as data entry being too boring or the use of colors being unattractive. Any of these could be a clue to ways to provide a more rewarding user experience. Also, be open minded and creative in this phase; even if a note implies a need that is technologically difficult to address, record it. You can revisit these later to assess feasibility and constraints.

10.3.6.2 Questions about missing data

Sometimes, as you go deeper into the implications of usage research data, you realize there are still some open questions. For example, in our usage data elicitation for MUTTS, while we were putting together requirements for the accounting system to aggregate sales at the end of the day, we had to face the fact that the existing business manages tickets from two independent systems. One is the local ticket office sales and the other is from the national affiliate, Tickets4ever.com. During our usage data elicitation and analysis, we neglected to probe the dependencies and connections between those two and how they reconciled sales across those two systems.

10.3.6.3 System support needs

You may also occasionally encounter system requirements for issues outside the user experience or software domains, such as expandability, reliability, security, and communications bandwidth. These are dealt with in a manner similar to that used for the software requirement inputs.

Example: System Support Requirements for TKS

A few examples from the TKS WAAD illustrate:

> Work activity note: "Identity theft and credit card fraud are huge concerns for me."
> System requirement: "System shall have specific features to address protecting ticket buyers from identity theft and credit card fraud." (This "requirement" is vague but it is really only a note for us to contact the systems people to figure out potential solutions to this problem.)

Another systems constraint for the existing working environment of MUTTS is the necessity of keeping the secure credit card server continuously operational. An inability of the ticket office to process credit card transactions would essentially bring their business to a halt. That constraint will be even more important in the transition to TKS, where human operators won't be present to notice or fix such problems.

Here is another example of how a UX requirement also creates a system support requirement, which you should capture here:

> UX requirement: "Ticket buyers shall be able to see a real-time preview of available seating for a venue."
> Corresponding system requirement: "System shall have networked infrastructure and a common database to 'lock and release' selected seats in a given venue for a given date and time and to update ticket and seat availability as kiosk transactions occur."

This is a good time for the software team members to work in parallel with your team to capture those inputs to software and system requirements so they are not lost.

10.3.6.4 Constraints as requirements

Constraints, such as from legacy systems, implementation platforms, and system architecture, are a kind of requirement in real-world development

MUTTS

MUTTS is the acronym for Middleburg University Ticket Transaction Service, our running example for most of the process chapters (Section 5.5).

Legacy System

An old process, technology, computer system, or application program, of, relating to, or being a previous or outdated computer system with maintenance problems that date back possibly many years (Section 3.2.4).

projects. Although, as we have said, much of the UX design can and should be done independently from concerns about software design and implementation, your UX design must eventually be considered as an input to software requirements and design.

Therefore, eventually, you and your UX design must be reconciled with constraints coming from systems engineering, hardware engineering, software engineering, management, and marketing. Not the least of which includes development cost and schedule as well as profitability in selling the product.

What restrictions will these constraints impose on the product? Will kiosk size or weight be taken into account if, for example, the product will be on portable or mobile equipment? Does your system have to be integrated with existing or other developing systems? Are there compliance issues that mandate certain features?

Example: Physical Hardware Requirements for TKS

Consider this TKS example about privacy:

> Work activity note: "When I am getting tickets for, say, a controversial political speaker, I do not want people in line behind me to know what I am doing."

> Physical hardware requirement: "Physical design of kiosk shall address protecting privacy of a ticket buyer from others nearby."

Here are some other example physical hardware requirements that might be anticipated in the TKS:

- Special-purpose hardware needed for the kiosk.
- Rugged, "hardened" vandal-proof outer shell.
- All hardware to be durable, reliable.
- Touchscreen interaction, no keyboard.
- Network communications possibly specialized for efficiency and reliability.
- If have a printer for tickets (likely), maintenance must be an extremely high priority; cannot have any customers pay and not get tickets (e.g., from paper or ink running out).
- Need a "hotline" communication feature as a backup, a way for customers to contact company representatives in case this does happen.

Exercise 10.1: Constraints for Your Product or System

Goal: Get a little experience in specifying constraints for system development.
Activities: Extract and deduce what you can about development and implementation constraints from contextual data for the product or system of your choice.
Deliverables: A short list of same.
Schedule: A half hour should do it.

Example: UX Design Requirements for the TKS

Here are some example UX requirements for the TKS, along with their first- and second-level structural headings. Space limitations preclude listing the huge number of requirements for the TKS, but you should get the idea.

User Accounts

Existence of accounts

User shall be able to create accounts through a web interface and access them through the kiosk. (optional, future?).

Shopping Cart

Existence of feature

Ticket buyer shall have a shopping cart concept with which they can buy multiple items and pay only once.

Reserved Seat Selection

Existence of feature

Ticket buyer shall have a shopping cart concept with which they can buy multiple items and pay only once, and be able to select seats from all available seats in various price categories.

Implied requirements: Display of seat layout within event venue. Display seating availability and to be able to filter that list of available seats by categories such as price.

Another important implied requirement: Seat selection requires the existence of a lock-and-release mechanism of some sort, something we perhaps did not yet have in the requirements structure. This is a technical requirement to give the buyer a temporary option on the selected seats until the transaction is completed or abandoned.

User Checkout

Use of cash, credit cards

Ticket buyer shall be able to use cash, credit cart, or debit card for payment.

Notes: Cash transactions have several drawbacks: Cash denominations are difficult to recognize, counterfeit bills are difficult to identify, dispensing change can be problematic, and cash in the kiosk can attract vandals and thieves.

Exercise 10.2: Writing Requirement Statements for Your Product or System

Following the descriptions in this chapter, write a few formal requirements statements for the product or system of your choice.

Goal: Get some practice with requirements extraction.

Activities: Assemble your UX team in your UX studio with:

■ The elemental data notes you have set aside as inputs to requirement statements.

■ Your WAAD for your product or system.

Choose a leader and recorder.

Do a walkthrough of the elemental data notes and the WAAD.

For each work activity note in the WAAD, work as a team to deduce user need(s) and UX design requirements to support the need(s).

As you go, have the recorder capture requirements in the format shown in this chapter, including extrapolation requirements and rationale statements, where appropriate.

To speed things up, you might consider having each person be responsible for writing the requirement statements extracted from a different subtree in the WAAD structure. Set aside any work activity notes that require additional thought or discussion to be dealt with at the end by the team as a whole.

If time permits, have the whole team read all requirement statements to assure agreement.

Deliverables: A requirements document covering at least one subtree of the WAAD for your system.

Notes and lists of the other kinds of information (discussed in this section) that come out of this process.

Schedule: We expect that this exercise could take at least a couple of hours. If you simply do not have that kind of time to devote to it, do as much as you can to at least get a flavor of how this exercise works.

10.4 VALIDATING USER STORIES AND REQUIREMENTS

After the user stories are gathered and organized into a hierarchical user story structure, it's a good time to take them back to users and other stakeholders to be sure they are the right ones. It's also a good time to coordinate between the UX and SE teams.

10.4.1 Coordinating Requirements, Terminology, and Consistency

Many UX requirements for tasks imply an SE (backend) requirement for functionality, and vice versa. Both teams need to be working toward the same set of tasks/functions. This is also a key time to standardize terminology and build consistency. Your usage research data will be full of user comments about usage and design concepts and issues. It is natural that they will not all use exactly the same terms for the same concepts. The same is true for the SE and systems people and other stakeholders.

For example, users of a calendar system might use the terms "alarm," "reminder," "alert," and "notification" for essentially the same idea. Sometimes differences in terminology may reflect subtle differences in usage, too. So it is your responsibility to sort out these differences and act to help standardize the terminology for consistency issues in the requirements statements.

10.4.2 Take User Stories and Requirements Back to Customers and Users for Validation

Your structured sets of user stories and requirements offer you, your client, and your users a lens through which you can contemplate and discuss groups of related user stories and requirements at various levels of abstraction. This is an important step for you both because it gives you a chance to get inputs and to correct misconceptions before you get into design. It also helps solidify your relationship as partners in the process.

For each work role, schedule a meeting with interested client representatives and representative users, preferably some from the ones you have interviewed or otherwise interacted with before. Walk them through the requirements to make sure your interpretation of user stories and requirements is accurate and relatively complete.

10.4.3 Resolve Organizational, Social, and Personal Issues Arising Out of Work Practice Changes

When you take your user stories and requirements to the customer for validation, it is also a good opportunity to resolve organizational, social, and personal issues that might arise out of work practice changes in the new design. Because your requirements reflect what you intend to put into the design, if heeded, they can flash early warning signs to customers and users about issues of which your team may be unaware, even after thorough usage data elicitation. Especially if your requirements are pointing toward a design that changes the work environment, the way work is done, or the job descriptions of workers, your requirements may give rise to issues of territoriality, fear, and control.

Changes in the workflow may challenge established responsibilities and authorities. There may also be legal requirements or platform constraints for doing things in a certain way, a way you cannot change regardless of arguments for efficiency or a better user experience. Organizational, social, and personal

Abstraction

The process of removing extraneous details of something and focusing on its irreducible constructs to identify what is really going on, ignoring everything else (Section 14.2.8.2).

issues can catch your team by surprise because they may well be thinking mostly about technical aspects and UX design at this point.

For a discussion of how user stories and requirements are used to drive design, see Chapter 14 on design creation. See also Chapter 29 (on UX + SE) for how user stories are the focus of how the UX designers and the SE team communicate to synchronize design and implementation in agile sprints.

Background: Understand Needs

11

11.1 THIS IS A REFERENCE CHAPTER

This chapter contains reference material relevant to the other chapters of Part 2. This chapter is not intended to be read through as a regular chapter, but each section is supposed to be read when a reference to it in the main chapters is encountered.

11.2 A TRUE STORY: VOTING TROUBLE EXPERIENCED BY A SENIOR CITIZEN

In southwest Virginia, somewhat remote from urban centers, when the first-time computer-based touchscreen voting machines were used, we heard that quite a few voters had difficulty in using them. Although an official gave instructions as people entered one particular voting area, a school gymnasium, he did it in a confusing way.

One of the voters in line was an elderly woman with poor eyesight, obvious from her thick eyeglasses. As she entered the voting booth, one could just imagine her leaning her head down very close to the screen, struggling to read the words, even though the font was reasonably large.

Her voice was heard floating above her voting booth, as she gave some unsolicited user feedback. She was saying that she had trouble distinguishing the colors (the screen was in primary colors: red, green, and blue). A bystander said aloud to himself, as if to answer the woman, that he thought there was an option to set the screen to black and white. But oddly, no one actually told this, if it was true, to the woman.

In time, the woman emerged with a huge smile, proclaiming victory over the evil machine. She then immediately wanted to tell everyone how the design should be improved. Remember, this is an elderly woman who probably knew nothing about technology or user experience but who is quite naturally willing to offer valuable user feedback.

It was easy to imagine a scenario in which the supervisors of the voting process quickly flocked about the voter and duly took notes, pledging to pass this important information on to the higher-ups who could influence the next design. But as you might guess, she was roundly humored and ignored.

There are a few things to note in this story. First, the feedback was rich, detailed, and informative about design. This level of feedback was possible only because it occurred in real usage and real context.

Second, this woman represented a particular type of user belonging to a specific age group and had some associated visual limitations. She was also naturally articulate in describing her usage experience, which is somewhat uncommon in public situations.

So what does this have to do with user research inquiry? If you do user research inquiry in a real environment like this, you might get lucky and find rich user data. It is certain, however, that if you do not do user research inquiry, you will never get this kind of information about situated usage.

11.3 HISTORY OF CONTEXTUAL INQUIRY

The terms contextual inquiry, contextual design, and contextual studies are early terms for what we are now calling usage research.

11.3.1 Roots in Activity Theory

First of all, we owe a great acknowledgment to those who pioneered, developed, and promoted the concepts and techniques of contextual design. Early foundations go back to Scandinavian work activity theory (Bjerknes, Ehn, & Kyng, 1987; Bødker, 1991; Ehn, 1988).

In our context, activity theory is an abstract adaptation for HCI of a theoretical descriptive framework based on the Soviet psychological activity theory as adapted by Scandinavian researchers in the mid-1980s.

The goal seems to have been to understand people (users of the systems) as complex human beings and not information processors or system components. People's actions are influenced by their social and cultural setting. This theory is based on learning what motivates people to take actions. Human activities, especially in the context of interacting with machines and systems, are seen as social actions, taking into account the individual characteristics and abilities of the human operators.

The activity theory work was conducted for quite some time in Scandinavia, in parallel with the task analysis work in Europe and the United Kingdom. More recent conferences and special issues have been devoted to the topic (Lantz & Gulliksen, 2003). Much of the initial work in this "school" was directed at the impact of computer-based systems on human labor and democracy within the organizations of the affected workers. This singular focus on human work activities shines through into contextual inquiry and analysis.

11.3.2 Roots in Ethnography

A second essential foundation for contextual inquiry is ethnography, an investigative field rooted in anthropology (LeCompte & Preissle, 1993). Anthropologists spend significant amounts of time living with and studying a particular group of humans or other possibly more intelligent animals, usually in social settings of primitive cultures. The goal is to study and document details of their daily lives and existence.

The Understand Needs lifecycle activity in UX derives from ethnography, a branch of anthropology that focuses on the study and systematic description of various human cultures.

In a trend toward design driven by work practice in context, quick and dirty varieties of ethnography, along with other hermeneutic approaches (concerned with ways to explain, translate, and interpret perceived reality) (Carroll, Mack, & Kellogg, 1988), have been adapted into HCI practice as qualitative tools for understanding design requirements. Contextual inquiry and analysis are examples of an adaptation of this kind of approach as part of the evolution of requirement elicitation techniques.

The characteristics that define ethnography in anthropology are what make it just right for adaptation in HCI, where it takes place in the natural setting of the people being studied. It also involves observation of user activities, listening to what users say, asking questions, and discussing the work with the people who do it; and it is based on the holistic view of understanding behavior in its context.

In contrast to long-term field studies of "pure" ethnography, with its cultural, anthropological, and social perspectives, the "quick and dirty" version of ethnography has been adapted for HCI. Although involving significantly shorter time with subjects and correspondingly less depth of analysis, this version still requires observation of subjects in their own environment and still requires attending to the sociality of the subjects in their work context (Hughes, King, Rodden, & Andersen, 1995). For example, Hughes, King, Rodden, and Andersen (1994) describe the application of ethnography in the area of computer-supported cooperative work (CSCW), a subarea of HCI.

Lewis, Mateas, Palmiter, and Lynch (1996) described an ethnographic-based approach to system requirements and design that parallels much of the contextual inquiry process described here. Rogers and Bellotti (1997) tell how they harnessed ethnography as a research tool to serve as a practical requirements and design process. Blythin, Rouncefield, and Hughes (1997) address the adaptation of ethnography from research to commercial system development.

11.3.3 Getting Contextual Studies into HCI

The foundations for contextual design in HCI were laid by researchers at Digital Equipment Corporation (Whiteside & Wixon, 1987; Wixon, 1995; Wixon, Holtzblatt, & Knox, 1990). By 1988, several groups in academia and industry were already reporting on early contextual field studies (Good, 1989) in the United States and the United Kingdom (notably the work of Andrew Monk). Similar trends were also beginning in the software world (Suchman, 1987). Almost a decade later, Wixon and Ramey (1996) produced an edited collection of much more in-depth reports on case studies of real application of contextual studies in the field. Whiteside, Bennett, and Holtzblatt (1988) helped integrate the concept of contextual studies into the UX process.

11.3.4 Connections to Participatory Design

Participatory design is a democratic process for UX design actively involving all stakeholders (e.g., employees, partners, customers, citizens, users) in the process to help ensure the result meets their needs and is usable. Underlying participatory design are the arguments that users should be involved in designs they will be using, and that all stakeholders, including and especially users, have equal inputs into UX design.[1]

---

[1]https://en.wikipedia.org/wiki/Participatory_design.

Contextual inquiry and analysis are part of a collection of collaborative and participatory methods that evolved in parallel courses over the past couple of decades. These methods share the characteristic that they directly involve users not trained in specialized methods, such as task analysis. Among these are participatory design and collaborative analysis of requirements and design developed by Muller and associates (Muller & Kuhn, 1993; Muller, Wildman, & White, 1993a, 1993b) and collaborative users' task analysis (Lafrenière, 1996).

11.4 THE SSA MODEL DISTRICT OFFICE—AN EXTREME AND SUCCESSFUL EXAMPLE OF AN ENVIRONMENT FOR DATA ELICITATION

In the mid-1990s, we worked extensively with the Social Security Administration in Baltimore, mainly in usability engineering (what UX used to be called then) lifecycle training. We worked with a small group pioneering the introduction of usability engineering techniques into an "old school," Waterfall-oriented, mainframe software development environment. Large Social Security systems were slowly migrating from mainframes (in Baltimore) plus terminals (by the thousands over the country) to client-server applications, some starting to run on PCs, and they wanted usability to be a high priority. Sean Wheeler was the group sparkplug and usability champion, strongly supported by Annette Bryce and Pat Stoos.

What impressed us the most about this organization was the Model District Office (MDO). A decade earlier, as part of a large Claims Modernization Project, a program of system design and training to "revolutionize the way that SSA serves the public," they had built a complete and detailed model of a district office from middle America right in the middle of SSA headquarters in Baltimore. The MDO was indistinguishable from a typical agency office in a typical town, with its carpeting, office furniture, and computer terminals, right down to the office lamps and pictures on the wall. They brought in real SSA employees from field offices all over the United States to sit in the MDO to test and pilot new systems and procedures.

Although the MDO was originally intended for developing and refining the ways agents interact with clients, when SSA was ready to focus on usability, the existing MDO was the perfect environment for developing ways that agents interact with computer systems and for usability testing of those designs. Simply put, it was an extreme and successful example of leveraging ecological validity (the extent to which your UX evaluation setup matches the user's real work context) for application development and testing as well as for user training. In the end, the group created a usability success story amid the inertia and enormous weight of the rest of the Social Security Administration. As a result of their work, this group won a federal award for quality and usability in a large and important software application.

As a testament to their seriousness about ecological validity and usability, by the mid- to late-1990s, the SSA was spending $1 million a year to bring in employees to stay and work at the MDO, sometimes for a few months at a time. Their cost justification calculations proved the activity was saving many times more.

11.5 ROOTS OF ESSENTIAL USE CASES IN SOFTWARE ENGINEERING

A use case is not a user experience lifecycle artifact, but a software engineering and systems engineering artifact for documenting functional requirements, especially for object-oriented development, of a system. "Use cases, stated simply, allow description of sequences of events that, taken together, lead to a system doing something useful" (Bittner & Spence, 2003). They include outside roles—end users and external entities such as database servers or bank authorization modules—and internal system responses to outside actions.

Although a use case can represent the user view, the bottom-line focus is on functional, not interaction, requirements. Sometimes use cases are thought of as an object-oriented approach to user modeling, but in practice they are usually created by developers and systems analysts without any user research data from users.

Use cases are formalized usage scenarios, narratives of "black box" functionality in the context of user-system interaction (Constantine & Lockwood, 1999, p. 101). Use cases are often used as a component of software requirements. Their strong software orientation means that use cases lean in the direction of software implementation and away from user interaction design. As Meads (2010) says, in use cases, the user is an external object, not a person with human needs and limitations. This view leads to system requirements, but not to usage or UX requirements.

Use cases describe the major business requirements, features, and functions that the envisioned system must support. A use case "describes a sequence of actions that are performed by a human in work roles or other entities such as a machine or another system as they interact with the software" (Pressman, 2009);

"use cases help to identify the scope of the project and provide a basis for project planning" (Pressman, 2009).

In answer to the need for something more effective than use cases in identifying interaction design requirements, Constantine (1994a, 1995) created a variation he calls "essential use cases."

UX Design

3

Part 3 contains several chapters about UX design, starting with a description of the nature of design and a discussion of the critical difference between bottom-up design and top-down design. Next is the ideation, sketching, and critiquing activities in generative design and a chapter on how designer and user mental models come together in the conceptual design.

Three chapters are devoted to design in each layer of the UX design pyramid: for designing the ecology, the interaction, and for emotional impact.

The Nature of UX Design

12

Highlights

- Switch in mode of thinking from usage research to design.
- Universality of design and relationships to other fields.
- Definition of design as a noun and as a verb.
- The purpose of design: To satisfy human needs.
- Information, information design, information architecture, and their role in UX design.
- The overall design creation lifecycle to illustrate expanding fidelity (the substance and richness of detail) through iterations of:
  - Generative design.
  - Intermediate design.
  - Detailed design.
  - Design refinement.

12.1 INTRODUCTION

12.1.1 You Are Here

We begin each process chapter with a "you are here" picture of the chapter topic in the context of The Wheel, the overall UX design lifecycle template (Fig. 12-1). In this chapter, we introduce the UX Design Solutions lifecycle activity with a discussion of the nature of design.

While user research data elicitation (Chapter 7) is empirical, user research data analysis (Chapter 8) is inductive, and user story and requirements extraction (Chapter 10) is deductive, design is integrative.

This chapter contains a descriptive discussion of the characteristics of design, especially UX design. The how-to part of design is in subsequent chapters.

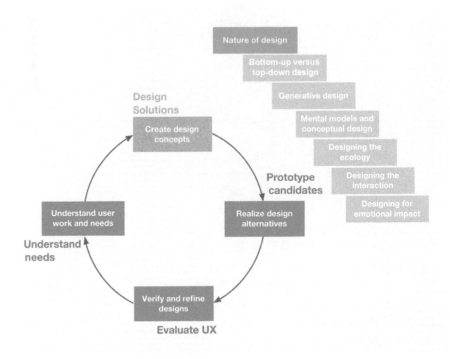

Fig. 12-1

You are here in the chapter describing the nature of design within the Design Solutions lifecycle activity, in the context of the overall Wheel UX lifecycle.

12.1.2 Moving Across the Gap from Analysis to Design

In this part of the book, we switch our focus from usage research to design. This involves changing our perspective from the existing work domain and work practice to an envisioned design domain and work practice. The transition to design is often regarded as the most difficult step in the UX lifecycle process, and we should expect it to be difficult. Beyer and Holtzblatt (1998, p. 218) remind us that, "The design isn't explicit in the data. The data guides, constrains, and suggests directions" that design "can respond to."

Another way to say this is that design is not simply a translation exercise; it is not about taking workflows in existing work practice and recreating them using technology artifacts. That would not address any of the existing breakdowns, problems, or inefficiencies, and would only add more constraints because of the newly introduced technology. There needs to be a switch in the mindset to focus on creating new solutions.

Larry Wood calls the transition to design a step where magic happens (Wood, 1998). In this same book, a number of authors share their own experiences and methods at making that transition.

12.1.3 Universality of Design and Relationship to Other Fields

Design is universal; it is about creating products and experiences using different media with the goal of helping humans satisfy a variety of needs.

Design is the core activity in many other creative fields. Fashion is about the design of clothes, which at a functional level is about protecting humans from the elements. But it is also about much more. Clothing designers use colors, fabrics, and shapes to create fashion experiences in infinite variations.

Of all the design fields, perhaps industrial design is the one closest to what we do in UX. In the last decade, with the proliferation of affordable technology in the form of hand-held and wearable devices, industrial design and UX have become inextricably bound. The user experience of a smartphone or smartwatch is derived not just from the software user interface but also the shape, texture, materials, and the form factor of the product that "houses" that user interface.

No matter what the field, all these design endeavors share the same fundamental process activities of understanding, creating, prototyping, and evaluating. Each discipline's vocabulary and domain knowledge may be different but they are all ultimately about creating products to solve problems and satisfy human needs.

12.1.4 Relationship to Design in Architecture

Architecture is a field in which design is foremost, a field that stands as an inspiration for UX. Architecture is a discipline about designing spaces to support humans and their needs, to sustain— and even glorify—living and working. Spaces in this context include everything from cities, neighborhoods, houses, community places, and offices as well as the infrastructure that connects them.

Great designs in architecture do not just provide shelter; they have the potential to spawn vibrant communities and induce strong emotional responses. For example, when people walk on the sixth floor of Bloomberg's Global Headquarters in New York City (where Pardha used to work) and see the scene in this image (Fig. 12-2), they encounter a feeling of movement and awe.

Visitors to the Bloomberg building say they experience a feeling of high energy and fast pace. This is because every element in this space was carefully designed by architects to evoke that experience of dynamism and connectedness. The constant movement of people through the space and digital displays showing the latest financial indicators, weather, and breaking news create a sense of energy as you walk into this central atrium. The expansive space and high ceilings combined with the curved glass surrounding an imposing courtyard injects a sense of grandness.

Fig. 12-2

Beautiful space in the Bloomberg building designed to evoke dynamic energy.

12.1.5 The Interdisciplinary Nature of Design

In Section 1.2.5.2, we said that user experience "is the sum total of all the effects felt by the user from what the user sees, does, hears, and feels and all the behaviors of the artifact during contact and communication between them." Given this breadth, it is expected that UX design teams have a wide variety of skills and backgrounds, including:

- Expertise in problem solving, analysis, and reasoning.
- Expertise in constraint solving and optimization.
- Expertise in product development, including estimation, budgeting, and timelines.
- Subject matter expertise in work domains and design platforms.
- Design expertise in particular technologies.
- Expertise in art, culture, liberal arts, and social sciences.

12.2 WHAT IS DESIGN?

The topics of design, what it is, and how to do it have all been studied in many different domains. It is perhaps the original embodied skill of humans, starting with the fashioning of artifacts into tools.

The study of design has retained its relevance through time, as manifest in a wide variety of perspectives, practices, and issues. A graphic or visual designer on the design team may think about design in terms of emotion, joy, and art.

A usability analyst may think about design from a diagnostic perspective. Consultants and design agencies may look at design from the perspective of what sells, who is going to pay for it, and how to budget for it. Another common view is that design is about form (shape of the product) and function (purpose of the product). These perspectives aside, in this book we focus on two ways of thinking about design.

12.2.1 Two Ways the Word "Design" is Used

Most English dictionaries define the word design along two main dimensions: as a verb (the act of creating) and as a noun (the resulting concept of, or plan for, a product or system). For example, the click wheel on an iPod Classic is an element (design as a noun) that was created as the result of a process of creation (design as a verb). Fig. 12-3 shows the simple relationship between these ways of using the term "design."

12.2.1.1 Design as a noun

A definition of *design as a noun is the concept or plan for a product or system.* It is about the organization, composition, or structure of elements to be executed or constructed.[1] When we hear someone say, "I like this design" or "this design is bad," they are referring to the design concept behind the product. Unpacking this definition further, design as a noun is specifically about an abstract

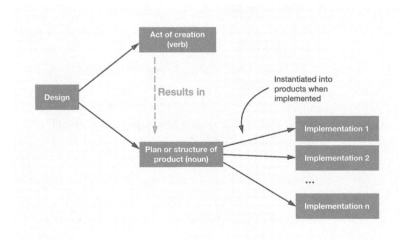

Fig. 12-3

Design as a noun and design as a verb.

---

[1]https://www.merriam-webster.com/dictionary/design.

construct that represents the way a product is conceived by its designer, a *description* of the plan or structure of the product.

It is *not* about an *instantiation* of that construct in the form of a tangible object or system, which can be thought of as one possible implementation of the design. In fact, not all designs come to fruition when instantiation is attempted. Some plans are flawed, or are revealed as such, when put into action (either by simulating the result using a prototype or by constructing a real implementation). Unexpected constraints, unforeseen technical limitations, or other omissions yet to be discovered may force revisions to these plans.

12.2.1.2 Design as a verb

Design as a verb refers to *the act of creating something that did not exist before—solutions to known problems and solutions looking for problems.* This is the Design Solutions box in the overall lifecycle, within which designs are created.

This box can be viewed using two perspectives:

- The fundamental nature of activities involved.
- The increasing fidelity (increasing depth of detail) of outputs with each subsequent iteration of this activity.

In the first perspective, the design box is a sublifecycle, a microcosm of the larger lifecycle, which follows the following fundamental activities (top of Fig. 12-4):

- Considering inputs and synthesizing them (act of analysis).
- Ideation to facilitate the genesis of design proposals or ideas (act of creation).
- Capture of these ideas in the form of sketches (act of lowest fidelity prototyping).
- Critiquing the tradeoffs and feasibility of design proposals or ideas (act of evaluation).

Metaphor

An analogy used in design to communicate and explain unfamiliar concepts using familiar conventional knowledge. A central metaphor often becomes the theme of a product, the motif behind the conceptual design (Section 15.3.6).

We cover this perspective in the chapter on "generative design" (Chapter 14).

In the second perspective, the design box is also a sublifecycle, this time of the expanding scope and fidelity of the designs (noun) created (Fig. 12-6):

- Generating ideas for features, capabilities, concepts, metaphors, and themes for the design (Chapter 14).
- Developing promising ideas further in the form of conceptual designs (Chapter 15).
- Increasing the fidelity and detail of the leading candidates in the form of intermediate design.
- Generating detailed design specifications of the chosen candidates to hand off to software engineering (SE) roles for implementation.

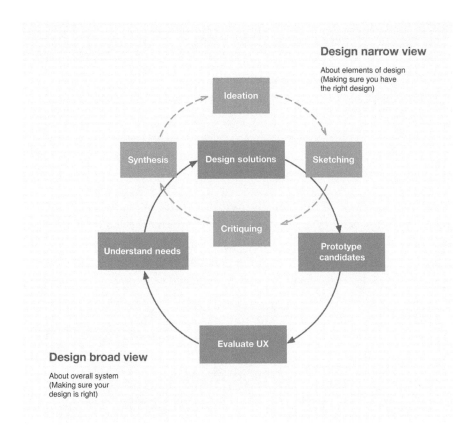

Design narrow view

About elements of design
(Making sure you have
the right design)

Ideation

Synthesis   Design solutions   Sketching

Critiquing

Understand needs   Prototype candidates

Evaluate UX

Design broad view

About overall system
(Making sure your
design is right)

Fig. 12-4

*The sublifecycle for doing
synthesis, ideation, sketching,
and critiquing within the
Design Solutions lifecycle
activity.*

12.3 THE PURPOSE OF DESIGN: SATISFYING HUMAN NEEDS

We talk about design along these two contexts:

- The kinds of human needs to satisfy with design (next section).
- The design aspects to focus on in order to meet these needs (later chapters).

12.3.1 A Pyramid of Human Needs

The purpose of design is, ultimately, about what it does for the user in the context of a work practice. It includes aid, support, capabilities, service, and even the joy the system provides the user. In this section, we provide a model for thinking about user needs with the objective of setting the stage for later discussion where we will talk about designing for those needs.

There are at least these three categories of human needs that must be met by a design:

- Ecological: Needs to be able to participate and thrive in the ecology of the work domain.
- Interaction: Needs to be able to perform required tasks in the ecology of the work domain.
- Emotional: Needs to be emotionally and culturally satisfied and enriched as they use the product, including the need to be able to form long-term emotional relationships with the product, which we call meaningfulness.

Designers often have to think about these categories in that order because these categories build on each other, as shown in what we call the pyramid of human needs in the context of UX design (Fig. 12-5). When designers work in one of these layers, they operate in the perspective of that layer: *the ecological perspective, the interaction perspective, and the emotional perspective.*

Fig. 12-5

Pyramid of human needs that are the purpose of UX design.

Meeting ecological needs is a prerequisite for meeting any other type of needs and is the foundational layer of the pyramid. Similarly, a design cannot satisfy users' emotional needs without first meeting ecological and interaction needs.

We will talk about designing the ecology (designing for a network or system of devices, physical locations, users, and information across which interactions can span) in Chapter 16, designing the interaction in Chapter 17, and designing for emotional impact in Chapter 18.

12.4 INFORMATION, INFORMATION DESIGN, AND INFORMATION ARCHITECTURE

We cannot discuss the nature of design without also talking about information, information design, and information architecture. These concepts are deeply intertwined and offer overlapping perspectives originating from different fields of study.

12.4.1 What is Information?

There are many definitions but, in the broadest sense and as the word implies, it is *anything that informs*. Taking an ecological perspective, this includes everything users sense, perceive, understand, and act on, in the environment. In this sense, the study of information is extremely broad. In this book, we take a similarly broad view of UX, and use a design-specific view of information surrounding the user.

There are other, narrower discussions of information, including but not limited to:

- Information encoding: About what symbols are used to represent information and how they are transmitted.
- Information detection: Identifying the presence or absence of a stimulus in the environment versus missing or making a false positive judgment (Wickens & Hollands, 2000, Chapter 2).
- Information processing: Looking at how humans sense stimuli in the environment, perception, cognition, memory, attention, and actions (Wickens & Hollands, 2000, Chapter 1).

12.4.2 Information Science

In the context of design, there is another area of study called information science, a sibling-concern of UX, focused on "the analysis, collection, classification, manipulation, storage, retrieval, movement, dissemination, and protection of information" (Stock & Stock, 2015).

This discipline predates HCI and UX and shares the goal of helping users with their needs, but from an information perspective. Some UX professionals trained in this discipline take the broad view that everything in the users' environment is information in some form or the other and therefore UX design is fundamentally about information. They even consider the field of architecture to be about information in the sense that issues such as how wide a corridor or a doorway should be in a building are information because users perceive and use that space accordingly.

12.4.3 Information Architecture

Another area of study that owes its roots to information science and the field of architecture is information architecture. Richard Saul Wurman, an architect by training and a graphic designer by choice, is regarded to be the inventor of the term information architecture.

Ecological Perspective

The design viewpoint taken from the ecological layer at the base of the pyramid of user needs, which is about how a system or product works within, interacts, and communicates with the context of its external environment. It is about how users can participate and thrive in the ecology of the work domain (Section 12.4.1).

The Information Architecture Institutes defines information architecture as *"the practice of deciding how to arrange the parts of something to be understandable."*[2] Note the emphasis on facilitating understanding and the breadth of situations where this can apply, including nondigital situations. The understanding part of this definition covers everything the users sense in an environment or a design, buttons that can be clicked, levers that can be pulled, audio prompts that can be heard, and displays that can be read.

Morville and Rosenfeld (2006) define information architecture as the design of information structures for organizing, storing, retrieving, displaying, manipulating, and sharing. Information architecture also includes design for labeling, searching, and navigating information.

12.4.4 Pervasive IA

Ecological Design

Design that pertains to the foundational layer of the needs pyramid, focused on designing for the overarching system needs of users and how they are supported in broader work practice. Includes designing for activities, the flow, sharing, and communication within the network of devices, other users, systems, and a pervasive information infrastructure (Section 16.2.1).

Information architects refer to the structure and design of information spanning multiple devices that users interact with as *pervasive information architecture* (Resmini & Rosati, 2011). *A pervasive information architecture is a structure for organizing, storing, retrieving, displaying, manipulating, and sharing information that provides ever-present information availability spanning parts of a broad ecology.*

Using our own vocabulary, we refer to those concerns as "ecological design." See Section 16.2.3 for further definition of pervasive IA and Section 16.5 for an extended example of ecological design as a pervasive information architecture.

12.4.5 Information Architecture is so Much More

We cannot begin to cover the many topics under the heading of information architecture. Readers should refer to other books in those areas.

12.4.6 Information Design

Information design is concerned with how "the objects and actions possible in a system are represented and arranged in a way that facilitates perception and understanding" (Rosson & Carroll, 2002, p. 109). As such, this is a core area of UX practice and focuses on helping users make sense of the information inherent in the system and its ecology. This includes everything from screens, dialogue boxes, icons, and voice prompts to tactile feedback (Rosson & Carroll, 2002).

---

[2]https://www.iainstitute.org/what-is-ia.

Traditionally, this area focused on how humans perceive and make sense of the information and included topics such as gestalt psychology, information visualizations, and visual metaphors. We cover some design guidelines pertaining to information design in Chapter 32.

12.5 ITERATION IN THE DESIGN CREATION SUBLIFECYCLE

Before we wrap up this chapter on the nature of design, here is a preview of chapters to come.

As a practical matter, the design creation box in the overall UX lifecycle (Fig. 12-6) unfolds as a series of iterative sublifecycles or activities. Among the very first to talk about iteration for interaction design were Buxton and Sniderman (1980).

In Fig. 12-6, we show a sequence of those activities.

The observant reader will note that the progressive series of iterative loops in Fig. 12-6 can be thought of as a kind of spiral lifecycle concept (Boehm, 1988). Each loop, in turn, addresses an increasing level of detail and fidelity.

12.5.1 Deciding on the Design Goal

The focus of this step is to agree on the goal for all subsequent design iterations. The question to answer is this: Is the goal of design to create a solution that will support existing work practice, or is it to create a solution that will radically transform the work practice (for the better)? (Chapter 13).

12.5.2 Generative Design Iteration

The focus of this phase of design creation is to generate as many design ideas and proposals as possible. In Fig. 12-7, we show the iteration for generative design—a fast, loosely structured activity for the purpose of exploring design ideas. This activity, a micro lifecycle within itself, includes synthesis, ideation, sketching, and critiquing.

The role of prototype is played by sketches, and the role of evaluation is carried out by discussion and critiquing. The output of generative design is a set of alternatives for conceptual designs and other capabilities or patterns for each level of the needs pyramid, mostly in the form of annotated rough sketches or storyboards.

We cover generative design (design creation) in Chapter 14.

Generative Design

An approach to design creation involving ideation, sketching, and critiquing in a tightly coupled but not necessarily structured iterative loop for exploring design ideas (Section 14.1.4).

Critiquing

An activity in which design ideas are assessed to identify advantages, disadvantages, constraints, and tradeoffs (Section 14.4).

Storyboard

A visual scenario in the form of a series of sketches or graphical clips, often annotated, in cartoon-like frames, illustrating the interplay between a user and an envisioned ecology or device (Section 17.4.1).

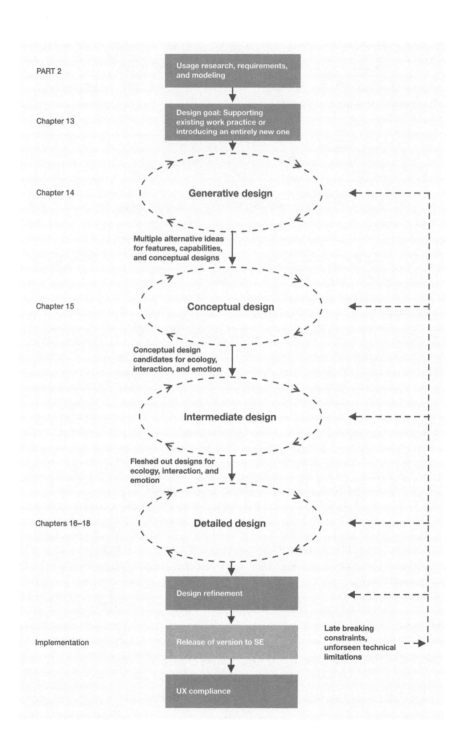

Fig. 12-6
Macro view of lifecycle activities in design.

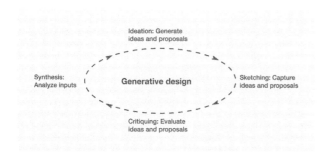

Fig. 12-7
Generative design iteration.

12.5.3 Conceptual Design Iteration

This iteration includes fleshing out the details of the high-level design theme or metaphor for each layer of the needs pyramid that came out of the generative design phase.

In Fig. 12-8, we show the early part of this phase, where you iterate on conceptual design candidates (Chapter 15). The role of prototype is played by storyboards and early wireframes. Wireframes, which will be described in more detail in Chapter 20, are essentially stick figure-like sketches of interaction screens made of lines, arcs, vertices, text, and (sometimes) simple graphics.

Depending on the project context, conceptual designs for one or more layers of the pyramid may be emphasized in storyboards. This is usually the stage where key stakeholders such as users or their representatives, business, software engineering, and marketing must be heavily involved. You are planting the seeds for what the entire design will be for the system going forward.

The type of evaluation here is usually in the form of storytelling via storyboards to key stakeholders. We discuss conceptual design (a high-level model or theme of how the system works acting as a framework to aid users to acquire their own mental model of how the system behaves) in Chapter 15.

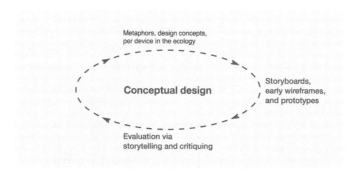

Fig. 12-8
Conceptual design iteration.

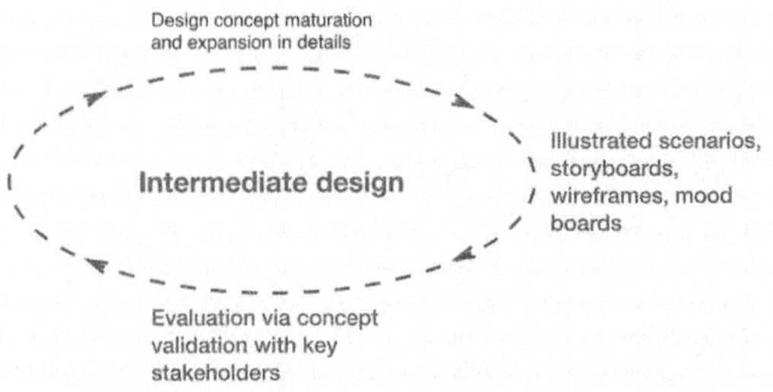

Fig. 12-9
Intermediate design
iteration.

12.5.4 Intermediate Design Iteration

In Fig. 12-9, we show intermediate design iteration. The initial purpose of intermediate design is to sort out possible multiple conceptual design candidates and to arrive at the one most viable for ecological, interaction, and emotional designs. Once candidate conceptual designs are identified, in intermediate design, we proceed to flesh out the details of each candidate (more below).

For example, for the Ticket Kiosk System, at least two conceptual design candidates for the kiosk's interaction design were explored further. One is a traditional "drill-in" concept where users are shown available categories (e.g., movies, concerts, MU athletics) from which they choose one. Based on the choice on this first screen, the user is shown further options and details, navigating with a back button and/or "bread crumb" trail, if necessary, to come back to the category view. A second conceptual design is the one using the three-panel idea described in Fig. 17.2.

Intermediate design is the activity that usually takes the longest. The goal of intermediate design is to work out the details of the envisioned ecology, create logical flows of intermediate-level navigational structure and screen designs for interaction, and flesh out themes for emotional impact.

During this phase, all layout and navigation elements become fully developed. The role of prototypes is played by wireflows, illustrated scenarios, click-through mockups, and mood boards. Using wireflows, or sequences of wireframes, key workflows are represented while describing what happens when the user interacts with the various user interface objects in the design. It is not uncommon to have wireframe sets represent part of the workflow or each task sequence using click-through prototypes.

Similarly, all emotional impact issues such as visual design styles, iconography, tone, typography, animation frameworks, and auditory styles are all fleshed out.

Mood Board

A collage of artifacts and images showcasing a theme of emotional impact to be embraced within a UX design (Section 18.3.2.1).

One of the best ways to describe parts of your intermediate interaction design in a document is through illustrated scenarios, which combine the visual communication capability of storyboards and screen sketches with the capability of textual scenarios to communicate details. The result is an excellent vehicle for sharing and communicating designs to the rest of the team, and to management, marketing, and all other stakeholders.

Making illustrated scenarios is simple; just intersperse graphical storyboard frames and/or screen sketches as figures in the appropriate places to illustrate the narrative text of a design scenario. The storyboards in initial illustrated scenarios can be sketches or early wireframes.

The best way to communicate intermediate designs for emotional impact is through mood boards, visuals of sample screens, typographic palettes, and sound libraries.

12.5.5 Detailed Design Iteration

In Fig. 12-10, we show the detailed design iteration, often called design production. You iterate on the details of the design and finalize screen and layout details, including "visual comps" of the "skin" for the look and feel appearance for each screen on each device type in the ecology.

The prototypes at this stage are usually detailed and annotated wireframes and/or high-fidelity interactive mockups. They include all user interface objects and data elements, represented with higher fidelity and annotated with call-out text.

As a parallel activity, a visual designer who has been involved in ideation, sketching, and conceptual design now produces what we call visual "comps," meaning variously comprehensive or composite layout (a term originating in the printing industry). All user interface elements are represented, now with a very specific and detailed graphical look and feel.

A visual comp is a pixel-perfect mockup of the graphical "skin," including objects, colors, sizes, shapes, fonts, spacing, and location, plus visual "assets" for

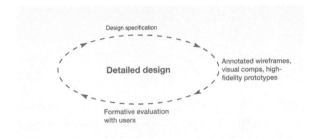

Fig. 12-10
Detailed design iteration.

user interface elements. An asset is a visual element along with all its defining characteristics as expressed in style definitions such as cascading style sheets for a website. The visual designer casts all of this to be consistent with company branding, style guides, and best practices in visual design.

At this stage, the design will be fully specified with complete descriptions of behavior, look and feel, and information on how all workflows, exception cases, and settings will be handled.

12.5.6 Design Refinement Iteration

The goal of the design refinement iteration is to make modifications, or adjust details of, the ecological, interaction, and emotional designs in response to findings from the formative evaluation (UX evaluation for the purpose of finding and fixing UX problems and thereby refining the design, Chapter 21) activity. In practice, if the previous iterations were conducted with the right amount of evaluation and involvement of key stakeholders, this phase usually does not result in drastic changes. This is also the last iteration within the UX lifecycle, before we merge into the larger SE+UX lifecycle (Chapter 29).

As part of this stage, the designs are presented to SE developers to get feedback about feasibility, platform constraints, etc., plus any necessary changes before an official "hand off" to them in the next phase.

12.5.7 SE Implementation

In this phase, the SE counterparts start the implementation. In early funnel, the UX output would be a large system-level specification. In late funnel, it would be at a feature level (see next section for more).

In practice, late-breaking constraints or unforeseen technical limitations may be discovered by the SE role that kick the design specifications back to the UX team. Depending on the severity of the issue, UX designers may need to make changes and go back to an earlier iteration stage. For deep system-level issues, the UX team might have to go as far back as revisiting the conceptual design decisions and make adjustments. The most common changes at this stage, however, tend to be at the detailed design level and require small adjustments.

12.5.8 UX Compliance Phase

After the SE role completes the implementation, the UX role checks the final implementation to ensure that SE faithfully implemented the UX design they were given in the "hand off." The objective of this phase is to ensure that there

Early Funnel

The part of the funnel (agile UX model) for large-scope activity, usually for conceptual design, before syncing with software engineering (Section 4.4.4).

Late Funnel

The part of the funnel (agile UX model) for small-scope activity, for syncing with agile software engineering sprints (Section 4.4.3).

were no misunderstandings and misinterpretations of the UX specifications as they got implemented. Any deviations from the specification will be caught and corrected in this phase before releasing to users.

12.6 DESIGN LIFECYCLE FOR THE AGILE UX FUNNEL

How does this design creation sublifecycle fit into the agile UX funnel concept we discussed in Section 4.4? In Fig. 12-11, we show another variation in the design sublifecycle: iteration in each slice of the agile UX funnel.

As you can see in the figure, designing each slice of functionality in the funnel entails an iteration of the steps in Fig. 12-6. Work in the early funnel addresses a global view of the product or system and, therefore, has a large (system-wide) scope. This translates to more time spent on the generative design and conceptual design phases because the decisions of these iterations will have a major impact on the later slices of the funnel.

As we progress to the narrower end of the funnel, the focus of generative design and other iterations will be on smaller slices of functionality (smaller scope features), further constrained by conceptual design decisions already made in previous slices.

Scope (of Delivery)

Describes how the target system or product is "chunked" (broken into what size pieces) in each iteration or sprint for delivery to the client and users for feedback and to the software engineering team for agile implementation (Section 3.3).

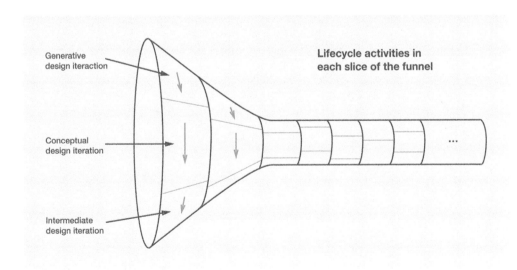

Fig. 12-11

Design creation sublifecycle in the agile UX funnel.

Bottom-Up Versus Top-Down Design

13

- Bottom-up design is designing for existing work practice.
- The role of biases and constraints in design.
- Abstract work activities.
- Top-down design is designing for an abstract work activity.
- Bottom-up design and top-down design are both appropriate in different situations.

13.1 INTRODUCTION

13.1.1 You Are Here

We begin each process chapter with a "you are here" picture of the chapter topic in the context of The Wheel, the overall UX design lifecycle template (Fig. 13-1). In this chapter, we set the stage for the Design Solutions UX design lifecycle activity.

Before we get to the next chapter on generative design, we discuss two quite different approaches to design creation: bottom-up design and top-down design.

13.2 BOTTOM-UP DESIGN: DESIGNING FOR EXISTING WORK PRACTICE

Bottom-up design is an approach to design that starts with the details known about the work domain, work practice, and how a product or system is being used and will be used. The design is then built up in a way that will support this known usage behavior.

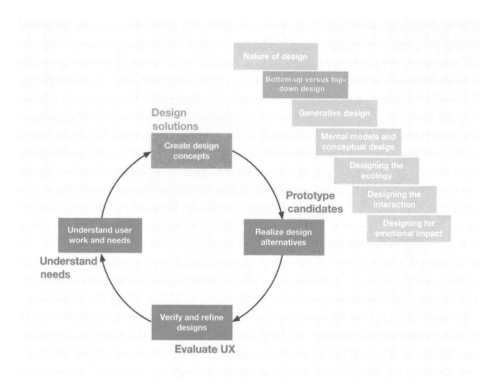

Fig. 13-1

You are here in the chapter describing two approaches to the subactivity of creating a UX design within the Design Solutions lifecycle activity, in the context of the overall Wheel UX lifecycle.

13.2.1 Recap of Our Process Steps Thus Far

So far in our discussion, the act of UX design covered the following steps:

- Project briefing and kick off: Client approaches design team with a "problem."
- Usage research data elicitation: Inquire into the users (e.g., work roles), the nature of work, artifacts used, challenges faced, and the breakdowns encountered.
- Usage research data analysis and modeling: Represent what designers learned about current work practice.
- Usage research user stories and requirements: Extracted actionable user needs to support in design.

13.2.2 The Process so far is Bottom Up

As the summary of the steps above shows, what we have done so far in this book is to immerse ourselves in the current work practice with the objective of designing a solution in a bottom-up way. We call this approach bottom up because we based all our investigations and analyses on data gathered from users in the existing work practice, avoiding other insights and inputs. We involved

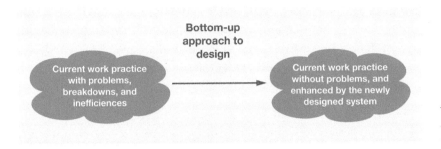

Fig. 13-2

Fig. 13-2

Nature of a bottom-up approach to UX design.

users (in the form of walkthroughs of the artifacts we produced) to ensure that what we are doing is consistent with the way they get work done.

This bottom-up approach is predominantly a translation exercise done through a series of transformations on a path from work activity notes to models to UX requirements to design. The premise is that these requirements, if met in the new design solution, will solve the problems of the users in this work practice, help users be more productive, and satisfy business mandates (Fig. 13-2).

13.2.3 Human-Centered Design or User-Centered Design: Common Names for Bottom-Up Design

"Human-centered design" (HCD) and "user-centered design" (UCD) are established terms in the discipline of human-computer interaction. "User-centered design" was coined by Norman and Draper back in 1986 (Norman & Draper, 1986). The plain English meaning of the term "user-centered design" puts the central focus of design on the user, which of course is true in some way for all approaches to UX design. No UX designer would deny this goal. So the term at face value does little to distinguish approaches.

But, as with so many other terms arising in the discipline, much more meaning is packed into the term by various researchers and practitioners.

To start with, HCD/UCD philosophy is based on understanding user needs and emphasizes empathy toward their goals and aspirations. It's about fitting technology to the user, rather than vice versa. As Wikipedia[1] defines it: UCD is "a framework of processes… in which the needs, wants, and limitations of end users of a product, service, or process are given extensive attention at each stage of the design process."

And many define HCD/UCD more in terms of a process than a focus on users. UCD is popularly characterized as being driven by usage research

> **Work Activity Note**
>
> A brief, clear, concise, and elemental (relating to exactly one concept, idea, fact, or topic) statement used to document a single point about the work practice as synthesized from raw usage research data (Section 8.1.2).

---

[1]https://en.wikipedia.org/wiki/User-centered_design.

(contextual inquiry (Beyer & Holtzblatt, 1998)), and guided by UX evaluation/testing. This means that most of what is known as UCD is about a bottom-up approach based on existing work practice. And, despite the word "design" being in the name, there is usually little emphasis on design.

13.2.4 Designing for Existing Work Practice is Practical

Bottom-up design, designing for existing work practice, is often the most practical approach. It does not create conflicts or friction with stakeholders because the introduction of the design solution only solves problems and removes breakdowns in the existing work practice. There are no disruptions in, or undue transformation of, how work currently gets done.

The philosophy underlying this approach is that users and current stakeholders are the experts in that work domain and they know best how work should be structured. We as designers are only to support that broader work structure with the solution we are introducing.

It is easy to understand why, when the discipline of HCI started, there was a strong push for user-centeredness. There was a need to get designers (who were all engineers at that time) to prioritize users and their needs over all else. The fear was that introducing ideas that are not substantiated by user data will take us to a place where designers create solutions that they think are good for users, but are in fact not.

This weight of history and tradition continues to exert great influence on even experienced designers in limiting their purview to creating solutions that support existing users and how they do work. As we move on to the discussion of constraints and biases, keep in mind that it is easier and more practical to just design something as called for by the initial design brief as compared to risking something boldly different.

13.2.5 The Role of Biases and Constraints

A bias in the UX design process is an influence on the data, how it is collected, or how it is viewed and analyzed, based on something the analyst knows outside the data.

13.2.5.1 Bias and inertia from existing usage and user preferences

When designing for the existing work practice, the ceiling is set through the lens of current user behavior and work practice, current revenue, current product, and current organizational biases and ways of doing things.

The bias of customer preference can subdue even an experienced designer's enthusiasm to adopt what they think is a better design. Going against such strong preference also goes against the "you are not the user" tenet and the need to have empathy toward users. And your whole team, the product people, the developers, and the sales specialists all need to be convinced as to why you are going with an idea that is counter to what users want.

Consider the example of the Blackberry smartphone. Before the introduction of the iPhone, the Blackberry phones were by far the market leaders in smartphones. While they were never known for their ease of use (in fact, they were pretty difficult to use with convoluted interaction patterns), they became the smartphone of choice in the corporate world. Their rise was predominantly due to three things: the first truly capable smartphone for a working professional, unbreakable security, and physical keyboards.

If Apple did usage research and analysis of existing work practice, they would have found a consistent and almost unanimous preference for a physical keyboard. This preference was so strong that it was widely reported that Blackberry users would never adopt the iPhone, considered by many to be a toy. It must have taken superhuman persuasive powers to convince the Apple design team, sales, engineering, and senior executives that, despite current preferences for the familiar, the touch paradigm is the future!

The designer who normally works in a framework of centering everything around satisfying customers and users will find it incredibly hard to not succumb to the biases and pressures of the usage data and other organizational and cultural trends in place.

And how does a designer know when it's the right thing to do, to break from relying entirely on usage research data about the existing work practice? It takes a special vision, a bold sense about the future, and an ability to close your eyes to risk. And, after all, what if the designers turn out to be wrong?

13.2.5.2 Bias and inertia from market success

When a product becomes successful and popular in the market, there is a natural tendency to stick with what works and continue that same line of design with incremental refinements over time. This introduces a design complacency that can block innovation. The downfall of Blackberry is a good example for existing market success acting as a bias against continuing to be innovative in design.

Perhaps the most striking example of this kind of bias is the case of Kodak, which was the market leader in film photography and the inventor of the digital camera. The work practice of film photography was less flexible and more expensive than the subsequent digital work practice, which allowed instantaneous feedback and an immediate opportunity to fix any problems.

But Kodak had bias and inertia from market success, so they didn't embrace the new digital technology. They couldn't bring themselves to risk their hugely successful business of selling the film, paper, and other supplies for film photography, a business that had been their bread and butter for almost a century. So they missed out on what could have been an amazing future. The rest, sadly, is history. Kodak is, for the most part, irrelevant in today's photography market.

13.2.5.3 Effects from advances in technology

Existing work practice is often limited by what was possible with yesterday's technology. Advances in technology can open up the work practice to a new world of usage possibilities. At the time of this writing, solid-state battery technology is just becoming a reliable power source and is beginning to upend traditional fuel sources in a wide range of devices, including home lawn mowers, snow blowers, recreation vehicles, and automobiles. But they are more expensive and difficult to get repaired compared to the ubiquitous internal combustion engines.

Of course, incremental advances in existing technology can hit a threshold point needed to make a product idea feasible, practical, and profitable. The iPhone and iPod were not the first attempts at these kinds of devices, but they emerged when advances in technology favored increased reliability of touchscreens, reduction of device size and weight, enhanced battery life, and greatly increased storage capacity.

13.2.6 Bottom-Up Design is Less Likely to Lead to Innovative Possibilities

While any introduction of a system into a work practice will change that practice, in bottom-up design it is only about changes to accommodate that system. It was never a goal of bottom-up design to see if the practice can or should be changed at a fundamental level.

13.3 ABSTRACT WORK ACTIVITIES

To create a new design that does more than just improve an existing work practice, we must approach the problem differently, from the top down. To understand this, we need to unpack the nature of work and work practice. In particular, much of the understanding of top-down design depends on the concept of an abstract work activity.

Abstract Work Activity

A description of the fundamental nature of work in a particular work domain, stripping it to its essentials (Section 13.3.2).

Top-Down Design

A UX design approach starting with abstract descriptions of work activities, stripped of information about existing work practice and working toward a best design solution independent of current perspectives and biases (Section 13.4).

13.3.1 Nature of Work and Work Practice

We have used the term "work practice" extensively in Part 2 (Understand Needs) of the book. As we have seen, the term work practice includes two aspects:

- The nature of what needs to be done.
- How it gets done.

The nature of what needs to be done. This is *the problem*, the essence of the work itself. It is a distillation and abstraction of why the work practice exists. It includes the end goal of the practice.

How this work gets done. This is the *solution*, a question of procedure and protocol that is shaped by factors such as tradition, history, regulations, constraints, available tools, business goals, culture, people, and evolution.

The nature of work might be similar in two different work sites, each with an entirely different work practice. To expand on this difference, we introduce the idea of an abstract work activity.

> **Abstraction**
>
> The process of removing extraneous details of something and focusing on its irreducible constructs to identify what is really going on, ignoring everything else (Section 14.2.8.2).

13.3.2 Abstract Work Activity

An abstract work activity is a description of the fundamental nature of a work activity in a particular domain, stripping it to its essentials. It is the essence of work in that domain involving only the central work roles, the simplest description without variations and modifications due to biases and constraints due to historical, business, political, or other influences.

It's about the work and not about work practice—the *what* of the work, not the *how*. For example, the abstract view of the act of voting is simply about people making choices among candidates.

13.3.3 Work Activity Instances

An abstract work activity can be instantiated into multiple different work practices. Each is one solution to the abstract work activity problem, one way of doing the work. It is how that work gets done in a given concrete context.

A work activity instance (work practice) is richer and more concrete, including all work roles, something we try to capture in those detailed and even overlapping models that we build during our user research phase.

13.3.4 Why is it Useful to Start Top-Down Design with Abstract Work Activities?

Abstract work activities are a useful way to start into top-down design by:

- Providing a clearer understanding of work.
- Illuminating possible design targets.

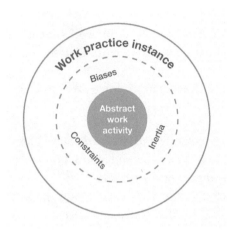

Fig. 13-3

The abstract work activity as work kernel.

13.3.4.1 Provide a clearer understanding of the essence of work

Abstract work activity descriptions help understand the work domain at a level where the layers of constraints and biases are removed. The process of describing the abstract work activity gets at the very kernel of the work (Fig. 13-3).

13.3.4.2 Illuminate possible design targets

A bottom-up design approach will generally lead to a design target supporting existing work practice. Top-down design will generally lead to design targets with the potential for radically different work practice (Fig. 13-4).

13.4 TOP-DOWN DESIGN: DESIGNING FOR THE ABSTRACT WORK ACTIVITY

In a top-down UX design approach, you start with abstract descriptions of work activities, stripped of information about existing work practice and work toward a best design solution independent of current perspectives and biases.

13.4.1 Top-Down Design Goal

In top-down UX design creation, the goal is to create the best design solution that enhances and supports the fundamental nature of work irrespective of current practices, preferences, traditions, or constraints. The primary driver in the top-down approach to design is the designer and the designer's knowledge, skills, experience, and intuition.

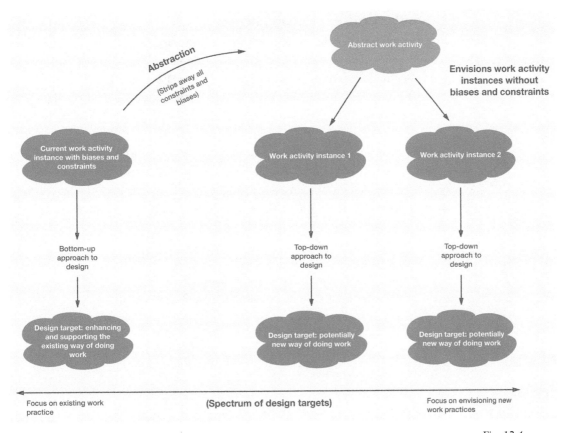

Fig. 13-4

*Different design targets:
Bottom-up design based on
existing work practice
versus top-down design
based on an abstract work
activity description.*

As a general matter, however, user/work/usage/domain knowledge still can
be, and is, used to inform design creation but does not *drive* the process. Both
approaches need usage research, but it is used in different ways:

- In bottom-up design, usage research is to analyze and model the existing work practice to
  improve it.
- In top-down design, usage research is to formulate and understand the abstract
  conceptualization of underlying essentials of the work.

Example: Voting in a Democracy

Imagine a business brief to design a voting booth for the state of Virginia in the United States. The state is in the process of updating their systems and is interested in going digital with touchscreen voting booths. This is a typical design brief where a client asks for a solution to support or solve specific problems facing a known practice.

The bottom-up approach: Designing for the existing work practice. In a bottom-up approach, we would conduct usage research studies of voting with election booths to understand the current voting work practice in Virginia. We create work activity affinity diagrams, flow models, and other models to describe:

- Prevoting preparation:
    - How citizens register to vote.
    - How they find the nearest voting stations.
    - What they need when they show up at the voting stations.
- The onsite configuration:
    - How voting booths are set up.
    - How voters interact with the booths.
- The workflow of voting:
    - Voter identification.
    - Checking voters off the rolls.
    - Guiding voters to the appropriate booths.
- Postvoting follow-up:
    - Counting ballots.
    - Combining tallies from all sites.
    - Announcing winners.

The design activity focuses on specifics of this particular work practice:

- Physical design of the voting booth.
- Clear labels on the touchscreen, accessibility issues with the booth, color contrasts and other sensory issues, ergonomics of the booth, error avoidance and recovery in case of user mistakes during voting, materials for the booth, etc.
- Making sure it all fits with the already established ecology.

The top-down approach. Using a top-down approach based on an abstract work activity, we would:

- Focus on designing the best way to get eligible users to elect someone from a list of candidates.

Work Activity Affinity Diagram (WAAD)

A hierarchical bottom-up technique for organizing disparate pieces of data, used to sort and organize work activity notes in usage research analysis, pulling together work activity notes with similarities and common themes to highlight common work patterns and shared strategies across all users (Section 8.7).

Flow Model

A simple graphical diagram giving a big picture or overview of work by representing how information, artifacts, and work products flow among work roles and system components within the work practice of an organization (Section 9.5).

Ecology

In the setting of UX design, the ecology is the entire set of surrounding parts of the world, including networks, other users, devices, and information structures, with which a user, product, or system interacts (Section 16.2.1).

- Bring into consideration all ways, including voting booths, to make this work happen.
- Consider a smartphone app or a website to vote from the comfort of the home?
- Or a 1-800 number where citizens can call and cast their votes?
- An Internet-connected device in the home that could be used for voting and that could also be used for other expressions of opinions, including petitions, surveys, and likes or dislikes of products.
- Allow for possibilities where citizens can vote over a period of time leading up to a deadline.
- Even provides for flexibility, allowing citizens to change their vote after it is cast up to the deadline—something mail-in ballots do not allow:
  - Perhaps new information about a candidate was unearthed in the interim.
- Emphasize designing for a very different envisioned ecology (in fact, defining the ecology is part of the design).
- Design for the interaction (workflows, etc.), information needs (for example, full display of candidates and their party affiliations, which offices a given voter can cast ballots for, full description of each side of all issues and proposals up for a vote) and emotional needs after ecological design is completed.

Abstraction redirects designer thinking. Many questions can be uncovered by this new way of thinking of work. Designing for the abstract work activity can result in a system that is significantly better at supporting the act of voting. It even questions the need for a voting booth. Whereas in the bottom-up case, the discussion for the most part centered on one particular way of casting a vote.

Although it is almost certainly apocryphal, Henry Ford is reputed to have once said, "If I'd asked people what they wanted, they would have asked for a better (or faster) horse." Regardless of the pedigree of attribution, the quote does point out the lack of regard Ford had for bottom-up inputs from customers and, to an extent, his genius at top-down design.

Indeed, cars have become much more than highly improved horses and carriages and, through a shift in technology and lots of design, more than even horseless carriages. Ford knew to interpret what the users were saying not as needs and not as design solutions but as inputs to inform and inspire a new concept.

The point of this example is to illustrate how thinking of the abstract work activity provides a different design target than that of a specific work activity instance.

13.4.2 Characteristics of Top-Down Design

Top-down design can be perceived as visionary. Because top-down designs are not constrained by current work practice, they can turn out startlingly different and even futuristic designs, which shows how top-down design can be visionary.

Ecological Design

Design that pertains to the foundational layer of the needs pyramid, focused on designing for the overarching system needs of users and how they are supported in broader work practice. Includes designing for activities, the flow, sharing, and communication within the network of devices, other users, systems, and a pervasive information infrastructure (Section 16.2.1).

Abstraction

The process of removing extraneous details of something and focusing on its irreducible constructs to identify what is really going on, ignoring everything else (Section 14.2.8.2).

Top-down design is heavily driven by domain knowledge. Designers need extensive domain knowledge to be able to abstract the nature of work in that domain. This usually translates to the need for designers to envision multiple work activity instances in that domain.

Being a potential user in the domain is good for a designer. An important factor in the success of Apple designers practicing top-down design is the fact that they could see themselves as users of the iPod and iPad, etc.

Another example of a domain in which designers can see themselves as users is photography. To design a photo editing and management application, it would help, perhaps even be essential, for designers to be experts in photography and even avid users of such a product, which would help with immersion necessary to be able to creatively think about the problem.

13.4.3 Top-Down Design is not Always Practical

Sometimes, however, constraints, conventions, regulations, history, and traditions that we discussed as biases in Section 13.2.6 can be too difficult to overcome in practice. They may even be decreed by law.

Business constraints can take priority. As an example of business "constraints," all parties that benefit from the current practice such as the booth vendors, the electronic voting machine manufacturers, and perhaps even the candidates on the ballot will resist any new ideas.

Can conflict with human comfort from familiarity. Humans are not naturally open to drastic changes. It unsettles and perturbs comfortable routines and practices. Our evolutionary biology prefers harmony and consistency to change and disruption.

Can work against short-term goals. Because of the upheaval of the work practice, designing for the abstract work activity usually results in disruption. It can be more expensive and take longer to introduce. This flies directly in the face of the unyielding push toward shorter-term returns and the reluctance to tackle larger projects, a mindset of business these days.

Technology constraints can limit innovation. Sometimes the requisite technology is not quite ready. UX designers must do a thorough exploration of the available technology (Gajendar, 2012).

13.4.4 Easing the Transition for Customers and Users

Tread carefully; ease potential trauma. Redesigning work practice can be traumatic to clients and users who value stability and naturally resist change. And that can put you in a position of defending your plans to all stakeholders.

You are changing something important in the lives of clients and users, taking them dramatically, and even traumatically, out of their comfort zones, which can be chaotic, disruptive, expensive, and offputting for employees. Tread with care and respect. You *have* to get buy-in before proceeding.

13.4.5 Hedging Against Risks of Top-Down Design

In top-down design, you need to be cautious because you have to recognize the high risk (and high potential for a huge payoff). You need to hedge against the risk through follow-up validation activities, such as usage research, prototyping, and evaluation to get user feedback early and often.

13.4.6 Extreme Top-Down Design is the Path to Disruptive Design

Top-down design can be disruptively innovative. The top-down approach carries a high risk because the envisioned solution may not be embraced by existing users because of the potential disruption to their work practice. Sometimes, when a design comes along at the right time and place in such a way that the benefits of going through the upheaval outweigh the discomfort of going through change, it becomes a disruptive idea that moves the status quo to the next step in the innovation ladder. Therefore, top-down design sometimes results in an innovative next-generation product (e.g., the iPod) where bottom-up design would have ended up solving problems people don't even yet know they have (Moore, 2017). Another way to put it is a good bottom-up design fills a niche, but a good top-down design can *create* a niche.

Example: Top-Down Design in Architecture

Frank Lloyd Wright serves as an archetypal example of a disruptive top-down design practitioner in architecture. He was supremely confident that he, as designer, knew best what was good for the user. Wright and Kevin Costner agree, "If you build it, they will come." Wright took top-down design to the extreme. It was no longer about what users thought: "I don't build a house without predicting the end of the present social order. Every building is a missionary... It's their [the users] duty to understand, to appreciate, and conform insofar as possible to the idea of the house" (Lubow, 2009).

Generative Design: Ideation, Sketching, and Critiquing

14

In the beginning the Universe was created. This has made a lot of people very angry and been widely regarded as a bad move.

– Douglas Adams, The Restaurant at the End of the Universe

Highlights

- Preparing for design via immersion.
- The role of synthesis.
- Ideas: the building blocks of design.
- Ideation:
  - Ideation informers.
  - Ideation catalysts.
  - Ideation techniques.
- Sketching.
- Critiquing.
  - Rules of engagement.

14.1 INTRODUCTION

14.1.1 You Are Here

We begin each process chapter with a "you are here" picture of the chapter topic in the context of The Wheel, the overall UX design lifecycle template (Fig. 14-1). In this chapter, we get into the UX design process, starting with generative design or design creation.

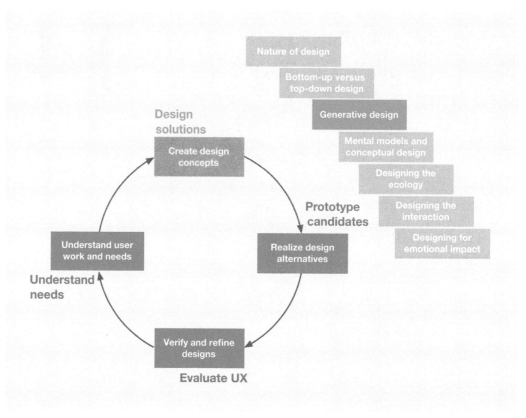

Fig. 14-1

You are here in the chapter on the subactivity of creating UX designs within the Design Solutions lifecycle activity, in the context of the overall Wheel UX lifecycle.

In this chapter we describe processes, methods, and techniques relating to design creation. The overarching objective of design creation is to formulate a plan for how the system will be structured to satisfy the ecological, interaction, and emotional needs of users (Section 12.3).

Compared to the usage research in Part 2, design is a less procedural and a more creative activity. While usage research was about observation and understanding things as they currently are, design is about lateral thinking and generating new ideas to make things better.

14.1.2 Preparing for Design Creation: Immersion

Designers, like usage researchers, need immersion—a form of deep thought and analysis—to understand a problem and to be able to make connections among the different aspects of it.

To set the stage for ideation, immerse yourself within a design-support milieu, a "war room" of working artifacts as inputs and inspiration to ideation. Get it all out there in front of you to point to, discuss, and critique. Fill your walls, shelves, and work tables with artifacts, representations of ideas, images, props, toys, notes, posters, sketches, diagrams, mood boards, and images of other good designs.

Immersion starts by getting reacquainted with all the models and inputs to design we created during usage research. It is a prerequisite to participating in activities for generating new ideas and concepts.

Now the UX studio really shines. The UX studio (Section 5.3) is a good way to house your immersive environment. The different artifacts trigger ideas and bring to surface the connections and relationships among various entities in the work domain. Any questions designers may have about the work domain can be readily answered by walking up to the appropriate model on the studio walls. The very context of a design studio puts you in a creative frame of mind.

Mood Board

A collage of artifacts and images showcasing a theme of emotional impact to be embraced within a UX design (Section 18.3.2.1).

14.1.3 The Role of Synthesis

At its base, design is an approach to problem solving based on synthesis, which involves integrating disparate inputs and insights; satisfying a variety of technical, business, and cultural constraints; achieving a variety of stakeholder goals; managing tradeoffs; etc., to create a single unified design.

It's about putting together known or existing ideas in new ways to form new concepts. While an analytic approach can suffice to improve existing designs, synthesis is required to make the leap to brand new ideas. Design synthesis is "… the epitome of the breakthrough idea, the ability to pull together disconnected ideas and arrive at something new and meaningful" (Baty, 2010).

Synthesis

The process of integrating diverse inputs, facts, insights, and observations of parts of a concept to make conclusions that characterize and aid understanding of the whole concept (Section 8.9).

14.1.4 Overview of Generative Design: Intertwining of Ideation, Sketching, and Critiquing

Following immersion into usage data and the synthesis of other design inputs, designers perform *generative design, an approach to design creation involving ideation, sketching, and critiquing in a tightly coupled, but not necessarily structured, iterative loop for exploring a design idea* (Fig. 14-2).

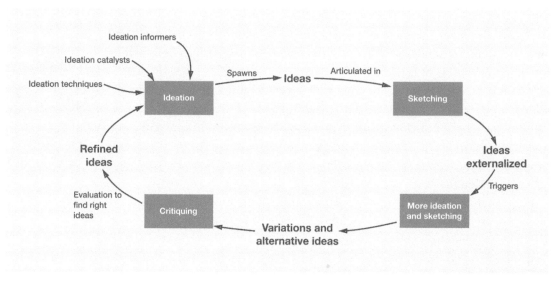

Fig. 14-2

Ideation, sketching, and critiquing activities for exploring design ideas.

These generative design activities include:

- Ideation: The activity where ideas are spawned. A cognitive technique to create varying and innovative design possibilities (Section 14.2).
- Sketching: An externalization activity that captures those ideas in concrete representations (Section 14.3).
- Critiquing: An analysis activity to evaluate the emergent design ideas for tradeoffs (Section 14.4).
- Refining: An activity (usually iterative) where ideas are adopted, modified, or discarded.

When people think of ideation they also think of the term "brainstorming," which is another term for this process of ideation, sketching, and critiquing. And, even though we describe these activities separately for clarity, they are inextricably intertwined and occur as a rapid iteration of tightly coupled and overlapping activities, often essentially performed simultaneously. Each of these activities supports and stimulates the others.

For example, the activity of sketching is a simple and immediate way to capture an idea, which in itself can incite further ideas. A sketch gives something tangible to refer to in discussion (critiquing). Similarly, the postulation (genesis) of an idea, for example, is often followed by a burst of reasoning or analysis (critiquing).

14.2 IDEATION

14.2.1 The Creative Role of Ideation in Design

If the roof doesn't leak, the architect hasn't been creative enough.

– Frank Lloyd Wright (Donohue, 1989)

Ideation is the most important generative aspect of design; it is the leading edge of the act of creation. Ideation is the process of creating various and innovative proposals for ecological, interaction, and emotional designs. This is a hugely creative and fun phase.

Diversity in the design team helps with ideation because it brings varied perspectives. If only team members with similar backgrounds participate in ideation, they will bring to the table only ideas, concepts, and constructs from that background and experience.

Ideation is the time to get clients and users to participate, too. There have been a number of participatory design (Muller, 2003) schemes in the past to actively involve all stakeholders to get the broadest range of design ideas and to be sure all needs are considered. For more about participatory design and its history in human-computer interaction, see Section 19.2.

14.2.2 Ideas: The Building Blocks of Design
14.2.2.1 What is an idea?

In this context, *an idea is a visualized design proposal that can include visions of new ecologies, interactions, emotional responses, and capabilities in a system or product.*

Ideas are conjured by the human mind or borrowed from observations of nature, and are triggered by focused activity or unexpected catalysts. For example, looking at a breakdown in a flow model can trigger ideas on how to circumvent or mitigate it. Similarly, looking at an inspiring image or artifact in the design studio can trigger a new idea about colors or graphics for the visual design of a product.

Sometimes ideas occur as "eureka moments," springing up at unexpected places and unexpected times. They can even occur when we are not actively seeking them (during idea "incubation").

Whatever their provenance, ideas by their very nature are delicate and need to be cultivated to grow. They need to be captured as soon as they occur or they may be lost forever. And they need to be nurtured. Without an environment or culture of openness, ideas can be cut down by premature judgment.

Participatory Design

A democratic process for UX design actively involving all stakeholders (e.g., employees, partners, customers, citizens, users) to help ensure that the result meets their needs and is usable. Based on the argument that users should be involved in designs they will be using, and that all stakeholders, including and especially users, have equal input into UX design (Section 11.3.4).

Incubation

Continuation of work in the background by the brain on a problem during a break after a period of deep thinking about the problem. Can result in fresh perspectives after returning to focus on the problem (Section 14.2.8.4).

Ideas can work together to generate a single design concept. For example, having a circular ring that is touch sensitive is an idea. Using that ring to scroll through a list of items is another idea. These two ideas were instantiated into a design feature on the iPod Classic.

And finally, some ideas can be reused in different situations; we call such ideas design patterns.

14.2.3 Ideation Scope

In the early part of the agile UX funnel, ideation is usually wide in scope because the goal is to create the overarching conceptual designs for the entire system. In the latter part of the funnel, ideation can be localized to focus on the designs for a particular sprint. The constraints of the broader conceptual design and what was delivered in previous sprints usually reduce the scope of ideation during these latter sprints.

14.2.4 Ideation Informers, Catalysts, and Techniques

There are three types of inputs to ideation (Fig. 14-2): ideation informers, catalysts, and techniques (Sections 2.4–2.6 and 14.2.4).

Ideation informers. Ideation informers provide information about usage, requirements, targets, and goals, and are part of immersion. Ideation informers are not building blocks; you don't just take them and put them together to make a design. Rather, they inform by pointing to design-oriented aspects, such as task descriptions or user personas, to consider or take into account in the design. Ideation informers are usually derived from the usage research data as a process step and manifest themselves as usage data models and, possibly, an affinity diagram of work activity notes (Section 8.7). See Section 14.2.4 for more on ideation informers.

Ideation catalysts. In contrast, ideation catalysts are design inspirers, design-oriented flashes that inspire creative design solutions. A catalyst in general is something that precipitates an event or change without itself being affected or changed. An ideation catalyst is not something a designer can do; it just happens and that happening can spawn a new design idea. See Section 14.2.4 for more on ideation catalysts.

Ideation techniques. In contrast, an ideation technique is something a designer can do to foster the spawning or nurturing of a design idea. Brainstorming, framing, and storytelling are examples of ideation techniques. See Section 14.2.8 for more on ideation techniques.

14.2.5 Doing Ideation

Setting the stage with immersion. As we said in Section 14.1.2, immerse yourself within a design-support milieu.

Ideation as a group activity. Even though ideation can be performed by designers on their own, it can be more effective when undertaken as a group with members from different backgrounds. When undertaken as a group activity, it is a common to start with an overview discussion to establish background and parameters and agreement on goals of the ideation exercise.

Mechanics of ideation. The goal here is to have intense rapid interactions to spawn and accumulate large numbers of ideas about characteristics and features. Write ideas on a whiteboard or use marking pens on flip charts. Or write your ideas on sheets of paper so that you can move them around to organize them.

Start with the ideation. The social, flow, artifact, and physical models are all visual, which makes them ideal for informing and inspiring design. We suggest that you organize some of your ideation sessions around each of these models by making each the focal point of design thinking and ideation before moving on to the next.

Proceed to ideation techniques. For example, ask yourself what the design would create if you had a magic wand. Look at the abstract work activity to see what ideas it triggers.

Use teamwork and play off each other's ideas while "living the part of the user." Talk in scenarios, keeping customers and users in the middle, telling stories of their experience as your team weaves a fabric of new ideas for design solutions.

Make the outputs of your ideation as visual and tangible as possible. Intersperse an outline with sketches, sketches, and more sketches. Post and display everything all around the room as your visual working context. Where appropriate, build physical mockups as embodied sketches. You can include examples of other systems, conceptual ideas, considerations, design features, marketing ideas, and experience goals. Get all your whacky, creative, and off-the-wall ideas out there. The flow should be a mix of verbal and visual.

When the fountain of new ideas seems to have run dry for the moment, the group can switch to critiquing mode.

Example: Ideation at IDEO

In IDEO's "deep dive" approach, a cross-disciplinary group works in total immersion without consideration of rank or job title. In their modus operandi of focused chaos (not organized chaos), "enlightened trial and error succeeds over

---

Ideation Informer

Informative inputs to design that help establish designs appropriate to the work practice, including all the usage research data models and user personas (Section 14.2.6).

Design Thinking

The mindset of getting organizations to think like designers; applying design principles and practice to businesses and business processes (Section 1.8.1).

Ideation

An active, creative, exploratory, highly iterative, fast-moving, and usually collaborative brainstorming process for forming ideas for design (Section 14.2).

Abstract Work Activity

A description of the fundamental nature of work in a particular work domain, stripping it to its essentials (Section 13.3.2).

Physical Mockup

A tangible, three-
dimensional prototype or
model of a physical device
or product, often one that
can be held in the hand
and often crafted rapidly
out of materials at hand,
used during exploration
and evaluation to at least
simulate physical
interaction
(Section 20.6.1).

Critiquing

An activity in which design
ideas are assessed to
identify advantages,
disadvantages,
constraints, and tradeoffs
(Section 14.4).

the planning of lone genius." Their designing process was illustrated in a well-known *ABC News* documentary (ABC News Nightline, 1999) with a new design for supermarket shopping carts, starting with a brief user research inquiry where team members visited different stores to understand the work domain of shopping and issues with existing shopping cart designs and use.

Then, in an abbreviated user research analysis process, they regrouped and engaged in debriefing, synthesizing different themes that emerged in their user research inquiry. This analysis fed parallel brainstorming sessions in which they captured all ideas, however unconventional. At the end of this stage they indulged in another debriefing session, combining the best ideas from brainstorming to assemble a design prototype. This alternation of brainstorming, prototyping, and review, driven by their "failing often to succeed sooner" philosophy, is a good approach for anyone wishing to create a good user experience.

Example: Ideation for the Ticket Kiosk System

We brainstormed with potential ticket buyers, students, MU representatives, and civic leaders. Here we show selected results of that ideation session with our Ticket Kiosk System design team as a consolidated list with related categories in the spirit of "verbal sketching." As in any ideation session, ideas were accompanied with sketches. We show the idea part of the session here separately to focus on the topic of this section.

Thought questions to get started:

What does "an event" mean? How do people treat events in real life?

An event is more than something that happens and maybe you attend.

An event can have emotional meanings, can be thought provoking, can have meaning that causes you to go out and do something.

Data artifacts:

Tickets, events, event sponsors, MU student ID, kiosk.

Things people might want to do with tickets:

People might want to email tickets to friends.

Possible features and breadth of coverage:

We might want to feature customized tickets for keepsake editions.

Homecoming events.

Parents weekend events.

Visiting speakers on current topics.

Visitor's guide to what's happening in town and the university.

Christmas tour of Middleburg.

View Christmas decorations on historic homes.

Walk Main Street to see decorations and festive shops.

Types of events:

Action movies, comedy (plays, stand-up), concerts, athletic events, specials.

Special themes and motifs:

Motif for the Ticket Kiosk System could be "Adventures in Entertainment," which would show up in the physical design (the shape, images and colors, the aesthetic appearance) of the kiosk itself and would carry through to the metaphor pervading the screen, dialogue, buttons, and so on in the interaction design.

Complete theme package: Football game theme: brunch, tailgating parties, game tickets, postgame celebrations over drinks at select places in town, followed by a good football movie.

Date night theme: Dinner and a movie, restaurant ads with movie/event tickets, proximity information and driving/public transportation directions, romantic evening, flowers from D'Rose, dinner at Chateau Morrisette, tour some of the setting for the movie *Dirty Dancing*, stroll down Draper Road under a full moon (calendar and weather driven), watch *Dirty Dancing* at The Lyric Theater, tickets for late-night wine tasting at The Vintage Cellar, wedding planner consultation (optional).

Business consideration:

Because it is a college town, if we make a good design, it can be reused in other college towns.

Competition: Because we are up against ubiquitous websites, we have to make the kiosk experience something way beyond what you can get on a website.

Emotional impact:

Emotional aspect about good times with good friends.

Emphasize MU team spirit, logos, etc.

Entertainment event tickets are a gateway to fun and adventure.

Combine social and civic participation.

Indoor locations could have immersive themes with video and surround sound.

Immersive experience: For example, indoor kiosk (where security is less of a problem) at the University Mall, offer an experience "they cannot refuse," support with surrounding immersive visuals and audio, ATM-like installation with wraparound display walls and surround sound, between ticket buyers, run preview of theme and its mood.

Minority Report style UIs.

Rock concerts for group euphoria.

Monster trucks or racing: ambience of power and noise, appeals to the more primal instincts and thrill-seeking.

Metaphor

An analogy used in design to communicate and explain unfamiliar concepts using familiar conventional knowledge. A central metaphor often becomes the theme of a product, the motif behind the conceptual design (Section 15.3.6).

Other desired impact:

Part of university and community "family."

Ride on the emerging visibility of and talent at MU.

Collective success and pride.

Leverage different competencies of MU and community technologies.

Patron-of-the-arts feeling: classiness, sophistication, erudition, feeling special.

Community outreach:

Create public service arrangements with local government (e.g., could help advertise and sell T-shirts for annual street art fair).

Advertise adult education opportunities, martial arts classes, kids camps, art and welding courses.

Ubiquitous locations:

Bus stops.

Library.

Major dorms.

Student center.

City Hall building.

Shopping malls.

Food courts.

Inside buses.

Major academic and administrative buildings.

Design Thinking

The mindset of getting organizations to think like designers, applying design principles and practice to businesses and business processes (Section 1.8.1).

Exercise 14-1: Ideation About Aircraft Flight Recorders

This is a team design thinking exercise, so gather into your team, go to a quiet place (your UX studio, if you have one) and start ideation and sketching, using what you know of the domain.

When planes crash, we often hear that the flight recorder box, which has the most recent flight and pilot data on magnetic tape, is the key to understanding the cause. However, we also often hear that the flight recorder box cannot be found or is found in damaged condition.

Taking into account available technology and the broadest context and ecosystem in which planes and flight recorders operate, come up with a conceptual design of a much better way to do it.

14.2.6 Ideation Informers

Ideation informers are informative inputs to design that help establish designs appropriate to the work practice. They include all the usage research data models and user personas.

14.2.6.1 User work roles

User work roles help identify the types of users and work that the design should support and a way to carve out subsystems in the overall ecology. For example, the ticket buyer work role and the event manager work role help designers think of two separate designs and capabilities. The work these two roles do has almost no overlap and consequently the designs for these roles will not either. This points to two subsystems that need to be built, each with different interaction designs and emotional impact aspects but sharing the same overall ecology.

14.2.6.2 Personas

We talked about constructing personas in Section 7.5.4.1. Personas work best to channel the act of creation toward supporting a particular archetype of a work role in the work domain. Without personas, the inputs designers need to deal with could be overwhelming and often competing or contradictory.

Where personas work best. Personas work best in design situations where the work domain is broad and unconstrained (i.e., projects on the left side of the system complexity space of Fig. 3.1). When personas are used in designing commercial products or systems in such situations, they help account for the nuances and activities in the personal lives of the various work roles.

In such systems, personas provide inferences that take the conclusion a bit beyond just what is explicit in the raw data. For example, Mary is a very busy 35-year-old soccer mom who balances the management of three kids, a household, and a career. You know immediately that a design solution for a calendar management app, for example, cannot require her to focus for long periods, sitting in front of a computer. The solution needs to have mobile components and we need to include various kinds of alerts (calendar alarms, text messages) because she is already overstretched in terms of time management and will be at risk of forgetting important calendar events responsibilities.

Goals for using personas in design. As we will see, designers often come up with more than one possible user persona for a work role (Cooper, 2004). The idea behind designing for these multiple personas is that the design must make the primary persona very happy while not making any of the selected personas unhappy. Buster will love it and it still works satisfactorily for the others.

Personas also provide inputs into emotional aspects because they describe personal traits and preferences of users.

Personas also provide a way to evaluate whether the design matches the target user. It is a concrete way of level setting as we develop designs. It is a way to check evolving design plans.

Using personas in design. Start by making your design as though Rachel, your primary persona, is the only user. Team members tell stories about how Rachel would handle a given usage situation. As more and more of her stories are told, Rachel becomes more real and more useful as a medium for conveying requirements.

In Fig. 14-3, let us assume that we have chosen persona P3 as the primary persona out of four selected candidate personas. Because Design(P3) is a design specific to just P3, Design(P3) will work perfectly for P3. Now we have to make adjustments to Design(P3) to make it suffice for P1.

Then, in turn, we adjust it to suffice for P2 and P4. As you converge on the final design, the nonprimary personas will be accounted for via Design(P1), Design(P2), and Design(P4), but will defer to the primary persona, Design (P3), in case of conflict. If there is a design tradeoff, you will resolve the tradeoff to benefit the primary persona and still make it work for the other selected personas.

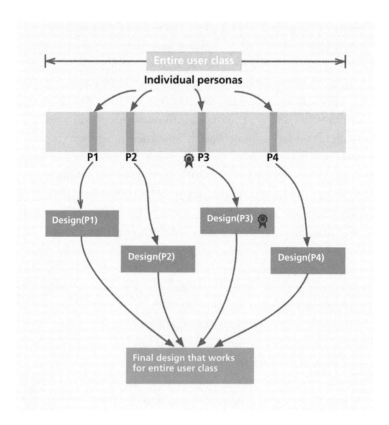

Fig. 14-3

Adjusting a design for the primary persona to work for all the selected personas.

Example: Cooper's In-Flight Entertainment System

Cooper (2004, p. 138) describes the successful use of personas in a Sony design project for an in-flight entertainment system called P@ssport. In addition to the work roles for system maintenance and the flight attendants who set up and operate the entertainment system, the main users are passengers on flights. We call this main work role the Traveler.

The user population that takes on the role of Traveler is just about the broadest possible population you can imagine, including essentially all the people who travel by air—almost everyone. Users will have very diverse characteristics. Cooper showed how the use of personas helped mitigate the breadth, vagueness, and openness of the various Traveler user class characteristics.

You could come up with dozens or more personas to represent the Traveler, but in that project the team got it down to four personas, each very different. Three were quite specialized to match the characteristics of a particular type of traveler while the fourth was more general: An older guy who was not technology savvy and was not into exploring user interface structures or features—essentially the opposite of most of the characteristics of the other personas.

They considered designs for each of the first three personas, but none of those designs would have worked for the fourth. In the end, they came up with an initial design for the fourth persona and then adapted it to work well for all the other personas without sacrificing its effectiveness for the target persona.

Exercise 14-2: Creating a User Persona for Your System

Goal: Get some experience at writing a persona.

Activities: Select an important work role within your system. At least one user class for this work role must be very broad, with the user population coming from a large and diverse group such as the general public.

- Using your user-related contextual data, create a persona, give it a name, and get a photo to go with it.
- Write the text for the persona description.

Deliverables: One- or two-page persona write-up.

Schedule: You should be able to do what you need to learn from this in about an hour.

14.2.6.3 Flow models and physical models

Flow models and, in some cases, physical models, provide insights into envisioning a new ecology for the work practice. Using them as guides, look for ideas to eliminate flows, roles, and redundant data entry. For those flows that cannot be eliminated, look for ideas to make them more efficient and to avoid ecology-level breakdowns and constraints.

14.2.6.4 Activity-based interaction and design

As we said in Section 1.6.2, an activity is one or more task thread(s), a set or possibly sequences of multiple overlapping tasks that go together in a way they is seen in real usage. It can involve a set of related tasks performed on one device or interaction across devices in the user's ecology.

Look at activity-based interaction for ideas to support workflows that span multiple devices in the ecology. For each device in the ecology, look for interaction design ideas. For example, what is the best way for a user to "access" event tickets? Does it require interacting with physical tickets or can the user somehow get them on their phones? What are some ideas for the buyer to pay for the tickets?

14.2.6.5 Task structure and sequence models

Look in these models for ideas for interaction design flows. What are different ways to support the different tasks in a sequence model? How should the design support interruption of a sequence? What are the best interaction design patterns for each task sequence in these models?

From the task interaction models, look for ideas to reduce and automate steps while avoiding redundant data entry and unnecessary physical motions.

These models can also provide clues toward emotional design concerns. For example, for repetitive and monotonous tasks, think of ideas such as gamification and positive reinforcement with task milestones in the interaction design.

14.2.6.6 Artifact model

Look at the artifacts in the artifact model and design requirements (Chapter 10). Identify metaphors that can relate the system to the artifacts people see and use daily in the work practice.

In Section 7.5.4.1, we talked about the student team that collected restaurant order-form artifacts. They can be a great start for an ideation exercise by asking questions such as: How can we make the experience for the customer placing an order in the restaurant more fun, engaging, and informed? Wouldn't it be cool if each dining table contained an embedded interactive touch screen? Diners can even browse the menu or read the biosketch of the new chef. Users could also pass time by playing games or surfing the web.

This interactive table feature can also help overcome an important problem in ordering food: Textual descriptions on a paper menu don't convey what the eating experience will be like. Paper menus do not leverage the potentially rich human sensual connection to the food! Why not let the customer, using an interactive tabletop, ask questions about ingredients and see images of the dish being served? Then it's only a small step to let customers place their orders themselves.

14.2.6.7 Information architecture model

An information object is an internally stored, structured or simple, article or piece of information or data that serves as a work object. Information objects are often data entities central to work flow being operated on by users; they are organized, shared, labeled, navigated, searched and browsed for, accessed and displayed, modified and manipulated, and stored back again, all within a system ecology.

Look for all the information objects in the current work practice that need to be managed in the design. As these information objects move within the envisioned ecology, they are accessed and manipulated by people in various work roles. In an enterprise human resources application, for example, information objects might be employee work history forms and other objects such as paychecks that are created, modified, and processed by users. Look for ideas on how to structure the various information objects in the design (i.e., ideas for the information architecture of the objects). Think about what kinds of operations or manipulations will be performed.

What are the different points in the ecology where a certain information object will be accessed? What aspects of that object will be preserved in each of the devices in the ecology? This is where you start defining it and laying out the information structure for the ecology. This is called pervasive information architecture (Resmini & Rosati, 2011), which provides ever-present information availability across devices, users, and other parts of a broad ecology.

14.2.6.8 Social models

Look for ideas to help with emotional needs. What are some concerns and issues you identified with the culture and inter-actor influences in the work practice? Think of ideas to mitigate them in the design. In your user research data, look for work activity notes about places in the work practice that are drudgery so you can invent fun ways to overcome these feelings. Use these issues as springboards to your design scenarios, sketches, and storyboarding. Find ways, using the social model as a guide, to increase communication, reinforce positive values, address concerns of people in work roles, and accommodate influences.

System-Spanning Interaction

A kind of activity-based interaction, often involving multiple parties in multiple work/play roles, multiple devices, and multiple locations (Section 1.6.3).

Artifact Model

A representation showing how users employ, manipulate, and share key tangible objects (physical or electronic work practice artifacts) as part of the flow in their work practice (Section 9.8).

Work Artifact

An object, usually tangible, that plays a role in the work flow of a system or enterprise—for example, a printed receipt in a restaurant (Section 9.8).

Metaphor

An analogy used in design to communicate and explain unfamiliar concepts using familiar conventional knowledge. A central metaphor often becomes the theme of a product, the motif behind the conceptual design (Section 15.3.6).

14.2.6.9 Requirements

In Chapter 10, we talked about capturing design requirements from the usage research data. The statement of a requirement in itself can trigger or inform a design idea. How do other systems support such a requirement? What are some problems or downsides with such an idea. Is there a better idea to support that requirement?

14.2.7 Ideation Catalysts

Ideation catalysts are phenomena that incite the creation of ideas. An ideation catalyst is not something a designer can willfully plan for and do, but something that arises spontaneously, possibly from brainstorming or storytelling. A catalyst can trigger a spark or inspiration that can lead to a "eureka moment," unlocking the power of ideation and making it fruitful. Ideation catalysts were important inputs for great inventors like Thomas Edison and great thinkers like Albert Einstein.

Example of a Design Idea Catalyst: Velcro

A good example of this is seen in the now well-known story (Brown, 2008) of George de Mestral, an engineer who, on a walk in the country, got those little round burrs stuck to his sweater. The nondesign thinker just gets irritated. But this guy was thinking like a designer and he envisioned a material that could stick together and be pulled apart many times without damage. And so he invents Velcro.[1]

The burrs were a design catalyst. They just happened and that spawned a design idea.

14.2.7.1 The eureka moment

Boling and Smith (2012), citing Krippendorff (2006), describe a crucial event in design creation: "When designers work, no matter what process they follow or type of thinking they employ, *they inevitably face the moment of invention* [emphasis ours]. This is the point at which no theory, guideline, example, or statement of best practice can tell the designer or the design team specifically what to do." This moment of invention is precisely the point where a design idea is created, something is conceived that didn't exist before. A design catalyst facilitates this moment of invention to help spawn the genesis of an idea.

Sometimes ideas occur spontaneously or involve a "muse," something that inspires or guides creativity. It definitely involves insight, instinct, intuition, and a natural ability to think outside the box and see "it," an aptitude Malcolm Gladwell (2007) says can be honed in a designer.

---

[1]https://en.wikipedia.org/wiki/George_de_Mestral.

When "it" happens, something triggers an "aha" moment and a design idea emerges. For example, sitting in a bath tub is supposed to have produced the spark that triggered Archimedes' idea of how to measure the volume of an irregular solid.[2]

Example: An Industrial Engineering Story

This is a story about the production line in a toothpaste factory. Credit goes to an unknown person who started this (possibly apocryphal but illustrative) story circulating through the Internet.

The factory had a problem: They sometimes shipped empty boxes, without the tube inside. This was due to the way the production line was set up, and people with experience in designing production lines will tell you how difficult it is to have everything happen with timing so precise that every single unit coming out of it is perfect. Small variations in the environment (which can't be controlled in a cost-effective fashion) mean you must have quality assurance checks smartly distributed across the line so that customers all the way down to the supermarket don't get upset and buy another product instead.

Understanding how important that was, the CEO of the toothpaste factory got the top people in the company together. They decided to start a new project in which they would hire an external engineering company to solve their empty box problem, as their own engineering department was already too stretched to take on any extra effort.

The project followed the usual process: budget and project sponsor allocated, RFP issued, third-parties selected, and six months (and $180,000) later they had a fantastic solution—on time, on budget, high quality. and everyone in the project had a great time.

They solved the problem by using high-tech precision scales that would sound a bell and flash lights whenever a toothpaste box weighed less than it should. The line would stop; someone would walk over and yank the defective box off it, pressing another button when done to restart the line.

A while later, the CEO decides to have a look at the return on investment of the project: amazing results! No empty boxes ever shipped out of the factory after the scales were put in place. Very few customer complaints, and they were gaining market share. "That's some money well spent!" he said, before looking closely at the other statistics in the report.

---

[2]https://en.wikipedia.org/wiki/Archimedes%27_principle.

It turns out that, after three weeks of production use, the number of defects picked up by the scales was zero. It should have picked up at least a dozen a day, so maybe there was something wrong with the report. He requested an inquiry, and after some investigation, the engineers come back saying the report was actually correct. The scales really weren't picking up any defects because all boxes that got to that point in the conveyor belt were good.

Puzzled, the CEO traveled down to the factory, and walked up to the part of the line where the precision scales were installed. A few feet before the scale, there was a cheap desk fan, blowing the empty boxes off the belt and into a bin.

"Oh, that," says one of the workers, "one of the guys put it there because he was tired of walking over here every time the bell rang." Sometimes the best idea is spawned in the simplest way.

14.2.8 Ideation Techniques

Ideation techniques are skill-based UX practices that UX designers can do to support ideation, sketching, and critiquing while fostering new design ideas. Ideation techniques are the more general UX design techniques (Section 2.4) as applied to ideation.

14.2.8.1 Framing and reframing

Framing

The practice of posing a problem within a particular perspective based on a pattern or theme that structures the problem and highlights the aspects you will explore (Section 2.4.10).

Framing and reframing represent a design technique that poses the design problem along a particular dimension to spark a hitherto-unconsidered analysis of tradeoffs. It is a technique to look at an aspect of the work domain along a particular dimension, making it easy to talk about that aspect of the problem. Framing acts as scaffolding because it has a structure and you use that structure to help in analysis.

As Cross (2006) puts it: "Designers tend to use solution conjectures as the means of developing their understanding of the problem." Creating frames is a way to focus not on the generation of solutions but on the ability to create new approaches to the problem situation itself (Dorst, 2015).

14.2.8.2 Abstraction: Getting back to the basics

In Chapter 13, we talked about using *abstraction, which is the process of removing extraneous details of a work activity and focusing on the irreducible constructs of the problem to identify what is really going on, ignoring everything else.*

14.2.8.3 Magic wand: Asking "what if?"

Another ideation technique is the magic wand technique where you ask "what-if" questions to temporarily set aside known constraints. This technique helps with lateral thinking and to generate ideas that, while impossible as is, shed light on other related ideas that are possible.

In the toothpaste factory example, if we had a magic wand, what would we do? We might ask for the ability to see through the cardboard box to know if it is empty. This idea of seeing through a box can now be modified to bring it out of the realm of magic by ideating on techniques to make this possible. An X-ray or sonogram machine mounted on the belt would provide the same outcome as the magical see-through idea.

14.2.8.4 Incubation

Another kind of ideation technique is incubation. Idea incubation can occur if you take a break after a period of deep thinking about a problem. Your brain can work on the problem in the background as you back off and give it a rest, resulting in fresh perspectives after you return to the problem. Even though we are not actively working on the problem during this break, our brains have the capacity to incubate ideas in the background and come up with ideas at unexpected times, typically while doing some other activity.

14.2.8.5 Design patterns and experience

A *design pattern is a repeatable solution to a common design problem that emerges as a best practice, encouraging sharing, reuse, and consistency.* See also Section 17.3.4. Sometimes design patterns from other disciplines help trigger ideas. For example, when Rex and I were discussing the problem of the toothpaste factory, we thought of another domain that solves a different problem using weighing scales that could be used here. We remembered how Amazon packing centers use exact weight calculation to know if a package being prepared on an automated conveyor belt has all the products the customer purchased. If the calculation was off more than a small margin of error, the package is pushed off the conveyor belt and flagged for further analysis and human intervention. When we reuse that knowledge, we call it a design pattern and it can be applied to the problem of the toothpaste factory, proposing a solution that pushes off a toothpaste box that doesn't weigh enough.

14.2.8.6 Traverse the different dimensions of the problem space

This ideation technique is to methodically traverse each dimension of the problem space to look for ideas that were previously missed. In this technique, designers systematically traverse the design space in search of ideas.

In the toothpaste factory example, one can traverse the different dimensions of the problem, such as mass/weight, volume, and opacity, to lead us to the following ideas:

- Mass of the product:
    - Ascertaining the mass is what it should be by weighing.
    - Ascertaining the mass is what it should be through resistance to force.
- Volume occupancy:
    - Internal sensor in the box.
    - Displacement of fluid (air) in the box.
- Seeing inside:
    - Visual inspection by manually opening each box.
    - Sensing by X-ray.
    - Sensing by sonogram.

Note how this traversal was done by framing the problem around the toothpaste box. Another framing could be the manufacturing process itself. Perhaps there is a different technique that wraps the box around a tube instead of building them separately and inserting one into the other?

14.2.8.7 Seek opportunities for embodied and tangible interaction

This ideation technique is about bringing physicality and embodiment into design. It is about weaving the fabric of interaction to include not just the digital realm with its windows, icons, and menus but also the physical world where things can be touched, grabbed, turned, held, and otherwise manipulated using noncognitive senses.

Simply stated, embodiment means having a body. So, taken literally, embodied interaction is about using one's physical body while interacting with the surrounding technology. But, as Dourish (2001) explains, embodiment does not simply refer to physical reality but "the way that physical and social phenomena unfold in real time and real space as a part of the world in which we are situated, right alongside and around us."

As a result, embodiment is not about people or systems per se. As Dourish puts it, "embodiment is not a property of systems, technologies, or artifacts; it is a property of interaction. Cartesian approaches separate mind, body, and thought from action, but embodied interaction emphasizes their duality."

Although tangible interaction (Ishii & Ullmer, 1997) seems to have a following of its own, it is very closely related to embodied interaction. You could say that they are complements to each other. Tangible design is about interactions

Embodied Interaction

Interaction with technology that involves a user's body in a natural and significant way, such as by using gestures (Section 6.2.6.3).

Tangible Interaction

Interaction involving physical actions between human users and physical objects. A key area of focus in Industrial design, pertaining to designing objects and products to be held, felt, and manipulated by humans. Closely related to embodied interaction (Section 6.2.6.3).

between human users and physical objects. Industrial designers have been dealing with it for years, designing objects and products to be held, felt, and manipulated by humans. The difference now is that the object involves some kind of computation. Also, there is a strong emphasis on physicality, form, and tactile interaction (Baskinger & Gross, 2010).

More than ever before, tangible and embodied interaction calls for physical prototypes as sketches to inspire the ideation and design process. Through physical prototypes, we can collaborate, communicate, and make meaning through physically shared objects in the real world.

In designing for embodied interaction (Tungare et al., 2006), ideate on how to involve hands, eyes, and other physical aspects of the human body in the interaction. Supplement the pure cognitive actions that designers have considered in the past and take advantage of the user's mind and body as they potentiate each other in problem solving.

Example: Embodied and Tangible Interaction in a Board Game

If we were to try to make a digital version of a game such as SCRABBLE (example shown below), one way to do it is by creating a desktop application where people operate in their own window to type in letters or words. This makes it an interactive game but not embodied.

Another way to make SCRABBLE digital is the way Hasbro did it in SCRABBLE Flash Cubes (Fig. 14-4). Hasbro Games has used embedded technology in producing an electronic version of the SCRABBLE. They made the game pieces into real physical objects with built-in technology. Because you can hold these objects in your hands, it makes them very natural and tangible and contributes to emotional impact because there is something fundamentally natural about that.

The fact that players hold the cubes, SmartLink letter tiles, in their hands and manipulate and arrange them with their fingers makes this a good example of embodied and tangible interaction.

At the start of a player's turn, the tiles each generate their own letter for the turn. The tiles can read each other's letters as they touch as a player physically shuffles them around. When the string of between two and five letters makes up a word, the tiles light up and beep and the player can try for another word with the same tiles until time is up.

The tiles also work together to time each player's turn, flag duplicates, and display scores. And, of course, it has a built-in dictionary as an authority (however arbitrary it may be) on what comprises a real word.

For more about embodied interaction (interaction with technology that involves a user's body in a natural and significant way, such as in gestures) and tangible interaction (interaction that involves physicality in user actions), see Section 19.3.

Physicality

Referring to real direct physical interaction with real physical (hardware) devices like in the grasping and moving of knobs and levers (Section 30.3.2.4).

Tangible Interaction

Interaction involving physical actions between human users and physical objects. A key area of focus in Industrial design, pertaining to designing objects and products to be held, felt, and manipulated by humans. Closely related to embodied interaction (Section 6.2.6.3).

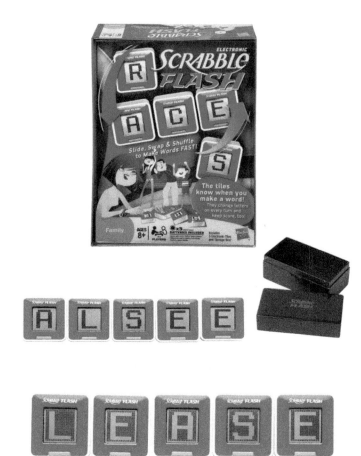

Fig. 14-4
The SCRABBLE Flash
Cube game.

14.3 SKETCHING

The idea of sketching as an indispensable part of design goes back at least to the
Middle Ages. Consider da Vinci and his famous sketchbooks. Nilsson and
Ottersten (1998) describe sketching as an essential visual language for
brainstorming and discussion.

14.3.1 Characteristics of Sketching

*Sketching is the rapid creation of freehand drawings expressing preliminary design
ideas, focusing on concepts rather than details.* We credit Buxton (2007b) as the
champion for sketching; much of what we say about sketching can be
credited to him.

Here are some more defining characteristics of sketching (Buxton, 2007b; Tohidi, Buxton, Baecker, & Sellen, 2006):

- Everyone can sketch; you do not have to be artistic.
- Most ideas are conveyed more effectively with a sketch than with words.
- Sketches are quick and inexpensive to create; they do not inhibit early exploration.
- Sketches are disposable; there is no real investment in the sketch itself.
- Sketches are timely; they can be made just in time, done in the moment, provided when needed.
- Sketches should be plentiful; entertain a large number of ideas and make multiple sketches of each idea.
- Textual annotations play an essential support role, explaining what is going on in each part of the sketch and how.

14.3.1.1 Sketching is essential to ideation and design

Sketching is an indispensable part of design. As Buxton (2007b) puts it, if you're not sketching, you're not doing design. Design is a process of creation and exploration, and sketching is a visual medium for exploration.

Sketching captures ideas into an embodied and tangible form; it externalizes the mental description of an idea for sharing, analysis, and archiving. By opening up new pathways to create new ideas, sketching acts as a multiplier in ideation.

By adding visualization to ideation, sketching adds cognitive supercharging, boosting creativity by bringing in more human senses to the task (Buxton, 2007b).

14.3.1.2 Sketching is a conversation about user experience

Sketching is not art. Sketching is not about putting pen to paper in the act of drawing, nor is it about artistic ability. A sketch is not about making a drawing or picture of a product to document a design.

A sketch is a conversation. A sketch is not just an artifact that you look at; *a sketch is a conversation* about design. A sketch is a medium to support a conversation among the design team.

A sketch is about the user experience, not the product. In a talk at Stanford, Buxton (2007a) challenges his audience to draw his mobile phone. But he does not mean a drawing of the phone as a product. He means something much harder—a sketch that reveals the interaction, the experience of using the phone in a situated context where the product and its physical affordances encourage one type of behavior and experience over another.

Fig. 14-5

A sketch to think about design (photo courtesy of Akshay Sharma, of the Virginia Tech Department of Industrial Design).

14.3.1.3 Sketching is embodied cognition to aid invention

Designers invent while sketching. A sketch is not just a way to represent your thinking; the act of making the sketch is part of the thinking (Fig. 14-5). In fact, the sketch itself is less important than the process of making it.

The importance of involving your hands in sketching. The kinesthetics of sketching, pointing, holding, and touching bring the entire hand-eye-brain coordination feedback loop to bear on the problem solving. Your physical motor movements are coupled with visual and cognitive activity; the designer's mind and body potentiate each other in invention (Baskinger, 2008).

14.3.2 Doing Sketching
14.3.2.1 Stock up on sketching and mockup supplies

Physical Mockup

A tangible, three-dimensional prototype or model of a physical device or product, often one that can be held in the hand and often crafted rapidly out of materials at hand, used during exploration and evaluation to at least simulate physical interaction (Section 20.6.1).

Stock the ideation studio with sketching supplies such as whiteboards, blackboards, corkboards, flip chart easels, Post-it labels, tape, and marking pens. Be sure to include supplies for constructing physical mockups, including scissors, hobby knives, cardboard, foam core board, duct tape, wooden blocks, push pins, string, bits of cloth, rubber, other flexible materials, crayons, and spray paint.

14.3.2.2 Use the language of sketching

The vocabulary of sketching. To be effective at sketching for design, you must use a particular vocabulary that has not changed much over the centuries. One of the most important language features is the vocabulary of lines, which are made as freehand "open" gestures. Instead of being mechanically correct and perfectly straight, lines in sketches are roughed in and not connected precisely.

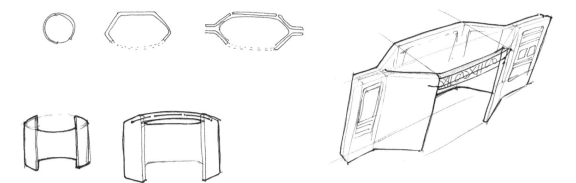

Fig. 14-6

*Freehand gestural sketches
for the Ticket Kiosk System
(sketches courtesy of Akshay
Sharma, of the Virginia
Tech Department of
Industrial Design).*

In this language, lines overlap, often extending a bit beyond the corner. Sometimes they "miss" intersecting and leave the corner open a little bit. *An unfinished appearance proposes exploration*. The low resolution and detail of a sketch suggest it is a concept in the making, not a finished design. It needs to look disposable and inexpensive to make. Sketches are deliberately ambiguous and abstract, leaving "holes" for the imagination about other aspects of the design. You can see this unfinished look in the sketches of Figs. 14-6 and 14-7. *Keep sketches open to interpretation*. Sketches can be interpreted in different ways, fostering new relationships to be seen within them, even by the person who drew them. In other words, avoid the appearance of precision; if everything is specified and the design looks finished, then the message is that you are telling something, "This is the design," not proposing exploration, "Let us play with this and see what comes up."

In Fig. 14-8, we show examples of designers doing sketching.

Example: Sketching for a Laptop Projector Project

The following figures show sample sketches for the K-YAN project (K-yan means "vehicle for knowledge"), an exploratory collaboration by the Virginia Tech Industrial Design Department and IL&FS.4.[3] The objective is to develop a combination laptop and projector in a single portable device for use in rural India. Thanks to Akshay Sharma of the Virginia Tech Industrial Design Department for these sketches. See Figs. 14-9–14-12 for different kinds of exploratory sketches for this project.

---

[3]www.ilfsindia.com.

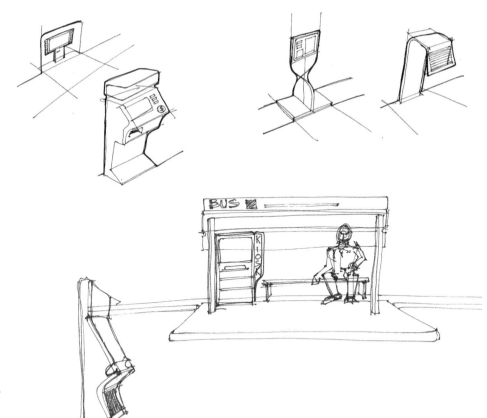

Fig. 14-7

*Ideation and design
exploration sketches for the
Ticket Kiosk System (sketches
courtesy of Akshay Sharma, of
the Virginia Tech Department
of Industrial Design).*

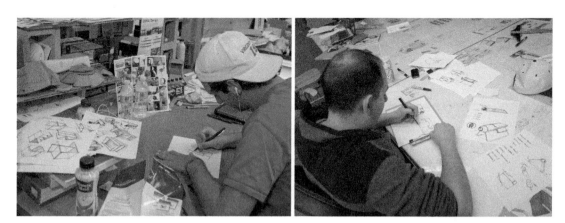

Fig. 14-8

*Designers doing sketching
(photos courtesy of Akshay
Sharma, of the Virginia
Tech Department of
Industrial Design).*

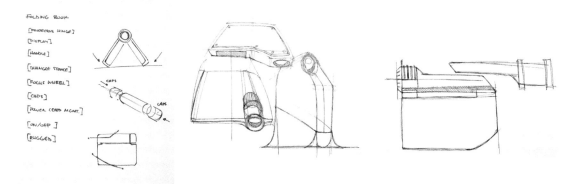

FOLDING BOOK

[PROJECTOR HINGE]

[DISPLAY]

[HANDLE]

[TRIANGLE STANCE]

[FOCUS WHEEL]

[CAPS]

[POWER CORD MGMT.]

[ON/OFF]

[RUGGED]

CAPS

Fig. 14-9

Early ideation sketches of K-YAN (sketches courtesy of Akshay Sharma, of the Virginia Tech Department of Industrial Design).

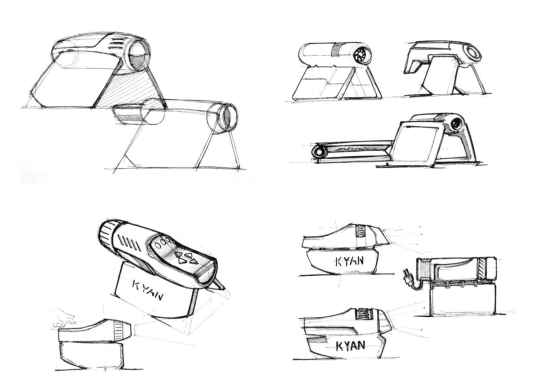

Fig. 14-10

Midfidelity exploration sketches of K-YAN (sketches courtesy of Akshay Sharma, of the Virginia Tech Department of Industrial Design).

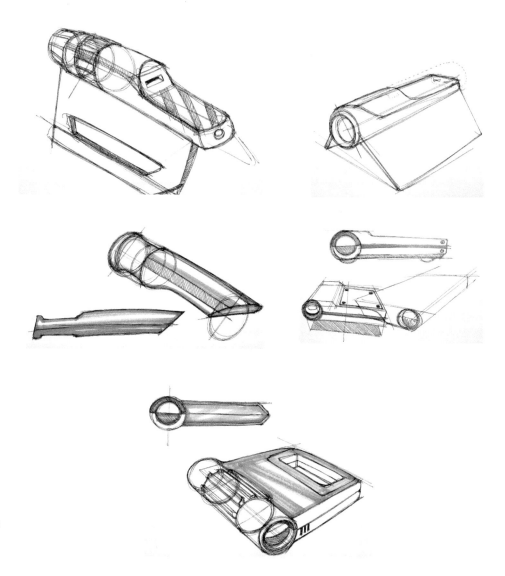

Fig. 14-11

Sketches to explore flip-open mechanism of K-YAN (sketches courtesy of Akshay Sharma, of the Virginia Tech Department of Industrial Design).

14.3.3 Exercise 14-3: Practice in Ideation and Sketching

Goal: To get practice in ideation and sketching for design.

Activities: Doing this in a small group is strongly preferable, but you can do it with one other person.

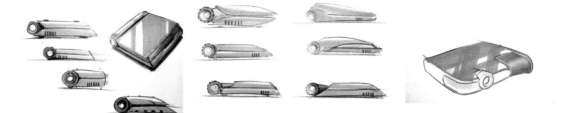

Fig. 14-12

Sketches to explore the emotional impact of the form for K-YAN (sketches courtesy of Akshay Sharma, of the Virginia Tech Department of Industrial Design).

- Get out blank paper, appropriate marking pens, and any other supplies you might need for sketching.
- Pick a topic, a system, or device. Our recommendation is something familiar, such as a dishwasher.
- Start with some free-flow ideation about ways to design a new and improved concept of a dishwasher. Do not limit yourself to conventional designs.
- Go with the flow and see what happens.
- Remember that this is an exercise about the process, so what you come up with for the product is not that crucial.
- Everyone should make sketches of the ideas that arise about a dishwasher design, as you go in the ideation.
- Start with design sketches in the ecological perspective. For a dishwasher, this might include your dining room, kitchen, and the flow of dishes in their daily cycle. You could include something unorthodox: sketch a conveyor belt from the dinner table through your appliance and out into the dish cabinets. Sketch how avoiding the use of paper plates can save resources and not fill the trash dumps.
- Make some sketches from an interaction perspective showing different ways you can operate the dishwasher: how you load and unload it and how you set wash cycle parameters and turn it on.
- Make sketches that project the emotional perspective of a user experience with your product. This might be more difficult, but it is worth taking some time to try.
- Ideate. Sketch, sketch, and sketch. Brainstorm and discuss.

Deliverables: A brief written description of the ideation process and its results, along with all your supporting sketches.

Schedule: Give yourself enough time to really get engaged in this activity.

Exercise 14-4: Ideation and Sketching for Your System

Goal: More practice in ideation and sketching for design. Do the same as you did in the previous exercise, only this time for your own system.

14.3.4 Physical Mockups as Embodied Sketches

Just as sketches are two-dimensional visual vehicles for invention, a physical mockup for ideation about a physical device or product is a three-dimensional sketch. Physical mockups as sketches, like all sketches, are made quickly, are highly disposable, and are made from at-hand materials to create tangible props for exploring design visions and alternatives.

A physical mockup is an embodied sketch because it is even more of a physical manifestation of a design idea and it is a tangible artifact for touching, holding, and acting out usage (Fig. 14-13).

For later in the process, after design exploration is done, you may want a more finished-looking three-dimensional design representation (Fig. 14-14) to show clients, customers, and implementers.

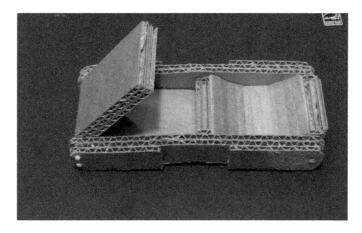

Fig. 14-13

Example of rough physical mockups (courtesy of Akshay Sharma, of the Virginia Tech Department of Industrial Design).

14.4 CRITIQUING

Critiquing is the activity where design ideas are assessed to identify advantages, disadvantages, and constraints and tradeoffs are evaluated for each idea.

At a high level, the goal of critiquing is to analyze if the design:

◾ Meets design goals?

Fig. 14-14

Example of a more finished looking physical mockup (courtesy of Akshay Sharma, of the Virginia Tech Department of Industrial Design).

- Fits well with the ecology? Communicates seamlessly with other devices in the environment?
- Supports the interaction needed with other devices?
- Provides good usability?
- Evokes positive emotional impact?
- Engenders meaningfulness for users?

This evaluation part of generative design is never formal; there are no established methods. It is a fast, furious, and freewheeling comparison of many alternatives and inspiration for further alternatives.

14.4.1 Include Users in the Critiquing Activity

Pull together the best of all the different brainstorming ideas into a single big-picture redesign of how work gets done and communicate the new vision to customers and users.

For this critical analysis, bring in a huge cross-section of people with broadly varying backgrounds, perspectives, and personalities.

- Show off your ideas and sketches along with other mockups and models.
- Let them talk, argue, and criticize.
- Your job is to listen.

Fig. 14-15

Critiquing within the Virginia Tech ideation studio, Kiva (photo courtesy of Akshay Sharma, of the Virginia Tech Department of Industrial Design).

In Fig. 14-15, we show an example of critiquing in midprocess within the Virginia Tech ideation studio.

14.5 "RULES OF ENGAGEMENT" FOR IDEATION, SKETCHING, AND CRITIQUING

14.5.1 Behave Yourself

The process should be democratic:

- Every idea valued the same.
- Ego-free process.
- No ownership of ideas:
  - All ideas belong to the group.

14.5.2 Be Aware of Which Mode You Are In

Back in graduate school, I (Rex) read a simple paper on "stop-and-go thinking" (Mason, 1968) that has affected my outlook on problem-solving and brainstorming ever since. This paper suggests that, if you keep the creative mindset of ideation separate from the judicial mindset of critiquing, you will get better ideas and make wiser judgments.

Although you will interweave ideation and critiquing throughout the design process, you should know which mode you are in at any given time and not mix the modes. Ideation should result in a pure flow of ideas regardless of feasibility, in the classic tradition of brainstorming. Although we know that, at the end of the day, practical implementation constraints must be considered and allowed to carry weight in the final overall design, saying "Hey, wait a minute!" too early can stifle innovation.

Mason (1968) calls this separation of ideation and critiquing "go-mode and stop-mode thinking." In idea-creation (go) mode, you adopt a freewheeling mental attitude that will permit ideas to flourish. In critiquing (stop) mode, you revert to a cold-blooded, critical attitude that will bring your judgment into full play.

Ideation gives you permission to be radical; you get to play outside the safe zone and no one can shoot you down. Allowing early cries of "that will never work," "they have already tried that," "it will cost too much," "we do not have a widget for that," or "it will not work on our implementation platform" will unfairly hobble and frustrate this first step of creativity.

The design teams at IDEO (ABC News Nightline, 1999) signal premature critiquing by ringing a wrist-mounted bicycle bell to signal the foul of being judgmental too early in design discussions.

14.5.3 Iterate to Explore

Finding the best design ideas requires exploring a large number of possibilities and candidate designs. The best tools for exploring ideas are ideation, sketching, and critiquing, combined with extensive iteration (Buxton, 2007b). Be ready to try, try, try, and try again, rapidly. Think about Thomas Edison and his more than 10,000 experiments to create a usable and useful light bulb.

Mental Models and Conceptual Design

15

15.1 INTRODUCTION

15.1.1 You Are Here

We begin each process chapter with a "you are here" picture of the chapter topic in the context of The Wheel, the overall UX design lifecycle template (Fig. 15-1). In this chapter, we continue the UX design process with conceptual design to communicate the designer's mental model to users.

15.1.2 Mental Models

A mental model is a description, understanding, or explanation of someone's thought process about how something works. As applied in UX, a mental model is how someone (e.g., designer or user) thinks a product or system works.

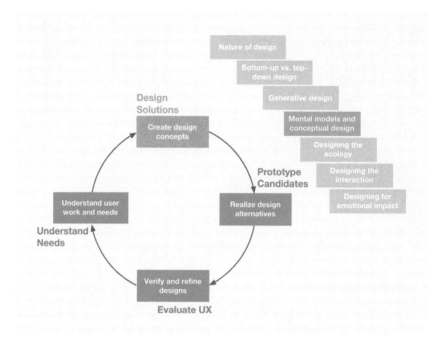

Fig. 15-1

You are here in the chapter describing the role of mental models and conceptual design within the Design Solutions lifecycle activity, in the context of the overall Wheel UX lifecycle.

Designers have mental models that, hopefully, are correct. Users, who may not completely understand a system, will have their own mental models, correct or not, of how a product or system works. If the user's mental model is correct, the user will know how to use the system. It is up to the designer to create a conceptual design capable of conveying a correct mental model to users.

For an example of how a mistaken mental model can make for entertainment, see Section 19.3.

15.2 HOW A CONCEPTUAL DESIGN WORKS AS A CONNECTION OF MENTAL MODELS

Fig. 15-2 shows how the conceptual design (in the center of the figure) is a kind of mapping from the designer's mental model (near the top) to the user's mental model (near the bottom).

Here's how it works:

1. The ideal mental model represents the reality of how something like a thermostat works "out there" in the world.

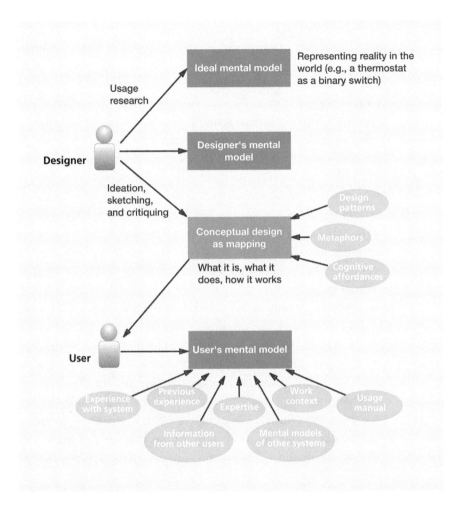

Fig. 15-2

The conceptual design as a mapping of the designer's mental model to the user's mental model.

2. The designer studies this reality via usage research, interactions with subject matter experts (SMEs), analysis, etc.

3. The designer develops a (possibly partial and/or not quite correct) mental model based on understanding of the reality thus captured.

4. The designer builds this mental model into the conceptual design.

5. The conceptual design conveys that knowledge of the designer's understanding to users.

6. If users had some a priori understanding of the reality, the conceptual design can either affirm or challenge that understanding. Otherwise, the user (hopefully) learns how this system or product works from the conceptual design.

We will explain the parts of this diagram in the sections that follow.

15.2.1 The Ideal Mental Model in Context

An ideal mental model is a theoretically correct description of the reality of a given design and a given implementation of a given system or product and how it works. The ideal mental model is a hypothetical abstraction of knowledge in the world and includes subject matter expertise and complete knowledge about the work domain. This complete knowledge will be held by a backend system designer or shared among the system design team, and for most domain simple systems, the UX designer may have this knowledge too.

Continuing with a common house thermostat as an example, the user's manual would probably say something to the effect that you turn it up and down to make it warmer or cooler, but would probably fall short of the full explanation of how a thermostat works. But the service manual will contain documentation about the complete knowledge about thermostat internals, including what type of thermally sensitive material is used, what its expansion profile is, what the material tolerances are, etc.

Thermostats are very simple devices, and their ideal mental model is widely known and understood. Most thermostats, as Norman explains in his famous book, *The Design of Everyday Things* (Norman, 1990, pp. 38–39), are binary switches that are simply either on or off. When the sensed ambient temperature is below the target value, the heating system switch closes and the thermostat turns the heat on. When the temperature then climbs to the target value, the switch opens and the thermostat turns the heat source off. It is, therefore, an incorrect mental model to believe (taken just as an example) that you can make a room warm up faster by turning the thermostat up higher than the target temperature.

15.2.2 The Designer's Mental Model in Context

The designer's mental model, sometimes called a conceptual model (Johnson & Henderson, 2002, p. 26), is the designer's understanding of the how the envisioned system is organized, what it does, and how it works. If anyone should know these things, it is the designer who is creating the system. But it is not uncommon for systems to get built without a clear mental model upfront.

The results can be a poorly focused design that fails as a mapping (middle of Fig. 15-2), causing users frustration.

15.2.3 The User's Mental Model in Context

Veer and Melguizo (2003), citing Carroll and Olson (1987), define a user's mental model as the "mental representation that reflects the user's understanding of the system." It's an internal explanation a user has built about how a particular system works. As Norman (1990) says, it is a natural human response to an unfamiliar situation to begin building an explanatory model a piece at a time. We look for cause-and-effect relationships and form theories to explain what we observe and why, which then helps guide our behavior and actions in task performance.

As shown in Fig. 15-2, each user's mental model is a product of many different inputs, including, as Norman has often said, knowledge in the head and knowledge in the world. Knowledge in the head comes from mental models of other systems, user expertise, and previous experience. Knowledge in the world comes from other users, work context, shared cultural conventions, documentation, and the conceptual design of the system itself. This latter source of user knowledge is the responsibility of the UX designer.

15.2.4 The Conceptual Design as Mapping Between Mental Models

A conceptual design is the part of a design containing a theme, metaphor, notion, or idea with the purpose of communicating a design vision about a system or product, corresponding to what Norman calls the "system image" of the designer's mental model (Norman, 1990, pp. 16, 189–190). The goal of a conceptual design (second box from the bottom in Fig. 15-2) is to communicate the designer's mental model to users.

A conceptual design must convey the designer's mental model in a way that the user can acquire or form a similar mental model and, thereby, know how to use the system. Without an effective conceptual design, users cannot leverage any experience they gain from interacting with one part of the system while interacting with another.

Example: The Washington, DC, Metro Ticket Kiosk

The Washington, DC, Metro ticket kiosk (Fig. 15-3) is an example of a system that lacks a good conceptual design, and it does not look like any other kiosk. It is what we call a "show up and throw up" user interface. This type of design is also sometimes called "information flooding." The designers didn't determine what information users needed and when, so they show everything at once and let the users take it from there.

A bewildering array of buttons and displays meets the user who walks up to this kiosk. Remember the context of interaction here: the users are in a hurry to purchase a fare to get on the train. Add to that the fact that a significant portion of these users are tourists having no prior experience with this system to rely

Metaphor

An analogy used in design to communicate and explain unfamiliar concepts using familiar conventional knowledge. A central metaphor often becomes the theme of a product, the motif behind the conceptual design (Section 15.3.6).

Fig. 15-3

A Washington, DC, Metro ticket kiosk.

upon. And finally, there is usually a line of people waiting behind the current user, so the pressure is on to get the fare and not hold up the line.

If the user is trying to purchase a one-time fare card, they have to first figure out how much the fare is by reading the small text at the top of the kiosk. If they are successful, they have to select one of the three options next to the "Select Purchase" section at the top to get started with the type of card they are purchasing. This option, thankfully, is at the top of the screen, a reasonable location the user will look for to get started. However, if the user already has a rechargeable "Smartrip" fare card, they have to start first by tapping their card on the circular widget in the bottom center part of the kiosk, to the lower right of the "Insert Payment" label. Then, they have to select an option from the "Select Purchase" step at the top. Then, they pay using one of the available options in the center and then touch the circular card again in the center. It is an arbitrary sequence of steps that is only explained through small text in the center of the kiosk.

Even if designers had a clear mental model, they didn't articulate it in an effective conceptual design, and, consequently, the users have no way of forming a mental model of how the system works. The three steps of the workflow are not supported consistently for all types of transactions. For example, the Smartrip users or users trying to combine their existing fare card balances into a single card do not start in the "Select Purchase" step. Similarly, not all payment steps are organized in the payment section in the middle (note the "coin return" at the bottom). Because people struggle with this so much, the Metro system had to post (and pay for) Metro employees onsite to help, but this defeats the purpose of having a kiosk in the first place.

Compare this to the NYC ticket kiosk where the user is guided through a task flow using a touch screen user interface and not overwhelmed with all options at once.

15.3 DESIGN STARTS WITH CONCEPTUAL DESIGN

A clear and consistent conceptual design assures that the rest of the product or system design presents a unified and coherent appearance to the user.

After doing usage research, many designers jump right into sketching out screens, menu structures, and widgets. But Johnson and Henderson (2002) will tell you to start with conceptual design before sketching any screen or user interface objects. As they put it, screen sketches are designs of "how the system presents itself to users. It is better to start by designing what the system is to them." Screen designs and widgets will come, but time and effort spent on interaction details can be wasted without a well-defined underlying conceptual structure. Norman (2008) puts it this way: "What people want is usable devices, *which translates into understandable ones*" (final emphasis ours).

Conceptual design is where you innovate and brainstorm to plant and first nurture the user experience seed to build this understanding. Without an effective conceptual design upfront, you can never iterate the design later to yield a good user experience. Conceptual design is where you establish the metaphor or the theme of the product—in a word, the concept.

It's a general rule in creating a conceptual design that the designer's mental model must be articulated clearly, precisely, and completely in the conceptual design. To paraphrase Johnson and Henderson's rule for the conceptual design: *If something is not in the conceptual design, which represents the designer's mental model, the system should not require users to be aware of it.*

15.3.1 Need for a Conceptual Design Component at Every Level in the User Needs Pyramid

Before we start to design for the ecology, interaction, and emotional impact, we must create a component of the conceptual design for each layer in the user needs pyramid (Section 12.3.1); see Fig. 15-4:

- An ecological component that helps users understand how the product or system fits into its ecology and works together with other products and systems in that ecology.
- An interaction component that helps users understand how to use the product or system.
- An emotional component that conveys the intended emotional impact.

The components of the conceptual design that address these three layers are described in the following sections.

15.3.2 Conceptual Design for Work Practice Ecology: Describing Full Usage Context

The mental model for the system ecology helps users understand how the product or system fits into its ecology and works together with other products and systems in that ecology. Let us expand the explanation of thermostats to include their ecological setting.

A thermostat ecology includes a heating (and/or cooling) system consisting of three major parts: a heating source or cooling unit, a heating or cooling distribution network, and a control unit, the latter being the thermostat and some other hidden circuitry. The heat source could be gas, electric, or wood burning, for example. The cooling unit might use electric power to run a

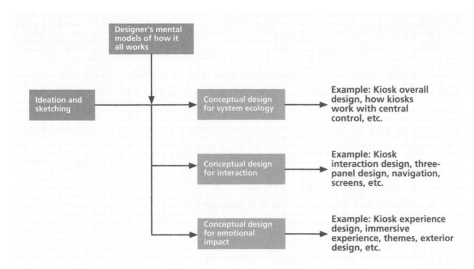

Fig. 15-4

*Designer workflow
and connections
among the three layers of the
user needs pyramid.*

compressor. The heating or cooling distribution network would use fans or air
blowers to send heated or cooled air through hot air ducts, or a pump would
send heated or cooled water through subfloor pipes. Finally, there is a living
space being heated or cooled, and its ambient temperature.

Next, we address what a thermostat does within its ecology by noting that it is for
controlling the temperature in a room or other space. It does this by turning
on the heating or cooling source until the temperature in the living space stays
near a user-settable value to keep people comfortable. In other words, the model
for a thermostat design is a controller that checks the ambient temperature and
keeps a thermal or cooling source on or off until a desired value is detected.

If the designers are planning to create a smart thermostat, their mental
model will also include a way to sense users in the house to ascertain
occupancy, conserving energy when the house is unoccupied. This includes
sensor locations, how the data from those sensors will be communicated to the
thermostat, and how users will be able to control the system when they are
away from the house. Thus, the conceptual design will expand to include
connectivity with the Internet, whether the data are saved over a period of
time for trend analysis, and whether the system provides other types of
feedback such as comparing with energy consumption averages in the
neighborhood or of friends and family.

15.3.3 Conceptual Design for Interaction: Describing How Users Will Operate It

For interaction, a conceptual design is a task-oriented view about how a user operates the system or product. There will need to be a different model for the different platforms and different devices for interacting with the system. For example, the thermostat could be a traditional physical device on the wall or it could be a smartphone app that interfaces with the physical device via the Internet.

In the physical device case, a user can see two numerical temperature displays, either analog or digital. One value is for the current ambient temperature, and the other is the setting for the target temperature. There will be a rotatable knob, slider, or other value-setting mechanism to set the desired target temperature. This covers the sensory and physical user actions for operating a thermostat. User cognition and proper formation of intentions with respect to user actions during thermostat operation, however, depend on understanding the mental model of its behavior.

A second possible interaction design, one that reveals the conceptual design, might have a display unit that provides feedback messages such as "checking ambient temperature," "temperature lower than target; turning heat on," and "temperature at desired level; shutting off." This latter design might suffer from being unnecessarily complex to produce, and the added display is likely to be a distraction to experienced users (i.e., most users). However, this does illustrate a design that helps project the designer's mental model to the user through the conceptual design in the interaction perspective.

The conceptual design must also include descriptions of interactions required for users to set up the ecology by connecting the thermostat to the Internet, accessing it via a smartphone app, logging into any required accounts, etc.

15.3.4 Conceptual Design in the Emotional Perspective: Describing Intended Emotional Impact

For emotional aspects, the conceptual design is a description of the expected overarching emotional response. Regarding the thermostat example, this could be about the emotional effect of a modern and sleek aesthetic with steel and glass components in contrast to traditional designs made with plastic materials. The conceptual design for emotion will also include physical design, how it fits in with the house décor, and the craftsmanship of its construction. The designers may also have specific plans for the visual design of the display on the device, including the type of LED to use and whether there will be color options available. A traditional

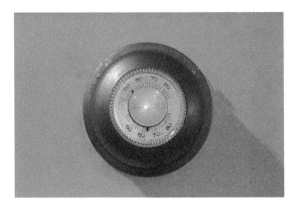

Fig. 15-5

The appearance of an old thermostat versus that of a Nest.

plain appearance gives up emotional ground to the sophisticated look of a Nest thermostat (Fig. 15-5), especially when that stylish exterior carries with it the knowledge that the Nest is really cool because of what it can do inside.

15.3.5 Leveraging Design Patterns in Conceptual Design

A design pattern is a repeatable solution to a common design problem that emerges as a best practice, encouraging sharing, reuse, and consistency (Sections 14.2.8.5, 17.3.4, and 15.3.5). Design patterns are design styles that entail reuse of interaction structures, color schemes, fonts, physical layout, look and feel, and locations of interaction objects. They help with consistency and ease of learning. As an example of designers leveraging the design patterns of conceptual designs from known applications to new ones, consider a well-known application such as Microsoft Outlook. People are familiar with the navigation bar on the left side, the list view at the top right side, and a preview of the selected item below the list. When designers use that same idea in the conceptual design of a new mail application, the familiarity carries over.

15.3.6 Leveraging Metaphors in Conceptual Design

A metaphor is an analogy used in design to communicate and explain unfamiliar concepts using familiar conventional knowledge. A central metaphor often becomes the theme of a product, the concept behind the conceptual design. Metaphors control complexity by allowing users to adapt what they already know in learning how to use new system features.

Metaphors are analogies for communication and explanations of the unfamiliar using familiar conventional knowledge. This familiarity becomes the foundation underlying and pervading the rest of the design.

What users already know about an existing system or existing phenomena can be adapted in learning how to use a new system (Carroll & Thomas, 1982). We use metaphors to control design complexity, making it easier to learn and easier to use instead of trying to reduce the overall complexity (Carroll, Mack, & Kellogg, 1988).

A good example is the now-pervasive desktop metaphor. When the idea of graphical user interfaces in personal computers became an economic feasibility, the designers at Xerox Parc were faced with an interesting UX design challenge: how to communicate to the users, most of whom were going to see this kind of computer for the first time, how the interaction design works.

In response, they created the powerful "desktop" metaphor. The design leveraged the familiarity people had with how a desktop works; it has files, folders, a space where current work documents are placed, and a "trash can" where documents can be discarded (and later recovered, until the trash can itself is emptied). This analogy of a simple everyday desk was brilliant in its simplicity and made it possible to communicate the complexity of a brand-new technology.

Another great example of a metaphor for interaction conceptual design can be found in the Time Machine feature on the Macintosh operating system. It is a backup feature where the user can take a "time machine" to go back to older backups—by flying through time as guided by the user interface—to retrieve lost or accidentally deleted files.

The designers of this feature use animation to represent traveling back through time to points where the user made backups. Any files from that backup can be selected and brought back to the present to recover lost files. This conceptual design is effective because it uses a familiar metaphor to simplify and explain the complexity of data backup. Other backup products provide similar capabilities but are more difficult to interact with because they lack a similar metaphor to reflect how it works.

Example: Physics as a Metaphor in UX Conceptual Designs

Scrolling through lists on an iOS device such as an iPad, done by swiping the finger up or down, demonstrates a phenomenon called physics in interaction. The scrolling is done as though the display was on a large wheel that you spin with your finger. This display *exhibits* significant mass, so it has inertia that keeps it spinning after you release your finger. But it also exhibits friction that soon slows it down and stops it.

Physicality

Referring to real direct physical interaction with real physical (hardware) devices like in the grasping and moving of knobs and levers (Section 30.3.2.4).

So, this display involves mass, inertia, and friction, all parameters of physics. The way the mass and inertia are exhibited is so real that it actually *feels* like a real wheel to the finger. It's a kind of artificial physicality. And if the users spin it past where they want to be, that is technically considered an "error" by most definitions, but it doesn't feel like an error. It feels normal for a wheel with mass, and they just *naturally* spin it back a bit.

See how natural that interaction is when the "physics" work as the user expects? Other examples include rubber-banding when reaching the end of a list and tactile feedback on buttons.

15.3.6.1 Metaphors can cause confusion if not used properly

As critical components of a conceptual design, metaphors set the theme of how the design works, establishing an agreement between the designer's vision and the user's expectations. But metaphors, like any analogy, can break down when the existing knowledge and the new design do not match.

When a metaphor breaks down, it is a violation of the agreement implicit in a conceptual design. The famous criticism of the Macintosh platform's design of ejecting an external disk by dragging its icon into the trash can is a well-known illustration of how a metaphor breakdown attracts attention. It might have been more faithful to the desktop metaphor if the system would discard an external disk, or at least delete its contents, when it is dragged and dropped onto the trash can, instead of ejecting it. However, that would be too dangerous. Maybe ejection could have been better portrayed by pulling a device symbol out of a computer symbol.

15.3.7 Conceptual Design for Subsystems by Work Role

In Section 8.7.3, we discussed how an overall product or system can be divided into subpieces by work role. Each such subsystem will have its own user needs within the pyramid: ecology, interaction, and emotional. That is, for each work role that corresponds to a subsystem, we must think of ecological, interaction, and emotional conceptual designs (Fig. 15-6).

We cover designing (including creating conceptual designs) for each of the layers of the pyramid in the following three chapters.

Exercise 15.1: Conceptual Design for Your System

Goal: Get a little practice in initial conceptual design.

Activities: Think about your system and usage research data and envision a conceptual design, including any metaphors, for how your overall system works.

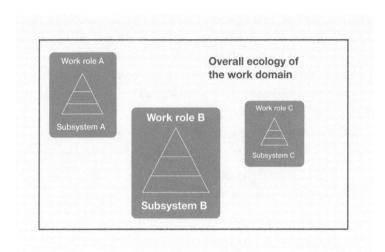

Fig. 15-6

Two dimensions of conceptual design: subsystems defined by different work roles and addressing the layers of the user needs pyramid.

Try to communicate the designer's mental model, or a design vision, of how the system works.

Deliverables: Brief written descriptions of your conceptual design and/or a few presentation slides of the same to share with others.

Schedule: You decide how much time you can afford to give this.

Designing the Ecology and Pervasive Information Architecture

16

Highlights

- Designing for ecological needs.
- Creating an ecological design.
- Example: An ecology for a shopping application within a pervasive information architecture.

16.1 INTRODUCTION

16.1.1 You Are Here

We begin each process chapter with a "you are here" picture of the chapter topic in the context of The Wheel, the overall UX design lifecycle template (Fig. 16-1). In this chapter, we describe how to design for the foundational layer of the human needs pyramid—the ecology.

In Section 12.3, we discussed how ecological needs are about the overarching and encompassing requirements, constraints, and activities of the work practice beyond just the product or system being designed. In this chapter, we go about designing the ecology to satisfy those needs of users.

> **Pyramid of user needs**
>
> An abstract representation as a pyramid shape with the bottom layer as ecological needs, the middle layer as interaction needs, and the top layer as emotional needs (Section 12.3.1).

16.2 DESIGNING FOR ECOLOGICAL NEEDS

16.2.1 Ecological Design: Foundational Layer of the Needs Pyramid Often Overlooked

In the setting of UX design, *the ecology is the entire set of surrounding parts of the world, including networks, other users, devices, and information structures with which a user, product, or system interact*s. Designing for ecological needs is one of the

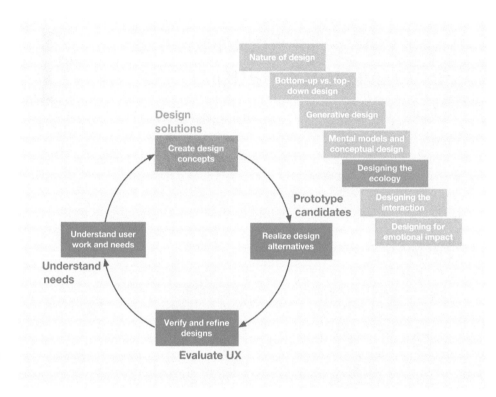

Fig. 16-1

You are here in the chapter describing designing the ecology within the Design Solutions lifecycle activity, in the context of the overall Wheel UX lifecycle.

most overlooked aspects in UX practice. The lure to get a sense of progress by diving right into interaction design (screen and visual designs) is often strong because it is easier to translate the tactical needs of the user at a task level to corresponding widgets or patterns in the UI. However, in order for users to be productive in the work practice, they need to first:

- Understand the broader ecology.
- Be able to participate in it.

Designing the ecology forces us to think about the overall system and how it addresses broader work activities.

Example: iTunes: Satisfying Ecological Needs First

Consider the "work" practice of listening to music. If a user is handed a brand-new music device such as an iPod and asked to listen to their favorite song, she will not be able to do that directly without first understanding how the Apple ecology works and doing some activities to set it up.

Understanding the ecology entails determining how to participate in Apple's ecosystem by accumulating, organizing, classifying, manipulating, sharing, listening to music, and syncing various devices to the user's music library.

She might start by setting up an Apple account and Apple ID if she doesn't have one. Then she links her iPod to iTunes through her Apple ID. Then she needs to look for her favorite song in her existing music library or in a music streaming service if she has one. If she doesn't, she needs to browse or search for it on Apple's or some other compatible music store, then buy and download or stream that piece of music. Interacting with the iPod to listen to music only happens after these ecological needs are satisfied.

In this example, the ecological needs are complex and can be a significant barrier to the desire to listen to music. But that is the nature of this work activity because of a variety of ecological requirements and constraints ranging from legal (music industry's antipiracy requirements) to platform (Apple's convoluted ecosystem requiring you to deal with iTunes, Apple ID, Apple Music) to device (iPod's connectivity Wi-Fi or cellular capabilities) to user (existing music library saved in a device vs. subscriptions and playlist setup on streaming services).

16.2.2 Designing the Ecology is about Usage Context

Designing the ecology is about envisioning and planning how work gets done in the broadest context of the user and system. This means looking at all the different:

- Devices users employ to get work done.
- Variations in their form factors and capabilities (e.g., watches, phones, tablets, laptops, desktops, wall displays, and ambient sensors).
- Usage contexts (e.g., usage while sitting at a desk vs. on the move).
- Infrastructure constraints (e.g., with connectivity vs. without).

16.2.3 Pervasive Information Architecture

Pervasive information architecture is a structure for organizing, storing, retrieving, displaying, manipulating, and sharing information that provides ever-present information availability spanning parts of a broad ecology.

UX design for the ecology almost always depends on pervasive information architecture, which provides ever-present information availability across devices, users, and other parts of a broad ecology. This allows users to interact with the same information, perhaps in different forms and accessed and displayed in different ways, on different devices at different times and in different places.

16.2.4 Ecological Design Spans Multiple Interaction Channels

An interaction channel is a means, mode, or medium through which users and parts of a system interact and communicate, including sensory modes such as visual communication as well as voice and tactile interaction. The concept also includes devices such as desktop computers, smartphones, and system-oriented channels such as the Internet, Wi-Fi connections, and even Bluetooth.

Ecological design is sometimes referred to as cross-channel information design or pervasive information design (Resmini & Rosati, 2011) (in the information architecture community) or multiplatform user interfaces (Pyla, Tungare, & Pérez-Quiñones, 2006) or continuous user interfaces (Pyla, Tungare, & Pérez-Quiñones, 2006) (in the human-computer interaction community).

When we are working at a computer, we are essentially doing single-platform computing. When we add in working on our tablets and smartphones, it extends to multiplatform computing.

In an ecology, a single service and the associated pervasive information architecture can be spread across multiple platforms, all of which are required to make it work (Houben et al., 2017). As an example, your bank sends a text message referring to a transaction you started online but have to come into the bank to finish.

The work on ubiquitous computing (Weiser, 1991) and tangible (Ishii & Ullmer, 1997) or embedded interaction has been a strong influence on making information available pervasively. Information objects have abilities to exhibit behavior and act according to external conditions. Also, the environment itself has the capability to act upon information objects.

For more about ubiquitous computing (interaction with transparent technology embedded in our everyday surroundings), tangible interaction (interaction that involves physicality in user actions), and embedded interaction, see Section 19.3.

16.2.5 A Single Platform in an Ecology Can Have Multiple Interaction Channels

Sometimes, within the same platform there is a need to consider different channels. While this is technically an interaction design concern (the focus of our next chapter), we discuss it here for continuity. Consider a user interacting with a typical laptop computer where interaction channels include:

- Text entry channel via a keyboard.
- A touch channel accessed via a touch pad or "joystick."

Information object

An internally stored structured or simple article, piece of information, or data that serves as a work object. Often data entities are central to work flow, being operated on by users; they are organized, shared, labeled, navigated, searched and browsed for, accessed and displayed, modified and manipulated, and stored back again, all within a system ecology (Section 14.2.6.7).

Ubiquitous computing/interaction

Technology (and interaction with that technology) that resides almost anywhere in a user's ecology, including in appliances, homes, offices, stereos and entertainment systems, vehicles, roads, and objects they carry (briefcases, purses, wallets, wrist watches) (Section 6.2.6.2).

- A touch channel if the screen is touch-enabled.
- A tactile channel if the touch pad can provide that kind of feedback.
- An audio channel through the computer's speakers.

16.2.6 For the User, the Entire Ecology Is a Single Service

Consider this example of how an extensive ecology provides a single user service. Suppose a user orders something online using a computer and the Internet, opting for free shipping to the local store. Shortly thereafter, the user gets an automated email with a purchase confirmation and a copy of the invoice. Sometime later, the customer gets an email saying that the item had been shipped, giving a tracking number. The user clicks on this tracking number a few times in the next day or two and sees the progress of the shipment.

An email and a text message later announce the arrival of the item at the store and soon the person goes to the store physically to pick it up. The user takes a copy of the email on his smartphone and the person at the store scans the barcode. The user signs a tablet at the store, confirming pickup. Sometimes another email confirms the pickup and closes out the transaction. Lots of different interactions, platforms, and devices, all serving one user transaction.

While we might think of goods and services as separate things, Norman shows how the real value in a product or service is to offer a great experience to the customer/user. Norman (2009) calls us to systems thinking, what we call ecological design, to provide that value to users.

Example: A Flawed Ecological Design Can Cause User Frustration

A good ecological design empowers users to perform whole activities in the work domain (high-level support to work activities) and not just specific work flows or tasks. A flawed ecological design results in inconsistent experiences for the users as they navigate the work domain in the ecology. Consider this issue we recently encountered that illustrates the difference between thinking about ecology versus just interaction, in the context of Apple's ecological design.

A user's ecology in the Apple world contains desktops, laptops, tablets, phones, and smart watches. Depending on the context of interaction, the user may use any one of these devices to access their information. When Rex wanted to look for some details from a previous doctor's appointment on his iPhone, the search came up with no results. He was surprised because he knew all his annual appointments for medical checkups are tracked in his calendar application. Just as a check, he tried the calendar on his desktop and, surprise, it was there.

It so happens that, by the default setting on his iPhone, only appointments from the last one month are saved and his last appointment fell out of that window. There was no indication on the search results page that this was the case; this constraint on the search results is hidden somewhere many levels deep in the device settings. On the desktop calendar application, however, there is no such restriction. The designers at Apple probably made this choice because of the limited storage available on the iPhone.

The problem is not with that choice but the way designers failed to reflect it or explain it. It appears the designers responsible for the iPhone search capability just focused on the interaction design on the phone (how search results are handled and the default calendar scope). But from the user's perspective, the phone was not different from the desktop when it came to their calendar information. It was supposed to be just a different device in the same ecology and, for the user, complete calendar information should have spanned that ecosystem.

This is a small example that clearly illustrates the difference between designing for the ecology and designing for just the interaction. If Apple designers thought of the ecological design, they would have supported the search task more effectively while still taking into account the constraints of the smartphone device. Perhaps they could have offered an option along the lines of "No search results found in the last 30 days. Continue the search on the server?" or something similar.

16.3 CREATING AN ECOLOGICAL DESIGN

The ecological perspective. The ecological design perspective is a viewpoint that looks at how a system or product works within its external environment. It is about how the system or product is used in its context and how the system or product interacts or communicates with all the components of its environment.

Representing ecological design. An ecology's design is usually represented using a concept diagram that looks like a flow model, identifying:

- System entities.
- Work roles.
- Propagated information.
- User tasks.
- Ecology boundaries.
- External dependencies.

- A description of the underlying metaphor or theme of the concept (e.g., a central mothership-like service coordinating a set of connected mobile devices).
- How they all fit together.

Start by identifying the subsystems by work role. In Section 9.6.7, we talked about work roles and how the work flow of certain work roles has little or no overlap with those of others. In many systems, these parts of the overall design are almost mutually exclusive, allowing for a logical partitioning of the target system.

For example, in the MUTTS work practice, the nature of work done by a ticket buyer is different from that of the event manager. They rarely, if ever, interact within the ecology of MUTTS. Each work role can be thought of as associated with a subsystem or an ecology in itself. This means, the overall ecology of the work practice can be thought of as having a set of ecologies, one for each subsystem. This separation provides us a way to reduce overall design complexity through a divide-and-conquer approach.

The subsystems themselves are connected via information exchange (for example, through a central database) and specialized work roles responsible for that exchange at their boundaries. For example, there are work roles such as systems or IT engineers responsible for ensuring that the ticket information from event vendors is correctly stored in a database that is available accurately and reliably to ticket buyers.

Proceed with generative design. Using ideation and sketching techniques we discussed in Chapter 14, synthesize ideas for what the ecology is, what it contains, including devices and channels, features, capabilities, and most importantly, a conceptual design to explain how it works. The goal is to create as many ideas as possible for the overall theme or metaphor of the ecological conceptual design. After the ideas are generated and captured as sketches, the team will critique each idea and concept for tradeoffs.

Establish a conceptual design for the ecology. For example, maybe the ecology will feature a "mothership" concept where there is a central entity that acts as the brain and information exchange for all other entities and devices in the ecology. Or is the ecology better served by a peer-to-peer architecture without a central repository concept? How will such a concept address the breakdowns, constraints, or other deficiencies in the work practice?

As part of this phase, you should also come up with ideas on the pervasive information architecture.

The issue of self-sufficiency. An ecology's self-sufficiency comes down to how the ecology is structured and whether it provides everything the user needs to thrive in the ecology without depending on other ecologies.

Metaphor

An analogy used in design to communicate and explain unfamiliar concepts using familiar conventional knowledge. A central metaphor often becomes the theme of a product, the motif behind the conceptual design (Section 15.3.6).

MUTTS

MUTTS is the acronym for Middleburg University Ticket Transaction Service, our running example for most of the process chapters (Section 5.5).

Pervasive information architecture

A structure for organizing, storing, retrieving, displaying, manipulating, and sharing information that provides ever-present information availability spanning parts of a broad ecology (Sections 12.4.4 and 16.2.3).

As an example, Norman (2009) cites the Amazon Kindle—a good example of a self-sufficient ecology. The product is for reading books, magazines, or any textual material. You don't need a computer to download or use it; the device can live as its own independent ecology. Browsing, buying, downloading books, and more is a pleasurable flow of activity. The Kindle is mobile, self-sufficient, and works synergistically with an existing Amazon account to keep track of the books you have bought through Amazon.com. It connects to its ecology through the Internet for downloading and sharing books and other documents. Each Kindle has its own email address so that you and others can send lots of materials in lots of formats to it for later reading.

A self-sufficient ecology has fewer dependencies and because it fully encompasses the users, gives more control to curate the experience. In contrast, gated ecologies like Apple's tend to come with their own tradeoffs with respect to how users can operate within the ecology.

Example: Conceptual Design for the Ticket Kiosk System Ecology

For the Ticket Kiosk System, we envision a central control system that acts as a hub for all transactions. This is necessary to keep track of ticket inventory and for managing temporary locking of tickets while users are in the middle of a buying transaction. If the transaction was abandoned or times out, those tickets will be released for other customers. One downside of this concept is that the central hub can become a single point of failure. If there is a breakdown, all kiosks and websites would go down together.

In Fig. 16-2, we show an early conceptual design sketch for the Ticket Kiosk System from the ecological perspective. All transactions from all kiosks and the website where tickets are sold are served by the control center. Users bring their own personal ecologies into the overall flow when they use laptops, tablets, and phones to search, browse, and buy tickets. At least some of these user devices can be used to contain e-tickets in lieu of physical tickets. This means that each ticket must have an ID number that can be scanned by the Ticket Kiosk System devices at event venues.

The team came up with other ideas such as smart tickets that were aware of a venue's layout (Fig. 16-3.) During the critiquing phase, several feasibility issues were brought up with available technology. The idea was then modified to put small "seat location finder" kiosks at the entrance of the venue. These finder kiosks scan the ticket and show a path on the screen for the location of the seats.

In Fig. 16-3, we show ideas from an ecological conceptual design for the Ticket Kiosk System focusing on a feature for a smart ticket to guide users to seating.

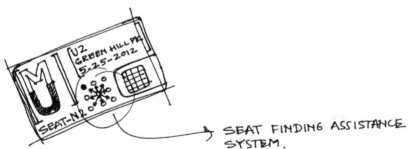

Fig. 16-2

An early conceptual design idea from the ecological perspective (sketch courtesy of Akshay Sharma, formerly of Virginia Tech Department of Industrial Design).

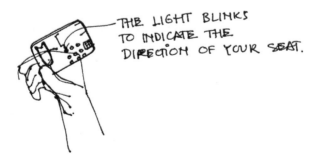

Fig. 16-3

Ecological conceptual design ideas focusing on a feature for a smart ticket to guide users to seating (sketch courtesy of Akshay Sharma, formerly of Virginia Tech Department of Industrial Design).

In Fig. 16-4, we show ecological conceptual design ideas for the Ticket Kiosk System focusing on a feature showing communication connection with a smartphone. You can have a virtual ticket sent from a kiosk to your mobile device and use that to enter the event.

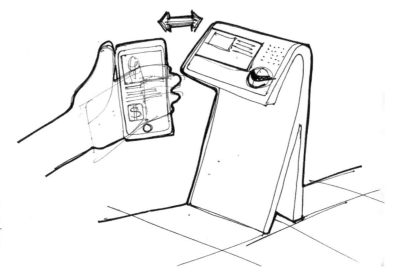

Fig. 16-4

Ecological conceptual design ideas focusing on a feature showing communication with a smartphone (sketch courtesy of Akshay Sharma, formerly of Virginia Tech Department of Industrial Design).

Ecological perspective

The design viewpoint taken from the ecological layer at the base of the pyramid of user needs, which is about how a system or product works within, interacts, and communicates with the context of its external environment. It is about how users can participate and thrive in the ecology of the work domain (Section 12.3.1).

In Fig. 16-5, we show an ecological conceptual design idea for the Ticket Kiosk System focusing on the features for communicating and social networking to share information about event attendance.

Exercise 16-1: Conceptual Design for the Ecology of Your System

Think about your system and contextual data and envision a conceptual design, including any metaphors, in the ecological perspective. Try to communicate the designer's mental model, or a design vision, of how the system works as a black box within its environment.

16.4 DESIGNING AN ECOLOGY TO INFLUENCE USER BEHAVIOR

Beale (2007) introduces the interesting concept of slanty design. "Slanty design is an approach that extends user-centered design by focusing on the things people should (and should not) be able to do with the product(s) behind the design."

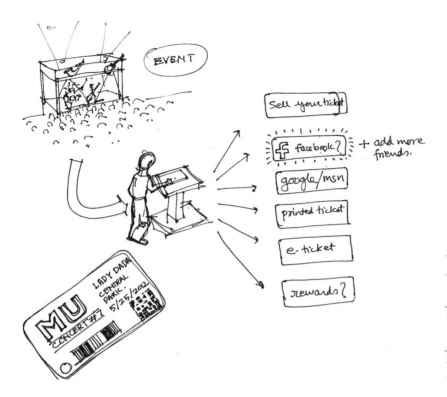

Fig. 16-5

Ecological conceptual design idea focusing on the features for communicating and social networking (sketch courtesy of Akshay Sharma, formerly of Virginia Tech Department of Industrial Design).

Design is a conversation between designers and users about both desired and undesired usage outcomes. But user-centered design, for example, using contextual inquiry and analysis, is grounded in the user's current behavior, which is not always optimal. Sometimes, it is desirable to change, or even control, the user's behavior (Chapter 13).

One such idea is to make a design that works best for all users taken together and for the enterprise at large within the ecological perspective. This can work against what an individual user wants. In essence, it is about controlling user behavior through designs that attenuate usability from the individual user's interaction perspective, making it difficult to do things not in the interest of other users or the enterprise in the ecological perspective, but still allowing the individual users to accomplish the necessary basic functionality and tasks.

One example is sloped reading desks in a library, which still allow reading but make it difficult to place food or drink on the desk or, worse, on the documents. Beale's similar example in the domain of airport baggage claims is marvelously simple and effective. People stand next to the baggage conveyor belt and many people even bring their carts with them. This behavior increases usability of the system for them because the best ease of use occurs when you can just pluck the baggage from the belt directly onto the cart.

However, crowds of people and carts cause congestion, reducing the accessibility and usability of other users with similar needs. Signs politely requesting users to remain away from the belt except at the moment of luggage retrieval are regrettably ineffective. A slanty design for the baggage carousel, however, solves the problem nicely. In this case, it involves something that is physically slanty; the surrounding floor slopes down away from the baggage carousel.

This interferes with bringing carts close to the belt and significantly reduces the comfort of people standing near the belt by forcing people to remain away from the carousel and then make a dash for the bags when they arrive within grasping distance. This reduces one aspect of individual usability somewhat, but it works best overall for everyone in the ecological perspective. Slanty design includes evaluation to eliminate unforeseen and unwanted side effects.

Pervasive information architecture

A structure for organizing, storing, retrieving, displaying, manipulating, and sharing information that provides ever-present information availability spanning parts of a broad ecology (Sections 12.4.4 and 16.2.3).

16.5 EXAMPLE: AN ECOLOGY FOR A SMART SHOPPING APPLICATION

We conclude this chapter with an extended example of designing the ecology for a shopping application based on what the information architecture people call pervasive information architecture, which we adapted from Resmini and Rosati (2011). This is also a good example of an activity-based design.

Activity-based interaction

Interaction in the context of one or more task thread(s), a set of, or possibly sequences of, multiple, overlapping, and related tasks, often involving more than one device in an ecology (Sections 1.6.2 and 14.2.6.4).

16.5.1 Some High-Level Issues

Who is the client? It might seem we are designing for shoppers, and we are. But our client is the store management. We're designing to help our client's customers have a good shopping experience. You can't make an app to help customers unless the store participates in the ecology. And that can't happen unless store management is the client. Let's assume the store is onboard.

It's hard work to find things in a store. Even after shopping the same large store dozens of times, many shoppers don't feel they know where things are, and there is seldom enough staff on hand to assist. As a result of just this one factor, the experience of shopping in a large physical retail store can often be frustrating and exhausting.

The dilemma of impulse buying. The UX team came up with a design idea that makes it easy for customers to locate products within the store, an efficient customer shopping experience that should be welcomed by all. But you are probably aware that typical store management doesn't want shoppers to know where everything is—at least not immediately, without having to browse through the store to find it. As you may know, many large stores actually design their merchandise layouts to slow shoppers down, exposing them to impulse buying "opportunities"—displays of items they hadn't planned on buying, but might find interesting enough to buy anyway.

Also, the layout of some stores is deliberately changed periodically to offset shoppers learning about where things are. Even experienced shoppers are now forced to browse large portions of the store layout, including the impulse item "traps."

How can designers support the user need for efficiency in the face of this behavior by store management? The answer goes back to basics. During usage research, you have to explore the store perspective of the shopping activity. And, through usage research, your team might recognize that impulse buying is not necessarily always bad for the shopper. Customers might occasionally buy one of these items that is really nice, useful, or even fun—good for both customer and store.

So you need a design to sell store management on streamlining the shopping experience while still retaining impulse sales. Your design challenge is to:

- Replace the usual frustrating and exhausting shopping experience with one that is efficient and actually fun.
- Convince store management that this alone can bring customers back more often, offsetting any lost impulse sales.
- Find ways to include impulse shopping in other ways in our design.

16.5.2 Key Parts of the Design

The SmartFridge. We will be designing a shopping experience for a customer that starts with a smart fridge in the home, a fridge that knows about its contents and learns about user needs and food preferences. It can, for example, tell when the milk supply is dwindling and suggest putting milk on the shopping list. The ecology can include a smart pantry that notifies when the last item of a type is removed from its shelves.

Mobile device and app. We will assume that users savvy enough to be using a SmartFridge will almost always carry a mobile device, such as a smartphone. As part of our ecology, we will design a smartphone app, called SmartShop.

The SmartKart. A large part of this project is to design a SmartKart that helps the user find things in the store. The SmartKart will contain a built-in mobile device with a touchscreen display, connected to the store ecology via a special Wi-Fi setup. The SmartKart processor can also be used offline for mundane tasks such as doing price/unit (e.g., price per ounce) cost comparisons.

16.5.3 How it Works

Preshopping activities. These activities have to occur before the actual shopping can begin:

1. Accumulate a generic list of things to buy.
2. Match the generic items to specific products in the store:
   a. SmartShop app finds candidate matches.
   b. User mediates by selecting best match among the candidates.
3. Generate a specific shopping list.
4. Download the specific shopping list to the SmartKart at the store.

Accumulating a generic list. Step 1 of the process is the accumulation over time of a generic shopping list, expressed with as much or as little detail and specificity as desired. An example of a generic item is "orange juice." We will make it easy for users to grab the phone to do Step 1 and enter a new item into the current generic list in SmartShop whenever they think of something to buy (left-most in Fig. 16-6).

Matching generic list items to specific store products. In Step 2, SmartShop is used to match each generic list item to a specific product known to be in the store (lower left in Fig. 16-6) by:

▪ Step 2a: SmartShop searches for a generic item using inexact database matching, leading to a set of candidate-specific matches.
▪ Step 2b: User selects desired specific item from possible matches in search results.

For example, for a generic item of "orange juice," a specific product might be "UPC code = xxxxx, Green Valley brand, fresh (not from concentrate), one quart, with pulp."

Generate specific shopping list. As each specific product is selected, in Step 3 it is added to the accumulating specific shopping list in the app (bottom next to far right in Fig. 16-6).

Through usage research, we also learned that users occasionally look through online ads and emails from stores about sales, specials, discounts, or

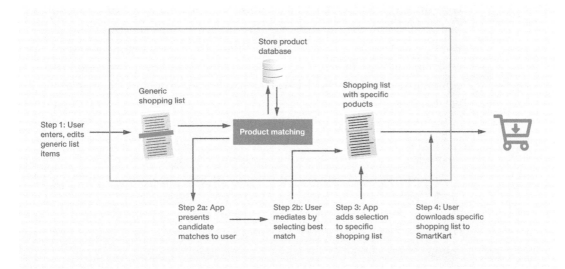

Fig. 16-6
Preshopping-trip activities.

coupons. Clicking on the Add to my shopping list button while viewing one of these items will add that item to the specific list in the app.

Download the specific shopping list to the SmartKart at the store. Upon arrival at the store, the shoppers perform Step 4 by launching the SmartShop app on a mobile phone and tapping the phone on the shopping cart. This establishes a connection to the built-in mobile device of the SmartKart, which automatically syncs to the current specific shopping list (extreme bottom right in Fig. 16-6), making the specific shopping list pervasive in the ecology.

16.5.3.1 Finding things in the store

If a design goal is to help customers locate items efficiently, where is the information needed to make that happen?

This is a good example of embodied information. Product-location information is embodied in the physical ecology of the store itself and in the items themselves. Each item could be aware of its location in terms of aisle, section, shelf, and so on. Conversely, each shelf could know what items are located there. Any number of existing technologies can capture this location information in a database.

In-store location awareness of products on the shelf. SmartKart browsing (sensing products as you pass them in the aisles) could be enough to help the user find things in the store. But we can do better if somehow the shelves themselves are embodied physical devices that know something about the products they contain. Perhaps something involving RFID sensors and/or bar code scanners built into the shelves. Awareness by the shelves of their contents will provide us with the necessary accurate product location information, even if there are errors in stocking. In addition, of course, the shelves must now be able to communicate (via the special Wi-Fi) what they know to carts and to the store database system.

Shelf-awareness of products offers a bonus—a continuous capability for keeping inventory information accurately up to date, eliminating the expensive, inconvenient, and labor-intensive hassle of periodic store inventories.

Another potential benefit to the store is, as Resmini and Rosati (2011, p. 217) say in their grocery store example, that a product-location system will be liberating to the store. First, sales associates on the floor no longer have to help customers find things. Also, if the layout no longer has to be constrained by how customers find things in the store, it opens the door to innovative and dramatically different store layouts.

With these critical ecological design innovations, the act of moving the cart through the store can be mapped to moving the cart through items on the shopping list—almost.

Cart awareness of its location in store. The next capability we need is obvious: The cart has to know where it is within the store. This could be accomplished by shelf-to-cart wireless communication, but perhaps a more flexible solution is a capability within the cart processor somewhat analogous to a localized GPS system and an internal map of the store. The in-store location system won't be a real GPS, however, but will be implemented via some kind of locating network strung (perhaps in the ceiling) along each aisle. So this introduces into the store information architecture a key new information object: the current location of each cart.

Cart ability to find a product. Now we have what we need for matching cart location to the location of products on the shopping list. In our pseudo-GPS app, the screen on the SmartKart shows a map of the internal layout of the store, showing aisles as "roads" on which to "drive" the cart. The GPS display shows where the cart is within the store and it knows the "addresses" of each item on the shopping list. The GPS will treat each item on your shopping list as a "destination," dropping "pins" for your items on the store map and ordering the list so that each item can be found in a single pass through the aisles of the store.

As the cart approaches a store location containing an item on the shopping list, the cart display will indicate where to look to pick it up. As the item is put in the cart, it will be checked off the shopping list and a running total of the cost can be updated, using cost information obtained via the UPC bar code. All of this is the perfect cross-channel mapping from one device to another that connects customer needs to store services.

And, of course, it's starting to happen in reality. Walmart has recently (as of this writing) unveiled a self-checkout mechanism[1] that allows customers to skip the checkout lines by:

- Scanning items as you shop.
- Paying via a smartphone app.
- Showing your e-receipt on the way out.

Similarly, Amazon has been evaluating a grocery store technology in which the system logs items as they are put in the cart[2] so shoppers can avoid traditional checkout lines. The system senses when the customer leaves the store, totals the bill, and charges it to that customer's Amazon account. Cashiers are replaced by hundreds of cameras that track purchases.[3]

16.5.4 Impulse Buying

Remember our discussion of the dilemma of impulse buying and the difficulties it posed to helping shoppers find things in the store? We can brainstorm about how the SmartKart display can make shoppers aware of items on special as they push the cart past them on the shelves, bringing up special offers and alerting customers to discounts, sale items, promotions, additional coupons, and impulse buying opportunities as shoppers pass them with their SmartKarts.

By this same token, the SmartKart display can suggest buying additional items or accessories related to items on the list and expanding the shopping list accordingly. For example, if the shopper is buying a vacuum cleaner, this feature will serve as a reminder: Don't forget to get some extra vacuum cleaner bags. Not only is this a good marketing idea but it can be a helpful reminder to shoppers, too (as long as it isn't overdone or doesn't become annoying).

Customers will come back in droves because, at last, someone has done something to make their shopping experience fun and easy instead of a

---

[1] https://www.androidpolice.com/2017/01/09/walmart-finally-rolls-scan-go-app-android/

[2] https://www.geekwire.com/2016/amazon-go-works-technology-behind-online-retailers-groundbreaking-new-grocery-store/

[3] https://www.npr.org/sections/thetwo-way/2018/01/22/579640565/amazons-cashier-less-seattle-grocery-opens-to-the-public

brain-deadening, loathsome experience. Now, who is going to a store that doesn't have this service?

Exercise 16-2: Pursue this SmartKart Design Idea Further

This is definitely a group assignment. Engage your team in ideation, sketching, critiquing, designing, prototyping, and evaluation to come up with further innovative ideas for the SmartKart.

Designing the Interaction

17

17.1 INTRODUCTION

17.1.1 You Are Here

We begin each process chapter with a "you are here" picture of the chapter topic in the context of The Wheel, the overall UX design lifecycle template (Fig. 17-1). In this chapter, we describe how to design for the middle layer of the human needs pyramid—the interaction.

In Section 12.3, we discussed how interaction needs are about being able to perform required tasks in the work domain using the product or system being designed. In this chapter, we go about designing the interaction to satisfy those user needs.

17.2 DESIGNING FOR INTERACTION NEEDS

17.2.1 Designing for Interaction Needs Is about Supporting Tasks

In practical terms, interaction design is about how people use the system or product to perform tasks within the broader work practice and covers all touch points where the user interacts with the ecology. It is where users look at displays and manipulate controls, doing sensory, cognitive, and physical actions. Examples of interaction design in Apple's iTunes ecology include

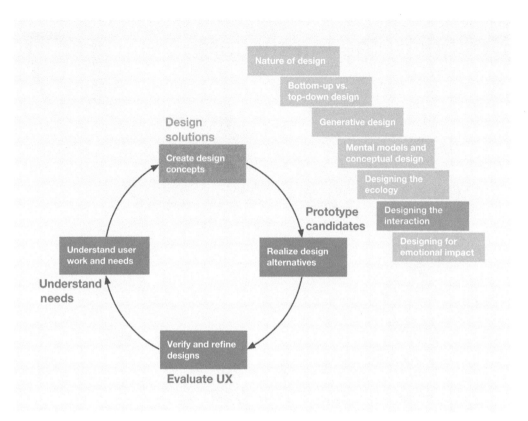

Fig. 17-1

You are here in the chapter describing designing the interaction, within the Design Solutions lifecycle activity, in the context of the overall Wheel UX lifecycle.

Ecology

In the setting of UX design, the ecology is the entire set of surrounding parts of the world, including networks, other users, devices, and information structures, with which a user, product, or system interacts (Section 16.2.1).

supporting users with signing up, logging in, searching or browsing for songs by artist, title, album, and rating, selecting, playing, pausing, rating, and manipulating songs.

17.2.2 Different Device Types in the Ecology Require Different Interaction Designs

Different devices have different form factors, usage conventions, constraints, and capabilities, each requiring an appropriate design for interaction with that device. For example, the interaction design for a search task will be different for desktops, phones, tablets, and watches—with smaller and less capable devices providing fewer options and more constrained results. Even within the same device category, such as a phone, interaction designs will differ to accommodate the various target platform's conventions. For example, the interaction design of an application on the Android platform will be different from that for the Apple or Microsoft platforms.

17.3 CREATING AN INTERACTION DESIGN

17.3.1 Start by Identifying All Devices and Their Roles in the Ecology

With your UX team, start by enumerating all the devices that are envisioned for the ecology. What role will each of these devices play? For example, depending on the nature of work practice, you can think of a smart watch as mostly a tracking and notification device whereas a desktop can be the central hub where the majority of the content is generated. Other devices such as phones and tablets can be used for the combination of both content generation and consumption tasks.

17.3.2 Proceed with Generative Design

Get immersed in the task-related models, requirements, and user stories and involve the team in ideation and sketching using the techniques we discussed in Chapter 14. The first goal is to create as many ideas as possible for the overall theme or metaphor of the interaction conceptual design (next section) for each device in the ecology. Then switch to generating ideas for interaction patterns and how the structure of the dialogue between user and system will proceed for each device. Think of how a given task sequence can be handled by multiple devices as the user switches contexts in the ecology.

After the ideas are generated and captured as sketches, the team will critique each idea and concept for tradeoffs.

17.3.3 Establish a Good Conceptual Design for the Interaction

A conceptual design for the interaction can be based on a design pattern (repeatable solution to a common design problem that emerges as best practice, encouraging sharing and reuse) or a metaphor to describe how the interaction design works for a given device.

Metaphor

An analogy used in design to communicate and explain unfamiliar concepts using familiar conventional knowledge. A central metaphor often becomes the theme of a product, the motif behind the conceptual design (Section 15.3.6).

An example is a calendar application on a desktop in which user actions look and behave like writing on a real calendar. A more modern example is the metaphor of reading a book on an iPad. As the user moves a finger across the display to push the page aside, the display takes on the appearance of a real paper page turning. Most users find it comfortingly familiar.

Also recall from Section 15.3.6 the example of using a "time machine" metaphor in the conceptual design of a backup feature available in Apple's Mac operating system. That metaphor explains the somewhat technical and cumbersome activity of data backup and recovery to everyday users.

17.3.4 Leverage Interaction Design Patterns

Design patterns (Borchers, 2001; Tidwell, 2011; Welie & Hallvard, 2000) are repeatable solutions to common design problems that emerge as best practices, encouraging sharing and reuse and promoting consistency. Much of what we see in modern GUIs and mobile interfaces today is built up of design patterns—for example, the way a button looks and acts or a search feature.

A pattern library (Schleifer, 2008) is like a beefed-up style guide. Like style guides, they help you avoid having to reinvent designs for common repetitive local design situations within the greater scope of interaction designs. They are a way of sharing design experience about widget-level design that has been evaluated and refined and that has worked.

Leverage design patterns, concepts from the work domain, interaction ideas, and work flows for each device. Some domains and products have established patterns that can be embraced. For example, suppose you are working on an email communication system. If you want to take advantage of an established standard interaction design concept that we know works for desktop systems, you will feature a three-way split pane pattern with a list of mailboxes as one pane, a list of messages of the selected mailbox in the second pane, and the preview of the selected message in the third pane.

However if the goal is to set yourself apart from the crowded space of email systems, you will break with the established pattern and come up with a better and more innovative design concept.

Another example of using a concept or idea from the target work domain in an interaction design is the use of a shopping cart on an online shopping website. This pattern communicates how the design works in the digital realm. As users shop, they can click on the cart icon to see what is in their cart, just like shopping in the physical world.

17.3.5 Establish the Information Architecture for Each Device

In the previous chapter, we talked about establishing the pervasive information architecture (which provides ever-present information availability across devices and users) for the entire ecology. Now, for each device, you also need to decide on the information architecture. What information will be available for interaction on each device? How will it be structured? What happens when a user tries to access information not available on that device? What is the best way to represent that information in the design? What are the modalities with which users can access that information (voice, touch, etc.)?

Example: Interaction Conceptual Design for the Ticket Kiosk System

There is a common perception of a ticket kiosk that includes a box on a pedestal and a touchscreen with colorful displays showing choices of events. If you give an assignment to a team of students, even most UX students, to come up with a conceptual design of a ticket kiosk in 30 minutes, nine times out of 10 you will get something like this. But if you teach them to approach it with ideation and sketching, they can come up with amazingly creative and varied results.

In our ideation about the Ticket Kiosk System, someone mentioned making it an immersive experience. That triggered more ideas and sketches on how to make it immersive, until we came up with a three-panel overall design that literally surrounds and immerses the user (Fig. 17-2).

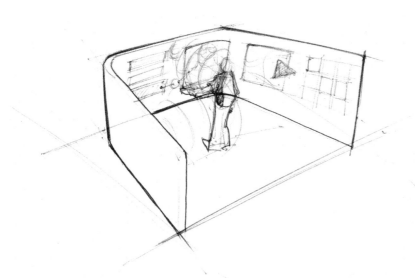

Fig. 17-2

Part of a conceptual design showing immersion in the emotional perspective (sketch courtesy of Akshay Sharma, formerly of Virginia Tech Department of Industrial Design).

Here is a brief description of the concept, in outline form.

- The center screen is the interaction area, where immersion and ticket-buying action occur.
- The left screen contains available options or possible next steps; for example, this screen might provide a listing of all required steps to complete a transaction, including letting the user access these steps out of sequence.
- The right screen contains contextual support, such as interaction history and related actions; for example, this screen might provide a summary of the current transaction so far and related information such as reviews and ratings.
- Each next step selection from the left panel puts the user in a new kind of immersion in the center screen, and the previous immersion situation becomes part of the interaction history on the right panel.
- Addressing privacy and enhancing the impression of immersion: When the ticket buyer steps in, rounded shields made of classy materials gently wrap around.
- An "Occupied" sign glows on the outside.
- The inside of the two rounded half-shells of the shield become the left and right interaction panels.
- Note: We might need to evaluate whether this could induce feelings of being "trapped by the machine."

Interaction perspective

The design viewpoint taken within the interaction layer of the pyramid of user needs, between the ecological layer at the base and the emotional layer on top. The interaction perspective is about how users operate the system or product. It is a task and intention view, in which user and system come together. It is where users look at displays and manipulate controls, and do sensory, cognitive, and physical actions (Section 12.3.1).

In Fig. 17-3, we show part of a conceptual design for the Ticket Kiosk System in the interaction perspective for a kiosk. The available categories of tickets are displayed as a menu, as the starting point. When the user selects a category, they go to a screen for that category and a curated set of "featured" events is displayed in a list. The details of navigating among these choices and accessing the full list of available events in this category are to be fleshed out in further rounds of ideation.

Exercise 17-1: Conceptual Design for Interaction for Your System

Think about your system and contextual data and envision a conceptual design in the interaction perspective. Try to communicate the designer's mental model of how the user operates the system.

17.3.6 Envision Interaction Flows Across Different Devices in the Ecology

Even though we design interactions based on device type, users don't think about their work that way. For users, work gets done in an ecology. So, it is important to support the overarching goals of the user as they transition from one device to another. For example, a user's high-level goal of buying a product may involve searching for it on a desktop using a website, placing an order,

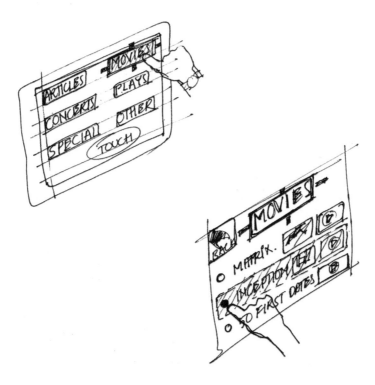

Fig. 17-3

Part of a conceptual design in the interaction perspective (sketch courtesy of Akshay Sharma, formerly of Virginia Tech Department of Industrial Design).

getting an email confirmation with details on when it will be available for pickup, getting a text message to notify that it is ready for pickup at a local store, and needing a confirmation message to show in the store during item pickup.

It is important for interaction designers to keep in mind this high-level user goal of buying a product as they go about designing for each individual device. In the e-commerce example, designing the interaction on the smartphone may include a feature to use location awareness capability to show the order confirmation when the user is detected to be at one of the company's stores. So, when the user opens the application on the phone to pull up the confirmation, the system anticipates the need and shows the "latest order" information by default.

One way to think about and model such work goals is through the use of storyboards, which we discuss next.

17.4 STORYBOARDS

17.4.1 What Are Storyboards?

A storyboard is a sequence of visual "frames" illustrating the interplay between a user and an envisioned ecology or device. Storyboards bring the design to life in graphical "clips," freeze-frame sketches of stories of how people will work with the system. This narrative description can come in many forms and at different levels of detail.

Storyboards for representing interaction sequence designs are like visual scenario sketches, depicting envisioned interaction design solutions. A storyboard might be thought of as a "comic-book" style illustration of a scenario, with actors, screens, interaction, and dialogue showing sequences of flow from frame to frame.

17.4.2 Storyboards Can Cover All Layers of the Pyramid

Even though storyboards are predominantly about how the users interact with the envisioned system, they cover aspects of the other two layers too. After all, interaction design touches all touch points the users have with the ecology and the design of the ecology, and interaction is a major contributor to emotional needs. Start by creating illustrated sequences that show users interacting with the system in a narrative style.

Include things such as these in your storyboards:

- Hand-sketched pictures annotated with a few words.
- All the work practice that is part of the task, not just interaction with the system. For example, include phone conversations with agents or roles outside the system.
- Sketches of devices and screens.
- Any connections with system internals, for example, flow to and from a database.
- Physical user actions.
- Cognitive user actions in "thought balloons."
- Extrasystem activities, such as talking with a friend about what ticket to buy.

Because storyboards illustrate how users go about meeting their goals while envisioning the high-level interplay among human users, the different devices in the ecology, and the surrounding context, they are great at demonstrating the potential of the system in a context where it solves particular problems. To do this, you might show a device in the hands of a user and connect its usage to the context. As an example, you might show how a handheld device could be used while waiting for a flight in an airport.

Storyboards can also focus exclusively on interaction designs and show screens, user actions, transitions, and user reactions for each device. You might still show the user, but now it is in the context of user thoughts, intentions, and actions upon user interface objects in operating the device. Here is where you get down to concrete task details. Select key tasks from the HTI, design scenarios, and task-sequence models to feature in your interaction perspective storyboards.

Storyboards can also be used to envision emotional design aspects and to illustrate deeper user experience phenomena such as fun, joy, and aesthetics (focus of our next chapter). They can show the experience itself—remember the excitement of actually riding the mountain bike in the example from Buxton (Section 1.4.4.3).

Example: Ticket Kiosk System Storyboard Sketches

See Fig. 17-4 for an example of a sequence of sketches as a storyboard depicting a sequence using the Ticket Kiosk System. This storyboard depicts how a kiosk at a bus stop can facilitate opportunistic interactions with users as they wait for the bus.

Example: More Ticket Kiosk System Storyboard Sketches

In Fig. 17-5, we show part of a different Ticket Kiosk System storyboard. This storyboard depicts a similar interaction in a mall context, and how a kiosk can potentially trigger a planning activity with friends involving entertainment events.

Example: Ticket Kiosk System Storyboard Sketches Focusing on the Interaction with the Kiosk

In Fig. 17-6, we have shown sample storyboard sketches that might go with the scenario below.

The following is one possible scenario that came out of an ideation session for an interaction sequence for a town resident buying a concert ticket from the Ticket Kiosk System to which the three-screen storyboard sketches in Fig. 17-6 roughly correspond. This example is a good illustration of the breadth we intend for the scope of the term "interaction," including a person walking with respect to the kiosk, radio-frequency identification at a distance, and audio sounds being made and heard.

- Ticket buyer walks up to the kiosk.
- Sensor detects user presence and starts the immersive protocol.
- Activates "Occupied" sign on the wraparound case.
- Detects people with MU passports.
- Center screen: Greets buyer and asks for PIN.
- Center screen: Shows recommendations and most popular current offering based on buyer's category.
- Screen on right: Shows buyer's profile if one exists on MU system.
- Screen on left: Lists options such as browse events, buy tickets, and search.
- Center screen: Buyer selects "Boston Symphony at Burruss Hall" from the recommendations.
- Screen on right: "Boston Symphony at Burruss Hall" title, information, and images.
- Surround sound: Plays music from that symphony.
- Center screen: Shows "pick date and time."

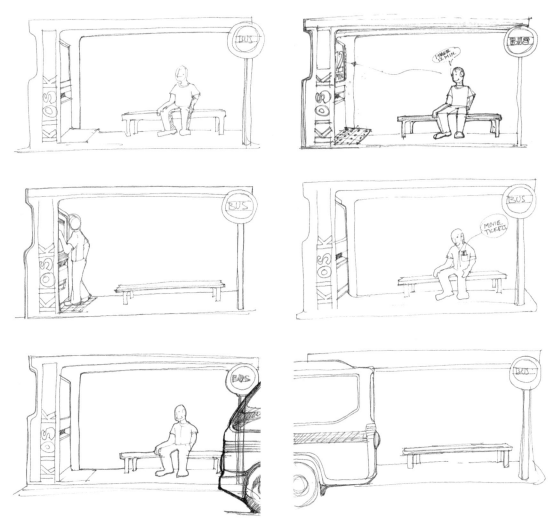

Fig. 17-4

Example of a sequence of sketches as a storyboard (sketches courtesy of Akshay Sharma, Virginia Tech Department of Industrial Design).

- Center screen: Buyer selects date from the month view of the calendar (can be changed to week view).
- Screen on right: The entire context selected so far, including date.
- Center screen: A day view with times, such as matinee or evening. The rest of the slots in the day show related events such as wine tasting or special dinner events.
- Screen on left: Options for making reservations at these special events.

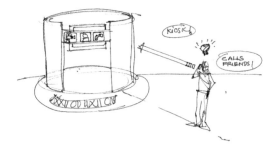

Fig. 17-5

Part of a different Ticket Kiosk System storyboard (sketches courtesy of Akshay Sharma, Virginia Tech Department of Industrial Design).

- Center screen: Buyer selects a time.
- Center screen: Available seating chart with names for sections/categories and aggregate number of available seats per each section.
- Screen on left: Categories of tickets and prices.
- Center screen: Buyer selects category/section.
- Screen on right: Updates context with time and selected category/section.
- Center screen: Immerses user from a perspective of that section. Expands that section to show individual available seats. Has a call to action "Click on open seats to select" and an option to specify number of seats.
- Screen on left: Options to go back to see all sections or exit.
- Center screen: Buyer selects one or more seats by touching on available slots.
- Center screen: Shows payment options and a virtual representation of selected tickets.
- Screen on left: Provides options with discounts, coupons, sign up for mailing lists, etc.
- Center screen: Buyer selects a payment option.
- Center screen: Provided with a prompt to put credit card in slot.
- Center screen: Animates to show a representation of the card on screen.
- Center screen: Buyer completes payment.
- Screen on left: Options for related events, happy hour and dinner reservations, etc. These are contextualized to the event for which they just bought tickets.
- Center screen: Animates with tickets and CC coming back out of their respective slots.

17.4.3 Importance of Between-Frame Transitions

Storyboard frames show individual states as static screenshots. Through a series of such snapshots, storyboards show the progression of interaction over time. However, the important part of storyboards is the spaces between the frames, which is where the transitions are made (Buxton, 2007b). And these transitions

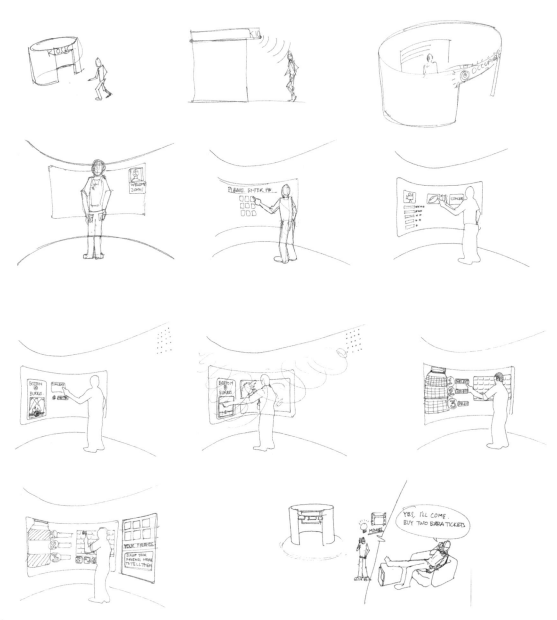

Fig. 17-6

*Sample sketches for a
concert ticket purchase
storyboard (sketches
courtesy of Akshay Sharma,
Virginia Tech Department
of Industrial Design).*

are where the user experience lives. Therefore, the actions between frames should be part of what is sketched. The transitions are where the cognitive affordances in your design earn their keep, where most problems for users exist, and where the challenges lie for designers.

We can augment the value of our storyboards greatly to inform design by showing the circumstances that lead to and cause the transitions and the context, situation, or location of those actions. These include user thoughts, words, gestures, reactions, expressions, and other experiential aspects of interaction. Is the screen difficult to see? Is the user too busy with other things to pay attention to the screen? Does a phone call lead to a different interaction sequence?

In Fig. 17-7, we show a transition frame with a user thought bubble explaining the change between the two adjacent state frames.

Cognitive affordance

A design feature that helps users with their cognitive actions: thinking, deciding, learning, understanding, remembering, and knowing about things (Section 30.2).

Fig. 17-7

Storyboard transition frame with thought bubble explaining state change (sketches courtesy of Akshay Sharma, Virginia Tech Department of Industrial Design).

Exercise 17-2: Storyboard for Your System

Goal: Get a little practice in sketching storyboards.

Activities: Sketch storyboard frames illustrating narrative sequences of action in each of the three perspectives.

- Include things such as these in your storyboards: Hand-sketched pictures annotated with a few words.
- All the work practice that is part of the task, not just interaction with the system. For example, include telephone conversations with agents or roles outside the system.

- Sketches of devices and screens.
- Any connections with system internals, for example, flow to and from a database.
- Physical user actions.
- Cognitive user actions in "thought balloons."
- Extrasystem activities, such as talking with a friend about what ticket to buy.
- For the ecological perspective, illustrate high-level interplay among human users, the system as a whole, and the surrounding context.
- In the interaction perspective, show screens, user actions, transitions, and user reactions.

Use storyboards in the emotional perspective to illustrate deeper user experience phenomena such as fun, joy, and aesthetics.

Schedule: You decide how much time you can afford to give this. If you cannot do this exercise in all three perspectives, just pick one, perhaps the ecological perspective.

17.5 WIREFRAMES

Because a wireframe (a line-drawing representation of the UX design, especially the interaction design, of a screen) is a kind of prototype, the major place we describe wireframes is in Section 20.4 in our prototyping chapter. However, because of the intertwining of prototyping in design, we need to introduce wireframes here.

17.5.1 The Path to Wireframes

In Fig. 17-8, we show the path from ideation and sketching, task interaction models, and envisioned design scenarios to wireframes as representations of your designs for screen layout and navigational flow.

Along with ideation, sketching, and critiquing, task interaction models and design scenarios are the principal inputs to storytelling and communication of designs. As sequences of sketches, storyboards are a natural extension of sketching. Storyboards, like scenarios, represent only selected task threads. Fortunately, it is a short and natural step from storyboards to wireframes.

To be sure, nothing beats pencil/pen and paper or a whiteboard for the sketching needed in ideation (brainstorming for design creation, Chapter 14), but, at some point, when the design concept emerges from ideation, it must be communicated to others who pursue the rest of the lifecycle process. Wireframes have long been the choice in the field for documenting, communicating, and prototyping interaction designs.

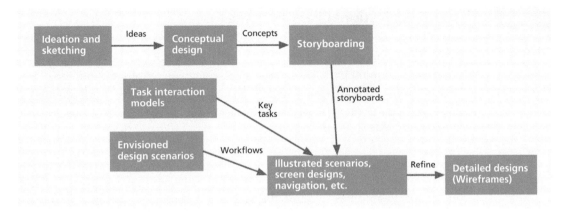

Fig. 17-8

The path from ideation and sketching, task interaction models, and envisioned design scenarios to wireframes.

17.5.2 What Are Wireframes?

Wireframes comprise lines and outlines (hence the name "wireframe") of boxes and other shapes to represent emerging interaction designs. They are:

- Schematic diagrams and "sketches" that define a webpage or screen content and navigational flow.
- Used to illustrate high-level concepts, approximate visual layout, and behavior.
- Sometimes used to show look and feel for an interaction design.
- Embodiments of screen or other state transitions during usage, depicting envisioned task flows in terms of user actions on user interface objects.

The drawing aspects of wireframes are often simple, involving rectangular objects that can be labeled, moved, and resized. Text and graphics representing content and data in the design are placed in those objects. Drawing templates are used to provide quick means to represent the more common kinds of user interface objects (more on this in the following sections).

In the early stages of design, typical wireframes are deliberately unfinished looking; they may not even be to scale. They usually don't contain much visual content, such as graphics, colors, or font choices. The idea is to create design representations quickly and inexpensively by just drawing boxes, lines, and other shapes.

Example: National Park Website

Introducing a national park website example. To illustrate the progression of design fidelity common in interaction design, we introduce a new example: A website for a fictitious national park where users can browse attractions and outdoor activities and can reserve park resources such as campsites. We show examples of interaction design for this product on a smartphone and desktop devices.

17.6 INTERMEDIATE INTERACTION DESIGN

As the team continues to refine the interaction design, the workflows explored using high-level storyboards are put to critique and analysis. This results in any necessary adjustments and whittling down of ideas under consideration. The team then focuses on the most promising ideas by increasing the fidelity of the designs and fleshing out more details of the flows.

In Fig. 17-9, we show early stage intermediate design wireframes depicting the workflow for reserving a campsite on a smartphone.

After entering parameters such as the dates desired, type of camping equipment (e.g., RV or tent), number of occupants, and facilities wanted (e.g., water and/or electric plug-ins) for a particular park or campground, the user sees Screen 1 in Fig. 17-9, which is a list of available campsite locations, vertically scrollable. Selecting a location takes the user to that location's page (Screen 2) with an image and a brief description followed by a list of available campsites at that location that meet the selection criteria. A map view of this location can be viewed by selecting the map icon on the top right of the screen, which takes you to Screen 3, with callouts for each available campsite.

Selection of a campsite from this page takes users to the campsite's page (Screen 4) with images and description of the site. A "reserve campsite" option on this page takes the user to a reservation form that spans multiple pages (Screen 5).

Screen 6 depicts the navigation menu that is accessible from the top left of Screen 1. This menu lists the different areas of this application, including locations saved as favorites. Selecting the "Saved" option gives users a list of their current reservations and any other bookmarked locations, as shown on Screen 7.

Note how a simple sequence of wireframes bring into focus details about the application. Even in this intermediate stage of design, it raises questions on how this design supports this work practice. What if the park has more than a handful of locations? How will the users browse them? This discussion uncovered a missing capability, namely a search feature, and raised the question of where such a capability should be manifest in the interaction design.

MAIN WORKFLOW

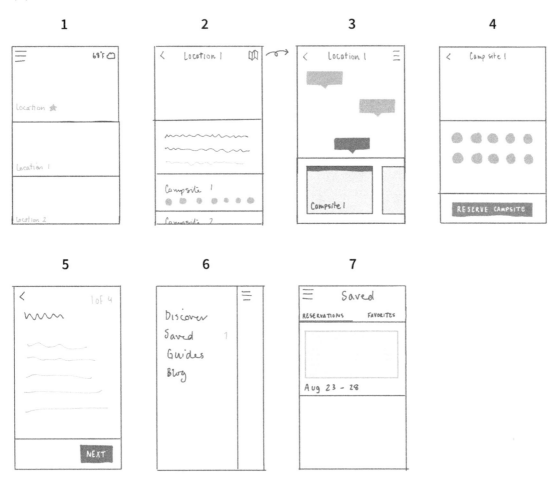

Fig. 17-9

Wireframe sketches depicting a workflow for exploring campsites (wireframes courtesy of Ame Wongsa, User Experience Design Lead, Cloudistics, Inc.).

Other questions that arose include how will the interaction in Screen 3 work if the camp sites on the map are too close to one another? Will the users have enough of a tap area to select one versus another (especially on a smartphone)? How can the design help the user make a choice of campsites? What criteria should be available to users to filter a list of campsites? Answering these questions in design is a journey toward higher fidelity.

Sometimes a particular aspect of design is explored further with more detailed wireframes. For example, in Fig. 17-10, we asked ourselves what to show when a campsite on a map is explored. In Screen 1, a small thumbnail image (shown as the green shaded area) and a brief description are shown anchored at the bottom. In Screen 2, a more detailed preview with a larger image and description idea is shown. In Screen 3, a smaller campsite location pin was explored in the shape of a circle instead of a callout.

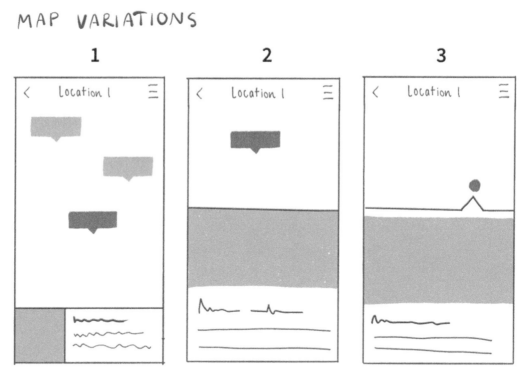

Fig. 17-10

Wireframe sketches exploring interaction pattern for seeing details of a campsite (wireframes courtesy of Ame Wongsa, User Experience Design Lead, Cloudistics, Inc.).

These wireframes also raise questions when subjected to critiquing. How much information can be provided in the description portion of the campsite preview at the bottom of Screen 1? Will that be enough for the user to make a decision on that site? In Screen 3, we are able to provide more context on the map by making the marker for a campsite small, but how will the campsite be identified in this idea if the marker is too small to hold the site number (which could have up to three digits)?

As the design team answers these questions through iteration, they slowly start filling in more details for the design. If the underlying design concept holds up to critiquing via these iterations, the team ends up with a final interaction design candidate for that device.

In Fig. 17-11, we show a resulting final interaction design for viewing camping areas on the phone. From the explore screen (top left frame), selecting a park shows the details of the park (top right frame) including a sliding tab of camp areas at that park (bottom of the frame). Selecting the map option on the top right of the frame shows the camp areas on a map (bottom left frame). Tapping on a camp area on the map (represented as pins) shows a preview of the area with name and other key information (bottom center frame). Users can see the full details of the camp area (bottom right frame) by tapping on the preview.

In Fig. 17-12, we show the final interaction design for reserving a campsite at a camp area on the phone. Users pick the dates for camping and number of occupants (top center frame) and are shown available campsites at that area. After confirming the reservation, users are provided with a confirmation page (bottom right frame). (The final interaction designs for the payment flows are not shown.)

17.7 INTERACTION DESIGN PRODUCTION

The final candidates for interaction are prototyped and subjected to evaluation (Part 5 of this book). Any issues identified in the evaluation kick off another round of design modifications and prototyping. Once the design is finalized, it's described in detail in a phase called design production. The objective of this phase is to define the design in enough detail so it becomes a specification for software engineers to implement.

In Fig. 17-13, we show the detailed design specification for a park page of the desktop device interaction design. Note the annotations in the bottom defining details such as how many lines the preview of the description should be and what happens when a user hovers over certain elements on the screen.

VIEW A CAMPING AREA

Fig. 17-11

High-fidelity wireframes showing workflow for viewing a camp area (wireframes and visual designs courtesy of Ame Wongsa, User Experience Design Lead, and Christina Janczak, UX Designer, of Cloudistics, Inc.).

RESERVE A CAMPSITE

Fig. 17-12

High-fidelity wireframes showing workflow for reserving a campsite in a camp area (wireframes and visual designs courtesy of Ame Wongsa, User Experience Design Lead, and Christina Janczak, UX Designer, of Cloudistics, Inc.).

Mount Cook National Park

AORAKI

People have been drawn to the rugged coast of Maine throughout history. Awed by its beauty and diversity, early 20th-century visionaries donated the land that became Acadia National Park. The park is home to many plants and animals, and the tallest mountain on the U.S. Atlantic coast. Today visitors come to Acadia to hike granite peaks, bike historic carriage roads, or relax and enjoy the scenery.

ACTIVITIES AND AMENITIES

Campground	First Aid
Trailer parking	Fishing
Cafe	Swimming
Trails	Fire pits

Campgrounds

SCHOODIC WOODS
281 Campsites   May 1 - Sept 14

SEAWALL
281 Campsites   May 1 - Sept 14

BLACKWOODS
281 Campsites   May 1 - Sept 14

Notes

1 Descriptions

Show 5 lines of text. On click, expand to show the full description and push down the next section.

2 Campgrounds

List all campgrounds in the location.

When the user mouses-over an entry in the campgrounds list, show a marker indicating the campgrounds location on the mini-map.

3 Mini Map

Shows a mini map of the location.

The map sticks to the top of the view when the screen scrolls.

A marker indicates the location of a highlighted campground

Fig. 17-13

Detailed design specification for the park page of the desktop device interaction design (wireframes and visual designs courtesy of Ame Wongsa, User Experience Design Lead, and Christina Janczak, UX Designer, of Cloudistics, Inc.).

EXERCISE 17-3: INTERMEDIATE AND DETAILED DESIGN FOR YOUR SYSTEM

Goal: Get some practice in developing a few parts of the intermediate and detailed design

Activities: If you are working with a team, get together with your team.

- Choose just one principal work role for your system (e.g., the customer).
- Choose just one key task that work role is expected to perform.
- For that work role and task, make a few illustrated scenarios to show some of the associated interaction.
- Sketch some annotated screen layouts (wireframes) to support your scenarios, along with some representation of the navigational structure.
- Go for a little depth, but not much breadth.

Hints, cautions, and assumptions:

- Do not get too involved in design details yet (e.g., icon appearance or menu placement).
- Control time spent arguing; learn the process!
- Base your screen designs on the usage research and design you have done so far.

Deliverables: Just the work products that naturally result from these activities.
Schedule: Whatever you can afford. At least give it an honest try.

17.8 MAINTAIN A CUSTOM STYLE GUIDE

As you get into detailed interaction design, it is important to maintain consistency of design vocabulary and styles within and across the various devices. Custom style guides are the way to ensure such consistency.

17.8.1 What is a Custom Style Guide?

A custom style guide is a document that is fashioned and maintained by designers to capture and describe details of visual and other general design decisions, especially about screen designs, font choices, iconography, and color usage, which can be applied in multiple places. Its contents can be specific to one project or an umbrella guide across all projects on a given platform or over a whole organization. A style guide helps with consistency and reuse of design decisions. Every project needs one.

Because your design decisions continue to be made throughout the project and because you sometimes change your mind about design decisions, the custom style guide is a living document that grows and is refined along with the design. Typically, this document is private to the project team and is used only internally within the development organization.

17.8.2 Why Use a Custom Style Guide?

Among the reasons for designers to use a custom style guide within a project are:

- It helps with project control and communication. Without documentation of the large numbers of design decisions, projects—especially large projects—get out of control. Everyone invents and introduces his or her own design patterns, possibly different each day. The result almost inevitably is poor design and a maintenance nightmare.
- It is a reliable force toward design consistency. An effective custom style guide helps reduce variations of the details of widget design, layout, formatting, color choices, and so on, giving you consistency of details throughout a product and across product lines.
- A custom style guide is a productivity booster through reuse of well-considered design patterns. It helps avoid the waste of reinvention.

17.8.3 What to Put in a Custom Style Guide?

Your custom style guide should include all the kinds of user interface objects and design situations where your organization cares the most about consistency (Meads, 2010). Most style guides are very detailed, spelling out the parameters of graphic layouts and grids, including the size, location, and spacing of user interface elements. This includes widget (e.g., buttons, dialogue boxes, menus, message windows, toolbars) usage, position, and design. Also important are the layouts of forms, including the fields, their formatting, and their location on forms.

Your style guide is the appropriate place to standardize fonts, color schemes, background graphics, and other common design elements. Other elements of a style guide include interaction procedures, interaction styles, message and dialogue fonts, text styles and tone, labeling standards, vocabulary control for terminology and message and label wording, and schemes for deciding how to use defaults and what defaults to use. It should be worded very specifically, and you should spell out interpretations and conditions of applicability.

You should include as many sample design sketches and pictures taken from designs on screens as possible to make it communicate visually. Supplement with clear explanatory text. Incorporate lots of examples of good and bad design, including specific examples of UX problems found in evaluation related to style guide violations.

Your style guide is also an excellent place to catalog design patterns (Borchers, 2001), your "standard" ways of constructing and placing menus, buttons, icons,

Design pattern

A repeatable solution to a common design problem that emerges as a best practice, encouraging sharing, reuse, and consistency (Sections 14.2.8.5, 17.3.4, and 15.3.5).

and dialogue boxes, and your use of color for UI objects such as buttons. Perhaps one of the most important parts of a style guide is rules for organizational branding.

Example: Style Guide for National Park Project

In Fig. 17-14, we show a small part of the style guide that was created for the national parks product. The top left column shows the various styles for checkboxes, including the color and typography specification in default, selected, and indeterminate states of the widget when it is active and inactive. The bottom row on the style sheet depicts input boxes, including the state of the box when it is in focus (left), not in focus (center), and when there is an error with the entered value (right).

A complete style guide will include all widgets available for the design team and their states.

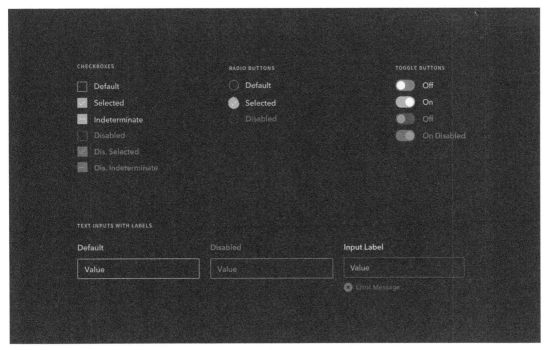

Fig. 17-14

A small part of a style guide for the national parks product (style guide courtesy of Christina Janczak, UX Designer, Cloudistics, Inc.).

Designing for Emotional Impact

18

Highlights

- Designing for emotional needs.
- Creating an emotional impact design.
- Mood boards.

18.1 INTRODUCTION

18.1.1 You Are Here

We begin each process chapter with a "you are here" picture of the chapter topic in the context of The Wheel, the overall UX design lifecycle template (Fig. 18-1). In this chapter, we describe how to design for the top layer of the human needs pyramid—for emotional impact.

In Section 12.3, we discussed how emotional needs occupy the top layer of the user needs pyramid and are about being satisfied, enriched, and being able to form long-term emotional relationships with a product or system. In this chapter, we go about designing for emotional impact to satisfy those needs.

18.2 DESIGNING FOR EMOTIONAL NEEDS

18.2.1 What Designing for Emotional Needs Is About

Designing for emotional needs means designing for satisfaction, meaningfulness, aesthetics, and joy. A design that satisfies emotional needs is endearing and timeless, with the potential for becoming a meaningful part of users' lives.

Pyramid of User Needs

An abstract representation as a pyramid shape with the bottom layer as ecological needs, the middle layer as interaction needs, and the top layer as emotional needs (Section 12.3.1).

Emotional perspective

The design viewpoint taken from the emotional layer of the user needs pyramid, on top of the interaction layer and the ecological layer at the base. The emotional perspective focuses on emotional impact and value-sensitive aspects of design, including aesthetics and joy of use and how users are emotionally and culturally satisfied and enriched as they use the product (Section 12.3.1).

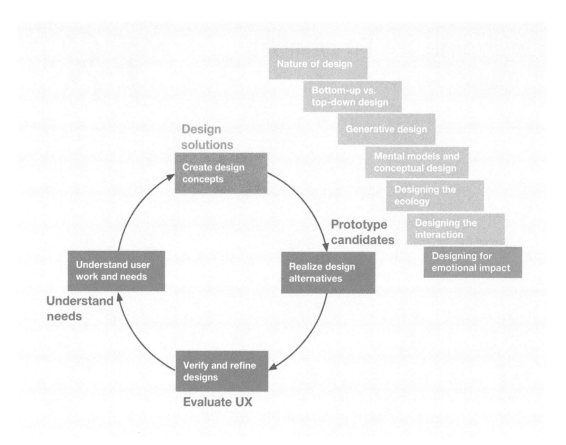

Fig. 18-1

You are here in the chapter describing designing for emotional impact within the Design Solutions lifecycle activity in the context of the overall Wheel UX lifecycle.

18.2.1.1 What users feel when interacting with the system

Humans have a broad range of feelings that are informed by what we see, hear, touch, smell, and taste. In the design of digital products with today's technology, we focus on influencing how users feel by designing what they see, hear, and touch.

For example, if the goal of the design is to delight the user, say, for a children's tablet app, a playful visual palette with bold colors combined with the right animations and screen transitions and generous use of audio cues can induce that emotion. On the other hand, if the goal is to communicate stability and reliability, say, for a stock trading application, a more restrained visual style where colors are used only for encoding information can induce an emotion of seriousness and being productive. For example, you could use green to show gains in the price of a financial instrument and red to show losses. In such systems, the use of audio will also be relegated to task-focused issues such as communicating error states and notifications.

18.2.1.2 Distinctiveness is a factor when designing for emotional impact

For some products, the goal is to elicit an emotional response in users by producing something different and noticeable, to craft an artistic design for the coolest and best piece of art a product can be. Examples include furniture, jewelry, fashion clothing, and architecture. These domains are full of everyday products that satisfy ecological and interaction needs, but what the world adores are the creations by designers who infuse unique emotional perspectives into their work. Who wouldn't like the cachet of owning custom designer clothing? Or a home designed by Frank Lloyd Wright? Or an original Charles Eames chair?

The emotional perspective in UX design. *The emotional UX design perspective is a point of view that focuses on emotional impact and value-sensitive aspects of design. It is about social and cultural implications as well as the aesthetics and joy of use.*

18.2.2 Designing for Emotional Impact Is Often Neglected But can be a Market Differentiator

In the day-to-day designs for products and systems, particularly enterprise software, business stakeholders focus on supporting the middle (interaction) tier of the needs pyramid, and to a lesser extent the bottom (ecological) tier. The top (emotional) tier is usually neglected. Designing for emotional needs may not even be mandated in the design brief, but it may end up becoming the differentiator that offers the potential to be a market leader.

A product or system that satisfies the emotional needs can distinguish good from "insanely great" products.

18.3 CREATING AN EMOTIONAL IMPACT DESIGN

Of the three types we discussed, designing for emotional impact is perhaps the most difficult to operationalize and externalize as a process. Unlike the ecological or interaction design efforts, there are no straightforward work activity models that directly inform emotional impact attributes. These must be carefully gleaned and nurtured from the users and the usage research data.

Moreover, emotional response targets vary—for example, in consumer products, responses such as delight and joy are important whereas in institutional or enterprise products, the goals are more toward reducing boredom in repetitive tasks and engendering satisfaction during task performance.

18.3.1 Start with Inputs for Emotional Impacts

In Fig. 18-2, we show a few common factors to think about while designing for emotional impact.

The purpose of the model in Fig. 18-2 is to get started on identifying and organizing user needs of various kinds. So, we need to express user needs in the indicated subareas of emotional impact. In this model, for each "ray" coming into the center, we identify the specific kinds of needs for users with respect to this product. For example, for the fashion factor, what is important to users about this product? Is it being avant garde? Being retro? Being modern? Once this is identified, designers can address in ideation, sketching, and critiquing how to achieve each specifically in the design.

Fig. 18-2

Inputs for emotional impact and meaningfulness.

18.3.2 Conceptual Design for Emotional Aspects

Conceptual designs for emotional aspects are often more abstract and difficult to articulate. They span concepts for branding, visual or graphic design, sound, motion, and even the tone of language used. It is an abstract theme centered around an idea or a factor.

For example, take the Mini Cooper automobile. The small boxy look could have ended up being plain and utilitarian. But they made it a distinguishing feature. The very idea of the car engenders fun and excitement with its distinctive looks and interior design. The designers use controls and toggle switches that are inspired by airplane cockpits. The location and shape of the central information console follows this concept as well. The result is a fun and adventurous theme that is consistent with their famous "go-cart like handling." Ask any Mini driver about what their Mini means to them and they are likely to describe it in these terms.

Metaphors can be used to articulate an emotional conceptual design. An example is seen in advertising in *Backpacker* magazine for the Garmin handheld GPS as a hiking companion. In wording that ties the human value of self-identity with orienteering, Garmin uses the metaphor of companionship: "Find yourself, then get back." It highlights emotional qualities such as comfort, cozy familiarity, and companionship: "Like an old pair of boots and your favorite fleece, GPSMAP 62ST is the ideal hiking companion."

> **Metaphor**
>
> An analogy used in design to communicate and explain unfamiliar concepts using familiar conventional knowledge. A central metaphor often becomes the theme of a product, the motif behind the conceptual design (Section 15.3.6).

18.3.2.1 Mood boards: Creating a conceptual design for emotional aspects

Use ideation to come up with the various themes and metaphors you think are appropriate for the product being designed. For each theme, create a "mood" board—a collage of artifacts and images showcasing or illustrating different aspects of that theme. Create a mood board for each emotional impact theme under consideration for the design. A mood board can include sketches of shapes, colors samples, pictures, sounds, typefaces, or any other artifacts. There are no rules on how it should be structured; the goal is for the various elements together to carry the feeling of the abstract idea being communicated.

Example: Mood Boards for the National Parks Website

See Fig. 18-3 for an example of a mood board based on the theme "vibrant nature." This mood board was constructed for the national parks product introduced in Section 17.5.2. This is one of the many themes the design team explored for this exercise. The various pictures and sights depicted in this mood board illustrate the vibrancy and energy of nature, making it attractive for potential park visitors and campers.

Fig. 18-3

Mood board for the theme "vibrant nature," to be used as a concept for the visual design of a national park website (mood board courtesy of Christina Janczak, UX Designer, Cloudistics, Inc.).

18.3.3 Intermediate Design for Emotional Impact

After a conceptual design is adopted, develop it further by elaborating each channel of the concept (e.g., visual, auditory, tactile) through more detailed mood boards, ideation, and sketching.

18.3.3.1 Define the visual language and vocabulary

Visual design is perhaps the most common channel used in practice for emotional impact. In this case, mood boards are modeled and represented to give a flavor of the visual language to be used in the system.

We were once tasked to design for an emotional response of boldness and dynamism for a mobile application. One of the themes we considered was New York City. We created a visual mood board with images of iconic New York City themes: yellow cabs, metro signs, skyscrapers, and movement (captured via blurry shots of people on the street and Times Square). This was later developed into specific visual aspects such as typography by using the font families found on the city subway signage.

Start defining your overall visual theme by creating a mood board for each of the themes you think are appropriate for the system being designed. Make sure it includes typography and iconography.

The typography styles include font families, how and if they will be different across different devices in the ecology, and how the various styles such as headings, body, callouts, and button labels will look. A team member with a strong graphic design background is an asset for this.

Identify all ideas that will be represented as icons or other images in the design and define the style for iconography. Create sample views of key screens if appropriate to get a sense of how the visual style contributes to the overall concept for the emotional design.

> **Ecology**
>
> In the setting of UX design, the ecology is the entire set of surrounding parts of the world, including networks, other users, devices, and information structures, with which a user, product, or system interacts (Section 16.2.1).

Example: Color Scheme for the National Parks Website

In Fig. 18-4, we show how the color scheme was derived from the mood board in Fig. 18-3. The designer picked a key image of the mood board and extracted various aspects such as the green color of the leaf, the white color of a full flower petal, the yellow color of the flower center, and the dark shadow of the water to derive the primary color palette (top left of the image).

Another set of colors was picked from other images in the mood board to create the secondary (extended) palette (center left of the image). The designer also derived textures (center right in the image) from other areas in the mood board that will be used in the design to evoke the theme of tranquil nature.

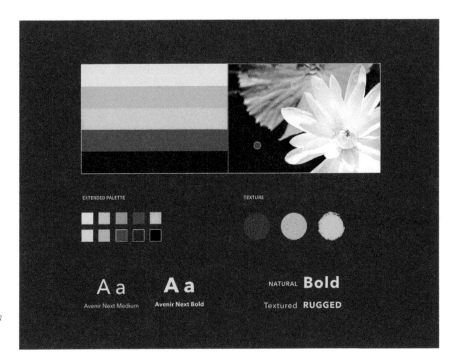

Fig. 18-4

Formulating color palette, typography, and visual language from the "vibrant nature" mood board (courtesy of Christina Janczak, UX Designer, Cloudistics, Inc.).

Example: Iconography for the National Parks Website

In Fig. 18-5, we show the iconography the designer created as the next step.

As these designs were critiqued, the issue of texture was brought up as a way to "make the visual language more organic." The result was the icons shown in Fig. 18-6.

18.3.3.2 Define the motion styles and physics of interaction for each design

For each device in the ecology, define the styles and physics for the animations and other transitions to be used. This will include ideas on using animations, scrolling, and screen transitions as well as descriptions of how the motions will occur. Having people with a motion design background on the team helps. They sketch ideas for these kinds of motion to describe accelerations, timing, etc.

We talked about the use of animation in an iPad iBooks app that simulates physically turning a page in Section 17.3.3. What are the opportunities for using animations in your application? For example, look for places where the system is performing long operations, places where a loading animation can help.

Think of how the physics of the interaction will work (Section 15.3.6). If there are two panes of content, which one is the primary and which is the secondary?

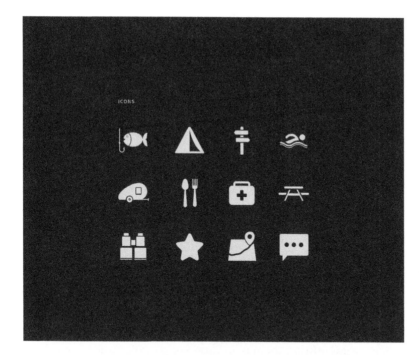

Fig. 18-5

Iconography for the national parks product, using the visual themes from the "tranquil nature" mood board (courtesy of Christina Janczak, UX Designer, Cloudistics, Inc.).

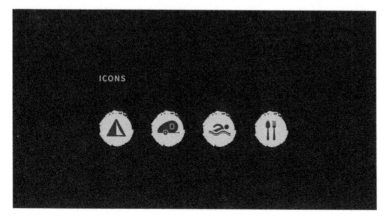

Fig. 18-6

Applying texture to icons to make them seem more natural (courtesy of Christina Janczak, UX Designer, Cloudistics, Inc.).

Which pane will slide over the other? Will it slide in from the left or the right? Which is more consistent with the way the application widgets are arranged?

18.3.3.3 Define the tone of the language to be used in the design

Another avenue that designers use for emotional impact is the tone and style of the language. Use of humor and anthropomorphism to imbue a personality in certain domains such as kids learning, adult gaming, and entertainment is common. This is captured using samples and textual descriptions of the tone to be achieved on a mood board.

For the overall ecology, what is the tone of the language used in all dialogue with the user (UI, video, and audio interactions)? Will it be conversational and informal or terse and formal? Will it use humor? Will it have a "personality" or will it be neutral?

Keep updating the product's style guide for language and tone. List words, phrases, and themes that should be avoided and examples of what should be used.

Style guide

A document fashioned and maintained by designers to capture and describe details of visual and other general design decisions, especially about screen designs, font choices, iconography, and color usage, which can be applied in multiple places. A style guide helps with consistency and reuse of design decisions (Section 17.8.1).

18.3.3.4 Define the audio characteristics to be used in the design

For the design of sounds, come up with ideas for appropriate actions that can be augmented by using sounds. The enclosed user space of a kiosk is perfect for gentle surround sound, which will add much to the feeling of immersion. What are the opportunities for providing feedback to the user during interactions? What is the overall theme of the sounds? Uplifting and playful? Or sober and serious?

Start by identifying themes and use samples of music to put together a palette of sounds corresponding to the different categories of tasks. For example, alerts will have one tone whereas positive feedback for actions will have another. For the national parks application, the nature mood board can include a variety of nature sounds, and those sounds can then be used to derive the audio vocabulary for the design.

18.3.3.5 Leverage social and psychological aspects in the design

Designers should be on the lookout for opportunities from the usage research phase through the evaluation activity to structure the design to take advantage of social and psychological factors. For example, if we are designing a fitness application, aspects in the work domain such as motivation and feedback can be structured to help the user succeed emotionally by showing the number of steps they take each day and comparing it with friends and family.

18.3.4 Emotional Impact Design Production

The final design candidates for emotional impact are subjected to evaluation (Part 5). Any ideas identified in the evaluation kick off another round of refinements and modifications. Once the design is finalized, it is described in detail in a phase called design production. The objective of this phase is to define the design in enough detail so that it becomes a specification for software engineers to implement.

In Fig. 18-7, we show the detailed design specification of a part of the visual design for the national parks application. Details such as padding, sizes, and exact color specifications are detailed for all visual elements used in the design.

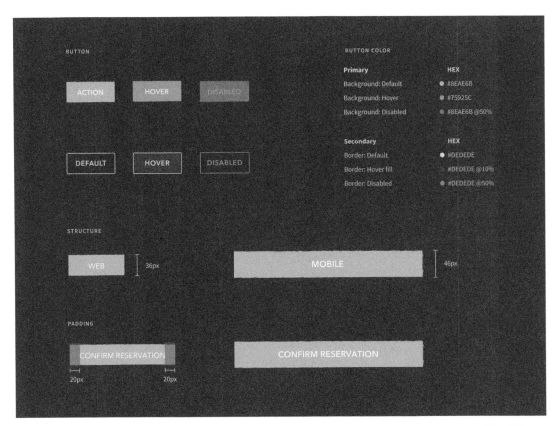

Fig. 18-7
Part of detailed visual design specification of the national parks application (courtesy of Christina Janczak, UX Designer, Cloudistics, Inc.).

Exercise 18-1: Conceptual Design for Emotional Response for Your System

Think about your system and contextual data and envision a conceptual design in the emotional perspective. Try to communicate a vision of how the design elements will evoke emotional impact in users.

Background: Design

19

- An example of how mental models can make for entertainment.
- Embodied, ubiquitous, embedded, ambient, and situated interaction.
- Participatory design.

19.1 THIS IS A REFERENCE CHAPTER

This chapter contains reference material relevant to the other chapters of Part 3. This chapter is not intended to be read through as a regular chapter, but each section is supposed to be read when a reference to it in the main chapters is encountered.

19.2 PARTICIPATORY DESIGN

19.2.1 Overview

Although we did not describe participatory design as a specific technique in Chapter 14 (on generative design creation), we wholeheartedly support user and client participation in the entire design process, starting from ideation and sketching through to refinement. Because the specific technique of participatory design is an important part of HCI history and literature, we touch on it here.

At the very beginning of a design project, you often have the user and customers on one side and system designers on the other. Participatory design is a way to combine the knowledge of work practice of the users and customers with the process, technology, and design skills of the UX and software engineering (SE) teams.

A participatory design session usually starts with reciprocal learning in which the users and the designers learn about each other's roles; designers learn about work practices and users learn about technical constraints (Carmel, Whitaker, &

Participatory design

A democratic process for UX design actively involving all stakeholders (e.g., employees, partners, customers, citizens, users) to help ensure that the result meets their needs and is usable. Based on the argument that users should be involved in designs they will be using, and that all stakeholders, including and especially users, have equal input into UX design (Section 11.3.4).

George, 1993). The session itself is a democratic process. Rank or job title has no effect; anyone can post a new design idea or change an existing feature. Only positive and supportive attitudes are tolerated. No one can criticize or attack another person or their ideas. This leads to an atmosphere of freedom to express even the farthest out ideas; creativity rules.

In our own experience, we have found participatory design very effective for specific kinds of interaction situations. For example, we think it could be a good approach, especially if used in conjunction with design scenarios, for sketching out the first few levels of screens of the Ticket Kiosk System interaction. These first screens are very important to the user experience, where first impressions are formed by users and where we can least afford to have users get lost and customers turn away. However, in our experience, the technique sometimes does not scale up well to complete designs of large and complex systems.

For information on the history and origins of participatory design, see the next section.

For a description of PICTIVE, an example of an approach to participatory design, see the section after next.

19.2.2 History and Origins of Participatory Design

Participatory design entails user participation in design for work practice. Participatory design is a democratic process for design (social and technological) of systems involving human work, based on the argument that users should be involved in designs they will be using, and that all stakeholders, including and especially users, have equal input into interaction design (Muller & Kuhn, 1993).

The idea of user participation in system design harkens back (as does the work on contextual studies) at least to a body of effort called work activity theory (Bødker, 1991; Ehn, 1990). Originating in Russia and Germany, it flourished in Scandinavia in the 1980s where it was closely related to the workplace democracy movement. These early versions of participatory design embraced a view of design based on work practice situated in a worker's own complete environment, but also espoused empowerment of workers to "codetermine the development of the information system and of their workplace" (Clement & Besselaar, 1993).

Going back to the 1980s and earlier, probably the most well-known participatory design project was the Scandinavian project called UTOPIA (Bødker, Ehn, Kammersgaard, Kyng, & Sundblad, 1987). A main goal of Project UTOPIA was to overcome limitations on opportunities for workers to affect workplace technology and organizational work practices. UTOPIA was one of the first such projects intended to produce a commercial product at the end of the day.

Participatory design has been practiced in many different forms with different rules of engagement. In some projects, participatory design limits user power to creating only inputs for the professional designers to consider, an approach called consultative design by Mumford (1981). Other approaches give the users full power to share in the responsibility for the final outcome, in what Mumford calls consensus design.

Also beginning in the 1970s and 1980s, an approach to user involvement in design (but probably developed apart from the participatory design history in Scandinavia) called Joint Application Design was emerging from IBM in the United States and Canada (August 1991). Joint Application Design falls between consultative design and consensus design in the category of representative design (Mumford, 1981), a commonly used approach in industry in which user representatives become official members of the design teams, often for the duration of the project. In comparison with participatory design, Joint Application Design is often a bit more about group dynamics, brainstorming, and organized group meetings.

In the early 1990s, the Scandinavian approach to democratic design was adapted and extended within the HCI community in the form of participatory design. Muller's (1991) vision of participatory design as embodied in his PICTIVE approach is the most well-known adaptation of the general concept specifically to HCI. The first Participatory Design Conference met in 1990 and it has been held biannually ever since. Participatory design has since been codified for practice (Greenbaum & Kyng, 1991), reviewed (Clement & Besselaar, 1993), and summarized (Muller, 2003).

19.2.3 PICTIVE[1]—An Example of an Approach to Participatory Design

Inspired by the mockup methods of the Scandinavian project called UTOPIA (Bødker et al., 1987), which provided opportunities for workers to give input to workplace technology and organizational work practices, PICTIVE (Muller, 1991; Muller, Wildman, & White, 1993b) is an example of how participatory design has been operationalized in HCI. PICTIVE supports rapid group prototype design using paper and pencil and other "low technology" materials on a large tabletop in combination with video recording.

The objective is for the group to work together to find technological design solutions to support work practice and, sometimes, to redesign the work practice

---

[1]Plastic Interface for Collaborative Technology Initiatives through Video Exploration.

in the process. Video recording is used to chronicle and communicate the design process and to record walkthroughs used to summarize the designs.

PICTIVE is, as are most participatory design approaches, a hands-on design-by-doing technique using low-tech tools, such as those used for paper prototyping: blackboards, large sheets of paper, bulletin boards, push pins, Post-it notes, colored marking pens, index cards, scissors, and tape. PICTIVE deliberately uses these low-tech (noncomputer, nonsoftware) representations to level the playing field between users and technical design team members. Otherwise, using even the most primitive programming tools for building prototypes on the fly can cast the users as outsiders and the design practitioners as intermediaries through whom all user ideas must flow. It then is no longer a collaborative storytelling activity.

After the mutual introduction to each others' backgrounds and perspectives, the group typically discusses the task at hand and the design objectives to get on the same page for doing the design. Then they gather around a table on which there is a large paper representation of a generic computer "window." Anyone can step forward and "post" a design feature, for example, button, icon, menu, dialogue box, or message, by writing or drawing it on a Post-it note or similar piece of paper, sticking it on the "window" working space, and explaining the rationale. The group can then discuss refinements and improvements. Someone else can edit the text on the object, for example, and change its location in the window.

The group works collaboratively to expand and modify, adding new objects, changing objects, and moving objects to create new layouts and groupings and changing wording of labels and messages, and so on, all the while communicating their thinking and reasons behind each change. The results can be evaluated immediately as low-fidelity prototypes with walkthroughs (usually recorded as video for further sharing and evaluation). In most project environments that use this kind of participatory design, it is often used in the consultative design mode, where users participate in forming parts of the design but the professional design practitioners have the final responsibility for the overall design.

PICTIVE has been evaluated informally in the context of several real product design projects (Muller, 1992). User participants report getting enjoyment from the process and great satisfaction in having a receptive audience for their own design ideas and, especially, in seeing those design ideas included in the group's output.

19.3 MENTAL MODELS: AN EXAMPLE OF HOW THEY CAN MAKE FOR ENTERTAINMENT

Lack of a correct user mental model can be the stuff of comedy curve balls. An example is the scene in the 1992 movie, *My Cousin Vinny*, where Marisa Tomei—as Vinny's fiancée, Mona Lisa Vito—tries to make a simple phone call. This fish-out-of-water scene pits a brash young woman from New York against a rotary dial telephone in a backwater Southern town. You cannot help but reflect on the mismatch in the mapping between her mental model of touch-tone operation and the reality of old-fashioned rotary dials as she pokes vigorously at the numbers through the finger holes.

But, lest you dismiss her as completely out of touch, we remind you that it was she who solved the case with her esoteric automobile knowledge, proving that the suspects' 1964 Buick Skylark could not have left the two tire tracks found outside the convenience store because it did not have a limited-slip differential.

Prototype Candidate Designs

Part 4 is a brief treatment of how to make UX design prototypes. Different types of prototypes are presented, to suit different types of design situations. Wireframe prototypes, the de facto standard of agile UX design, are described in depth. We discuss how to build increasing levels of fidelity in prototypes and show how to develop prototypes for each level of the UX design pyramid: ecology, interaction, and emotional impact.

Prototyping

20

Highlights

- ▪ Depth and breadth of prototypes.
- ▪ Fidelity of prototypes.
- ▪ Wireframe prototypes.
- ▪ Wireflow prototypes.
- ▪ Building up increasing levels of fidelity.
- ▪ Specialized prototypes.

20.1 INTRODUCTION

20.1.1 You Are Here

We begin each process chapter with a "you are here" picture of the chapter topic in the context of The Wheel, the overall UX design lifecycle template (Fig. 20-1). In this chapter, we describe how to perform the Prototype Candidates UX design lifecycle activity.

This is the chapter describing types of prototypes and how to make wireflow and wireframe prototypes within the Prototype Candidates lifecycle activity.

20.1.2 Prototyping Intertwines with Other UX Activities

Back in Chapter 5, the *Prelude to the process chapters*, we said that we have to describe each lifecycle activity separately in its own chapter(s), but they actually all go together and happen in combination—closely intertwined and interleaved throughout the lifecycle.

Prototyping is a good example of this intertwining. See Chapter 14 on generative design where prototyping occurs right from the start of design creation in the form of sketches and continues to occur as wireframes and other forms throughout much of the remaining design process.

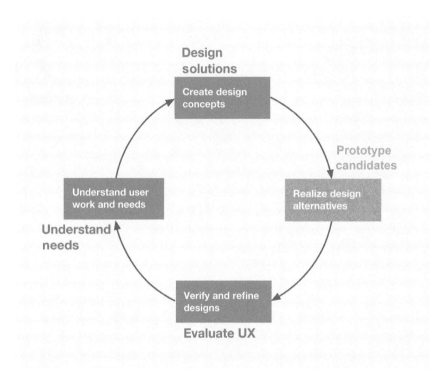

Fig. 20-1

You are here in the chapter on the Prototype Candidates lifecycle activity in the context of the overall Wheel UX lifecycle process.

20.1.3 A Dilemma and a Solution

The only way to be sure that your design is the right design and the best design it can be is to subject it to UX evaluation. However, at some early point, you will have a design but no product or system yet to evaluate. But if you wait until after it is implemented, changes are much more difficult and expensive to make.

A prototype gives you something to evaluate before you have to commit resources to build the real thing. Prototypes allow you to fail faster, learn sooner, and succeed earlier.

20.1.4 Advantages of Prototyping

Prototypes have these advantages:

- Provide a platform to support UX evaluation with users.
- Offer concrete baseline for communication between users and designers.
- Provide a conversational "prop" to support communication of concepts not easily conveyed verbally.

▪ Allow users to "take the design for a spin" (who would buy a car without taking it for a test drive or buy a stereo system without first listening to it?).

▪ Give project visibility and buy-in within customer and developer organizations.

▪ Encourage early user participation and involvement.

▪ Give the impression that design is easy to change because a prototype is obviously not finished.

▪ Afford designers immediate observation of user performance and consequences of design decisions.

▪ Help sell management on an idea for new product.

▪ Help affect a paradigm shift from an existing system to a new system.

20.1.5 Universality of Prototyping

The idea of prototyping is timeless and universal. Automobile designers build and test mockups, architects and sculptors make models, circuit designers use "bread-boards," artists work with sketches, and aircraft designers build and fly experimental designs. Even Leonardo da Vinci and Alexander Graham Bell made prototypes.

Thomas Edison is famous for making thousands of prototypes before getting just the right design. In each case, the concept of a prototype was the key to affording the design team and others an early ability to observe something about the final product—evaluating ideas, weighing alternatives, and seeing what works and what does not.

Alfred Hitchcock, master of dramatic dialogue design, is known for using prototyping to refine the plots of his movies. Hitchcock would tell variations of stories at cocktail parties and observe the reactions of his listeners. He would experiment with various sequences and mechanisms for revealing the storyline. Refinement of the story was based on listener reactions as an evaluation criterion. The movie *Psycho* is a notable example of the results of this technique.

20.1.6 Scandinavian Origins of Prototyping

Like a large number of other parts of this overall lifecycle process, the origins of prototyping in UX, especially low-fidelity prototyping, go back to the Scandinavian work activity theory research and practice of Ehn, Kyng, and others (Bjerknes, Ehn, & Kyng, 1987; Ehn, 1988) as well as participatory design work (Kyng, 1994). These formative works emphasized the need to foster early and detailed communication about design and participation in understanding the requirements for that design.

20.2 DEPTH AND BREADTH OF A PROTOTYPE

The idea behind prototypes is to provide fast and easily changed early views of an envisioned UX design. *Because it must be quickly and easily changed, a prototype is a design representation that is in some way(s) less than a full implementation.* The choices for your approach to prototyping are about *how* to make it less. One way you can make it less is by focusing on just the breadth or just the depth of the system.

When you slice the features and functionality of a system by breadth, you get a horizontal prototype. And when you slice by depth, you get a vertical prototype (Hartson & Smith, 1991). In his usability engineering book, Nielsen (1993) illustrates the relative concepts of horizontal and vertical prototyping, which we show as Fig. 20-2.

20.2.1 Horizontal Prototypes

A horizontal prototype (top "bar" in Fig. 20-2) is very broad in the features it incorporates, but offers less depth in its coverage of how that functionality works. A horizontal prototype is a good place to start with your prototyping, as it provides an overview on which you can base a top-down approach. A horizontal prototype is effective in demonstrating the product concept and for conveying an early product overview to managers, customers, and users (Kensing & Munk-Madsen, 1993). However, because of the lack of details in depth, horizontal prototypes usually do not support complete workflows, and user experience evaluation with this kind of prototype is generally less realistic. For these reasons, prototyping in the early funnel tends to be horizontal in nature.

Early funnel

The part of the funnel (agile UX model) for large-scope activity, usually for conceptual design, before syncing with software engineering (Section 4.4.4).

20.2.2 Vertical Prototypes

A vertical prototype (upright "bar" in Fig. 20-2) contains more depth of detail for some functionality, but only for a narrow selection of features. A vertical prototype allows testing a limited range of features but those functions

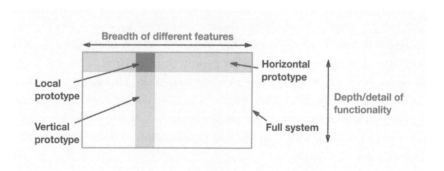

Fig. 20-2

Horizontal and vertical prototyping concepts, adapted from Nielsen (1993), with permission.

that are included are evolved in enough detail to support realistic user experience evaluation. Often the functionality of a vertical prototype can include a stub for or a connection to an actual working backend database.

A vertical prototype is ideal for times when you need to represent completely the details of an isolated part of an individual interaction workflow in order to understand how those details play out in actual usage. For example, you may wish to study a new design for the checkout part of the workflow for an e-commerce website. A vertical prototype might show that one task sequence and associated user actions, in depth. Because vertical prototypes are usually about individual features, they are most commonly used in the late funnel part of the process.

20.2.3 Local Prototypes

Sometimes you need a "local prototype," a prototype that is narrow in both dimensions, limiting its focus to a localized interaction design issue. A local prototype is used to evaluate design alternatives for particular isolated interaction details, such as one dialogue box, the appearance of an icon, the wording of a message, or the behavior of an individual interaction object.

A local prototype is the solution for those times when your design team encounters an impasse in design discussions where, after a while, there is no agreement and people are starting to repeat themselves. Perhaps usage research data are not clear on the question and further arguing is a waste of time. It is time to put the specific design issue on a list for testing, letting the user or customer speak to it in a kind of "feature face-off" to help decide among the alternatives.

Because of their role in deciding specific issues, local prototypes are used independently from other prototypes and are temporary and disposable, having short life spans.

20.2.4 "T" Prototypes

A "T" prototype combines advantages of both the horizontal and vertical prototypes (see the T-shaped shaded area of Fig. 20-2), offering a good compromise for design evaluation. Much of the feature breadth is realized at a shallow level (the top of the T), but a few parts are done in depth (the vertical part of the T).

In the early going, we recommend the T prototype because it provides a nice balance between the two extremes, giving you some advantages of each. Once you have established a system overview in your horizontal prototype, as a practical matter the T prototype is the next step toward achieving some depth. In time, the horizontal foundation supports evolving vertical growth across the whole prototype.

Late funnel

The part of the funnel (agile UX model) for small-scope activity and for syncing with agile software engineering sprints (Section 4.4.3).

20.3 FIDELITY OF PROTOTYPES

In addition to depth and breadth, the level of fidelity of a prototype is another dimension along which there are tradeoffs with respect to completeness and cost/time. *The fidelity of a prototype reflects how "finished" it is perceived to be by customers and users* (Tullis, 1990). Being "finished" applies to completeness of content and functionality as well as how refined it is in appearance.

In general, lower fidelity prototypes are less finished but more flexible and can be constructed more rapidly and at less cost. But, as you progress through stages of development in your project, your need for fidelity in prototypes increases. The level of fidelity to aim for depends on your current stage of progress in the project and the purpose for which you plan to use the prototype.

There are many ways that levels of fidelity in a prototype have been described and used in the past. Here we focus on the practical role they play in an agile UX process. In Section 20.5 we describe these levels of prototype fidelity in the context of their various purposes.

20.4 WIREFRAME PROTOTYPES

Wireframes are now the go-to prototyping technique in UX practice. The bulk of the wireframe prototypes will be made during interaction design creation (Chapter 14).

20.4.1 What is a Wireframe?

A wireframe is a sketch, image, or prototype of a single interaction page or screen (in the broadest sense of "screen").

As we said in Section 17.5, wireframes are described as two-dimensional sketches or drawings consisting of lines, arcs, and vertices (thus the name wireframe), plus some text for labels, representing the layout of an interaction design for a page or screen. These wireframes are best generated with a software tool (such as Sketch).[1]

20.4.2 Wireframe Design Elements

Low-fidelity wireframes usually do not have graphical design elements such as images or specific colors or typography. Typical elements represented in a wireframe can include:

---

[1]https://www.sketchapp.com/

- Header.
- Footer.
- Content areas.
- Labeling.
- Menus.
- Tabs (possibly with drop-downs).
- Buttons.
- Icons.
- Pop-ups.
- Messages.
- Navigation bar, navigation links.
- Placeholders for logo and branding images.
- Search field.

Draw on everything you have worked on so far for the design. Use your conceptual design, design scenarios, ideation, personas, storyboards, and everything else you have created in working up to this first real materialization of your design ideas.

20.4.3 Wireflow Prototypes

The most common term UX professionals use in the context of prototyping using boxes, arrows, and other simple shapes is a wireframe. Even though in industry practice, the plural form of that term, _wireframes_, is used to denote flows and sequences of individual wireframes, the more accurate term is a wireflow.

20.4.3.1 What is a wireflow prototype?

Simply put, a wireflow[2] prototype (Fig. 20-3), or wireflow for short, is a prototype that illustrates navigational flow within an interaction design. Structurally, a wireflow is a directed graph in which:

- The nodes are wireframes.
- The arcs are arrows representing navigational flow among the wireframes.

As we will describe soon in more detail, a wireflow prototype is, at its base, a state diagram of user workflow.

Notice that the flow arrows go from interaction objects (such as a button or icon) that users can act upon (e.g., click) within one wireframe to navigate to subsequent wireframes.

---

[2]http:/nform.com/cards/wireflow/, https:/www.nngroup.com/articles/wireflows/

Storyboard

A visual scenario in the form of a series of sketches or graphical clips, often annotated, in cartoon-like frames, illustrating the interplay between a user and an envisioned ecology or device (Section 17.4.1).

State diagram (in UX)

A directed graph in which nodes are states which correspond to screens (in the broadest sense), and arcs (or arrows) are transitions between states resulting from user actions or system events. Used in wireflow and wireframe prototypes to show navigation among screens (Sections 9.7.6 and 20.4.4.2).

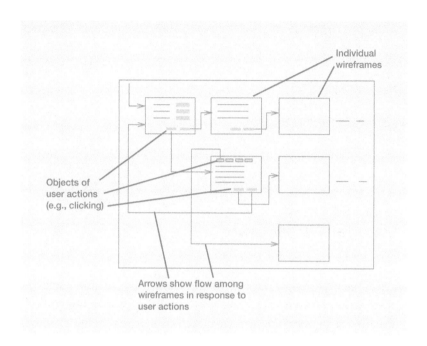

Fig. 20-3

Generic wireflow diagram.

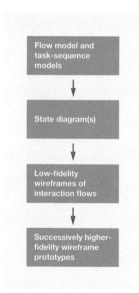

Fig. 20-4

The general evolutionary process of going from usage research models to wireframes.

Most of the configurations of wireframes that serve as UX prototypes are actually wireflow prototypes, which include both the individual wireframes and the navigational arrows connecting them. To simplify the terminology, we will mostly use the industry term "wireframes" or "wireframe deck" instead of "wireflow" to refer to the whole prototype.

20.4.4 General Process of Representing Interaction

The evolutionary process of establishing the interaction design for the set of related tasks of a feature is summarized in Fig. 20-4.

20.4.4.1 Focus on user workflow

Start by looking in detail at user workflow and navigation (in the most general sense). The flow model (a simple graphical representation giving an overview of how information, artifacts, and work products flow among user work roles and parts of the product or system, as the result of user actions, Section 9.5) is a starting point. More detailed task sequence models will fill in specifics about user actions and resulting navigation paths (top of Fig. 20-4).

20.4.4.2 Represent flow and navigation with state diagrams

Using your task-sequencing models, the next step in prototyping task sequencing and navigation is the creation of one or more state diagrams (next node down in Fig. 20-4), which take us a step closer to design by helping us represent details of flow and navigation in the interaction view of design.

Start with the main navigational paths, the essence of the flow, and initially leave out unnecessary detail, special conditions, and edge cases, such as error checking, confirmation dialogue, etc.

Example: State Diagram for Bundling Network Services[3]

The Network Infrastructure and Services group, part of the IT organization at Virginia Tech, is responsible for providing network and communications services to faculty, staff, and students. They maintain systems for ordering, billing, and maintaining services such as wireless Internet access for buildings and classrooms and wired ethernet for faculty offices and laboratories. Services also include all campus telephones and cable TV for classrooms.

As part of their mission, hardware, software, and UX people develop systems to support customers in ordering of network services. This example is about a web-based feature for bundling services together in popular configurations. To understand this example, you need to know that each service can be offered in a "plan" (e.g., a choice of ethernet connection speed) and each plan can have what they call "add ons," which are additional related features. A specialist in the Network Infrastructure and Services group is authorized to create these bundles, which can then be ordered by customers.

The system feature that supports bundle creation was the target of agile UX design. Starting with raw usage research data from interviews with these specialists, we created a flow model and several task sequence models. These were used to create an early state diagram (Fig. 20-5) to illustrate the main sequencing of workflow for this user task.

Starting at the "Bundles Landing Page," users can view, delete, or edit an existing bundle or create a new bundle. Editing a bundle includes editing bundle attributes (e.g., name, cost) and editing bundle contents (e.g., services, plans, and add ons in the bundle). Once those changes are saved, the user is taken back to the "Bundles Landing Page." It looks straightforward in this diagram and maybe that is a testimony to the power of a good state diagram because it took

---

[3]Thanks for permission to use this example to Joe Hutson and Mathew Mathai, Network Infrastructure and Services, Virginia Tech.

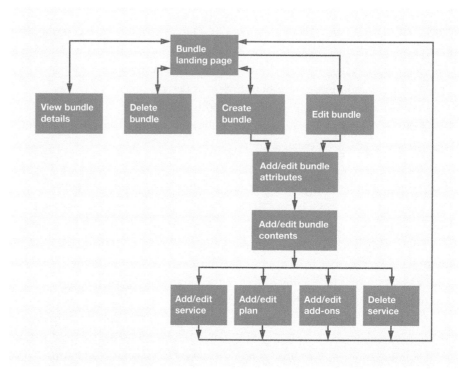

Fig. 20-5

Early state diagram for service bundling (Thanks for permission to use this example to Joe Hutson and Mathew Mathai, Network Infrastructure and Services, Virginia Tech).

quite a bit of analysis and synthesis of the disparate pieces of usage research data to get to this tidy representation.

In early design, your state diagrams can be translated almost directly into the structure of a wireframe deck (next section).

20.4.5 Create a Wireframe for Each State

Each state of the state diagram or box in the wireflow diagram becomes a low-fidelity wireframe design for one "screen." Within that screen, you are designing for things that "live" in that state, including the work spaces and dialogue to support the related task. Arcs of the state diagram will guide you in adding the controls (e.g., buttons) to support navigation among the wireframes.

As you work, you will probably have to add new states and the corresponding navigation to handle nonmainstream dialogue (e.g., to handle confirmation requests such as "Are you sure you want to delete this service?").

After you have fleshed out the details of the individual screens, you get a higher-fidelity version to see the wireframes in the navigational context (Fig. 20-6). Space limitations prevent showing this large enough to read the text, but you get the idea.

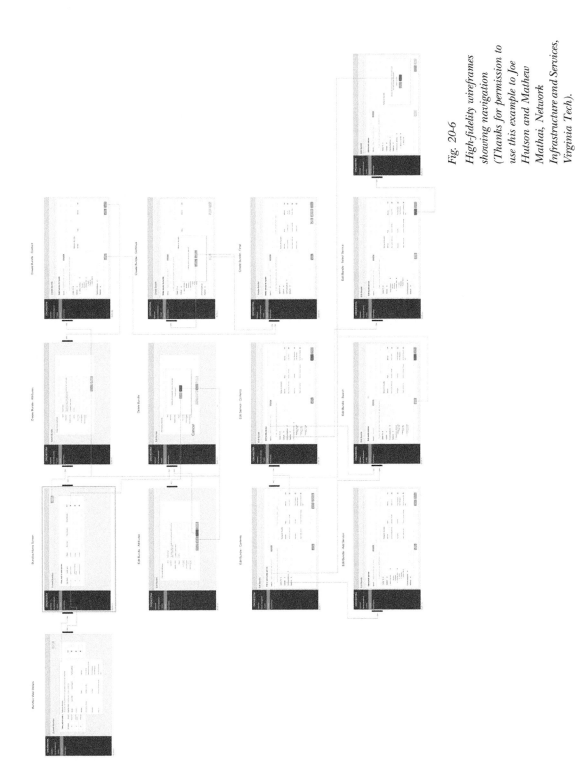

Fig. 20-6
*High-fidelity wireframes
showing navigation
(Thanks for permission to
use this example to Joe
Hutson and Mathew
Mathai, Network
Infrastructure and Services,
Virginia Tech).*

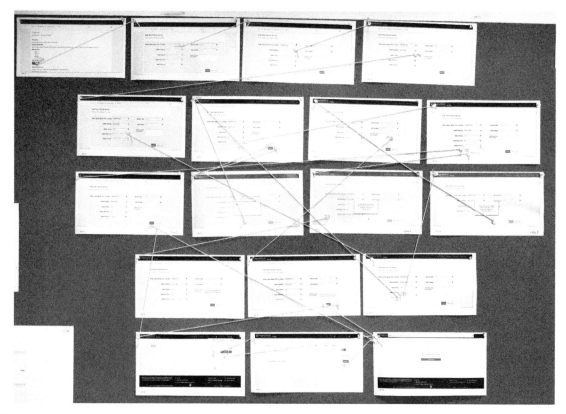

Fig. 20-7

Posting a readable wireflow diagram using colored yarn to represent navigational connections between individual wireframes (Thanks for permission to use this example to Joe Hutson and Mathew Mathai, Network Infrastructure and Services, Virginia Tech).

We posted this high-fidelity wireframe deck in our UX studio as a work artifact around which we had design discussions. To print the diagram large enough for everyone to read, we printed each wireframe on a sheet of paper and taped them together.

Another technique we have used is to print each wireframe on a separate sheet of paper, post them on a cork board, and represent the navigational connections with yarn held in place by push pins (Figs. 20-7 and 20-8).

20.5 BUILD UP PROTOTYPES IN INCREASING LEVELS OF FIDELITY

In this section we develop a sequence of the kind of prototypes we would use in a typical UX project to illustrate an increasing level of fidelity in the context of a UX design.

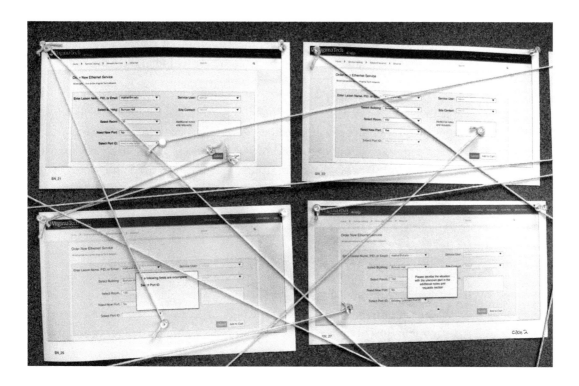

20.5.1 High-Level Task Context

In the previous section, we talked about state diagrams and interaction flow wireframes. Such broad representations of the design are helpful to envision high-level conceptual design and the breadth of the emerging design. This will take the user from the "home page" or beginning of an application down into the task hierarchy to the context of where they will be performing individual tasks of the feature being designed. This part in itself has no detailed task representation, just context.

In much of what we do with adding to or updating existing systems, this is unnecessary because the context is already well established.

20.5.2 Very Low-Fidelity Wireframe Sketches to Support Design Idea Exploration in Generative Design
20.5.2.1 The nature of low-fidelity prototypes

Low-fidelity prototypes are, as the term implies, prototypes that are not faithful representations of the details of look, feel, and behavior, but instead give rather high-level, more abstract impressions of the intended design. The low-fidelity versions usually do not have set graphical design elements such as images, color, or typography. Low-fidelity prototypes are appropriate when design details have

Fig. 20-8

Close-up of wireflow diagram using colored yarn to represent navigational connections (Thanks for permission to use this example to Joe Hutson and Mathew Mathai, Network Infrastructure and Services, Virginia Tech).

not been decided or when they are likely to change. They are flexible and easy to change, costing almost nothing to iterate. Therefore, these are essentially sketches that come and go as part of ideation, sketching, and critiquing.

20.5.2.2 The first level of fidelity

At the first level of fidelity in prototypes are very-low-fidelity wireframe sketches to support ideation and sketching as the UX design team explores design ideas in generative design. These quick and "dirty" design representations are almost always just hand sketches. They are disposable and short lived and are changing and evolving rapidly.

20.5.2.3 Decks of wireframes

If you group related wireframes in a sequence, we call this a *deck* of wireframes. When demonstrating the flow of this design, you can move through the deck one wireframe at a time, simulating a potential scenario by pretending to click on interaction widgets on the screen. These page sequences can represent the flow of user activity within a scenario, but cannot show all possible navigational paths.

A designer can narrate a design scenario where user actions cause the navigation to progress through the corresponding images in a deck.

20.5.3 Static Low-Fidelity Wireframes to Summarize and Solidify Design with UX Team

Once you get through initial generative design for a set of screens and have at least initially settled on the most promising candidate design, you create a deck of slightly higher fidelity wireframes that represents where you think you are with that design, to summarize and clarify it for yourselves in the UX team. To simulate navigation, you can just say "click here" and move manually to the next wireframe on your laptop.

While these are a little higher fidelity than the design exploration sketches, these low-fidelity wireframes are still just static sketches of screens in that there is no interaction or navigation.

Sometimes it is convenient to use paper printouts of wireframes and move them around on the tabletop to show the design ideas to the UX team and others. During your early design reviews and walk-throughs, a prototype "executor" can manipulate the paper pages to respond to simulated user actions. If you show your stakeholders the prototype on paper (which we often do), UX team members can write redesign suggestions directly on the paper.

As an alternative, you can go directly to showing the screens on a laptop displayed for discussion via a projector.

20.5.3.1 Lower fidelity means initial cost effectiveness

It is at the lowest end of the fidelity spectrum where you often get the most value from evaluation in terms of user experience gained per unit of effort expended. For finding and fixing most of the really obvious usability and UX problems early on, we believe this kind of paper wireframe prototype can be enormously effective. A low-fidelity prototype is much less evolved and therefore far less expensive. It can be constructed and iterated in a fraction of the time it takes to produce a good high-fidelity prototype. And yet, while there can be a big difference between a prototype and the finished product, low-fidelity prototypes can be surprisingly effective at finding UX problems in the design.

But, because of the low-fidelity prototype's simplicity and obvious lack of fidelity, many UX designers overlook its potential. The facility of wireframe prototypes enables you to create a design for a set of related user tasks, implement them in a low-fidelity wireflow prototype, evaluate with users, and modify the whole design—all within a day or so.

Example: Low-Fidelity Sketched Wireframes for Ordering Ethernet Service

Fig. 20-9 shows a low-fidelity sketched wireframe for a new design to order ethernet service, designed by the Network Infrastructure and Services UX team at Virginia Tech.

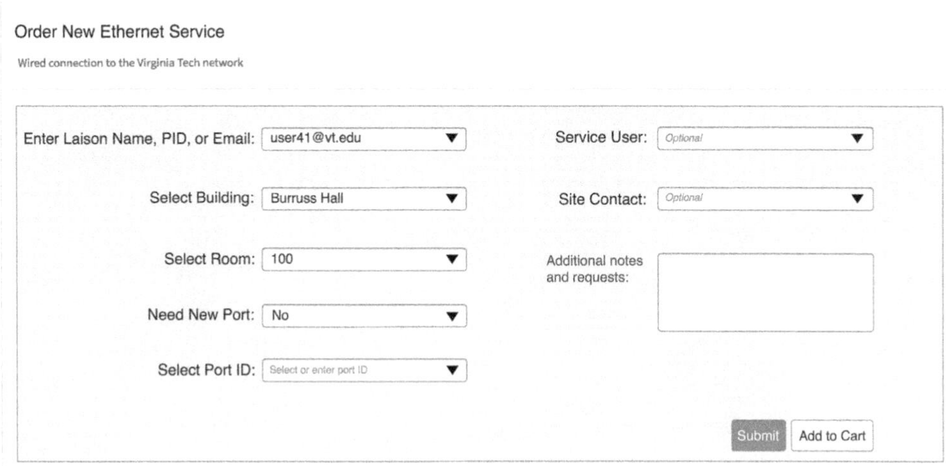

Fig. 20-9

Low-fidelity sketched wireframe for ethernet service ordering (Thanks for permission to use this example to Joe Hutson and Mathew Mathai, Network Infrastructure and Services, Virginia Tech).

20.5.4 Increased Fidelity Wireframes for Subsequent Design Reviews and Walkthroughs

As you work with the design and go back to stakeholders with more refined versions, you will want to steadily increase the fidelity of the wireframes, which you can accomplish by adding more screens and more detail to each screen. You can add some color and some appearance of branding. Add increased fidelity by using a static image (e.g., JPEG) as a basic template containing background, color schemes, and styles in a fairly high-fidelity appearance.

Example: Increasing Fidelity of a Wireframe for Ordering Ethernet Service

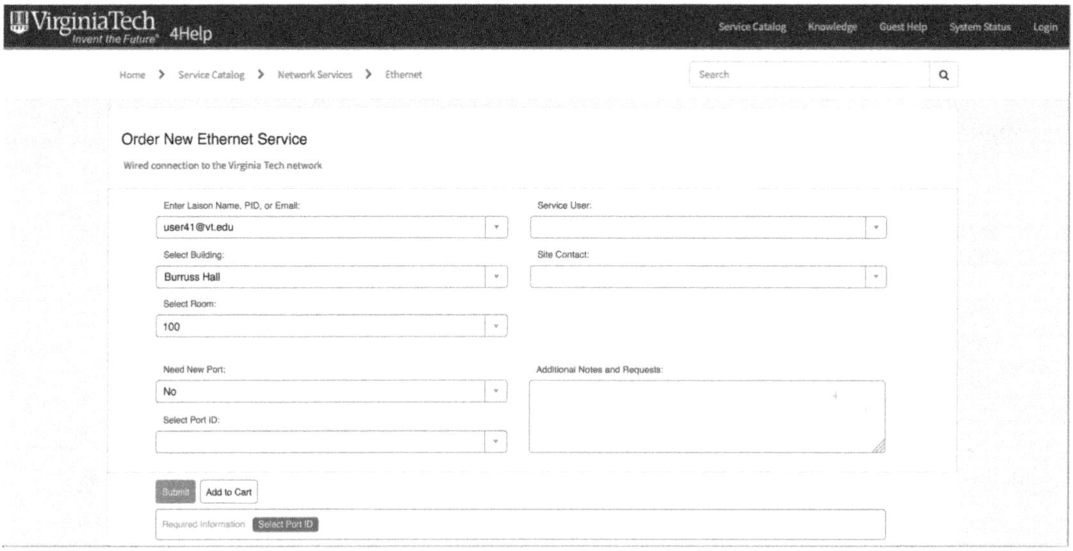

Fig. 20-10

Higher-fidelity wireframe for ethernet service ordering showing expected colors and style (Thanks for permission to use this example to Joe Hutson and Mathew Mathai, Network Infrastructure and Services, Virginia Tech).

The static image used in Fig. 20-10 is an example of an increased fidelity version of the same screen design as shown in Fig. 20-9, containing the background, colors, and styles that are starting to approach the desired look and feel. In this case, this design style template was obtained from people higher up in the organization who were responsible for making the official design appearance. We took a JPEG screenshot of that template, opened it in the Sketch app, and saved it as a background image to be used for all screens. We used the Sketch drawing tool to duplicate the colors, background, and styles in wireframe designs.

SN_21_HF

Work fast and efficiently. Reuse widgets by establishing a "library" of reusable forms and templates and predefined UI objects. You can even set yourself up with a library of particular styles—for example, Windows or Mac styles or your own branded style. In fact, you don't even have to use "real" widgets, just pick something that looks close from your library of UI objects.

The goal is for the client and users to see some of the UX design very quickly, usually by way of the design review and walkthrough evaluation techniques. Because of the low fidelity, UX people will have to do the "driving" to operate the prototypes. The wireframe identifiers are essential for "connecting" user actions on interaction objects to subsequent wireframes in the workflow. The UX team can annotate the paper wireframes with UX problems observed in the early rounds of evaluation. You can even hand sketch possible design solutions directly on the prototype and get feedback on those from the users.

Always trade off fidelity (when it is not needed) for efficiency (that is always needed). As an example, if it is not important to have the days and dates on your calendar correspond to the real-world calendar, you can even reuse the calendar grid with the dates already on it.

20.5.4.1 Establish a library of templates for interaction objects in your sketching tool

You can add efficiency as you build up the fidelity of look and feel through tools with libraries of interaction and UI styles and UI objects such as icons, buttons, menu bars, pull-down menus, pop ups, etc. Don't waste time by repeatedly building these interaction objects.

Reusing templates of design objects from a library can help you with consistency across designs and certainly increases your efficiency. Tools such as Sketch allow you to build libraries of such widgets, called symbols, and reuse them. Symbols can be nested and defined to specify aspects that can be overridden when instantiated. This allows designers, for example, to create a button symbol with a generic text label, and override that label every time that symbol is instantiated on the screen. For example, two instances of the same button symbol can have two different labels: "Save changes" and "Discard changes." Furthermore, updating a symbol will automatically update all instances of that symbol in the wireframe deck. For example, if the shape or color of that button symbol is updated, those changes are automatically propagated to all instances of that symbol.

Once you define your symbol library for your target platform, or choose to use one of the popular ones already built and available as a download, you can be very efficient and quick in generating detailed wireframe decks. Even large-scale changes to large wireframe decks can be made rather quickly because of the capabilities of modern tools such as Sketch.

20.5.5 Medium-Fidelity Wireframes with Some Navigational Behavior to Support Early Design Reviews and Walkthroughs

When you are ready for your earliest design reviews with the client, users, and other stakeholders, you connect these low-fidelity wireframes in a deck by way of some initial "hotspots," links or active buttons that allow sequencing through screens by clicking to demonstrate interaction flow by simulating navigational behavior. These prototypes do not usually have more functionality than that. With this added capability, these wireframes are called *click-through prototypes*, which are fast and easy to create and modify and, because they are machine-readable, they are easily sharable.

Click-through wireframe prototypes are used for evaluation via design reviews and walkthroughs with UX team and other stakeholders. This is really still just moving from one static visual wireframe to another but, because some links now work, the prototype can be operated on a laptop by anyone in the group, projecting it onto a screen or TV for group viewing and discussion.

The addition of links takes more effort to create, and even more to maintain as the deck changes, but the added realism is worth it. We have had users and clients exclaim that these are so realistic that they look just like the real thing.

These earliest design reviews usually result in going back to the UX studio, modifying the design, and returning to the same audience for confirmation and/or more feedback.

20.5.6 Medium- to High-Fidelity Click-Through Prototypes to Support Empirical Evaluation

Once you have the layout of each wireframe settled and have decided on the colors, with all the text, labels, boxes, widgets, and links in place, you might be ready to consider moving on from design review and walkthrough evaluations to empirical testing with real users who will do the driving and operate the prototype.

These days a user-based empirical evaluation is not something you always have time to do but, if you need to, you should have the right prototype to support it. To support user-based empirical evaluation or analytic evaluation, you may need to move to a medium- to high-fidelity programmed prototype with more detailed representations of designs, including details of appearance and interaction behavior and possibly even connections to system functionality. HTML5 and

CSS3 are common technologies for programmed prototypes and are often developed by a dedicated "prototyper" embedded in the UX team.

You can use prototypes containing scripts (written in scripting languages) to give a set of wireframes more ability to respond to user actions, such as links to pieces of real or simulated functionality. This added behavior is limited only by the power of the scripting language, but now you are getting into prototype programming, usually not a cost-effective path to follow very far.

Scripting languages can be relatively easy to learn and use and, being high-level languages, can be used to produce some kinds of behavior, mostly navigational behavior, very rapidly. But they are still not effective tools for implementing much functionality.

Preparing for an evaluation session with users will probably require elaborating all the states of the design relevant to the workflow that is the focus of the evaluation.

In projects requiring high rigor and where the stakes for getting it right are high, a high-fidelity prototype, although more expensive and time consuming, can lead to the insight you need; it is still less expensive and faster than building the final product. High-fidelity prototypes can also be useful as advance sales demos for marketing and even as demos for raising venture capital for the company. Aside from these possibilities, high-fidelity prototypes are beyond what you need in most projects, especially in agile development projects.

20.5.6.1 Include "decoy" user interface objects

If the goal is empirical evaluation with real users, you need to make sure the prototypes are representative of the real design. This means they have horizontal coverage. If you include only user interface objects needed to do your initial benchmark tasks, it may be unrealistically easy for users to do just those tasks. Doing user experience testing with this kind of initial interaction design does not give a good idea of the ease of use of the design compared to when it is complete. It also contains many user interface objects to choose from and many other choices to make during a task.

Therefore, you should include many other "decoy" buttons, menu choices, etc., even if they do not do anything—so that participants see more than just the "happy path" for their benchmark tasks. Your decoy objects should look plausible and should, as much as possible, anticipate other tasks and other paths. Users performing tasks with your prototype will be faced with a more realistic array of user interface objects about which they will have to think as they make choices about what user actions are next. When a user clicks on a decoy object, you get to use your "not implemented" message (next section). It's also an opportunity to probe users on why they clicked on that object when it is not part of your envisioned task sequence.

20.5.6.2 Make a "this feature not yet implemented" message

This is the prototype's response to a user action that was not anticipated or that has not yet been included in the design. You will be surprised how often you may use this in user experience evaluation with early prototypes. See Fig. 20-11.

20.5.7 Medium- to High-Fidelity Prototypes Refined Through Evaluation and Iteration to Hand Off to Software Developers

Finally, after the design ideas are iterated and agreed upon by relevant stakeholders, wireframes (and in rare cases programmed prototypes) can be used as a part of interaction design specifications and for design production. Annotate them with details to describe the different states of the design and widgets, including mouse-over states, keyboard inputs, and active focus states. Edge cases and transition effects can now also be described. The goal here is completeness to enable a developer to implement the designs without the need for any interpretation.

If the developers don't have control over color and branding schemes, such UX design specifications can be accompanied by high-fidelity visual comps (pixel-perfect application "skins") from graphic designers (Section 12.5.5).

Fig. 20-11

"Not yet implemented" message (Thanks for permission to use this example to Joe Hutson and Mathew Mathai, Network Infrastructure and Services, Virginia Tech).

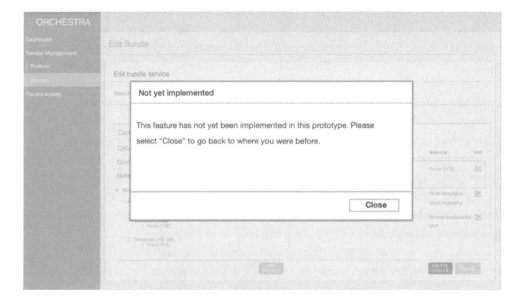

When you hand this prototype off to the software developers for implementation, the process requires collaboration across the UX-SE (software engineering) aisle. The UX people "own" the UX design but not the software that implements it. It is a little like owning a home but not the land it sits on. The "hand-off" point is a serious nexus in the two lifecycles (Chapter 29).

This is the time to go over it with a developer. This prototype:

- Acts as a kind of "contract" for what is to be built.
- Provides the mock-up for:
  - Discussing implementation feasibility.
  - Checking against software platform constraints.
  - Checking for consistency with other features already implemented.

Make it clear that you will be back to check the implemented version against this design.

20.5.7.1 Do not think the UX team is now done

Because preserving a hard-earned quality user experience in the design is not in the purview of the SE people, the UX people have a strong responsibility to ensure that their UX design comes through with fidelity. This checking of the implementation against the final design is something for which we borrowed the term quality assurance (QA), an essential part of the agile UX lifecycle in the late funnel. If the SE people are the sole interpreters of this process, there is no way to predict whether the user experience you worked so hard to achieve will still be there in the final product.

20.5.8 Visually High-Fidelity Prototypes to Support Graphic Design

It is usually not important for even high-fidelity wireframes to have exactly the right graphical appearance and exact colors at this point. Most of the time the UX team will already have worked out the colors and templates necessary for visual comps for the various styles used in the design. Wireframes usually don't have to be produced to those standards.

Visual comp

A pixel-perfect mockup of the graphical "skin," including objects, colors, sizes, shapes, fonts, spacing, and location, plus visual "assets" for user interface elements (Section 12.5.5).

Exercise 20-1: Building a Low- to Mid-Fidelity Wireframe Prototype Deck for Your System

Goal: To obtain experience with rapid construction of a low- to mid-fidelity wireframe prototype deck for some selected user tasks in your system.

Activities: This should be one of your most fun exercises, but it can also be quite a bit of work.

Make sure that the prototype will support at least the benchmark tasks (You might have to read ahead in Section 22.6 to learn a little bit about benchmark tasks for this).

Add in some other "decoy" interaction design "features," widgets, and objects so that the prototype does not look tailored to just your benchmark tasks.

Hints and cautions: It is normal for you to have to do more design work during this exercise to complete details that were not fully designed in previous exercises.

Remember: You are learning the process, not creating a perfect design or prototype.

Assuming you are doing this as a team: Get everyone on your team involved in drawing or using the wireframe sketching tool, not just one or two people. You will be done much faster if everyone pitches in.

If you are sketching the wireframes by hand, this is not art class so don't worry too much about straight lines, exact details, etc.

Pilot test to be sure it will support your benchmark tasks for evaluation.

Deliverables: A right, smart, "executable" wireframe prototype deck that will support your benchmark tasks in user experience testing.

Schedule: It could take several hours, but it is essential for the exercises that follow.

20.6 SPECIALIZED PROTOTYPES

In addition to the wireframe prototypes that are the bread and butter of today's UX design, for completeness we describe a few other kinds of prototypes to consider in specialized situations.

20.6.1 Physical Mockups for Physical Interactivity

A physical mockup is a tangible, three-dimensional prototype or model of a physical device or product, often one that can be held and often crafted rapidly out of materials at hand, used during exploration and evaluation to at least simulate physical interaction.

If a primary characteristic of a product or system is physicality, such as you have with a handheld device, then an effective prototype will also offer the same kind of physicality in its interaction. Programming new applications on physical devices with real software means complex and lengthy implementation on a challenging hardware and software platform. Physical prototypes are an inexpensive way to afford designers and others insight into the product look and feel.

Some products are "physical" in the sense that they are a tangible device that users might hold in their hands. A physical prototype for such products goes

Physicality

Referring to real direct physical interaction with real physical (hardware) devices like in the grasping and moving of knobs and levers (Section 30.3.2.4).

beyond screen simulation on a computer, encompassing the whole device. Pering (2002) describes an older case study of such an approach for a handheld communicator device that combines the functionality of a PDA and a cellphone. If the product is to be handheld, make a prototype from cardboard, wood, or metal that can also be handheld.

Or a system might be "physical" like a kiosk. The TKS kiosk is an ideal candidate for physical prototyping. Brainstorm the physical design through ideation and sketches and then build some cardboard mockups that sit on the floor or the ground, add some physical buttons, and have a cutout for the screen about head height. After homing in on the overall look and feel with cardboard, you can make a wooden version to be sturdier, then add physical buttons and attach a touchscreen (e.g., an iPad or a detachable laptop touchscreen) from the inside to fill the cutout and allow some real interaction.

You can use materials at hand and/or craft physical prototypes with realistic hardware. Start off with glued-on shirt buttons and progress to real push-button switches. Scrounge up hardware buttons and other controls that are as close to those in your envisioned design as possible: push buttons, sliders (for example, from a light dimmer), knobs and dials, a rocker switch, or a joystick from an old Nintendo game.

Even if details are low fidelity, these prototypes are higher fidelity in some ways because they are typically three-dimensional, embodied, and tangible. You can touch them and manipulate them physically. If they are small, you can hold them in your hands. Also, physical prototypes are excellent media for supporting evaluation of emotional impact and other user experience characteristics beyond just usability.

Designers of the original Palm PDA carried around a block of wood as a physical prototype of the envisioned personal digital assistant. They used it to explore the physical feel and other requirements for such a device and its interaction possibilities (Moggridge, 2007, p. 204). Fig. 20-12 shows an example of a rough physical mockup of a design for a "rickshaw"-style cart for transporting people in developing countries.

Physical prototyping is now being used for cellphones, consumer electronics, and products beyond interactive electronics, employing found objects, "junk" (paper plates, pipe cleaners, and other playful materials) from the recycle bin, thrift stores, dollar stores, and school supply shops (Frishberg, 2006). Perhaps IDEO[4] is the company most famous for its physical prototyping for product

Embodied interaction

Interaction with technology that involves a user's body in a natural and significant way, such as by using gestures (Section 6.2.6.3).

Tangible interaction

Interaction involving physical actions between human users and physical objects. A key area of focus in Industrial design, pertaining to designing objects and products to be held, felt, and manipulated by humans. Closely related to embodied interaction (Section 6.2.6.3).

Emotional impact

An affective component of user experience that influences user feelings. Includes such effects as enjoyment, pleasure, fun, satisfaction, aesthetics, coolness, engagement, and novelty and can involve deeper emotional factors such as self-expression, self-identity, a feeling of contribution to the world, and pride of ownership (Section 1.4.4).

---

[4]http://www.ideo.com

Fig. 20-12

Example of a rough physical mockup (courtesy of Akshay Sharma, Virginia Tech Department of Industrial Design).

ideation; see their shopping cart project video (ABC News Nightline, 1999) for a good example.

Wright (2005) describes the power of a physical mockup that users can see and hold as a real object over just pictures on a screen, however powerful and fancy the screen graphics. Users get a real feeling that this *is* the product. The kind of embodied user experience projected by this approach can lead to a product that generates user surprise and delight, product praise in the media, and must-have cachet in the market.

Heller and Borchers (2012) created a physical mechanism for individual electric consumers to be visually aware of their levels of electric consumption at any moment as a simple but compelling example of a physical mockup. By integrating a display where the power is consumed, right at the household outlet, they fashioned a display that is there all the time, not something the consumer has to choose to use or must attach.

Iterating through a series of software and hardware prototypes, the final step was to add a DIY hardware design printed circuit board behind the outlet, making it a fully functional model. The amount of power being consumed at any moment is displayed very simply by a band of color surrounding the outlet socket—green for low consumption, yellow for medium, and red for high.

See more about physical mockups as embodied sketches (physical embodiments of design ideas) in Section 14.3.3.

20.6.2 Paper-in-Device Mockup Prototype, Especially for Mobile Applications

Prototypes can be very effective for apps on mobile devices, but a paper prototype of a mobile app needs an "executor," a person playing computer to change screens and do all the other actions of the system in response to a user's actions. This role of mediator between user and device will necessarily interfere with the usage experience, especially when a large part of that experience involves holding, feeling, and manipulating the device itself.

Bolchini, Pulido, and Faiola (2009) and others devised a solution by which they placed the paper prototype inside the device, leveraging the advantages of paper prototyping in evaluating mobile device interfaces with the real physical device. They drew the prototype screens on paper, scanned them, and loaded them into the device as a sequence of digital images that the device can display. During evaluation, users can move through this sequential navigation by making touches or gestures that the device can already recognize.

(This kind of realism can be achieved without needing a sequential series of screens by click-through wireframe prototypes where hotspots on the screen take you to different screens. The prototype is then loaded as a pdf file into a mobile device.)

This is an agile and inexpensive technique, and the authors reported that their testing showed that even this limited amount of interactivity generated useful feedback and discussion with evaluation users. Also, by adding page annotations about user interactions, possible user thoughts, and other behind-the-scenes information, the progression of pages can become a design storyboard.

> **Storyboard**
>
> A visual scenario in the form of a series of sketches or graphical clips, often annotated, in cartoon-like frames, illustrating the interplay between a user and an envisioned ecology or device (Section 17.4.1).

20.6.3 Animated Prototypes

Most prototypes are static in that they depend on user interaction to show what they can do. Video animation can bring a prototype to life for concept demos, to visualize new UX designs, and to communicate design ideas. While animated prototypes are not interactive, they are at least active. *An animated prototype is a prototype in which the interaction objects are brought to life via animation, usually in video, to demonstrate dynamically and visually what the interaction looks like.*

Löwgren (2004) shows how video animations based on a series of sketches can carry the advantages of low-fidelity prototypes to new dimensions where a static paper prototype cannot tread. Animated sketches are still "rough" enough to invite engagement and design suggestions but, being more like scenarios or storyboards, animations can convey flow and sequencing better in the context of usage.

HCI designers have been using video to bring prototypes to life as early as the 1980s (Vertelney, 1989). A simple approach is to use storyboard frames in a flip book-style sequence on video or, if you already have a fairly complete low-fidelity prototype, you can film it in motion by making a kind of "claymation" frame-by-frame video of its parts moving within an interaction task.

20.6.4 Experience Prototyping, the Goal of High-Fidelity Physical Prototyping

As Buchenau and Suri (2000) point out, if you are told something, you forget it. If you see something for yourself, you remember it. But if you do something for yourself, you understand it.

For some domains, then, for participants to understand the design situation and context well enough to give effective feedback, the prototype they use must allow them to actually do the activity being designed for, to become engaged and immersed in the subjective experience. To appreciate what users will feel, participants need to get beyond being passively exposed to a demo or walkthrough of a prototype and become actively engaged (Buchenau & Suri, 2000, p. 425).

A very good example that everyone can understand is a full flight simulator for a specific airplane. It's not enough to just look at screens and have someone tell you what would be happening. The pilot in training must experience flight situations in as close a way as possible to the real thing.

But aircraft flight simulators are a special case that can be almost as complex as the aircraft themselves. Buchenau and Suri are talking about experience prototypes that succeed in domains not nearly as expensive or as complex. For example, in a project to design for an Internet-enabled cardiac telemetry system that included a device to deliver a defibrillating shock to heart patients in the field (Buchenau & Suri, 2000, p. 426), participants had to simulate usage of several device designs set in the usage context to give full contextual feedback.

In this case, an experience prototype was used in support of usage research. Participants were given a pager to carry with them on weekends. Getting a page on this device represented a patient getting a rather large electrical shock, with the aim of stopping fibrillation that had been detected by the remote device. They were also given a camera to photograph their immediate surroundings at the time of the "shock" and a notebook in which to describe the experience, what were they doing, and what it would have been like to be stunned by a real defibrillating shock at that exact moment in time.

Participants quickly understood the necessity for getting a warning before such a shock is administered—if only for safety (in case they were holding a baby or operating a power tool, for example) and to prepare themselves psychologically. Plus, a way was needed to explain the patient's condition to bystanders. In this approach, "high fidelity" means bringing the participant close to the experience of the real thing.

20.6.5 "Wizard of Oz" Prototypes

Even though we rarely see this type of prototyping in practice these days, we cover it here for completeness. The Wizard of Oz prototyping technique is a deceptively simple approach that gives the *appearance* of a high degree of interactivity. It can be a rapid way to produce highly flexible prototype behavior in complex situations where user inputs are unpredictable. The setup requires two connected computers, each in a different room. The user's computer is connected as a "slave" to the evaluator's computer. The user makes input actions on one computer, which are sent directly to a human team member at the evaluator's computer, hidden in the second room. The human evaluator sees the user inputs on the hidden computer and sends appropriate simulated output back to the user's computer.

This approach has the advantage of an apparently high level of interactivity as seen by the user. It is especially effective when flexible and adaptive "computer" behavior is of the essence, as with artificial intelligence and other difficult-to-implement systems. Within the limits of the cleverness of the human evaluator, the "system" should never break down or crash.

In one of the earliest uses of the Wizard of Oz technique that we know of, Good, Whiteside, Wixon, and Jones (1984) designed empirically a command-driven email interface to accommodate natural novice user actions. Users were given no menus, help, documentation, or instruction.

Users were unaware that a hidden operator was intercepting commands when the system itself could not interpret the input. The design was modified iteratively so that it would have recognized and responded to previously intercepted inputs.

The design progressed from recognizing only 7% of inputs to recognizing about 76% of user commands.

The Wizard of Oz prototyping technique is especially useful when your design ideas are still wide open and you want to see how users behave naturally in the course of simulated interaction. It could work well, for example, with a kiosk.

You would set up the general scope of usage expected and let users at it. You will see what they want to do. Because you have a human at the other end, you do not have to worry about whether you programmed the application to handle any given situation.

20.7 SOFTWARE TOOLS FOR MAKING WIREFRAMES

Wireframes can be sketched using any drawing or word processing software package that supports creating and manipulating shapes. While many applications suffice for simple wireframing, we recommend tools designed specifically for this purpose. We use Sketch, a drawing app, to do all the drawing. Craft is a plug-in to Sketch that connects it to InVision, allowing you to export Sketch screen designs to InVision to incorporate hotspots as working links.

In the "Build mode" of InVision, you work on one screen at a time, adding rectangular overlays that are the hotspots. For each hotspot, you specify what other screen you go to when someone clicks on that hotspot in "Preview mode." You get a nice bonus using InVision: In the "operate" mode, you, or the user, can click anywhere in an open space in the prototype and it highlights all the available links. These tools are available only on Mac computers, but similar tools are available under Windows.

Beyond this discussion, it's not wise to try to cover software tools for making prototypes in this kind of textbook. The field is changing fast and whatever we could say here would be out of date by the time you read this. Plus, it wouldn't be fair to the numerous other perfectly good tools that didn't get cited. To get the latest on software tools for prototyping, it's better to ask an experienced UX professional or to do your research online.

UX Evaluation

5

Part 5 is about evaluating UX designs, via their prototypes, to explore alternative designs and to refine selected candidate designs. A full discussion of UX evaluation methods and techniques comes to a focus on formative evaluation methods for finding and fixing UX problems in designs. Chapters elaborate on preparation for evaluation, empirical data collection, analytic data collection, evaluation data analysis, and reporting of results.

UX Evaluation Methods and Techniques

21

- Types of UX evaluation data:
  - Quantitative versus qualitative data.
  - Objective versus subjective data.
- Formative versus summative evaluation.
- Informal versus formal summative evaluation versus engineering UX evaluation.
- Analytic versus empirical UX evaluation methods.
- Rigor versus rapidness in UX evaluation methods.
- Rapid UX evaluation methods.
- UX evaluation data collection techniques.
- Specialized UX evaluation methods and techniques.
- UX evaluation goals and constraints determine method choices.

21.1 INTRODUCTION

21.1.1 You Are Here

We begin each process chapter with a "you are here" picture of the chapter topic in the context of The Wheel, the overall UX design lifecycle template (Fig. 21-1). In this chapter, the first of the chapters about the Evaluate UX lifecycle activity, we begin by introducing UX evaluation methods and techniques.

This chapter is to introduce UX evaluation methods and techniques, associated terminology, distinctions among the methods and techniques, strengths of each, and how to choose the UX evaluation methods and techniques based on evaluation goals. The how-to details for applying each method and technique are coming later in Chapters 24 and 25 on UX evaluation data collection.

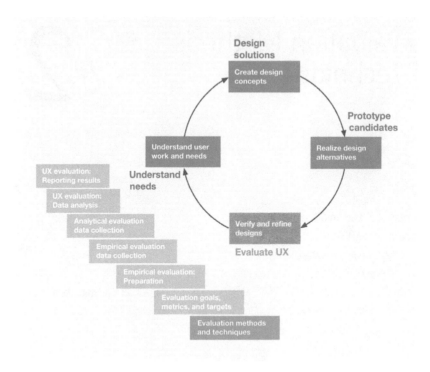

Fig. 21-1

You are here in the upfront chapter on UX evaluation methods and techniques for evaluation within the Evaluate UX lifecycle activity in the context of the overall Wheel lifecycle template.

Lab-based UX evaluation

An empirical UX evaluation method based on observing user participants performing tasks in a UX laboratory setting. Employs critical incident identification and think-aloud techniques for qualitative, and sometimes other quantitative, data collection (Section 21.2.4.1).

21.1.2 Methods versus Techniques

The concepts of methods and techniques were already established in Chapter 2. We review and interpret them here specifically in the context of UX evaluation.

There is not a clear-cut definition of the difference between a method and a technique in our practice, with the main difference being level. An evaluation method is a high-level overall way of doing UX evaluation and a technique is usually a lower-level way of doing specific steps within a method.

For example, lab-based empirical testing with users is an evaluation method. One of the techniques used to collect data about UX problems within that method is critical incident identification. Don't worry if these terms don't mean much to you now; we'll get to them soon.

In this chapter, we introduce some selected UX evaluation methods and techniques to get you familiar with the range of possibilities.

21.1.3 User Testing? No!

You know what "user testing" means, but it's not really an accurate term and no user will like the idea of being tested and, thereby, possibly made to look ridiculous. Users are participants who help us test or evaluate UX designs for usability or user experience, but *we are not testing the user.*

Traditionally, studies in psychology and human factors have referred to "subjects" as the people who perform the tasks while others observe and measure. In UX, we wish to invite these volunteers to join our team and help us evaluate designs. Because we want them to participate, we use the terms "participant" or "user participant" instead of "subject."

21.1.4 Types of UX Evaluation Data

UX evaluation data can be objective or subjective and it can be quantitative or qualitative. Practically, the two dimensions are orthogonal, so both objective and subjective data can be either qualitative or quantitative. For example, questionnaire results (Section 24.3.2) are usually both subjective and quantitative.

21.1.4.1 Quantitative versus qualitative data

Quantitative data are numeric data, usually from measurements, used to assess a level of achievement. The two most common kinds of quantitative data collected most often in formative evaluation are objective user performance data measured using benchmark tasks and subjective user opinion data measured using questionnaires. Quantitative data are the basis of the informal summative evaluation component and help the team assess UX achievements and monitor convergence toward UX targets, usually in comparison with the specified levels set in the UX targets (Chapter 22).

Qualitative data are nonnumeric descriptive data used to find and fix UX problems. Qualitative data from UX evaluation are usually descriptions of UX problems or issues observed or experienced during usage. Qualitative data, the key to identifying UX problems and their causes, are usually collected via critical incident identification, the think-aloud technique, and UX inspections methods.

21.1.4.2 Objective versus subjective data

Objective UX data are data observed directly. Objective data arise from observations by either the UX evaluator or the participant. Objective data are always associated with empirical methods.

Subjective UX data represent opinions, judgments, and other feedback. Subjective data originate from opinions of either UX evaluator or participant, concerning

---

Objective UX evaluation data

Qualitative or quantitative data acquired through direct empirical observation, usually of user performance (Section 21.1.4.2).

Formal summative evaluation

A formal, statistically rigorous summative (quantitative) empirical UX evaluation that produces statistically significant results (Section 21.1.5.1).

Critical incident

An event that occurs during user task performance or other user interaction that indicate possible UX problem(s). Critical incident identification, an empirical UX evaluation data collection technique based on the participant and/or evaluator detecting and analyzing critical incidents, is arguably the single most important qualitative data collection technique (Section 24.2.1).

the user experience and satisfaction with the design. Analytic UX evaluation methods (Chapter 25) yield only qualitative subjective data (UX problem identification based on an expert opinion of the UX inspector). Questionnaires (Section 24.3.2) yield data that are quantitative and subjective (data on numeric scales based on opinions of users).

21.1.5 Formative Evaluation versus Summative Evaluation

The distinction between formative evaluation and summative evaluation is based on a long-standing dichotomy:

- *Formative UX evaluation is diagnostic UX evaluation using qualitative data collection with the objective to form a design, that is, for finding and fixing UX problems and thereby refining the design.*
- *Summative UX evaluation is defined to be UX evaluation with the objective to sum up or assess the success of a UX design.*

A cute, but apropos, way to look at the difference: "When the cook tastes the soup, that's formative; when the guests taste the soup, that's summative" (Stake, 2004, p. 17).

The earliest reference to the terms formative evaluation and summative evaluation we know of stems from their use by Scriven (1967) in education and curriculum evaluation. Perhaps more well known is the follow-up usage by Dick and Carey (1978) in the area of instructional design. Williges (1984) and Carroll, Singley, and Rosson (1992) were among the first to use the terms in an HCI context.

Formative evaluation is primarily diagnostic, with the aim of identifying and fixing UX problems and their causes in the design. Summative evaluation is primarily rating or scoring; it is about collecting quantitative data for assessing a level of quality due to a design.

21.1.5.1 Formal summative evaluation

Summative UX evaluation includes both formal and informal methods. *A formal summative (quantitative) UX evaluation method is an empirical method that produces statistically significant results.* The term "formal" is used because the process is statistically rigorous.

In science, there is no substitute for formal summative studies, inferential statistics, and statistically significant results to find the "truth" in answers to science and research questions. But most of the work we do in UX evaluation is more engineering than science, where getting at "truth" is a more practical and less exact business. In many ways, engineering is about judgment based on hunches and intuition that are, in turn, based on skill and experience.

Formal summative evaluation is based on an experimental design for controlled comparative hypothesis testing using an m by n factorial design with y independent variables, the results of which are subjected to statistical tests for significance. This takes special training and skills, so don't promise summative evaluation if you can't deliver. In addition, it's expensive and time consuming to do a proper summative evaluation. In sum, formal summative evaluation is an important HCI research skill, but in our view it is not part of UX practice.

As an example of a design change that is probably not (by itself) measurably better in terms of usability but is arguably better, consider a particular button label. If the whole team agrees that the old button label was vague and confusing and the new button label is clear and easily understood, then the team probably should make that design change.

Formal summative evaluation is outside the scope of the rest of this book.

For more discussion of why we don't consider formal summative evaluation as part of UX practice, see Section 28.2.

21.1.5.2 Informal summative evaluation

An *informal summative UX evaluation method is a quantitative summative UX evaluation method that is not statistically rigorous and does not produce statistically significant results.* Informal summative evaluation is used in support of formative evaluation, as an engineering technique to help assess how well you are achieving good usability and UX.

Informal summative evaluation is done without experimental controls, with smaller numbers of user participants, and with only summary descriptive statistics (such as average values). At the end of each iteration for a product version, the informal summative evaluation can be used as a kind of acceptance test to compare with our UX targets (Chapter 22) and help ensure that we meet our UX and business goals with the product design.

Table 21-1 highlights the differences between formal and informal summative UX evaluation methods.

21.1.5.3 Engineering UX evaluation: Formative plus informal summative

As an engineering method, UX evaluation can include formative evaluation plus an optional informal summative component (Fig. 21-2). The summative part can't be used to *prove* anything, but it is a valuable guide to the UX design process. Evaluation methods such as design reviews, heuristic methods, and other UX

Participant

A participant, or user participant, is a user, potential, or user surrogate who helps evaluate UX designs for usability and user experience. These are the people who perform tasks and give feedback while we observe and measure. Because we wish to invite these volunteers to join our team and help us evaluate designs (i.e., we want them to participate), we use the term "participant" instead of "subject" (Section 21.1.3).

Table 21-1

Some differences between formal and informal summative UX evaluation methods

Formal Summative UX Evaluation	Informal Summative UX Evaluation
Science	Engineering
Randomly chosen subjects/participants	Deliberately nonrandom participant selection to get most formative information
Concerned with having large enough sample size (number of subjects)	Deliberately uses relatively small number of participants
Uses rigorous and powerful statistical techniques	Deliberately simple, low-power statistical techniques (e.g., simple mean and, sometimes, standard deviation)
Results can be used to make claims about "truth" in a scientific sense	Results cannot be used to make claims, but are used to make engineering judgments
Relatively expensive and time consuming to perform	Relatively inexpensive and rapid to perform
Rigorous constraints on methods and procedures	Methods and procedures open to innovation and adaptation
Tends to yield "truth" about very specific scientific questions (A vs. B)	Can yield insight about broader range of questions regarding levels of UX achieved and the need for further improvement
Not used within a UX design process	Intended to be used within a UX design process in support of formative methods

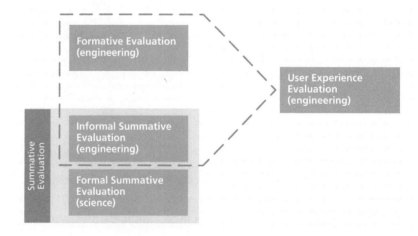

Fig. 21-2

Engineering UX evaluation is a combination of formative evaluation and informal summative evaluation.

inspection methods are good examples of purely formative evaluation methods (without a summative component).

Empirical methods such as testing with user participants can also be limited to a formative evaluation component, especially in early stages, when we are defining and refining the design and are not yet interested in performance indicators.

21.1.6 Our Goal-Oriented Approach

We will describe our approach in which UX evaluation goals determine the choices of methods and techniques needed to achieve the goals. But first we need to establish some terminology.

21.2 UX EVALUATION METHODS

For formative UX evaluation, you can use either empirical or analytic UX evaluation methods (Hartson, Andre, & Williges, 2003).

21.2.1 Empirical UX Evaluation Methods

Empirical methods, by definition, depend on data observed in the performance of real user participants and data coming directly from user participants. These data include critical incident data observed in empirical evaluation and comments from users while "thinking aloud" and/or in their questionnaire responses.

Empirical methods can be performed in a UX laboratory setting, at a conference table, or in the field. Empirical testing can produce both quantitative and qualitative data from the same measuring instrument, such as user task performance.

The UX lab is a more or less controlled environment, which is a plus in terms of limiting distractions, but testing in the real work context of a field setting can be more effective at ensuring realistic task conditions for ecological validity.

21.2.2 Analytic UX Evaluation Methods

Analytic methods are based on examining inherent attributes of the design rather than seeing the design in use. Except for numerical ratings and similar data, analytic methods yield qualitative subjective data. Although analytic UX evaluation methods (Chapter 25) can be applied rigorously and correspondingly more slowly, they were developed as faster and less expensive methods to produce approximations to or predictors of empirical results.

Empirical UX evaluation

A family of UX evaluation methods that depends on data observed in the performance of real user participants and data coming directly from user participants (Section 21.2.1).

Think-aloud technique

A qualitative empirical data collection technique in which participants verbally express thoughts about the interaction experience, including their motives, rationale, and perceptions of UX problems, especially to identify UX problems (Section 24.2.3).

Measuring instrument

The means of generating values for the particular UX measure, the vehicle through which values are measured for a UX character to be evaluated. Examples include benchmark tasks and questionnaires (Sections 22.6 and 22.7).

Ecological validity

Refers to the realism with
which a design of evaluation
setup matches the user's real
work context. It is about how
accurately the design or
evaluation reflects the
relevant characteristics of the
ecology of interaction, that
is, its context in the world or
its environment (Sections
16.3, 22.6.4.4).

Analytic methods include design reviews, design walkthroughs, and inspection methods, such as heuristic evaluation (HE).

21.2.3 Comparison

Empirical methods are sometimes called "payoff methods" (Carroll et al., 1992; Scriven, 1967) because they are based on how a design or design change pays off in real observable usage. Analytic methods are sometimes called "intrinsic methods" because they are based on analyzing intrinsic characteristics of the design.

Some methods in practice are a mix of analytic and empirical. For example, expert UX inspection can involve "simulated empirical" aspects in which the expert plays the user role, simultaneously performing tasks and "observing" UX problems.

In describing the distinction between payoff and intrinsic approaches to evaluation, Scriven wrote an oft-quoted (Carroll et al., 1992; Gray & Salzman, 1998, p. 215) analogy featuring an axe (Scriven, 1967, p. 53): "If you want to evaluate a tool, say an axe, you might study the design of the bit, the weight distribution, the steel alloy used, the grade of hickory in the handle, etc., or you might just study the kind and speed of the cuts it makes in the hands of a good axeman." He was speaking of intrinsic and payoff evaluation, respectively. In Hartson et al. (2003) we added our own embellishments, which we paraphrase here.

Although this example served Scriven's purpose well, it also offers us a chance to make a point about the need to identify UX goals carefully before establishing evaluation criteria. Giving a UX perspective to the axe example, we note that user performance observation in payoff evaluation does not necessarily require a *good* axeman (or axeperson). UX goals (and, therefore, evaluation goals) depend on expected user classes of key work roles and the expected kind of usage.

Subjective UX
evaluation data

Data based on opinion or
judgment, of evaluator or
user (Section 21.1.4.2).

For example, an axe design that gives optimum performance in the hands of an expert might be too dangerous for a novice user. For the inexperienced user, safety might be a UX goal that transcends firewood production, calling for a safer design that might necessarily sacrifice some efficiency.

21.2.4 Some Specific Empirical UX Evaluation Methods
21.2.4.1 Lab-based evaluation

Lab-based UX evaluation is an empirical UX evaluation method based on observing user participants performing tasks in a UX laboratory setting. It employs critical incident identification and think-aloud techniques for qualitative, and sometimes quantitative, data collection.

Lab-based empirical UX evaluation relies on observing user participants performing representative tasks. Qualitative data lead to identifying UX problems to fix and quantitative data, if collected, lead to assessment of how well users perform with a given design.

In Chapter 22, we discuss quantitative lab-based evaluation goals and metrics. Chapter 23 is about preparing for empirical design. Chapter 24 covers empirical evaluation data collection methods and techniques.

21.2.4.2 RITE

The approach called Rapid Iterative Test and Evaluation (RITE) (Medlock, Wixon, McGee, & Welsh, 2005; Medlock, Wixon, Terrano, Romero, & Fulton, 2002), a fast user-based UX evaluation approach designed to pick the low-hanging fruit at relatively low cost, is one of the best rapid empirical evaluation methods. The key to fast iteration with RITE is fixing the problems as soon as they are identified. This fast turnaround of qualitative evaluation results and problem fixing makes RITE one of the most agile empirical methods. Problem reporting occurs while the team is still there, so they are already informed and immersed in the process. More details about RITE are in Section 24.6.1.

21.2.4.3 Quasiempirical evaluation

Quasiempirical UX evaluation methods are hybrid approaches arising when UX professionals develop their own methods with shortcuts, explained in more detail in Section 24.6.2.

21.2.5 Weaknesses of UX Evaluation Methods
21.2.5.1 Measurability of user experience: A problem on the empirical quantitative side

Quantitative evaluation of an attribute such as usability or UX implies some kind of measurement. But can you measure usability or user experience? This may come as a surprise, but neither usability nor user experience is directly measurable. In fact, most interesting phenomena, such as teaching and learning, share the same difficulty. So we resort to measuring things we *can* measure and use those measurements as *indicators* of our more abstract and less measurable notions. For example, we can understand usability effects such as productivity or ease of use by measuring observable user performance-based *indicators* such as time to complete a task and counts of errors encountered by users within task performance.

Quasiempirical UX evaluation

Hybrid approaches arising when UX professionals develop their own methods with shortcuts. They are empirical because they involve data collection using participants or participant surrogates. But they are "quasi" because they are informal and flexible with respect to process and protocol and the UX evaluator can play a significant analytic role (Section 24.6.2).

Questionnaires also provide indicators of user satisfaction through answers to questions we think are closely related to their perceived performance and satisfaction. Similarly, emotional impact factors such as satisfaction and joy of use also cannot be measured directly but only through indirect indicators.

21.2.5.2 Reliability of UX evaluation methods: A problem on the qualitative side

In simple terms, the reliability of a UX evaluation method means *repeatability*, and it's a problem with both empirical and analytic methods (Hartson et al., 2003). It means that, if you use the same formative evaluation method with several different user participants (for empirical methods) or several different UX inspectors (for analytic methods), you won't get the same list of UX problems each time. In fact, the differences can be fairly large. We have to live with imperfect reliability. For more about UX evaluation reliability, see Section 28.3.

The good news is that even UX evaluation methods and techniques with low reliability can still be very effective—i.e., the methods still find UX problems that need fixing and often they find the most important problems (Hartson et al., 2003). Low reliability is not always a serious drawback; much of each iteration of formative evaluation in UX practice is about learning as much about the design as you can at the lowest cost and then moving on.

So, while it would be nice to have perfect reliability, as a practical matter if the method is reasonably effective, the process still works. Each time you do formative evaluation, you will get some list of UX problems. If you apply more rigor in the evaluation method, your list will be more complete and accurate. If you fix all those problems and do formative evaluation again, you'll get another list (of some of the remaining UX problems). Eventually, you can find and fix most of the UX problems, especially the important ones. This kind of approximation to the ideal is what engineering is all about.

21.2.6 Some Specific Analytic UX Evaluation Methods
21.2.6.1 Early design reviews and design walkthroughs

Early design reviews and design walkthroughs are demos of the design by the UX team to get early reactions and feedback from team members and other stakeholders, including users and people in the client organization. We classify these as analytic methods because they are based on descriptions of how the design works rather than real usage by users.

Earliest presentations might employ scenarios and storyboards for evaluating the ecological view or conceptual design and screen sketches for task-level evaluation—nothing interactive. These media will rapidly evolve into

Design review

A slightly more comprehensive UX evaluation technique than design walkthroughs, usually done with click-through wireframe prototypes to demonstrate workflow and navigation. Often the primary evaluation method for task-level UX designs in the fast iteration of the late funnel (Section 25.2.2).

Design walkthrough

Informal technique for getting initial reactions to design concepts, usually employing only scenarios, storyboards, screen sketches, and/or some wireframes. No real interaction capability, so UX designer has to do the "driving" (Section 25.2.1).

click-through wireframe prototypes. You, the UX team, have to do the "driving" to demonstrate interaction and navigation; it's too early for anyone else in a user role to engage in real interaction.

The leader walks the group through key workflow patterns that the design is intended to support. In the early funnel part of the lifecycle process, this will involve an overview, the flow model, and the conceptual design. In the late funnel part, this will be centered on mostly the interaction design of one feature at a time (focusing on a small set of tasks). As the team follows the scenarios, looking systematically at parts of the design and discussing the merits and potential problems, the leader tells stories about users and usage, user intentions and actions, and expected outcomes.

21.2.6.2 Expert UX inspection

The expert UX inspection is a rapid analytic evaluation method. Expert UX inspectors use their professional experience and knowledge of UX design guidelines to spot UX problems during an in-depth inspection of the design. They also often simulate real usage by playing the part of users and carrying out key tasks in search of problems.

Although the UX inspector may be an expert in UX, he or she may not be an expert at all in the system in question or its associated work domain. In these cases, the UX inspector can leverage this unfamiliarity to find problems for novice users, or the UX inspector can team up with a subject matter expert.

21.2.6.3 Heuristic evaluation (HE)

The heuristic evaluation (HE) method (Nielsen, 1992; Nielsen & Molich, 1990) is the best known and most popular of the inspection methods. In the HE method, inspectors are guided by an empirically derived list of about 20 "heuristics" or rules that govern good UX design. The UX professionals on the team do an expert UX inspection, asking how well each of these rules is followed in the design. The HE method has the advantages of being inexpensive, intuitive, and easy to motivate practitioners to do, and is especially effective for use early in the UX process.

21.3 RIGOR VERSUS RAPIDNESS IN UX EVALUATION METHODS AND TECHNIQUES

The relationship between method rigor and rapidness (Section 3.2.7) is multifaceted:

Wireframe prototype

A prototype composed of wireframes, which are line-drawing representations of UX designs, especially the interaction design of screens (Section 20.4).

Inspection (UX)

An analytical evaluation method in which a UX expert evaluates an interaction design by looking at it or trying it out, sometimes in the context of a set of abstracted design guidelines. Expert evaluators are both participant surrogates and observers, asking themselves questions about what would cause users problems and giving an expert opinion predicting UX problems (Section 25.4).

Subject matter expert (SME)

Someone with a deep understanding of a specific work domain and the range of work practices within that domain (Section 7.4.4.1).

Heuristic evaluation

An analytic evaluation method based on expert UX inspection guided by a set of heuristics, general high-level UX design guidelines (Section 25.5).

- There is a tradeoff between the rigor with which you apply any method and the rapidness that can be achieved.
- All methods can span a range of rigor (and, therefore, rapidness).
- High rigor is not always a goal.
- Some methods were invented to favor rapidness over rigor.

21.3.1 There Is a Tradeoff between Rapidness and Achievable Rigor

In general, applying an evaluation method (or any method) with more rigor can achieve more complete and more accurate results, but will take more time and be more costly. Similarly, by taking shortcuts you can usually increase speed and reduce the cost of almost any UX evaluation method, but at the price of reduced rigor. See Section 3.2.7 for more discussion of rapidness versus rigor.

21.3.2 All Methods Can Span a Range of Rigor and Speed

Each UX evaluation method has its own range of potential rigor. For example, you can perform a lab-based empirical method in a highly rigorous way that will maximize effectiveness and minimize the risk of errors by refraining from shortcuts and by retaining all the data.

When high rigor is not required, you can also perform lab-based empirical evaluation rapidly and with many shortcuts. By filtering and abstracting the evaluation data down to the most important points, you can gain efficiency (higher speed and lower cost).

Similarly, an analytic method can be performed rapidly and at a low level of rigor or it can be performed with a high level of rigor, paying careful attention to the sources, completeness, and purity of the data.

21.3.3 High Rigor Is not Always a Goal

In many design situations, such as early project stages where things are changing rapidly, rigor isn't a priority. It's more important to be agile to iterate and learn quickly.

21.3.4 Some Methods were Invented to Favor Rapidness Over Rigor

Not all methods cover the same range of potential rigor, so there are choices to be made to match your need for rigor. While certainly not perfect, empirical UX evaluation methods performed at a high level of rigor have long been considered the standard of comparison with respect to effectiveness of methods.

Some other UX evaluation methods, including analytic methods (Chapter 25), were invented specifically to be faster and more cost-effective substitutes for the fully rigorous empirical methods. Analytic methods are designed to be shortcut methods for approximating what really counts, UX problems that could be found empirically.

So, there are two ways you can view the rigor of a UX evaluation method:

- The rigor with which any given method is applied.
- The range of rigor inherent in the method itself.

Because design reviews, walkthroughs, and UX inspections can be performed rapidly, they are the frequent choice in late-funnel task-level evaluation. There are also some empirical methods specifically designed to be rapid, including RITE and quasiempirical methods.

21.4 UX EVALUATION DATA COLLECTION TECHNIQUES

21.4.1 Quantitative Data Collection Techniques

21.4.1.1 Objective data: User performance measures

Some quantitative data collection techniques employ user performance measures taken during empirical UX testing with user participants. Users perform benchmark tasks and UX evaluators take objective measures, such as the time to complete a task.

21.4.1.2 Subjective data: User questionnaires

Other quantitative data collection techniques employ questionnaires or user surveys to gather subjective data about how users view the design (Section 24.3.2). Questionnaires can be used as an evaluation method on their own or to supplement your objective UX evaluation data with subjective data directly from the user. Questionnaires are simple to use, for both analyst and participant, and can be used with or without a lab. Questionnaires are good for evaluating specific targeted aspects of the user experience, including perceived usability, usefulness, and emotional impact.

21.4.1.3 Warning: Modifying a questionnaire can damage its validity

The validity of a questionnaire is a statistical characteristic more of concern to summative studies. Ready-made questionnaires are usually created and tested carefully for statistical validity. A number of already developed and validated

RITE

Rapid Iterative Test and Evaluation (Medlock et al., 2005; Medlock et al., 2002), a fast user-based UX evaluation approach designed to pick low-hanging fruit at relatively low cost. Based on fast iteration and fixing the problems as soon as they are identified. One of the best rapid empirical evaluation methods (Section 21.2.4.2).

Quasiempirical UX evaluation

Hybrid approaches arising when UX professionals develop their own methods with shortcuts. They are empirical because they involve data collection using participants or participant surrogates. But they are "quasi" because they are informal and flexible with respect to process and protocol and the UX evaluator can play a significant analytic role (Section 24.6.2).

Participant

A participant, or user participant, is a user, potential, or user surrogate who helps evaluate UX designs for usability and user experience. These are the people who perform tasks and give feedback while we observe and measure. Because we wish to invite these volunteers to join our team and help us evaluate designs (i.e., we want them to participate), we use the term "participant" instead of "subject" (Section 21.1.3).

Benchmark task

A task description devised for a participant to perform during UX evaluation so that UX measures such as time on task and error rates can be obtained and compared to a baseline value across the performances of multiple participants (Section 22.6).

Usefulness

A component of user experience based on utility, system functionality that gives users the ability to accomplish the goals of work (or play) through using the system or product (Section 1.4.3).

questionnaires are available for assessing usability, usefulness, and emotional impact.

However, if you want or need to modify an existing questionnaire to suit specific needs, don't worry that modifying an existing, already validated, questionnaire might affect its validity; questionnaire validity is rarely a practical concern in UX practice.

For most things in this book, we encourage you to improvise and adapt, and that includes questionnaires. However, you must do so armed with the knowledge that any modification, especially by one not expert in making questionnaires, carries the risk of undoing the questionnaire validity. The more modifications, the more the risk. The methods for and issues concerning questionnaire validation are beyond the scope of this book.

Because of this risk to validity, homemade questionnaires and unvalidated modifications to questionnaires are not allowed in summative evaluation but are often used in formative evaluation. This is not an invitation to be slipshod; we are just allowing ourselves to not have to go through validation for sensible modifications made responsibly.

21.4.2 Qualitative Data Collection Techniques

Qualitative data collection techniques are used to capture data for UX problem identification. Critical incident identification, think aloud, and codiscovery, described next, are among the most popular qualitative data collection techniques.

21.4.2.1 Critical incident identification

Critical incident identification is a qualitative UX data collection technique that involves the UX team observing user participants performing tasks and detecting "critical incidents," or occurrences where users encounter UX problems. Problems thus identified are traced to their causes in the UX design and put on a list to be fixed in subsequent iterations (Section 26.4.9).

21.4.2.2 User think-aloud techniques

The think-aloud technique is usually applied together with critical incident identification as a second way of spotting UX problems during user task performance. In this technique, users are encouraged to express their thoughts verbally as they perform tasks and exercise the UX design, thus revealing otherwise possible hidden qualitative data about UX problems. The think-aloud technique is perhaps the most useful of all UX evaluation techniques as it gets at the user's state of mind precisely at the time of use.

21.4.2.3 Codiscovery

You can use two or more participants in a team approach to the think-aloud technique (O'Malley, Draper, & Riley, 1984), an approach that Kennedy (1989) called "codiscovery" (Section 24.2.3.3). Multiple participants sometimes offer the natural ease of talking in conversation with another person (Wildman, 1995), leading to data from multiple viewpoints.

21.5 SPECIALIZED UX EVALUATION METHODS

In addition to the "standard" UX evaluation methods and techniques of the previous sections, there are a number of specialized methods and techniques. We briefly describe a few here.

21.5.1 Alpha and Beta Testing and Field Surveys

Alpha and beta testing are useful postdeployment evaluation methods. After almost all development is complete, manufacturers of software applications sometimes send out alpha and beta (prerelease) versions of the application software to select users, experts, customers, and professional reviewers as a preview. In exchange for the early preview, users try it out and give feedback on the experience. Often little or no guidance is given for the review process beyond just survey questions such as "tell us what you think is good and bad and what needs fixing, what additional features you would like to see, etc."

An alpha version of a product is an earlier, less polished version, usually with a smaller and more trusted "audience." Beta is as close to the final product as they can make it and is sent out to a larger community. Most companies develop a beta trial mailing list of a community of early adopters and expert users, mostly known to be friendly to the company and its products and helpful in their comments.

Alpha and beta testing are easy and inexpensive ways to get high-level feedback, and they are based on real usage. But alpha and beta testing barely qualify as formative evaluation because:

- You don't get the kind of detailed UX problem data you get from a mainstream formative evaluation process.
- It is usually too late to change the design in any significant way if problems are identified.

Alpha and beta testing are very much individualized to a given development organization and environment. Full descriptions of how to do alpha and beta testing are beyond our scope.

Like alpha and beta testing, user field survey information is retrospective and, while it can be good for getting at user satisfaction, it does not capture the details of use within the usage experience.

Anything is better than nothing, but please don't let these after-the-fact methods be the only formative evaluation used within the product lifecycle in your given organization.

21.5.2 Remote UX Evaluation

Remote UX evaluation methods (Dray & Siegel, 2004; Hartson & Castillo, 1998) are good for evaluating systems after they have been deployed in the field. Methods include:

- Simulating lab-based UX testing using the Internet as a long extension cord to the user (e.g., UserVue by TechSmith).
- Online surveys for getting after-the-fact feedback.
- Software instrumentation of clickstream and usage event information.
- Software plug-ins to capture user self-reporting of UX issues.

The latter approach (Hartson & Castillo, 1998) uses self-reporting of UX problems by users as the problems occur during their normal usage, allowing you to get at the perishable details of the usage experience, especially in real-life daily work usage. As always, the best feedback for design improvement is feedback deriving from Carter's (2007) "inquiry within experience," or formative data given concurrent with usage rather than retrospective recollection.

21.5.3 Automatic UX Evaluation

Lab-based and UX inspection methods are labor intensive and, therefore, limited in scope (small number of users exercising small portions of large systems). But large and complex systems with large numbers of users offer the potential for a vast volume of usage data. Think of "observing" a hundred thousand users using Microsoft Word. Automatic methods have been devised to take advantage of this boundless pool of data, collecting and analyzing usage data without need for UX specialists to deal with each individual action. Sometimes multiple versions of the product are released to different sets of users and resulting data are compared to ascertain which version is better. This type of evaluation is often called A-B testing, where A and B are two variations of the design.

The result is a massive amount of data about keystrokes, clickstreams, and pause/idle times. But all data are at the low level of user actions, without any information about tasks, user intentions, cognitive processes, etc. There are no direct indications of when the user is having a UX problem somewhere in the midst of that torrent of user action data. Basing redesign on click counts and low-level user navigation within a large software application could well lead to low-level optimization of a system with a bad high-level design. A full description of how to do automatic usability evaluation is beyond our scope.

21.6 ADAPTING AND APPROPRIATING UX EVALUATION METHODS AND TECHNIQUES

It's not enough to choose the "standard" UX evaluation methods and techniques that fit your goals and constraints. You will find it very natural to tailor and tune the methods and techniques to the nuances of your team and project until you have appropriated them as your own for each different design situation. This aspect of choosing methods and techniques is discussed at length in Section 2.5.

For UX evaluation, as perhaps for most UX work, our motto echoes that old military imperative: improvise, adapt, and overcome! Be flexible and customize your methods and techniques, creating variations to fit your evaluation goals and needs. This includes adapting any method by leaving out steps, adding new steps, and changing the details of a step.

Empirical UX Evaluation: UX Goals, Metrics, and Targets

22

22.1 INTRODUCTION

22.1.1 You Are Here

We begin each process chapter with a "you are here" picture of the chapter topic in the context of The Wheel, the overall UX design lifecycle template (Fig. 22-1). In this chapter, we establish operational targets for user experience to assess the level of success in your designs so that you know when you can move on to the next iteration.

UX goals, metrics, and targets help build scaffolding to support planning for evaluation that will successfully reveal problems with user performance and emotional satisfaction. If used, UX goals, metrics, and targets are set up early as part of preparation for evaluation, and can serve to guide much of the process from analysis through evaluation.

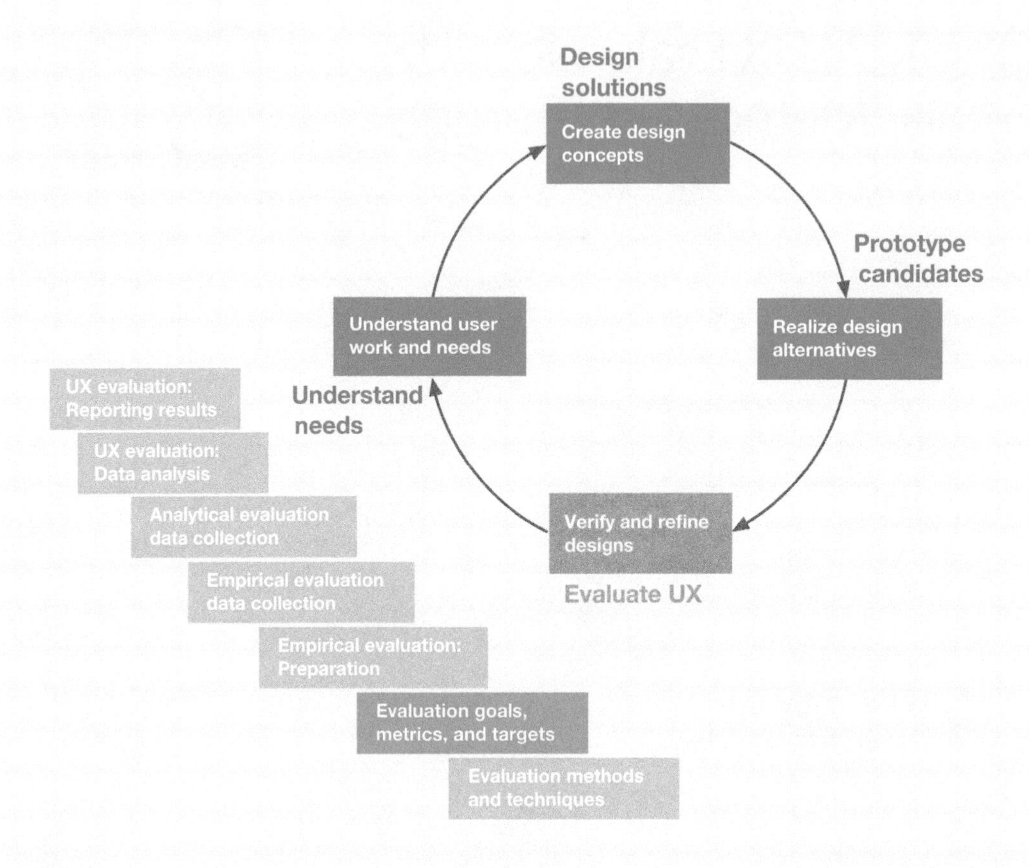

Fig. 22-1

You are here in the chapter on UX evaluation goals, metrics, and targets within the Evaluate UX lifecycle activity in the context of the overall Wheel lifecycle process.

22.1.2 Project Context for UX Metrics and Targets

In the early stages, evaluation usually focuses on qualitative data for finding UX problems. In these early evaluations, the absence of quantitative data precludes the use of UX metrics and targets. But you can start to establish them at any point if you intend to use them in later evaluations.

However, you might wish to forego UX metrics and targets altogether. In most practical contexts, specifying UX metrics and targets and following up with the correspondingly rigorous evaluation may be too expensive. This level of completeness is only possible in a few organizations where there are significant established UX resources. In many projects, one round of evaluation is all you get. Also, as designers, we can know which parts of the design need further investigation just by looking at the results of the first round of evaluation. In such cases, quantitative UX metrics and targets may not be useful but benchmark tasks are still useful as vehicles for driving evaluation.

Regardless, the trend in the UX field is moving away from a focus on quantitative user performance measures and more toward rapid qualitative evaluation of usability, user satisfaction, and enjoyment. Nonetheless, we include the full treatment of UX goals, metrics, and targets here and quantitative data collection and analysis in the later UX evaluation chapters for completeness. This is because some readers and practitioners still want or need coverage of the topic.

In any case, we find that specifying UX goals, metrics, and targets is often overlooked, either because of lack of knowledge or because of lack of time. Sometimes this can be unfortunate because it can diminish the potential of what can be accomplished with the resources you will be putting into user experience evaluation. This chapter can help you avoid that pitfall.

Fortunately, creating UX metrics and targets, after a little practice, does not take much time. You will then have specific quantified UX goals against which to test rather than just waiting to see what happens when you put users in front of your UX design. Because UX metrics and targets provide feasible objectives for formative evaluation efforts, the results can help you pinpoint where to focus on redesign most profitably.

And, finally, UX goals, metrics, and targets offer a way to help manage the lifecycle by defining a quantifiable end to what can otherwise seem like endless iteration. Of course, designers and managers can run out of time, money, and patience before they meet their UX targets—sometimes after just one round of evaluation—but at least then they know where things stand.

For a bit more discussion about the historical roots of UX metrics and targets, see Section 28.7.

22.2 UX TARGET TABLES

Through years of working with real-world UX professionals and doing our own user experience evaluations, we have refined the concept of a UX target table, in the form shown in Table 22-1, from the original conception of a usability

Table 22-1

Our UX target table, as evolved from the Whiteside, Bennett, and Holtzblatt (1988) usability specification table

Work Role: User Class	UX Goal	UX Measure	Measuring Instrument	UX Metric	Baseline Level	Target Level	Observed Results

User class

A description of the relevant characteristics of the user population who can take on a particular work role. User class descriptions can include such characteristics as demographics, skills, knowledge, experience, and special needs—for example, because of physical limitations (Section 9.3.4).

specification table as presented by Whiteside et al. (1988). A spreadsheet is an obvious way to implement these tables.

For convenience, one row in the table is called a "UX target." The first column is for the work role and related user class to which this UX target applies. The next two columns are for the related UX goal and the associated UX measure. These all go together because each UX measure is aimed at supporting a UX goal and is specified with respect to a work role and user class combination. Next, you will see where you get the information for these three columns.

As a running example to illustrate the use of each column in the UX target table, we will progressively set some UX targets for the new Ticket Kiosk System.

22.3 WORK ROLE AND USER CLASSES

Because UX targets are aimed at specific work roles, we label each UX target by work role. Recall that different work roles in the user models perform different task sets.

So the key task sets for a given work role will have associated usage scenarios or other task sequence representations, which will inform benchmark task descriptions we create as measuring instruments to go with UX targets. Within a given work role, different user classes will generally be expected to perform to different standards, that is, at different target levels.

Example: A Work Role and User Class for the Ticket Kiosk System

For the Ticket Kiosk System, let's begin by focusing on the user work role of the ticket buyer. As we saw earlier, user class definitions for a work role can be based on, among other things, level of expertise, disabilities and limitations, and other demographics. For this work role, user classes could include a casual town resident user from Middleburg and a student user from Middleburg University. In this example, we feature the casual town user, as shown in Table 22-2.

Table 22-2

Choosing a work role and a user class for a UX target

Work Role: User Class	UX Goal	UX Measure	Measuring Instrument	UX Metric	Baseline Level	Target Level	Observed Results
Ticket buyer: Casual new user, for occasional personal use							

22.4 UX GOALS

UX goals are high-level objectives for a UX design, stated in terms of user experience objectives. UX goals can be driven by business goals and reflect real use of a product and identify what is important to an organization, its customers, and its users. They are expressed as desired effects to be experienced in usage by users of features in the design and they translate into a set of UX measures to be assessed in evaluation.

You can extract UX goals from user concerns captured in work activity notes, the flow model, social models, and work objectives, some of which will be market driven, reflecting competitive imperatives for the product. User experience goals can be stated for all users in general, in terms of a specific work role or user class, or for specific kinds of tasks.

Examples of user experience goals include ease of use for all users, ease of remembering for intermittent users, power performance for experts, avoiding errors for safety-critical systems, high customer satisfaction, walk-up-and-use learnability for new users, and so on.

Example: User Experience Goals for the Ticket Kiosk System

From our usage research data, we can define the primary high-level UX goals for the ticket buyer to include:

- Fast and easy walk-up-and-use user experience, with absolutely no user training.
- Fast learning so new user performance (after limited experience) is on par with that of an experienced user.
- High customer satisfaction leading to high rate of repeat customers.

Some other possibilities:

- High learnability for more advanced tasks.
- Draw, engagement, attraction.
- Low error rate for completing transactions correctly, especially in the interaction for payment.

Table 22-3

Choosing a work role and a user class for a UX target

Work Role: User Class	UX Goal	UX Measure	Measuring Instrument	UX Metric	Baseline Level	Target Level	Observed Results
Ticket buyer: Casual new user, for occasional personal use	Walk-up ease of use for new user						

Translating the goal of "fast-and-easy walk-up-and-use user experience" into a UX target table entry for the UX goal is straightforward. This goal refers to the ability of a typical occasional user to do at least the basic tasks on the first try, certainly without training or manuals. We see the beginnings of a UX target in Table 22-3.

Exercise 22-1: Identify UX Evaluation Goals for Your System

Goal: A little experience in stating user experience goals.

Activities: Review the work activity affinity diagram (WAAD) and user concerns in the social model for the system of your choice, noting user or customer concerns relating to UX goals.

Deliverables: A short list of UX goals for one user class of the system of your choice.

Schedule: A half hour or so (it should be easy by now).

22.5 UX MEASURES

Within a UX target, *the UX measure is the general user experience characteristic to be measured with respect to usage of your UX design.* The choice of UX measure implies something about which types of measuring instruments and UX metrics are appropriate.

UX targets are based on quantitative data—both objective data, such as observable user performance, and subjective data, such as user opinion and satisfaction.

Some common UX measures that can be paired with quantitative metrics include:

- Objective UX measures (directly measurable by evaluators):
  - Initial performance.
  - Long-term performance (longitudinal, experienced, steady state).
  - Learnability.

- Retainability.
- Advanced feature usage.
- Subjective UX measures (based on user opinions):
  - First impression (initial opinion, initial satisfaction).
  - Long-term (longitudinal) user satisfaction.
  - Emotional impact.
  - Meaningfulness to user.

Initial performance refers to a user's performance during the very first use (somewhere between the first few minutes and the first few hours, depending on the complexity of the system). Initial performance is a key UX measure because any user of a system must, at some point, use it for the first time.

Long-term performance typically refers to performance during more constant use over a longer period of time (fairly regular use over several weeks, perhaps). Long-term usage usually implies a steady-state learning plateau by the user; the user has become familiar with the system and is no longer constantly in a learning state.

Learnability and retainability refer, respectively, to how quickly and easily users can learn to use a system and how well they retain what they have learned over some period of time.

Advanced feature usage is a UX measure that helps determine the user experience of more complicated functions of a system. The user's initial opinion of the system can be captured by a first impression UX measure, whereas long-term user satisfaction refers, as the term implies, to the user's opinion after using the system for some greater period of time, after some allowance for learning.

Initial performance and first impression are appropriate UX measures for virtually every UX design. Other UX measures often play support roles to address more specialized UX needs. Conflicts among UX measures are not unheard of. For example, you may need both good learnability and good expert performance. In the design, those requirements can work against each other. This, however, just reflects a normal kind of design tradeoff. UX targets based on the two different UX measures imply user performance requirements pulling in two different directions, forcing the designers to stretch the design and face the tradeoff honestly.

Example: UX Measures for the Ticket Kiosk System

For the walk-up ease-of-use goal of our casual new user, let us start simply with just two UX measures: initial performance and first impression. Each UX measure will appear in a separate UX target in the UX target table, with the work role and user class repeated, as in Table 22-4.

Table 22-4

Choosing initial performance and first impression as UX measures

Work Role: User Class	UX Goal	UX Measure	Measuring Instrument	UX Metric	Baseline Level	Target Level	Observed Results
Ticket buyer: Casual new user, for occasional personal use	Walk-up ease of use for new user	Initial user performance					
Ticket buyer: Casual new user, for occasional personal use	Initial customer satisfaction	First impression					

22.6 MEASURING INSTRUMENTS: BENCHMARK TASKS

Within a UX target, *a measuring instrument is the means of generating values for the particular UX measure*; it's the vehicle through which values are measured for the UX measure.

Although you can get creative in choosing your measuring instruments, objective measures are commonly associated with a benchmark task—for example, a time-on-task measure as timed on a stopwatch, or an error rate measure made by counting user errors—and subjective measures are commonly associated with a user questionnaire—for example, the average user rating-scale scores for a specific set of questions.

For example, we will see that the objective "initial user performance" UX measure in the UX target table for the Ticket Kiosk System is associated with a benchmark task and the "first impression" UX measure is associated with a questionnaire. Both subjective and objective measures and data can be important for establishing and evaluating user experience coming from a design.

22.6.1 What Is a Benchmark Task?

As a measuring instrument for an objective UX measure, a benchmark task is a representative task that you will have user participants attempt to accomplish in evaluation while you observe their performance and behavior. As such, a benchmark task is a "standardized" task that can be used to compare performance among different users and across different design versions.

22.6.2 Selecting Benchmark Tasks

Here are some guidelines for choosing kinds of benchmark tasks.

22.6.2.1 Address designer questions with benchmark tasks and UX targets

As designers work on UX designs, questions arise constantly. Sometimes the design team simply cannot decide an issue for themselves and they defer it to UX testing ("let the users decide").

Or maybe you do agree on the design for a feature, but you are very curious about how it will play out with real users. If you have kept a list of such design questions as they came up in design activities, they now play a role in setting benchmark tasks to get feedback from users.

22.6.2.2 Create benchmark tasks for a representative spectrum of user tasks

Choose realistic tasks intended to be used by each user class of a work role across the system. To get the best coverage for your evaluation investment, your choices should represent the cross section of real tasks with respect to frequency of performance and criticality to goals of the users of the envisioned product. Benchmark tasks are also selected to evaluate new features, "edge cases," and business-critical or mission-critical tasks. While some of these tasks may not be performed frequently, getting them wrong could cause serious consequences.

22.6.2.3 Start with short and easy tasks and then increase difficulty progressively

In most cases, it's best to start with relatively easy tasks to get users accustomed to the design and feeling comfortable in their role as evaluators. After building user confidence and engagement, especially with the tasks for the "initial performance" UX measure, you can introduce more features, more breadth, variety, complexity, and higher levels of difficulty.

Example: Initial Benchmark Task Choice for the Ticket Kiosk System

For our ticket kiosk system, maybe start with finding a movie that is currently playing. Then follow with searching for and reserving tickets for a movie that is to be showing 20 days from now and then go to more complex tasks such as purchasing concert tickets with seat and ticket selection.

22.6.2.4 Include some navigation where appropriate

In real usage, because users usually have to navigate to get to where they will do the operations specific to performing a task, you want to include the need for this navigation even in your earliest benchmark tasks. It tests their knowledge of the fact that they do need to go elsewhere, where they need to go, and how to get there.

22.6.2.5 Avoid large amounts of typing (unless typing skill is being evaluated)

Avoid anything such as extensive typing in your benchmark task descriptions that can cause large user performance variation not related to user experience in the design.

22.6.2.6 Match the benchmark task to the UX measure

Obviously, if the UX measure is "initial user performance," the task should be among those a first-time user realistically would face. If the UX measure is about advanced feature usage, then, of course, the task should involve use of that feature to match this requirement. If the UX measure is "long-term usage," then the benchmark task should be faced by the user after considerable practice with the system. For a UX measure of "learnability," a set of benchmark tasks of increasing complexity might be appropriate.

22.6.2.7 Adapt scenarios or other task sequence representations already developed for design

Design scenarios clearly represent important tasks to evaluate because they have already been selected as key tasks in the design. However, you *must* remember to remove information about how to perform the tasks, which is usually abundant in a scenario. See guideline "Tell the user *what* task to do, but not *how* to do it" in the next section for more discussion.

22.6.2.8 Use tasks in realistic combinations to evaluate task flow

To measure user performance related to task flow, use combinations of tasks and activities such as those that will occur together frequently. In these cases, you should set UX targets for such combinations because difficulties related to user experience that appear during performance of the combined tasks can be different than for the same tasks performed separately. For example, in the Ticket Kiosk System, you may wish to measure user performance on the task thread of searching for an event and then buying tickets for that event.

Example: Benchmark Task for the Ticket Kiosk System

As another example, a benchmark task might require users to buy four tickets for a concert under a total of $200 while showing tickets in this price range for the upcoming few days as sold out. This would force users to perform the task of searching through other future concert days, looking for the first available day with tickets in this price range.

22.6.2.9 Pick tasks where you think or know the design has weaknesses

In general, of course, the benchmark tasks you choose as measuring instruments should closely represent tasks real users will perform in a real work context. Avoiding such tasks where you know there might be design problems violates the spirit of UX targets and user experience evaluation, which is about finding user experience problems so that you can fix them, not about proving you are the best designer.

22.6.2.10 Don't forget to evaluate with your power users

Often, user experience for power users is addressed inadequately in product testing (Karn, Perry, & Krolczyk, 1997). Do your product business and UX goals include power use by a trained user population? Do they require support for rapid repetition of tasks or complex and possibly very long tasks? Does their need for productivity demand shortcuts and direct commands over interactive hand-holding?

   If any of these are true, you must include benchmark tasks that match this kind of skilled and demanding power use. And, of course, these benchmark tasks must be used as the measuring instrument in UX targets that match up with the corresponding user classes and UX goals.

22.6.2.11 To evaluate error recovery, a benchmark task can begin in an error state

Effective error recovery is a kind of "feature" that designers and evaluators can easily forget to include. Yet no UX design can guarantee error-free usage, and trying to recover from errors is something most users are familiar with and can relate to. A "forgiving" design will allow users to recover from errors relatively effortlessly. This ability is definitely an aspect of your design that should be evaluated by one or more benchmark tasks.

22.6.2.12 Consider tasks to evaluate performance in "degraded modes" due to partial equipment failure

In large interconnected networked systems such as military systems or large commercial banking systems, especially involving multiple kinds of hardware, subsystems can sometimes fail. When this happens, will your part of the system give up and die or can it at least continue some of its intended functionality and give partial service in a "degraded mode?" If your application fits this description, you should include benchmark tasks to evaluate the user's perspective of this ability accordingly.

22.6.2.13 Don't try to make a benchmark task for everything

Evaluation driven by UX targets is only an engineering sampling process. It will not be possible to establish UX targets for all possible classes of users doing all possible tasks. It is often stated that about 20% of the tasks in an interactive system account for 80% of the usage and vice versa. While these figures are obviously folkloric guesses, they carry a grain of truth to guide in targeting users and tasks in establishing UX targets.

Example: Benchmark Tasks as Measuring Instruments for the Ticket Kiosk System

For the Ticket Kiosk System, the first UX target in Table 22-4 contains an objective UX measure for "Initial user performance." An obvious choice for the corresponding measuring instrument is a benchmark task. Here we need a simple and frequently used task that can be done in a short time by a casual new user in a walk-up ease-of-use situation. An appropriate benchmark task would involve buying tickets to an event. Here is a possible description to give the user participant:

> BT1: Go to the Ticket Kiosk System and buy three tickets for the Monster Truck Pull on February 28 at 7 p.m. Get three seats together as close to the front as possible. Pay with a major credit card.

In Table 22-5, we add this to the table as the measuring instrument for the first UX target.

Let us say we want to add another UX target for the "initial performance" UX measure, but this time we want to add some variety and use a different

Table 22-5

Choosing "buy special event ticket" benchmark task as a measuring instrument for "initial performance" UX measure in first UX target

Work Role: User Class	UX Goal	UX Measure	Measuring Instrument	UX Metric	Baseline Level	Target Level	Observed Results
Ticket buyer: Casual new user, for occasional personal use	Walk-up ease of use for new user	Initial user performance	BT1: Buy special event ticket				
Ticket buyer: Casual new user, for occasional personal use	Initial customer satisfaction	First impression					

Table 22-6

Choosing "buy movie ticket" benchmark task as a measuring instrument for second initial performance UX measure

Work Role: User Class	UX Goal	UX Measure	Measuring Instrument	UX Metric	Baseline Level	Target Level	Observed Results
Ticket buyer: Casual new user, for occasional personal use	Walk-up ease of use for new user	Initial user performance	BT1: Buy special event ticket				
Ticket buyer: Casual new user, for occasional personal use	Walk-up ease of use for new user	Initial user performance	BT2: Buy movie ticket				
Ticket buyer: Casual new user, for occasional personal use	Initial customer satisfaction	First impression					

benchmark task as the measuring instrument—namely, the task of buying a movie ticket. In Table 22-6, we have entered this benchmark task in the second UX target, pushing the "first impression" UX target down by one.

22.6.3 Crafting Benchmark Task Contents

22.6.3.1 Remove any ambiguities with clear, precise, specific, and repeatable instructions

Unless resolving ambiguity is what we want users to do as part of the task, we must make the instructions in benchmark task descriptions clear and not confusing. Unambiguous benchmark tasks are necessary for consistent results; we want differences in user performance to be due to differences in users or differences in designs but usually not due to different interpretations of the same benchmark task.

As a subtle example, consider this "add appointment" benchmark task for the "initial performance" UX measure for an interdepartmental event scheduling system: "Schedule a meeting with Dr. Ehrich for a month from today at 10 a.m. in 133 McBryde Hall concerning the HCI research project."

For some users, the phrase "a month from today" can be ambiguous. Why? It can mean, for example, on the same date next month or it can mean exactly four weeks from now, putting it on the same day of the week. If that difference in meaning can make a difference in user task performance, you need to make the wording more specific to the intended meaning.

You also want to make your benchmark tasks specific so that participants don't get sidetracked on irrelevant details during testing. If, for example, a "find event" benchmark task is stated simply as "Find an entertainment event for sometime next week," some participants might make it a long, elaborate task, searching around for some "best" combination of event type and date, whereas others would do the minimum and take the first event they see on the screen. To mitigate such differences, add specific information about event selection criteria.

22.6.3.2 Tell the user what task to do, but not how to do it

This guideline is very important; the success of your evaluation based on this task will depend on it. Sometimes we find students in early evaluation exercises presenting users with task instructions that spell out a series of steps to perform. They should not be surprised when the evaluation session leads to uninteresting results.

The users are just giving a rote performance of the steps as they read them from the benchmark task description. If you wish to test whether your UX design helps users discover how to do a given task on their own, you must avoid giving any information about *how* to do it. Just tell them *what* task to do and let them figure out how.

Examples: Instructional Wording in Benchmark Task for the Ticket Kiosk System

Example (to do): "Buy two student tickets for available adjacent seats as close to the stage as possible for the upcoming Iris Dement concert and pay with a credit card."

Example (*not* to do): "Click on the Special Events button on the home screen; then select More at the bottom of the screen. Select the Iris Dement concert and click on Seating Options..."

Example (*not* to do): "Starting at the Main Menu, go to the Music Menu and set it as a Bookmark. Then go back to the Main Menu and use the Bookmark feature to jump back to the Music Menu."

22.6.3.3 Don't use words in benchmark tasks that appear specifically in the UX design

In your benchmark task descriptions, you must avoid using any words that appear in menu headings, menu choices, button labels, icon pop ups, or any place in the UX design itself. For example, don't say "Find the first event (that has such and such a characteristic)" when there is a button in the UX design labeled "Find." Instead, you should use words such as "Look for…" or "Locate…"

Otherwise, it is very convenient for your users to use a button labeled "Find" when they are told to "Find" something. It does not require them to think and, therefore, does not evaluate whether the design would have helped them find the right button on their own in the course of real usage.

22.6.3.4 Use work context and usage-centered wording, not system-oriented wording

Because benchmark task descriptions are, in fact, descriptions of user tasks and not system functionality, you should use usage-centered words from the user's work context and not system-centered wording. For example, "Find information about xyz" is better than "Submit query about xyz." The former is task oriented; the latter is more about a system view of the task.

22.6.3.5 Have clear start and end points for timing

In your own mind, be sure that you have clearly observable and distinguishable start and end points for each benchmark task and make sure you word the benchmark task description to use these end points effectively. These will ensure your ability to measure the time on task accurately, for example.

At evaluation time, not only must the evaluators know for sure when the task is completed, but *the participant must know when the task is completed.* For purposes of evaluation, the task cannot be considered completed until the user experiences closure.

The evaluator must also know when the user knows that the task has been completed. Don't depend on the user to say when the task is done, even if you explicitly ask for that in the benchmark task description or user instructions. Therefore, rather than ending task performance with a mental or sensory state (i.e., the user knowing or seeing something), it is better to incorporate a user action confirming the end of the task, as in the (to do) examples that follow.

Examples: Clear Starting and End Points in Benchmark Tasks

Example (*not* to do): "Find out how to set the orientation of the printer paper to 'landscape'." Completion of this task depends on the user knowing something and that is not a directly observable state. Instead, you could have the user actually set the paper orientation; this is something you can observe directly.

Example (*not* to do): "View next week's events." Completion of this task depends on the user seeing something, an action that you may not be able to confirm. Perhaps you could have the user view and read aloud the contents of the first music event next week. Then you know whether and when the user has seen the correct event.

Example (to do): "Find next week's music event featuring Rachel Snow and add it to the shopping cart."

Example (to do): Or, to include knowing or learning how to select seats, "Find the closest available seat to the stage and add to shopping cart."

Example (to do): "Find the local weather forecast for tomorrow and read it aloud."

22.6.3.6 Keep some mystery in it for the user

Don't always be too specific about what the users will see or the parameters they will encounter. Remember that real first-time users will approach your application without necessarily knowing how it works. Sometimes try to use benchmark tasks that give approximate values for some parameters to look for, letting the rest be up to the user. You can still create a prototype in such a way that there is only one possible "solution" to this task if you want to avoid different users in the evaluation ending in a different state in the system.

Example (to do): "Purchase two movie tickets to *Bee Movie* within 1.5 hours of the current time and showing at a theater within five miles of this kiosk location."

22.6.3.7 Annotate situations where evaluators must ensure preconditions for running benchmark tasks

Suppose you write this benchmark task: "Your dog, Mutt, seems perfectly healthy and energetic. Delete your appointment with the vet for Mutt's annual checkup from your calendar."

Every time a user performs this task during evaluation, the prototype calendar must start on the same "current" date and it must contain an existing appointment at some future date in the calendar so that each user can find it and delete it. You must attach a note in the form of rubrics (next point later) to this benchmark task to that effect—a note that will be read and followed in the evaluation activity.

22.6.3.8 Use "rubrics" for special instructions to evaluators

Ecological validity

Refers to the realism with which a design of evaluation setup matches the user's real work context. It is about how accurately the design or evaluation reflects the relevant characteristics of the ecology of interaction, that is, its context in the world or its environment (Sections 16.3 and 22.6.4.4).

When necessary or useful, add a "rubrics" section to your benchmark task descriptions as special instructions to evaluators, not to be given to participants in evaluation sessions. Use these rubrics to communicate a heads up about anything that needs to be done or set up in advance to establish task preconditions, such as an existing event in the kiosk system, work context for ecological validity, or a particular starting state for a task.

Benchmark tasks for addressing designer questions are especially good candidates for rubrics. In a note accompanying your benchmark task, you can alert evaluators to watch for user performance or behavior that might shed light on these specific designer questions.

22.6.4 Other Benchmark Task Mechanics
22.6.4.1 Put each benchmark task description on a separate sheet of paper

Yes, we want to save trees but, in this case, it is necessary to present the benchmark tasks to the participant only one at a time. Otherwise, the participant will surely read ahead, if only out of curiosity, and can become distracted from the task at hand.

As another reason for separate task descriptions, it is possible that not all participants will complete all tasks. There is no need for anyone to see that they have not accomplished them all. If they see only one at a time, they will never know and never feel bad.

Finally, if a task has a surprise step, such as a mid-task change of intention, that step should also be on a separate piece of paper, not shown to the participant initially. To save trees you can cut (with scissors) a list of benchmark tasks so that only one task appears on one smaller piece of paper.

22.6.4.2 Write a "task script" for each benchmark task

Sometimes it's useful to write a "task script" describing the steps of a representative or typical way to do the task and include it in the benchmark task document "package." This is just for use by the evaluator and is definitely not given to the participant. The evaluator may not have been a member of the design team and initially may not be too familiar with how to perform the benchmark tasks, and it helps the evaluator to be able to anticipate a possible task performance path. This is especially useful in cases where the participant cannot determine a way to do the task; then, the evaluation facilitator knows at least one way.

22.6.4.3 How many benchmark tasks and UX targets do you need?

As in most things UX, it depends. The size and complexity of the system should be reflected in the quantity and complexity of the benchmark tasks and UX targets. We cannot even give you an estimate of a typical number of benchmark tasks.

You have to use your engineering judgment and make enough benchmark tasks for reasonable, representative coverage without overburdening the evaluation process. If you are new to this, we can say that we have often seen a dozen UX targets, but 50 would probably be too much—not worth the cost to pursue in evaluation.

How long should your benchmark tasks be (in terms of time to perform)? The typical benchmark task takes a range of a couple of minutes to 10–15 minutes. Some short and some long are good. Longer sequences of related tasks are needed to evaluate transitions among tasks. Try to avoid really long benchmark tasks because they may be tiring to participants and evaluators during testing.

22.6.4.4 Ensure ecological validity

The extent to which your UX evaluation setup matches the user's real work context is called *ecological validity* (Thomas & Kellogg, 1989). One of the valid criticisms of lab-based user experience testing is that a UX lab can be kind of a sterile environment, not a realistic setting for the user and the tasks. But you can take steps to add ecological validity by asking yourself, as you write your benchmark task descriptions, how can the setting be made more realistic?

- What are the constraints in the user or work context?
- Does the task involve more than one person or role?
- Does the task require a telephone or other physical props?
- Does the task involve background noise?
- Does the task involve interference or interruption?
- Does the user have to deal with multiple simultaneous inputs, for example, multiple audio feeds through headsets?

As an example for a task that might be triggered by a telephone call, instead of writing your benchmark task description on a piece of paper, try calling the participant on a telephone with a request that will trigger the desired task. Rarely do task triggers arrive written on a piece of paper someone hands you. Of course, you will have to translate the usual boring imperative statements of the benchmark task description to a more lively and realistic dialogue: "Hi, I am Fred Ferbergen and I have an appointment with Dr. Strangeglove for a physical exam tomorrow, but I have to be out of town. Can you change my appointment to next week?"

Telephones can be used in other ways, too, to add realism to work context. A second telephone ringing incessantly at the desk next door or someone talking loudly on the phone next door can add realistic task distraction that you would not get from a "pure" lab-based evaluation.

For an anecdote about the need for ecological validity (the extent to which your UX evaluation setup matches the user's real work context) in the early testing of the early A330 Airbus, see Section 28.5.

Example: Ecological Validity in Benchmark Tasks for the Ticket Kiosk System

To evaluate use of the Ticket Kiosk System to manage the work activity of ticket buying, you can make good use of physical prototypes and representative locations to enhance ecological validity. By this we mean building a touchscreen display into a cardboard or wooden kiosk structure and placing it in the hallway of a relatively busy work area. Users will be subject to the gawking and questions of curiosity seekers. Having coworkers join the kiosk queue will add extra realism.

Exercise 22.2: Create Benchmark Tasks and UX Targets for Your System

Goal: To gain experience in writing effective benchmark tasks and measurable UX targets.

Activities: We have shown you a rather complete set of examples of benchmark tasks and UX targets for the Ticket Kiosk System. Your job is to do something similar for the system of your choice.

Begin by identifying which work roles and user classes you are targeting in evaluation (brief description is enough).

Write three or more UX table entries (rows), including your choices for each column. Have at least two UX targets based on a benchmark task and at least one based on a questionnaire.

Create and write a set of about three benchmark tasks to go with the UX targets in the table. Do NOT make the tasks too easy.

Make tasks increasingly complex.

Include some navigation.

Create tasks that you can later "implement" in your low-fidelity rapid prototype.

The expected average performance time for each task should be no more than about 3 minutes, just to keep it short and simple for you during evaluation.

Include the questionnaire question numbers in the measuring instrument column of the appropriate UX target.

Cautions and hints:

Do not spend any time on design in this exercise; there will be time for detailed design in an upcoming exercise.

Do not plan to give users any training.

Deliverables:

Two user benchmark tasks, each on a separate sheet of paper.

Three or more UX targets entered into a blank UX target table on your laptop or on paper.

If you are doing this exercise in a classroom environment, finish up by reading your benchmark tasks to the class for critique and discussion.

Schedule: Work efficiently and complete in about an hour and a half.

*Subjective UX
evaluation data*

Data based on opinion or
judgment, of evaluator or
user (Section 21.1.4.2).

22.7 MEASURING INSTRUMENT: USER SATISFACTION QUESTIONNAIRES

As a measuring instrument for a subjective UX measure, a questionnaire related to various user UX design features can be used to determine a user's satisfaction with the UX design. Measuring a user's satisfaction provides a subjective, but still quantitative, UX metric for the related UX measure. As an aside, we should point out that objective and subjective measures are not always orthogonal. For example, very low user satisfaction can degrade user performance over a long period of time. In the following examples, we use the QUIS questionnaire (Section 24.3.2.4), but there are other excellent choices, including the System Usability Scale or SUS (Section 24.3.2.5).

Example: Questionnaire as Measuring Instrument for the Ticket Kiosk System

If you think the first two benchmark tasks (buying tickets) make a good foundation for assessing the "first-impression" UX measure, then you can specify that a particular user satisfaction questionnaire or a specific subset thereof be administered following those two initial tasks, stipulating it as the measuring instrument in the third UX target of the growing UX target table, as we have done in Table 22-7.

Example: Goals, Measures, and Measuring Instruments

Before moving on to UX metrics, in Table 22-8 we show some examples of the close connections among UX goals, UX measures, and measuring instruments.

Table 22-7

Choosing a questionnaire as the measuring instrument for first-impression UX measure

Work Role: User Class	UX Goal	UX Measure	Measuring Instrument	UX Metric	Baseline Level	Target Level	Observed Results
Ticket buyer: Casual new user, for occasional personal use	Walk-up ease of use for new user	Initial user performance	BT1: Buy special event ticket				
Ticket buyer: Casual new user, for occasional personal use	Walk-up ease of use for new user	Initial user performance	BT2: Buy movie ticket				
Ticket buyer: Casual new user, for occasional personal use	Initial customer satisfaction	First impression	Questions Q1–Q10 in the QUIS questionnaire				

Table 22-8

Connections among UX goals, UX measures, and measuring instruments

UX Goal	UX Measure	Potential Metrics
Ease of first-time use	Initial performance	Time on task
Ease of learning	Learnability	Time on task or error rate, after given amount of use and compared with initial performance
High performance for experienced users	Long-term performance	Time and error rates
Low error rates	Error-related performance	Error rates
Error avoidance in safety critical tasks	Task-specific error performance	Error count, with strict target levels (much more important than time on task)
Error recovery performance	Task-specific time performance	Time on recovery portion of the task
Overall user satisfaction	User satisfaction	Average score on questionnaire
User attraction to product	User opinion of attractiveness	Average score on questionnaire, with questions focused on the effectiveness of the "draw" factor
Quality of user experience	User opinion of overall experience	Average score on questionnaire, with questions focused on quality of the overall user experience, including specific points about your product that might be associated most closely with emotional impact factors
Overall user satisfaction	User satisfaction	Average score on questionnaire, with questions focusing on willingness to be a repeat customer and to recommend product to others
Continuing ability of users to perform without relearning	Retainability	Time on task and error rates reevaluated after a period of time off (e.g., a week)
Avoid having user walk away in dissatisfaction	User satisfaction, especially initial satisfaction	Average score on questionnaire, with questions focusing on initial impressions and satisfaction

22.8 UX METRICS

A *UX metric* describes the kind of value to be obtained for a UX measure. It states what is being measured. There can be more than one metric for a given measure. As an example from the software engineering world, software complexity is a measure; one metric for the software complexity measure (one way to obtain values for the measure) is "counting lines of code."

Probably the most common UX metrics are objective, performance-oriented, and taken while the participant is doing a benchmark task. Other UX metrics can be subjective, based on a rating or score computed from questionnaire results. Typical objective UX metrics include time to complete task[1] and number of errors made by the user. Others include frequency of help or documentation use; time spent in errors and recovery; number of repetitions of failed commands (what are users trying to tell us by repeating an action that did not work before?); and the number of commands, mouse clicks, or other user actions to perform task(s).

If you are feeling adventurous, you can use a count of the number of times the user expresses frustration or satisfaction (the "aha and cuss count") during his or her first session as an indicator of his or her initial impression of the UX design. Of course, because the number of remarks is directly related to the length of the session, plan your levels accordingly or you can set your levels as a count per unit time, such as comments per minute, to factor out the time differences. Admittedly, this measuring instrument is rather participant-dependent, depending on how demonstrative a participant feels during a session, whether a participant is generally a complainer, and so on, but this metric can produce some interesting results.

Typically, subjective UX metrics will represent the kind of numeric outcome you want from a questionnaire, usually based on simple arithmetic statistical measures such as the numeric average. Remember that you are going only for an engineering indicator of user experience, not for statistical significance.

And don't overlook a combination of measures for situations where you have performance tradeoffs. If you specify your UX metric as some function, such as a sum or an average, of two other performance-related metrics, for example, time on task and error rate, you are saying that you are willing to give up some performance in one area if you get more in the other.

---

[1]Although the time on task often makes a useful UX metric, it clearly is not appropriate in some cases. For example, if the task performance time is affected by factors beyond the user's control, then time on task is not a good measure of user performance. This exception includes cases of long and/or unpredictable communication and response-time delays, such as might be experienced in some website usage.

We hope you will explore many other possibilities for UX metrics, extending beyond what we have mentioned here, including:

- Percentage of task completed in a given time.
- Ratio of successes to failures.
- Time spent moving cursor (would have to be measured using software instrumentation, but would give information about the efficiency of such physical actions, necessary for some specialized applications).
- For visibility and other issues, fixations on the screen, cognitive load as indicated by correlation to pupil diameter, and so on using eye tracking.

Finally, be sure you match up your UX measures, measuring instruments, and metrics to make sense in a UX target. For example, if you plan to use a questionnaire in a UX target, don't call the UX measure "initial performance." A questionnaire does not measure performance; it measures user satisfaction or opinion.

Example: UX Metrics for the Ticket Kiosk System

For the initial performance UX measure in the first UX target of Table 22-8, as already discussed in the previous section, the length of time to buy a special event ticket is an appropriate value to measure. We specify this by adding average "time on task" as the metric in the first UX target of Table 22-9.

As a different objective performance measure, you might measure the average number of errors a user makes while buying a movie ticket. This was chosen as the

Table 22-9

Choosing UX metrics for UX measures

Work Role: User Class	UX Goal	UX Measure	Measuring Instrument	UX Metric	Baseline Level	Target Level	Observed Results
Ticket buyer: Casual new user, for occasional personal use	Walk-up ease of use for new user	Initial user performance	BT1: Buy special event ticket	Average time on task			
Ticket buyer: Casual new user, for occasional personal use	Walk-up ease of use for new user	Initial user performance	BT2: Buy movie ticket	Average number of errors			
Ticket buyer: Casual new user, for occasional personal use	Initial customer satisfaction	First impression	Questions Q1– Q10 in the QUIS questionnaire	Average rating across users and across questions			

value to measure in the second UX target of Table 22-9. You will often want to measure both these metrics during a participant's single performance of the same single task. A participant does not, for example, need to perform one "buy ticket" task while you time performance and then do a different (or repeat the same) "buy ticket" task while you count errors.

Finally, for the UX metric in the third UX target of Table 22-9, the subjective UX target for the first impression UX measure, let us use the simple average of the numeric ratings given across all users and across all the questions for which ratings were given (i.e., Q1–Q10).

22.9 BASELINE LEVEL

The baseline level is the benchmark level of the UX metric; it is the "talking point" level against which other levels are compared. It is often the level that has been measured for the current version of the system (automated or manual).

22.10 TARGET LEVEL

The target-level specification is a quantitative statement of an aimed-at or hoped-for value for a UX metric. The target level is an operationally defined criterion for success of the expected user experience. The target level for a UX metric is the minimum value indicating attainment of user experience success. Target levels not met in evaluation serve as focal points for improvement by designers.

22.11 SETTING LEVELS

The baseline level and target level in the UX target table are key to *quantifying user experience metrics*. But sometimes setting baseline and target levels can be a challenge. The answer requires determining what level of user performance and user experience the system is to support.

Obviously, level values are often "best guesses" but with practice, UX people become quite skilled at establishing reasonable and credible target levels and setting reasonable values.

Among the yardsticks you can use to set both baseline and target levels are:

- An existing system or previous version of the new system being designed.
- Competing systems, such as those with a large market share or with a widely acclaimed user experience.

Table 22-10

Setting baseline levels for UX measures

Work Role: User Class	UX Goal	UX Measure	Measuring Instrument	UX Metric	Baseline Level	Target Level	Observed Results
Ticket buyer: Casual new user, for occasional personal use	Walk-up ease of use for new user	Initial user performance	BT1: Buy special event ticket	Average time on task	Three minutes		
Ticket buyer: Casual new user, for occasional personal use	Walk-up ease of use for new user	Initial user performance	BT2: Buy movie ticket	Average number of errors	<1		
Ticket buyer: Casual new user, for occasional personal use	Initial customer satisfaction	First impression	Questions Q1–Q10 in questionnaire XYZ	Average rating across users and across questions	7.5/10		

Although it may not always be explicitly indicated in a UX target table, the baseline and target *levels shown refer to the mean over all participants* of the corresponding measure. That is, the levels shown don't have to be achieved by every participant in every session. So, for example, if we specify a target level of four errors for benchmark task BT 2 in the second UX target of Table 22-10 as a worst acceptable level of performance, there must be no more than *an average of* four errors, as averaged across all participants who perform the "buy movie ticket" task.

22.11.1 Setting the Baseline Level

Example: Baseline Level Values for the Ticket Kiosk System

To determine the values for the first two UX target baseline levels for the Ticket Kiosk System, we can have someone perform the benchmark tasks for buying a ticket for a special event and a movie using the MUTTS ticket counter. That might be quite different from what you expect users will be able to achieve using our new system, but it is a stake in the sand, something for comparison. Measuring a baseline level helps ensure that the UX metric is, in fact, measurable.

Suppose that buying a ticket for a special event takes about 3 minutes. If so, this value, 3 minutes, makes a plausible baseline level for the first UX target in Table 22-10. Because most people are already experienced with ticket offices, this value is not really for initial performance, but it gives some idea for that value.

MUTTS

MUTTS is the acronym for Middleburg University Ticket Transaction Service, our running example for most of the process chapters (Section 5.5).

To set a baseline value for the second UX target, for buying a movie ticket, it can be assumed that almost no one should make any errors doing this at a ticket counter, so let us set the baseline level as less than 1, as in Table 22-10.

To establish a baseline value for the first impression UX measure in the third UX target, we could administer the questionnaire to some users of MUTTS. Let us say we have done that and got an average score of 7.5 out of 10 for the first impression UX measure (a value we put in Table 22-10).

22.11.2 Setting the Target Level

Because "passing" the user experience test means meeting all your target levels simultaneously, you have to ensure that the target levels for all UX measures in the entire table must be, in fact, simultaneously attainable. That is, don't build in tradeoffs of the kind where meeting one target level goal might make it much more difficult to meet another related target level.

So how do you come up with reasonable values for your target levels? As a general rule of thumb, a target level is usually set to be an improvement over the corresponding baseline level. Why build a new system if it is not going to be better? Of course, improved user performance is not the only motivation for building a new system; increased functionality or just meeting user needs at a higher level in the design can also be motivating factors. However, the focus here is on improving user experience, which often means improving user performance and satisfaction.

For initial performance measures, you should set target levels that allow enough time, for example, for unfamiliar users to read menus and labels, think a bit, and look around each screen to get their bearings. So don't use levels for initial performance measures that assume users are familiar with the design.

Example: Target Level Values for the Ticket Kiosk System

In Table 22-11, for the first initial performance UX measure, let us set the target level to 2.5 minutes. In the absence of anything else to go on, this is a reasonable choice with respect to our baseline level of 3 minutes. We enter this value into the "Target level" column for the first UX target of the UX target table in Table 22-11.

With a baseline level of less than one error for the "Buy movie ticket" task, it would again be tempting to set the target level at zero, but that does not allow for *anyone ever* to commit an error. So let us retain the existing level, <1, as the target level for error rates, as entered into the second UX target of Table 22-11.

For the first impression UX measure, let us be somewhat conservative and set a target level of a mean score of 8 out of 10 on the questionnaire. Surely 80% is passing in most anyone's book or course. This goes in the third UX target of Table 22-11.

Table 22-11

Setting target levels for UX metrics

Work Role: User Class	UX Goal	UX Measure	Measuring Instrument	UX Metric	Baseline Level	Target Level	Observed Results
Ticket buyer: Casual new user, for occasional personal use	Walk-up ease of use	Initial user performance	BT1: Buy special event ticket	Average time on task	Three minutes, as measured at the MUTTS ticket counter	2.5 minutes	
Ticket buyer: Casual new user, for occasional personal use	Walk-up ease of use for new user	Initial user performance	BT2: Buy movie ticket	Average number of errors	<1	<1	
Ticket buyer: Casual new user, for occasional personal use	Initial customer satisfaction	First impression	Questions Q1–Q10 in questionnaire XYZ	Average rating across users and across questions	7.5/10	8/10	
Ticket buyer: Frequent music patron	Accuracy	Experienced usage error rate	BT3: Buy concert ticket	Average number of errors	<1	<1	
Casual public ticket buyer	Walk-up ease of use for new user	Initial user performance	BT4: Buy Monster Truck Pull tickets	Average time on task	Five minutes (online system)	2.5 minutes	
Casual public ticket buyer	Walk-up ease of use for new user	Initial user performance	BT4: Buy Monster Truck Pull tickets	Average number of errors	<1	<1	
Casual public ticket buyer	Initial customer satisfaction	First impression	QUIS questions 4–7, 10, 13	Average rating across users and across questions	6/10	8/10	
Casual public ticket buyer	Walk-up ease of use for user with a little experience	Just postinitial performance	BT5: Buy Dunkirk movie tickets	Average time on task	Five minutes (including review)	Two minutes	
Casual public ticket buyer	Walk-up ease of use for user with a little experience	Just postinitial performance	BT6: Buy Ben Harper concert tickets	Average number of errors	<1	<1	

22.11.3 A Few Additional Targets

Just for illustration purposes, we have added a few additional UX targets to Table 22-11. The UX target in the fourth row is for a regular music patron's task of buying a concert ticket using a frequent-customer discount coupon. The UX measure for this one is to measure experienced usage error rates using the "Buy concert ticket" benchmark task, with a target level of 0.5 (average).

Additional benchmark tasks used in the last two UX targets of the table are:

> BT5: You want to buy a ticket for the movie *Dunkirk* for between 7–8 p.m. tonight at a theater within a 10-minute walk from the Metro station. First check to be sure this movie is rated PG-13 because you will be with your 15-year-old son. Then go to the reviews for this movie (to show us you can find the reviews, but you don't have to spend time reading them now) and then buy two general admission tickets.
>
> BT6: Buy three tickets to the Ben Harper concert on any of the nights on the weekend of Sep. 29–Oct. 1. Get the best seats you can for up to $50 per ticket. Print out the directions for taking the Metro to the concert.

22.12 OBSERVED RESULTS

The final column in Table 22-11 is for *observed results*, a space reserved for recording values measured while observing users performing the prescribed tasks during formative evaluation sessions. As part of the UX target table, this column affords direct comparisons between specified levels and results of testing.

Because you typically will have more than one user from which observed results are obtained, you can either record multiple values in a single observed results column or, if desired, add more columns for observed results and use this column for the average of the observed values. If you maintain your UX target tables in spreadsheets, as we recommend, it is easier to manage observed data and results later in UX evaluation analysis (Chapter 26).

Exercise 22-3: Creating Benchmark Tasks and UX Targets for Your System

Write out descriptions of a few (3–4) key/interesting user tasks for your product or system. Say what to do, but not how. Using these as measuring instruments, and anything else appropriate, fill out a UX target table.

22.13 PRACTICAL TIPS AND CAUTIONS FOR CREATING UX TARGETS

Here we present some hints about filling out your UX target table:

- Be prepared to adjust your target level values based on initial observed results.

Sometimes in evaluation, you observe that users perform dramatically differently than you had expected when you set the levels. These results can mean serious problems with the design, but they can help you refine the target levels in UX targets, too. While it is possible to set the levels too leniently, it is also possible that you make your initial UX targets too demanding, especially in early cycles of iteration.

- Don't set nearly impossible average goals such as zero errors.

Because the target-level value is an average, even one error occurring anywhere in the session will prevent the result value from being zero.

- What about UX goals, metrics, and targets for usefulness and emotional impact?

Questionnaires and interviews can also be used to assess usefulness, emotional impact (such as branding issues), and meaningfulness.

> *Usefulness*
>
> A component of user experience based on utility, system functionality that gives users the ability to accomplish the goals of work (or play) through using the system or product (Section 1.4.3).

22.14 RAPID APPROACH TO UX GOALS, METRICS, AND TARGETS

As in most of the other process chapters, the process here can be abridged, trading rigor (e.g., completeness) for speed and lower cost. Possible steps of increasing abridgement include:

- Eliminate objective UX measures and metrics, but retain UX goals and quantitative subjective measures. Metrics obtained with questionnaires are easier and far less costly than metrics requiring empirical testing, lab-based or in the field.
- Eliminate all UX measures and metrics and UX target tables. Retain benchmark tasks as a basis for user task performance and behavior to observe in limited empirical testing for gathering qualitative data (UX problem data).
- Ignore UX goals, metrics, and targets altogether and use only rapid evaluation methods that later produce only qualitative data.

Empirical UX Evaluation: Preparation

23

Be prepared; that's the Boy Scouts' marching song… Don't be nervous, don't be flustered, don't be scared; Be prepared!

– Tom Lehrer

Highlights

- Empirical UX evaluation plan.
- Evaluation scope and rigor.
- Goals for empirical UX evaluation.
- Select team roles for empirical UX evaluation.
- Prepare an effective range of user tasks.
- Recruit participants.
- Prepare for the session.
- The UX evaluation session work package.
- Do final pilot testing before evaluation.

23.1 INTRODUCTION

23.1.1 You Are Here

We begin each process chapter with a "you are here" picture of the chapter topic in the context of The Wheel, the overall UX design lifecycle template (Fig. 23-1). This chapter is about how to prepare for empirical UX evaluation. Much of this will apply to planning for other kinds of evaluation, too.

Although, for completeness, we include quantitative UX data collection techniques in Chapter 24 and quantitative data analysis in Chapter 26, this is emphasized less than it used to be in previous usability engineering books

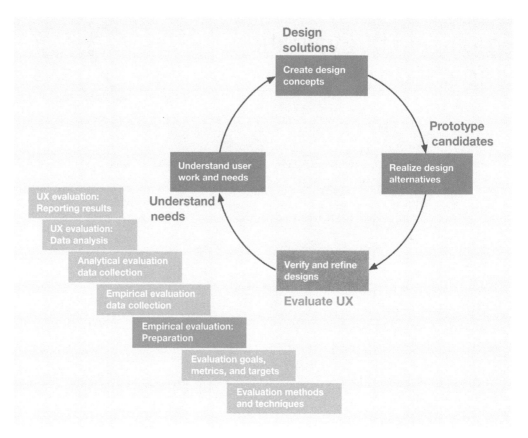

Fig. 23-1

You are here in the chapter on preparing for empirical evaluation within the Evaluate UX lifecycle activity in the context of the overall Wheel lifecycle template.

because of less focus in practice on quantitative user performance measures and more emphasis on qualitative evaluation to reveal UX problems to be fixed.

23.1.2 A Plan for the Empirical UX Evaluation Session

Empirical UX evaluation methods (Chapter 24) entail data observed in the performance of real user participants and data coming directly from participants. The purpose of your plan for empirical UX evaluation is to identify the most appropriate evaluation goals, methods, activities, conditions, constraints, and expectations for your project. If the plan will be read by people outside your immediate project group, you might want an upfront "boilerplate" introduction with some topics such as these, described very concisely:

- Overview of plan.
- Overview of product or parts of product being evaluated (for people outside the group).
- Goals of the product user interface (i.e., what will make for a successful user experience).
- Description of the intended user population.
- Overview of approach to informed consent.
- Overview of how this evaluation fits into the overall iterative UX process lifecycle.
- Overview of the UX evaluation process in general (e.g., preparation, data collection, analysis, reporting, iteration).
- General evaluation methods and activities planned for this session.
- Estimated schedule.
- Responsible personnel.

The body of the plan should start with evaluation goals (next section) and should also include a description of your approach and mechanics:

- Description of resources and constraints (e.g., time needed/available, state of prototype, lab facilities, and equipment).
- Pilot testing plan.
- Approach to evaluation, choices of data collection techniques.
- Mechanics of the evaluation (e.g., materials used, informed consent, location of evaluation, UX goals and metrics involved, tasks to be explored, including applicable benchmark tasks).
- All instruments to be used (e.g., benchmark task descriptions, questionnaires).
- Approaches to data analysis.
- Specifics of your approach to evaluate emotional impact and, if appropriate, long-term emotional aspects of interaction.

23.2 EVALUATION SCOPE AND RIGOR

23.2.1 Evaluation Scope

You can perform UX evaluation at any scope. A large-scope approach is best for the early part of the agile UX funnel, where you would evaluate the overall product or system architecture and user workflow, and the conceptual design—addressing the ecological layer of the needs pyramid.

Participant

A participant, or user participant, is a user, potential, or user surrogate who helps evaluate UX designs for usability and user experience. These are the people who perform tasks and give feedback while we observe and measure. Because we wish to invite these volunteers to join our team and help us evaluate designs (i.e., we want them to participate), we use the term "participant" instead of "subject" (Section 21.1.3).

Emotional Impact

An affective component of user experience that influences user feelings. Includes such effects as enjoyment, pleasure, fun, satisfaction, aesthetics, coolness, engagement, and novelty and can involve deeper emotional factors such as self-expression, self-identity, a feeling of contribution to the world, and pride of ownership (Section 1.4.4).

Scope (of Delivery)

Describes how the target system or product is "chunked" (broken into what size pieces) in each iteration or sprint for delivery to the client and users for feedback and to the software engineering team for agile implementation (Section 3.3).

A small-scope approach is best for frequent iterations within the sprints of the late agile UX funnel. Small-scope evaluation is used to address task-level design in the interaction level of the pyramid.

As you might guess, you can address the emotional-needs layer of the pyramid at any scope.

23.2.2 Evaluation Rigor

You can perform UX evaluation at any level of rigor. You can perform low-rigor evaluation in early design stages when the design is changing rapidly and careful attention to preserving detail in the data would be wasted. You might also have to perform your UX evaluation at a relatively low level of rigor in the late funnel simply because of the pressure to keep up with the agile sprints.

Larger organizations used to devote huge resources to do rigorous UX evaluation and rigorous methods still have a place in projects that demand it. However, with the shift of attention toward agile methods, it is more difficult to justify the time and cost in most projects. High rigor in UX evaluation requires careful attention to detail and full preservation of the data—both data purity and data completeness. Because of the amount of detail we give for completeness, our descriptions may appear to represent a very rigorous view of the process. But, in fact, what you read here can be applied at any level of rigor.

23.3 GOALS FOR AN EMPIRICAL UX EVALUATION SESSION

One of the first things to do in an evaluation plan is to set and prioritize your evaluation goals specific to this project. Identify the most important design issues and user tasks to investigate. Decide which parts of the system or functionality you simply will not have time to look at.

Your evaluation goals can include:

- Evaluation range (parts of the system to be covered by this evaluation).
- Scope (size of chunk) at which evaluation will be applied (Section 23.2.1).
- Rigor (level of formality and completeness) to be applied (Section 23.2.2).
- Layers of the needs pyramid to be addressed (from the top: emotional, interaction, and ecological needs, Section 12.3.1).
- Types of data to collect (Section 21.1.4), especially whether it will involve quantitative data.

- UX goals, targets, and metrics, if any, to be addressed (Chapter 22).
- Matching this evaluation to the current stage of product design evolution (early design ideas to explore versus near-final prototype).

23.4 SELECT TEAM ROLES

23.4.1 Participation and Buy-In

Encourage your whole project team to participate in at least some evaluation. Broad participation begets buy-in and ownership, necessary for your results to be taken as a serious mandate to fix problems. Roles include the facilitator, the prototype "executor," all data collectors, and other supporting roles. Anyone on the team can learn as an observer.

23.4.2 Facilitator

Your facilitator is the leader of the evaluation team, the orchestrator, and the one who makes sure it all works right. The facilitator has the primary responsibility for planning and executing the evaluation sessions, and the final responsibility to make sure the laboratory is set up properly. Because the facilitator will be the principal contact for participants during a session and responsible for putting the participant at ease, you should select someone with good "people skills."

23.4.3 Prototype Executor

If you are using a low-fidelity click-through wireframe prototype, you need to select a prototype executor, a person to "execute" the prototype and move it through its paces as users interact.

The prototype executor must have a thorough technical knowledge of how the design works. So that the prototype executor responds only to participant actions, he or she must have a steady Vulcan sense of logic. The executor must also have the discipline to maintain a poker face and not speak a single word throughout the entire session.

23.4.4 Quantitative Data Collectors

If you plan to include quantitative data collection, you'll need people to do it. Depending on your UX metrics and quantitative data collection instruments, people designated to collect quantitative data may be walking around with stopwatches and counters (mechanical, electronic, or paper and pencil). These people must be ready to record the quantitative data as it occurs. Because quantitative metrics usually involve simple descriptive statistics (e.g., averages), the data collector may wish to enter performance and other data directly into a spreadsheet.

23.4.5 Qualitative Data Collectors

Select as many team members as possible to serve as qualitative data collectors and recorders. No evaluation team member should be idle during a session. Thoroughness will improve with more people doing the job. Everyone should be ready to collect qualitative data, especially critical incident data.

23.4.6 Supporting Actors

Sometimes you need someone to interact with the participant as part of the task setting or to manage the props needed in the evaluation. For example, for task realism you may need someone to call the participant on a telephone in the participant room or, if your user participant is an "agent" of some kind, you may need a "client" to walk in with a specific need involving an agent task using the system. Select team members to play supporting roles and handle props.

23.5 PREPARE AN EFFECTIVE RANGE OF USER TASKS

If evaluation is to be task based, including task-driven UX inspection methods, select appropriate tasks to support evaluation. Select different kinds of tasks for different evaluation purposes.

23.5.1 Benchmark Tasks to Generate Quantitative Measures

Benchmark tasks portray representative, frequent, and critical tasks that apply to the key work role and user class represented by each participant. If you have defined a benchmark task to generate quantitative measures, you should now have the corresponding task description and UX target metrics ready and waiting to guide your data collection and to compare with observed results.

Also, the benchmark task description should be printed and ready to use by participants to generate data to be measured. Make sure each task description says only *what* to do, with no hints about *how* to do it. Also, don't use any language that telegraphs any part of the design (e.g., names of user interface objects or user actions, or words from labels or menus).

23.5.2 Unmeasured Tasks

You might also like to have descriptions for unmeasured tasks, tasks for which participant performance will not be measured quantitatively. Evaluators can use these representative tasks to add breadth to qualitative evaluation by addressing aspects of the design not covered in some way by the benchmark tasks.

Inspection (UX)

An analytical evaluation method in which a UX expert evaluates an interaction design by looking at it or trying it out, sometimes in the context of a set of abstracted design guidelines. Expert evaluators are both participant surrogates and observers, asking themselves questions about what would cause users problems and giving an expert opinion predicting UX problems (Section 25.4).

Benchmark Task

A task description devised for a participant to perform during UX evaluation so that UX measures such as time on task and error rates can be obtained and compared to a baseline value across the performances of multiple participants (Section 22.6).

In early stages, you might employ only unmeasured tasks, the sole goal of which is to observe critical incidents and identify initial UX problems to root out and fix at least the most obvious and most severe problems before any measured user performance data is useful.

Just as for benchmark tasks created for evaluation UX attributes, you should print out representative unmeasured task descriptions, which should be just as specific as the benchmark task descriptions to give to the participant to perform in the evaluation sessions.

23.5.3 Exploratory Free "Use"

In addition to strictly specified benchmark and unmeasured tasks, the evaluator may also find it useful to observe the participant in informal interaction with the design, a free-play period without the constraints of predefined tasks. This does not necessarily mean that they are even doing tasks, maybe just exploring.

To engage a participant in free use, the evaluator might simply say "play around with the interface for a while, doing anything you would like to, and talk aloud while you are playing." Free use is valuable for revealing participant expectations and system behavior in situations not anticipated by designers, often situations that can break a poor design.

23.5.4 User-Defined Tasks

Sometimes tasks that users come up with will address unexpected aspects of your design (Cordes, 2001). You can include user-defined tasks by giving your participants a system description in advance of the evaluation sessions and ask them to write down some tasks they think are appropriate to try. Otherwise, you can wait until the session is under way and ask each participant extemporaneously to come up with tasks to try.

If you want a more uniform task set over your participants but still wish to include user-defined tasks, you can ask a different set of potential users to come up with a number of candidate task descriptions before starting any evaluation session. This is a good assignment for a focus group. You can vet, edit, and merge these into a set of user-defined tasks to be given to each participant as part of each evaluation session.

> **Focus Group (in UX Practice)**
>
> A small discussion group of representative users or stakeholders aimed at identifying broad themes and issues in a work practice (Section 7.4.4.3).

23.6 RECRUIT PARTICIPANTS

The next step in preparing for empirical UX evaluation is selection and recruitment of participants—finding representative users, usually outside your team and often outside your project organization, to help with evaluation.

This section is mainly focused on participants for empirical UX evaluation, but also applies to other situations where user participants are needed.

23.6.1 Establish Budget and Schedule for Recruiting User Participants Upfront

Finding and recruiting evaluation participants might be part of the process where you are tempted to cut corners and save a little on the budget or might be something you think to do at the last minute. But, to protect the larger investment already made in the UX lifecycle process and in setting up formative evaluation so far, you need to secure a reasonable amount of resources—money in the budget to pay the participants and time in the schedule to recruit the full range and number of evaluation participants you will need. If you do this kind of evaluation infrequently, you can engage the services of a professional recruiter to do your participant recruiting or even the UX evaluation consulting group to do the whole evaluation.

23.6.2 Identify the Right Kinds of Participants

Formal Summative Evaluation

A formal, statistically rigorous summative (quantitative) empirical UX evaluation that produces statistically significant results (Section 21.1.5.1).

In formal summative evaluation, the process of selecting participants is referred to as "sampling," but that term is not appropriate here because what we are doing has nothing to do with the implied statistical relationships and constraints. In fact, it's quite the opposite. You're trying to learn the most about your design with the smallest number of participants and with exactly the right selected (not random) participants. Look for participants who are "representative users," that is, participants who match your target work role's user class descriptions and who are knowledgeable of the general target system domain. If you have multiple work roles and user classes, you should try to recruit participants representing *each* category. If you want to be certain your participants are representative, you can prepare a short written demographic survey to administer to participants to confirm that each one meets the requirements of your intended work activity role's user class characteristics.

In fact, participants must match the user class attributes in any UX targets they will help evaluate. So, for example, if initial usage is specified, you need participants unfamiliar with your design.

23.6.2.1 "Expert" participants

If you have a session calling for experienced usage, it's obvious that you should recruit an expert user, someone who knows the system domain and knows your particular system. Expert users are good at thinking aloud to generate qualitative data. These expert users will understand the tasks and can tell you what they don't like about the design. But you cannot necessarily depend on them to tell you how to make the design better.

Recruit a UX expert if you need a participant with broad UX knowledge and who can speak to design flaws in terms of design guidelines. As participants, these experts may not know the system domain as well and the tasks might not make as much sense to them, but they can analyze user experience, find subtle problems (e.g., small inconsistencies, poor use of color, confusing navigation), and offer suggestions for solutions.

Or you can consider recruiting a so-called "double expert," a UX expert who also knows your system very well, perhaps the most valuable kind of participant.

23.6.3 Determine the Right Number of Participants

The question of how many participants you need is entirely dependent on the kind of evaluation you are doing and the conditions under which you are doing it. There are some rules of thumb, such as the famous "three to five participants is enough" maxim, which is quoted so often out of context as to be almost meaningless. However, it is a good starting point until you learn more about what you need. For further discussion about the "three to five users" rule and its limitations, see Section 28.6.

The good news is that your experience and intuition will be effective touchstones for knowing when you have gotten the most out of an iteration of UX evaluation and when to move on. One telltale sign of having used enough participants is the lack of many new critical incidents or UX problems being discovered with additional participants.

You have to decide for yourself every time you do empirical UX evaluation—how many participants you can or want to afford. Sometimes it is just about achieving your UX targets, regardless of how many participants and iterations it takes. More often it is about getting in, getting some insight, and getting out.

23.6.4 Consider Recruiting Methods and Screening

Now the question arises as to where to find participants. Inform your customer early on about how your evaluation process will proceed so you will have the best chance of getting representative users from the customer organization at appropriate times.

Here are some hints for successful participant recruiting:

- Try to get the people around you (coworkers, colleagues elsewhere in your organization, spouses, children, and so on) to volunteer their time to act as participants, but be sure their characteristics fit your key work role and the corresponding user class needs.
- Newspaper ads and emails can work to recruit participants, but these methods are usually inefficient.

- If the average person off the street fits your participant profile (e.g., for a consumer software application), hand out leaflets in shopping malls and parking lots or post notices in grocery stores or in other public places (e.g., libraries).
- Use announcements at meetings of user groups and professional organizations if the cross section of the groups matches your user class needs.
- Recruit students at universities, community colleges, or even K-12, if appropriate.
- Consider temporary employment agencies as another source for finding participants.

A possible pitfall with temporary employment agencies is that they usually know nothing about UX evaluation, nor do they understand why it is so important to choose appropriate people as participants. The agency goal, after all, is to keep their pool of temporary workers employed, so it will be up to you to screen their candidates against your user class characteristics.

23.6.5 Use a Participant Recruiting Database

If you are going to be doing evaluation often, you should maintain a recruiting database of contact information for your potential participants. Because all the participants you have used in the past should be in this database, you can draw on the good ones for repeat performances.

You can also sometimes use your own customer base or your customer's contact lists as a participant recruiting source. Perhaps your marketing department has its own contact database.

23.6.6 Decide on Incentives and Remuneration

Generally, you should not ask your participants to work for free, so you will usually have to advertise some kind of remuneration. You will usually pay a modest hourly fee (e.g., about a dollar above minimum wage for an off-the-street volunteer). Expert participants cost more, depending on your specialized requirements. Don't try to get by too cheaply; you might get what you pay for.

Instead of, or in addition to, money, you can offer various kinds of premium gifts, such as coffee mugs with your company logo, gift certificates for local restaurants and shops, T-shirts proclaiming they survived your UX tests, free pizza, or even chocolate chip cookies! Sometimes just having a chance to learn about a new product before it is released or to help shape the design of some new technology is motivation enough.

23.6.7 Don't Give Up on Difficult-To-Find User Participants

Be creative in arranging for hard-to-find participant types. Sometimes, the customer—for whatever reasons—simply will not let the developer organization have access to representative users. The navy, for example, can be rightfully hesitant about calling in its ships and shipboard personnel from the high seas to evaluate a system being developed to go onboard.

Specialized roles (such as an ER physician) have demands on their time that make if difficult, or impossible, to schedule them in advance. Sometimes you can have an "on call" agreement through which they call you if they have some free time and you do your best to work them in.

Sometimes when you cannot get a representative user, you can find a user representative, someone who is not exactly in the same role but who knows the role from some other angle. A domain expert is not necessarily the same as a user, but might serve as a participant, especially in an early evaluation cycle. We once were looking for a particular kind of agent of an organization who worked with the public, but had to settle, at least at the beginning, for supervisors of those agents.

23.6.8 Recruit for Codiscovery

Consider recruiting pairs of participants specifically for codiscovery evaluation. Your goal is to find people who will work well together during evaluation and, as a practical matter, who are available at the same time. We have found it best not to use two people who are close friends or who work together on a daily basis; such close relationships can lead to too much wisecracking and acting out.

Look for people whose skills, work styles, and personality traits complement each other. Sometimes this is a good place to give them the Myers-Briggs test (Myers, McCaulley, Quenk, & Hammer, 1998) for collaborative personality types.

Codiscovery

A qualitative data collection technique employing two or more participants interacting in a team approach to evaluation, usually with a think-aloud data collection technique. Two people can verbalize more naturally, yielding multiple viewpoints expressed within conversational interplay (Sections 21.4.2.3 and 24.2.3.3).

23.6.9 Manage Participants as Any Other Valuable Resource

Once you have gone through the trouble and expense to recruit participants, don't let the process fail because a participant forgot to show up. Devise a mechanism to manage participant contact to keep in touch, remind in advance of appointments, and to follow up, if useful, afterward.

You need a standard procedure and a foolproof way to remind you to follow it for calling your participants in advance to remind them of their appointment, just as they do in doctor's offices. No-show participants cost money in unused lab facilities, evaluator frustration, wasted time, and schedule delays.

23.6.10 Select Participants for Subsequent Iterations

A question that commonly arises is whether you should use the same participants for more than one cycle of formative evaluation. Of course you would not use a repeat participant for tasks addressing an "initial use" UX attribute.

But sometimes reusing a participant (maybe one out of three to five) can make sense. This way, you can get a reaction to design changes from the previous cycle in addition to a new set of data on the modified design from the two new participants. Calling on a previously used participant tells them you value their help and gives them a kind of empowerment, a feeling that they are helping to make a difference in your design.

23.7 PREPARE FOR THE SESSION

23.7.1 Lab and Equipment

If you are planning lab-based evaluation, the most obvious aspect of preparation is to have the lab available and configured for your needs. If you plan to collect quantitative UX data, prepare by having on hand the right kind of timers for tasks and counters for errors, from simple stopwatches to instrumented software for automatically extracting timing data.

If you think you should evaluate outside the lab or with special props or environmental conditions, see Section 22.6.4.4 for more on this topic.

Example: A Modern UX Lab at Bloomberg LP

Bloomberg LP, a leader in financial informatics, employs a modern UX evaluation lab with two areas—a participant room and an observation room—each with an independent entrance and separated by a one-way mirror. The participant room has a multimonitor workstation (Fig. 23-2) on which Bloomberg's desktop applications are evaluated.

Fig. 23-2

Desktop evaluation in the Bloomberg UX evaluation lab.

On the other side of this participant room, there is another station designed for evaluations with paper prototypes (Fig. 23-3) or mobile devices (Fig. 23-4).

The left part of Fig. 23-4 shows this station being used during an evaluation of Bloomberg's mobile application. The right part shows a close up of the mobile device holder with a mounted camera, allowing the participant to hold and move

Fig. 23-3

Paper prototype evaluation in the Bloomberg UX evaluation lab.

Fig. 23-4

Mobile devices evaluation in the Bloomberg UX evaluation lab.

the mobile device as she interacts while the mounted camera captures the user interface and her actions.

Fig. 23-5 is a view of the observation room, which is kept dark to prevent people in the participant room from seeing through. In this image you can see the participant room showing through the one-way mirror. The lab is set up to stream up to five selections of the seven video sources and four screen capture sources from the participant room to the large screens seen at the top in the observation room.

Fig. 23-5

The observation room in the Bloomberg UX evaluation lab.

This lab has been instrumental in defining the UX designs of Bloomberg's flagship desktop and mobile applications. Special thanks to Shawn Edwards, the CTO; Fahd Arshad, the head of UX Design; Pam Snook; and Vera Newhouse at Bloomberg LP for providing us these lab photos.

23.7.2 Session Parameters

Evaluators must determine protocol and procedures for conducting the evaluation—exactly what will happen and for how long during an evaluation session with a participant.

23.7.2.1 Task and session lengths

The typical length of time of an evaluation session for one participant is anywhere from 30 minutes to two hours. However, it is possible that a real-world UX evaluation session can become a day-long experience for a participant. The idea is to get as much as possible from each user without burning out the participant.

If you require sessions longer than a couple of hours, it will be more difficult for participants. In such cases, you should:

- Prepare participants for possible fatigue in long sessions by warning them in advance.
- Mitigate fatigue by scheduling breaks between tasks where participants can get up and walk around, leave the participant room, get some coffee or other refreshments.
- Have some granola bars and/or fruit available in case hunger becomes an issue.
- Always have water and possibly other beverages.

23.7.2.2 Number of full lifecycle iterations

Just as a loose rule of thumb from our experience, an ideal number of full UX engineering cycle iterations per version or release is about three, but resource constraints often limit it to fewer. In many projects, you can expect only one iteration. Of course, any iterations are better than none.

23.7.3 Informed Consent

Informed consent is formal and signed permission is given to UX professionals by usage research and evaluation participants to use the data gathered within the UX lifecycle activities, usually with certain stipulated limits.

When we collect empirical data involving human subjects, we have certain legal and ethical responsibilities, even though there is very little risk of a participant being harmed in UX evaluation.

We still have professional obligations, which center on the informed consent form, a document to establish explicitly the rights of your participants and which also serves as legal protection for you and your organization. Therefore, you should always have all participants, anyone from who you collect data of any kind, sign an informed consent form.

23.7.3.1 Informed consent permission application

Your preparation for informed consent begins with an application to your institutional review board (IRB), an official group within your organization responsible for the legal and ethical aspects of informed consent. The evaluator or project manager should prepare an IRB application that typically will include:

- Summary of the evaluation plan.
- Statement of complete evaluation protocol.
- Statement of exactly how human subjects will be involved.
- Your written subject/participant instructions.
- A copy of your informed consent form.
- Any other standard IRB forms for your organization.

Because most UX evaluation does not put participants at risk, the applications are usually approved without question. The details of the approval process vary by organization, but it can take up to weeks and can require changes in the documents. The approval process is based on a review of the ethical and legal issues, not the quality of the proposed evaluation plan.

23.7.3.2 Informed consent form

The informed consent form, an important part of your IRB application and an important part of your empirical UX evaluation, is a requirement; it is not optional. The informed consent form, which is to be read and signed by each participant, should state in clear understandable language:

- That the participant is volunteering to participate in your evaluation.
- The expected length of time for the evaluation session (the evaluator should have some idea of how long a session will take after performing pilot testing).
- That the participant can withdraw anytime, for any reason, or for no reason at all.
- That you are taking data that the participant helps generate.
- That the data are taken anonymously (neither the name of the participant nor any other kind of identification will be associated with data after it has been collected).
- That the participant understands any foreseeable risks or discomforts, which should be minimal to zero for UX evaluation.
- That the participant understands any benefits (e.g., educational benefit or just the satisfaction of helping make a good design) and/or compensation to participants (if there is payment, state exactly how much; if not, say so explicitly).
- All project/evaluator contact information.
- That they can ask the evaluator questions at any time.
- Whether any kind of recording (e.g., video, audio, photographic, or holodeck) involving the participant will be made and how you intend to use it, who will view it (and not), and by what date it will be erased or otherwise destroyed.
- A statement that, if you want to use a video clip (for example) from the recording for any other purpose, you will get their additional approval in writing.

The consent form may also include nondisclosure requirements. This form must spell out participant rights and what you expect the participants to do, even if there is overlap with the general instruction sheet. The form they sign must be self-standing and must tell the whole story.

Although informed consent may not be required in the case where your participants are also organization employees, this is an area where you should err on the side of caution. In any case, you should have two copies of the consent form ready for reading and signing by participants when they arrive. One copy is for the participant to keep.

Example: Simple Informed Consent Form

Informed Consent for Participant of Development Project

<Name of your development organization> <Date or version number of form> Title of Project: <Project title>

Project team member(s) directly involved: <Team member names> Project manager: <Project manager name>

I. THE PURPOSE OF YOUR PARTICIPATION IN THIS PROJECT As part of the <project title> project, you are invited to participate in evaluating and improving various designs of <name of system or product>, <description of system or product>.

II. PROCEDURES You will be asked to perform a set of tasks using the <name of system or product>. These tasks consist of <description of range of tasks>. Your role in these tests is to help us evaluate the designs. We are not evaluating you or your performance in any way. As you perform various tasks with the system, your actions and comments will be noted and you will be asked to describe verbally your learning process. You may be asked questions during and after the evaluation in order to clarify our understanding of your evaluation. You may also be asked to fill out a questionnaire relating to your usage of the system.

The evaluation session will last no more than four hours, with the typical session being about two hours. The tasks are not very tiring, but you are welcome to take rest breaks as needed. If you prefer, the session may be divided into two shorter sessions.

III. RISKS There are no known risks to the participants of this study.

IV. BENEFITS OF THIS PROJECT Your participation in this project will provide information that may be used to improve our designs for <name of system or product>. No guarantee of further benefits has been made to encourage you to participate (Change this if a benefit such as a payment or a gift is offered). You are requested to refrain from discussing the evaluation with other people who might be in the candidate pool from which other participants might be drawn.

V. EXTENT OF ANONYMITY AND CONFIDENTIALITY The results of this study will be kept strictly confidential. Your written consent is required for the researchers to release any data identified with you as an individual to anyone other than personnel working on the project. The information you provide will have your name removed and only a subject number will identify you during analyses and any written reports of the research.

The session may be recorded. If it is recorded, the recordings will be stored securely, viewed only by the project team members and erased after three months. If the project team members wish to use a portion of your recording for any other purpose, they will get your written permission before using it. Your signature on this form does not give them permission to show your recording to anyone else.

VI. COMPENSATION Your participation is voluntary and unpaid (Change this if a benefit such as a payment or a gift is offered).

VII. FREEDOM TO WITHDRAW You are free to withdraw from this study at any time for any reason.

VIII. APPROVAL OF RESEARCH This research has been approved, as required, by the Institutional Review Board <or the name of your review committee> for projects involving human subjects at <your organization>.

IX. PARTICIPANT RESPONSIBILITIES AND PERMISSION I voluntarily agree to participate in this study, and I know of no reason I cannot participate. I have read and understand the informed consent and conditions of this project. I have had all my questions answered. I hereby acknowledge the above and give my voluntary consent for participation in this project. If I participate, I may withdraw at any time without penalty. I agree to abide by the rules of this project.

Signature   Date

Name (please print) Contact: phone or email

23.7.4 Other Paperwork

User instructions

Overview. In conjunction with developing evaluation procedures, you, as the evaluator, should write *introductory instructional remarks* that will be read uniformly by each participant at the beginning of the session. All participants thereby start with the same level of knowledge about the system and the tasks they are to perform. This uniform instruction for each participant will help ensure consistency across the test sessions.

Specifics. These introductory instructions should explain briefly the purpose of the evaluation and tell a little bit about the system the participant will be using as well as describe what the participant will be expected to do and the procedure to be followed by the participant. For example, instructions might state that a participant will be:

- Asked to perform some benchmark tasks that will be given by the evaluator.
- Allowed to use the system freely for a while.
- Given some more benchmark tasks to perform.
- Asked to complete an exit questionnaire.

Make it clear that you are not evaluating the participant. In your general instructions to participants, make it clear that the purpose of the session is to evaluate the system, not to evaluate them. You should say explicitly *"You are helping us evaluate the system—we are not evaluating you!"* Some participants may be fearful that somehow their performance might not be up to "expectations" or that participation in this kind of test session could reflect poorly on them or even be used in their employment performance evaluations (if, for example, they work for the same organization that is designing the interface they are helping evaluate). They should be reassured that this is not the case. This is where it is important for you to reiterate your guarantee of confidentiality with respect to individual information and anonymity of data.

Prepare the participant for thinking aloud. The instructions may inform participants that you want them to think aloud while working. Explain what this is and how to do it and offer a very brief trial run for learning.

Print out and copy the general instructions so that you can give one to each participant.

23.7.4.1 Nondisclosure agreements (NDAs)

Sometimes an NDA is required by the developer or customer organizations to protect the intellectual property contained in the design. If you have an NDA, print out copies for reading, signing, and sharing with the participant.

23.7.4.2 Questionnaires and surveys

If your evaluation plan includes administration of one or more participant questionnaires, make sure that you have a good supply available. It is best to keep blank questionnaires in the control room or away from where a newly arriving participant could read them in advance.

23.7.4.3 Data collection forms

If appropriate, make up a simple data collection form in advance. Your data collection form(s) should contain fields suitable for all types of quantitative data you collect and, probably separate, data collection forms for recording critical incidents and UX problems observed during the sessions. The latter should include spaces for the kind of supplementary data you like to keep, including associated tasks, effect on user (e.g., minor or task-blocking), guidelines involved, potential cause of problems in design, relevant designer knowledge (e.g., how it was supposed to work), etc. Keep your data collection forms simple and easy to use on the fly. Consider a spreadsheet form on a laptop.

23.7.5 Training Materials

Use training materials for participants only if you anticipate that a user's manual, quick reference cards, or any sort of training material will be available and needed by users of the final system.

23.7.6 The UX Evaluation Session Work Package

To summarize, as you do the evaluation preparation and planning described in this chapter, you need to gather your evaluation session work package, all the materials you will need in each evaluation session.

Examples of package contents can include:

- The evaluation configuration plan, including diagrams of rooms, equipment, and people in evaluation roles.
- General instruction sheets.
- Informed consent forms, with participant names and date entered.
- Any nondisclosure agreements.
- All questionnaires and surveys, including any demographic survey.
- All printed benchmark task descriptions, one task per sheet of paper (Section 22.6.4.1).
- All printed unmeasured task descriptions (these can be listed several to a page).
- Any special instructions to watch out for particular parts of the design, evaluation scripts, things to do before each participant session (e.g., to reset browser caches so that no auto complete entries from previous participant's session interfere with the current session), etc.
- For each evaluator, a printout (or laptop version) of the UX targets associated with the day's sessions.
- All data collection forms, on paper or on laptops.
- Any props needed to support tasks.
- Any training materials to be used as part of the evaluation.
- Any compensation to be given out (e.g., money, gift cards, T-shirts, coffee mugs, used cars).

Exercise 23-1: Empirical UX Evaluation Preparation for Your System

Goal: To get some practice in preparation for a simple empirical evaluation.
Activities: If you are working with a team, get together with your team.

Decide roles for team members. Include at least a facilitator and a prototype executor, plus a quantitative data recorder and one or more critical incident recorders.

In addition, if you are doing this exercise in a classroom with other teams, assign two team members as participants to trade to another team when you start data collection in the next exercise.

The prototype executor should get out the wireframe prototype deck you made in a previous exercise and become familiar with the navigation.

This activity works well for a team of about four. If you have more or fewer members in your team, it is easy to make adjustments. If there are only two of you, for example, one person can be the executor and the other person can record critical incidents and time the benchmark tasks. If there are four or five of you, the extra people will be valuable in helping record critical incidents. If you have been working alone on all the previous exercises, you may want find a couple of other people to help you run the evaluation. In addition and in any case, you need to recruit two people to serve as participants to evaluate your prototype.

Get out the UX target table you made in a previous exercise.

Have at least two benchmark tasks that you created in a previous exercise, each written on a separate piece of paper.

Assuming you used a questionnaire for subjective data in your evaluation session, get out copies of the questionnaire, one for each participant you will be using, and circle the questions you want participants to answer.

Review your evaluation protocols.

Deliverables: Just have everything ready for the next exercise, data collection.

Schedule: It should not take too long to get ready for evaluation.

Subjective UX Evaluation Data

Data based on opinion or judgment, of evaluator or user (Section 21.1.4.2).

23.7.7 Do Final Pilot Testing: Fix Your Wobbly Wheels

If your UX evaluation plan involves using a prototype, give it a final shakedown to be sure it is robust enough to support evaluation without breaking. This step really applies to any level of fidelity if your prototype will be seen by people beyond your UX team.

In addition to shaking down your prototype, think of your pilot testing as a dress rehearsal to be sure of your lab equipment, benchmark tasks, procedures, and personnel roles.

You don't want to "use up" a user participant by getting them started only to discover the prototype dies and prevents benchmark task performance.

Simulate user experience evaluation conditions by having one member of your team "execute" the prototype while another member plays "user" and tries out all benchmark tasks. The user person should go through each task in as many ways as anyone thinks possible to head off unexpected problems. Don't assume error-free performance by your users; try to have appropriate error messages where user errors might occur.

Empirical UX Evaluation: Data Collection Methods and Techniques

24

24.1 INTRODUCTION

24.1.1 You Are Here

We begin each process chapter with a "you are here" picture of the chapter topic in the context of The Wheel, the overall UX design lifecycle template (Fig. 24-1). In this chapter, we elaborate on how to collect data for empirical UX evaluation.

24.1.2 Empirical Ways of Generating and Collecting Data Within the Needs Pyramid

As a reminder, the UX needs pyramid has these layers (bottom to top):

- Ecological.

- Interaction.
- Emotional.

Almost all the empirical data collection methods and techniques in this chapter can be used to conduct UX evaluation within any layer of the needs pyramid, at any scope, and any level of rigor.

Foremost, essentially everything in the UX evaluation chapters (Chapters 21–27) applies to the interaction level. Many topics in this chapter are generally relevant to evaluating the emotional level, too, and those instances

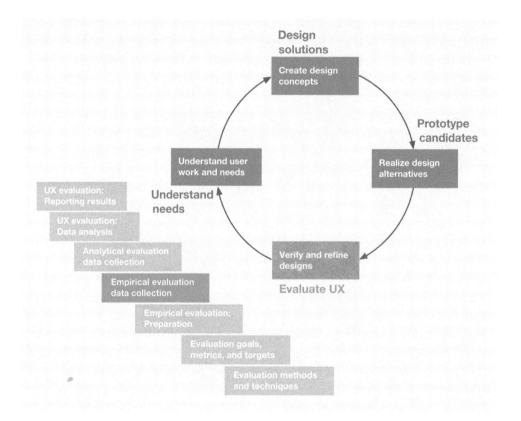

Fig. 24-1

You are here in the chapter on data collection within the Evaluate UX lifecycle activity in the context of the overall Wheel lifecycle process.

are pointed out as such. In addition, there is an entire section (Section 24.4) devoted to specific ways to evaluate the emotional level. That leaves the ecological level, which is the subject of the next section.

As usual, the early funnel is best for evaluating in the ecological layer, where you have a large scope to embrace the product or system ecology and its conceptual design. The late funnel is best for evaluating within the interaction layer, where you address user actions in task-level design.

24.1.2.1 Empirical methods and techniques for generating and collecting UX evaluation data in the ecological layer

Ecological concepts are sometimes difficult to evaluate. Because ecology is about how the broader system works, and the various devices and contexts it encompasses, the issues with its design tend to be high-level in nature and generally abstract. Therefore, evaluating the conceptual design of an ecology requires measuring instruments that bring into focus the themes and structures of how the overarching system works.

There are two main goals for evaluating the design of an ecology:

- Ascertain whether users *understand* how the ecology is structured:
  - Evaluate whether the designers' mental model is communicated clearly through the conceptual design.
  - Evaluate whether users are able to form a clear mental model as a result.
- Ensure the users are able to get work done in the new ecology. Evaluate whether the conceptual design of the ecology is *appropriate* for their work context.

Evaluate user understanding. An effective way to evaluate the first goal is to first introduce the system's ecology to users and allow them to get familiar by performing benchmark tasks on individual designs. This usually involves prototypes of the UX designs on all devices that constitute the ecology. After they get familiar with the various devices and their capabilities, address the first goal by asking them to articulate how the overall system works. A specific task asking them to explain how the system works to a new colleague who joined their team is a good way to get at their understanding.

Specifically, you can ask questions such as "How would you describe this system to someone who has never seen it before? What is the underlying "model" for this system? Is that model appropriate? Where does it deviate? Does it meet your expectations? Why and how? These questions get to the root of determining the user's mental model for the system.

Ecology

In the setting of UX design, the ecology is the entire set of surrounding parts of the world, including networks, other users, devices, and information structures, with which a user, product, or system interacts (Section 16.2.1).

Another way to evaluate understanding is by following benchmark tasks on a device with questions on expectations of what the consequences will be on another device. This probes their mental model on how the two devices work together. For example, asking what they expect to see on the phone or watch when they save a record on the desktop gets to their understanding on what data they expect to be available on what platforms.

Evaluate appropriateness to work context. The second goal of evaluating appropriateness of the design to a given work practice is a more task-centric issue—about how well users can get work done in the ecology. For this, you need benchmark tasks that require the user to switch among various devices in the ecology. This second goal also requires tasks pertaining to participating in the ecology (e.g., sign up or create an account). Tasks that start on one device, are interrupted, and then resume on another device help evaluate user expectations on what context is maintained across devices. Questionnaires are another evaluation instrument that probes the users about capabilities they expect on each of the devices in the ecology.

24.2 EMPIRICAL METHODS AND TECHNIQUES FOR GENERATING AND COLLECTING QUALITATIVE UX DATA

Qualitative data collection is by far the most important kind of evaluation data across all UX practice. The defining formative UX evaluation goal is to identify UX problems and their causes so the design can be improved. In empirical testing with participants, this goal is achieved through qualitative UX data collected primarily through observation and recording of critical incidents (next section) and use of the think-aloud technique.

24.2.1 Critical Incident Identification

Along with the think-aloud technique, critical incident identification is arguably the real workhorse of empirical data collection techniques. Critical incident identification is an empirical data collection technique based on the participant or evaluator detecting and analyzing occurrences of events that indicate a (usually) bad user experience.

24.2.1.1 What is a critical incident?

Despite many variations in procedures for gathering and analyzing critical incidents, researchers and practitioners agree about the definition of a critical incident. *A critical incident is an event occurring within usage that reveals a barrier, problem, or difficulty encountered by the user, or simply something the user did not like* (Castillo and Hartson, 2000; del Galdo, Williges, Williges, and Wixon, 1986).

For more on the history and background of the critical incident identification technique, see Section 28.7.

24.2.1.2 Mostly used as a variation

In today's practice, there is no single critical incident identification technique, but each UX evaluator adapts a variation most suitable to the needs at hand. For more about how the application of this technique varies, see Section 28.7.2.

24.2.1.3 Who identifies critical incidents?

For simplicity, in our interpretation of the critical incident data collection technique, the UX evaluator is the one who identifies and records critical incident data. For more about who identifies critical incidents, see Section 28.7.3.

24.2.2 Critical Incident Data Capture

The way that you collect and document critical incident data as you go will have much to say about the accuracy and efficiency of your subsequent data analysis. Write concise but detailed critical incident and UX problem descriptions as clearly, precisely, and completely as you can in real time. Terse notes will be more difficult to interpret later.

The best kind of critical incident data are:

- Detailed.
- Observed during usage.
- Captured immediately.
- Associated closely with specific task performance.

Critical incident data are perishable. The biggest reason why empirical UX evaluation is effective is that it allows the capture of detailed usage-related data as it occurs. These detailed data, perishable if not captured immediately and precisely as they arise during usage, are essential for isolating specific problems with the user UX design.

Sometimes critical incident data are subtle. Experienced UX evaluators will know how to see critical incidents in subtle user behavior—a user hesitation, a participant comment in passing, a head shaking, a slight shrugging of the shoulders, or drumming of fingers on the table. A timely request for clarification might help determine if any of these subtle observations should be considered a symptom of a UX problem.

For a discussion about the timing of critical incident data capture and the evaluator's awareness zone, see Section 28.7.4.

24.2.2.1 What's in critical incident data?

Critical incident data about a UX problem should contain as much detail as possible, including usage research information such as:

- The user's general activity or task.
- Objects or artifacts involved.
- The specific user intention and action that led immediately to the critical incident.
- Expectations of the user about what the system was supposed to do when the critical incident occurred.
- What happened instead.
- As much as possible about the mental and emotional state of the user.
- Indication of whether the user could recover from the critical incident and, if so, a description of how the user did so.
- Additional comments or suggested solutions to the problem.

24.2.2.2 Avoid video recording

In past years, some UX labs used video recording routinely to capture all user and screen actions and facilitator and participant comments and, thereby, captured the raw data necessary to identify critical incidents. However, most videotaping setups were cumbersome, complicated, expensive, and often unreliable. And reviewing the video was time consuming and expensive. Today's UX practice calls for more lightweight and nimble techniques for data collection.

24.2.2.3 Manual note taking for critical incident data collection

Instead, manual note taking is the most basic critical incident capture technique and is the most useful and efficient approach. Evaluators take comprehensive, real-time raw critical incident notes with a laptop or with pencil and paper. When thoughts come faster than they can write, they might make audio notes to themselves on a handheld digital voice recorder—anything to capture raw data while it is still fresh.

24.2.2.4 Follow up on hunches

If you get an intuitive feeling during UX evaluation that something is wrong with the design that is not coming out explicitly in the data, you should not let it go but you should follow up on it.

24.2.3 The Think-Aloud Data Collection Technique

Also called "verbal protocol" in the early human factors literature, the think-aloud technique is a qualitative data collection technique in which user participants, as the name implies, verbally express their thoughts about their interaction experience, including their motives, rationale, and perceptions of UX problems. By this method, participants let us in on their thinking, giving us access to a precious understanding of their perspective of the task and the UX design, their expectations, strategies, biases, likes, and dislikes. Variations of this simple technique are rooted in psychological and human factors experimentation well before it was used in usability engineering (Lewis, 1982).

24.2.3.1 Why use the think-aloud technique?

The think-aloud technique is simple to use for both analyst and participant. It is most useful during empirical evaluation of user task performance, but it is also useful when a participant walks through a prototype or helps you with a UX inspection. Nielsen (1993, p. 195) says "thinking aloud may be the single most valuable usability engineering method." It is effective in accessing user intentions, what they are doing or are trying to do, and their motivations, the reasons why they are doing any particular actions. The think-aloud technique is also effective in assessing emotional impact because emotional impact is felt internally and the internal thoughts and feelings of the user are exactly what the think-aloud technique accesses for you.

Observational data are important during an evaluation session with a participant attempting to perform a task. But often quite a bit of the real UX problem data is hidden from observation in the mind of the participant. What is really causing a hesitation and why does this participant perceive it as a problem or barrier? The goal of the think-aloud technique is to tap into this data hidden in the participant's mind.

24.2.3.2 How to manage the participant in the think-aloud technique

Although there are some points to watch for, in its simplest form this technique could not be easier. It simply entails having participants think out loud and share their thoughts verbally while they perform tasks or otherwise interact with a product or system you want to evaluate. Here's what to do with the participants involved:

- At the beginning, explain the concept of thinking aloud.
- Explain that this means you will expect them to talk while they work and think, sharing their thoughts by verbalizing them to you.

Inspection (UX)

An analytical evaluation method in which a UX expert evaluates an interaction design by looking at it or trying it out, sometimes in the context of a set of abstracted design guidelines. Expert evaluators are both participant surrogates and observers, asking themselves questions about what would cause users problems and giving an expert opinion predicting UX problems (Section 25.4).

Emotional Impact

An affective component of user experience that influences user feelings. Includes such effects as enjoyment, pleasure, fun, satisfaction, aesthetics, coolness, engagement, and novelty and can involve deeper emotional factors such as self-expression, self-identity, a feeling of contribution to the world, and pride of ownership (Section 1.4.4).

- Ask participants to tell you what they are thinking and not describing what they are doing.
- You might start with a little exercise or practice session to get warmed up and to get participants acclimated to thinking aloud.
- Among the thoughts you should encourage participants to express are descriptions of their intentions, what they are doing or are trying to do, and their motivations, the reasons why they are doing any particular actions.
- Encourage them to get past the chatty stage and get down to real engagement and introspection.
- You especially want them to speak out when they get confused, frustrated, or blocked.
- Actively elicit participant thoughts if they are not forthcoming.

Depending on the individual, thinking aloud usually comes quite naturally; it does not take much practice. Occasionally you might have to encourage or remind the participant to keep up the flow of thinking aloud.

24.2.3.3 Codiscovery think-aloud techniques

You may wish to try using two or more participants in a team approach, a technique that originated with O'Malley, Draper, and Riley (1984) and was named "codiscovery" by Kennedy (1989).

While it can seem unnatural and inhibiting to a lone participant to be thinking aloud, essentially talking to oneself, there is more ease in talking in a natural conversation with another person (Wildman, 1995). A single individual participant can have trouble remembering to verbalize, but it is just natural with a partner.

Hackman and Biers (1992) found that using multiple participants, while slightly more expensive, resulted in more time spent in verbalizing and, more importantly, participant teams spent more time verbalizing statements that had high value as feedback for designers.

24.2.3.4 Does thinking aloud affect quantitative task performance metrics in empirical evaluation?

It depends on the participant. Some participants can naturally chat about what they are doing as they work. For these participants, the concurrent think-aloud technique usually does not affect task performance when used with measured benchmark tasks.

24.3 EMPIRICAL METHODS AND TECHNIQUES FOR GENERATING AND COLLECTING QUANTITATIVE UX DATA

As we have said, quantitative measures are not used much anymore in UX evaluation.

24.3.1 Objective Quantitative Data for User Performance Measurement

If you do need quantitative data, though, the most popular quantitative data collection techniques involve measurement of user performance of benchmark tasks, usually at the same time you collect qualitative data.

For example, an evaluator may measure the time it takes the participant to perform a task, count the number of errors a participant makes while performing a task, count the number of tasks a participant can perform within a given time period, and so on, depending on the measures established in your UX targets (Chapter 22).

24.3.1.1 Timing task performance

By far the simplest way to measure time on task is by manually using a stopwatch. It is really the only sensible way for low-fidelity prototypes, such as click-through wireframe prototypes.

For the rare times when precise timing measurements are required, it is possible to embed software timers to instrument the software internally.

24.3.1.2 Counting user errors

The simplest way to count user errors during task performance is to use a manual event counter such as a handheld "clicker" for counting people coming through a gate for an event. Manual counters are perfect for low-fidelity, especially paper, prototypes.

The key to counting errors correctly is in knowing what constitutes an error. Not everything that goes wrong, not even everything a user does wrong, during task performance should be counted as a user error. So what are we looking for? A user error is usually considered to have occurred when the participant takes *any action that does not lead to progress in performing the desired task within the boundaries of the intended design (and not, for example, gaps in a prototype's functionality).*

24.3.1.3 What generally does not count as a user error?

Typically, we don't count accessing online help or other documentation as an error. As a practical matter, we also want to exclude any random act of curiosity or exploration that might be interjected by the user (e.g., "I know this is not right, but I am curious what will happen if I click this"). Also a different successful path "invented" by the user is not really an error, but probably should be noted as an important observation.

And we don't usually include "oops" errors, what Norman (1990, p. 105) calls "slips." These are errors that users make by accident when, in fact, they know better. For example, the user knows the right button to click but clicks the wrong one, perhaps through a slip of the hand, a brain burp, or being too hasty. Finally, we don't usually include typing errors, unless their cause could somehow be traced to a problem in the design or unless the application is about typing (Section 22.6.2.5).

24.3.2 Subjective Quantitative Data Collection: Questionnaires

A questionnaire is a fast and easy way to collect subjective UX data, either as a supplement to any other rapid UX evaluation method or as a method on its own.

Questionnaires with good track records, such as the Questionnaire for User Interface Satisfaction (QUIS), the System Usability Scale (SUS), or Usefulness, Satisfaction, and Ease of Use (USE), are all easy and inexpensive to use and can yield varying degrees of UX data. Perhaps the AttrakDiff questionnaire might be the best choice for a rapid standalone method, as it is designed to address both pragmatic (usability and usefulness) and emotional impact issues. All these questionnaires are discussed further at the end of this section.

24.3.2.1 Questionnaires as supplements to lab-based sessions

Postsession questionnaires can be used to supplement what you have discovered objectively in the session. Most questionnaire responses are written, but you might also consider asking survey questions orally to gather postsession information. The direct verbal exchange allows you to pursue issues of interest with impromptu follow-up questions.

24.3.2.2 Questionnaires as an evaluation method on their own

A questionnaire can also be used as the primary UX data collection instrument when used as an evaluation method on its own. A questionnaire can contain probing questions about the total user experience. Although questionnaires have been used primarily to assess user satisfaction, they can also contain effective

---

Subjective UX Evaluation Data

Data based on opinion or judgment, of evaluator or user (Section 21.1.4.2).

Emotional Impact

An affective component of user experience that influences user feelings. Includes such effects as enjoyment, pleasure, fun, satisfaction, aesthetics, coolness, engagement, and novelty and can involve deeper emotional factors such as self-expression, self-identity, a feeling of contribution to the world, and pride of ownership (Section 1.4.4).

Usefulness

A component of user experience based on utility, system functionality that gives users the ability to accomplish the goals of work (or play) through using the system or product (Section 1.4.3).

questions oriented specifically toward evaluating broader emotional impact and usefulness of the design.

Questionnaires are a self-reporting data collection technique and, as Shih and Liu (2007) say, semantic differential questionnaires (see next section) are used most commonly because they are a product-independent method that can yield reliable quantitative subjective data. This kind of questionnaire is inexpensive to administer but requires skill to create so that data are valid and reliable.

24.3.2.3 Semantic differential scales

A semantic differential scale, or Likert scale (1932), is a range of semantic values describing an attribute. Each value on the scale represents a different level of that attribute. The most extreme value in each direction on the scale is called an anchor. The scale is then divided, usually in equal divisions, with points between the anchors that divide up the difference between the meanings of the two anchors.

The number of discrete points we have on the scale between and including the anchors is the granularity of the scale, or the number of choices we allow users in expressing their own levels of the attribute. It is helpful to also include verbal (or pictorial) labels associated with each numeric value.

For example, consider the following statement for which we wish to get an assessment of agreement by the user: "The checkout process on this website was easy to use." A corresponding semantic differential scale might have these labels: strongly agree, agree, neutral, disagree, and strongly disagree, with the associated numeric values, respectively, of +2, +1, 0, −1, and −2.

24.3.2.4 The Questionnaire for User Interface Satisfaction (QUIS)

The QUIS, developed at the University of Maryland (Chin, Diehl, and Norman, 1988), is one of the earliest available questionnaires for evaluating user satisfaction. It was the most extensive and most thoroughly validated questionnaire at the time of its development for determining subjective interaction design usability.

The QUIS is organized around such general categories as *screen, terminology and system information, learning,* and *system capabilities.* Within each of these general categories are sets of questions about detailed features, with Likert scales from which a participant chooses a rating. It also elicits some demographic information as well as general user comments about the interaction design being evaluated. Many practitioners supplement the QUIS with some of their own questions, specific to the interaction design being evaluated.

The original QUIS had 27 questions (Tullis and Stetson, 2004), but there have been many extensions and variations. Although developed originally for screen-based designs, QUIS is resilient and can be extended easily, for example, by replacing the term "system" with "website" and "screen" with "webpage."

Practitioners are free to use the results of a QUIS questionnaire in any reasonable way. In much of our use of this instrument, we calculated the average scores, averaged over all the participants and all the questions in a specified subset of the questionnaire. Each such subset was selected to correspond to the goal of a UX target, and the numeric value of this score averaged over the subset of questions was compared to the target performance values stated in the UX target table.

Although the QUIS is quite thorough, it can be administered in a relatively short time. For many years, a subset of the QUIS was our own choice as the questionnaire to use in both teaching and consulting.

Last we heard, QUIS is still being updated and maintained and can be licensed[1] for a modest fee from the University of Maryland Office of Technology Liaison. In Table 24-1, we show a sample excerpted and adapted with permission from the QUIS with fairly general applicability, at least to desktop applications. The columns represent the UX attribute being evaluated and the semantic anchors.

Table 24-1

An excerpt adapted from QUIS, with permission

1. Terminology relates to task domain	Distantly—closely
2. Instructions describing tasks	Confusing—clear
3. Instructions are consistent	Never—always
4. Operations relate to tasks	Distantly—closely
5. Informative feedback	Never—always
6. Display layouts simplify tasks	Never—always
7. Sequence of displays	Confusing—clear
8. Error messages are helpful	Never—always
9. Error correction	Confusing—clear
10. Learning the operation	Difficult—easy

[1] http:/lap.umd.edu/quis/.

Table 24-1 An excerpt adapted from QUIS, with permission —cont'd

11. Human memory limitations	Overwhelmed—are respected
12. Exploration of features	Discouraged—encouraged
13. Overall reactions	Terrible—wonderful
Overall reactions	Frustrating—satisfying
Overall reactions	Uninteresting—interesting
Overall reactions	Dull—stimulating
Overall reactions	Difficult—easy

24.3.2.5 The System Usability Scale (SUS)

The SUS was developed by John Brooke while at Digital Equipment Corporation (Brooke, 1996) in the United Kingdom. The SUS questionnaire contains 10 questions. As an interesting variation from the usual questionnaire, the SUS alternates positively worded questions with negatively worded questions to prevent quick answers without the responder really considering the questions.

The questions are presented as simple declarative statements, each with a five-point Likert scale anchored with "strongly disagree" and "strongly agree" and with values of 1–5. These 10 statements are (used with permission):

- I think that I would like to use this system frequently.
- I found the system unnecessarily complex.
- I thought the system was easy to use.
- I think that I would need the support of a technical person to be able to use this system.
- I found the various functions in this system were well integrated.
- I thought there was too much inconsistency in this system.
- I would imagine that most people would learn to use this system very quickly.
- I found the system very cumbersome to use.
- I felt very confident using the system.
- I needed to learn a lot of things before I could get going with this system.

The 10 items in the SUS were selected from a list of 50 possibilities, chosen for their perceived discriminating power.

The bottom line for the SUS is that it is robust, extensively used, widely adapted, and in the public domain. It has been a very popular questionnaire for complementing objective UX data because it can be applied at any stage in the UX lifecycle and is intended for practical use in an industry context. The SUS is

Objective UX
Evaluation Data

Qualitative or quantitative
data acquired through
direct empirical
observation, usually of
user performance
(Section 21.1.4.2).

technology independent; can be used across a broad range of kinds of systems, products, and interaction styles; and is fast and easy for both analyst and participant. The single numeric score (see later) is easy to understand by everyone. According to Usability Net (2006), it was the most highly recommended of all the publicly available questionnaires.

24.3.2.6 The Usefulness, Satisfaction, and Ease of Use (USE) questionnaire

With the goal of measuring the most important dimensions of usability for users across many different domains, Lund (2001, 2004) developed USE, a questionnaire for evaluating the user experience on three dimensions: usefulness, satisfaction, and ease of use. USE is based on a seven-point Likert scale.

According to Lund, questions were chosen for inclusion in USE through a process of factor analysis and partial correlation.

USE has been applied successfully to systems, products, and websites. It is available in the public domain and has good face validity for both users and practitioners, that is, it looks right intuitively, and people agree that it should work.

Here is an abbreviated version of the USE questionnaire questions:

Usefulness

- It helps me be more effective.
- It helps me be more productive.
- It is useful.
- It gives me more control over the activities in my life.
- It makes the things I want to accomplish easier to get done.
- It saves me time when I use it.
- It meets my needs.
- It does everything I would expect it to do.

Ease of use

- It is easy to use.
- It is simple to use.
- It is user-friendly.
- It requires the fewest steps possible to accomplish what I want to do with it.
- It is flexible.
- Using it is effortless.
- I can use it without written instructions.
- I do not notice any inconsistencies as I use it.

- Both occasional and regular users would like it.
- I can recover from mistakes quickly and easily.
- I can use it successfully every time.

Ease of learning

- I learned to use it quickly.
- I easily remember how to use it.
- It is easy to learn to use it.
- I quickly became skillful with it.

Satisfaction

- I am satisfied with it.
- I would recommend it to a friend.
- It is fun to use.
- It works the way I want it to work.
- It is wonderful.
- I feel I need to have it.
- It is pleasant to use.

24.3.2.7 Other questionnaires

Here are some other questionnaires that are beyond our scope but might be of interest to some readers.

General-purpose usability questionnaires:

- Computer System Usability Questionnaire (CSUQ), developed by James Lewis (Lewis, 1995, 2002) at IBM, is well regarded and available in the public domain.
- Software Usability Measurement Inventory (SUMI)[2] is "a rigorously tested and proven method of measuring software quality from the end user's point of view." According to Usability Net,[3] SUMI is "a mature questionnaire whose standardization base and manual have been regularly updated." It is applicable to a range of application types from desktop applications to large domain-complex applications.
- After Scenario Questionnaire (ASQ), developed by IBM, is available in the public domain (Bangor, Kortum, and Miller, 2008, p. 575).
- Post-Study System Usability Questionnaire (PSSUQ), developed by IBM, is available in the public domain (Bangor et al., 2008, p. 575).

---

[2]Human Factors Research Group (http:/www.ucc.ie/hfrg/) questionnaires are available commercially as a service, on a per report basis or for purchase, including scoring and report-generating software.
[3]http:/www.usabilitynet.org/tools/r_questionnaire.htm.

Web evaluation questionnaires:

- Website Analysis and MeasureMent Inventory (WAMMI) is "a short but very reliable questionnaire that tells you what your visitors think about your website" Human Factor Research Group (2010).

Multimedia system evaluation questionnaires:

- Measuring the Usability of Multi-Media Systems (MUMMS) is a questionnaire "designed for evaluating quality of use of multimedia software products" Human Factor Research Group (1996).

Evaluation questionnaires that address emotional impact:

- The Lavie and Tractinsky (2004) questionnaire.
- The Kim and Moon (1998) questionnaire with differential emotions scale.

24.3.2.8 Modifying questionnaires for your evaluation

As an example of adapting a data collection technique, you can make up a questionnaire of your own or you can modify an existing questionnaire for your own use by:

- Choosing a subset of the questions.
- Changing the wording in some of the questions.
- Adding questions of your own to address specific areas of concern.
- Using different scale values.

On any questionnaire that does not already have its scale values centered on zero, you might consider making the scale something such as $-2, -1, 0, 1, 2$ to center it on the neutral value of zero. If the existing scale has an odd number of rating points, you can change it to an even number to force respondents to choose one side or the other of a middle value, but that is not essential here.

Finally, one of the downsides of any questionnaire based only on semantic differential scales is that it does not allow the participant to give indications of *why* any rating is given, which is important for understanding what design features work and which ones don't and how to improve designs. Therefore, we recommend you consider adding to each question a free-form space, labeled as "If notable, please describe why you gave that rating."

24.3.2.9 Modifying the Questionnaire for User Interface Satisfaction

We have found an adaptation of the QUIS to work well. In this adaptation, we reduce the granularity of the scale from 12 choices (0–10 and NA) to 6 (−2, −1, 0, 1, 2, and NA) for each question, reducing the number of choices faced by the participant. We felt a midscale value of zero was an appropriately neutral value while negative scale values corresponded to negative user opinions and positive scale values corresponded to positive user opinions.

24.3.2.10 Modifying the System Usability Scale

In the course of their study of SUS, Bangor et al. (2008) provided an additional useful item for the questionnaire that you can use as an overall quality question, based on an adjective description. Getting away from the "strongly disagree" and "strongly agree" anchors, this adjective rating statement is: "Overall, I would rate the user-friendliness of this product as worst imaginable, awful, poor, ok, good, excellent, or best imaginable."

Not caring for the term "user-friendliness," we would add the recommendation to change that phrase to something else such as "usability" or "UX quality." In studies by Bangor et al. (2008), ratings assigned to this one additional item correlated well with scores of the original 10 items in the questionnaire. So, for the ultimate in inexpensive evaluation, this one questionnaire item could be used as a soft estimator of SUS scores.

If you are concerned about questionnaire validity, see Section 21.4.1.3.

24.3.3 Methods and Techniques for Generating and Collecting Emotional Impact and Meaningfulness Data

In this section we describe a series of techniques for collecting data about emotional impact and meaningfulness, given in order of increasing specialization. You may never need to use some of the more painstaking of these techniques in your practice of UX evaluation, but they are here for completeness.

24.3.4 The Most Important Technique: Direct Observation

Before looking to the upcoming more specialized techniques for emotional impact and meaningfulness, your best practical approach is to pick up on indications of emotional impact and meaningfulness during your regular use of critical incident identification and think-aloud techniques.

In contrast to self-reporting techniques, UX practitioners can obtain emotional impact indicator data through direct observation of participant physiological responses to emotional impact encounters as usage occurs. Usage can be teeming with user behaviors that indicate emotional impact, including gestures and facial expressions, such as ephemeral grimaces or smiles; and body language, such as tapping of fingers, fidgeting, or scratching one's head.

You will identify emotional impact through its indicators: "verbal and nonverbal languages, facial expressions, behaviors, and so on" (Shih and Liu, 2007, citing Dormann, 2003). For a "Usability Test Observation Form," a comprehensive list of verbal and nonverbal behaviors to be noted during observation, see Tullis and Albert (2008, p. 170).

One difficulty in any observation or measurement of physiological reactions to usage events is that often there is no way to connect the physiological response to a particular emotion and its cause within the interaction.

For more on direct observation of physiological responses as indicators of emotional impact, see Section 28.8.1.

24.3.5 Verbal Self-Reporting Techniques for Collecting Emotional Impact Data

Beyond observing indicators of emotional impact and meaningfulness in your usual qualitative data collection, the more commonly used and less complex techniques involve indicators that are self-reported via verbal techniques such as the think-aloud technique or questionnaires.

24.3.5.1 Using the think-aloud technique to evaluate emotional impact

We have already talked about using the think-aloud technique for capturing the participant's view of interaction, critical incidents, and UX problems. The think-aloud technique can also be excellent as a window into the mind of the user with respect to emotional feelings as they occur. Because user think-aloud is a kind of self-reporting technique, we add some detail here.

Depending on the nature of the interaction, emotional impact indicators may be infrequent in the flow of task performance user actions, and you may see them mainly as a by-product of your hunt for other UX problem indicators. So, when you do encounter an emotional impact indicator during observation in task performance, you certainly should make a note of it. You can also make emotional impact factors the primary focus during the think-aloud technique:

- When you explain the concept of thinking aloud, be sure participants understand that you want to include emotional feelings resulting from interaction and usage.

- Explain that this means you will expect them to share their emotions and feelings while they work and think by talking about them to you.
- As you did when you used the think-aloud technique to capture qualitative UX data, you may wish to begin with a little exercise to be sure participants are on the same page about the technique.
- As before, you will mainly capture think-aloud data by written or typed notes.
- Also, as before, you may have to remind participants occasionally to keep the thinking aloud flowing.

During the flow of interaction:

- You can direct participants to focus their thinking aloud on comments about joy of use, aesthetics, fun, and so on.
- You should observe and note the more obvious manifestations of emotional impact, such as expressions like "I love this" and "this is really cool" and "wow" expressions, annoyances, or irritation.
- You should be sensitive to detecting when emotional impact goes flat, when there is no real joy of use; ask participants about it in terms of causes and how it can be improved.

Finally, a caution about cultural dependency. Most emotions themselves are pretty much the same across cultures, and nonverbal expressions of emotion, such as facial expressions and gestures, are fairly universal. But cultural and social factors can govern an individual's willingness to communicate about emotions. Different cultures may also have different vocabularies and different perspectives on the meaning of emotions and the appropriateness of sharing and revealing them to others.

24.3.5.2 Questionnaires as a self-reporting technique for collecting emotional impact data

Questionnaires about emotional impact allow you to pose to participants probing questions based on any of the emotional impact factors, such as joy of use, fun, and aesthetics, offering a way for users to express their feelings about this part of the user experience.

Being subjective, quantitative, and product independent, questionnaires as a self-reporting technique have the advantages of being easy to use for both practitioners and users as well as being inexpensive, applicable from the earliest design sketches and mockups to fully operational systems, and high in face validity, which means that intuitively they seem as though they should work (Westerman, Gardner, and Sutherland, 2006).

24.3.5.3 The AttrakDiff questionnaire as a verbal self-reporting technique for collecting emotional impact data

AttrakDiff (now AttrakDiff2), developed by Hassenzahl, Burmester, and Koller (2003), is an example of a questionnaire based on Likert (semantic differential) scales especially developed for getting at user perceptions of emotional impact.

Reasons for considering the AttrakDiff questionnaire include:

- AttrakDiff is freely available.
- AttrakDiff is short and easy to administer, and the verbal scale is easy to understand (Hassenzahl, Beu, and Burmester, 2001; Hassenzahl, Platz, Burmester, and Lehner, 2000).
- AttrakDiff is backed with research and statistical validation; although only the German-language version of AttrakDiff was validated, there is no reason to believe that the English version will not also be effective.
- AttrakDiff has a track record of successful application.

Example: AttrakDiff Questionnaire and a Variation of Same

With permission, here we show the full AttrakDiff questionnaire as taken from Hassenzahl, Schöbel, and Trautman (2008, Table 1), with semantic anchors for each scale item:

- Pragmatic Quality 1: Comprehensible—Incomprehensible.
- Pragmatic Quality 2: Supporting—Obstructing.
- Pragmatic Quality 3: Simple—Complex.
- Pragmatic Quality 4: Predictable—Unpredictable.
- Pragmatic Quality 5: Clear—Confusing.
- Pragmatic Quality 6: Trustworthy—Shady.
- Pragmatic Quality 7: Controllable—Uncontrollable.
- Hedonic Quality 1: Interesting—Boring.
- Hedonic Quality 2: Costly—Cheap.
- Hedonic Quality 3: Exciting—Dull.
- Hedonic Quality 4: Exclusive—Standard.
- Hedonic Quality 5: Impressive—Nondescript.
- Hedonic Quality 6: Original—Ordinary.
- Hedonic Quality 7: Innovative—Conservative.
- Appeal 1: Pleasant—Unpleasant.
- Appeal 2: Good—Bad.
- Appeal 3: Aesthetic—Unaesthetic.
- Appeal 4: Inviting—Rejecting.
- Appeal 5: Attractive—Unattractive.
- Appeal 6: Sympathetic—Unsympathetic.
- Appeal 7: Motivating—Discouraging.
- Appeal 8: Desirable—Undesirable.

Across the many versions of AttrakDiff that have been used and studied, there are broad variations in the number of questionnaire items, the questions used, and the language for expressing the questions (Hassenzahl et al., 2000). Schrepp, Held, and Laugwitz (2006) developed a variation, reordered to group related items together.

24.3.5.4 Scoring ATTRAKDIFF questionnaires

Once an AttrakDiff questionnaire has been administered to participants, it is time to calculate the average scores. Begin by adding all the values given by the participant, excluding all unanswered questions. If you used a numeric scale of 1–7 between the anchors for each question, the total will be in the range of 1–7 times the number of questions the participant answered.

For example, because there are 22 questions, as shown by the sample AttrakDiff questionnaire items above, the total summed-up score will be in the range of 22–154 if all questions were answered. If you used a scale from −3 to + 3 centered on zero, the range for the sum of 22 question scores would be −66 to +66. The final result for the questionnaire is the average score per question.

24.3.5.5 Alternatives to AttrakDiff

Hassenzahl, Beu, and Burmester

As an alternative to the AttrakDiff questionnaire, Hassenzahl et al. (2001) have created a simple questionnaire of their own for evaluating emotional impact, also based on semantic differential scales. Their scales have the following easy-to-apply anchors (from their Fig. 1):

- Outstanding versus second rate.
- Exclusive versus standard.
- Impressive versus nondescript.
- Unique versus ordinary.
- Innovative versus conservative.
- Exciting versus dull.
- Interesting versus boring.

Like AttrakDiff, each scale in this questionnaire has seven possible ratings, including these end points, and the words were originally in German.

PrEmo

Verbal emotion measurement instruments, such as questionnaires, can assess mixed emotions because questions and scales in a questionnaire or images in pictorial tools can be made to represent sets of emotions (Desmet, 2003). PrEmo, developed by Desmet, uses seven animated pictorial representations of pleasant emotions and seven unpleasant ones. Desmet concludes that "PrEmo is a satisfactory, reliable emotion measurement instrument in terms of applying it across cultures."

There is a limitation, however. Verbal instruments tend to be language dependent and, sometimes, culture dependent. For example, the vocabulary for different dimensions of a questionnaire and their end points is difficult to translate precisely. Pictorial tools can be the exception, as the language of pictures is more universal. Pictograms of facial expressions can sometimes express emotions elicited more effectively than verbal expression, but the question of how to draw the various pictograms most effectively is still an unresolved research challenge.

Self-Assessment Manikin

An example of another emotional impact measuring instrument is the Self-Assessment Manikin (SAM) (Bradley and Lang, 1994). SAM contains nine symbols indicating positive emotions and nine indicating negative emotions. Often used for websites and print advertisements, the SAM is administered during or immediately after user interaction. One problem with application after usage is that emotions can be fleeting and perishable.

24.3.6 Direct Detection of Physiological Responses as Indicators of Emotional Impact

Beyond direct observation or self-reporting, there is a genre of techniques, called biometrics, for detecting emotional impact by directly measuring physiological responses in participants. These nonverbal techniques, which usually entail deploying probes and instrumentation, are beyond what almost any UX design project needs or wants and are almost exclusively in the realm of UX research. For a discussion of physiological measurements, see Section 28.8.2.

24.3.7 Generating and Collecting Meaningfulness Evaluation Data

Meaningfulness, or long-term emotional impact, occurs when users invite the product into their lives, giving it a presence in daily activities.

As an example of a product with a presence in someone's life, we know someone who carries a digital voice recorder in his pocket everywhere he goes. He uses it to capture thoughts, notes, and reminders for just about everything. He keeps it at his bedside while sleeping and always has it in his car when driving. It is an essential part of his lifestyle. He feels lost without it.

If it is a goal to understand the meaningfulness of a product, its adoption into human lifestyles, and how it impacts user lives over long periods of time, you should plan ways to study these phenomena situated in the real activities of users over time from the earliest thinking about the product to adoption into their lifestyles. Most choices for data collection techniques will include some kind of self-reporting by users, because you will not be able to be with your participants all the time.

As you collect data, you will be looking for indicators of all the different ways your users involve the product in their lives; the high points of joy in use; how the basic mode of usage changes, evolves, or emerges over time; and especially how usage is adapted to emerge as new and unusual kinds of usage. As we said earlier, you want to be able to tell stories of usage and emotional impact over time.

24.3.7.1 Long-term studies to evaluate meaningfulness

As users experience a product over time, they build perceptions and judgment through exploration and learning as usage expands and emerges (Thomas and Macredie, 2002). Thus, meaningfulness is not about tasks but about human activities. So, naturally, meaningfulness must be studied longitudinally and not just in the snapshots of usage that you might be used to observing in other kinds of UX evaluation.

The timeline defining meaningfulness within the user experience starts even before first meeting the product, perhaps with the desire to own or use the product, researching the product and comparing similar products, visiting a store (physical or online), shopping for it, and beholding the packaging and product presentation. By the time long-term meaningfulness studies are done, they really end up being case studies. The length of these studies does not necessarily mean large amounts of person hours, but it can mean significant calendar time. Therefore, the technique will not fit with an agile method or any other approach based on a short turnaround time.

It is clear that methods for studying and evaluating the meaningfulness aspects of usage must be situated in the real activities of users to encounter a broad range of user experiences occurring "in the wild." This means that you cannot just schedule a session, bring in user participants, have them "perform," and take your data. Rather, this deeper importance of context usually means collecting data in the field rather than in the lab.

The iPad is an example of a device that illustrates how usage can expand over time. At first it might be mostly a novelty to play with and to show friends.

Then the user will add some applications, let us say the *iBird Explorer: An Interactive Field Guide to Birds of North America.*[4] Suddenly usage is extended out to the deck and perhaps eventually into the woods.

Finally, of course, the user will start loading it up with all kinds of music and books on audio. This latter usage activity, which might come along after several months of product ownership, could become the most fun and most enjoyable part of the whole usage experience.

24.3.7.2 Goals of meaningfulness data collection techniques

Regardless of which technique is used for data collection about meaningfulness, the objective is to look for occurrences within long-term usage that are indicators of:

- Ways people tend to use the product.
- High points of joy in use, revealing what it is in the design that yields joy of use and opportunities to make it even better.
- Problems and difficulties people have in usage that interfere with a high-quality user experience.
- Usage people want but is not supported by the product.
- How the basic mode of usage changes, evolves, or emerges over time.
- How their original impressions and expectations of the product evolve over time, and why.
- How usage is adapted; new and unusual kinds of usage people come up with on their own.
- How important the product has become in the life of the user.

The idea is to be able to tell stories of usage and emotional impact over time.

24.3.7.3 Direct observation and interviews in simulated real usage situations

Before we get into the techniques of self reporting, triggered reporting, and periodic questionnaires as ways of sampling meaningfulness within usage activity, let's look at a more direct approach. The analyst team can simulate real long-term usage within a series of direct observations and interviews. The idea is to meet with participant(s) periodically, each time setting up conditions to encourage episodes showing emotional impact to occur during these

---

[4]http:/www.ibird.com/.

observational periods. The primary techniques for data collection during these simulated real usage sessions are direct observation and interviews. You will need to create conditions to encourage episodes of long-term usage activity to occur during these observational periods. The idea is to set up conditions so you can capture the essence of real usage and reflect real usage in a tractable time frame.

As an example of using this technique, Petersen, Madsen, and Kjaer (2002) conducted a longitudinal study of the use of a TV and video recorder by two families in their own homes. During the time of usage, periodic interviews were scheduled in the analysts' office, except in cases where users had difficulty in getting there and, then, the interviews were conducted in the users' homes. Within these interviews, the evaluators posed numerous usage scenarios and had the participants do their best to enact the usage while giving their feedback, especially about emotional impact. The idea is to set up conditions so that you can capture the essence of real usage and reflect real usage in a tractable time frame.

Here are some tips for success with this approach:

- Establish the interview schedule to take into account learning through usage by implementing a sequence of sessions longitudinally over time.
- As in usage research, it is necessary to observe user activities in addition to asking about them; as we know, the way people talk about what they do is often not the same as what they actually do.
- If you must make video recordings, be cautious and discreet in more private settings (such as the participant's home) usually found in this kind of usage context.

24.3.7.4 The importance of self-reporting

The best raw meaningfulness data would come from constant attention to the user and usage, but it is not possible to live with a participant 24/7 and be in all the places that a busy life takes a participant. Even if you could be with the participant all the time, you would find that most of the time you will observe just dead time when nothing interesting or useful is happening or when the participants are not even using the product. When events of interest do happen, they tend to be episodic, requiring special techniques to capture meaningfulness data.

But, in fact, the only ones who can be there all the times and places where usage occurs are the participants themselves. Therefore, most of the collection techniques for meaningfulness data are self-reporting techniques or at least have self-reporting components—the participants report on their own activities, thoughts, emotions, problems, and kinds of usage. Self-reporting techniques are not as objective as direct observation, but they do offer practical solutions to the problems of accessing data that occur in your absence.

24.3.7.5 Periodic questionnaires to sample meaningfulness

Another way you could choose to sample data about meaningfulness is by periodic questionnaires over time. You can use a series of such questionnaires to elicit understanding of major changes in usage over those time periods.

Questionnaires can be used efficiently with a large number of participants and can yield both quantitative and qualitative data. This is a less costly method that can get answers to predefined questions, but it cannot be easily used to give you a window into the more revealing details of usage in context to reveal growth and emergence of use over time.

24.3.7.6 Diary-based self-reporting by users

We encourage you to improvise a self-reporting technique yourself, but you should definitely consider a diary-based technique in which each participant maintains a "diary," documenting problems, experiences, and occurrences of meaningfulness within usage. Diaries can be kept via paper and pencil notes, online reports, cell-phone messages, or voice recorders. Diaries are an effective and efficient technique for meaningfulness data collection, but analysis of the data can take time and effort.

For a diary-based technique to be effective, participants must be primed in advance:

- Give your users a list of the kinds of things to report, including problems, experiences, and occurrences of meaningfulness within long-term usage.
- Give them some practice exercises in identifying relevant situations and reporting on them.
- Get them to internalize the need to post a report whenever they confront a usage problem, use a new feature, or encounter anything interesting or fun within usage.

There are many ways to facilitate this kind of data capture within self-reporting, including:

- Paper and pencil notes.
- Online reporting, such as in a blog.
- Cellphone voicemail messages.
- Pocket digital voice recorder.

24.3.7.7 Voicemail to capture user reports

Because of its flexibility and convenience and the ability of a user to make a phone call at almost any time, the use of voicemail is a meaningfulness data collection technique to consider for self-reporting on usage.

In one study (Petersen et al., 2002), phone reporting proved more successful than paper diaries because it could occur in the moment and had a much lower incremental effort for the participant. The key to this success is readiness at hand.

A mobile phone can be kept ready to use at all times. Participants don't need to carry paper forms and a pen or pencil and can make the calls any time day or night and under conditions not conducive to writing reports by hand. Cellphones keep users in control during reporting; they can control the amount of time they devote to each report.

To encourage participants to use voicemail for reporting, consider paying them a per-call monetary compensation (in addition to whatever payment you give them for participating in the study). In the Palen and Salzman (2002) study, they found that a per-call payment encouraged participants to make calls. There is a possibility, however, that this incentive might bias participants into making some unnecessary calls, but that did not seem to happen in this study.

As Palen and Salzman (2002) learned, the mobile phone voicemail method of data collection over time is also low in cost for analysts. Unlike paper reports, recorded voice reports are available immediately after their creation and systematic transcription is fairly easy. They found that unstructured verbal data from voicemails supplemented their other data very well and helped explain some of the observations or measurements they made.

These verbal reports, made at the crucial time following an incident, often mentioned issues that users forgot to bring up in later interviews, making voicemail reports a rich source of issues to follow up on in subsequent in-person interviews.

If a mobile phone is not an option for self-reporting, a compact and portable handheld digital voice recorder is a viable alternative. If you can train the participants to carry it essentially at all times, a dedicated personal digital recorder is an effective and low-cost tool for self-reporting usage phenomena in a long-term study.

24.3.7.8 Evaluator-triggered reporting to control timing

Regardless of the reporting medium, there is still the question of when the self-reporting is to be done during meaningfulness evaluation. If you allow the participant to decide when to report, it could bias reporting toward times when it is convenient or times when things are going well with the product, or the participant might forget and you will lose opportunities to collect data.

You might choose to trigger reporting to control the timing of self-reporting to make it a bit more randomly timed and according to your choice of frequency. This approach to timing could result in a more random sampling of the occurrence of meaningfulness within long-term usage. Buchenau and Suri (2000) suggest that the participant be given a dedicated pager to carry at all times. You can then use the pager to signal randomly timed "events" to the participant "in the wild." As soon as possible after receiving the pager signal, the participant is to report on current or most recent product usage, including specific real-world usage context and any emotional impact being felt.

For other methods to evaluate emotional impact and meaningfulness, see Section 28.8.

24.4 PROCEDURES FOR EMPIRICAL DATA COLLECTION SESSIONS

24.4.1 Preliminaries with Participants

24.4.1.1 Introduce yourself and the lab: Be sure participants know what to expect

Informed Consent

A formal and signed permission given to UX professionals by usage research and evaluation participants to use the data gathered within the UX lifecycle activities, usually with certain stipulated limits (Section 23.7.3).

If you have a separate reception room in your UX facility, this is where you meet your participants before getting down to business with evaluation. Greet and welcome each participant and thank him or her for helping. Bring them in and show them around.

Introduce them to the setup and show them the lab. If you have one-way glass, explain it and how it will be used and show them the other side—what happens "behind the curtain." Openly declare any video recording you will do, which should have been explained in the consent form, too. Make participants feel that they are partners in this endeavor.

Tell your participants all about the design being evaluated and about the process in which they are participating. For example, you might say "We have early screen designs for our product in the form of a low-fidelity prototype of a new system for …" Tell them how they can help and what you want them to do.

Do your best to relieve anxiety and satisfy curiosity. Be sure that your participants have all their questions about the process answered before you proceed into evaluation. Make it very clear that they are helping you evaluate and you are not evaluating them in any way.

24.4.1.2 Paperwork

While still in the reception room or as soon as the user has entered the participant room:

- Have each participant read the general instructions (Section 23.7.4.1) and explain anything verbally, as needed.
- Have the participant read the institutional review board consent form (Section 23.7.3.2) and explain the consent form verbally as well.
- Have the participant sign the consent form (two copies); it must be signed "without duress." You keep one signed copy and give the participant the other signed copy; your copy must be retained for at least three years (the period may vary by organization).
- Have the participant sign a nondisclosure form (Section 23.7.4.2), if needed.
- Have the participant fill out any demographic survey you have prepared (to ensure they meet the requirements of your intended work activity role and corresponding user class characteristics).

24.4.2 Session Protocol and Your Relationship with Participants

Session protocol is about the mechanical details of session setup, your relationship with participants, and how you handle them throughout each session.

24.4.2.1 Your attitude toward UX problems

Before you actually do evaluation, it is easy to agree that this UX testing is a positive thing and we are all working together to improve the design. However, once you start hearing about problems participants are having with the design, it can trigger unhelpful reactions in your ego, instincts, and pride and you might feel inclined to be defensive about the design. Resist that temptation and proceed in your testing with a positive attitude; it will pay off.

24.4.2.2 Cultivating a partnership with participants

Take the time to build rapport with your participants. More important to the success of your UX evaluation sessions than facilities and equipment is the relationship you establish with participants as partners in helping you evaluate and improve the product design. Once in the participant room, the facilitator should take a little time to "socialize" with the participant. If you have taken the participant on a "tour" of your facilities, that will have been a good start.

If you are using codiscovery techniques, allow some time for codiscovery partners to get to know each other and do a little bonding, perhaps while you are

Codiscovery

A qualitative data collection technique employing two or more participants interacting in a team approach to evaluation, usually with a think-aloud data collection technique. Two people can verbalize more naturally, yielding multiple viewpoints expressed within conversational interplay (Sections 21.4.2.3 and 24.2.3.3).

setting things up. Starting the session as total strangers can make them feel awkward and can interfere with their performance.

24.4.3 Prepare Yourself for Evaluating with Low-Fidelity Prototypes

If your wireframe prototype deck is printed on paper, lay it out, and have it ready to go (see example in Fig. 24-2). If your wireframe prototype deck is on a laptop, have it ready to operate (by you or by the user participant). We'll describe the process in terms of a paper wireframe prototype deck but it works the same way on a laptop.

Before each participant enters, the "executor" should "boot up" the prototype by putting the initial "screen" (wireframe) on the table. Arrange everything necessary for running the prototype, including the deck of subsequent wireframes.

Have the whole evaluation team ready to assume their roles and be ready to carry them out in the session.

- Evaluation *facilitator*, to keep the session moving, to interact with participants, and to possibly take notes on critical incidents (pick a person who has leadership abilities and "people" skills).
- Mark each page of the wireframe deck with an identifier of its role in the expected interaction sequence; it also helps to mark each object within a wireframe with the identifier of the destination wireframe should the user make an action on that object.

Fig. 24-2

Typical setup with participant at the end of a table for evaluation with the prototype deck printed on paper.

- Prototype *executor*, to move through the wireframes in response to user actions (pick a person who knows the design well).
- User performance *timer*, to time participants performing tasks and/or count errors (to collect quantitative data)—the timer person may want to practice with a stopwatch a bit before getting into a real session.
- Critical incident note takers (for spotting and recording critical incidents and UX problems).

Review your own in-session protocol. Some of the "rules" we suggest include:

- Team members *must not coach* participants as they perform tasks.
- The executor *must not anticipate user actions* and especially must not give the correct computer response for a wrong user action. The person playing computer must respond only to what the user actually does!
- The person playing computer may not speak, make gestures, etc.
- You may not change the design on the fly, unless that is a declared part of your process.

24.4.4 The Data Collection Session
24.4.4.1 The session begins
If you are using benchmark tasks, after the preliminaries and when you both are ready to start, have the participant read the first benchmark or other task description and ask if there are any questions. If you are taking timing data, don't include the benchmark task reading time as part of the task.

Once the evaluation session is under way, interesting things can happen quickly. Data you need to collect may start arriving in a flood. It can be overwhelming, but, by being prepared, you can make it easy and fun, especially if you know what kinds of data to collect.

24.4.4.2 Interacting with participants during the session
Now is the time to administer the benchmark tasks and do critical incidents identification, use the user think-aloud technique, and apply what you have learned here about the data collection techniques. Gather up your lists of critical incidents, UX problems, and user performance measures, as appropriate.

The facilitator is responsible for ensuring that the session runs smoothly and efficiently. It is generally the job of the facilitator to listen and not talk. But at key junctures you might elicit important data, if it does not interfere with task timing or if you are focusing on qualitative data. You can ask brief questions, such as "What are you trying to do?" "What did you expect to happen when you clicked on the such-and-such icon?" "What made you think that approach would work?"

If you are focusing on qualitative data, the evaluator may also ask leading questions, such as "How would you like to perform that task?" "What would make that icon easier to recognize?" If you are using the "think-aloud" technique for qualitative data gathering, encourage the participant by prompting occasionally: "Remember to tell us what you are thinking as you go."

If participants show signs of stress or fatigue, give them a break. Let them leave the participant room, walk around, and/or have some refreshments. Don't be too uptight about the session schedule.

24.4.4.3 To help the participant or not to help the participant?

When using participants for the critical incident technique and/or the think-aloud technique, you may be asked by the participant for a hint to help decide what to do next. Sometimes when participants are not making progress, they can benefit from a hint to get them back on track, but direct help almost always works against the goals of the session. You want to see whether the *participant* can determine how to perform the task, so don't tell them how to do it. It's often best to lead them to answer their own questions.

For example, don't answer questions such as "Is this right?" or "What if I click on this?" directly, but by asking your own questions, directing them to think it through for themselves, asking back what they think will happen.

24.4.4.4 Keeping your participant at ease

Remind yourself and your whole team that you should never, never laugh at anything during a UX evaluation session. You may be in a control room and think you have a soundproof setup but laughter has a way of piercing the glass. Because participants cannot see people behind the glass, it is easy for participants to assume that someone is laughing at them.

If participants become visibly flustered, frustrated, "zoned out," or blame themselves continually for problems in task performance, they may be suffering from stress and you should intervene. Take a short break and reassure and calm them. If participants become so discouraged that they want to quit the entire session, there is little you can or should do but thank them, pay them, and let them go.

24.4.5 Wrapping Up an Evaluation Session
24.4.5.1 Postsession probing via interviews and questionnaires

Immediately after each session, ask probing questions to clear up any confusion you have about critical incidents or UX problems. Conduct postsession interviews and administrator questionnaires to capture user thoughts and feelings while they are fresh.

Facilitators often start with some kind of standard *structured interview*, asking a series of preplanned questions aimed at probing the participant's thoughts about the product and the user experience. A typical postsession interview might include, for example, the following general questions. "What did you like best about the interface?" "What did you like least?" "How would you change so-and-so?" An interesting question to ask is "What are the three most important pieces of information that you must know to make the best use of this interface?"

For example, in one design, some of the results of a database query were presented graphically to the user as a data plot, the data points of which were displayed as small circles. Because most users did not at first realize that they could get more information about a particular data point if they clicked on the corresponding circle, one very important piece of information users needed to know about the design was that they should treat a circle as an icon and that they could manipulate it accordingly. Find out if your users got this.

24.4.5.2 Reset for the next participant

After running an evaluation session with one participant, you should organize the wireframe prototype to be ready for the next participant.

For web-based evaluation, clear out the browser history and browser cache, delete temporary files, remove any saved passwords, and so on. For a software prototype, save and back up any data you want to keep. Then reset the prototype state and remove any artifacts introduced in the previous session.

Finally, give the participant(s) their pay, gifts, and/or premiums, thank them, and send them on their way.

24.5 RAPID EMPIRICAL METHODS FOR GENERATING AND COLLECTING QUALITATIVE UX EVALUATION DATA

Empirical methods can be time-consuming and expensive. So some methods have evolved that are still empirical but are specifically designed with shortcuts to speed them up.

24.5.1 The Rapid Iterative Testing and Evaluation (RITE) UX Evaluation Method
24.5.1.1 Introduction

The approach called RITE (Medlock, Wixon, Terrano, Romero, and Fulton, 2002; Medlock, Wixon, McGee, and Welsh, 2005), a fast user-based testing approach, is representative of the category of rapid empirical UX evaluation methods and is one of the best.

RITE employs a fast collaborative (team members and participants) test-and-fix cycle designed to pick the low-hanging fruit at relatively low cost. The whole team is involved in arriving at the results.

The defining feature of RITE is fast turnaround—fixing key UX problems as soon as they are identified. Immediately after the product is evaluated, the whole project team, including the participants, analyzes the problems and decides on which changes to make. Changes are then implemented straightaway. If warranted, another immediate iteration of testing and fixing might ensue.

Because changes are included in all testing that occurs after that point, further testing can determine the effectiveness of the changes—whether the problem is, in fact, fixed and whether the fix introduces any new problems. Fixing a problem immediately also gives access to any aspects of the product that could not be tested earlier because they were blocked by that problem.

In his inimitable Wixonian wisdom, our friend Dennis reminds us that, "In practice, the goal is to produce, in the quickest time, a successful product that meets specifications with the fewest resources while minimizing risk" (Wixon, 2003).

24.5.1.2 How to do it: The RITE UX evaluation method

This description of the RITE UX evaluation method is based mainly on Medlock et al. (2002, 2005).

The project team starts by selecting a UX practitioner, whom we call the facilitator, to direct the testing session. The UX facilitator and the team prepare by:

- Identifying the characteristics needed in participants.
- Deciding on which tasks they will have the participants perform.
- Agreeing on critical tasks, the set of tasks that every user must be able to perform.
- Constructing a test script based on those tasks.
- Deciding how to collect qualitative user behavior data.
- Recruiting participants (Section 23.6) and scheduling them to come into the lab.

The UX facilitator and the team conduct the evaluation session with one to three participants, one at a time:

- Gathering the entire project team and any other relevant project stakeholders, either in the observation room of a UX lab or around a table in a conference room.
- Bringing in the participant playing the role of user.
- Introducing everyone and setting the stage, explaining the process and expected outcomes.

- Making sure that everyone knows the participant is helping evaluate the system and the team is not in any way evaluating the participant.
- Having the participant perform a small number of selected tasks while all project stakeholders observe silently.
- Having the participants think aloud as they work.
- Working together with the participants to find UX problems and ways the design should be improved.
- Taking thorough notes on problem indicators, such as task blocking and user errors.
- Focusing session notes on finding usability problems and noting their severity.

The UX facilitator and other UX practitioners:

- Identify from session notes the main UX problems observed and their causes in the design.
- Give everyone on the team the list of UX problems and causes.

The UX practitioner and the team, including the participants, address problems:

- Identifying problems with obvious causes and obvious solutions, such as those involving wording or labeling, to be fixed first.
- Determining which other problems can also reasonably be fixed.
- Determining which problems need more discussion.
- Determining which problems require more data (from more participants) to be sure they are real problems.
- Sorting out which problems they cannot afford to fix right now.
- Deciding on feasible solutions for the problems to be addressed.
- Implementing fixes for problems with obvious causes and obvious solutions.
- Starting to implement other fixes and bringing them into the current prototype as soon as feasible.

The UX practitioner and the team immediately conduct follow-up evaluation by:

- Bringing in new participants.
- Having them perform the tasks associated with the fixed problems, using the modified design.
- Working with the participants to see if the fixes worked and to be sure the fixes did not introduce any new UX problems.

The entire process just described is repeated until you run out of resources or the team decides it is done (all major problems found and addressed).

24.5.1.3 Variations in RITE data collection

The flexibility of RITE allows consideration of alternative data collection techniques. For example, instead of testing with user participants, the team could employ a UX inspection method, heuristic evaluation, or otherwise for data collection while retaining the fast analysis and fixing parts of the cycle.

24.5.2 Quasiempirical UX Evaluation

Quasiempirical UX evaluation methods are hybrid approaches arising when UX professionals develop their own methods with shortcuts. They are empirical because they involve data collection using participants or participant surrogates. But they are "quasi" because they are informal and flexible with respect to process and protocol and the UX evaluator can play a significant analytic role.

24.5.2.1 Introduction to quasiempirical UX evaluation

Quasiempirical UX evaluation methods:

- Are still empirical, using volunteer participants (or an evaluator emulating a user).
- Are defined by the freedom given to the practitioner to innovate, to make it up as they go while being flexible about goals and approaches.
- Are very informal with respect to protocol—evaluators are encouraged to interrupt and intervene at opportune moments to elicit more thinking aloud and to ask for explanations and specifics.
- Do not involve any quantitative data.
- Can take place anywhere—UX lab, conference room, office, cafeteria, in the field.
- Are often punctuated with impromptu changes of pace, changes of direction, and changes of focus.
- Are characterized by jumping on issues as they arise and milking them to get the most information about problems, their effects on users, and potential solutions.
- Are not based on predefined "benchmark tasks," but a session can be task-driven, drawing on usage scenarios, essential use cases, step-by-step task interaction models, or other task data or task models.
- Can be driven by exploration of features, screens, widgets, or whatever suits.

24.5.2.2 Preparing for a quasiempirical evaluation session

Begin by ensuring that you have a set of representative, frequently used, and mission-critical tasks for your participants to explore. Have some exploratory questions ready.

Assign your UX evaluation team roles effectively, including participant, facilitator, and data collectors. If useful, try two evaluators for codiscovery. Further prepare for your quasiempirical session the same way you would for a full empirical session, only less formally and less thoroughly, to match the more rapid and more opportunistic nature of the quasiempirical approach.

24.5.2.3 Conduct a quasiempirical session, collecting data

As you, the facilitator, sit with each participant:

- Cultivate a partnership with the participant; you get the best results from working closely in collaboration.
- Make extensive use of the think-aloud data collection technique; encourage the participant by prompting occasionally: "Remember to tell us what you are thinking as you go."
- Encourage the participant to explore the system for a few minutes and get familiarized with it.
- Use some of the tasks that you have at hand, from the preparation step given earlier, more or less as props to support the action and the conversation; you are not interested in user performance times or other quantitative data.
- Work together with the participant to find UX problems and ways the design should be improved; take thorough notes—they are the sole raw data from the process.
- Let the user choose some tasks to do.
- Be ready to follow threads that arise rather than just following prescripted activities.
- Listen as much as you can to the participant; most of the time it is your job to listen, not talk.
- It is also your job to lead the session, which means saying the right thing at the right time to keep it on track and to switch tracks when useful.

At any time during the session, you can interact with the participant with questions such as:

- Ask participants to describe initial reactions as they interact with this system.
- Ask what parts of the design are not clear and why.
- Inquire about how the system compares with others they have used in the past.
- Ask if they have any suggestions for changing the designs.
- To place them in the context of their own work, ask them how they would use this system in their daily work; in other words, ask them to walk you through some tasks they would perform using this system in a typical workday.

Exercise 24-1: Empirical UX Evaluation Data Collection for Your System

Goal: To get a little practice in empirical data collection for a very simple formative UX evaluation using a wireframe prototype deck.

Activities: This is perhaps the most fun and most rewarding of all the exercises when you finally get to see some users in action with your UX design.

New team formation: This is described in terms of multiple teams in a classroom setting. For other setups, make appropriate adjustments.

- After all the teams are gathered and sitting around a table, make the switch of participants with another team. You send the two people in the participant role from your team to another team. Curb the potential confusion here by doing the swap in an orderly circular fashion among the teams.
- You will now have new participants from a different team who are unfamiliar with your design. These new participants are now permanently on your team for the rest of these exercises, including data collection, analysis, and reporting.
- As an alternative, if you do not have multiple teams, try recruiting a couple of coworkers or friends as participants.
- Sitting together in your newly formed teams, get out your UX target table form, your benchmark task descriptions, and your questionnaires.
- Dismiss your two participants (the new team members you just got) to the hallway or other waiting area.

Data collection:

- "Boot up" your prototype.
- Call in your first participant into the "lab," greet the participant, and explain the evaluation session.
- Have this first participant perform your first benchmark task for your UX targets. Have the participant read the first benchmark task aloud.
- Ask the participant to perform that task while thinking aloud.
- The executor moves prototype parts in response to participant actions.
- The facilitator directs the session and keeps it moving.
- Timer(s) writes down or enters timing and error count data as indicated in UX targets as the user performs the task (do not count participant's reading aloud of task in task timing).
- Everyone else available should be used to take notes on critical incidents and UX problems.
- Remember the rules about not coaching or anticipating user actions. And the computer may not speak!
- Have the participant read the second task aloud and ask any questions that might exist.
- Perform it.
- Be ready to collect data according to your UX targets.

- Have this first participant perform your second benchmark task while thinking aloud.
- How much data to collect? You need to collect a dozen or more critical incidents in this overall exercise (i.e., from both participants doing both benchmark tasks). If you do not get at least a half dozen from each participant, continue with that participant doing exploratory use of your prototype until you get enough critical incidents. For example, have them browse through each screen, looking at each object (button, menu, etc.), commenting on and giving their opinion about the quality of the user experience relating to various features.
- Have this participant complete your questionnaire and then give them their "reward."
- Keep your first participant as a new member of the rest of the team to help with observations.
- Bring in the second participant and perform the same session again.

Deliverables: All your data.

Schedule: Complete by end of class (about an hour and a half, if you are efficient).

Analytic UX Evaluation: Data Collection Methods and Techniques

25

- Design walk-throughs and reviews as early analytic evaluation methods.
- Focus groups.
- UX inspection.
- Heuristic evaluation.
- Our practical approach to UX inspection.

25.1 INTRODUCTION

25.1.1 You Are Here

We begin each process chapter with a "you are here" picture of the chapter topic in the context of The Wheel, overall UX design lifecycle template (Fig. 25-1). As an alternative approach to the empirical data collection methods of the previous chapter, this chapter is about analytic data collection methods.

25.1.2 Adding Analytic Methods to the Mix

Some projects, especially large domain-complex system projects, can benefit greatly from the potential for high rigor offered by empirical UX evaluation (Chapters 23 and 24).

For most other kinds of projects, analytic UX evaluation methods offer an alternative. Although analytic methods can be performed with high rigor and, therefore, less speed, they were developed as faster and less expensive methods to produce approximations to or predictors of empirical results.

Therefore, in practice, analytic methods tend to be more rapid and less expensive because you don't need to:

Analytic UX Evaluation

Evaluation methods based on examining inherent attributes of the design rather than seeing the design in use (Section 21.2.2).

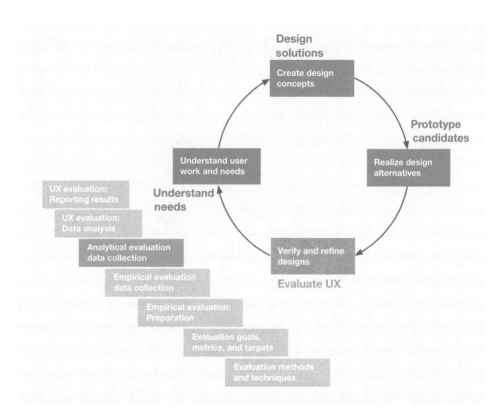

Fig. 25-1

You are here, in the chapter on analytic UX evaluation data collection within the Evaluate UX activity, in the context of the overall Wheel lifecycle process.

- Identify and recruit user participants.
- Schedule participant sessions and bring in participants (or go to visit them).
- Run long task-based evaluation sessions.

Analytic methods are based on deconstructing a UX design and examining its inherent attributes rather than seeing the design in use, producing primarily qualitative, subjective data. The analytic methods of this chapter, especially suitable for smaller fast-track projects, agile environments, and product development, include design reviews, design walk-throughs, and inspection methods, such as heuristic evaluation.

Here are some general characteristics of analytic evaluation methods:

- Because they are based on expert opinions rather than empirical usage data, they require experts in both UX and the subject-matter domain.
- They are aimed almost exclusively at finding the most important qualitative data, the UX problems that are cost-effective to fix.

- There is a heavy dependency on practical techniques.
- Usually they are less formal, with less protocol and fewer rules.
- There is much more variability in the process, with almost every evaluation "session" being different, tailored to the prevailing conditions.
- This freedom to adapt to conditions creates more room for spontaneous ingenuity, something experienced UX professionals do best.

In early stages of a project, your prototype may not be developed well enough for interacting with customers or users. Still, you can use design reviews, focus groups, and walk-throughs for early design evaluation.

Beyond these early approaches, when you have an interactive prototype, at least a click-through wireframe prototype, you will usually employ some variation of the UX inspection methods.

25.1.3 Criticism of Analytic Methods

Analytic UX evaluation methods, including most inspection methods, have been criticized In HCI literature of the past. Sometimes disparagingly called "discount methods," analytic methods have been criticized for not being thorough and for being unscientific. Although these two claims are, in fact, true, the rapid methods we discuss in this chapter are the result of simply trading off the thoroughness of high rigor for low cost and fast application. These methods are the bread and butter of agile UX practice. For more about "discount" evaluation methods, see Section 28.3.3.

25.2 DESIGN WALK-THROUGHS AND REVIEWS

25.2.1 Design Walk-Throughs

Design reviews and walk-throughs are not as deeply analytic as the UX inspection methods described later in this chapter, but we consider them as analytic methods because they are based on looking at design (as presented by the designers) rather than on empirical data from usage.

A design walk-through is an informal way to get initial reactions to design concepts. At this point you usually have only scenarios, storyboards, screen sketches, and/or some wireframes. So, you may have to do the "driving," if it's too early for anyone else in a user role to engage in real interaction.

Walk-throughs are an important way to get early feedback from the rest of the design team, customers, potential users, subject matter experts, and other stakeholders.

Inspection (UX)

An analytical evaluation method in which a UX expert evaluates an interaction design by looking at it or trying it out, sometimes in the context of a set of abstracted design guidelines. Expert evaluators are both participant surrogates and observers, asking themselves questions about what would cause users problems and giving an expert opinion predicting UX problems (Section 25.4).

Heuristic Evaluation

An analytic evaluation method based on expert UX inspection guided by a set of heuristics, general high-level UX design guidelines (Section 25.5).

Design Review

A slightly more comprehensive UX evaluation technique than design walkthroughs, usually done with click-through wireframe prototypes to demonstrate workflow and navigation. Often the primary evaluation method for task-level UX designs in the fast iteration of the late funnel (Section 25.2.2).

25.2.2 Design Reviews

Design reviews, a bit more advanced than early walk-throughs, tend to be a bit more comprehensive and are usually done with click-through wireframe prototypes to demo the workflow and navigation. Design reviews are often the primary evaluation method for task-level UX designs in the fast iteration of the late funnel. In this kind of use, the reviews often amount to a team-based UX inspection. And, even though these are click-through prototypes, they are usually not interactive enough to support someone else doing the clicking, so, again, usually you have to do the driving.

Memmel, Gundelsweiler, and Reiterer (2007, Table 8) declare that design reviews are less time-consuming and more cost-effective than participant-based testing, and that their flexibility and scalability mean the effort can be adjusted to match the needs of the situation.

The goal of a design walk-through or design review, as with almost any kind of analytic method, is to explore a design on behalf of users to simulate the user's view of moving through the design, but to see it with an expert's eye. The team is trying to anticipate problems that users might have if they were the ones using the design.

25.2.3 Prepare for a Design Review

Prepare for a design review or walk-through by doing these things:

- Test your prototype for completeness, consistency, glitches, flaws, inconsistencies, and breakdowns (don't use up other people's valuable time to fix your own mistakes).
- If useful, start with storyboards to illustrate flow.
- Have at hand descriptions of relevant users, work roles, and user classes.
- Practice with your design scenarios or user stories to drive the walk-through.
- Schedule the session with the appropriate users and stakeholders:
  - Set a beginning and end time.
  - Your UX studio is a good venue for this.
- Decide who will take the role of leader and who will run the prototype.
- Decide who will take the role of note-taker to record UX problems discovered and changes needed.

25.2.4 Conduct a Design Review Session

Informal session protocol can include:

- The leader introduces the design and its purpose and context.
- The leader does the clicking and navigation in a guided tour of the design in action:

- First, cover the main workflow and navigational paths.
- Then, cover edge cases, exceptions, error and recovery.
- Comments and discussion are invited from the entire group.
- The note-taker records UX problems discovered (this is data collection for this method).
  - Each note should be referenced to the wireframe numbers involved.
- End on time; stick to your announced end time (if you chronically allow sessions to run overtime, your group will be less likely to return and help with the many more design reviews yet to come).

To be realistic and engaging, UX evaluators explore early UX designs through the lens of usage or design scenarios. The leader walks the group through key workflow patterns that the system is intended to support.

As the team follows the scenarios, looking systematically at parts of the design and discussing the merits and potential problems, the leader tells stories about users and usage, user intentions and actions, and expected outcomes. The leader explains what the user will be doing, what the user might be thinking, and how the task fits in the work practice, workflow, and context. Other team members think about how well all of that might work for users. As potential UX problems arise, someone records them on a list for further consideration.

Reviews may also include considerations of compliance with design guidelines and style guides as well as questions about emotional impact, including aesthetics and fun. Beyond just the details of UX and other design problems that might emerge, it is a good way to communicate about the design and keep on the same page within the project.

25.2.5 After the Session

Make changes needed and update wireframes to fix the problems identified. Decide if enough has been changed to require you to reconvene the group for a follow-up review of the updated design.

25.3 FOCUS GROUPS

Focus groups, composed of a moderator and, say, a half-dozen other participants, are an analytic method for (in our practice) early evaluation of UX designs. As Martin and Hanington (2012) say, "The power of focus groups lies in the group dynamic that it creates." Group members share opinions and collaboratively discuss the pros and cons as peers. As the group members describe their experiences and feelings, they will tell stories and use metaphors and analogies. At the end of a session, the moderator leads the group in creating a summary of the discussion.

25.4 EXPERT UX INSPECTION

25.4.1 What is UX Inspection?

A UX inspection is an analytic evaluation method in that it involves evaluating by looking at and trying out the design yourself as a UX expert instead of having participants exercise it while you observe. The evaluator is both participant surrogate and observer. Inspectors ask themselves questions about what would cause users problems. So, the essence of these methods is the inspector giving an opinion predicting UX problems.

25.4.2 Inspection is a Valuable Tool in the UX Toolbox

UX professionals have been using UX inspection methods for years with great success. In our own practice, we now use it as our main go-to evaluation approach, falling back on empirical methods only when we need more rigor. UX inspection is especially useful:

- When applied in early stages and early design iterations.
- When you are brought in to evaluate an existing system that has not undergone previous UX evaluation and iterative redesign.
- When you cannot afford or cannot do empirical testing for some reason but still want to do *some* evaluation.

UX inspection can still do a good job for you when you do not have the time or other resources for a rigorous empirical evaluation (which, these days, is most of the time). However, there is a tradeoff, in that there will always be some UX problems showing up in real live user-based interaction that you will not see in an inspection or design review.

25.4.3 How Many Inspectors are Needed?

In empirical UX testing, you can improve evaluation effectiveness by adding more participants until you get diminishing returns. Similarly, in UX inspection, to improve effectiveness, you can add more inspectors. A team approach is beneficial, maybe even necessary, because low individual problem detection rates preclude finding enough problems by one person.

Research and experience have shown that different evaluators (even experts) find different problems, and this diversity of skills is valuable because the union of problems found over a group of inspectors is usually much larger than the set of problems found by any individual. Most heuristic inspections are done by a team of UX inspectors, typically two or three inspectors.

But what is the optimal number? It depends on conditions and a great deal on the system you are inspecting. Nielsen and Landauer (1993) found that, under some conditions, a small set of experts, in the range of three to five, is optimal before diminishing returns. For further discussion about the "three-to-five-users" rule and its limitations, see Section 28.6.3. As a practical matter, as with almost any kind of evaluation, some is better than none. For early project stages, we often have to be satisfied with a single inspection by one or two inspectors working together.

25.4.4 What Kind of Inspectors are Needed?

Not surprisingly, Nielsen (1992) found that UX experts (UX practitioners or consultants) make the best inspection evaluators, which is why this kind of evaluation method is also sometimes called "expert evaluation" or "expert inspection" (Section 25.4).

Sometimes, it is best to get a fresh view by using an expert evaluator who is not on the project team. If those UX experts also have knowledge in the subject-matter domain of the interface being evaluated, all the better. Those people are called dual experts and can evaluate through both a design guidelines perspective and a work activity, workflow, and task perspective. The equivalent of having a dual expert can be approximated by pairing up a UX expert with a work domain expert.

25.5 HEURISTIC EVALUATION, A UX INSPECTION METHOD

Heuristic UX evaluation is an analytic evaluation method based on expert UX inspection in which the evaluator compares aspects of the design against a set of heuristics, general high-level UX design guidelines.

25.5.1 Introduction

As Nielsen (Nielsen, 1992; Nielsen & Molich, 1990) states, the heuristic evaluation (HE) method has the advantages of being inexpensive, intuitive, and easy to motivate practitioners to do, and it is effective for use early in the UX process. It is no surprise that, of all the inspection methods, the HE method is the best known and the most popular.

25.5.1.1 The heuristics

For a list of the original Molich and Nielsen heuristics (Molich & Nielsen, 1990; Nielsen & Molich, 1990), see Section 28.9. Following publication of the original heuristics, Nielsen enhanced the heuristics with a study based on factor analysis of a large number of real usability problems. The resulting refined heuristics (Nielsen, 1994) are these (from "10 Usability Heuristics for User Interface Design" by Jakob Nielsen (January 1, 1995; https://www.nngroup.com/articles/ten-usability-heuristics)):

1. Visibility of system status

    The system should always keep users informed about what is going on through appropriate feedback within reasonable time.

2. Match between system and the real world

    The system should speak the users' language, with words, phrases, and concepts familiar to the user rather than system-oriented terms. Follow real-world conventions, making information appear in a natural and logical order.

3. User control and freedom

    Users often choose system functions by mistake and will need a clearly marked "emergency exit" to leave the unwanted state without having to go through an extended dialogue. Support undo and redo.

4. Consistency and standards

    Users should not have to wonder whether different words, situations, or actions mean the same thing. Follow platform conventions.

5. Error prevention

    Even better than good error messages is a careful design that prevents a problem from occurring in the first place. Either eliminate error-prone conditions or check for them and present users with a confirmation option before they commit to the action.

6. Recognition rather than recall

    Minimize the user's memory load by making objects, actions, and options visible. The user should not have to remember information from one part of the dialogue to another. Instructions for use of the system should be visible or easily retrievable whenever appropriate.

7. Flexibility and efficiency of use

    Accelerators—unseen by the novice user—may often speed up the interaction for the expert user such that the system can cater to both inexperienced and experienced users. Allow users to tailor frequent actions.

8. Aesthetic and minimalist design

    Dialogues should not contain information that is irrelevant or rarely needed. Every extra unit of information in a dialogue competes with the relevant units of information and diminishes their relative visibility.

9. Help users recognize, diagnose, and recover from errors

    Error messages should be expressed in plain language (no codes), indicate the problem precisely, and suggest a solution constructively.

10. Help and documentation

    Even though it is better if the system can be used without documentation, it may be necessary to provide help and documentation. Any such information should be easy to search, focused on the user's task, list concrete steps to be carried out, and not be too large.

25.5.1.2 The procedure

Despite the large number of variations in practice, we endeavor to describe what roughly represents the "plain" or "standard" version. These inspection sessions can take from a couple of hours for small systems to several days for larger systems. Here is how to do it:

- The project team or manager selects a set of evaluators, typically three to five.
- The team selects a small, tractable set, about 10, of "heuristics," generalized and simplified design guidelines in the form of inspection questions, for example, "Does the interaction design use the natural language that is familiar to the target user?"
  - The set of heuristics given in the previous section are a good start.
- Each inspector individually browses through each part of the interaction design, asking the heuristic questions about that part and, for each heuristic question:
  - Assesses the compliance of each part of the design.
  - Notes places where a heuristic is violated as candidate usability problems.
  - Notes places where heuristics are supported (things done well).
  - Identifies the context of each instance noted previously, usually by capturing an image of the screen or part of the screen where the problem or good design feature occurs.
- All the inspectors get together and, as a team, they:
  - Merge their problem lists.
  - Select the most important ones to fix.
  - Brainstorm suggested solutions.
  - Decide on recommendations for the designers based on the most frequently visited screens, screens with the most usability problems, guidelines violated most often, and resources available to make changes.
  - Issue a group report.

A heuristic evaluation report should:

- Start with an overview of the system being evaluated.
- Give an overview explanation of inspection process.
- List the inspection questions based on heuristics used.

- ▪ Report on potential usability problems revealed by the inspection:
  - ▪ By heuristic: for each heuristic, give examples of design violations and of ways the design supports the heuristic.
  - ▪ Or by part of the design: for each part, give specific examples of heuristics violated and/or supported.
- ▪ Include as many illustrative screen images or other visual examples as possible.

The team then puts forward the recommendations they agreed on for design modifications, using language that will motivate others to want to make these changes. They highlight a realistic list of the "Top 3" (or 4 or 5) suggestions for modifications and prioritize suggestions, to give the biggest improvement in usability for the least cost (perhaps using the cost-importance analysis of Section 26.4).

25.5.1.3 Documenting UX problems

We have found it best to keep HE problem documentation simple. Long forms with lots of fields can capture more information, but tend to be tedious for UX professionals who have to deal with large numbers of problems. Table 25-1 is a simple HE data capture form that we have adapted, with permission, from one developed by Brad Myers.

Be specific and insightful; include subtlety and depth. Saying, "The system does not have good color choices because it does not use color," is pretty trivial and is not helpful. Also, if you evaluated a prototype, saying that functions are not implemented is obvious and unhelpful.

25.5.1.4 Variations abound

The one "constant" about the HE method and most other analytic methods is the variation with which they are used in practice. These methods are adapted and customized by almost every team that ever uses them usually in undocumented and unpublished ways.

Task-based or heuristic-based expert UX inspections can be conducted with just one evaluator or with two or more evaluators, each acting independently or all working together. Other expert UX inspections can be scenario-based, persona-based, checklist-based, or as a kind of "Can you break it?" test.

As an example of a variation that was described in the literature, participatory heuristic evaluation extends the HE method with additional heuristics to address broader issues of task and workflow, beyond just the design of user interface artifacts to "consider how the system can contribute to human goals and human

Table 25-1

Simple HE reporting form, adapted from Brad Myers

Heuristic Evaluation Report

Dated: mm/dd/yyyy

Prepared By: Name: Signature:

Problem number: 1

Name of heuristic violated or supported: Consistency

Prototype screen, page, location of problem:

Reason for reporting as negative or positive: Inconsistent placement of "Add to Cart" buttons: The "Add to Cart" button is below the item in CDW but above in CDW-G

Scope of problem: Every product page

Severity of problem (high/medium/low): Low—minor, cosmetic problem

Justification for severity rating: Unlikely that users will have trouble with finding or recognizing the button

Suggestions to fix: Move the button on one of the sites to be in the same place as on the other site

Possible tradeoffs (why fix might not work): This may result in an inconsistency with something else, but unknown what that might be

---

experience" (Muller, Matheson, Page, & Gallup, 1998, p. 16). The definitive difference in participatory HE is the addition of users, work domain experts, to the inspection team.

Sears (1997) extended the HE method with what he calls heuristic walk-throughs. Several lists are prepared and given to each practitioner doing the inspection: user tasks, inspection heuristics, and "thought-focusing questions." Each inspector performs two inspections, one using the tasks as a guide and supported by the thought-focusing questions. The second inspection is the more traditional kind, using the heuristics. Their studies showed that "heuristic walk-throughs resulted in finding more problems than cognitive walk-throughs and fewer false positives than heuristic evaluations."

Perspective-based usability inspection (Zhang, Basili, & Shneiderman, 1999) is another published variation on the HE method. Because a large system can present a scope too broad for any given inspection session, Zhang et al. (1999) proposed "perspective-based usability inspection," allowing inspectors to focus on a subset of usability issues in each inspection. The resulting focus of attention afforded a higher problem detection rate within that narrower perspective.

Examples of perspectives that can be used to guide usability inspections are novice use, expert use, and error handling. In their study, Zhang et al. (1999) found that their perspective-based approach did lead to significant improvement in detection of usability problems in a web-based application. Persona-based UX inspection is a variation on the perspective-based inspection in that it includes consideration of context of use via the needs of personas (Wilson, 2011).

As our final example, Cockton, Lavery, and Woolrych (2003) developed an extended problem-reporting format that improves heuristic inspection methods by finding and eliminating many of the false positives typical of the usability inspection approach. Their Discovery and Analysis Resource (DARe) model allows analysts to bring distinct discovery and analysis resources to bear to isolate and analyze false negatives as well as false positives.

25.5.1.5 Limitations

While a helpful guide for inexperienced practitioners, we find that heuristics usually get in the way of the experts. To be fair to the heuristic method, the heuristic method was intended as a kind of "scaffolding" to help novice practitioners do usability inspections, so it should not really be compared with expert usability inspection methods, anyway.

It was perhaps self-confirming when we read that others found the actual heuristics to be similarly unhelpful (Cockton et al., 2003; Cockton & Woolrych, 2001). In their studies, Cockton et al. (2003) found that it is experts who find problems with inspection, not experts using heuristics. Cockton and Woolrych (2002, p. 15) also claim that the "inspection methods do not encourage analysts to take a rich or comprehensive view of interaction." While this may be true for heuristic methods, it does not have to be true for all inspection methods.

A major drawback with any inspection method, including the HE method, is the danger that novice practitioners will get too comfortable with it and think the heuristics are enough for any evaluation situation. There are few indications in its usage that let the novice practitioner know when it is not working well, and when a different method should be tried.

Also, like all UX inspection methods, the HE method can generate numerous false negatives, situations in which inspectors identified "problems" that turned out to be not real problems or not very important UX problems. Finally, like most other analytic UX evaluation methods, the HE method is not particularly effective in finding usability problems below the surface—problems about sequencing and workflow.

25.6 OUR PRACTICAL APPROACH TO UX INSPECTION

We have synthesized existing UX inspection methods into a relatively simple and straightforward method that, unlike the heuristic method, is definitely for UX experts and not for novices. Sometimes, we have novices sit in and observe the process as a kind of apprentice training, but they do not perform these inspections on their own.

25.6.1 The Knock on Your Door

It is the boss. You, the UX professional, are being called in and asked to do a quick UX assessment of a prototype, an early product, or an existing product being considered for revision. You have 1 or 2 days to check it out and give feedback. You feel that if you can give some valuable feedback on UX flaws, you will gain some credibility and maybe get a bigger role in the project next time.

What method should you use? No time to go to the lab, and even the "standard" inspection techniques will take too long, with too much overhead. What you need is a practical, fast, and efficient approach to UX inspection. As a solution, we offer an approach that evolved over time in our own practice. You can apply this approach at almost any stage of progress, but it usually works better in the early stages. We believe that most real-world UX inspections are more like our approach than like the somewhat more elaborate techniques to inspection described in the literature.

25.6.2 Guided by Insight and Experience

We don't directly or explicitly use a list of heuristics to drive this kind of UX inspection. In our own industry and consulting experience, we have just not found specific heuristics as useful as we would like. We drive our inspection process with usage in context by focusing on tasks and work activities. But, we do, however, bring our expert knowledge of UX design guidelines (Chapter 32) to bear to decide what issues are real problems and to understand the underlying nature of the problems and potential solutions.

We like a usage-based approach because it allows the practitioner to better take on the role of user. Using this approach, and our UX intuition honed over the years, we can see, and even anticipate, UX problems, many of which might not have been revealed under the purely heuristic spotlight.

25.6.3 Use a Codiscovery or Team Approach in UX Inspection

Expert UX professionals as inspectors are in the role of "UX detectives." To aid the detective work, it can help to use two practitioners, working together as mutual sounding boards in a give-and-take interplay, potentiating each other's efforts to keep the juices flowing, to promote a constant flow of think-aloud comments from the inspectors, and to maintain a barrage of problem notes flying.

It is also often useful to team up with customers, users, designers, and other people familiar with the overall system, who can help make up for any lack of system knowledge on your part, especially if you have not been with the team during the entire project. Work domain experts can reinforce your user-surrogate role and bring in more subject-matter expertise (Muller et al., 1998).

25.6.4 Explore Systematically With a Rich and Comprehensive Usage-Oriented View

As an inspector, you should not just look for individual little problems associated with individual tasks or functions. Use all your experience and knowledge to see the big picture. Keep an expert eye on the high-level view of workflow, the overall integration of functionality, and emotional impact factors that go beyond usability.

Usage scenarios and design scenarios (Section 9.7.1) are fruitful places to look to focus on key user work roles and key user tasks that must be supported in the design.

25.6.5 Inspection is Driven by Tasks and by the Design Itself

Representative user tasks help us put ourselves in the users' shoes. By exploring the tasks ourselves and taking our own think-aloud data, we can imagine what real users might encounter in their usage. A hierarchical task inventory (Section 9.6) is helpful in attaining a good understanding of the task structure and ensuring broad coverage of the range of tasks.

Driving the inspection with the interaction design itself means trying all possible actions on all the user interface artifacts, trying out all user interface objects such as buttons, icons, and menus. It also means being opportunistic in following leads and hunches triggered by parts of the design.

How much time to spend? The time and effort required for a good inspection are more or less proportional to the size of the system (i.e., the number of user tasks, choices, and system functions). System complexity can have an even bigger impact on inspection time and effort.

Codiscovery

A qualitative data collection technique employing two or more participants interacting in a team approach to evaluation, usually with a think-aloud data collection technique. Two people can verbalize more naturally, yielding multiple viewpoints expressed within conversational interplay (Sections 21.4.2.3 and 24.2.3.3).

Emotional Impact

An affective component of user experience that influences user feelings. Includes such effects as enjoyment, pleasure, fun, satisfaction, aesthetics, coolness, engagement, and novelty and can involve deeper emotional factors such as self-expression, self-identity, a feeling of contribution to the world, and pride of ownership (Section 1.4.4).

Skills needed. The main skill you need for finding UX problems as you inspect the design is your detective's "eagle eye" for curious or suspicious incidents or phenomena. The knowledge requirement centers on design guidelines and principles and your mental inventory of typical interaction design flaws you have seen before. You really have to know the design guidelines cold, and your mental storehouse of problem examples helps you anticipate and rapidly spot new occurrences of the same types of problems.

Soon, you will find the inspection process blossoming into a fast-moving narration of critical incidents, UX problems, and guidelines. By following various threads of UX clues, you can even uncover problems that you do not encounter directly within the tasks.

25.6.6 Analytic UX Evaluation in the Layers of the Needs Pyramid

In whatever analytic UX evaluation method you use, there are certain basic questions to ask to help evaluate UX in the layers of the needs pyramid:

- Ecological layer.
- Interaction layer.
- Emotional layer.

25.6.7 Ecological-Layer Inspection

Does the system ecology make sense? Is the conceptual design appropriate for envisioned work in that domain? If you are not confident in your own ability to assess the conceptual design by inspection, you can use focus groups and similar methods to evaluate the ecological level and effectiveness of the conceptual design in the early funnel.

25.6.8 Interaction-Layer Inspection

The interaction layer is the most common focus of analytic UX evaluation methods, usually in the context of finding UX problems in task-level evaluation within the iterations of the late funnel.

25.6.9 Emotional-Layer Inspection

In the past, inspections for evaluating UX designs have been almost exclusively usability inspections at the interaction level. But this kind of evaluation can easily be extended to a more complete UX inspection by addressing issues of emotional impact, too. The process is essentially the same, but you need to look beyond a task view to the overall usage experience. Ask additional questions.

Pyramid of User Needs

An abstract representation as a pyramid shape with the bottom layer as ecological needs, the middle layer as interaction needs, and the top layer as emotional needs (Section 12.3.1).

Ecology

In the setting of UX design, the ecology is the entire set of surrounding parts of the world, including networks, other users, devices, and information structures, with which a user, product, or system interacts (Section 16.2.1).

Among the emotional impact questions to have in mind in a UX inspection are:

- Is usage fun?
- Is the visual design attractive (e.g., colors, shapes, layout) and creative?
- Will the design delight the user visually, aurally, or tactilely?
- If the target is a product:
  - Is the packaging and product presentation aesthetic?
  - Is the out-of-the-box experience exciting?
  - Does the product feel robust and good to hold?
  - Can the product add to the user's self-esteem?
  - Does the product embody environmental and sustainable practices?
  - Does the product convey the branding of the organization?
  - Does the brand stand for progressive, social, and civic values?
  - Are there opportunities to improve emotional impact in any of the aforementioned areas?

Codiscovery

A qualitative data collection technique employing two or more participants interacting in a team approach to evaluation, usually with a think-aloud data collection technique. Two people can verbalize more naturally, yielding multiple viewpoints expressed within conversational interplay (Sections 21.4.2.3 and 24.2.3.3).

You can also use focus groups (Section 25.3) and/or codiscovery to evaluate the emotional layer.

Most of the questions in a questionnaire for assessing emotional impact are also applicable as inspection questions here. As an example, using attributes from AttrakDiff:

- Is the system or product interesting?
- Is it exciting?
- Is it innovative?
- Is it engaging?
- Is it motivating?
- Is it desirable?

Exercise 13-1: UX Inspection of Your System

Goal: Get a little practice in doing a UX inspection.

Activities: It is strongly preferred that you use the wireframe prototype deck you built in a previous exercise. If your prototype is not suitable for an effective exercise in UX inspection, select an application or appropriate website as the target of your inspection.

Perform a team-based UX inspection as described in this chapter.

Deliverables: A list of UX problems identified by your UX inspection.

Schedule: An hour and a half.

UX Evaluation: Data Analysis

26

If it ain't broke, it probably doesn't have enough features.

– Anonymous

Highlights

- Analyzing quantitative data:
  - Comparing results with usability targets.
  - Deciding whether you can stop iterating.
- Analyzing qualitative UX problem data.
- Cost-importance analysis to prioritize UX problems to fix.
- Lessons from the field.

26.1 INTRODUCTION

26.1.1 You Are Here

We begin each process chapter with a "you are here" picture of the chapter topic in the context of The Wheel, overall UX design lifecycle template (Fig. 26-1). In this chapter, we show how to analyze the UX evaluation data you collected. The techniques described here generally apply regardless of the evaluation method used to obtain the data.

26.2 ANALYZE QUANTITATIVE DATA

If you collected quantitative UX data from informal summative evaluation, now is the time to analyze it.

Informal Summative Evaluation

A quantitative summative UX evaluation method that is not statistically rigorous and does not produce statistically significant results (Section 21.1.5.2).

Summative Evaluation

Quantitative evaluation with a goal to assess, determine, or compare a level achieved of a parameter (such as usability), especially for assessing improvement in the user experience due to formative evaluation (Section 21.1.5).

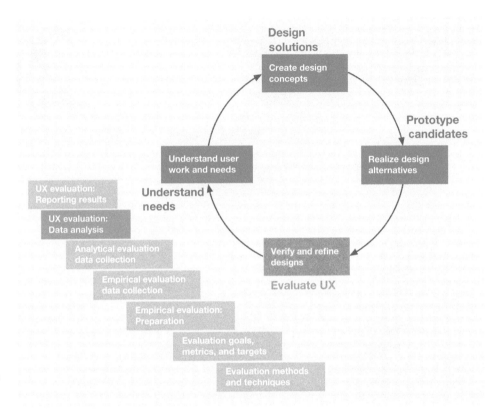

Fig. 26-1

You are here, in the chapter on data analysis within the Evaluate UX lifecycle activity, in the context of the overall Wheel lifecycle process.

26.2.1 Use Simple Descriptive Statistics

As we have said, our informal quantitative data analysis does not include inferential statistical analyses. Rather, it uses simple "descriptive" statistics (such as averages) to make an engineering determination as to whether the UX design has met the UX target levels. If the design has not yet met those targets, qualitative analysis will indicate how to modify the design to improve the UX ratings and help converge toward those goals in subsequent cycles of formative evaluation.

The first step in analyzing quantitative data is to compute averages, or whatever metrics you are using, for timing, error counts, questionnaire ratings, and so on, as stated in the UX targets (Section 22.10).

You don't usually need to worry about standard deviation values. For example, if three participants are all very close in performance times for a particular task or three questionnaires have nearly the same values for a question, the numbers should give you pretty good confidence; those averages are meaningful. If there is a big spread, however, you should find out why there is such a variance (e.g., one user spent a huge amount of time in an error situation). Sometimes, it can mean that you should try to run a few more participants.

26.2.2 Treat Subjective Quantitative Questionnaire Data as Simply as Possible

There are many different questionnaires and some (the System Usability Scale, for example [Bangor, Kortum, & Miller, 2008]) have specialized ways of assessing and interpreting the results. For our purposes we like to use just averages. As an example, to obtain a single numerical result for a questionnaire-based metric, we might use the average of scores on questions 1, 2, 5, and 8 as averaged over all the parts. Or, more often, we'll average the scores over all the questions and over all the participants.

26.2.3 Lining Up Your Quantitative Ducks
26.2.3.1 Filling in the "observed results"

After you compute summary statistics of quantitative data across all your users, put the results in the "Observed Results" column at the end of the UX target table. As an example, partial results from a hypothetical evaluation of the Ticket Kiosk System are shown in Table 26-1 using some of the UX targets established in Chapter 22. The first two targets are based on user performance metrics and the values entered are "3.5 minutes," a count of "2" errors, and an average questionnaire score for Questions 1 through 10 of "7.5," respectively.

Participant

A participant, or user participant, is a user, potential, or user surrogate who helps evaluate UX designs for usability and user experience. These are the people who perform tasks and give feedback while we observe and measure. Because we wish to invite these volunteers to join our team and help us evaluate designs (i.e., we want them to participate), we use the term "participant" instead of "subject" (Section 21.1.3).

Subjective UX Evaluation Data

Data based on opinion or judgment, of evaluator or user (Section 21.1.4.2).

Table 26-1

Example of partial informal quantitative testing results for the Ticket Kiosk System

Work Role: User Class	UX Goal	UX Measure	Measuring Instrument	UX Metric	Baseline Level	Target Level	Observed Results	Meet Target?
Ticket buyer: Casual new user, for occasional personal use	Walk-up ease of use	Initial user performance	BT1: Buy special event ticket	Average time on task	3 min as measured at the kiosk	2.5 min	3.5 min	No
Ticket buyer: Casual new user, for occasional personal use	Walk-up ease of use for new user	Initial user performance	BT2: Buy movie ticket	Average number of errors	<1	<1	2	No
Ticket buyer: Casual new user, for occasional personal use	Initial customer satisfaction	First impression	Questions Q1–Q10 in questionnaire XYZ	Average rating across users and across questions	7.5/10	8/10	7.5	No

26.2.3.2 Filling in the "meet target?" column

Next, by directly comparing the observed results with the specified target levels, you can tell immediately which UX targets have been met, and which have not, during this cycle of formative evaluation. It is useful to add, as we have done in Table 26-1, yet one more column to the right-hand end of the UX target table, for "Did you meet UX target?" Entries can be Yes, No, or Almost.

In looking at the example results in Table 26-1, in this round of evaluation, you can see that we didn't meet any of these three UX evaluation targets. This is not unusual for an early evaluation of a still-evolving design.

26.2.4 The Big Decision: Can We Stop Iterating?

Now it is time for a major project management decision: Should you continue to iterate? This decision should be a team affair and made at a global level, not just considering quantitative data. Here are some questions to consider:

- Did you simultaneously meet all your target-level goals?
- What is your general team feeling about the conceptual design, the overall UX design, the metaphor, and the user experiences they have observed?
- What role does pressure from management and marketing play in this decision?

If your answers to these questions tell you that you can accept the design as is, you can stop iterating. Or resource limitations also can force you to stop iterating and get on with pushing this version out in the hope of fixing known flaws in the next version. If and when you do decide to stop iterating, don't throw your *qualitative* data away, though; you paid to get it, so keep this round of problem data for next time.

If your UX targets were not met—the most likely situation after the first cycle(s) of testing—and resources permit (e.g., you are not out of time or money), you need to iterate. This means analyzing the UX problems and going back through the lifecycle again to find a way to solve them in order of their cost and effect on the user experience.

26.2.4.1 Convergence toward a quality user experience

Following our recurring theme of using your own thinking and experience in addition to following a process, we point out that this is a good place to use your intuition. As you iterate, you should keep an eye on the quantitative results over multiple iterations: Is your design at least moving in the right direction?

It is always possible for UX levels to get worse with any round of design changes. If you are not converging toward improvement, why not? Are UX problem fixes uncovering problems that existed but could not be seen before, or are UX problem fixes causing new problems?

26.3 ANALYZE QUALITATIVE UX DATA

26.3.1 Overview

Our friend Whitney Quesenbery gave us this nutshell digest of her approach to usability problem analysis, which she, in turn, adapted from someone else:

> *The team usually includes all the stakeholders, not just UX folks, and we rarely have much time. First, we agree on what we saw. No interpretation, just observation. This gets us all on the same page. Then we brainstorm until we agree on "what it means." Then we brainstorm design solutions.*

Formative analysis of qualitative data is the bread and butter of UX evaluation. The goal of formative data analysis is to identify UX problems and causes (design flaws) so that they can be fixed, thereby improving product user experience. The process of determining how to convert collected data into scheduled design and implementation solutions is essentially one of negotiation in which, at various times, all members of the project team are involved.

26.3.2 Analysis Preparation Steps

26.3.2.1 Keep a participant around to help with early analysis

In a typical way of doing things, it isn't until the final participant for data collection data analysis is dismissed before the team turns its attention to data analysis. But this approach can put the problem analyst at a disadvantage when the need inevitably arises to ask the participant questions. So, we suggest that you start analyzing qualitative data for each participant while that participant is still present to fill in missing data and clarify ambiguous issues.

26.3.2.2 Multiple sources of raw UX data

Regardless of the source of the raw evaluation data, most of the data analysis we do in this chapter is essentially the same.

Qualitative UX data notes can include:

- Critical incident comment.
- User think-aloud comment.
- UX inspection note.

Qualitative UX Evaluation Data

Nonnumeric descriptive data taken, for example, while observing user task performance, used to find and fix UX problems (Section 21.1.4.1).

Inspection (UX)

An analytical evaluation method in which a UX expert evaluates an interaction design by looking at it or trying it out, sometimes in the context of a set of abstracted design guidelines. Expert evaluators are both participant surrogates and observers, asking themselves questions about what would cause users problems and giving an expert opinion predicting UX problems (Section 25.4).

26.3.2.3 Clean up the raw data before your memory fades

However you get data, you probably still have a large number of raw data notes at this point. Many of your notes are likely to be terse observational comments that will be difficult to expand and interpret if:

- There is a delay between data collection and analysis.
- The person performing UX problem analysis is not the same person who observed the incidents and recorded the comments.

Therefore, it is essential to go through your UX data notes to clean up and flesh out the raw data, especially emotional impact data, as soon after data collection as possible, while perishable detailed data are still fresh.

26.3.3 Qualitative UX Data Analysis Steps

Fig. 26-2 illustrates the steps of qualitative data analysis, each of which is discussed in the following sections:

1. Gather up your raw qualitative UX data notes.
2. Extract elemental data notes (just as we did in analysis for usage research).
   a. Each elemental data note should be about exactly one UX problem.
3. Edit elemental data notes into UX problem.
4. Consolidate multiple notes about the same UX problem description.
5. Group related UX problem descriptions so they can be fixed together.

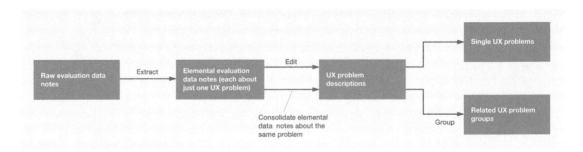

Fig. 26-2

Extracting, editing, consolidating, and grouping elemental UX evaluation data notes into UX problem descriptions.

26.3.3.1 Gather up your raw qualitative UX data notes

Didn't find many UX problems? Better look again at your data collection process. We seldom, if ever, see a UX design for which UX testing does not reveal lots of UX problems. Absence of evidence is not evidence of absence.

26.3.3.2 Extract elemental data notes: Each refers to just one problem

On occasion, participants can experience more than one distinct UX problem at the same time and a resulting UX data note can refer to all of those problems. Look through your data notes for any such notes about more than one UX problem, and separate them into multiple elemental data notes, each about a single UX problem. This is the same way we distilled the essence of raw usage research data notes in Section 8.2.

Here is an example from one of our UX evaluation sessions for a companion website for the Ticket Kiosk. The participant was in the middle of a benchmark task that required her to order three tickets to a Three Tenors concert. As she proceeded through the task, at one point she could not locate the button (which was below the "fold") to complete the transaction.

When she finally scrolled down and saw the button, the button label said, "Submit." At this point, she remarked, "I am not sure if clicking on this button will let me review my order or just send it in immediately." This is an example of a critical incident note that needs to be divided into separate elemental notes:

1. The button is located where it is not immediately visible.
2. The label is not clear enough to help the user make a confident decision.

26.3.3.3 Edit raw UX data notes into UX problem descriptions

In UX data analysis, we have to sort through the raw UX data notes and extract the essential associated UX problem information. In editing from UX data notes to UX problem descriptions, you are cleaning up the wordings, getting rid of fluff and noise, filling in missing words, making complete sentences, and generally making the descriptions readable to all team members. This is also a good time for a reality check on the value of this problem description, keeping only ones that represent "real" UX problems that are worth fixing.

Depending on the size and complexity of your project, you can keep management of your UX problem descriptions simple by typing them into a word processor or spreadsheet. The earlier you can get your raw critical incident notes packaged as data records, the more expedient the transition to subsequent data analysis.

<div class="sidebar">

Elemental Data Note

A data note from either usage research or UX evaluation that is brief, clear, concise, and refers to or relates to exactly one concept, idea, fact, or topic (Section 8.2.2).

</div>

As you create each UX problem description, think not only of the user but also of the UX team. This means including enough information to make the UX problem description as useful as possible for data analysis so team members can:

- Understand the problem in its usage context.
- Glean insight into its causes and possible solutions.
- Be conscious of relationships among similar problems.
- Come up with suitable redesign solutions.

To that end, we suggest that you consider including these kinds of information:

Problem name: So people can refer to it in other contexts and discussions

Problem statement: Terse one-sentence summary of the problem as an effect or outcome experienced by the user, but not as a suggested solution. You want to keep your options flexible when you do get to considering solutions.

User goals and task information: This information provides problem context to know what the user was trying to do when the problem was encountered.

What the user tried to do, what happened instead, and why: It's important to explain what actually happened and what incorrect assumptions about the design or misunderstandings of how the design works led to it. Explain what the user should have done.

Causes and potential solutions: Although you may not know the problem causes or potential solutions at first, you should explain it if you do know or have any ideas.

26.3.3.4 Consolidate congruent data notes

You are likely to encounter some different data notes about the same UX problem, especially if you have used multiple participants to perform the same tasks. We use the term *congruent* to refer to multiple UX data notes that are about the same underlying UX problem (not just similar problems or problems in the same category).

As you are editing these notes into UX problem descriptions, if a UX problem description already exists for this data note, consolidate and merge it into the existing problem description.

If you have trouble knowing if two problem descriptions are about the same underlying problem, Capra (2006, p. 41) suggests a practical solution-based criterion: "Two problems, A and B, were considered the same [congruent] if fixing problem A also fixes problem B, and fixing problem B also fixes problem A." Capra's approach is based on criteria used in the analysis of UX reports collected in CUE-4 (Molich & Dumas, 2008). The symmetric aspect of this criterion rules out a case where one problem is a subset of the other.

As an example, from our Ticket Kiosk System evaluation, one UX problem description states that the participant was confused about the button labeled "Submit" and didn't know that this button should be clicked to move on in the transaction to pay for the tickets. Another (congruent) UX problem description (as encountered by a different participant) said that the participant complained about the wording of the button label "Submit," saying it didn't help understand where one would go if one clicked on that button.

26.3.3.5 Group related UX problem descriptions to be fixed together

UX problems can be related in many different ways that call for you to consider fixing them at the same time:

- Problems may be in physical or logical proximity (e.g., may involve objects or actions within the same dialogue box).
- Problems may involve objects or actions used in the same task.
- Problems may be in the same category of issues or design features but scattered throughout the UX design.
- Problems may have consistency (or other) issues that require similar treatments.
- Observed problem descriptions are indirect symptoms of common, more deeply rooted, UX problems.
  - A telling indicator of such a deeply rooted problem is complexity and difficulty in its analysis.

The idea is to create a common solution that might be more general than required for a single problem, but which will be the most efficient and consistent for the whole group.

Example: Grouping Related Problems for the Ticket Kiosk System

Consider Table 26-2, adapted with permission, from a student team in one of our classes. In the second column, we list five UX problems, all related to distinguishability of seat categories (e.g., availability). The right-hand column contains corresponding suggested solutions.

These problems may be indicative of a much broader design problem: a lack of effective visual design elements in seat selection part of the workflow. We can group and label all these problems into a problem group, along with a group solution (Table 26-2):

Table 26-2

A group of related UX problems and solutions in a spreadsheet (thanks to Sirong Lin and her student project team)

Seat category distinguishability usability problem	9. User expected graphic of seat layout but missed seeing the button for that at first; kept missing "View Seats"	Group "View Seats" button in layout with other seat purchase task controls
	13. For "Selected seats," no way to distinguish balcony from floor seats because they use the same numbering scheme	Distinguish balcony seats and floor seats with different numbering schemes
	20. In "View Seats" view, participant couldn't determine which seats were already sold, because color choices were confusing	Use different icons or colors to distinguish which seats are already sold
	25. Missed fact that blue seat sections are clickable to zoom in on detailed view of available seats. User left thinking that blue seat section wasn't enough information about *which* seats are available	Show clearly that blue seat sections are clickable. When one is clicked, display the detailed seat information, like location, price, etc. Add legend to explain color usage
	26. Seat availability color-coding scheme problematic. Colors not distinguishable (color blindness?). In detailed seat view, purple wasn't distinguishable as separate between red and blue. Labels in this view not legible enough. Probably should have thicker font (maybe bold would do it)	Change the colors to a better combination with which the user can distinguish the different categories of seats clearly. Use a thicker font

Group 1: Visual designs for seat selection workflow.
Group 1 Solution: Comprehensively revise all visual design elements for seat selection workflow. Update style guide accordingly.

26.3.3.6 Usage research analysis tools work here, too

For projects with large numbers of UX data notes, you might need a way to organize the resulting UX problem descriptions to make logical sense of them. This usually means organize them by category—by feature, area of functionality, task, user activity, etc. Putting your problem descriptions into an affinity diagram can help you:

- Find congruencies.
- Find problem descriptions to be grouped for fixing together.

26.3.3.7 Higher level common issues within groups

When UX problem data include a number of critical incidents or problems that are quite similar, you will group these descriptions together because they are closely related. Then, you usually look for common issues among the problems in the group.

But sometimes, the real problem is not explicit in the commonality within the group, but the problems only represent symptoms of a higher-level problem. You might have to deduce that this higher-level problem is the real underlying cause of these common critical incidents.

For example, in one application we evaluated, users were having trouble understanding several different quirky and application-specific labels. We first tried changing the label wordings, but eventually we realized that the reason they didn't "get" these labels was that they didn't understand an important aspect of the conceptual design. Changing the labels without improving their understanding of the model didn't solve the problem.

26.3.4 UX Problem Data Management

In large projects, management of the sheer numbers of UX problem descriptions can be a challenge, and you might have to adopt a database management approach. We leave it up to you to work this out in a way that works for your project. For more about UX problem data management, see Section 28.10.

26.3.5 Rapid Qualitative Data Analysis

As a rapid approach to qualitative data analysis:

- Just take notes about UX problems in real time during the data collection session.
- Immediately after session, make UX problem records from the notes.

As an alternative, if you have the necessary simple tools for creating UX problem records:

- Create UX problem records as you encounter each UX problem during the session.
- Immediately after the session, expand and fill in missing information in the records.
- Analyze each problem, focusing on the real essence of the problem and noting causes (design flaws) and possible solutions.

26.4 COST-IMPORTANCE ANALYSIS: PRIORITIZING PROBLEMS TO FIX

Cost-importance analysis is an approach to prioritizing the time and effort of fixing UX problems found in UX evaluation based on priority ratios, which are calculated by dividing the importance of making a change by the cost.

Of course, we want to fix all known UX problems after each iteration of evaluation. However, because resources are limited, and time is short, we have to take the engineering approach of prioritizing problems to fix.

We call this cost-importance analysis because it is based on calculating tradeoffs between the cost to fix a problem and the importance of getting it fixed. Cost-importance analysis applies to any UX problem list regardless of what evaluation method or data collection technique was used.

Although these simple calculations can be done manually, this analysis lends itself nicely to the use of a simple spreadsheet. The basic form we will use is the cost-importance table shown in Table 26-3.

26.4.1 Problem

Starting with the left-most column in Table 26-3, we enter a concise description of the problem. Analysts needing to review further details can consult the original problem data notes. We will use some sample UX problems from the Ticket Kiosk System to illustrate how we fill out the entries in the cost-importance table.

Table 26-3

Basic form of the cost-importance table

Problem	Imp.	Solution	Cost	Prio. Ratio	Prio. Rank	Cuml. Cost	Resolution

In our first example problem, the user had decided on an event to buy tickets for and had established the parameters (date, venue, seats, price, etc.) but didn't realize that it was then necessary to click on the "Submit" button to finish up the event-related choices and move to the screen for making payment. So, we enter a brief description of this problem in the first column of Table 26-4.

Table 26-4

Problem description entered into cost-importance table

Problem	Imp.	Solution	Cost	Prio. Ratio	Prio. Rank	Cuml. Cost	Resolution
User unaware of the need to click on the "Submit" button to proceed to payment							

26.4.2 Importance to Fix

The next column is for an estimate of the importance to fix the problem, independent of cost. While importance includes severity or criticality of the problem, most commonly used by other authors, this parameter can also include other considerations. The idea is to capture the effect of a problem on user performance, user experience, and overall system integrity and consistency. Importance can also include intangibles such as management and marketing "feelings" and consideration of the cost of not fixing the problem (e.g., in terms of lower user satisfaction).

Because an importance rating is just an estimate, we use a simple scale for the values:

- Importance = M: Must fix, regardless
- Importance = 5: The most important problems to fix after the "Must fix" category
  - The UX feature involved is mission critical.
  - The UX problem has a major impact on task performance or user satisfaction (e.g., user cannot complete key task or can do so only with great difficulty).
  - The UX problem is expected to occur frequently and/or could cause costly errors.
- Importance = 3: Moderate impact problems
  - The user can complete the task, but with some difficulty (e.g., it caused confusion and required some extra effort).
  - The problem was a source of moderate dissatisfaction.
- Importance = 1: Low impact problems
  - The problem didn't impact task performance or dissatisfaction much (e.g., mild user confusion or irritation or a cosmetic problem), but is still worth listing.

This fairly coarse gradation of values has proven to work for us. You can customize it to suit your project needs.

26.4.2.1 Importance rating adjustments

We also need some flexibility to assign intermediate values, so we allow for importance rating adjustment factors, the primary one of which is estimated frequency of occurrence. If this problem is expected to occur very often, you might adjust your importance rating upward by one value.

Conversely, if it is not expected to occur very often, you could downgrade your rating by one or more values. As Karat, Campbell, and Fiegel (1992) relate frequency of occurrence to problem severity classification, they ask: Over all the affected user classes, how often will the user encounter this problem?

For example, consider the Ticket Kiosk System problem about users being confused by the button label "Submit" to proceed to payment in the ticket-purchasing transaction. Because this was not shown to be a show-stopper, we initially assigned it an importance of 3. But because it will be encountered by almost every user in almost every transaction, we "promoted" it to a 4, as shown in Table 26-5.

Table 26-5

Estimate of importance to fix entered into cost-importance table

Problem	Imp.	Solution	Cost	Prio. Ratio	Prio. Rank	Cuml. Cost	Resolution
User unaware of the need to click on the "Submit" button to proceed to payment	4						

Learnability can also be an importance adjustment factor. Some problems have most of their impact on the first encounter. After that, users learn quickly to overcome (work around) the problem, so it does not have much effect in subsequent usage. That could call for an importance rating reduction.

26.4.3 Solutions

The next column in the cost-importance table is for one or more candidate solutions to the problems. Solving a UX problem is redesign, a kind of design, so you should use the same approach and resources as we did for the original design, including consulting your usage research data. Other resources and activities that might help include design principles and guidelines, ideation and sketching, study of other similar designs, and solutions suggested by users and experts. It is almost never a good idea to think of more training or better documentation as a UX problem solution–that is fixing the user, not the UX design.

Example: Solution for Ticket Kiosk System Problem

Coming back to the confusing button label in the Ticket Kiosk System, one obvious and inexpensive solution is to change the label wording to better represent where the interaction will go if the user clicks on that button. Maybe "Proceed to payment" would make more sense to most users.

We wrote a concise description of our proposed fix in the Solution column in Table 26-6.

Table 26-6

Potential problem solution entered into cost-importance table

Problem	Imp.	Solution	Cost	Prio. Ratio	Prio. Rank	Cuml. Cost	Resolution
User unaware of the need to click on the "Submit" button to proceed to payment	4	Change label wording to "Proceed to Payment"					

26.4.4 Cost to Fix

The Cost column is where you enter your estimate of the cost to fix this problem. You should use the cost to fix the design at the current stage of development in the project. For example, the cost to fix almost any problem in a paper prototype is low, even including the cost to brainstorm a solution. But, in later stages, with medium- to high-fidelity prototypes and programmed prototypes, costs can be substantially higher.

Making accurate estimates of the cost to fix a given UX problem takes practice; it is an acquired engineering skill. But it is nothing new; it is part of our job to make cost estimates in all kinds of engineering and budget situations. For our analysis, costs are stated in terms of resources needed, which almost always translates to person-hours required.

Because this is an inexact process, we usually round up fractional values just to keep it simple. When you make your cost estimates, don't make the mistake of including only the cost to implement the change; you must include the cost of redesign and discussion and, sometimes, even some prototyping and experimentation. If you have a programmed prototype, you might need help from your software developers to estimate implementation costs.

Because it is very easy to change label wordings in our Ticket Kiosk System, we have entered a value of just one person-hour into the Cost column in Table 26-7.

Table 26-7

Estimate of cost to fix entered into cost-importance table

Problem	Imp.	Solution	Cost	Prio. Ratio	Prio. Rank	Cuml. Cost	Resolution
User unaware of the need to click on the "Submit" button to proceed to payment	4	Change the label wording to "Proceed to Payment"	1				

26.4.4.1 Cost values for problem groups

Table 26-8 shows an example of including a problem group in the cost-importance table. Note that the cost for the group is higher than that of either individual problem, but lower than their sum.

26.4.4.2 Calibration feedback from down the road: Comparing actual with predicted costs

To learn more about making cost estimates and to calibrate your engineering ability to estimate costs to fix problems, we recommend that you add a column to your cost-importance table for actual cost. After you have done the redesign and implementation for your solutions, you should record the actual cost of each and compare with your predicted estimates. It can tell you how you are doing and help you improve your estimates.

26.4.5 Priority Ratio

The next column in the cost-importance table, the priority ratio, is a metric we use to establish priorities for fixing problems. We want a metric that will reward high importance but penalize high costs. A simple ratio of importance to cost fits this bill. Intuitively, a high importance will boost up the priority but a high cost will bring it down. Because the units of cost and importance will usually yield a fractional value for the priority ratio, we scale it up to the integer range by multiplying it by an arbitrary factor, say, 1000.

If the importance rating is "M" (for "must fix regardless"), the priority ratio is also "M." For all numerical values of importance, the priority ratio becomes:

$$\text{Priority ratio} = (\text{importance}/\text{cost}) \times 1000$$

Table 26-8

Cost entries for problem groups entered into cost-importance table

Problem Group	Problem	Imp.	Solution	Group Solution	Single Costs	Group Cost
Transaction flow for purchasing tickets	7. The user wanted to enter or choose date and venue first and then click "Purchase Tickets," but the UX design required them to click on "Purchase Tickets" before entering specific ticket information	3	Change flow to allow actions in either order and label it so	Establish a comprehensive and more flexible model of transaction flow and add labeling to explain it	3	5
	17. The "Purchase Tickets" button took user to screen to select tickets and commit to them, but then users didn't realize they had to continue on to another screen to pay for them		Provide better labeling for this flow		3	

Example: Priority Ratios for Ticket Kiosk System Problems

For our first Ticket Kiosk System problem, the priority ratio is $(4/1) \times 1000 = 4000$, which we have entered into the cost-importance table in Table 26-9.

Table 26-9

Priority ratio calculation entered into cost-importance table

Problem	Imp.	Solution	Cost	Prio. Ratio	Prio. Rank	Cuml. Cost	Resolution
User unaware of the need to click on the "Submit" button to proceed to payment	4	Change the label wording to "Proceed to Payment"	1	4000			

In the next part of this example, shown in Table 26-10, we have added several more Ticket Kiosk System UX problems to fill out the table a bit more realistically.

Table 26-10

Priority ratios for more Ticket Kiosk System problems

Problem	Imp.	Solution	Cost	Prio. Ratio	Prio. Rank	Cuml. Cost	Resolution
User unaware of the need to click on the "Submit" button to proceed to payment	4	Change the label wording to "Proceed to Payment"	1	4000			
Didn't recognize the "counter" as being for the number of tickets. As a result, user failed to even think about how many tickets he needed	M	Move quantity information and label it	2	M			
Unsure of current date and what date he was purchasing tickets for	5	Add current date field and label all dates precisely	2	2500			
Users were concerned about their work being left for others to see	5	Add a timeout feature that clears the screens	3	1667			
User confused about "Theatre" on the "Choose a domain" screen. Thought it meant choosing a physical theater (as a venue) rather than the category of theatre arts	3	Improve the wording to "Theatre Arts"	1	3000			
Ability to find events hampered by lack of a search capability	4	Design and implement a search function	40	100			
Didn't recognize what geographical area theater information was being displayed for	4	Redesign graphical representation to show search radius	12	333			

Continued

Table 26-10 Priority ratios for more Ticket Kiosk System problems —cont'd

Problem	Imp.	Solution	Cost	Prio. Ratio	Prio. Rank	Cuml. Cost	Resolution
Didn't like having a "Back" button on second screen because first screen was only a "Welcome"	2	Remove it	1	2000			
Transaction flow for purchasing tickets (group problem; see Table 26-8)	3	Establish a comprehensive and more flexible model of transaction flow and add labeling to explain it	5	600			

Note that although fixing the lack of a search function (the sixth row in Table 26-10) has a high importance, its high cost is keeping the priority ratio low. This is one problem to consider for an Importance = M rating in the future. At the other end of things, the next-to-last problem (about the Back button to the Welcome screen) is only Importance = 2, but the low cost boosts the priority ratio quite high. Fixing this will not cost much and will get it out of the way.

26.4.6 Priority Rankings

The next step is to sort the cost-importance table by priority ratios to get the final priority rankings, the order in which to fix the problems.

First, move all problems with a priority ratio value of "M" to the top of the table. These are the problems you must fix, regardless of cost. Then sort the rest of the table in descending order by priority ratio. This puts high-importance, low-cost problems (shown at **A** in the upper left-hand quadrant of Fig. 26-3) at the top of the priority list. These are the problems to fix first, the fixes that will give the biggest bang for the buck.

You might think that, in the real world, you won't see many problems having high importance in combination with low cost. You're thinking you have to pay for what you get. But, in fact, we often find many problems of this kind in early iterations. A good example is a badly worded button label. It can completely confuse users, but usually costs almost nothing to fix.

In contrast, the UX problems that sort to the bottom of the priority list are costly to fix with relatively little gain in doing so. You will probably not bother to fix these problems, as shown at **B** in the lower right-hand quadrant of Fig. 26-3.

Quadrants **A** and **B** sort out nicely in the priority rankings. Quadrants **C** and **D**, however, may require more thought. Quadrant **C** represents problems for which fixes are low in cost and low in importance. You will usually just go ahead and fix them to get them off your plate. The most difficult choices appear in quadrant **D** because, although they are of high importance to fix, they are also the most expensive to fix.

No formula will help; you need good engineering judgment. Maybe it is time to request more resources so these important problems can be fixed. That is usually worth it in the long run.

A cost-importance table for sample UX problems in the Ticket Kiosk System, sorted by priority ratio, is shown in Table 26-11.

26.4.7 Cumulative Cost

The next step is simple. In the "Cuml. Cost" column of the table, sorted by priority ratio, is the cost of fixing each problem plus the cost of fixing all the problems above it in the table. See how we have done this for our example Ticket Kiosk System cost-importance table in Table 26-11.

26.4.8 The Line of Affordability

Your team leader or project manager should determine your "resource limit," in person-hours, that you can afford to allocate to making design changes for the current cycle of iteration. For example, suppose that for the Ticket Kiosk System, we have only a fairly small amount of time available in the schedule, about 16 person hours.

Draw the "line of affordability," a horizontal line in the cost-importance table just above the line in the table where the cumulative cost value first exceeds your resource limit. For the Ticket Kiosk System, the line of affordability appears just above the row in Table 26-11 where the cumulative cost hits 27.

If you have time for more learning about your process, it might be interesting to graph the problems in a cost-importance space like that of Fig. 26-3. Sometimes, this kind of graphical representation can give insight into your process, especially if your problems tend to appear in clusters. Your line of affordability will be a vertical line that cuts the cost axis at the amount you can afford to spend on fixing all problems in this iteration.

26.4.9 Drawing Conclusions: A Resolution for Each Problem

It's time for the payoff of your cost-importance analysis. It's time to decide how each problem will be addressed.

Table 26-11

The Ticket Kiosk System cost-importance table, sorted by priority ratio, with cumulative cost values entered, and the "line of affordability" showing the cutoff for this round of problem fixing

Problem	Imp.	Solution	Cost	Prio. Ratio	Prio. Rank	Cuml. Cost	Resolution
Didn't recognize the "counter" as being for the number of tickets. As a result, user failed to even think about how many tickets he needed	M	Move quantity information and label it	2	M	1	2	
User unaware of the need to click on the "Submit" button to proceed to payment	4	Change the label wording to "Proceed to Payment"	1	4000	2	3	
User confused about "Theatre" on the "Choose a domain" screen. Thought it meant choosing a physical theater (as a venue) rather than the category of theatre arts	3	Improve the wording to "Theatre Arts"	1	3000	3	4	
Unsure of current date and what date he was purchasing tickets for	5	Add current date field and label all dates precisely	2	2500	4	6	
Didn't like having a "Back" button on second screen because first screen was only a "Welcome"	2	Remove it	1	2000	5	7	
Users were concerned about their work being left for others to see	5	Add a timeout feature that clears the screens	3	1667	6	10	
Transaction flow for purchasing tickets (group problem; see Table 26-8)	3	Establish a comprehensive and more flexible model of transaction flow and add labeling to explain it	5	600	7	15	

Line of affordability (16 person-hours—2 work days)

Problem	Imp.	Solution	Cost	Prio. Ratio	Prio. Rank	Cuml. Cost	Resolution
Didn't recognize what geographical area theater information was being displayed for	4	Redesign graphical representation to show search radius.	12	333	8	27	
Ability to find events hampered by lack of a search capability	4	Design and implement a search function.	40	100	9	67	

First, you have to deal with your "Must fix" problems, the show-stoppers. If you have enough resources, that is, if all the "Must fix" problems are above the line of affordability, fix them all. If not, you already have a headache. Someone, such as the project manager, has to earn his or her pay today by making a difficult decision.

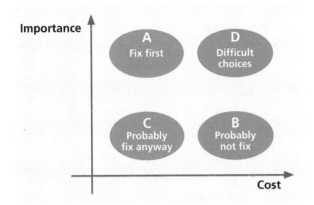

Fig. 26-3

The relationship of importance and cost in prioritizing which problems to fix first.

The extreme cost of a "Must fix" problem could make it infeasible to fix in the current version. Exceptions will surely result in cost overruns, but might have to be dictated by corporate policy, management, marketing, etc. It is an important time to be true to your principles and to everything you have done in the process so far. Don't throw it away now because of some perceived limit on how much you are willing to put into fixing problems that you have just spent good money to find. Quality is remembered long after budget and schedules are forgotten.

Sometimes you have resources to fix the "Must fix" problems, but no resources left for dealing with the other problems. Fortunately, in our example, we have enough resources to fix a few more problems. Depending on their relative proximity to the line of affordability, you have to decide among these choices as a resolution for all the other problems:

- Fix now.
- Fix, time permitting.
- Remand to the "wait-and-see list."
- Table until next version.
- Postpone indefinitely; probably never get to fix.

In the final column of the cost-importance table, write in your resolution for each problem, as we have done for the Ticket Kiosk System in Table 26-12.

Table 26-12

Problem resolutions for Ticket Kiosk System

Problem	Imp.	Solutions	Cost	Prio. Ratio	Prio. Rank	Cuml. Cost	Resolution
Didn't recognize the "counter" as being for the number of tickets. As a result, user failed to even think about how many tickets he needed	M	Move quantity information and label it	2	M	1	2	Fix in this version
User unaware of the need to click on the "Submit" button to proceed to payment	4	Change the label wording to "Proceed to Payment"	1	4000	2	3	Fix in this version
User confused about "Theatre" on the "Choose a domain" screen. Thought it meant choosing a physical theater (as a venue) rather than the category of theatre arts	3	Improve the wording to "Theatre Arts"	1	3000	3	4	Fix in this version
Unsure of current date and what date he was purchasing tickets for	5	Add current date field and label all dates precisely	2	2500	4	6	Fix in this version
Didn't like having a "Back" button on second screen because first screen was only a "Welcome"	2	Remove it	1	2000	5	7	Fix in this version
Users were concerned about their work being left for others to see	5	Add a timeout feature that clears the screens.	3	1667	6	10	Fix in this version
Transaction flow for purchasing tickets (group problem; see Table 26-8)	3	Establish a comprehensive and more flexible model of transaction flow and add labeling to explain it	5	600	7	15	Fix in this version
Line of affordability (16 person-hours—2 work days)							
Ability to find events hampered by lack of a search capability	4	Design and implement a search function	40	100	9	67	Defer to a future version

Finally, look at your table; see what is left below the line of affordability. Is it what you would expect? Can you live with not making fixes below that line? That is okay, as our engineering approach is aiming for cost-effectiveness, not perfection. You might even have to face the fact that some important problems cannot be fixed simply because they are too costly.

26.4.10 Special Cases
26.4.10.1 Tie-breakers

Sometimes you will get ties for priority rankings. If they don't occur near the line of affordability, it isn't necessary to do anything about them. In the rare case that they straddle the line of affordability, you can break the tie by almost any practical means, for example, your team members may have a personal preference.

In cases of more demanding target systems (e.g., an air traffic control system), where the importance of avoiding problems, especially dangerous user errors, is a bigger concern than cost, you might break priority ties by adjusting the priorities by weighting importance higher than cost in the priority ratio formula.

26.4.10.2 Cost-importance analysis involving multiple problem solutions

Sometimes, you can think of more than one solution for a problem. It is possible that, after a bit more thought, one solution will emerge as best. If, however, after careful consideration, you still have multiple possibilities for a problem solution, you can keep all solutions in the running and in the analysis until you see something that helps you decide.

If all solutions have the same cost to fix, then you and your team will just have to make an engineering decision. This might be the time to implement all of them and retest, using further prototyping to evaluate alternative design solutions for just this one feature.

Usually, though, solutions are distinguished by cost and/or effectiveness. Maybe one is less expensive but some other one is more desirable or more effective; in other words, you have a cost-benefit tradeoff to resolve before entering the chosen solution and its cost into the cost-importance table.

26.4.10.3 Problem groups straddling the line of affordability

If you have a group of related problems right at the line of affordability, the engineering answer is to do the best you can before you run out of resources. If necessary, break the group back apart and do as many pieces as possible. Give the rest of the group a higher importance in the next iteration.

26.4.10.4 Priorities for emotional impact problems

Priorities for fixing emotional impact problems can be difficult to assess. They are often very important because they can represent problems with product or system image and reputation in the market. They can also represent high costs to fix because they often require a broader view of redesign, not just focusing on one detail of the design as you might for a usability problem.

Also, emotional impact problems are often not just redesign problems but might require more understanding of the users and work or play context, which means going all the way back in the process to usage research and a new approach to the conceptual design. Because of business and marketing imperatives, you may have to move some emotional impact problems into the "Must fix" category and do what is necessary to produce an awesome user experience.

26.4.11 Rapid Cost-Importance Analysis

As a rapid version of the cost-importance analysis process:

- Put the problem list in a spreadsheet or similar document.
- Project it onto a screen in a room with pertinent team members to decide priorities for fixing the problems.
- Have a discussion about which problems to fix first based on a group feeling about the relative importance and cost to fix each problem, without assigning numeric values.
- Do a kind of group-driven "bubble sort" of problems in which problems to fix first will float toward the top of the list, and problems you probably cannot fix, at least in this iteration, will sink toward the bottom of the list.
- When you are satisfied with the relative ordering of problem priorities, start fixing problems from the top of the list downward, and stop when you run out of time or money.

26.5 FEEDBACK TO THE PROCESS

Now that you have been through an iteration of the UX process lifecycle, it is time to reflect not just on the design itself, but also on how well your process worked. If you have any suspicions after doing the testing that the quantitative criteria were not quite right, you might ask if your UX targets worked well.

For example, if all target levels were met or exceeded on the very first round of evaluation, it will almost certainly be the case that your UX targets were too lenient. Even in later iterations, if all UX targets are met, but observations during evaluation sessions indicate that participants were frustrated and performed tasks poorly, your intuition will probably tell you that the design is nevertheless not acceptable in terms of its quality of user experience. Then, obviously, the UX team should revisit and adjust the UX targets or add more considerations to your criteria for evaluation success.

Next, ask yourself whether the benchmark tasks supported the evaluation process in the most effective way. Should they have been simpler or more complex, narrower or broader? Should any benchmark task description be reworded for clarification or to give less information about how to do a task?

Finally, assess how well the overall process worked for the team. You will never be in a better position to sit down, discuss it, and document possible improvements for the next time.

26.6 LESSONS FROM THE FIELD

26.6.1 Onion-Layers Effect

There are many reasons to make more than one iteration of the design-evaluate-redesign part of the UX lifecycle. The main reason, of course, is to continue to uncover and fix UX problems until you meet your UX target values. Another reason is to be sure that your "fixes" have not caused new problems. The fixes are, after all, new and untested designs.

Also, in fixing a problem, you can uncover new UX problems obscured by the original problem, preventing participants and evaluators from seeing the new problem, until the top layer of the onion[1] is peeled off by solving that "outer" problem.

26.6.2 UX Problem Data as Feedback to Process Improvement

In our analysis, we are also always on the lookout for *process causes of the problem causes*. It sometimes pays off to look at your UX process to find causes of the design flaws that cause UX problems, places in your process where, if you could have done something differently, you might have avoided a particular kind of design flaw. If you suffer from an overabundance of a particular kind of UX problem and can determine how your process is letting them into the designs, maybe you can head off that kind of problem in future designs by fixing that part of the process.

For example, if you are finding a large number of UX problems involving confusing button or icon labels or menu choices, maybe you can address these in advance by providing a place in your design process where you look extra carefully at the precise use of words, semantics, and meanings of words. You might even consider hiring a professional writer to join the UX team. We ran into a case like this once. For expediency, one project team had been letting their

---

[1]Thanks to Wolmet Barendregt for the onion-layer analogy.

software programmers write error messages as they encountered the need for them in the code. This situation was a legacy from the days when programmers routinely did most of the user interface. As you can imagine, these error messages were not the most effective. We helped them incorporate a more structured approach to error message composition, involving UX practitioners, without unduly disrupting the rest of their process.

Similarly, large numbers of problems involving physical user actions are indicators of design problems that could be addressed by hiring an expert in ergonomics, human factors engineering, and physical device design. Finally, large numbers of problems involving visual aspects of design, such as color, shape, positioning, or gray shading, might indicate the need for hiring a graphic designer or layout artist.

Exercise 26-1: UX Data Analysis for Your System

Goal: To get some practice with the analysis part of a very simple formative UX evaluation.

Activities: If you are working with a team, get together with your team, including any new participants you picked up along the way.

Fill in the UX target table "Observed results" column.

Together, your team compiles and compares the quantitative results to determine whether UX targets were met.

Review your raw critical incident notes and write a UX problem list.

Organize the UX problem list and perform cost-importance analysis. Using a paper cost-importance table or laptop spreadsheet, list a dozen or more UX problems from critical incidents.

Assign an importance (to fix) rating to each observed problem.

Propose solutions (without doing all the work of redesign).

Group together any related problems and list as single problem.

Assign cost values (in person-hours) to each solution.

Compute priority ratios.

Compile your results:

Move your "Must fix" problems to the top of your cost-importance table.

Sort the remaining problems by decreasing priority ratios to determine the priority rank of UX problems.

Fill in the cumulative cost column.

Assume a hypothetical value for available time resources (something to make this exercise work).

Draw the cutoff, line of affordability.

Finalize your "management" decisions (resolution) about which changes to make now and in the next version.

Deliverables: Summary of quantitative results, written in "Observed results" column in your UX target table form (for comparison with UX targets).

List of raw critical incidents.

Cost-importance table form containing three UX problems selected as interesting to present to class or your work group (complete across all three rows).

Choose someone to give brief a report on your evaluation results.

Schedule: Given the simplicity of the domain, we expect this exercise to take about 30 to 60 minutes.

UX Evaluation: Reporting Results

27

27.1 INTRODUCTION

27.1.1 You Are Here

We begin each process chapter with a "you are here" picture of the chapter topic in the context of The Wheel, overall UX design lifecycle template (Fig. 27-1). This chapter is about reporting UX evaluation results and applies more or less regardless of the evaluation method or data collection technique.

27.1.2 Importance of Quality Communication

Evaluation reports are often required to communicate across discontinuities of time, location, and people. Redesign activities are often separated from UX evaluation by delays in time that can cause information loss due to human memory limitations. This is further aggravated if the people doing the redesign are not the ones who conducted the evaluation.

Finally, evaluation and redesign can occur at different physical locations, rendering all information not well communicated to be unrecoverable. UX evaluation reports with inadequate contextual information or incomplete UX

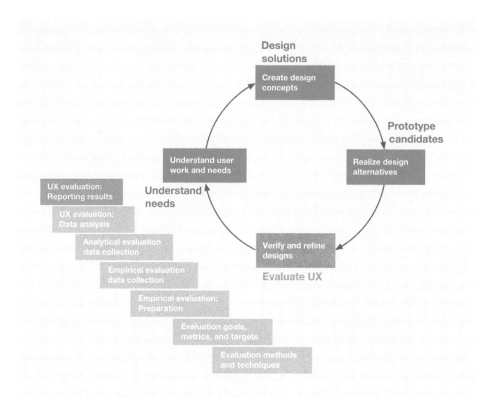

Fig. 27-1

You are here, in the chapter on the reporting subactivity within the Evaluate UX lifecycle activity, in the context of the overall Wheel lifecycle process.

problem descriptions will be too vague for designers who were not present for the evaluation.

To the project team, the report for an evaluation within an iteration is a redesign proposal. Hornbæk and Frøkjær (2005) show the need for usability evaluation reports that summarize and convey UX information, not just lists of problem descriptions by themselves.

All the effort and cost you invested thus far in UX evaluation can be wasted at the last minute if you don't follow up now to:

- Inform the team and project management about the UX problems in the current design.
- Persuade them of the need to invest even more in fixing those problems.

27.1.3 Participant Anonymity

We remind you, before we get into the details, that regardless of the kind of evaluation or reporting you are doing, you must preserve participant anonymity. You should have promised this on your informed consent form, and you have an ethical, and perhaps a legal, obligation to protect it religiously thereafter. The necessity for preserving participant anonymity extends especially to evaluation reporting.

27.2 REPORTING DIFFERENT KINDS OF DATA

27.2.1 Reporting Informal Summative Results

If we collect and analyze quantitative data in UX practice, it will always be informal summative evaluation. When you refer to quantitative UX data in a report, it should never be associated with anything that even remotely looks like a statistical claim. This is a nonnegotiable professional and ethical requirement.

Beyond this caveat, because any quantitative data collected during UX evaluation are for the UX team only, our coverage of the reporting of informal summative results will be limited.

27.2.1.1 What if you need to convince the team to fix the problems?

What good is doing the UX evaluation if no one is convinced the problems you found are "real" and, as a result, the design does not get changed? It may be part of the job of UX engineers to convince others in the project team to take action about poor UX, as revealed by UX evaluation. This part of the role is especially important in large organizations where people who collect data are not necessarily the same people (or even people who have a close working relationship with them) as those who make the decisions about design changes.

In your team evaluation report, you may want to explain why some of the changes are necessary. If statistical "proof" is requested, however, you will not be able to provide it. At its extreme, this kind of request could be indicative of an unfortunate management or organizational problem showing a lack of trust that the UX team can do its job.

27.2.2 Reporting Qualitative Results—The UX Problems

All UX practitioners should be able to write clear and effective reports about problems found but, in their "CUE-4" studies, Dumas, Molich, and Jeffries (2004) found that many cannot. They observed a large variation in reporting quality over teams of usability specialists, and that most reports were inadequate by their standards.

If you use rapid evaluation methods for data collection, it is especially important to communicate effectively about the analysis and results because this kind of data can otherwise be dismissed easily "as unreliable or inadequate to

> **Informal Summative Evaluation**
>
> A quantitative summative UX evaluation method that is not statistically rigorous and does not produce statistically significant results (Section 21.1.5.2).

inform design decisions" (Nayak, Mrazek, and Smith, 1995). Even in empirical evaluation, though, the primary type of data from formative evaluation is qualitative, and raw qualitative data must be skillfully distilled and interpreted to avoid the impression of being too "soft" and subjective.

27.2.2.1 Common Industry Format for reporting

We don't include formal summative evaluation in typical UX practice, but the US National Institute of Standards & Technology (NIST) did initially produce a Common Industry Format (CIF) for reporting formal summative UX evaluation results.

Following this initial effort, the group—under the direction of Mary Theofanos, Whitney Quesenbery, and others—organized two workshops in 2005 (Theofanos, Quesenbery, Snyder, Dayton, and Lewis, 2005), these aimed at a CIF for formative evaluation reports (Quesenbery, 2005; Theofanos and Quesenbery, 2005).

In this work, they recognized that, because most evaluations conducted by usability practitioners are formative, there was a need for an extension of the original CIF project to identify best practices for reporting formative results. They concluded that requirements for content, format, presentation style, and level of detail depended heavily on the audience, the business context, and the evaluation techniques used.

While their working definition of "formative testing" was based on having representative users, here we use the slightly broader term "formative evaluation" to include usability inspections and other methods for collecting formative usability and user experience data.

27.3 REPORT AUDIENCES

As Theofanos and Quesenbery (2005) say, choices about content, format, vocabulary, and tone are all about the relationship between the author and the audience. Authors of the 2005 UPA Workshop Report on formative evaluation reporting (Theofanos et al., 2005) stressed different reporting requirements for different business contexts and audiences.

27.3.1 Reporting to Inform Your Project Team
27.3.1.1 Convey UX problem results clearly

The primary audience for a report of UX problem details is your own project team—the designers and implementers who will fix the problems. The key goal is to convey results and product implications clearly and meaningfully to your workmates, informing them about UX flaws in the design and/or informally measured shortcomings in user performance with the purpose of understanding what needs to be done to improve the design in the next iteration. Your report can usually be short and to the point, with little need for embellishments.

27.3.1.2 Meet with UX team and software developers in person

You should try to meet with the UX team and software developers to present the results personally, so you can explain points and answer questions.

Start with a "boilerplate" summary of the basics, including evaluation goals, methods, and UX targets and benchmark tasks used. Screen shots illustrating actual problem encounters are always good for selling your points about problems.

Your audience will expect you to prioritize your redesign recommendations, and cost-importance analysis is a good way to do this. Assuming that your team has technical savvy, use tables to summarize your findings; don't make them plow through a volume of text for the essence. If your development schedule is short, and things are already moving fast, keep the report and your problem list short.

27.3.2 Explaining UX Evaluation to Stakeholders

Because your goal is to persuade stakeholders of the need to invest time and cost into taking action to fix problems discovered, you must include your audience in the process and reasoning that led from raw data to conclusions, so that your recommendations don't appear to be pulled out of the air. To include them in your process, you must explain the process.

This kind of audience requires a different kind of report from all the others. It is more like an evaluation report contained within a more general presentation about UX evaluation. First, you have to establish your credentials and credibility and gain their engagement.

The goals for reporting to this kind of audience include (more or less in this order):

- Engender awareness and appreciation.
- Teach concepts.
- Sell buy-in.
- Present results.

Building rapport. Start on the first goal by building rapport and empathy. You want to get them to appreciate the need for usability and a good user experience to

> ### Cost-Importance Analysis
>
> An approach to prioritizing the time and effort of fixing UX problems found in UX evaluation based on priority ratios, which are calculated by dividing the importance of making a change by the cost (Section 26.4).

appreciate the value of these things to them and their organization. This is basically a motivation for UX based on a business case.

Educating the audience. The next goal of your presentation is teaching, explaining terminology and concepts. Help them understand how to view evaluation results as a positive thing, an opportunity and a means to improve.

Persuading and selling UX. You want to get their buy-in to the idea of doing UX. You want them to want to include a UX component in their overall development process (and budgets and schedules).

27.3.3 Reporting to Inform and/or Influence Management

Reports to management have to be short and sweet. Be concise and get to the point. Start with an executive summary. Briefly explain the process, the evaluation goals, the methods, and the UX targets and benchmark tasks used. Because this can be counted as at least a partly "internal" audience, you can share high-level aspects of informal quantitative testing (e.g., user performance and satisfaction scores), but just trends observed, not numbers and no "claims," and remember not to call it a "study."

Define your priorities and relate them directly to business goals. This is easier if you used UX targets driven by UX goals, based on business and product goals. You need an "explicit connection between the business or test goals and the results" (Theofanos and Quesenbery, 2005; Theofanos et al., 2005). The team's key goal for reporting to this audience is to influence and convince them that this is part of the process and that the process is working.

Use cost-importance analysis to focus on UX problems that can be fixed within the number of people hours allocated in the budget, but paint a complete picture of your findings. Screen shots illustrating actual problem encounters might be useful in engaging them in the whole evaluation scene.

27.3.4 Reporting to Customer or Client

If your team did not create the design you evaluated, it is best to not start by hitting the client square on with what is wrong with the system. This audience needs first to understand the whole concept of designing for UX and the methods you use and how they help improve the product. You have to tell them tactfully that their baby is ugly, but can be fixed.

Explain that finding UX problems in evaluation is simply part of a process focused on *fixing* problems. Be selective and describe a few examples. Clients and customers will not want to hear that there is a whole list of problems with the design of their system. For clients, UX problems are best described with scenarios

---

UX Goal

High-level objectives for a UX design, stated in terms of user experience targets (Section 22.4).

and screen shots that tell stories of how design flaws affected users, and how your UX engineering process finds and fixes those problems.

27.4 REPORT CONTENT

In this section, we cover the different types of content that could go into a UX evaluation report.

27.4.1 Individual Problem Reporting Content

Many researchers and practitioners have suggested various content items that might prove useful for problem diagnosis and redesign. The idea is to provide all the essential facts a designer will need to understand and fix the problem. Of course, at this point, the evaluators would have had to collect sufficient data to be able to provide all this information. The basic information needed includes:

- The problem description.
- A best judgment of the causes of the problem in the design.
- An estimate of its severity or impact.
- Suggested solutions.

In the first of these items, be sure to describe each problem as a problem, not as a solution. Because the problems were experienced by users doing tasks, describe them in that context—users and tasks and the effects of the problems on users. This means saying, for example, "Users could not figure out what to do next because they did not notice the buttons," instead of "We need flashing red buttons."

The second item, the engineering judgment of the causes of the problem in the UX design, is an essential part of the diagnosis of a UX problem and perhaps the most important part of the report. Because the flaw in the design is what needs to be fixed, you should connect it with the appropriate design guidelines and/or heuristic violations as much as possible in terms of UX issues and principles.

Next is an estimate of severity or importance in terms of the impact on users. To be convincing, this must be well reasoned. Finally, to help designers act to fix the problems, recommend one or more possible design solutions, along with cost estimates and tradeoffs for each, especially if a solution has a downside. To justify the fixes, make compelling arguments for improved design and positive impact on users.

There are many other kinds of information that can be useful in a UX problem report content, including an indication of how many times each UX problem was encountered (by each user and by all users) to help convey its importance.

27.4.2 Give Some Coverage of the Ecological and Emotional Layers of the Needs Pyramid

Most of the UX problems you will find and report will occur at the interaction level. But you should also give some attention to the ecological and emotional layers. If there are problems with the design at the ecological level, especially problems with the conceptual design, be sure to stress the importance of this level of design. Unless the design is successful at the ecological level, evaluation at the other levels won't ever make it a good design.

Special discussion should be directed to reporting emotional impact problems, as those problems can be the most important for product improvement and marketing advantage, but these problems and their solutions can also be the most elusive. Emotional impact problems should be flagged as a somewhat different kind of problem with different kinds of recommendations for solutions.

Provide a holistic summary of the overall emotional impact on participants. Report specific positive and negative highlights with examples from particular episodes or incidents. If possible, try to inspire by comparing with products and systems having high emotional impact ratings.

27.4.3 Include Cost-Importance Data

Usually, cost-importance analysis is considered part of the nitty-gritty engineering details that would be beyond the interest or understanding of those outside the UX team and its process. However, cost-importance analysis, especially the prioritization process, can be of interest to those who have to fix the problems and those who have to pay for it.

Importance ratings and supporting rationale can be helpful in convincing designers to fix at least the most urgent problems. The cost-importance table, plus any discussion supporting the choice of table entries, will tell the story.

27.5 REPORT MECHANICS

27.5.1 Consistency Rules

Consistency in reporting UX problems is important for all audiences. Evaluation reports are, above all, a means of communication, and understanding is hampered by wildly varying vocabulary, differences among diagnoses and descriptions of the same kinds of problems, the language and style of expression in UX problem descriptions, and level of description contained (e.g., describing surface observables versus the use of abstraction to get at the nature of the underlying problem). Establishing your own standards for reporting results helps control broad variation in content, structure, and quality of UX problem reports.

Abstraction

The process of removing extraneous details of something and focusing on its irreducible constructs to identify what is really going on, ignoring everything else (Section 14.2.8.2).

27.5.2 Reporting Vocabulary
27.5.2.1 Precision and specificity

You are communicating with others to accomplish an outcome. To get the audience to share the vision of that outcome or to even understand what outcome you want, you need to communicate effectively; perhaps the first rule for effective communication is to be precise and specific. It takes more effort to write effective reports.

Sloppy terminology, vague directions, and lazy hand-waving are likely to be met with indifference, and the designers and other practitioners are less likely to understand the problems and solutions we propose in the report. This kind of effect of a problem report on our audience usually results in their being unconvinced that there is a real problem.

So, instead of saying a dialogue box message text is hard to understand and recommending that someone write it more clearly, you should, in fact, make your own best effort at rewording to clarify the text and say why your version is better. The criterion for effectiveness is whether the designer who receives your problem report will be able to make better design choices (Dumas et al., 2004).

27.5.2.2 Jargon

As UX professionals, we, like most others in technical disciplines, have our own jargon. But, as UX professionals, we must also know that our UX problem reports are like "error messages" to designers, and that guidelines for error message design apply to our reports as well. And one of those guidelines about messages is to avoid jargon.

So, while we might not put jargon in our UX designs, we might well be tempted to use our own technical language in our reports about UX. Yes, our audience is supposed to include UX professionals and UX designers, but you cannot be sure how much they share your specialized vocabulary. Spell things out in plain natural language.

27.5.3 Report Tone

The British are too polite to be honest, but the Dutch are too honest to be polite.

–Candid Dutch saying

All your audiences deserve respect in evaluation reports. In reporting to customers and clients, most UX professionals appreciate the need to temper reports with restraint. But even your own team should be addressed with courtesy.

27.5.3.1 Respect feelings

Whether the design you evaluated was created by your own team or by others, treat the work with respect. Don't attack. Don't demean. Don't insult. Your goal is not to get designers angry or resentful, but to get them to act on the report and fix the problems. As Dumas, Molich, and Jeffries put it: "Express your annoyance tactfully."

Some evaluators believe that design flaws must be stated in strong language to convey the message. But designers say they are insulted by emotional rants and that, "Being blunt is not helpful; it is simply rude" (Dumas et al., 2004).

27.5.3.2 Accentuate the positive and avoid blaming

Most UX professionals do realize that they should start with good things to say about the system being evaluated. However, even when encouraged to be positive, some practitioners in studies (Dumas et al., 2004) proved to be reticent in this regard. This may be because their usual audience is the project team who just want to know what the problems are so that they can start fixing them.

However, even if the report is mainly critical, it is best to start with *something* positive. Include information about places where participants did not have problems, where they were successful in task completion, and where users expressed great satisfaction or joy of use. Stories of good things happening can start things off with very positive feelings. The rest is, then: "We are on a roll: How can we make it even better?"

Present reports about design flaws as opportunities for design improvement, not as a criticism. A good way to do this is to remind them that the *goal* of formative evaluation is to find problems so that you can fix them. Therefore, a report containing information about problems found is an indication of success in the process. Congratulations, team; your process is working!

27.5.4 Reporting on Large Amounts of Qualitative Data

If you are reporting on a large amount of evaluation, about a large number of UX problems, you need to be well organized. If you ramble and jump around among different kinds of problems without an integrated perspective, it will be like a hodgepodge to your audience, and you will lose them, along with their support for making changes based on your evaluation.

One possible approach is to use an affinity diagram technique (a hierarchical diagram of evaluation notes, a bottom-up technique for organizing lots of disparate pieces of evaluation data, Section 8.7.1). We showed how to use an affinity diagram to organize work activity data, and you can use the same technique here to organize all your UX problem data for reporting. Post notes about each problem at the detailed level, and group them according to commonalities and categories, for example, with respect to task structure, organization of functionality, or other system structure.

27.5.5 Your Personal Presence in Reporting

Don't just write up a report and send it out, hoping that will do the job. If possible, you should be there to make a presentation when you deliver the report. The difference your personal presence at the time of reporting can make in reaching your goals, especially in influencing and convincing, is inestimable. Nothing beats face-to-face communication to set the desired tone and expectations. There is no substitute for being there to answer questions and head off costly misunderstandings. If the audience is distributed geographically, this is a good time to use videoconferencing or at least a teleconference.

Exercise 27-1: UX Evaluation Reporting for Your System

Goal: Write a report of the formative UX evaluation you did on the system of your choice.

Activities: Report on your informal summative evaluation results using a table showing UX targets, benchmark tasks, questionnaires, and so on used to gather data, along with target values and observed values.

Add brief statements about whether or not each UX target was met.

Write a full report on a selected subset (about half a dozen) of UX problems found in the qualitative part of your formative UX evaluation. Follow the guidelines in this chapter regarding content, tone, and format, being sure to include redesign proposals for each problem.

Report on the results of your cost-importance analysis, including problem resolutions, for all the problems you reported previously and, if appropriate, some others for context.

Deliverables: Your formative evaluation report.

Schedule: We expect this exercise to take about an hour.

Background: UX Evaluation

28

Highlights

- The dangers of trying to do summative evaluation in UX practice.
- Evaluation reliability.
- Variations in formative evaluation results.
- Roots for UX metrics and targets.
- The early A330 Airbus—An example of the need for ecological validity in testing.
- Determining the right number of participants.
- Roots of the critical incident data collection technique.
- More data collection techniques for emotional impact data.
- Nielsen and Molich's original heuristics.
- UX problem data management.

28.1 THIS IS A REFERENCE CHAPTER

This chapter contains reference material relevant to the other chapters of Part 5. This chapter is not intended to be read through as a regular chapter, but each section is supposed to be read when a reference to it in the main chapters is encountered.

28.2 THE DANGERS OF TRYING TO (OR EVEN APPEARING TO) DO FORMAL SUMMATIVE EVALUATION IN UX PRACTICE

28.2.1 Engineering Versus Science

> *It's all very well in practice but it will never work in theory.*
>
> — French management saying

Sometimes, empirical lab-based UX testing that includes informal quantitative metrics is the source of controversy with respect to "validity." Sometimes we hear,

Formal Summative Evaluation

Quantitative evaluation with a goal to assess, determine, or compare a level achieved of a parameter (such as usability), especially for assessing improvement in the user experience due to formative evaluation (Section 21.1.5).

"Because your informal summative evaluation was not controlled testing, why should we not dismiss your results as too 'soft'?" "Your informal studies aren't good science. You can't draw any conclusions."

These questions ignore the fundamental difference between formal and informal summative evaluation and the fact that they have completely different goals and methods. This may be due, in part, to the fact that the fields of HCI and UX were formed as a melting pot of people from widely varying backgrounds. From their own far-flung cultures in psychology, human factors engineering, systems engineering, software engineering, marketing, and management, they arrived at the docks of HCI with their baggage containing their own perspectives and mindsets.

Thus, it is known that formal summative evaluations are judged on a number of rigorous criteria, such as validity. But informal summative evaluation may be less known as an important engineering tool in the HCI bag, and that the *only* criterion for judging this kind of summative evaluation method is effectiveness within an *engineering* process.

28.2.2 What Happens in Engineering Stays in Engineering

Because informal summative evaluation is engineering, it comes with some very strict limitations, particularly on sharing informal summative results.

Informal summative evaluation results are only for internal use as engineering tools to do an engineering job by the project team and shouldn't be shared outside the team. Because of the lack of statistical rigor, these results especially can't be used to make any claims inside or outside the team. To make claims about UX levels achieved from informal summative results, for example, would be a violation of professional ethics.

We read of a case in which a high-level manager in a company got a UX report from a project team, but discounted the results because they were not statistically significant. This problem could have been avoided by following our simple rules and not distributing formative evaluation reports outside the team or by writing the report for a management audience with careful caveats.

28.3 UX EVALUATION RELIABILITY

The reliability of a UX evaluation method is about repeatability—how consistently can it be used to find the same results (UX problems to be fixed) across different evaluators and different designs being evaluated?

28.3.1 Individual Differences Naturally Cause Variations in Results

The literature contains many discussions and debates about the effectiveness and reliability of various UX evaluation methods. Effectiveness in the entire field of UX evaluation has been called into question. We can't hope to replicate that level of discussion here, but we do offer a few insights into the problem.

When the variation of UX evaluation results is due to using different evaluators, it is called the "evaluator effect" (Hertzum and Jacobsen, 2003; Vermeeren, van Kesteren, and Bekker, 2003). Different people see usage and problems differently and have different problem detection rates. They naturally see different UX problems in the same design. Different evaluators even report very different problems when observing the same evaluation session. Different UX teams interpret the same evaluation report in different ways. Even the same person can get different results in two successive evaluations of the same system.

28.3.2 Why So Much Variation? UX Evaluation is Difficult

In our humble opinion, the biggest reason for the limitations of our current methods is that evaluating UX, especially in large system designs, is very difficult.

No one has the resources to look everywhere and test every possible feature on every possible screen or web page in every possible task. You are just not going to find all the UX problems in all those places. One evaluator might find a problem in a place that other evaluators didn't even look. Why are we surprised that each evaluator doesn't come up with the same comprehensive problem list?

How can you ever hope to find your way through it all, let alone do a thorough job of UX evaluation? There are just so many issues and difficulties, so many places for UX problems to hide. It brings to mind the image of a person with a metal detector, searching over a large beach. There is no chance of finding all the detectable items.

28.3.3 "Discount" UX Evaluation Methods
28.3.3.1 What is a "discount" UX evaluation method?

A rapid UX evaluation method is a method that results simply from trading off the thoroughness of high rigor for low cost and fast application. The rapid methods include most of the analytic data collection, especially in their less rigorous forms. Because inspection techniques are less costly, they have been called "discount" evaluation techniques (Nielsen, 1989).

28.3.3.2 Criticism of discount methods

Rapid UX evaluation methods, especially inspection methods, have been criticized as "damaged merchandise" (Gray and Salzman, 1998) or "discount goods" (Cockton and Woolrych, 2002). The term "rapid" was intended as a positive reflection of the advantage of lower costs. However, the terms "damaged" and "discount" were used pejoratively to connote inferior, bargain-basement goods because of the reduced effectiveness and susceptibility to errors in identifying UX problems.

28.3.3.3 Real limitations

The major downsides of inspection methods, which do not employ real users, is that they can be error-prone and can tend to find a higher proportion of lower severity problems. They can suffer from validity problems, yielding some false positives (occurrences identified as UX issues but which turn out not to be real problems) and missing some UX problems because of false negatives.

Another potential drawback is that the UX experts doing the inspection may not know the subject-matter domain or the system in depth. This can lead to a less effective inspection but can be offset somewhat by including a subject-matter expert on the inspection team.

It might be some comfort, however, to know that these weaknesses are inherent in virtually all kinds of UX evaluation, including our venerable yardstick of performance, rigorous lab-based empirical formative evaluation (Molich et al., 1998; Molich et al., 1999; Newman, 1998; Spool and Schroeder, 2001). That is because many of the phenomena and principles are the same, and the working concepts are not that different. Formative evaluation, in general, just isn't very reliable or repeatable.

28.3.3.4 But do less rigorous methods work?

As in most things, the value of these methods depends on the context of their use and the most common use today is in agile UX practice, where the rapid evaluation methods are the de facto standard.

In the hands of an experienced evaluator, inspection methods can be relatively fast and very effective—you can get a significant portion of UX problems dealt with and out of the way at a low cost. Under the right conditions, you can do a UX inspection and its analysis, fix the major problems, and update the prototype design in a day!

28.3.3.5 Be practical

Approaching perfection is expensive. In engineering, the goal is to make it good enough. Wixon (2003) speaks up for the practitioner in the discussion of usability evaluation methods. From an applied perspective, he points out that a focus on validity and proper statistical analysis in these studies isn't serving the needs of practitioners in finding the most suitable usability evaluation method and best practices for their work context in the business world.

Wixon (2003) would like to see more emphasis on usability evaluation method comparison criteria that take into account factors that determine their success in real product development organizations. As an example, the value of a method might be less about absolute numbers of problems detected and more about how well a usability evaluation method fits into the work style and development process of the organization. And to this we can only say amen.

28.3.3.6 Sometimes you do have to pay more to get more

Where human lives are at risk, we are compelled to spend more resources to be more thorough in all our process activities and surely don't want an evaluation error to weaken the design in the end. In most applications, though, each error simply means that we missed an opportunity to improve usability in just one detail of the design.

28.3.3.7 At the end of the day, discount methods are the way forward

In sum, although criticized as false economy in the academic HCI literature, these so-called "discount" methods are practiced heavily and successfully in the field.

Hope. Among reasons we have to be optimistic in the long run about less rigorous UX evaluation methods are:

- Iteration helps close the gap.
- Evaluation methods can be backed up with UX expertise.
- Because evaluators have individual differences, adding evaluators really helps because one evaluator might detect a problem that others don't.
- We are using our experience as UX practitioners and not doing the process with our eyes closed.

Low reliability is acceptable. It's not that the facts uncovered in the studies critical of evaluation reliability are wrong but, in the context of UX practice, the conclusions are wrong. Despite the low reliability of methods, especially the rapid and low-cost methods; these methods work quite well enough to suffice. While our methods may not find all UX problems, we usually get some good ones. If we fix those, maybe we will get the others the next time.

So don't worry too much about evaluation reliability. Every problem you find and fix is one less barrier to a good user experience. It's an engineering process and we have to be happy with "good enough."

So, here we wholeheartedly affirm the value of discount UX evaluation methods among your UX engineering tools!

28.4 HISTORICAL ROOTS FOR UX METRICS AND TARGETS

The concept of formal UX measurement specifications in tabular form, with various metrics operationally defining success, was originally developed by Gilb (1987). The focus of Gilb's work was on using measurements in managing software development resources. Bennett (1984) adapted this approach to usability specifications as a technique for setting planned usability levels and managing the process to meet those levels.

These ideas were integrated into usability engineering practice by Good, Spine, Whiteside, and George (1986) and further refined by Whiteside, Bennett, and Holtzblatt (1988). Usability engineering, as defined by Good et al. (1986), is a process through which quantitative usability characteristics are specified early and measured throughout the lifecycle process.

28.5 THE EARLY A330 AIRBUS—AN EXAMPLE OF THE NEED FOR ECOLOGICAL VALIDITY IN TESTING

We experienced a real-world example of a product that could have benefited enormously from better ecological validity (the extent to which your UX evaluation setup matches the user's real work context) in its testing. We traveled in an A330 Airbus airplane when that model first came out; our plane was 1 week old. (Advice: for many reasons, do not be the first to travel in a new airplane design.) We were told that a human-centered approach was taken in the A330 Airbus design, including UX testing of buttons, layout, and so on of the passenger controls for the entertainment system. Apparently, though, they did not do enough in situ testing. Each passenger had a personal viewing screen for movies and other entertainment, considered an advantage over the screens hanging from the ceiling. The controls for each seat were more or less like a TV remote control, only tethered with a "pull-out" cord. When not in use, the remote control snapped into a recessed space on the seat arm rest. Cool, eh?

The LCD screen had nice color and brightness but a low acceptable viewing angle. Get far off the axis (away from perpendicular to the screen) and you lose all brightness, and, just before it disappears altogether, you see the picture as a color negative image. But the screen is right in front of you, so no problem, right? Right, until in a real flight, the person in front of you tilts back the seat. Then, we could barely see it. We could tell it was affecting others, too, because we could see many people leaning their heads down into an awkward position just to see the screen. After a period of fatigue, many people gave up, turned it off, and leaned back for comfort. If the display screen was used in UX testing, and we have to assume it was, the question of tilting the seat never entered the discussion, probably because the screen was propped up on a stand in front of each participant in the UX lab. Designers and evaluators just did not think about passengers in front of screen users tilting back their seats. Testing in a more realistic setting, better emulating the ecological conditions of real flight, would have revealed this major flaw.

It does not end there. Once the movie got going, most people stowed the remote control away in the arm rest. But, of course, what do you also rest on an arm rest? Your arm. And in so doing, it was easy to bump a button on the control and make some change in the "programming." The design of this clever feature almost always made the movie disappear at a crucial point in the plot. And because we were syncing our movie viewing, the other one of us had to pause the movie, while the first one had to go back through far too many button pushes to get the movie back and fast-forwarded to the current place.

It still does not end here. After the movie was over (or for some viewers, after they gave up) and we wanted to sleep, a bump of the arm on the remote caused the screen to light up brightly, instantly waking us to the wonderful world of entertainment. The flight attendant in just one week with this design had already come up with a creative workaround. She showed us how to pull the remote out on its cord and dangle it down out of the way of the arm rest. Soon, and this is the UX-gospel truth, almost everyone in the plane had a dangling remote control swinging gracefully in the aisle like so many synchronized reeds in the breeze as the plane moved about on its course.

28.6 DETERMINING THE RIGHT NUMBER OF PARTICIPANTS

One of your activities in preparing for formative evaluation is finding appropriate users for the evaluation sessions. In formal summative evaluation, this part of the process is referred to as "sampling," but that term isn't appropriate here because what we are doing has nothing to do with the implied statistical relationships and constraints.

28.6.1 How Many are Needed? A Difficult Question

How many participants are enough? This is one of those issues that some novice UX practitioners take so seriously, and yet, it is a question to which there is no definitive answer. Indeed, there can't be one answer. It depends so much on the specific context and parameters of your individual situation that you have to answer this question for yourself each time you do formative evaluation.

There are studies that lead UX gurus to proclaim various rules of thumb, such as, "three to five users are enough to find 80% of your UX problems," but when you see how many different assumptions are used to arrive at those "rules," and how few of those assumptions are valid within your project, you realize that this is one place in the process where it is most important for you to use your own head and not follow vague generalizations.

And, of course, cost is often a limiting factor. Sometimes, you just get one or two participants in each of one or two iterations, and you have to be satisfied with that because it is all you can afford. The good news is that you can accomplish a lot with only a few good participants. There is no statistical requirement for large numbers of "subjects" as there is for formal summative evaluation; rather, the goal is to focus on extracting as much information as possible from every participant.

28.6.2 Rules of Thumb Abound

There are bona fide studies that predict the optimum number of participants needed for UX testing under various conditions. Most "rules of thumb" are based empirically but, because they are quoted and applied so broadly without regard to the constraints and conditions under which the results were obtained, these rules have become among the most folklorish of folklore out there.

Nielsen and Molich (1990) had an early paper about the number of users/ participants needed to find enough UX problems and found that 80% of their known UX problems could be detected with four to five participants, and the most severe problems were usually found with the first few participants. Virzi (1990, 1992) more or less confirmed Nielsen and Molich's study.

Nielsen and Landauer (1993) found that detection of problems as a function of the number of participants is well modeled as a Poisson process, supporting the ability to use early results to estimate the number of problems left to be found and the number of additional participants needed to find a certain percentage.

Depending on the circumstances, though, some say that even five participants is no way near enough (Hudson, 2001; Spool and Schroeder, 2001), especially for complex applications or large websites. In practice, each of these numbers has proven to be right for some set of conditions, but the question is whether they will work for you in your evaluation.

28.6.3 An Analytic Basis for the Three-To-Five-Users Rule
28.6.3.1 The underlying probability function

In Fig. 28-1, you can see graphs, related to the binomial probability distribution, of cumulative percentages of problems likely to be found for a given number of participants used and at various detection rates, adapted from Lewis (1994).

Y-axis values in these curves are for "discovery likelihood," expressed as a cumulative percentage of problems likely to be found as a function of the

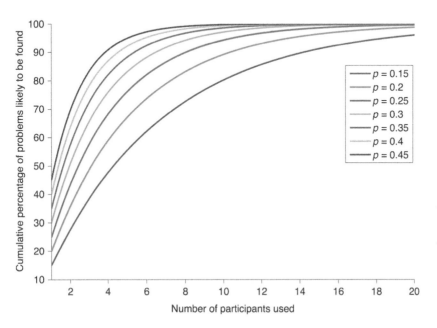

Fig. 28-1

Graphs of cumulative percentages of problems likely to be found for a given number of participants used and at various detection rates [adapted from (Lewis, 1994)].

number of participants or evaluators used. These curves are based on the probability formula:

discovery likelihood (cumulative percentage of problems likely to be found = 1 − (1 − p)^n,

where n is the number of participants used (X-axis values), and p is what we call the

"detection rate" of a certain category of participants.

As an example, this formula tells us that a sample size of five participant evaluators (*n*) with an individual detection rate (*p*) of at least 0.30 is sufficient to find approximately 80% of the UX problems in a system.

28.6.3.2 The old balls-in-an-urn analogy

Let us think of an interaction design containing flaws that cause UX problems as analogous to the old probability setting of an urn containing various colored balls. Among an unknown number of balls of all colors, suppose there are a number of red balls, each representing a different UX problem.

Suppose now that a participant or evaluator reaches in and grabs a big handful of balls from the urn. This is analogous to an evaluation session using a single expert evaluator, if it is a UX inspection evaluation, or a single participant, if it is a lab-based empirical session. The number of red balls in that handful is the number of UX problems identified in the session.

In a UX inspection, it is the expert evaluator, or inspector, who finds the UX problems. In an empirical UX test, participants are a catalyst for UX problem detection—not necessarily detecting problems themselves, but encountering critical incidents while performing tasks, enabling evaluators to identify the corresponding UX problems. Because the effect is essentially the same, for simplicity in this discussion we will use the term "participant" for both the inspector and the testing participant and "find problems" for whatever way the problems are found in a session.

28.6.3.3 Participant detection rates

The detection rate, *p*, of an individual participant is the percentage of existing problems that this participant can find in one session. This corresponds to the number of red balls a participant gets in one handful of balls. This is a function of the individual participant. For example, in the case of the balls in the urn, it might be related to the size of the participant's hand. In the UX domain, it is perhaps related to the participant's evaluation skills.

In any case, in this analysis, if a participant has a detection rate of *p* = 0.20, it means that this participant will find 20% of the UX problems existing in the design. The number of participants with that same individual detection rate who, in turn, reach into the urn is the value on the X axis. The curve shown with a green line is for a detection rate of $p = 0.20$. The other curves are for different detection rates, from $p = 0.15$ up to $p = 0.45$.

Most of the time, we do not even know the detections rates of our participants. To calculate the detection rate for a participant, we would have to know how many total UX problems exist in a design. But that is just what we are trying to find out with evaluation. You could, we guess, run a testing session with the participant against a design with a certain number of known flaws. But that would tell you that participant's detection rate for that day, in that context, and for that system. Unfortunately, a given participant's detection rate isn't constant.

28.6.3.4 Cumulative percentage of problems to be found

The Y axis represents values of the cumulative percentage of problems to be found. Let us look at this first for just one participant. The curve for $p = 0.20$, for example, has a Y axis value of 20%, for $n = 1$ (where the curve intersects the Y axis). This is consistent with our expectation that one participant with $p = 0.20$ will find 20% of the problems, or get 20% of the red balls, in the first session.

Now, what about the "cumulative" aspect? What happens when the second participant reaches into the urn depends on whether you replaced the balls from the first participant. This analysis is for the case where each participant returns all the balls to the urn after each "session"; that is, none of the UX problems are fixed between participants.

After the first participant has found some problems, there are fewer *new* problems left to find by the second participant. If you look at the results with the two participants independently, they each help you find a somewhat different 20% of the problems, but there is likely to be overlap, which reduces the cumulative effect (the union of the sets of problems) of the two.

This is what we see in the curves of Fig. 28-1 as the percentage of problems likely to be found drops off with each new participant (moving to the right on the X axis) because the marginal number of new problems found is decreasing. That accounts for the leveling off of the curves until, at some high number of participants, essentially no new problems are being found, and the curve is asymptotically flat.

28.6.3.5 Marginal added detection and cost-benefit

One thing we do notice in the curves of Fig. 28-1 is that, despite the drop-off of effective detection rates, as you continue to add more participants, you will continue to uncover more problems. At least for a while. Eventually, high detection rates coupled with high numbers of participants will yield results that asymptotically approach about 100% in the upper right-hand part of the figure, and virtually no new problems will be found with subsequent participants.

But what happens along the way? Each new participant helps you find fewer new problems, but because the cost to run each participant is about the same, with each successive participant, the process becomes less efficient (fewer new problems found for the same cost).

As a pretty good approximation of the cost to run a UX testing session with n participants, you have a fixed cost to set up the session plus a variable cost (or cost per participant) $= a + bn$. The benefit of running a UX testing session with n participants is the discovery likelihood. So, the cost benefit is the ratio benefit/cost, each as a function of n, or benefit/cost $= (1 - (1 - p^n))/(a + bn)$.

If you graph this function (with some specific values of a and b) against $n = 1, 2, \ldots$, you will see a curve that climbs for the first few values of n and then starts dropping off. The values of n around the peak of cost-benefit are the optimum (from a cost-benefit perspective) number of participants to use. The range of n for which the peak occurs depends on parameters a, b, and p of your setup; your mileage can vary.

Nielsen and Landauer (1993) showed that real data for both UX inspections and lab-based testing with participants did match this mathematical cost-benefit model. Their results showed that, for their parameters, the peak occurred for values of n around 3 to 5. Thus, the "three-to-five-users" rule of thumb.

28.6.3.6 Assumptions do not always apply in the real world

This three-to-five-users rule, with its tidy mathematical underpinning, can and does apply to many situations similar to the conditions Nielsen and Landauer (1993) used, and we believe their analysis brings insight into the discussion. However, we know there are many cases where it just does not apply.

For starters, all of this analysis, including the analogy with the balls-in-an-urn setting, depends on two assumptions:

- Each participant has a constant detection rate, p.
- Each UX problem is equally likely to be found in testing.

If UX problems were balls in an urn, our lives would be simpler. But neither of these assumptions is true, and the UX life isn't simple.

Assumptions about detection rates. Each curve in Fig. 28-1 is for a fixed detection rate, and the cost-benefit calculation given earlier was based on a fixed detection rate, p. But the "evaluator effect" tells us not only will different evaluators find different problems, but also the detection rate can vary widely over participants (Hertzum and Jacobsen, 2003).

In fact, a given individual does not even have a fixed "individual detection rate"; it can be influenced from day to day or even from moment to moment by how rested the participant is, blood caffeine and ethanol levels, attitude, the system, how the evaluators conduct the evaluation, what tasks are used, the evaluator's skills, and so on.

Also, what does it *really* mean for a testing participant to have a detection rate of $p = 0.20$? How long does it take in a session for that participant to achieve that 20% discovery? How many tasks? What kinds of tasks? What if that participant continues to perform more tasks? Will no more critical incidents be encountered after 20% detection is achieved?

Assumptions about problem detectability. The curves in Fig. 28-1 are also based on an assumption that all problems are equally detectable (like all red balls in the urn are equally likely to be drawn out). But, of course, we know that some problems are almost obvious on the surface, and other problems can be orders of magnitude more difficult to ferret out. So detectability, or likelihood of being found, can vary dramatically across various UX problems.

Task selection. One reason for the overlap in problems detected from one participant to another, causing the cumulative detection likelihood to fall off with additional participants, as it does in Fig. 28-1, is the use of prescribed tasks. Participants performing essentially the same sets of tasks are looking in the same places for problems and are, therefore, more likely to uncover many of the same problems.

However, if you employ user-directed tasks (Spool and Schroeder, 2001), participants will be looking in different places, and the overlap of problems found could be much less. This keeps the benefit part of the curves growing linearly for more participants, causing your optimum number of participants to be larger.

Application system effects. Another factor that can torpedo the three-to-five-users rule is the application system being evaluated. Some systems are much larger than others. For example, an enormous website or a large and complex word processor will harbor many more possibilities for UX problems than, say, a simple interoffice scheduling system. If each participant can explore only a small portion of such an application, the overlap of problems among participants may be insignificant. In such cases, the cost-benefit function will peak with many more participants than three to five.

Bottom line. You can't compute and graph all the theoretical curves and parameters we talk about here because you will never know how many UX problems exist in the design, so you will never know what percentage of the existing problems you have found. You do not have to use those curves, anyway, to have a pretty good intuitive feeling for whether you are still detecting useful new problems with each new participant. Look at the results from each participant and each iteration and ask if those results were worth it and whether it is worth investing a little more.

28.7 HISTORICAL ROOTS OF THE CRITICAL INCIDENT TECHNIQUE

28.7.1 Critical Incident Techniques Started Long Ago in Human Factors

Critical Incident

An event that occurs during user task performance or other user interaction that indicate possible UX problem(s). Critical incident identification, an empirical UX evaluation data collection technique based on the participant and/or evaluator detecting and analyzing critical incidents, is arguably the single most important qualitative data collection technique (Section 24.2.1).

The origins of the critical incident technique can be traced back at least to studies performed in the Aviation Psychology Program of the US Army Air Forces in World War II to analyze and classify pilot error experiences in reading and interpreting aircraft instruments. The technique was first formally codified by the work of Fitts and Jones (1947). Flanagan (1954) synthesized the landmark critical incident technique.

28.7.2 Mostly Used as a Variation

When Flanagan designed the critical incident technique in 1954, he did not see it as a single rigid procedure. He was in favor of modifying this technique to meet different needs as long as original criteria were met. The variation occurring over the years, however, may have been more than Flanagan anticipated. Forty years after the introduction of Flanagan's critical incident technique, Shattuck and Woods (1994) reported a study that revealed that this technique has rarely been used as originally published. In fact, numerous variations of the method were found, each suited to a particular field of interest. In HCI, we have continued this tradition of adaptation by using our own version of the critical incident technique as a primary UX evaluation technique to identify UX problems and their causes.

28.7.3 Who Identifies Critical Incidents?

In the original work by Fitts and Jones (1947), the user (an airplane pilot) was the one who reported critical incidents after task performance was completed. Later, Flanagan (1954) used trained observers (evaluators) to collect critical incident information while observing users performing tasks.

del Galdo, Williges, Williges, and Wixon (1986) involved users in identifying their own critical incidents, reporting during task performance. The technique was also used as a self-reporting mechanism by Hartson and Castillo (1998) as the basis for remote system or product usability evaluation. Further, Dzida, Wiethoff, and Arnold (1993) and Koenemann-Belliveau, Carroll, Rosson, and Singley (1994) adopted the stance that identifying critical incidents during task performance can be an individual process by either the user or an evaluator or a mutual process between the user and an evaluator.

28.7.4 Timing of Critical Incident Data Capture: The Evaluator's Awareness Zone

While users are known to report major UX problems in alpha and beta testing (sending software out for comments on how well it worked), one reason these methods can't be relied upon for thorough identification of UX problems to fix is the retrospective nature of that kind of data collection. Lab-based UX evaluation has the advantage of having the precious and volatile details right in front of you as they happen. The key to this kind of UX data is in the details, and details of these data are perishable; they must be captured immediately as they arise during usage.

The upshot: capture and document the details while they are fresh. If you capture them as they happen, we call it concurrent data capture. If you capture data immediately after the task, we call it contemporaneous data capture. If you try to capture data after the task is well over, through someone trying to remember the details in an interview or survey after the session, this is retrospective data capture, and many of the once-fresh details can be lost.

It isn't as easy, however, as just capturing critical incident data immediately upon its occurrence. A critical incident is often not immediately recognized for what it is. In Fig. 28-2, the evaluator's recognition of a critical incident will necessarily occur sometime after it begins to occur. And following the point of initial awareness, after confirming that it is a critical incident, the evaluator requires some time and thought in a kind of "awareness zone" to develop an understanding of the problem, possibly through discussion with the participant.

The optimum time to report the problem, the time when the potential for a quality problem report is highest, is at the peak of this problem understanding, as seen in Fig. 28-2. Before that point, the evaluator has not yet established a full understanding of the problem. After that optimum point, natural abstraction due to human memory limitations sets in and

Alpha and Beta Testing

Post-deployment evaluation methods in which near-final versions of a product are sent to select users, experts, customers, and professional reviewers as a preview, in exchange for which, they try it out and give feedback on the experience (Section 21.5.1).

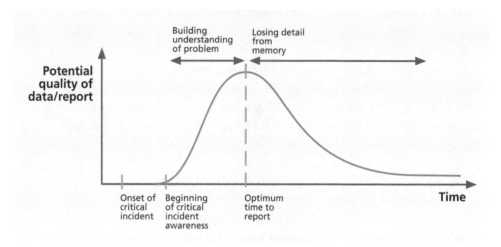

Fig. 28-2

Critical incident description detail versus time after critical incident.

details drop off rapidly with time, accelerated by proactive interference from any intervening tasks.

28.8 OTHER METHODS FOR IDENTIFYING EMOTIONAL RESPONSE TO UX DESIGNS

28.8.1 Direct Observation of Physiological Responses as Indicators of Emotional Impact

In contrast to self-reporting techniques, UX practitioners can obtain emotional impact indicator data through direct observation of participant physiological responses to emotional impact encounters as usage occurs. Usage can be teeming with user behaviors, including facial expressions (such as ephemeral grimaces or smiles) and body language (such as tapping of fingers, fidgeting, or scratching one's head) that indicate emotional impact. You will need to create conditions to encourage episodes of long-term usage activity to occur during these observational periods.

Physiological responses can be "captured" either by direct behavioral observation or by instrumented measurements. Behavioral observations include those of facial expressions, gestural behavior, and body posture. One difficulty in any observation or measurement of physiological reactions to usage events is that often there is no way to connect the physiological response to a particular emotion and its cause within the interaction.

The emotional "tells" of facial and bodily expressions can be fleeting and subliminal, easily missed in real-time observation. Therefore, to capture facial expressions data and other similar observational data reliably, practitioners usually need to make video recordings of participant usage behavior and do frame-by-frame analysis. Methods for interpreting facial expressions have been developed, including one called the Facial Action Coding System (Ekman and Friesen, 1975).

Kim et al. (2008) remind us that while we can measure physiological effects, it is difficult to connect the measurements with specific emotions and with causes within the interaction. Their solution is to supplement with traditional synchronized video-recording techniques to correlate measurements with usage occurrences and behavioral events. But this kind of video review has disadvantages: the reviewing process is usually tedious and time-consuming, you may need an analyst trained in identifying and interpreting these expressions often within a frame-by-frame analysis, and even a trained analyst can't always make the right call.

Fortunately, software-assisted recognition of facial expressions and gestures in video images is beginning to be feasible for practical applications. Software tools are now becoming available to automate real-time recognition and interpretation of facial expressions. A system called "faceAPI"[1] from Seeing Machines is advertised to both track and understand faces. It comes as a software module that you embed in your own product or application. An ordinary webcam, focused on the user's face, feeds both faceAPI and any digital video-recording program with software-accessible time stamps and/or frame numbers.

Facial expressions do seem to be mostly culture independent, and you can capture expressions without interruption of the usage. However, there are limitations that generally preclude their use. The main limitation is that they are useful for only a limited set of basic emotions such as anger or happiness, but not mixed emotions. Dormann (2003) says it is, therefore, difficult to be precise about what kind of emotion is being observed.

In order to identify facial expressions, faceAPI must track the user's face during head movement that occurs in 3D with usage. The head-tracking feature outputs X, Y, Z position and head orientation coordinates for every video frame. The facial feature detection component of faceAPI tracks three points on each eyebrow and eight points around the lips.

The detection algorithm is "robust to occlusions, fast movements, large head rotations, lighting, facial deformation, skin color, beards, and glasses." This part

---

[1]http:/www.seeingmachines.com/product/faceapi/.

of faceAPI outputs a real-time stream of facial feature data, time coordinated with the recorded video, that can be understood and interpreted via a suite of image-processing modules. The faceAPI system is a commercial product, but a free version is available to qualified users for noncommercial use.

28.8.2 Biometrics to Detect Physiological Responses to Emotional Impact

The use of instrumented measurement of physiological responses in participants is called biometrics. Biometrics are about detection and measurement of autonomic or involuntary bodily changes triggered by nervous system responses to emotional impact within interaction events. Examples include changes in heart rate, respiration, perspiration, and eye pupil dilation. Changes in perspiration are measured by galvanic skin response measurements to detect changes in electrical conductivity.

Such nervous system changes can be correlated with emotional responses to interaction events. Pupillary dilation is an autonomous indication especially of interest, engagement, and excitement and is known to correlate with a number of emotional states (Tullis and Albert, 2008).

The downside of biometrics is the need for specialized monitoring equipment. If you can get some good measuring instruments and are trained to use them to get good measures, it does not get more "embodied" than this. But most equipment for measuring physiological changes is out of reach for the average UX practitioner.

It is possible to adapt a polygraph or lie detector, for example, to detect changes in pulse, respiration, and skin conductivity that could be correlated with emotional responses to interaction events. However, the operation of most of this equipment requires skills and experience in medical technology, and interpretation of raw data can require specialized training in psychology, all beyond our scope. Finally, the extent of culture independence of facial expressions and other physiological responses isn't entirely known.

28.8.3 The HUMAINE Project—Physiological Techniques for Affective Measurements

The European community project HUMAINE (Human-Machine Interaction Network on Emotions) issued a technical report detailing a taxonomy of affective measurement techniques (Westerman, Gardner, and Sutherland, 2006). They point out that there is a history of physiological and psychophysiological measurement in human factors practice since the late 1970s to detect, for

Embodied Interaction

Interaction with technology that involves a user's body in a natural and significant way, such as by using gestures (Section 6.2.6.3).

example, stress due to operator overload, and an even longer history of this kind of measurement in psychological research.

In the HUMAINE report, the authors discuss the role of medicine in physiological measurement, including electroencephalograms and event-related potential, measured with electroencephalography, a technique that detects and measures electrical activity of the brain through the skull and scalp. Event-related potentials can be roughly correlated to cognitive functions involving memory and attention and changes in mental state.

As the authors say, these physiological measurements have the advantage over self-reporting methods in that they can monitor continuously, require no conscious user actions, and do not interrupt task performance or usage activity. To be meaningful, however, such physiological measurements have to be associated with time stamps on a video of user activity.

A major disadvantage, ruling the approach out for most routine UX evaluation, is the requirement for attached sensors. New, less intrusive instrumentation is being developed. For example, Kapoor, Picard, and Ivanov (2004) report being able to detect changes in user posture, for example, due to fidgeting, with pressure sensors attached to a chair.

28.9 NIELSEN AND MOLICH'S ORIGINAL HEURISTICS

The first set of heuristics that Nielsen and Molich developed for usability inspection (Molich and Nielsen, 1990; Nielsen and Molich, 1990) were 10 "general principles" for interaction design. They called them heuristics because they are not strict design guidelines. Here, we list the 10 original Nielsen and Molich heuristics from Nielsen's *Usability Engineering* book (Nielsen, 1993, Chapter 5).

Heuristic (in UX Design)

An analytic evaluation method based on expert UX inspection guided by a set of heuristics, general high-level UX design guidelines (Section 25.5).

- Simple and natural dialogue:
    - Good graphic design and use of color.
    - Screen layout by gestalt rules of human perception.
    - Less is more; avoid extraneous information.
- Speak the users' language:
    - User-centered terminology, not system or technology centered.
    - Use words with standard meanings.
    - Vocabulary and meaning from work domain.
    - Use mappings and metaphors to support learning.

- ▢ Minimize user memory load:
  - ▢ Clear labeling.
- ▢ Consistency:
  - ▢ Help avoid errors, especially by novices.
- ▢ Feedback:
  - ▢ Make it clear when an error has occurred.
  - ▢ Show user progress.
- ▢ Clearly marked exits:
  - ▢ Provide escape from all dialogue boxes.
- ▢ Shortcuts:
  - ▢ Help expert users without penalizing novices.
- ▢ Good error messages:
  - ▢ Clear language, not obscure codes.
  - ▢ Be precise rather than vague or general.
  - ▢ Be constructive to help solve problem.
  - ▢ Be polite and not intimidating.
- ▢ Prevent errors:
  - ▢ Many potential error situations can be avoided in design.
  - ▢ Select from lists, where possible, instead of requiring user to type in.
  - ▢ Avoid modes.
- ▢ Help and documentation:
  - ▢ When users want to read the manual, they are usually desperate.
  - ▢ Be specific with online help.

28.10 UX PROBLEM DATA MANAGEMENT

As time goes by, and you proceed further into the UX process lifecycle, the full life story of each UX problem grows, entailing slow expansion of data in the UX problem record. Each UX problem record will eventually contain information about the problem: diagnosis by problem type and subtype, interaction design flaws as problem causes, cost/importance data estimating severity, management decisions to fix (or not) the problem, costs, implementation efforts, and downstream effectiveness.

Most authors mention UX problems or problem reports but do not hint at the fact that a complete problem record can be a large and complex information object. Maintaining a complete record of this unit of UX data is surely one place where some kind of tool support, such as a database management system, is warranted. As an example of how your UX problem record structure and content

Information Object

An internally stored structured or simple article, piece of information, or data that serves as a work object. Often data entities are central to work flow, being operated on by users; they are organized, shared, labeled, navigated, searched and browsed for, accessed and displayed, modified and manipulated, and stored back again, all within a system ecology (Section 14.2.6.7).

can grow, here are some of the kinds of information that can eventually be attached to it. These are possibilities we have encountered; pick the ones that suit you:

- Problem name.
- Problem description.
- Task context.
- Effects on users (symptoms).
- Associated designer knowledge.
- Problem diagnosis (problem type and subtype and causes within the design).
- Links to constituent UX problem instances.
- Links for relationships to other UX problems (e.g., in groups to be fixed together).
- Links to project context.
- Project name.
- Version/release number.
- Project personnel.
- Link to evaluation session.
- Evaluation session date, location, etc.
- Session type (e.g., lab-based testing, UX inspection, remote evaluation).
- Links to evaluators.
- Links to participants.
- Cost-importance attributes for this iteration (next section).
- Candidate solutions.
- Estimated cost to fix.
- Importance to fix.
- Priority ratio.
- Priority ranking.
- Resolution.
- Treatment history.
- Solution used.
- Dates, personnel involved in redesign, implementation.
- Actual cost to fix.
- Results (e.g., based on retesting).

For more about representation schemes for UX problem data, see Lavery and Cockton (1997).

Part 6: Connecting Agile UX with Agile Software Engineering

6

Part 6 contains a single-chapter discourse on how to make agile UX processes and methods work with agile software engineering approaches. Beginning with the basics and the lifecycle aspects of agile SE (software engineering), we conclude with a synthesized approach to integrating agile UX and agile SE.

Connecting Agile UX With Agile Software Development

29

Highlights

- Basics of agile SE (software engineering) methods.
- Lifecycle aspects of agile SE.
- Planning in agile SE.
- Sprints in agile SE.
- Challenges in agile SE from the UX perspective.
- What is needed on the UX side?
- Problems to anticipate.
- A synthesized approach to integrating agile UX.
- Integrating UX into planning.
- Integrating UX into sprints.
- Synchronizing the two agile work flows.

Agile Software Engineering

A lifecycle process approach to software implementation based on delivering frequent small-scope operational and usable releases that can be evaluated to yield feedback (Section 29.2).

29.1 INTRODUCTION

In Chapter 4, we introduced the agile UX funnel model, and in all subsequent process chapters, we have assumed an agile UX process. Now, we discuss some details about how the agile UX process can connect to an agile SE process in real-world project environments.

Agile software engineering (SE) approaches, now well-known and commonly used, are incremental, iterative, and test-driven means of frequently delivering pieces of useful working software to customers. In the past, agile SE approaches have not taken UX into account. And, because traditional UX processes have not fit well within agile SE environments, the UX side has struggled to adjust their methods to fit SE constraints.

Funnel Model (of Agile UX)

A way of envisioning UX design activities before syncing with agile software engineering sprints (for overall conceptual design in the early funnel) and after syncing with software engineering (for individual feature design in the late funnel) (Section 4.4).

At the end of the day, the entire system development team needs an overall approach that includes agile UX while retaining the basics of agile SE approaches. In this chapter, we present a variation of our agile UX process methods that will integrate well with existing agile SE processes by accounting for the constraints imposed by those agile SE processes.

29.1.1.1 Agility is not (just) about being fast

Lots of people think the point of an agile approach is to be fast, but that misses the main point. Being agile means being light on your feet, nimble, and responsive to change during the process. Yes, an agile process is also considered fast. Compared to the old waterfall method, agile methods are very fast. But that is just a bonus side effect, not the essence of it. It's about *how* it is fast.

Agility is about being fast by not wasting time on things you don't need or will never use. It's about being fast by knowing what doesn't work before investing time and effort pursuing the wrong course. It's about being fast by focusing on the product or system rather than the process. But, more than anything else, it's about being nimble and responsive to change. A project is not a race; it's an obstacle course, or sometimes even a labyrinth. You can't know what will try to derail you from your course until you encounter it and have to react. In the old slow and careful waterfall method, you never get the feedback you need to even know there is a problem to respond to until the whole project is almost over.

Waterfall Lifecycle Process

One of the earliest formal software engineering lifecycle processes; an ordered linear sequence of lifecycle activities, each of which flowed into the next like a set of cascading tiers of a waterfall (Section 4.2).

Example: Working Too Fast Can Hurt You in the Marketplace

This is an extension of an example we started in Chapter 1 (Section 1.8.3). A number of years ago I (HRH) consulted for a small company that developed large e-commerce software systems. They had produced a new application in their line of software products, but they were having trouble with customer satisfaction. When we described the UX lifecycle process for understanding users and basing UX design on their needs and work context, we were quickly told there was no time for user research. They proudly mentioned that they were very agile organization and developed new products and systems in "internet time," working tirelessly to release products on an almost impossible schedule.

This latest system was no exception; they released it to their customers after an unbelievably short lifecycle, but it wasn't very good. But, fortunately, they had a cadre of loyal existing customers who bought essentially everything they released. Not surprisingly, they found the new system difficult to use, but they needed that functionality, so, they invested significant time and effort into learning how to use it. But this new version of the system got bad reviews and a bad reputation in the marketplace. Their marketing group became quite concerned that, although they sold a few units to existing customers, they were not able to bring in new customers.

So, they panicked, brought it back to the drawing board, and pulled everyone in to work on an improved version, this time applying some principles of UX design. The result was a system that, in fact, was better but quite different from the original version.

How did the marketplace react? Well, potential new customers did not take the bait. The company's reputation was already spoiled. What about the existing customers? Well, they were very angry and upset. They had gone through all the trouble and expense of learning the old system, and now it had changed completely. They now had to learn yet another new system. In the end, the company had managed to alienate almost all the existing and potential customers, and it was a real crisis for them. Therein lies a profound lesson about sacrificing quality for the sake of speed.

29.1.2 Don't Practice Agility Blindly

Finally, before we get into the discussion of agile SE methods, a word of caution: Some practitioners of agile software development have adopted it almost as a religion, applying it without considering the consequences and pushing it beyond its useful limits. And there is danger in agile UX practitioners following that trend. The agile process is a tool and shouldn't take on a cult-like life of its own. Use it when it works, but don't stop asking what's the best process for your project.

We begin by reviewing the essence of the agile SE approach and then identify what is needed for the two agile processes to fit together.

29.2 BASICS OF AGILE SE METHODS

Much of what is said here about agile methods in SE goes back to the fundamental work of Kent Beck (2000), one of the most authoritative sources on agile SE development methods as embodied in the approach called eXtreme Programming (XP).[1] We have taken words from Beck and other authors and tried to blend them into a summary of the practice. Accurate representations are credited to these authors, while errors in representation are on us.

---

[1] There are other "brands" of approaches to agile SE methods beyond XP, including Scrum (Rising & Janoff, 2000), but for convenience we focus on XP.

29.2.1 Goals and Principles of Agile SE

To establish agreement on early agile software methods, a group met at a workshop in Snowbird, Utah in February 2001 and worked out an "agile manifesto"[2] in which the following principles emerged:

- Our highest priority is to satisfy the customer through early and continuous delivery of valuable software.
- Welcome changing requirements, even late in development. Agile processes harness change for the customer's competitive advantage.
- Deliver working software frequently, from a couple of weeks to a couple of months, with a preference for the shorter timescale.
- Business people and developers must work together daily throughout the project.
- Build projects around motivated individuals. Give them the environment and support they need, and trust them to get the job done.
- The most efficient and effective method of conveying information to and within a development team is face-to-face conversation.
- Working software is the primary measure of progress.
- Agile processes promote sustainable development. The sponsors, developers, and users should be able to maintain a constant pace indefinitely.
- Continuous attention to technical excellence and good design enhances agility.
- Simplicity—the art of maximizing the amount of work not done—is essential.
- The best architectures, requirements, and designs emerge from self-organizing teams.
- At regular intervals, the team reflects on how to become more effective, then tunes and adjusts its behavior accordingly.

Also from that manifesto, practitioners of agile SE methods value:

- Individuals and interactions over processes and tools.
- Working software over comprehensive documentation.
- Customer collaboration over contract negotiation.
- Responding to change over following a plan.

29.2.2 Contrasting With the Waterfall Method

Such general principles can seem like platitudes, but it wasn't always so obvious. Perhaps the best way to understand the impact of these principles is through the most extreme contrast, a contrast with the old SE "waterfall" lifecycle development methodology (Royce, 1970). The waterfall model (Fig. 29-1) is a heavy process in the sense that it proceeds slowly and deliberately, finishing all of

---

[2]http://agilemanifesto.org/.

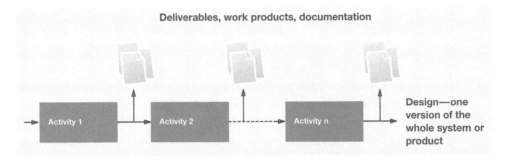

Fig. 29-1

Heavy waterfall process with deliverables and documentation after every process activity.

one process activity before starting the next, and thereby, not being responsive to change. By the end, needs and requirements have changed, and the product is off course and mostly irrelevant. Resources are wasted.

29.2.2.1 Operating in Silos

Each stage of the lifecycle was a complete enterprise in itself, occurring in its own more or less closed environment that came to be known as a silo. In each silo, a team of specialists for the work of that stage worked with its own management and produced its own deliverables. Each stage typically produces documentation, usually voluminous. You didn't get any working version of anything until the very end of the lifecycle, at which point, you got one version of the whole system or product. The problem often was, though, that it took so long to get there that, by the time you arrived, the design and even the basic concept were likely to be out of date. Certainly any requirements that had been painstakingly developed and documented in the requirements phase would no longer be complete or correct. And one long iteration wouldn't have been enough to get the design right, anyway.

29.2.3 Characteristics of Agile SE Methods

Agile SE development methods begin coding very early. Agile SE has a shorter, almost nonexistent, requirements engineering phase and far less documentation than that of traditional SE. As typified in XP, agile SE code implementation occurs in small increments and iterations.

Small releases are delivered to the customer after each short iteration, or development cycle. In most cases, these small releases, although limited in functionality, are intended to be working versions of the whole system that run by themselves and deliver some useful capability for the customer.

Silos

Major lifecycle activities in the waterfall model were sometimes called "silos," because they strongly compartmentalized the activities, a compartmentalization that was usually reflected in the developer or contractor's organization (Section 6.6).

In simplest terms, agile SE development methods "describe the problem simply in terms of small, distinct pieces, then implement these pieces in successive iterations" (Constantine, 2002, p. 3). Each piece is tested until it works and is then integrated into the rest. Next, the whole is tested in what Constantine calls "regression testing," until the new feature works with all the previously developed pieces. As a result, the next iteration always starts with something that works.

The agile software development methods are further characterized by a profound emphasis on communication, especially continuous communication with the customer. Informal communication is strongly preferred over formal. Close communication is emphasized to the point that they have an onsite customer as part of the team, giving feedback continuously.

29.2.3.1 Avoiding big design upfront

A main principle of agile SE methods is to avoid big design upfront. This means the approach generally eschews upfront ethnographic and field studies and extensive requirements engineering. The idea is to get code written as soon as possible and resolve problems by reacting to customer feedback later.

SE practitioners verify that they are writing the code correctly by the practice of pair programming. Code is written by two programmers working together and sharing one computer and one screen; that is, a colleague is always watching over each programmer's shoulder.

Of course, pair programming is not new with agile methods. Even outside agile SE methods (and before they existed, pair programming) was a proven technique with a solid track record (Constantine, 2002). Code is further verified by regular and continuous testing against an inventory of test cases.

29.3 LIFECYCLE ASPECTS OF AGILE SE

If this process were to be represented by a lifecycle diagram, it would not be a waterfall or even an iteration of stages, but a set of overlapping microdevelopment activities. In agile approaches developers do just enough—a microlevel of each activity—to support one small feature; Fig. 29-2 illustrates XP as an example agile method.

This shows that building an e-commerce website in the waterfall approach would require listing all requirements that must be supported in the website before starting a top-down design. In an agile approach, the same website would be built as a series of smaller features, such as a shopping cart or checkout module.

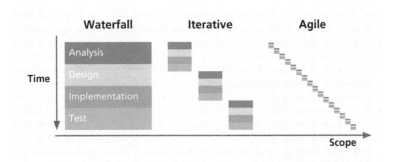

Fig. 29-2

Comparison of scope of development activities across methodologies, taken with permission from Beck (1999, Fig. 1).

29.3.1 Planning in Agile SE Methods

In our discussion of how an agile SE method works,[3] we are roughly following XP as a guide. As shown in Fig. 29-3, each iteration consists of two parts: planning and a sprint to implement and test the code for one release.

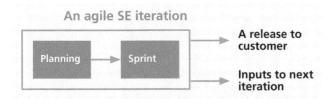

Fig. 29-3

Abstraction of an agile SE release iteration.

29.3.1.1 Customer stories

We have already been discussing user stories since Chapter 7, where the inputs to them are collected, Chapter 8, where the essence of user stories is extracted from the raw usage data, and Chapter 10, where user stories are written. Now, we show how they play a pivotal role in connecting the UX and SE in late funnel development activities.

For the moment, we will use the term "customer story," which has been used in the context of agile SE because they don't work with users. As we bring agile UX into this process, we will be switching to "user stories," which can include both sources.

> **Sprint**
>
> A relatively short (not more than a month) time period within an agile software engineering schedule in which a working and releasable product increment is implemented. It is a unit of work being done in an agile SE environment; an iteration associated with a release (to the client and/or users) (Sections 3.3, 29.3.2, and 29.7.2).

---

[3] This is the way things should work "in theory." As with most UX and SE methods, there are many variations in practice.

The planning part of each SE iteration in Fig. 29-3 yields a set of customer-written stories, prioritized by business value and cost to implement. A customer story has a role a bit like that of a use case, a scenario, or a requirement. A customer story, written on a story (index) card, is a description of a customer-requested feature. It is a narrative about how the system is supposed to solve a problem, representing a chunk of functionality that is coherent and useful in some way to the customer.

29.3.1.2 Story-based planning

Expanding the "planning" box of Fig. 29-3, we get the details of how customer stories are used in SE planning, as shown in Fig. 29-4.

As shown in Fig. 29-4, developers start the planning process by sitting down with onsite customer representatives. They ask customer representatives to think about the most useful chunks of functionality that can add business or enterprise value. The customer writes stories about the need for these pieces of functionality. This is the primary way that the developers understand "requirements," indirectly through the customer representatives.

Developers assess the stories and estimate the effort required to implement (program) a solution for each, writing the estimate on the story card. Typically, in XP, each story gets a 1-, 2-, or 3-week estimate in "ideal development time." More on how these estimates are created follows.

The customer sorts and prioritizes the story cards by choosing a small set for which the cost estimates are within a predetermined budget and which represent features they want to include in a "release." Prioritization might result in lists of stories or requirements labeled as "do first," "desired—do, if time," and "deferred—consider next time." Developers break down the stories into

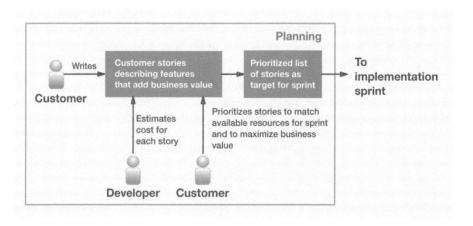

Fig. 29-4

Customer stories as the basis of agile SE planning.

development tasks, each written on a task (for the developers to do) card. Each such development task is giving a point count representing an estimate of the amount of development effort required to implement that task. Then, all tasks in a story card are totaled to arrive at the ideal development time.

The output of the planning box, which goes to the upcoming implementation sprint, is a set of customer-written stories, prioritized by cost to implement.

29.3.1.3 Managing customer stories and development tasks

The most popular project management system used in industry practice to manage stories and associated tasks is Atlassian's JIRA software.[4] This system provides product managers and SE roles capabilities to plan releases, manage user stories and associated tasks for current and future sprints, acceptance criteria for each user story, and the current status of each story. JIRA also provides a robust defect (bug) tracking capability including ability to plan which bugs will be fixed in a given release, including dependencies and other blockers for resolving those bugs.

29.3.1.4 Controlling scope

Customer stories are the local currency in what Beck (2000, p. 54) calls the "planning game" through which the customer and the developers negotiate the scope of each release. At the beginning, there is a time and effort "budget" of the person-hours or level of effort available for implementing all the stories, usually per release.

As the customer prioritizes story cards, the total of the work estimates is kept and, when it reaches the budget limit, the developers' "dance card" is full. Later, if the customer wants to "cut in" with another story, they have to decide which existing customer story with an equal or greater value must be removed to make room for the new one. So no one, not even the boss, can just add more features.

This approach gives the customer control of which stories will be implemented, but affords developers a tool to battle scope or feature creep. Developer estimates of effort can be way off, probably in most cases underestimating the effort necessary, but at least it lets them draw a line in the sand. With experience, developers get pretty good at this estimation, called team velocity, given a particular technology platform and application domain. The better developers get at estimation, the more smoothly the entire project will go.

Sprint

A relatively short (not more than a month) time period within an agile software engineering schedule in which a working and releasable product increment is implemented. It is a unit of work being done in an agile SE environment; an iteration associated with a release (to the client and/or users) (Sections 3.3, 29.3.2, and 29.7.2).

---

[4]https://www.atlassian.com/software/jira.

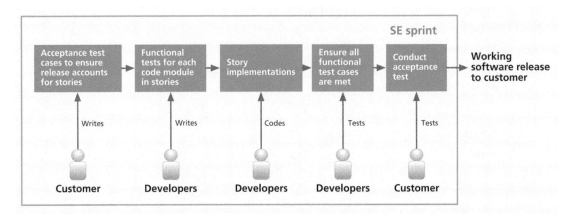

Fig. 29-5

An agile SE sprint.

29.3.2 Sprints in Agile SE Methods

In Fig. 29-5, we show an expansion of the "sprint" box of Fig. 29-3. Each agile SE sprint consists of activities that are described in the following sections.

29.3.2.1 Acceptance test creation

The customer writes the functional acceptance tests. There is no process for this, so it can be kind of fuzzy, but it does put the customer in control of acceptance of the eventual code. With experience, customers get good at this. Usually the acceptance criteria on which the acceptance tests are based are summarized in the corresponding customer stories as a list of feature capabilities that the customer has to be able to perform.

29.3.2.2 Unit code test creation

The team divides the work by assigning customer stories to be coded in the next sprint. A programmer picks a customer story card and finds a programming partner. Before any coding, together, the pair writes unit tests that can verify that functionality is present in the code that is yet to be written.

29.3.2.3 Implementation coding

The programming pairs work together to write the code for modules that support the functionality of selected customer stories. As they work, the partners do on-the-fly design. The agile SE literature says almost nothing about design.

The programmers do not worry about the higher level architecture; the system architecture supposedly evolves with each new slice of functionality added to the overall system. The programming pair integrates this code into the latest version.

29.3.2.4 Code testing

Next, the programming pair runs the unit code tests designed for the modules just implemented to make sure that the realization of this functionality in code is correct.

29.3.2.5 Regression testing

In addition to testing the code for the current features, the team runs all code tests again on all modules coded so far until all tests are passed, to ensure that the new module doesn't break any of the previously implemented modules. This allows developers to make code modifications based on changing requirements, while ensuring that all existing parts of the code continue to function properly.

29.3.2.6 Acceptance testing and deployment

Developers submit this potentially shippable product functionality to the customer for acceptance review. Upon acceptance, the team deploys this small iterative release to the customer.

29.4 CHALLENGES OF AGILE SE METHODS FROM THE UX PERSPECTIVE

Agile methods make SE practitioners feel productive and in control because they and their customers, and not some overarching design, drive the process. These methods are inexpensive, fast, and lightweight, with early deliverables. The pair-programming aspect also seems to produce high-reliability code with fewer bugs. Nonetheless, agile SE methods are programming methods developed by programmers for programmers, and they pose some challenges from the UX perspective.

Because big design upfront is shunned, there is no upfront analysis to glean general concepts of the system and associated work practice. The one customer representative on the team is not required even to be a real user and can't be expected to represent all viewpoints, needs and requirements, usage issues, or usage context. There may be no real user data at all upfront, and coding will end up being "based only on assumptions about user needs" (Memmel, Gundelsweiler, and Reiterer, 2007, p. 169). There is no identification of user tasks and no process for identifying user interaction or information needs.

Beyer, Holtzblatt, and Baker (2004) echo this criticism of using a customer representative as the only application domain expert. As they point out, under their Axiom 2, "Make the user the expert," many customer representatives are

Big Design Upfront

A lifecycle process approach that involves starting with ethnographic and field studies and extensive requirements engineering, of which the old Waterfall method is an archetype (Section 29.2.3.1).

not also users and, therefore, can't necessarily speak for the work practice of others.

Beyond these predesign drawbacks, the agile SE method does not involve design, so, there is no room in the process for design ideation.

29.5 WHAT IS NEEDED ON THE UX SIDE

Nonetheless, in some ways, the UX process lifecycle is a good candidate to fit with agile software methods because it is already iterative. But there is a big difference. The traditional UX lifecycle is built on starting with a complete understanding of users and their needs followed by extensive design activities, both missing in agile SE. Regarding the early agile usage research, Beyer et al. (2004) recommend devoting an iteration of usage research with real users to understand user needs. They say they have been able to get through quick usage research and early design with five to eight users in one to two weeks. (Our experience, even on medium complexity projects has been more in the order of 1–2 months.)

In this section, we discuss the considerations necessary to adjust traditional UX methods to adapt to agile SE approaches (Memmel et al., 2007).

To work in the UX domain, an agile method must involve some early analysis devoted to understanding user work activities and work context and gleaning general concepts of the system within its ecology. And some early design activities must also be retained in the process to give structure and coherence to how interaction and information fit into the design. And, if top-down design is needed for an innovative product design, it should take place before any involvement on the SE side. Early-funnel UX activities accommodate exactly those needs.

At the same time, to be compatible with the agile SE side of development, UX methods must:

- Be lightweight.
- Emphasize team collaboration and require colocation.
- Include effective customer and user representatives.
- Adjust UX lifecycle activities to be compatible with SE sprint-based incremental releases by switching focus from top-down holistic design to bottom-up feature design.
- Include ways to control scope.

Late-funnel UX activities are designed to accommodate these needs.

29.6 PROBLEMS TO ANTICIPATE

In a special-interest-group workshop at CHI 2009 (Miller and Sy, 2009), a group of UX practitioners met to share their experiences in trying to incorporate a user-centered design approach into the agile SE process. Among the difficulties experienced by these practitioners in their own environments were:

- Sprints too short; not enough time for customer contact, design, and evaluation.
- Inadequate opportunities for user feedback, and the user feedback they did get was ignored.
- Customer representative weak, not committed, and lack of colocation.
- No shared vision of broader conceptual design because focus is on details.
- Risk of piecemeal results in a bottom-up approach.

29.6.1 UX and SE Don't Always Work Together the Way They are Supposed To

In Fig. 29-6, we show a general picture of how UX and SE are supposed to work together in design and implementation.

In either the traditional or agile lifecycle, the UX team is supposed to provide a UX design as specifications to the SE team to implement and integrate with the corresponding functionality. If everyone on both sides of the project (and management as well) agrees to this simple model at the beginning, the matter of integrating UX and SE within the project will be well on its way to being solved.

In reality, however, the SE team is often well into its process when the UX team is introduced to the project, and the UX team is doomed to play catch-up for the rest of the project, and, of importance to all, the project can never benefit from

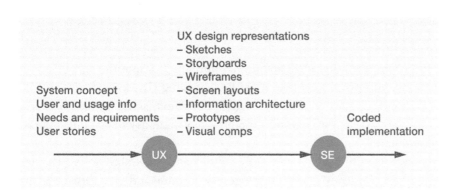

Fig. 29-6

How UX and SE work together.

what the UX team could have done. In the worst of scenarios, the UX team is called in to review and give feedback on the work done so far by the SE team.

While it is true that the SE team needs its own inputs in addition to those provided by the UX team, this must be done in an open and shared way. Both teams get some of the same kinds of inputs (e.g., customer or user stories) but use them in different ways to produce different kinds of designs. The main requirement is that all inputs obtained from the client or users are shared with both teams. The SE team does not gather requirements or design recommendations without involving the UX team from the beginning.

29.6.2 The Need for a Full Overview: The Software Side Versus the UX Side

Because the agile approach to SE is incremental and bottom-up, it precludes the luxury of seeing a full overview of the system upfront. In fact, some agile teams see not having an overview as a "badge" testifying to their correct use of the agile method, not being distracted from their feature-at-a-time emerging view of the system. The whole point of the agile approach is that they can't afford to establish a system overview upfront, nor do they really need to. That is mainly because the user doesn't see the software directly.

But building a system a little piece at a time can be risky, at least on the UX side. The user's view of the system is the user interface. This view, depending directly on the UX design, must look as though it is built around a well-integrated conceptual model, a single unified style or theme, and not a patchwork of different ideas and views. If not, it will lead to a confusing and disjointed user experience. It's almost impossible to develop a unified user interface exclusively by piecewise and bottom-up methods, one feature at a time. So, the UX team needs an overview to emerge as soon as possible.

29.7 A SYNTHESIZED APPROACH TO INTEGRATING AGILE UX AND AGILE SE

Most of the early literature about incorporating UX into the agile SE development process is based on either adjusting UX design methods to somehow keep pace with existing agile SE methods or trying to do just selected parts of UX design processes in the presence of an essentially inflexible agile SE method.

While it is possible that XP, for example, and some abbreviated UX design techniques can coexist and work together, in these add-on approaches, the two parts are not really combined (McInerney and Maurer, 2005; Patton, 2002, 2008). This creates a coping scenario on the UX side, as UX practitioners attempt to live with the constraints while trying to ply their own processes within an overall development environment driven solely by the agile SE method.

Here, we have tried to synthesize an approach to allow our agile UX process to mesh with an agile SE environment without compromising on essential UX needs.

We especially acknowledge the influence of Constantine and Lockwood (2003), Beyer et al. (2004), Meads (2010), and Lynn Miller (2010).

29.7.1 Integrating UX into Planning

Fig. 29-7 shows a scheme for integrating the UX role into the planning box of Fig. 29-3.

Planning in Fig. 29-7 features small upfront analysis and design by the UX designer, customer, and users, in the left-most box, producing a broad (if partial) understanding of the work domain, work practice, and conceptual model (next to left-most box). This upfront UX activity occurs in the early agile UX funnel.

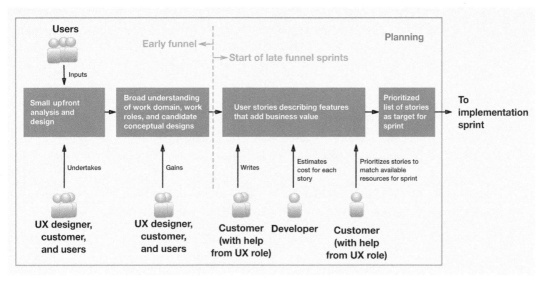

Fig. 29-7

Integrating the UX role into early agile UX funnel planning.

Scope (of Delivery)

Describes how the target
system or product is
"chunked" (broken into
what size pieces) in each
iteration or sprint for
delivery to the client and
users for feedback and to
the software engineering
team for agile
implementation
(Section 3.3).

Early Funnel

The part of the funnel
(agile UX model) for large-
scope activity, usually for
conceptual design, before
syncing with software
engineering
(Section 4.4.4).

29.7.1.1 Small upfront analysis and design

In Section 29.2.3.1, we described how SE practitioners avoid big design upfront, preferring instead to write *some* code as soon as possible and then fix problems by reacting to customer feedback later. In UX, we can't afford to operate this way. The integrity and consistency of all our designs, including the small-scope task-level designs of the late funnel, depend on first establishing a solid overall conceptual design in the early funnel. But the ground work necessary can't turn the whole process into a waterfall model. So, it has to be light on its feet, and that's where the small upfront analysis and design come in.

The small upfront analysis and design, in the left-most box of Fig. 29-7, is our way of including an initial abbreviated form of usage research and design that involves the customer and users. This is exactly what happens in the early agile UX funnel. And much of the "design" in the early funnel small upfront analysis and design is conceptual design to establish the high-level consistency overview.

Also, in planning, the UX person also assists the customer in other responsibilities, such as writing and prioritizing stories. These stories are now called user stories rather than customer stories because their substance came from users in the upfront analysis. Although this begins to change the basic agile pattern, it gives the UX team more traction in bringing UX into the overall process. Other authors (Constantine and Lockwood, 1999; Memmel et al., 2007) have agreed that adding a measure of user and/or task modeling is also a very useful supplement in that same spirit.

Goals of the small upfront analysis and design in the early agile UX funnel include:

- Understand the users' work and its context.
- Identify key work roles, work activities, and user tasks.
- Model workflow and activities in the existing enterprise and system.
- Forge an initial high-level conceptual design.
- Identify inputs for selected user stories that reflect user needs in the context of their work practice.

These early agile UX funnel small upfront analysis and design activities are what we describe in the early chapters (Part 2) of this edition of the book.

Data capture. Agile usage research can be as brief or as lengthy as desired or afforded. We suggest interviewing and observing the work practice of at least one or two people in each key work role. There is no recording and no transcript of interviews. The UX practitioners write notes by hand directly on small index cards—a Constantine hallmark—to discourage verbosity in the notes.

Aim toward effective user stories. We are looking for user stories to drive our small pieces of interaction design and prototyping. But what kind of user stories do we seek? Stories about work activities, roles, and tasks can still be a good way for designers to start. However, as Meads (2010) says, users are not interested in tasks per se, but are more interested in features. Following his advice, *we focus on features*, which can entail a substantial set of related user work activities and tasks within a work context. Therefore, we usually come up with a *set* of related user stories for a feature (for example, tasks to create, search for, display, modify, and delete subscriptions to a certain kind of service).

29.7.1.2 UX role helps customer write user stories

In the third box from the left in Fig. 29-7, the UX person helps the customer write user stories. As we said earlier, the UX person usually takes charge of user story writing to ensure completeness, appropriate scope, consistency, and cohesion.

Because UX team members, customers, and users participate in the early agile UX funnel small upfront analysis and design, user story writing will be easier, faster, and more representative of real user needs. The UX role influences the customer toward creating stories based on workflows revealed in the agile usage research part of small upfront analysis and design.

29.7.1.3 The truth about user stories

As we explained in Section 10.2.1, you can't depend on stories written by just users to be accurate, complete, or comprehensive. So, in real projects, UX analysts and designers take inputs from users collected in usage research and write small-scope user capability requirements as user stories, as though users had expressed them, so the whole collection has a uniform format. This is one important way process variations exist in practice.

29.7.1.4 UX role helps customer prioritize user stories

By helping the customer representative prioritize the user stories, the UX person can keep an eye on the overarching vision of user experience and a cohesive conceptual design, thereby steering the result toward an effective set of stories for an iteration.

29.7.2 Integrating UX into Sprints

In Fig. 29-8, we show UX counterpart activities occurring in the late funnel during an agile SE sprint of Fig. 29-5.

Sprint

A relatively short (not more than a month) time period within an agile software engineering schedule in which a working and releasable product increment is implemented. It is a unit of work being done in an agile SE environment; an iteration associated with a release (to the client and/or users) (Sections 3.3, 29.3.2, and 29.7.2).

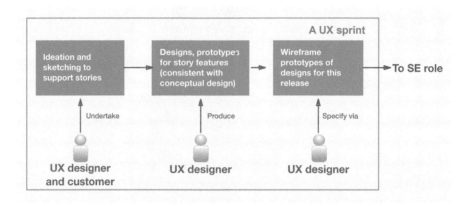

Fig. 29-8

UX counterpart of an agile SE sprint.

While the SE people are doing a sprint, the UX person and customer perform their own version of a sprint, which is shown in Fig. 29-8. They begin by picking a story or picking a feature with a set of related user stories.

With the conceptual design in mind, the UX designers start ideation and sketching of an interaction design to support the functionality of the user story. Initial static wireframe prototypes are used as sketches of interaction designs, leading to "interactive" click-through wireframe prototypes to demonstrate navigation within interaction sequences.

Design reviews, design walk-throughs, plus iterative design fixes. At this small scope, the tightly-coupled design creation-prototyping-evaluation cycle will often start with frequent multiple static wireframe sketches. These sketches are iteratively reviewed within the UX team for ideation in task-level design creation. This early design ideation and sketching can also involve brief focused returns to usage research to fill gaps and answer questions about the feature.

When the UX team is satisfied they have their best initial design, it is demonstrated in the form of a click-through wireframe prototype in a walk-through review with all stakeholders, including client/customers and users. The typical result is possibly multiple rounds of feedback, refinement, and further evaluation.

Then, the same kind of walk-through evaluation is done with SE developers, to get feedback on feasibility, consistency, platform issues, etc. This leads to possibly multiple rounds of fixing and refining, leading to a handoff to developers for implementation. By this time, UX designers and software developers should be on the same page about the feature.

After implementation, the UX designer should check the result against the UX designs for fidelity of implementation. Then, the whole team should submit the working feature to the customer for acceptance review.

Table 29-1 shows a mini-UX check-list developed while Hartson was working as a consultant at the Network Infrastructure and Services group at Virginia Tech.

29.7.3 Synchronizing the Two Agile Workflows

After describing agile SE planning, agile SE sprints, and UX integration in the late funnel, we now talk about how the UX and SE teams work together and synchronize the workflow in their respective parts of the agile process.

29.7.3.1 Dove-tailed work activities

Miller (2010) proposed a "staggered" approach to parallel track agile development that featured a "criss-cross" interplay between UX activities and SE activities across multiple cycles of agile development. As Patton (2008) put in his blog, the overall approach is characterized as "work ahead, follow behind."

As Patton says, UX people on agile teams "become masters of development time travel, nimbly moving back and forth through past, present, and future development work." Based roughly on Miller's idea, and adding our early funnel concept, we show a scheme in Fig. 29-9 for how UX people and SE people can synchronize their work via a dovetail alternation of activities across progressive iterations.

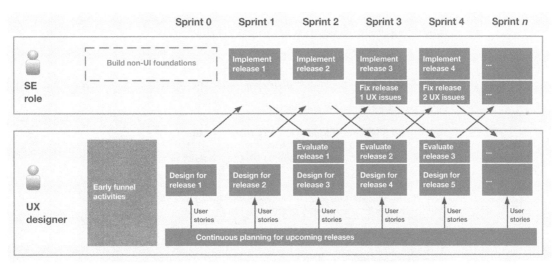

Fig. 29-9

Alternating UX and SE workflow in an agile process.

Table 29-1

Late-funnel mini-UX process checklist

Activity Step	Date Performed	Person
View user stories in JIRA (Section 29.3.1.3)		
Task-level usage research and modeling: Identify work roles, HTI (hierarchical task inventory) context, task sequences, business rules, relevant existing apps/screens, work flow		
As needed: Define terminology, database schemas		
Ideation and sketching of initial UX design		
Draw state diagram of flow, if appropriate		
Draw wireframes in Sketch		
Connect wireframes with navigation links in InVision and Craft		
Add link in JIRA to user story to wireframe prototype		
With UX group: Design review & walkthrough, iterate		
Get UX agreement		
With DEV: Initial (preimplementation) design review		
Update wireframe prototype with changes from DEV		
Increase prototype fidelity, if useful		
With non-UX stakeholders: Design review, iterate as needed		
With DEV: Design review and handoff		
UX: Create JIRA issue, add link to InVision, assign issue to DEV		
DEV: Create JIRA issue, assign issue to UX (dependency link to original issue)		
QA: Implementation fidelity check (UX responsibility)—What is built should reflect wireframe prototype exactly		
If no discrepancy, sign off (UX)		
Else: UX create JIRA issued "Update software with UX review feedback"		
Repeat until no discrepancy		

In the original agile SE approach, SE people started first with Sprint 1, taking a set of stories and building a release. That worked when the only thing that was happening was implementation. Now that we are bringing in UX design and evaluation into the mix, we need a few changes, starting with the early funnel activities before going on to initial Sprint 0 on the UX side.

Sprint 0 follows early funnel work on usage research and conceptual design on the UX side and is for beginning the synchronization with the SE cadence. The amount of time these early funnel activities will take depends on the size and complexity of the product or system and the familiarity of the UX team with the problem domain. At the end of Sprint 0, the UX team should have UX designs for the initial feature ready to give to the SE people for their Sprint 1. During this time, the SE people focus on other things, such as building the software infrastructure and services required to support the whole system, what Miller calls building the "high-development, low-UI features." When the UX people are done with their designs for Release 1, they hand them off to SE people for implementation in Sprint 1, which includes implementation of both functional stories and interaction design components for that cycle.

Not all UX design challenges are equal; sometimes, there is not enough time to address UX design adequately in a given sprint. Then, that design will have to evolve over the design and evaluation activities of more than one sprint. Also, sometimes in interaction design, we want to try out two variations because we are not sure, so that will have to take place over multiple sprints.

Because of the staggering or dovetailing of activities, people on each part of the team are typically working on multiple things at a time. For example, right after handing off the designs for Release 1 to the SE people, the UX people start on designs for Release 2 and continue doing this until the end of Sprint 1 (while the SE people are coding release 1). In any given sprint, say, Sprint n, the UX people are performing usage research and planning for Sprint $n + 2$, while doing design (and prototyping) for Sprint $n + 1$, and evaluation of the design for Sprint $n - 1$.

Following the "lifecycle" of a single release, Release n, we see that in Sprint $n - 1$, the UX role designs for Release n, to be implemented by the SE people in Sprint n. UX evaluates Release n in Sprint $n + 1$. SE fixes it in Sprint $n + 2$ and rereleases it at the end of that sprint.

29.7.3.2 The value of early delivery

As Memmel et al. (2007) say, you have the potential to deliver design visions extremely early in the process, resulting in amazingly early involvement of the customer.

Feedback for the first feature can go far beyond just that one feature and its usage. This is the first opportunity for the team to get *any* real feedback. Many additional things can come out of that, not specific to that feature. For example, you will get feedback on how the process is working. You will get feedback on the overall style of your design. You will hear other questions and issues that customers are thinking about that you would not have access to until much later in a nonagile process. Your customers may even reprioritize the story cards based on this interaction. This early feedback fits well with the agile principles of abundant communication and the expectation of early and frequent change.

29.7.3.3 Continuous delivery

Delivery to customers and users is continuous but in pieces. At the end of any given sprint (call it Sprint n), the customer sees a UX prototype of the upcoming release and in the next sprint, Sprint $n + 1$, they see the full functional implementation of that prototype. In Sprint $n + 2$, they see UX evaluation findings for that same prototype, and, in Sprint $n + 3$, they see the final redesign. Each of these points in time is an opportunity for the customer to give feedback on the interaction design.

29.7.3.4 The importance of regression testing

Regression testing is a step in the agile SE process used to integrate the most recent tested-and-passed feature with all those that have come before it. Without regression testing, the agile method is little more than an incremental waterfall method. You are stuck with decisions made in Sprints 0 and 1, with no ability to iterate major concepts. Unfortunately, time pressures of sprints in real practice can cause teams to short cut regression testing.

Furthermore, this kind of quick testing is easy, and for the most part, automated on the SE side. On the UX side it is a whole different story. Doing regression testing on the UX side would entail running an evaluation after each sprint and using all measuring instruments (e.g., benchmark tasks or surveys) from all previous sprints plus those for the current sprint before releasing it to the customer. In practice, there is almost never enough time to do this.

29.7.3.5 Planning across iterations

Fig. 29-9 shows planning in a single box at the bottom, continuously extending across all sprint cycles. That is to convey the idea that planning does not occur in discrete little boxes over time at a specific spot in the flow. Planning is more of an "umbrella" activity, distributed over time, and it is cumulative in that the process builds up a "knowledge base" founded on agile usage research with users. The planning process does not start over for the planning of each cycle.

Instead, the same knowledge base is consulted, updated, and massaged, working with the original small upfront analysis and design results and anything added to supplement those results. Because an overview and conceptual design are evolving in the process, this kind of UX planning brings some top-down benefits to an otherwise exclusively bottom-up process.

29.7.3.6 Communication during synchronization

This kind of interwoven development process brings with it the risk of falling apart if anything goes wrong. This intensifies the need for constant communication so that everyone remains aware of what everyone else is doing, what progress is being made by others, and what problems are being encountered.

Agile processes can be more fragile than their heavyweight counterparts. Because each part depends on the others in a tightly orchestrated overall activity, if something goes wrong in one place, there might be little time to react to surprises. Constant communication can help minimize this risk.

UX Affordances, the Interaction Cycle, and UX Design Guidelines

Part 7 contains a potpourri of related topics. Five different types of UX design affordances are defined and explained, and a method is described for combining them in UX design. The Interaction Cycle is a descriptive model for the different phases and kinds of user actions one goes through to interact with a product or system. The UX design guidelines are organized around the Interaction Cycle and give "rules" for using the affordances in UX designs.

Affordances in UX Design

30

Highlights

- The concept of affordance.
- Five different types of affordances and how each kind is used in UX design.
- Cognitive affordance:
  - How shared conventions affect the interpretation of cognitive affordances.
  - False cognitive affordances.
- Physical affordance.
- Sensory affordance.
- Functional affordance.
- Emotional affordance.
- Putting affordances together in UX design:
  - A UX design checklist of affordances.
- User-created affordances as a wake-up call to designers.

30.1 INTRODUCTION

30.1.1 Acknowledgement of Source

To begin, we gratefully acknowledge the kind permission of Taylor & Francis, Ltd., to use a paper published in *Behavior & Information Technology* (Hartson, 2003) as the primary source of material for this chapter.

30.1.2 The Concept of Affordance

The relevant part of what the dictionary says about "to afford" is that it means to offer, yield, provide, give, or furnish something. For example, a particular window in a house may afford a fine view of the outdoors; the window helps one see that nice view. In UX design, where we focus on helping the user, *a UX affordance is something in a UX design that helps the user do or feel something.*

For a brief discussion of the background and history of affordances, see Section 33.2.

30.1.3 The Importance of Affordance Issues in UX Design

Few topics in HCI or UX have been as misunderstood and misused as the notion of "affordance." Yet few concepts are as central to effective UX design. In fact, the concept of affordance is one of the most fundamental notions pervading all of UX design. Because affordances are all about helping users do things, you can imagine that the majority of usability and UX problems involve design issues about affordances in designs that don't help the user as much as they should. Likewise, the majority of HCI and UX design *guidelines* are also about affordances.

30.1.4 Demystifying Affordances

Although a crucially important and powerful concept, the notion of "affordance," as pointed out by Norman (1999), has suffered misunderstanding and misuse (or perhaps uninformed use) by researchers and practitioners alike and in the literature. Because of this confusion in the field about affordances, the concept can seem mysterious and elusive, so our goal for these chapters is to dispel this mystery and reveal it as an intriguing topic that can be fascinating, fun, and very useful in UX design. For more discussion of the confusion over affordances in the literature, see Section 33.3.

30.1.5 Five Different Kinds of Affordance in UX Design

In an effort to clarify the concept of affordance and how it is used in UX design, I (2003) defined four types of affordances, each of which plays a different role in supporting users during interaction, each reflecting user processes and the kinds of actions users make in task performance. Since that paper, we have added a fifth affordance type, resulting in this set of affordance types (as illustrated in Fig. 30-1):

Table 30-1 contains a summary of these affordance types and their roles in UX design.

For simplicity of understanding, in this chapter, we separate the human senses associated with each kind of affordance. But the human brain integrates the information we get from all our senses and uses each to mediate the other (Obrist et al., 2016; Rosenblum, 2013).

As Gaver (1991, p. 81) says, thinking of affordances in terms of design roles "allows us to consider affordances as properties that can be designed and analyzed in their own terms." Each type of affordance uses different mechanisms, corresponds to different kinds of user actions, and has different requirements for design and different implications in evaluation and problem diagnosis.

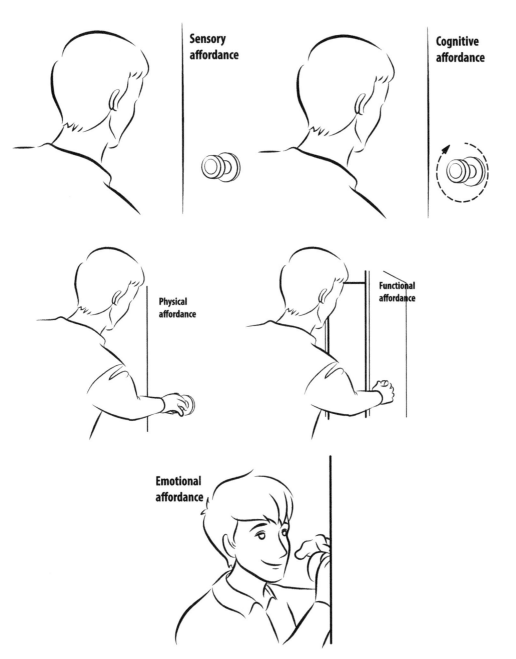

Fig. 30-1

Illustrating the kinds of affordances in UX design.

Table 30-1

Summary of affordance types

Affordance Type	Description	Example
Cognitive affordance	Design feature that helps users with their cognitive actions: Thinking, deciding, learning, remembering, and knowing about things	A button label that helps users know what will happen if they click on it
Physical affordance	Design feature that helps users with their physical actions: Clicking, touching, pointing, gesturing, and moving things	A button that is large enough so that users can click on it accurately
Sensory affordance	Design feature that helps users with their sensory actions: Seeing, hearing, and feeling (and tasting and smelling) things	A label font size large enough to be discerned
Functional affordance	Design feature that helps users employ a product or system to accomplish work (i.e., usefulness of a system function)	The internal system ability to sort a series of numbers (invoked by users clicking on the Sort button)
Emotional affordance	Design feature that adds emotional impact to the user experience and helps users appreciate and enjoy the interaction	Beautiful aesthetics on a webpage, something that makes interaction fun

As an example to get you started, consider a button available for clicking somewhere on a user interface. Sensory affordance helps you sense (in this case, see or notice) it. Sensory affordance can be supported in design by, for example, the color, size, and/or location of the button. Cognitive affordance helps you understand the button by comprehending what the button is used for, in this case via the meaning of its label. Physical affordance helps you reliably click on this button, so, its design support could include the size of the button or its distance from other related buttons.

30.2 COGNITIVE AFFORDANCES

30.2.1 Introduction

30.2.1.1 Definition of cognitive affordance

A cognitive affordance is a design feature that helps, aids, supports, facilitates, or enables thinking, learning, understanding, and knowing about something. Accordingly, cognitive affordances are among the most significant usage-centered design features in present-day interactive systems, screen based or otherwise. They are the key to answering Norman's question (1999, p. 39) on behalf of the user: "How do you know what to do?"

Cognitive affordance is associated with the semantics or meaning of user interface artifacts. As a simple example, the symbol of an icon that clearly conveys its meaning could be a cognitive affordance enabling users to understand the icon in terms of the functionality behind it and the consequences of clicking on it. Another cognitive affordance might be in the form of a clear and concise button label.

In this regard, cognitive affordance is used as *feed forward*. It is help with *a priori* knowledge, that is, knowledge used to predict the outcome before making an action on an object such as a button, icon, or menu choice that invokes that functionality.

Another use of cognitive affordance is in *feedback*—helping a user know what happened after a button click, for example, and execution of the corresponding system functionality. Feedback helps users in knowing whether the course of interaction has been successful so far or whether an error has occurred.

30.2.1.2 Starring role in UX design for new users

Cognitive affordances play a starring role in UX design, especially for less experienced users who need help with understanding and learning.

30.2.1.3 How do users acquire cognitive support information?

The whole point of cognitive affordances is that users need knowledge of how things work. What are the ways users can get that needed information about how to use or operate an object or a device?

Knowledge in the head. First, there is knowledge in the head of the user—it gets there by learning through training or experience.

Knowledge in the world. Then there is knowledge in the world—knowledge inherent in objects and devices that gives us clues as to their operation. This is the inherent kind of affordance in Gibson's ecological view (Gibson, 1977). Gibson was a perceptual psychologist who took an "ecological" approach to perception, meaning he studied the relationship between a living being (let's say a human being) and its environment, in particular what the environment offers or affords the person. Gibson's affordances are the properties and objects of the environment as reckoned relative to the person, and "the 'values' and 'meanings' of things in the environment [that] can be directly perceived" (Gibson, 1977) by the person. Here Gibson is talking about physical properties, giving an example of how a horizontal, flat, and rigid surface affords support for a person for standing or walking.

Knowledge in the design. Finally, there is knowledge that designers add by way of deliberately designed cognitive affordances, such as a label on a button or a message suggesting an action. This communication depends on a shared understanding between designer and user. See the next section for how we extract meaning from shared cultural conventions.

Example: Mail Icon as Cognitive Affordance

The icon in Fig. 30-2 shows an example of a graphical cognitive affordance. This icon is a clear and succinct way to use a simple image to convey the meaning behind the corresponding key—this is how you get email.

Fig. 30-2
Clear email icon.

30.2.1.4 The meaning of cognitive affordances as found in shared conventions

An important function of cognitive affordance is communication, which depends on agreement about meaning. But often the meaning of a cognitive affordance is not intrinsic to its appearance. The symbols themselves may have no inherent meaning, but a shared convention about the meaning of an image, icon, or symbol (e.g., the shape of a stop sign or an icon for an emergency exit)—even some words or phrases—can convey that meaning.

For examples of how cognitive affordances can be informed by shared cultural conventions, see Section 33.4.

Devices for opening doors

In the tradition of *The Design of Everyday Things* (Norman, 1990), we illustrate with a simple and ubiquitous noncomputer device, a device for opening doors. The hardware store carries both round doorknobs and lever-type door handles. The visual design of both kinds conveys a cognitive affordance, helping users think or know about usage through the implied message their appearance gives to users: "This is what you use to open the door." The doorknob and lever handle each suggests, in its own way, the grasping and rotating required for operation.

In cases where users must just push on the door to open it, designers often help users understand this by installing, for example, a brass plate to show that one should push and where to push. Even though this plate might also help avoid handprints on the door, it is a cognitive affordance and not a real physical affordance because it adds nothing to the door itself to help the user in the physical part of the pushing action. Sometimes the word "push" is engraved in the plate to augment the clarity of meaning as a cognitive affordance.

But perhaps the message of how to operate a door is so universally understood mainly because of shared conventions. Some people might find nothing intrinsic in the appearance of a doorknob that necessarily conveys this information. On another planet, it could seem mysterious and confusing, but for us, a doorknob is an excellent cognitive affordance because almost all users do share the same easily recognized convention.

Exercise 30-1: Understanding Meaning Based on Cultural Conventions

Can you think of any situation where the meaning of an object, according to shared conventions, is taken for granted in one culture but carries a completely different meaning in another culture? How would these differences affect the behavior of people from the other culture?

30.2.2 Cognitive Affordance Design Issues

Of all affordances, cognitive affordances are probably the most important in UX design and may require the most careful design. We look to cognitive affordances to ensure:

- Clarity of wording.
- Correctness of wording.
- Completeness of wording.
- Predictability of user actions.
- Distinguishability between meanings.
- User centeredness in expressions of meaning.

These cognitive affordance design issues and more will be covered in the UX design guidelines of Chapter 33.

30.2.2.1 Cognitive affordance to get the user started

In Fig. 30-3, we show a nice example of a very simple cognitive affordance that helps early users of Keynote on the Mac know what to do to get started and make a slide for presentation. This application, like its Windows counterpart,

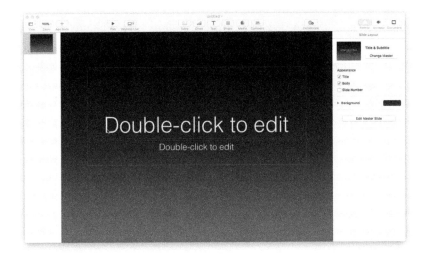

Fig. 30-3

*A cognitive affordance to help
user get started.*

PowerPoint, is typical of large applications where users often start out being faced
with a blank screen. All the power of the application is sitting there, but the user
doesn't know how to get started. Once you are started, it gets easier because you
can respond to feedback in the task thread.

30.2.2.2 Cognitive affordance to help users avoid task completion errors

Sometimes cognitive affordances can help users avoid task completion errors.
They're usually in the form of a simple reminder to do the last step, such as
"Please take your tickets and your receipt." In Fig. 30-4, we show an example of a
cognitive affordance as a reminder to include an email attachment.

Fig. 30-4

*Cognitive affordances used
to remind the user to make
an email attachment.*

If any variation of the word "attach" appears in an email, but it is sent without an attachment, the system asks if the sender intended to attach something.

30.2.2.3 False cognitive affordances misinform and mislead

There are also things that *shouldn't* be in a UX design—things we call *false cognitive affordances—things that look like cognitive affordances but are wrong and misinform, mislead, and confuse users.* Because of the power of cognitive affordances to influence users, misuse of cognitive affordances in design can be a force against usability and a good user experience. Gibson calls this "misinformation in affordances." As an example, consider a glass panel that appears to be a door but doesn't afford passage. Draper and Barton (1993) call this an "affordance bug."

Example: False Cognitive Affordance in a Door Sign

What do you think about the picture of a sign on the door of a local store in Fig. 30-5?

The explanation was that you should use this door only to enter from the outside and not to exit through the door from the inside. They were probably reusing an available design object, the "Do Not Enter" sign, instead of tailoring a sign more specific to the usage situation. The resulting mashup was nonsense.

Fig. 30-5

A door with a confusing sign containing conflicting cognitive affordances.

Example: False Cognitive Affordance in Links Masquerading as Buttons

A common example of a false cognitive affordance is seen in webpage links that are made to look like buttons, but don't behave like buttons. Here's one we found in an evaluation of a real digital library system. The gray background of the text in the top menu bar of a digital library website, Fig. 30-6, makes them seem like buttons acting as tabs from which to pick high-level functionality.

Simple search	Advanced search	Browse	Register	Help

Fig. 30-6

False cognitive affordances in a menu bar with links that look like buttons.

But, in fact, underneath, they are actually just textual hyperlinks, and the gray box around them is just graphical. A user might click on the background, assuming it is part of a button (something we saw more than once in our evaluations), and not get any result. When nothing happened, they were temporarily confused. Because the "button" is actually just a hyperlink, it requires clicking exactly on the text. This is a false cognitive affordance in that it looks like something it is not.

Example: False Cognitive Affordance in a Line That Looks Like the End of a Webpage

Below-the-fold issues on webpages can be compounded by having a horizontal line that happens to fall at the bottom of a screen. Users see the line and assume falsely that it is the bottom of the page and so don't scroll, missing possibly vital information below.

Example: False Cognitive Affordance in a Microwave Control

As another example, Fig. 30-7 is a photo of part of an old microwave.

The dial marks for power settings between the settings for DEFROST and COOK seem to indicate a range of possible settings but, in fact, it is a binary choice: either DEFROST or COOK, with nothing in between. Lots of microwaves

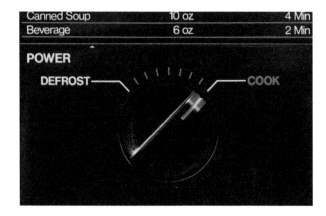

Fig. 30-7

Useless dial marks between power settings on a microwave.

do have many different settings for the power level between defrosting and full-on cooking. But it turns out this one does not. The designer couldn't resist the temptation to fill in the space between these choices with misleading "design details" that are false affordances.

30.3 PHYSICAL AFFORDANCES

30.3.1 Introduction

30.3.1.1 Definition of physical affordance

A physical affordance is a design feature that helps, aids, supports, facilitates, or enables doing something physically. Adequate size and an easy-to-access location could be physical affordance features of an interface button design, enabling users to click easily on the button. Physical actions include clicking, grabbing, dragging, touching, swiping, and so on. Physical affordances are associated with "operability" characteristics of UI artifacts, which can include software artifacts in computer interfaces or they can be real hardware buttons, knobs, handles, dials, or levers. They can be elevator or ATM buttons, or they can even be mechanisms for driving a car, like a steering wheel or brake pedal. Operability is often about physical characteristics of such devices and related human factor issues.

We usually treat active interface objects on a screen, for example, as real physical objects, as they can be on the receiving end of physical actions, such as clicking or dragging.

Example: Add to Cart Button as a Physical Affordance

In Fig. 30-8, we see an example of a physical affordance, the Add to Cart button.

When we analyze the button as a physical affordance, we ask, "How easy is it to click on this button?" The answer, of course, is it is *very* easy to click on this button—after all, they want you to add as much as possible to your cart.

Fig. 30-8

Add to Cart button as physical affordance.

30.3.1.2 Starring role in UX design for experienced or power users

As we said earlier, cognitive affordances play a starring role for novice users. Physical affordances also play a starring role, only for experienced or power users. Their productivity and task performance are all about the speed of physical actions, being able to make physical actions efficient—as rapid and as error-free as possible. Because power users already understand what actions to make, they have less need for cognitive affordances.

30.3.1.3 Some physical affordances are better than others; some depend on the user

The way you decide if one physical affordance is better than another can depend on the individual user. In Fig. 30-9 we show the old BlackBerry phone, one of the few smartphones that had a full hardware keyboard. Some people just liked having a real keyboard like this, one that gives tactile feedback. That is one reason why the makers of BlackBerry have kept it in their design for a long time.

But, of course, on a small device, the keys have to be tiny and close together. Speaking just for me, I think this crowded design makes for less-than-desirable physical affordance and can lead to lots of typing errors.

Fig. 30-9
The BlackBerry mobile phone with a physical keypad.

In contrast, other mobile devices such as the iPhone or iPod have soft touch keypads (Fig. 30-10). I didn't like that as much at first, but it didn't take me long to get used to it, and now, I kind of prefer it. I think the design earned my acceptance through its very good visual and audible feedback. I can see which key I am touching, and when contact is made, and that helps me avoid errors.

Fig. 30-10
Soft keypad on an old iPhone.

30.3.1.4 Physical affordances for opening doors

Here we return to devices for opening doors. As we look at these in Fig. 30-11, we see that each one is different from the others—different in appearance and even different in how they operate. Each one has its own way to afford physical grasping and rotating for door operation.

Some designs, such as a lever, are considered to give better physical affordance than that of a round knob because the lever is easier to use with slippery hands or with an elbow when the hands are full. The push bar on double doors is another example of a physical affordance helpful to door users with full hands.

Sometimes, the physical affordance to help a user open a door is provided by the door itself; people can open some swinging doors by just pushing on the door. Similarly, sometimes the user of a swinging door must open it by pulling. The door itself doesn't usually offer sufficient physical affordance for the pulling action, so a pull handle is added. A pull handle offers both cognitive and physical affordance, providing a physical means for pulling as well as a visual indication that pulling is required (Section 30.3.1.5).

Fig. 30-11

Physical affordances for opening doors.

Example: Some Physical Affordances are Better Than Others: Levers for opening Doors

A number of years ago, I had a chance to design my own home. One of the details I attended to was to be sure that every single doorknob in the house was the "lever" kind that you see in the upper left of Fig. 30-11. That's because, in my experience, that kind offers a better physical affordance under a wider range of usage conditions. For example, if your hands are full or wet and slippery, the lever-type handle affords operation, say, with your elbow. And people who have arthritis or other physical limitations preventing a solid grasp on a round doorknob, can find it difficult to grab and rotate a knob. The lever works much more easily.

30.3.1.5 Physical devices can also offer cognitive affordance

This kind of physical affordance can also act as a cognitive affordance. As you look at it, its appearance might suggest something about how to operate it. It has its own cognitive affordance built into its physical presence. This is an ecological cognitive affordance, in the J. J. Gibson sense, because the lever and the knob in the Fig. 30-12 in their natural state (without a label, for example) both call out and say, "Grab me, twist me; this is how you open the door."

Gibson's Ecological View of Affordances

Perspective on affordances that says knowledge inherent in objects and devices can give us clues as to their operation. Gibson (1977) studied the relationship between a living being (e.g., a human) and its environment, in particular what the environment offers or affords being— for example, how a horizontal rigid surface affords support for a person for standing (Section 30.2.1.3).

Fig. 30-12

Physical devices as cognitive affordances for how you open a door.

30.3.1.6 Physical devices can also offer emotional affordance

And some designs really *look* good, sometimes so much so that the appearance is a source of aesthetic pleasure and pride. Personally, I like the one in Fig. 30-13. To me, it's a simple design with beautiful sweeping lines.

It's up to you whether you think the one in Fig. 30-14 is aesthetic (or grotesque). At least I think it has emotional impact, one way or the other.

Fig. 30-13

*An aesthetic door lever
(according to the author).*

Fig. 30-14

*Does this door knob elicit
feelings?*

30.3.2 Physical Affordance Design Issues

Physical affordance design issues have to do with the following, each of which is explained in subsequent sections:

- Helping users perform physical actions.
- Accommodating physical disabilities.
- Awkwardness of physical actions.
- Human factors and ergonomic issues of device design.

- Physicality.
- Manual dexterity and Fitts' law (Fitts, 1954; MacKenzie, 1992).
- A special characteristic of physical actions that we call physical overshoot.

These physical affordance design issues and more are covered in the UX design guidelines of Chapter 33.

30.3.2.1 Helping user manipulate objects, do actions

Above all else, physical affordance design issues are about helping users perform physical actions, usually to manipulate user interface objects. It's about how easy it is for the user to make physical actions. This definitely applies in GUI design, but can also apply to hardware interfaces with real buttons and knobs.

30.3.2.2 Physical disabilities

Some human factors and UX designs require attention to physical disabilities and physical limitations of users, and this is at the core of what physical affordances are all about. Clearly, there are individual differences among human users in their physical abilities. For example, very young or older users might have difficulty with fine motor control in using the mouse or another pointing device.

Sometimes, users just naturally have limitations, while others develop disabilities from accidents or disease; it doesn't matter. The design of physical affordances is where you accommodate their needs.

30.3.2.3 Physical awkwardness

Awkwardness is something we may not often think about in UX design but, if we do, it can be one of the easiest difficulties to avoid. Designs that present physical awkwardness, such as in holding down the Ctrl, Shift, and Alt keys while dragging with the mouse button down, present an awkwardness that costs users time and energy.

Beyond that, a device that requires an awkward hand movement can lead to *fatigue* in repetitive usage. For example, a touchscreen mounted on the wall at eye level can cause arm fatigue from having to do interactions with one's hand up in the air.

Another example of awkwardness results from the user having to alternate constantly among multiple input devices, such as having to move between keyboard and mouse or between either device and the touchscreen. This kind of behavior involves constant "homing" actions, never getting a chance to "settle down" physically on one device, a time-consuming and effortful distraction of cognitive focus, visual attention, and physical action.

30.3.2.4 Physicality

Physicality is a term referring to real direct physical interaction with real physical (hardware) devices like in the grasping and moving of knobs and levers. This isn't about clicking on "soft" display controls like images of arrows, buttons, or sliders (e.g., to tune a radio or adjust the volume), but is about actually pushing, pulling, grasping, and/or turning real hardware devices such as knobs, buttons, and levers.

Example: Physicality in a Car Shifting Knob

Fig. 30-15 shows a gear-shift knob that is an archetypical example of physicality.

That knob just *looks* so graspable. It's just sticking out there and fits your hand so nicely. The leather exterior gives it a nice texture for grasping. Almost everyone likes the kind of physicality that this thing affords. It gives a sure grip and a satisfying feeling of control as you shift confidently through the gears.

Fig. 30-15

A car gear-shift knob that just says physicality.

Physicality has been an issue for human factors engineers for a long time; Don Norman (2007a) brought it to the attention of the HCI/UX community.

Example: Physicality in Controls for a Radio

Fig. 30-16 shows a car radio that illustrates the issue of physicality.

While this radio does have a physical volume control, there is no knob for tuning. Tuning is done by pushing the up and down arrows on the left-hand side. This design lacks the satisfying kind of physicality you get from the almost universally preferred grasping and turning of a knob.

Fig. 30-16

A car radio with limited physicality.

30.3.2.5 Manual dexterity and Fitts' law

Among the characteristics that affect physical affordance, especially in GUIs, are the size and location of the object to be manipulated. A large object is obviously easier to click on than a tiny one. And location of the object can determine how easy it is to get at the object to manipulate it.

These relationships are represented by Fitts' law, an empirically-based theory expressed as a set of mathematical formulae that govern certain physical actions in human behavior. As it applies in HCI/UX, Fitts' law governs physical movement (e.g., of the cursor) for object selection, moving, dragging, and dropping.

It's specifically about movement from an initial position to a target object at a terminal position. The formulas predict the time to make a movement as:

- Proportional to $\log_2$ of distance moved.
- Inversely proportional to $\log_2$ of target cross-section normal to the direction of motion.

Also (not expressed by Fitts' Law), the time to make a movement is also inversely proportional to the depth of the target along the path of movement.

The potential for errors is the same, namely, proportional to $\log_2$ of the distance moved and inversely proportional to $\log_2$ of target cross-section normal to direction of motion. And, similarly, accuracy is proportional to the depth of the target perpendicular to the path of movement.

In Table 31-2, we translate this to what it means for UX design.

Fitts' law is one of the elements of HCI theory and is the subject of numerous empirical studies in the early HCI literature (Fitts, 1954; MacKenzie, 1992).

Table 31-2

How Fitts' law plays out in UX design

Practical Conclusions	Design Implications
Longer distance movement takes more time (and produces more fatigue)	Group clickable objects related by task flow close together, but not so close that it could cause erroneous selection
Small objects are harder to click on than large ones	Make selectable objects large enough to be clicked on easily
Smaller (shallower) objects are harder to land on as targets of movement	Make target objects large enough for quick and accurate termination of cursor movement

30.3.2.6 Physical overshoot

What is physical overshoot?

Physical action overshoot is what occurs when you move an object, a cursor, a slider, a lever, a switch—and you go too far in making the physical action, beyond where you wanted to be. An example in a computer interface is the setting of a slider bar, when you pull the slider too far.

Example: Downshifting an Automatic Transmission

Fig. 30-17 shows the transmission gear indicator in an old pickup truck I used to have. Here you can see, from right to left at the bottom, the common linear progression of gears from low (number 1) to high (shown as a circle around "D," meaning drive or overdrive).

For general driving, it's a pretty good design, but when you are coming down a long hill, you might want to downshift to third gear on the fly, using engine drag to maintain the speed limit without wearing out the brakes.

Fig. 30-17

Gear shifting with an automatic transmission.

However, because the shifting movement is linear, when you pull that lever down from D, it is too easy to overshoot third gear and end up in second. The result of this error becomes immediately obvious from the engine straining at high RPM.

Exercise 30-2: Other Examples of Physical Overshoot

Can you think of any other examples of physical overshoot that you might encounter in your daily life?

Constraining physical actions to prevent overshoot

In noncomputer examples, you can design to control overshoot by building in physical constraints, as in the example just below. In computer applications, you can ameliorate the risk of overshoot with additional controls, such as using arrow keys to make final slide adjustments.

Example: Constraining a Gear Shift Pattern

Here is an example of introducing a "barrier" that blocks physical movement from going too far, in the shifting mechanism of a Toyota Sienna van, shown in Fig. 30-18.

Fig. 30-18

Constrained gear shifting in a Toyota Sienna van, helping prevent physical overshoot.

Let's say that, while in Drive (4-D in the figure), the driver pulls the lever down to downshift. The lever moves easily down to third gear (3 in the figure) but is blocked by the cutout "template" surrounding the shift lever, preventing it from overshooting and going down to second gear. It is very unlikely that a user will accidentally shift into second gear because that requires an extra action of moving the lever to the right and then further down.

So, here we have a case of consciously taking physical affordance into account in a design by using constraints on physical actions that help users stay within physical boundaries.

30.4 SENSORY AFFORDANCE

30.4.1 Introduction

30.4.1.1 Definition of sensory affordance

A sensory affordance is a design feature that helps, aids, supports, facilitates, or enables user in sensing (e.g., seeing, hearing, feeling) something. Sensory affordance is associated with the "sense-ability" characteristics of user interface artifacts—how well human users can sense (e.g., see) a given interaction object, especially a cognitive, physical, or emotional affordance. Design issues for sensory affordances are about the presentation of user interface objects and include noticeability, discernibility, legibility (in the case of text), and audibility (in the case of sound) of features or devices associated with visual, auditory, haptic/tactile, or other sensations.

While cognitive affordance and physical affordance are the stars of UX design, sensory affordance plays an important supporting role. As an example, the legibility of label text on a button is supported by an adequate size font and appropriate color contrast between text and background, so the label can be read.

Haptics

UX design issues that entail touch and feel in tactile interaction involving physical contact between user and machine (Section 30.4.4).

30.4.2 Visual Sensory Affordance Design Issues

Visual sensory affordance design issues are about characteristics relating to the user's ability to sense visually (i.e., to see), which include:

- Visibility.
- Noticeability.
- Discernibility.
- Text legibility.
- Distinguishability.

- Color.
- Presentation timing.

These sensory affordance design issues and more are covered in the UX design guidelines of Chapter 33.

30.4.2.1 Visibility

The characteristic of visibility is about whether an object important to the user is visible to the user. Sometimes when an object isn't visible, it's because it is blocked by another object. Or sometimes you can't see an object because it simply isn't on the screen. In such cases, the user may have to take some actions to access the object and bring it onto the screen.

Example: Store User Cannot Find the Deodorant

The setting for this noncomputer example is a local grocery store, where a shopper has the simple task of buying some deodorant. The store had been reorganized, so he couldn't rely on his memory to locate the deodorant. He went through the aisles, looking at overhead signs but nothing matched his search goal.

Upon his asking the clerk, he was told, "Oh, it is right over there," being pointed to one of the upfront aisles that he had just scanned. "But I don't see any sign for deodorant." "Oh, yeah, there is a sign," the clerk replied, "you just have to get up real close and look right behind that panel on the top of the end shelf." Fig. 30-19 shows what that panel looked like to someone scanning these upfront aisles.

In Fig. 30-20, you can see the "deodorant" sign revealed if you "just get up real close and look right behind that panel on the top of the end shelf."

The panels on top of the shelves are an aesthetic touch, but they were put in a location that exactly blocked the "deodorant" sign and others, rendering that important cognitive affordance invisible from most perspectives in the store.

30.4.2.2 Noticeability

Suppose an object important to the user is technically visible but not *noticeable?* Being somewhere on the screen isn't necessarily enough for an interaction object. For it to be useful, the user has to notice it. Noticeability is especially important in cases where the user might not even know the needed cognitive affordance exists and isn't necessarily looking for it. It's your job, as the UX

Fig. 30-19

Aesthetic panel blocks
visibility of sign as cognitive
affordance.

Fig. 30-20

The sign is visible if you look
carefully.

designer, to make it so the user will notice it. Your design has to foster user awareness of a necessary object.

The user's focus of attention

The most important design factor in getting an interaction object noticed is putting it right within their *focus* of attention.

A good computer example of an object that often suffers from poor noticeability is a status message line, say, at the bottom of the screen. Such message lines are notoriously unnoticeable because they are outside of most users' focus of attention.

At any point in time within task performance, a user typically has a narrow focus of attention, usually near where the cursor is located. So, a pop-up message next to the cursor will usually be far more noticeable than a message in a line at the bottom of the screen.

Object size

Larger objects are easier to notice.

Object color contrast and separation from clutter

Object color that makes good contrast with the background can make an interaction object noticeable. Another important factor affecting noticeability is the separation of the object of interest from the clutter of other user interface objects.

Example: Where is the "Start Presentation" Icon?

PowerPoint users with any experience know that the icon for getting into the presentation mode is the little icon that looks like a slide show screen. And, once you know where it is, it's no problem. But the inexperienced user might never find it without help because this icon is so small, and it's hidden.

In the partial screen image in Fig. 30-21 of a PowerPoint slide being edited, the red arrow points to the very tiny little "Start Presentation" icon—and yet showing the presentation is one of the most important actions in using PowerPoint!

30.4.2.3 Discernibility

It's not enough to make an important interaction object visible and noticeable; it also needs to be discernible. Can the user make out, detect, or recognize an important object? That is, can the user recognize the object, its shapes, and colors?

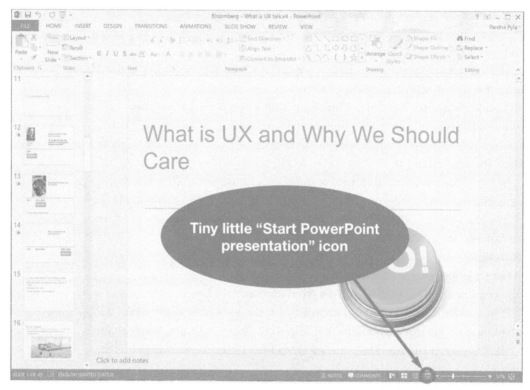

Fig. 30-21

How do you start a PowerPoint presentation?

Example: Black-on-Black in Stereo

Fig. 30-22 shows a picture of a panel on a CD player that used to be part of my stereo system. The controls, such as for play and stop, are black buttons embossed with black icons. Some designer must have thought it would be cool and aesthetic to use this black-on-black color scheme.

Fig. 30-22

Fashionable (?) design of gray-black icons on a gray-black background.

But these symbols are not easily discernible. You can't make them out very well visually, even in a good light. And the symbols aren't raised enough to be discernible as tactile inputs.

This is also a good example about designing for usage in context. Often you want to lower the lights and kick back while you're listening to music. While this may make for a relaxing ambience, it does nothing to help the visibility and discernibility of the symbols on these controls.

30.4.2.4 Text legibility

Legibility is about discernibility of text. Can the user make out text in order to read it? Legibility is about the text being presented so it can be read or sensed, not about whether the meaning of the words is understandable. The meaning is the same regardless of legibility.

The design factors affecting text legibility are obvious and include font type, size, color, and contrast.

Example: Small Font in Crowded Text, Poor Contrast With Background

Look at the sign in Fig. 30-23. This example shows a design (apparently by the systems people) using yellow text on a light background. And someone (a UX person?) left a clarifying note!

30.4.2.5 Distinguishability

Distinguishability applies to all the senses. It's about whether similar but different objects are recognizable as distinct. It's not enough to make an important interaction object visible, noticeable, and discernible. To avoid errors in operating on the wrong object, the interaction object of interest also needs to be distinguishable from other objects.

Example: Here's Soap in Your Eyes

Here is a good example of visual distinguishability and taking usage context into account. In the context of taking a shower, consider the two bottles in Fig. 30-24, one for shampoo and one for conditioner. These are different bottles for different purposes but they are so strikingly similar that users cannot easily tell them apart.

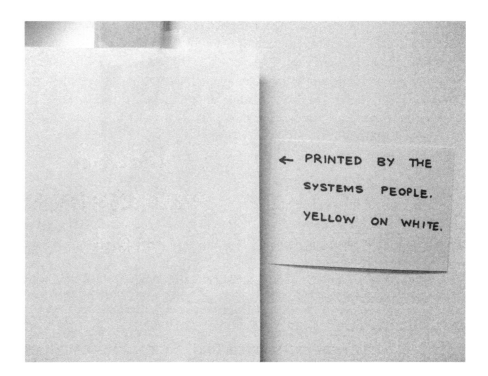

Fig. 30-23

Yellow text on a light background (a real sign on the door of a lab, credit unknown).

Fig. 30-24

Bottles for shampoo and conditioner are difficult to distinguish.

The important distinguishing labels, for shampoo and for conditioner, are "hidden" within other text and are in a very small font—indistinguishable, especially for users with soap in their eyes. And, remember, users who need eyeglasses cannot wear them in the shower.

So, users sometimes add their own affordances. In the case shown in Fig. 30-25, a user has added labels on the tops of these bottles to tell shampoo from conditioner in the shower.

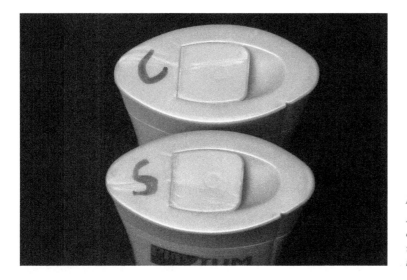

Fig. 30-25

Because of poor sensory affordance, a user had to mark the bottles to tell them apart.

You can see, in Fig. 30-26, an example of a kind of shampoo bottle design that would have avoided the problem in the first place.

Fig. 30-26

Better: A design to distinguish the bottles.

In this clever design, the shampoo, the first one you need, is right-side up, and the labeling on the conditioner bottle, the next one you need, is printed so that you stand the bottle "upside down."

30.4.2.6 Color

The use of color is an interesting facet of visual sensory design. Color decisions are often made by specialist graphic designers and constrained by organizational standards and branding requirements. For a bit more about guidelines for the use of color in UX design, see Section 32.10.7.

30.4.2.7 Presentation timing

Sometimes a user needs an affordance at a certain time during the interaction. In these cases, it just doesn't work if it isn't there when you need it.

Example: Just-In-Time Towel Dispenser Message

Fig. 30-27 is a photograph of a paper towel dispenser in a public bathroom. The next available towel is visible, and the cognitive affordance in the sketch on the cover of the dispenser clearly says "Pull the towel down with both hands."

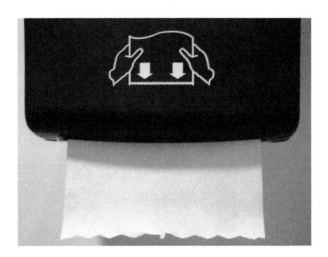

Fig. 30-27

The primary cognitive affordance for taking a paper towel.

But what if the next towel fails to drop down and users cannot grab it? Now a different user action is needed to get a towel, so a different cognitive affordance is required, as illustrated in Fig. 30-28.

Fig. 30-28

The backup cognitive affordance to help start a new paper towel.

Designers provided this new cognitive affordance, telling the user to push the lever to get the next towel started down into position. Normally this second cognitive affordance is obscured by the towel, but it becomes visible just when needed.

From the "wear marks" on the push bar, you can see that this "*exception*" case, and the need for this added cognitive affordance, have occurred quite often.

30.4.3 Auditory Sensory Issues

While the majority of objects in UX designs are visual, there are also auditory signals to users. Auditory sensory design issues are somewhat parallel to and similar to the *visual* sensory design issues, only they have to do with sound and how well users are able to hear sounds. Here is a summary of auditory issues for UX design.

- Audibility issues (counterpart to visibility issues):
  - Can users hear the sound?
- Noticeability of audio cues:
  - Volume of auditory cues (a major factor in noticeability).
  - Plus, ability of user to control volume.
- Intelligibility, discernibility, distinguishability of audio:
  - Has much to do with audio quality.
  - Can the user make out what is being said?

- Frequency, pitch (of sound):
  - Verbal messages should be centered in the mid-range of human hearing.
- Garbling.
- Interference from background noise.
- Timing of audio cue.
- Tone of audio cues.
  - Gentle tone can encourage, reduce stress.
  - Harsh tone can annoy, irritate.
  - But harsh tone can be used to get attention.
- Multiple audio cues can fragment user attention.
- Like visual branding, some audio can be subject to branding constraints.
  - Example: Iconic audio, such as the Microsoft chime at Windows startup.

Interaction Channel

A means or mode or medium through which users and parts of a system interact and communicate, including sensory modes such as visual, voice, and tactile interaction. The concept also includes devices such as desktop computers and smartphones and system-oriented channels such as the Internet, Wi-Fi connections, and even Bluetooth (Section 16.2.4).

Interaction designs involving auditory inputs and outputs are becoming more popular. Patel and Hughes (2012) make the case for moving beyond purely visual user interfaces to distribute tasks over other senses. They propose using auditory channels, in particular, to support the task of understanding of meaning and for decreasing cognitive load. One major advantage of auditory interaction components is that sound usually doesn't distract user attention from the visual channel.

They show that nonspeech sound, what they call sonification, is feasible as an interaction channel in certain situations. The challenge in making the sounds meaningful is designing them to be distinguishable in terms of pitch, intensity, and tempo.

30.4.4 Haptic and Tactile Sensory Issues

Issues of haptics and touch have been around in UX design discussions for a long time and, like auditory interactions, they are being used more often. An interesting example of one such design is the touchable virtual object, as manifest in a touchable hologram (Kugler, 2015). In this approach to haptic interaction, ultrasound is used to focus a shape that can be felt by the human hand.

Haptic and tactile issues (about touch and feel) are somewhat parallel and similar to visual and auditory issues, including:

- Noticeability: Is a tactile signal strong enough for users to feel it?
- Discernibility: Can users make out what a given tactile signal is?
- Distinguishability: Are there enough differences between two possibly similar tactile signals for users to tell the difference?

- Consistency: Are tactile and haptic representations consistent in meaning?
- Tone: As with other senses, we have to design tactile and haptic stimuli not to be harsh or irritating.

The factors of noticeability, discernibility, and distinguishability are often aided through some form of vibration (Thompson & Vandenbroucke, 2015) rather than just tactile pressure. One area where design work using tactile vibration is thriving is automotive user interfaces (Kern & Pfleging, 2013). Haptic feedback is a good match to the physical user actions needed for driving a car. Various kinds of vibrations felt in the steering wheel, the brake pedal, or the driver's seat allow users to receive feedback without having to look away from the driving task. These are especially effective for alerting the driver of situations needing immediate attention, such as an impending accident or drifting from the lane on a road.

30.5 FUNCTIONAL AFFORDANCE

30.5.1 Definition of Functional Affordance

A functional affordance is a design feature that helps users get work done by connecting physical user actions to system, or backend, functionality. Functional affordances are the reason why users will make an action; they want access to the functionality to do something. A functional affordance connects users to the usefulness component of the user experience via the power of the software behind the user interface.

For example, if you look at the button in Fig. 30-29 that says Add to cart, the functional affordance associated with that button is seated in the backend

Fig. 30-29

An Add to Cart button viewed as a physical affordance that leads to a functional affordance in the backend software.

application software that carries out the function implied by that button label—in this case, it puts the item selected for purchase into the virtual shopping cart.

For a discussion about how functional affordances fit in with Gibson's ecological view, see Section 33.5.

30.6 EMOTIONAL AFFORDANCE

30.6.1 Definition of Emotional Affordance

An emotional affordance is a design feature that helps a user make an emotional connection resulting in emotional impact within the user experience. Emotional affordances include design features that connect to our intuitive appreciation of fun, aesthetics, to our sense of identity, and challenges to personal growth.

Many UX designs meet all the functional requirements but are not very exciting or interesting. They tick all the boxes but don't light up the lights. The difference is emotional impact, which has become an important component of user experience in most UX designs. The mobile device world is leading attempts to leverage emotional affordances to attract customers. It is especially what new electronic products—like smartphones and personal music players—are all about. And some are proposing computers and devices that can sense and understand the emotions of users (Thompson, 2010).

Emotional impact is also a central concept in the automobile design world. Manufacturers of cars today compete over the pleasure of driving and the fun of using their electronic entertainment systems.

Example: Emotional Impact in the Hibu Image

In an advertisement for a Website Design service, hibu (see hibu.com) shows nothing but butterflies, saying, "Websites so stunning, they'll give you butterflies" (Fig. 30-30).

This is an ad for a high-tech web design company whose motto is "Made for business," and butterflies are the only image? The message is about design, emotional impact, and beauty! Their text begins with, "Our incredibly beautiful websites…" What a testimony to the importance of emotional impact in their view of UX Design.

Fig. 30-30
A hibu advertisement promising butterflies in the user experience (with permission).

30.6.2 Affordances to Support Meaningfulness

Meaningfulness is a phenomenon through which a product or artifact becomes meaningful in the life of a user. Meaningfulness comes out of emotional impact that develops into a personal relationship with the product, enduring over time. It is difficult to isolate a single design feature that instills meaningfulness; much of that long-term personal feeling of companionship, for example, can be traced to the conceptual design and to the daily usefulness of the product.

> **Meaningfulness**
>
> A personal relationship that develops and endures over time between human users and a product that has become a part of the user's lifestyle (Section 1.4.5).

30.7 PUTTING AFFORDANCES TOGETHER IN DESIGN

User work goals that require affordances to work together (Fig. 30-31):

- Users must *understand* the interaction objects (through cognitive affordances).
- Users must be able to *operate* the interaction objects (through physical affordances).
- Users must be able to *sense* interaction objects (through sensory affordances).
- Users must have *access* to functionality they need (through functional affordances).
- And it would be nice to *engender* a good emotional experience in the process (through emotional affordances).

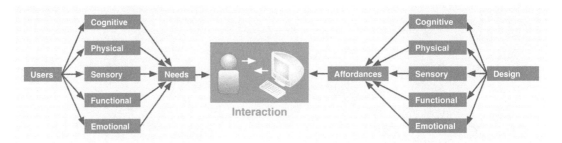

Fig. 30-31

User interaction needs relate directly to affordances in design.

30.7.1 Affordance Roles—An Alliance in Design

In most UX designs, the five types of affordance work together to help users accomplish work goals by sensing, understanding, and using affordances within a UX design. Each kind of affordance plays a different role in the design of specific attributes of the same artifact, including design of appearance, content, and manipulation characteristics.

An approach to UX design that integrates the different kinds of affordances compels us to consider all five affordance roles together in the design of an interaction artifact.

- Is the functionality to which this interaction object or artifact gives access useful in achieving user goals through task performance (functional affordance, or purpose of physical affordance)?
- Does the design include clear, understandable cues about how to use the artifact (cognitive affordance) or about system outcomes if the artifact is a feedback message?
- Can users easily sense visual (or other) cues about artifact operation (sensory affordance in support of cognitive affordance)?
- Is the artifact easy to manipulate by all users in the target user classes (physical affordance)?
- Can users easily sense the artifact for manipulation (sensory affordance in support of physical affordance)?

Considering one affordance role but ignoring another is likely to result in a flawed design. For example, if the wording for a feedback message is carefully crafted to be clear, complete, and helpful (good cognitive affordance), but users don't notice the message because it is displayed out of the users' focus of attention (poor sensory affordance), or users cannot read it because the font is too small, the net design is ineffective. A powerful drag-and-drop mechanism on a Mac may offer good physical and functional affordance for opening files (by dragging a file on to an application Icon on the Dock), but lack of a sufficient cognitive affordance to show how it works could mean that most users will not use it.

30.7.2 A UX Design Checklist of Affordances

The set of affordances will serve you well as a kind of UX design checklist (Fig. 30-32), against which each part of your design is checked.

Example: Affordances for a Sort Capability

Let's see how the checklist works with a very simple example, the design of a button to invoke, say, some kind of *Sort* function.

Functional affordance considerations

The first item on the checklist is functional affordance. The designer should ask if the intended functionality, the functional affordance, is appropriate, useful, and available to the user. If not, none of the other affordances will be useful in the end. Let's say functional affordance is OK, so we check this item off our list.

Cognitive affordance considerations

The next item on the list is cognitive affordance considerations. Is the meaning expressed clearly, in this case, in the label or menu choice that invokes the *Sort* function? Does the label advertise the purpose of the button by ensuring its meaning (in terms of a task-oriented view of its underlying functionality) is clear, unambiguous, and complete to help the user know when it is appropriate to click on the button?

As we say in Section 32.6.3.9, long labels are not necessarily bad. Short labels can be nice, but sometimes it takes more words to convey the full meaning. It's also nice to have both a verb and a noun—to indicate the action and the object.

✔ Functional affordance
✔ Cognitive affordance
✔ Physical affordance
✔ Sensory affordance
✔ Emotional affordance

Fig. 30-32

A UX design affordance checklist.

So, instead of just *Sort*, we could expand it to *Sort Records*. Sometimes even adding an adjective will help convey the meaning more fully, in this case giving us, *Sort Address Records*. Or an adverbial phrase might add information about how the sort will be done: *Sort By Last Name*.

Now, we can check cognitive affordance off the list.

Physical affordance considerations

The designer is next led to consider how physical affordance is to be supported in the button design. Does our *Sort* button design provide adequate physical affordance for easy clicking? Is the size of the button large enough to click on it easily? The button at the left of Fig. 30-33 is large enough so that a little accidental cursor movement during clicking won't move it off the button. But the button on the right is perhaps too small.

Is the button located near other artifacts used in the same and related tasks to minimize mouse movement between task actions? Is the button located far enough away from other, nonrelated, user interface objects to avoid clicking on them erroneously? The button on the left in Fig. 30-33 is isolated from others to reduce errors of clicking on the wrong ones. The button on the right is too close to ones you don't want to click on.

This is also the time to check on physical disabilities. You may not have thought of this, but even some people who don't appear to have physical disabilities may have trouble clicking.

Now, we can check physical affordances off our list.

Sensory affordance considerations

Now, the designer is asked to consider sensory affordance in support of both cognitive affordance and physical affordance in the button design.

In support of the physical affordance, the button must be a color, size, and shape that make it noticeable and, if possible, it should be located in the screen layout so that it is near enough to the user's focus of attention.

In support of cognitive affordance, the button label must have effective font size and color contrast, for example, to help the user discern the label text to read it.

Fig. 30-33

Different buttons have different physical affordances.

Fig. 30-34
*Different **Sort By** buttons with different sensory affordances.*

On the left side of Fig. 30-34 we have a nice ***Sort By*** button. But the low-contrast label in the middle is more difficult to read. And the font at the right-hand side is unnecessarily small. There's plenty of space; use it!

Now we can check sensory affordances off our list.

Emotional affordance considerations

Finally, we ask about emotional affordances in this design. Well, it's a little hard to get emotional about a ***Sort*** button or ***Sort*** function, I have to admit. But maybe you could make it a little more fun with an animation that shows how the sort works. Novice users might be intrigued by this. Or maybe you could find some interesting way to use sound. Challenge yourself and be creative!

In any case, let's check this off the list.

Exercise 30-3: Affordance Design Checklist

Now that we have shown you how to use a checklist of affordance types in the consideration of a design for a ***Sort*** button, your job in this exercise is to explain how to apply the same checklist when designing a feedback message indicating a "user error."

30.8 USER-CREATED AFFORDANCES AS A WAKE-UP CALL TO DESIGNERS

A user-created affordance (usually a cognitive affordance or physical affordance) is an affordance that is added to the original design (for example, by taping on a label) by a user who needs that affordance for a better user experience.

If a device in the everyday world doesn't suit the user, we will frequently see users modify the apparatus, briefly and unknowingly switching to the role of designer. We have all seen the little cognitive or physical affordances added to devices by users—Post-it notes added to a computer monitor or keyboard or a better grip taped to the handle of something. These trails of user-created artifacts blazed in the process of day-to-day usage are like wake-up messages, telling designers what the users think they missed in the design.

A common example of trails (literally) of user-made artifacts is seen in the paths worn by people as they walk. Sidewalk designers usually like to make the sidewalk patterns regular, symmetric, and rectilinear. However, the most efficient paths for people getting from one place to the other are often less tidy but more direct. Wear patterns in the grass show where people need or want to walk and, thus, where the sidewalks probably should have been located. The rare and creative sidewalk designer will wait until seeing the worn paths, employing the user-made artifacts as clues to drive the design.

Example: Confusing Glass Door

In Fig. 30-35, a photo of a glass door in a convenience store, we show an example of an added cognitive affordance. The glass and stainless-steel design is elegant: the perfectly symmetric layout and virtually unnoticeable hinges contribute to the uncluttered aesthetic appearance (good emotional affordance), but these same attributes work against cognitive affordance for its operation.

The storeowner noticed many people unsure about which side of the stainless-steel bar to push or pull to open the door, often trying the wrong side first. To help his customers with what should have been an easy task in the first place, he glued a bright yellow cardboard arrow to the glass, pointing out the correct place to operate the door.

Fig. 30-35

Glass door with a user-added cognitive affordance (arrow) indicating proper operation.

Example: Copier Darkness Icon

As another example of user-created affordances, consider the icons shown in Fig. 30-36. These are for lightness and darkness settings on a home office copier, icons with ambiguous meanings. The icon for lighter copies is whiter, but the white can be interpreted as part of the copy, and it seems denser than the icon for darker copies, so the user had to add his own label, as you can see in the figure.

These trails of often inelegant but usually effective artifacts added by frustrated users leave a record of affordance improvements that designers should consider for all their users. Perhaps if designers of the everyday things that Norman (1990) discusses had included usability testing in the field, they would have found these problems before the products went to market.

In the software world, most applications have only very limited capabilities for users to set their preferences. Would not it be much nicer for software users if they could modify UX designs as easily as applying a little duct tape, a Post-it, or extra paint here and there?

Fig. 30-36
A user-created cognitive affordance explaining copier darkness settings.

Example: Car Drink Holder

In Fig. 30-37, we show how a car owner created an artifact to replace an inadequate physical affordance—a built-in drink holder that was too small for today's super-sized drinks. During one trip, the user improvised with a shoe, resulting in this interesting example of a user-installed artifact.

Fig. 30-37

A user-made automobile cup-holder artifact, used with permission from Roundel *magazine, BMW Car Club of America, Inc. (Howarth, 2002).*

Example: Letterhead Printing

Consider a desktop printer used only occasionally to print on letterhead stationery. Inserting the stationery on top of the existing plain paper supply in the printer does this rather easily. The only problem is that it isn't easy to determine the correct orientation of the sheet to be inserted because:

- There is no clear mental model of how the sheet travels through in the interior mechanism of the printer.
- Printers can vary in this configuration.
- The design of the printer itself gives no cognitive affordance for loading a single sheet of letterhead.

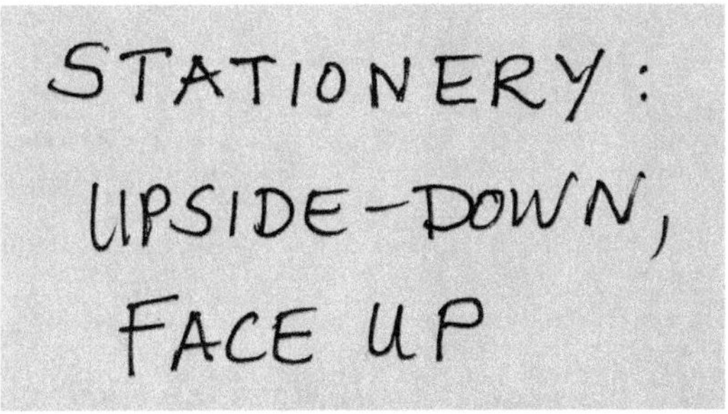

STATIONERY :
UPSIDE-DOWN,
FACE UP

Fig. 30-38

A user-created cognitive affordance to help users know how to insert blank letterhead stationery.

Thus, the user attached his own white adhesive label, shown in Fig. 30-38. As Norman (1990, p. 9) says, "When simple things need pictures, labels, or instructions, the design has failed."

More interesting and fun examples to come in Chapter 32, on UX design guidelines, but first, we stop and visit the Interaction Cycle in the next chapter.

The Interaction Cycle

31

31.1 INTRODUCTION

31.1.1 What is the Interaction Cycle?

The Interaction Cycle is our adaptation of Norman's (1986) "stages-of-action" model that characterizes sequences of user actions typically occurring in interaction between a human user and almost any kind of machine.

31.1.2 Need for a Theory-Based Conceptual Framework

As Gray and Salzman (1998, p. 241) have noted, "To the naïve observer it might seem obvious that the field of HCI would have a set of common categories with which to discuss one of its most basic concepts: Usability. We do not. Instead we have a hodgepodge collection of *do-it-yourself* categories and various collections of *rules-of-thumb*."

As Gray and Salzman (1998) continue, "Developing a common categorization scheme, preferably one grounded in theory, would allow us to compare types of usability problems across different types of software and interfaces." We believe our Interaction Cycle helps meet this need. It provides UX practitioners with a way to frame design issues and UX problem data within the structure of how designs support user actions and intentions.

31.2 NORMAN'S STAGES-OF-ACTION MODEL OF INTERACTION

Norman's stages-of-action model, illustrated in Fig. 31-1, shows a generic view of a typical sequence of user actions as a user interacts with almost any kind of machine.

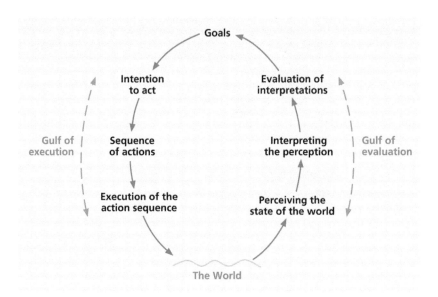

Fig. 31-1

Norman's (1990) stages-of-action model, adapted with permission.

The stages of action naturally divide into three major kinds of user activity. On the execution side (left side of Fig. 31-1), the user typically begins at the top of the figure by establishing a *goal*, decomposing goals into tasks and *intentions*, and mapping intentions to *action sequence* specifications. The user manipulates system controls by *executing the physical actions* (Fig. 31-1, bottom left), which cause internal system state changes (outcomes) in the world (the system) at the bottom of the figure.

On the evaluation side (right side of Fig. 31-1), users *perceive, interpret*, and *evaluate* the outcomes with respect to goals and intentions through perceiving the system state by sensing feedback from the system (state changes in "the world" or the system). Interaction success is evaluated by comparing outcomes with the original goals. The interaction is successful if the actions have brought the user closer to the goals.

Norman's model, along with the structure of the analytic evaluation method called the cognitive walkthrough (Lewis, Polson, Wharton, & Rieman, 1990), had an essential influence on our Interaction Cycle. Both ask questions about whether the user can determine what to do with the system to achieve a goal in the work domain, how to do it in terms of user actions, how easily the user can perform the required physical actions, and (to a lesser extent in the cognitive walkthrough method) how well the user can tell whether the actions were successful in moving toward task completion.

31.2.1 Gulfs between User and System

Originally conceived by Hutchins, Hollan, and Norman (1986), the gulfs of execution and evaluation were described further by Norman (1986). The two gulfs represent places where interaction can be most difficult for users, and where designers need to pay special attention to help users.

31.2.1.1 The gulf of execution

In the gulf of execution, on the left-hand side of the stages-of-action model in Fig. 31-1, users need help in knowing what actions to make on what objects. The gulf of execution, is a kind of language gap—from user to system. Users think of goals in the language of the work domain. In order to act upon the system to pursue these goals, intentions in the work domain language must be translated into the language of physical actions and the physical system.

As a simple example, consider a user composing a letter with a word processor. The letter is a work domain element, and the word processor is part of the system. The work domain goal of "creating a permanent record of the letter" translates to the system domain intention of "saving the file," which translates to the action of "clicking on the SAVE icon." A mapping or translation between the two domains is needed to bridge the gulf.

Let us revisit the example of a thermostat on a furnace from Section 15.2.2. Suppose that a user is feeling chilly while sitting at home. The user formulates a simple goal, expressed in the language of the work domain (in this case the daily living domain), "to feel warmer." To meet this goal, something must happen in the physical system domain. The ignition function and air blower, for example, of the furnace must be activated. To achieve this outcome in the physical domain, the user must translate the work domain goal into an action sequence in the physical (system) domain, namely, to set the thermostat to the desired temperature.

The gulf of execution lies between the user knowing the effect that is desired and what to do to the system to make it happen. In this example, there is a cognitive disconnect for the user in that the physical system variables to be controlled (burning fuel and blowing air) are not the ones the user cares about (being warm). The gulf of execution can be bridged from either direction—from the user and/or from the system. Bridging from the user's side means teaching the user about what has to happen in the system to achieve goals in the work domain. Bridging from the system's side means building help (cognitive affordances) to support the user into the design by hiding the need for translation, keeping the problem couched in work domain language. The thermostat does a little of each—its operation depends on a shared knowledge of how thermostats work, but it also shows a way to set the temperature visually.

To avoid having to train all users, the interaction designer can take responsibility to bridge the gulf of execution from the system's side by an effective conceptual design to help the user form a correct mental model. Failure of the interaction design to bridge the gulf of execution will be evidenced in observations of hesitation or task blockage *before* a user action because the user does not know what action to take or cannot predict the consequences of taking an action.

31.2.1.2 The gulf of evaluation

In the gulf of evaluation, on the right side of the stages-of-action model in Fig. 31-1, users need help in knowing whether their actions had the expected outcomes. The gulf of evaluation, is the same kind of language gap, only in the other direction. The ability of users to assess outcomes of their actions depends on how well the interaction design supports their comprehension of a change in the system state through their understanding of system feedback.

System state is a function of internal system variables, and it is the job of the interaction designer who creates the display of system feedback to bridge the gulf by translating a description of system state into the language of the user's work domain so that outcomes can be compared with the goals and intentions to assess the success of the interaction.

Failure of the interaction design to bridge the gulf of evaluation will be evidenced in observations of hesitation or task blockage *after* a user action because the user does not understand feedback and does not fully know what happened as a result of the action.

31.2.2 From Norman's Model to Our Interaction Cycle

We adapted and extended Norman's theory of action model of Fig. 31-1 into what we call the Interaction Cycle, which is also a model of user actions that occur in typical sequences of interaction between a human user and a machine.

31.2.2.1 Partitioning the model

Because the early part of Norman's execution side was about planning of goals and intentions, we call it the *planning* part of the cycle (Fig. 31-2). Planning includes formulating goal and task hierarchies, as well as decomposition and identification of specific intentions.

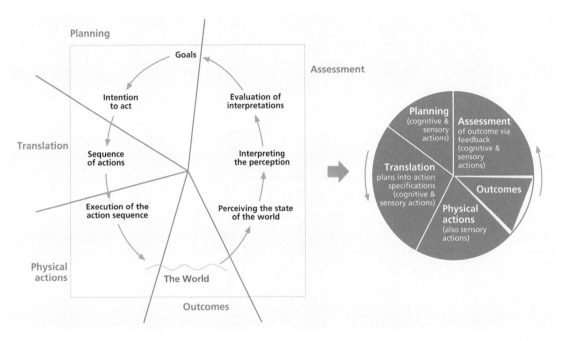

Fig. 31-2
Transition from Norman's model to our Interaction Cycle.

Planning is followed by formulation of the specific actions (on the system) to carry out each intention, a cognitive action we call *translation*, because it is here that the goals and plan are translated into action intentions.

Norman's "execution of the action sequence" component maps directly into what we call the *physical actions* part of the Interaction Cycle. Because Norman's evaluation side is where users assess the outcome of each physical action based on system feedback, we call it the *assessment* part.

31.2.2.2 Adding outcomes and system response and emphasizing translation

Finally, we added the concepts of *outcomes* and a system response, resulting in the mapping to the Interaction Cycle as shown in Fig. 31-2. Outcomes is represented as a "floating" sector between physical actions and assessment in the

Interaction Cycle because the Interaction Cycle is about user interaction, and what happens in outcomes is entirely internal to the system and not part of what the user sees or does. The system response, which includes all system feedback and which occurs at the beginning of and as an input to the assessment part, tells users about the outcomes.

Finally, the importance of translation to the Interaction Cycle and its significance in design for a high-quality user experience is, in fact, so great that we made the relative sizes of the "wedges" of the Interaction Cycle parts represent the weight of this importance visually.

31.3 INTERACTION CYCLE CATEGORIES OF UX DESIGN ISSUES

Here, we give just an overview of the kinds of UX design issues that come under each Interaction Cycle category. These categories and subcategories are used to organize the UX design guidelines in the next chapter. As an example of this kind of hierarchical structure, consider this breakdown of some translation topics:

Translation
    Presentation of a cognitive affordance to support translation
        Legibility, visibility, noticeability of the cognitive affordance
            Fonts, color, layout
            Font color, color contrast with background

31.3.1 Planning (Design Helping User Know What to Do)

Planning is the part of the Interaction Cycle containing all cognitive actions by users to determine "what to do?" or "what can I do?" using the system to achieve work domain goals.

Interaction design support for user planning is concerned with how well the design helps users understand the overall computer application relative to the perspective of work context, the work domain, and environmental requirements and constraints in order to determine in general how to use the system to solve problems and get work done. Planning support has to do with the system model, conceptual design, and metaphors, the user's awareness of system features and capabilities (what the user *can* do with the system), and the user's knowledge of possible system modalities. Planning is about user strategies for approaching the system to get work done.

31.3.2 Translation (Design Helping User Know How to Do Something)

Translation concerns the lowest level of task preparation. Translation includes anything that has to do with deciding how a user can or should make an action on an object, including thinking about which action to take or on what object to take it, or what might be best action to take next within a task.

Translation is the part of the Interaction Cycle that contains all cognitive actions by users to determine *how* to carry out the intentions that arise in planning, in terms of physical actions on interface objects, such as "click and drag the document file icon," using the computer to carry out an intention.

Here is a simple example about driving a car. Planning for a trip in the car involves thinking about traveling to get somewhere, involving questions such as, "where are you going," "by what route," and "do we need to stop and get gas and/or groceries first?" So *planning is in the work domain*, which is travel, not operating the car.

In contrast, translation takes the user into the system, machine, or physical world domain and is about formulating actions to operate the gas pedal, brake, and steering wheel to accomplish the tasks that will help you reach your planning, or travel, goals. Because steps such as, "turn on headlight switch," "push horn button," and "push brake pedal" are actions on objects, they are the stuff of translation.

Over the bulk of interaction that occurs in the real world, translation is arguably the single-most important part of the cycle because it is about how you do things. From our own experience over the years, we guess that the largest bulk of UX problems observed in UX evaluation, 75% or more, falls into this category.

31.3.3 Physical Actions (Design Helping User Do the Actions)

After users decide which actions to take, the physical actions part of the Interaction Cycle is *where users do the actions*. This part includes all user inputs acting on devices and user interface objects to manipulate the system, including typing, clicking, dragging, touching, gestures, and navigational actions, such as walking in virtual environments. The physical actions part of the Interaction Cycle *includes no cognitive actions*; thus, this part is not about thinking about the actions or determining which actions to do.

31.3.3.1 Physical actions—concepts

Physical actions are especially important for analysis of performance by expert users who have, to some extent, "automated" planning and translation associated with a task and for whom physical actions have become the limiting factor in task performance.

Physical affordance

A design feature that helps, aids, supports, facilitates, or enables user physical actions: clicking, touching, pointing, gesturing, and moving things (Section 30.3).

Physical affordance design factors include design of input/output devices (e.g., touchscreen design or keyboard layout), haptic devices, interaction styles and techniques, direct manipulation issues, gestural body movements, physical fatigue, and such physical human factors issues as manual dexterity, hand-eye coordination, layout, interaction using two hands and feet, and physical disabilities.

31.3.4 Outcomes (Internal, Invisible Effect/Result within System)

Physical user actions are seen by the system as inputs and usually trigger a system function that can lead to system state changes that we call *outcomes* of the interaction. The outcomes part of the Interaction Cycle represents the system's turn to do something that usually involves computation by the nonuser-interface software or, as it is sometimes called, core or back-end functionality. One possible outcome is a *failure* to achieve an expected or desired state change, as in the case of a user error.

A user action is not always required to produce a system response. The system can also autonomously produce an outcome, possibly in response to an internal event such as a disk becoming full; an event in the environment sensed by the system such as a process control alarm; or the physical actions of other users in a shared work environment.

The system functions that produce outcomes are purely internal to the system and do not involve the user. Consequently, outcomes are technically not part of the user's Interaction Cycle, and the only UX issues associated with outcomes might be about usefulness or functional affordance of the nonuser-interface system functionality.

Because internal system state changes are not directly visible to the user, outcomes must be revealed to the user via system feedback or a display of results, to be evaluated by the user in the assessment part of the Interaction Cycle.

Usefulness

A component of user experience based on utility, system functionality that gives users the ability to accomplish the goals of work (or play) through using the system or product (Section 1.4.3).

31.3.5 Assessment (Design Helping User Know If Interaction Was Successful)

The assessment part of the Interaction Cycle corresponds to Norman's evaluation side (Fig. 31-1) of interaction. A user in assessment performs sensory and cognitive actions needed to sense and understand system feedback and displays of results as a means to comprehend internal system changes or outcomes due to a previous physical action or other triggers to system change.

The user's objective in assessment is to determine whether the outcomes of all that previous planning, translation, and physical actions were favorable, meaning desirable or effective to the user. In particular, an outcome is favorable if it helps the user approach or achieve the current intention, task, and/or goal; that is, if the plan and action "worked."

The assessment part parallels much of the translation part, only focusing on system feedback. Assessment has to do with the existence of feedback, presentation of feedback, and content or meaning of feedback. Assessment is about whether users can know when an error occurred, and whether a user can sense a feedback message and understand its content.

31.3.5.1 Example: Creating a business report as a task within the interaction cycle

Let us say that the task of creating a quarterly report to management on the financial status of a company breaks down into these basic steps:

- Calculate monthly profits for last quarter.
- Write summary, including graphs, to show company performance.
- Create table of contents.
- Print the report.

In this kind of task decomposition, it is common that some steps are more or less granular than others, meaning that some steps will decompose into more substeps and more details than others. As an example, Step 1 might decompose into these substeps:

- Open spreadsheet program.
- Call accounting department and ask for numbers for each month.
- Create column headers in spreadsheet for expenses and revenues in each product category.
- Compute profits.

The first step here, to open a spreadsheet program, might correspond to a single simple pass through the Interaction Cycle. The second step is a nonsystem task that interrupts the workflow temporarily. The third and fourth steps could take several passes through the Interaction Cycle.

The first intention for the "Print report" task step is the "getting started intention"; the user intends to invoke the print function, taking the task from the work domain into the computer domain. In this particular case, the user does not do further planning at this point, expecting the feedback from acting on this intention to lead to the next natural intention.

To translate this first intention into an action specification in the language of the actions and objects within the computer interface, the user draws on experiential knowledge and/or the cognitive affordances provided by display of the Print choice in the File menu to create the action specification to select "Print." A more experienced user might translate the intention subconsciously or automatically to the shortcut actions of typing "Ctrl-P" or clicking on the Print icon.

The user then carries out this action specification by doing the corresponding physical action, the actual clicking on the Print menu choice. The system accepts the menu choice, changes state internally (the outcomes of the action), and displays the Print dialogue box as feedback. The user sees the feedback and uses it for assessment of the outcome so far. Because the dialogue box makes sense to the user at this point in the interaction, the outcome is considered to be favorable, that is, leading to accomplishment of the user's intention and indicating successful planning and action so far.

31.4 COOPERATIVE USER-SYSTEM TASK PERFORMANCE WITHIN THE INTERACTION CYCLE

31.4.1 Primary Tasks

Primary tasks are tasks that have direct work-related goals. The task in the previous example of creating a business report is a primary task, as is the small task of printing. Primary tasks can be user initiated or initiated by the environment, the system, or other users. Primary tasks usually represent simple, linear paths through the Interaction Cycle.

User-initiated tasks. The typical linear path of user-system turn taking starting at the top and going counterclockwise around the Interaction Cycle represents a user-initiated task because it starts with user planning and translation.

Tasks initiated by environment, system, or other users. When a user task is initiated by events that occur outside that user's Interaction Cycle, the user actions become reactive. The user's cycle of interaction begins at the outcomes part, followed by the user sensing the subsequent system response in a feedback output display and, thereafter, reacting to it.

31.4.2 Path Variations in the Interaction Cycle

For all but the simplest tasks, interaction can take alternative, possibly nonlinear, paths. Although user-initiated tasks usually begin with some kind of planning, Norman (1986) emphasizes that interaction does not necessarily follow a simple cycle of actions. Some activities will appear out of order or be omitted or repeated. In addition, the user's interaction process can flow around the Interaction Cycle at almost any level of task/action granularity.

Multiuser tasks. When the Interaction Cycles of two or more users interleave in a cooperative work environment, one user will enter inputs through physical actions (Fig. 31-3), and another user will assess (sense, interpret, and evaluate) the system response, as viewed in a shared workspace, revealing system outcomes due to the first user's actions. For the user who initiated the exchange, the cycle begins with planning, but for the other users, interaction begins by sensing the system response and goes through assessment of what happened before it becomes that second user's turn for planning for the next round of interaction.

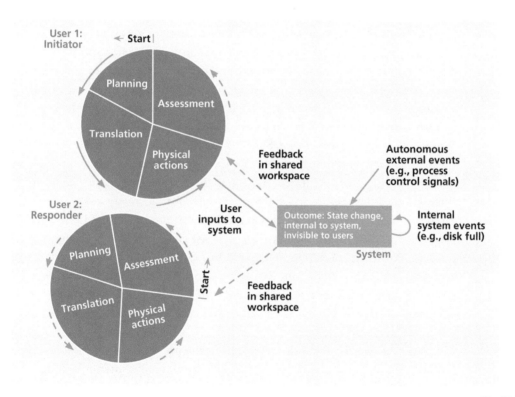

Fig. 31-3

Multiuser interaction, system events, and asynchronous external events within multiple Interaction Cycles.

31.4.3 Secondary Tasks, Intention Shifts, and Stacking

Secondary tasks and intention shifts. Kaur, Maiden, and Sutcliffe (1999), who based an inspection method primarily for virtual environment applications on Norman's stages of action, recognized the need to interrupt primary work-oriented tasks with secondary tasks to accommodate intention shifts, exploration, information seeking, and error handling. Kaur et al. (1999) created different and separate kinds of Interaction Cycles for these cases, but from our perspective, these cases are just variations in flow through the same Interaction Cycle.

Secondary tasks are "overhead" tasks in that the goals are less directly related to the work domain and usually oriented more toward dealing with the computer as an artifact, such as error recovery or learning about the interface. Secondary tasks often stem from changes of plans or intention shifts that arise during task performance; something happens that reminds the user of other things that need to be done or that arise out of the need for error recovery.

For example, the need to explore can arise in response to a specific information need, when users cannot translate an intention to an action specification because they cannot see an object that is appropriate for such an action. Then, they have to search for such an object or cognitive affordance, such as a label on a button or a menu choice that matches the desired action.

Stacking and restoring task context. Stacking and restoring of work context during the execution of a program is an established software concept. Humans must do the same during the execution of their tasks due to spontaneous intention shifts. Interaction Cycles required to support primary and secondary tasks are just variations of the basic Interaction Cycle. However, the storing and restoring of task contexts in the transition between such tasks impose a human memory load on the user, which could require explicit support in the interaction design. Secondary tasks also often require considerable judgment on the part of the user when it comes to assessment. For example, an exploration task might be considered "successful" when users are satisfied that they have had enough or get tired and give it up.

Example of stacking due to intention shift. To use the previous example of creating a business report to illustrate stacking due to a spontaneous intention shift, suppose the user has finished the task step "Print the report" and is ready to move on. However, upon looking at the printed report, the user does not like the way it turned out and decides to reformat the report. The user has to take some time to go learn more about how to format it better. The printing task is stacked temporarily while the user takes up the information-seeking task.

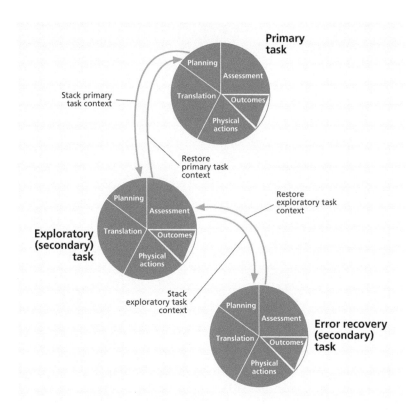

Fig. 31-4

Stacking and returning to Interaction Cycle task context instances.

Such a change of plan causes an interruption in the task flow and normal task planning, requiring the user mentally to "stack" the current goal, task, and/or intention while tending to the interrupting task, as shown in Fig. 31-4. As the primary task is suspended in mid-cycle, the user starts a new Interaction Cycle at planning for the secondary task. Eventually, the user can unstack each goal and task successively and return to the main task.

In the next chapter, we use the basic stages of the Interaction Cycle as a way to organize the UX design guidelines.

UX Design Guidelines

To err is human; forgive by design.

– Anonymous

Highlights

- Human memory limitations.
- Selected UX design guidelines and examples for user actions within the Interaction Cycle:
  - Planning.
  - Translation.
  - Physical actions.
  - Outcomes.
  - Assessment.
  - Overall.

32.1 INTRODUCTION

When properly interpreted in context, UX (or any) design guidelines help channel design per the collective wisdom of empirical studies and extensive practitioner experience.

32.1.1 Scope and Universality

Lots of design and design guidelines out there. There have been many books and articles on design guidelines for graphical user interfaces (GUIs) and other user interfaces and their widgets—how to create and employ windows, buttons, pull-down menus, pop-up menus, cascading menus, icons, dialogue boxes, check boxes, radio buttons, options menus, forms, and so on. But we want you to think about UX design and design guidelines much more broadly than that, well beyond GUIs, webpages, mobile devices, particular platforms, media, and devices.

There is a world of design out there, and, as Don Norman (1990) says, seeing the guidelines applied to the design of everyday things helps us understand the application of guidelines to interaction by humans with almost any kind of device or system.

Design principles behind the guidelines don't change over time. Although guidelines may change somewhat to remain specific to technology, **design principles have not changed over the years** (Soon, 2013). Changes in technology only affect the ways these design principles are applied.

Universality of design guidelines. The principles and guidelines in this chapter are universal; you will see in this chapter that the same issues apply to ATMs, elevator controls, hair dryers, and even highway signage. We, too, have a strong flavor of *The Design of Everyday Things* (Norman, 1990) in our guidelines and examples. We agree with Jokela (2004) that usability and a quality user experience are also essential in everyday consumer products.

Not everything is covered. We hope you will forgive us for excluding guidelines about internationalization or accessibility (as we advised in the Preface). This book, especially this chapter, is already large, and we cannot cover everything. Beyond that, because the collection of guidelines and examples is so large and diverse, we make no claim for completeness or even that they are consistent among themselves.

For more about where UX design guidelines came from, see Section 33.6.

32.1.2 Some of Our Examples Are Intentionally Old

We have been collecting examples of good and bad interaction and other kinds of design for decades. This means that some of these examples are old. Some of these systems no longer exist. Certainly, some of the problems have been fixed over time, but they are still good examples, and their age shows how we as a community have advanced and improved our designs. Many readers may think the interfaces of modern commercial software applications have always been as they are. Read on.

32.2 USING AND INTERPRETING UX DESIGN GUIDELINES

Are most UX design guidelines not obvious? When we teach these design guidelines, we usually get nods of agreement upon our statement of each guideline. There is very little controversy about most UX design guidelines stated absolutely, out of context. It's obvious; how else would you do it?

However, it's not always so easy to apply those same guidelines in specific usability design and evaluation situations. People are often unsure about which guidelines apply or how to apply, tailor, or interpret them in a specific design situation (Potosnak, 1988). Practitioners don't even agree on the meaning of some guidelines. As Lynn Truss (2003) says in the context of English grammar, that even considering people who are rabidly in favor of using the rules of grammar, it's impossible to get them all to agree on the rules and their interpretation and to pull in the same direction.

Bastien and Scapin (1995, p. 106) quote a study by de Souza and Bevan (1990), who "found that designers made errors, that they had difficulties with 91% of the guidelines, and that integrating detailed design guidelines with their existing experience was difficult for them."

You will not see guidelines here of the type: "Menus should not contain more than X items." That is because such guidelines are meaningless without interpretation within a design and usage context. In the presence of sweeping statements about what is right or wrong in UX design, we can only think of our long-time friend Jim Foley who said, "The only correct answer to any UX design question is: it depends."

We believe much of the difficulty stems from the broad generality, vagueness, and even contradiction within most sets of design guidelines. One of the guidelines near the top of almost any list is "be consistent," an all-time favorite UX platitude. But what does it mean? Consistency at what level; what kind of consistency? Consistency of layout or semantic descriptors such as labels or system support for workflow?

Another such overly general maxim is "keep it simple," certainly a shoo-in to the UX design guidelines hall of fame. But, again, what is simplicity? Minimize the things users can do? It depends on the kind of users, the complexity of their work domain, their skills and expertise.

To address this vagueness and difficulty in interpretation at high levels, we have organized the guidelines in a particular way. Rather than organize the guidelines by the obvious keywords such as consistency, simplicity, and the language of the user, we have tried to associate each guideline with a specific part of the user's Interaction Cycle (previous chapter). This allows specific guidelines to be linked to user actions for planning, knowing what actions to take, making physical actions, and assessing feedback.

Finally, we warn you to use your head and not follow guidelines blindly. While design guidelines and custom style guides are useful in supporting UX design, remember that there is no substitute for a competent, careful, and experienced practitioner.

Interaction cycle

Our adaptation of Norman's (1986) "stages-of-action" model that characterizes sequences of user actions typically occurring in interaction between a human user and almost any kind of machine (Section 31.1.1).

Style guide

A document fashioned and maintained by designers to capture and describe details of visual and other general design decisions, especially about screen designs, font choices, iconography, and color usage, which can be applied in multiple places. A style guide helps with consistency and reuse of design decisions (Section 17.8.1).

32.3 HUMAN MEMORY LIMITATIONS

Because some of the guidelines and much of practical user performance depend on the concepts of human working memory, we interject a short discussion of the same here, before we get into the guidelines themselves. We treat human memory here because:

- It applies to most of the Interaction Cycle parts.
- It's one of the few areas of psychology that has solid empirical data supporting knowledge that is directly usable in UX design.

Our discussion of human memory here is by no means complete or authoritative. Seek a good psychology book for that. We present a potpourri of concepts that should help your understanding in applying the design guidelines related to human memory limitations.

32.3.1 Short-Term or Working Memory

Short-term memory, which we usually call working memory, is the type we are primarily concerned with in UX and has a duration of about 30 seconds.[1] With a little rehearsal, you can stretch this duration out to 2 minutes or longer. Other intervening activities, sometimes called proactive interference, will cause the contents of working memory to fade even faster.

Working memory is a buffer storage that carries information of immediate use in performing tasks. Most of this information is called "throw-away data" because its usefulness is short term, and it's not even desirable to keep it longer. In his famous paper, George Miller (1956) showed experimentally that under certain conditions, the typical capacity of human short-term memory is about seven, plus or minus two items; often it's less.

32.3.1.1 Chunking

The items in short-term memory are often encodings that Simon (1974) has labeled "chunks." A chunk is a basic human memory unit containing one piece of data that is recognizable as a single gestalt. That means for spoken expressions, for example, a chunk is a word, not a phoneme, and in written expressions a chunk is a word or even a single sentence, not usually a letter.

Random strings of letters can be divided into groups which are remembered more easily. If the group is pronounceable, it's even easier to remember, even if it

---

[1] All of these quantifications are admittedly approximations and can vary with respect to the situation.

has no meaning. Duration trades off with capacity; all else being equal, the more chunks involved, the less time they can be retained in short-term memory.

Example: Phone Numbers Are Designed to be Remembered

Not counting the area code, a phone number has seven digits—not a coincidence that this exactly meets the Miller estimate of working memory capacity. If you look up a number in the phone book, you are loading your working memory with seven chunks. You should be able to retain the number if you use it within the next 30 seconds or so.

A telephone number is a classic example of working memory usage in daily life. If you get distracted between memory loading and usage, you may have to look the number up again, a scenario we all have experienced. If the prefix (the first three digits) is familiar, it's treated as a single chunk, making the task easier.

Sometimes items can be grouped or recoded into patterns that reduce the number of chunks. When grouping and recoding is involved, storage can trade off with processing, just as it does in computers. For example, think about keeping this pattern in your working memory:

001010110111000

On the surface, this is a string of 15 digits, beyond the working memory capacity of most people. But a clever user might notice that this is a binary number and the digits can be grouped into threes:

001 010 110 111 000

By converting this to octal digits: 12670, we have traded off a modicum of processing against memory requirements.

32.3.1.2 Stacking

One way user working memory limitations affect task performance is when task context stacking (storing away context information in the middle of a task, Section 31.4.3) is required due to a new situation arising in the middle of task performance. Before the user can continue with the original task, its context (a memory of where the user was in the task) must be put on a "stack" in the user's memory.

This same thing happens to the context of execution of a software program when an interrupt must be processed before proceeding: the program execution context is stacked in a last-in-first-out (LIFO) data structure. Later, when the system returns to the original program, its context is "popped" from the stack, and execution continues.

It's pretty much the same for a human user whose primary task is interrupted, only the stack is implemented in human working memory. This means that user task stacks are small in capacity and short in duration; people have leaky stacks. After enough time and interruptions, they forget what they were doing.

32.3.1.3 Cognitive load

Cognitive load is the load on working memory at any point in time (Cooper, 1998; Sweller, 1988, 1994). Cognitive load theory (Sweller, 1988, 1994) has been aimed primarily at improvement in teaching and learning through attention to the role and limitations of working memory, but, of course, it also applies directly to UX design. While working with the computer, users are often in danger of having their working memory overloaded. Users can get lost easily in cascading menus with lots of choices at each level or tasks that lead through large numbers of webpages.

If you could chart the load on working memory as a function of time through the performance of a task, you would be looking at variations in the cognitive load across the task steps. When users get to "pop" task context back off the stack, memory load reaches zero, and they get "closure," a feeling of cognitive relief they get from not having to retain information in their working memories.

By organizing tasks into smaller operations instead of one large hierarchical structure, you will reduce the average user cognitive load over time and achieve task closure more often.

32.3.1.4 Recognition versus recall

Because we know that computers are better at memory and humans are better at pattern recognition, we design interaction to play to each other's strengths. You hear people say, in many contexts, "I cannot remember it exactly, but I will recognize it when I see it." That is the basis for the guideline to use recognition over recall. In essence, it means letting the user choose from a list of possibilities rather than having to come up with the choice entirely from memory.

Recognition over recall does work better for initial or intermittent use where learning and remembering are the operational factors, but what happens to people who do learn? They migrate from novice to experienced userhood. In terms of the Interaction Cycle, they begin to remember how to make translations of frequent intentions into actions. They focus less on cognitive actions to know what to do and more on the physical actions of doing it. The cognitive affordances to help new users make these translations can now begin to become barriers to performance of the physical actions.

Moving the cursor and clicking to select items from lists of possibilities becomes more effortful than just typing short memorized commands. When more experienced users do recall the commands they need by virtue of their frequent usage, they find command typing a (legal) performance enhancer compared to the less efficient and, eventually, more boring and irritating physical actions required by those once-helpful GUI affordances.

Even command users get some memory help through command completion mechanisms, the "hum a few bars of it" approach. The user has to remember only the first few characters and the system provides possibilities for the whole command.

32.3.1.5 Shortcuts

When expert users get stuck with a GUI designed for translation affordances, it's time for shortcuts to come to the rescue. In GUIs, these shortcuts are physical affordances, mainly "hot key" equivalents of menu, icon, and button command choices, such as Ctrl-S for the Save command.

The addition of an indication of the shortcut version to the pull-down menu choice, for example, Ctrl+S added to the Save choice in the File menu, is a simple and subtle but remarkably effective design feature to remind all users of the menu about the corresponding shortcuts. All users can migrate seamlessly from using the shortcuts on the menus to learning and remembering the commands, bypassing the menus to use the shortcuts directly. This is true "as-needed" support of memory limitations in design.

32.3.2 Other Kinds of Human Memory

These other kinds of human memory are usually not important in UX, but we describe them briefly here for completeness.

32.3.2.1 Sensory memory

Sensory memory is of very brief duration. For example, the duration of visual memory ranges from a small fraction of a second to maybe 2 seconds and is primarily about visual (and other) patterns observed, not anything about identifying what was seen or what it means. It is raw sensory data that allow direct comparisons between stimuli, such as might occur in detecting voice inflection. Sensory persistence is the phenomenon of storage of the stimulus in the sensory organ, not the brain.

For example, visual persistence allows us to integrate the fast-moving sequences of individual image frames in movies or television, making them appear as a smooth integrated motion picture.

Physical affordance

A design feature that helps, aids, supports, facilitates, or enables user physical actions: clicking, touching, pointing, gesturing, and moving things (Section 30.3).

32.3.2.2 Muscle memory

Muscle memory is a little bit like sensory memory in that it's mostly stored locally (in the muscles in this case), and not the brain. Muscle memory is important for repetitive physical actions; it's about getting in a "rhythm." Thus, muscle memory is an essential aspect of learned skills of athletes. In UX, it's important in physical actions such as typing.

Example: Muscling Light Switches

In the United States at least, we use an arbitrary convention that moving an electrical switch up means "on," and down means "off." Over a lifetime of usage, we develop muscle memory because of this convention and hit the switch in an upward direction as we enter the room without pausing.

However, if you have lights on a three-way switch, "on" and "off" cannot be assigned consistently to any given direction of the switch. It depends on the state of the whole set of switches. If, out of habit, you find yourself hitting a three-way switch in an upward direction, sometimes the light fails to turn on because the switch was already up with the lights off. No amount of practice or trying to remember can overcome this conflict between muscle memory and this design.

32.3.2.3 Long-term memory

Information stored in short-term memory can be transferred to long-term memory by "learning," which may involve the hard work of rehearsal and repetition. Transfer to long-term memory relies heavily on organization and structure of information already in the brain. Items transfer more easily if associations exist with items already in long-term memory.

The capacity of long-term memory is almost unlimited—a lifetime of experiences. The duration of long-term memory is also almost unlimited, but retrieval is not always guaranteed. Learning, forgetting, and remembering are all intertwined with the vagaries of long-term memory. Sometimes, items can be classified in more than one way. Maybe one item of a certain type goes in one place, and another item of the same type goes elsewhere. As new items and new types of items come in, the classification system is revised to accommodate. Retrieval depends on being able to reconstruct the structural encoding used for storage.

When we forget, items become inaccessible, but probably not lost. Sometimes forgotten or repressed information can be recalled. Electric brain stimulation can trigger reconstructions of visual and auditory memories of past events. Hypnosis can help recall vivid experiences of years ago. Some evidence indicates that hypnosis increases willingness to recall rather than the ability to recall.

32.4 REVIEW OF THE INTERACTION CYCLE STRUCTURE

The selected UX design guidelines in this section are generally organized by the Interaction Cycle (previous chapter) structure.

To review the structure of the Interaction Cycle from the previous chapter, we show the simplest view of this cycle in Fig. 32-1, featuring these parts:

- Planning: How the UX design supports users in determining what to do?
- Translation: How the UX design supports users in determining how to do actions on objects?
- Physical actions: How the UX design supports users in doing those actions?
- Outcomes: How the noninteraction functionality of the system helps users achieve their work goals?
- Assessment of outcomes: How the UX design supports users in determining whether the interaction is turning out right?

32.5 PLANNING

Support for user planning (Fig. 32-2) is often a missing component of UX designs.

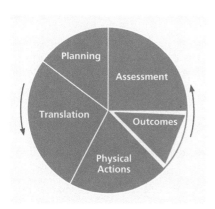

Fig. 32-1

Simplest view of the Interaction Cycle.

Planning guidelines are to support users as they plan how they will use the system to accomplish work in the application domain, including cognitive user actions to determine what tasks or steps to do. It's also about helping users understand what tasks they *can* do with the system and how well the design supports learning about the system for planning. If users cannot determine how

Fig. 32-2

The planning part of the Interaction Cycle.

to organize several related tasks in the work domain because the system doesn't help them understand exactly how it can help do these kinds of tasks, the design needs improvement in planning support.

32.5.1 Clear System Task Model for User

Support the user's ability to acquire an overall understanding of the system at a high level, including the system model, conceptual design, and metaphors.[2]

Help users plan goals, tasks by providing a clear model of how users should view system in terms of tasks.

Support user task decomposition by matching the design to users' concept of task decomposition and organization.

Example: Get Organized

The top of Fig. 32-3 shows tabs that occur on every page of a particular digital library website. These tabs are not well organized by task, having information-seeking tasks mixed in with other kinds of tasks. Part of the new tab bar in our suggested new design is shown in the bottom of Fig. 32-3.

Help users understand what system features exist and how they can be used in their work context.

---

[2]This special green font denotes a guideline.

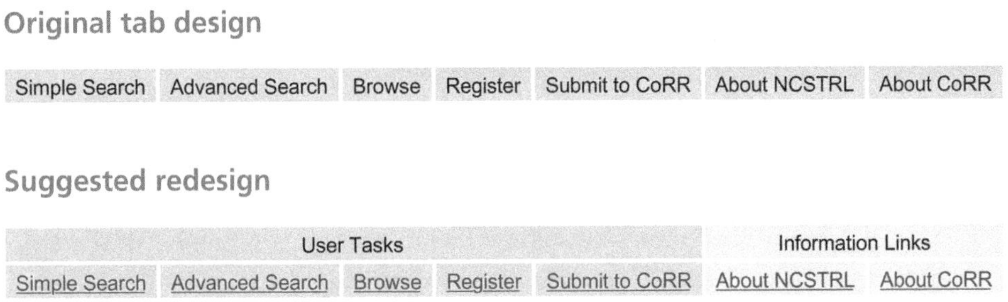

Original tab design

| Simple Search | Advanced Search | Browse | Register | Submit to CoRR | About NCSTRL | About CoRR |

Suggested redesign

User Tasks					Information Links	
Simple Search	Advanced Search	Browse	Register	Submit to CoRR	About NCSTRL	About CoRR

Fig. 32-3
Tab reorganization to match task structure.

Support user awareness of specific system features capabilities and understanding of how they can use those features to solve work domain problems in different work situations. Support user ability to attain awareness of specific system feature or capability.

Example: Mastering the Master Document Feature

Consider the case of the Master Document feature in Microsoft Word. For convenience and to keep file sizes manageable, users of Microsoft Word can maintain each part of a document in a separate file. At the end of the day, they can combine those individual files to achieve the effect of a single document for global editing and printing.

However, we have found this ability to treat several chapters in different files as a single document almost impossible to understand. The system doesn't help the user determine what can be done with it or how it might help with this task. Further, one wrong move, and "it can corrupt your entire document at the most inconvenient time possible."[3]

Help users decompose tasks, logically breaking long, complex tasks into smaller, simpler pieces.

Make clear all possibilities for what users can do at every point.

Keep users aware of system state for planning the next task.

Maintain and clearly display system state indicators when next actions are state dependent.

Keep the task context visible to minimize memory load.

To help users compare outcomes with goals, maintain and clearly display user request along with results.

---

[3] A comment on the Internet (and it has happened to us).

Example: Library Search by Author

In the search mode within a library information system, users can find themselves deep down many levels and screens into the task where card catalog information is being displayed. By the time they dig into the information structure that deeply, there is a chance users may have forgotten their exact original search intentions. Somewhere on the screen, it would be helpful to have a reminder of the task context, such as "You are *searching by author* for: Stephen King."

32.5.2 Planning for Efficient Task Paths

Help users plan the most efficient ways to complete their tasks.

Example: The Helpful Printing Command

This is an example of good design, rather than a design problem, and it's from an old version of Borland's 3-D Home Architect. Using this house-design program, when a user tries to print a large house plan, it results in an informative message in a dialogue box that says: "Current printer settings require 9 pages at this scale. Switching to Landscape mode allows the plan to be drawn with 6 pages. Click on Cancel if you wish to abort printing."

This tip can be most helpful, saving the time and paper involved in printing it incorrectly the first time, making the change, and printing again. As an aside here, this message still falls short of the mark. First, the term "abort" has overtones that could be interpreted as violent. Plus, the design could provide a button to change to landscape mode directly, without forcing the user to find out how to make that switch.

32.5.3 Progress Indicators

Support user planning with task progress indicators to help users manage task sequencing and keep track of what parts of the task are done and what parts are left to do.

During long tasks with multiple and possibly repetitive steps, users can lose track of where they are in the task. For these situations, task progress indicators or progress maps can be used to help users with planning based on knowing where they are in the task.

Example: Turbo-Tax Keeps You on Track

Filling out income tax forms is a good example of a lengthy multiple-step task. The designers of Turbo-Tax by Intuit used a "wizard-like" step-at-a-time prompter to help users understand where they are in the overall task, showing the user's progress through the steps while summarizing the net effect of the user's work at each point.

32.5.4 Avoiding Transaction Completion Slips

A transaction completion slip is a kind of error in which the user omits or forgets a final action, often a crucial action for consummating the task.

Provide cognitive affordances at the end of critical tasks to remind users to complete the transaction.

Example: Hey, Don't Forget Your Tickets

A transaction completion slip can occur in the Ticket Kiosk System when the user gets a feeling of closure at the end of the interaction for the transaction and fails to take the tickets just purchased. In this case, special attention is needed to provide a cognitive affordance to remind the user of the final step in the task plan and help prevent this kind of slip: "Please take your tickets (and your bank card and receipt)."

Example: Another Forgotten Email Attachment

As another example, almost everyone has sent or tried to send an email for which an attachment was intended but forgotten. Recent versions of Google's Gmail (and others, like the Mac) have a simple solution. If any variation of the word "attach" appears in an email but it's sent without an attachment, the system asks if the sender intended to attach something, as you can see in Fig. 32-4. Similarly, if the email author says something such as "I am copying …", and there is no address in the Copy field, the system could ask about that, too.

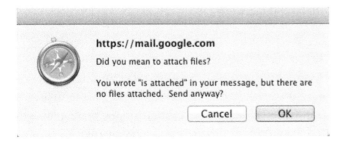

Fig. 32-4
Reminder to attach a file.

Example: Oops, You Didn't Finish Your Transaction

On one banking site, when users transfer money from their savings accounts to their checking accounts, they often think the transaction is complete when it's actually not. This is because, at the bottom right-hand corner of the last page in this transaction workflow, just below the "fold" on the screen, there is a small button labeled **Confirm** that is often completely missed.

Users close the window and go about their business of paying bills, unaware that they are possibly heading toward an overdraft. At least they should have gotten a pop-up message reminding them to click the Confirm button before letting them log out of the website.

Later, when one of the users called the bank to complain, they politely declined his suggestion that they should pay the overdraft fee because of their liability due to poor usability. We suspect they must have gotten other such complaints, however, because the flaw was fixed in the next version.

Example: Microwave Is Anxious to Help

As a final example of avoiding transaction completion slips, we cite a microwave oven. Because it takes time to defrost or cook the food, users often start it and do something else while waiting. Then, depending on their level of hunger, it's possible to forget to take out the food when it's done.

So, microwave designers usually include a reminder. At completion, the microwave usually beeps to signal the end of its part of the task. However, a user who has left the room or is otherwise occupied when it beeps may still not be mindful of the food waiting in the microwave. As a result, most oven designs call for the beep to repeat periodically until the door is opened to retrieve the food.

The design for one particular microwave, however, took this too far. It didn't wait long enough for the follow-up beep. Sometimes a user would be on the way to remove the food and it would beep. Some users found this so irritating that they would hurry to rescue the food before that "reminder" beep. To them, this machine seemed to be "impatient" and "bossy" to the point that it had been controlling the users by making them hurry.

32.6 TRANSLATION

Translation guidelines are to support users in sensory and cognitive actions needed to determine how to do a task step in terms of what actions to make on which objects and how. Translation, along with assessment, is one of the places in the Interaction Cycle where cognitive affordances play a major role.

Many of the principles and guidelines apply to more than one part of the Interaction Cycle and, therefore, to more than one section of this chapter. For example, "Use consistent wording" is a guideline that applies almost everywhere. Rather than repeat, we will put them in the most pertinent location and hope that our readers recognize the broader applicability.

Translation issues include:

- Existence (of cognitive affordance).
- Presentation (of cognitive affordance).
- Content and meaning (of cognitive affordance).
- Task structure.

32.6.1 Existence of Cognitive Affordance

Fig. 32-5 highlights the "existence of cognitive affordance" part within the breakdown of the translation part of the Interaction Cycle.

"Existence of a cognitive affordance" is about whether a needed cognitive affordance is provided in the first place. If UX designers don't provide needed cognitive affordances, such as labels and other cues, users will lack the support they need for learning and knowing what actions to make on what objects in order to carry out their task intentions. The existence of cognitive affordances is necessary to:

- Show which user interface object to manipulate.
- Show how to manipulate an object.

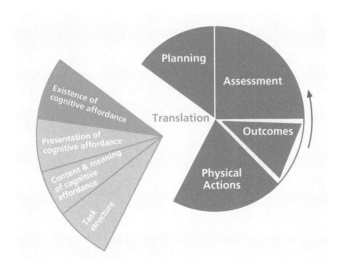

Fig. 32-5

Existence of a cognitive affordance within translation.

- Help users get started in a task.
- Guide data entry in formatted fields.
- Indicate active defaults to suggest choices and values.
- Indicate system states, modes, and parameters.
- Remind about steps the user might forget.
- Avoid inappropriate choices.
- Support error recovery.
- Help answer questions from the system.
- Deal with idioms that require rote learning.

Provide effective cognitive affordances that help users get access to system functionality.

Support users' cognitive needs to determine how to do something by ensuring the existence of an appropriate cognitive affordance.

It's possible to build in effective cognitive affordances that help novice users and don't get in the way of experienced users.

Help users know how to do something at the action/object level, to know/learn what actions are needed to carry out intentions.

Users get their operational knowledge from experience, training, *and cognitive affordances in the design.* It's our job to provide this latter source of user knowledge.

Be predictable; help users predict outcome of actions with feed-forward information in cognitive affordances.

Users need *feed-forward* cognitive affordances, such as labels, data field formats, and icons that explain the effects of physical actions, such as clicking on a button. Not giving feed-forward cues is what Cooper (2004, p. 140) calls "uninformed consent"; the user must proceed without understanding the consequences and possibly go down a rabbit hole. Predictability helps both learning and error avoidance.

Help users determine what to do to get started.

Users need support in understanding what actions to take for the first step of a particular task, the "getting started" step, often the most difficult part of a task.

Example: Helpful PowerPoint

In Fig. 32-6, we see a start-up screen of an early version of Microsoft PowerPoint. In applications where there is a wide variety of things a user can do, it's difficult to know what to do to get started when faced with a blank screen. The addition of one simple cognitive affordance: The advice to **Click to add first slide**, provides an easy way for an uncertain user to get started in creating a presentation.

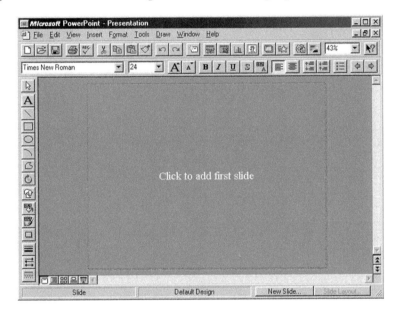

Fig. 32-6

Help in getting started in PowerPoint (screen image courtesy of Tobias Frans-Jan Theebe).

Similarly, in Fig. 32-7, we show other such helpful cues to continue, once a new slide is begun.

Provide a cognitive affordance for a step the user might forget.

Support user needs with cognitive affordances as prompts, reminders, cues, or warnings for a particular needed action that might get forgotten.

32.6.2 Presentation of Cognitive Affordance

In Fig. 32-8, we highlight the "presentation of cognitive affordance" portion of the translation part of the Interaction Cycle.

Presentation of cognitive affordances is about how cognitive affordances *appear* to users, not how they convey meaning. Users must be able to sense, for example, see or hear, a cognitive affordance before it can be useful to them. Therefore, presentation of cognitive affordances is primarily about sensory affordances.

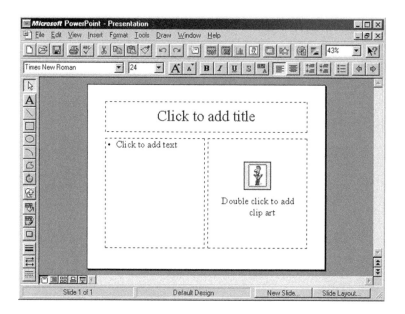

Fig. 32-7

More help in getting started (screen image courtesy of Tobias Frans-Jan Theebe).

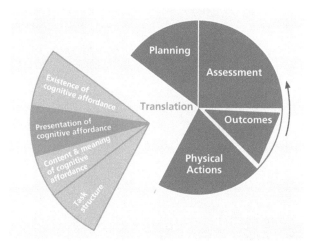

Fig. 32-8

Presentation of cognitive affordances within translation.

Support user sensory needs in seeing and hearing cognitive affordances by effective presentation or appearance.

This category is about issues such as legibility, noticeability, timing of presentation, layout, spatial grouping, complexity, consistency, and presentation medium, for example, audio, when needed. Sensory affordance issues also include text legibility and content contained in the appearance of a graphical feature, such as an icon, but only about whether the icon can be seen or discerned easily. For an audio medium, the volume and sound quality are presentation characteristics.

32.6.2.1 Cognitive affordance visibility

Obviously, a cognitive affordance cannot be an effective cue if it cannot be seen or heard when it's needed. Our first guideline in this category is conveyed by the sign in Fig. 32-9, if only we could be sure what it means.

Fig. 32-9
Good advice anytime.

Make cognitive affordances visible.

If a cognitive affordance is invisible, it could be because it's not (yet) displayed or because it's occluded by another object. A user aware of the existence of the cognitive affordance can often take some actions to summon an invisible cognitive affordance into view. It's the designer's job to be sure each cognitive affordance is visible, or easily made visible, when it's needed in the interaction.

See the example of shopping for deodorant in a grocery store in Section 30.4.2.1.

32.6.2.2 Cognitive affordance noticeability

Make cognitive affordances noticeable.

When a needed cognitive affordance exists and is visible, the next consideration is its noticeability or likelihood of being noticed or sensed. Just putting a cognitive affordance on the screen is not enough, especially if the user doesn't necessarily know it exists or is not necessarily looking for it. These design issues are largely about supporting awareness. Relevant cognitive affordances should come to users' attention without users seeking it. The primary design factor in this regard is location, putting the cognitive affordance within the users' focus of attention. It's also about contrast, size, and layout complexity and their effect on separation of the cognitive affordance from the background and from the clutter of other user interface objects.

Example: Status Lines Often Don't Work

Message lines, status lines, and title lines at the top or bottom of the screen are notoriously unnoticeable. Each user typically has a narrow focus of attention, usually near where the cursor is located. A pop-up message next to the cursor will be far more noticeable than a message in a line at the bottom of the screen.

Example: Where the Heck Is the Log-In?

For some reason, many websites have very small and inconspicuous log-in boxes, often mixed in with many objects most users don't even notice in the far top border of the page. Users have to waste time in searching visually over the whole page to find the way to log in.

32.6.2.3 Cognitive affordance legibility

Make text legible, readable.

Text legibility is about being discernable, not about the words being understandable. Text presentation issues include the way the text of a button label is presented so it can be read or sensed, including appearance or sensory characteristics of the text, such as font type, font size, font and background color, bolding, or italics, but it's not about the content or meaning of the words in the text. The meaning is the same regardless of the font or color.

32.6.2.4 Cognitive affordance presentation complexity

Control cognitive affordance presentation complexity with effective layout, organization, and grouping.

Support user needs to locate and be aware of cognitive affordances by controlling layout complexity of user interface objects. Screen clutter can obscure needed cognitive affordances such as icons, prompt messages, state indicators, dialogue box components, or menus and make it difficult for users to find them.

32.6.2.5 Cognitive affordance presentation timing

Support user needs to notice cognitive affordance with appropriate timing of appearance or display of cognitive affordances. Don't present a cognitive affordance too early or too late. Present with adequate persistence; that is, avoid "flashing."

Present cognitive affordance in time to help the user before the associated action.

Sometimes getting cognitive affordance presentation timing right means presenting at exactly the point in a task and under exactly the conditions when the cognitive affordance is needed.

See the example about the just-in-time towel dispenser message in Section 30.4.2.7.

Example: Special Pasting

When a user wishes to paste something from one Word document to another, there can be a question about formatting. Will the item retain its formatting, such as text or paragraph style, from the original document or will it adopt the formatting from the place of insertion in the new document? And how can the choice be controlled by the user? When you want more control of a paste operation, you might choose **Paste Special** … from the **Edit** menu.

But the choices in the **Paste Special** dialogue box say nothing about controlling formatting. Rather, the choices can seem system centered or too technical, for example, **Microsoft Office Word Document Object** or **Unformatted Unicode Text**, without an explanation of the resulting effect in the document. While these choices might be precise about the action and its results to some users, they are cryptic even to most regular users.

In some versions of Word, a small cognitive affordance, a tiny clipboard icon with a pop-up label **Paste Options** appears, but it appears *after* the paste operation. Many users don't notice this little object, mainly because by the time it appears, they have experienced closure on the paste operation and have already moved on mentally to the next task. If they don't like the resulting formatting, then changing it manually becomes their next task.

Even if users notice the little object, it's possible they might confuse it with something to do with undoing the action or something similar because Word uses that same object for in-context undo. However, if a user does notice this icon and does take the time to click on it, that user will be rewarded with a pull-down menu of useful options, such as **Keep Source Formatting**, **Match Destination**

Formatting, **Keep Text Only**, plus a choice to see a full selection of other formatting styles.

Just what users need! But it's made available too late; the chance to see this menu comes *after* the user action to which it applied. If choices on this after-the-fact menu were available on the **Paste Special** menu, it would be perfect for users.

32.6.2.6 Cognitive affordance presentation consistency

When a cognitive affordance is located within a user interface object that is also manipulated by physical actions, such as a label within a button, maintaining a consistent location of that object on the screen helps users find it quickly and helps them use muscle memory for fast clicking. Hansen (1971) used the term "display inertia" in reference to one of his top-level principles, optimize operations, to describe this business of minimizing display changes in response to user inputs, including displaying a given user interface object in the same place each time it's shown.

Give similar cognitive affordances consistent appearance in presentation.

Example: Archive Button Jumps Around

When users of an older version of Gmail were viewing the list of messages in the Inbox, the **Archive** button was at the far left at the top of the message pane, set off by the blue border, as shown in Fig. 32-10.

But on the screen for reading a message, Gmail had the **Archive** button as the second object from the left at the top. In the place where the **Archive** button was earlier, there was now a **Back to Inbox** link, as seen in Fig. 32-11. Using a link instead of a button in this position is a slight inconsistency, probably without

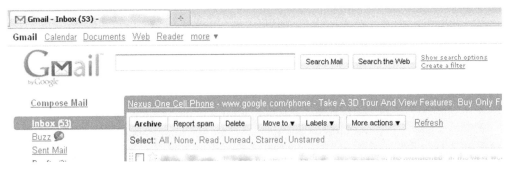

Fig. 32-10

*The **Archive** button in the Inbox view of an older version of Gmail.*

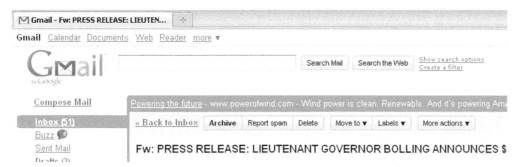

Fig. 32-11
*The **Archive** button in a different place in the message reading view.*

much effect on users. But users feel a larger effect from the inconsistent placement of the Archive button.

Selected messages can be archived from either view of the email by clicking on the **Archive** button. Further, when archiving messages from the Inbox list view, the user sometimes goes to the message-reading view to be sure. So, a user doing an archiving task could be going back and forth between the Inbox listing of Fig. 32-10 and message viewing of Fig. 32-11.

For this activity, the location of the **Archive** button is never certain. The user loses momentum and performance speed by having to look for the **Archive** button each time before clicking on it. Even though it moves only a short distance between the two views, it's enough to slow down users significantly because they cannot run the cursor up to the same spot every time to do multiple archive actions quickly. The lack of display inertia works against an efficient sensory action of finding the button, and it works against muscle memory in making the physical action of moving the cursor up to click.

It seems that Google people have fixed this problem in subsequent versions, as attested to by the same kinds of screens in Figs. 32-12 and 32-13.

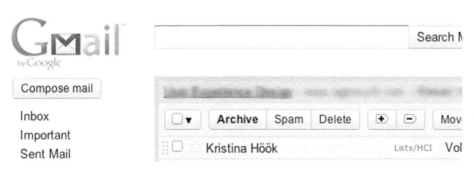

Fig. 32-12
*The **Archive** button in the Inbox view of a later version of Gmail.*

Fig. 32-13

*The **Archive** button in the same place in the new message reading view.*

32.6.3 Content and Meaning of Cognitive Affordance

Just what part of quantum theory do you not understand?

– Anonymous

Fig. 32-14 highlights the "content and meaning of cognitive affordance" portion of the translation part of the Interaction Cycle.

The content and meaning of a cognitive affordance are the knowledge that must be conveyed to users to be effective in helping them as affordances to think, learn, and know what they need to make correct actions. The cognitive affordance design concepts that support understanding of content and meaning include clarity, distinguishability from other cognitive affordances, consistency,

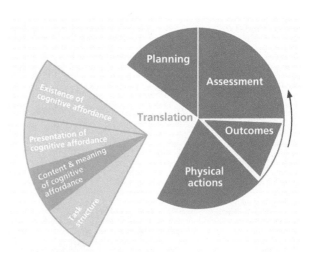

Fig. 32-14

Content/meaning within translation.

layout, and grouping to control complexity, usage centeredness, and techniques for avoiding errors.

Help user determine actions with effective content/meaning in cognitive affordances.

   Support user ability to determine what action(s) to make and on what object (s) for a task step through understanding and comprehension of cognitive affordance content and meaning: what it says, verbally or graphically.

32.6.3.1 Clarity of cognitive affordances
Design cognitive affordances for clarity.

Use precise wording, carefully chosen vocabulary, or meaningful graphics to create correct, complete, and sufficient expressions of content and meaning of cognitive affordances.

32.6.3.2 Precise wording
Support user understanding of cognitive affordance content by precise expression of meaning through precise word choices.

Precise word choices are especially important for short, command-like text, such as is found in button labels, menu choices, and verbal prompts. For example, the button label to dismiss a dialogue box could say "**Return to …**" where appropriate, instead of just **OK**.

Use precise wording in labels, menu titles, menu choices, icons, data fields.

   The imperative for clear and precise wording of button labels, menu choices, messages, and other text may seem obvious, at least in the abstract. Even experienced designers often don't take the time to choose their words carefully.
   In our own evaluation experience, this guideline is among the most violated in real-world practice. Others have shared this experience, including Johnson (2000). Because of the overwhelming importance of precise wording in UX designs and the apparent unmindful approach to wording by many designers in practice, we consider this to be one of the most important guidelines in the whole book.
   Part of the problem in the field is that wording is often considered a relatively unimportant part of UX design and is left to developers and software people not trained to construct precise wording and not even trained to think much about it.

Example: Wet Paint!

This is one of our favorite examples of precise wording, probably overdone: "Wet Paint. This is a warning, not an instruction."

This guideline represents a part of UX design where a great improvement can be accrued for only a small investment of extra time and effort. Even a few minutes devoted to getting just the right wording for a button label used frequently has an enormous potential payoff. Here are some related and helpful subguidelines:

Use a verb and noun and even an adjective in labels where appropriate.
Avoid vague, ambiguous terms.
Be as specific to the interaction situation as possible; avoid one-size-fits-all messages.
Clearly represent work domain concepts.

Example: Then, How Can We Use the Door?

As an example of matching the message to the reality of the work domain, signs such as "Keep this door closed at all times" (Fig. 32-15) probably should read something more like "Close this door immediately after use."

Use dynamically changing labels when toggling.

Fig. 32-15

Difficult to follow this instruction literally.

When using the same control object, such as a **Play/Pause** button on an mp3 music player, to control the toggling of a system state, change the object label to show that it's consistently a control the user can act on to get to the next state. Otherwise, the current system state can be unclear, and there can be confusion over whether the label represents an action the user can make or feedback about the current system state.

Example: Reusing a Button Label

In Fig. 32-16, we show an early prototype of a personal document retrieval system. The underlying model for deleting a document involves two steps: marking the document for deletion and later deleting all marked documents permanently. The small check box at the lower right is labeled: **Marked for Deletion**.

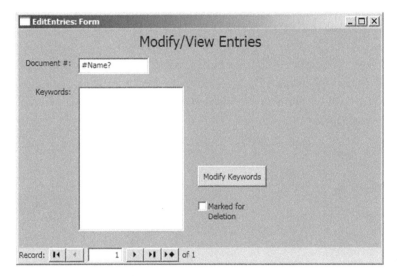

Fig. 32-16

The Marked for Deletion check box in a document retrieval screen (screen image courtesy of Raphael Summers).

The designer's idea was that users would check that box to signify the intention to delete the record. Thereafter, until a permanent purge of marked records, seeing a check in this box signifies that this record is, indeed, marked for deletion. The problem comes before the user checks the box.

The user wants to delete the record (or at least mark it for deletion), but this label seems to be a statement of system state rather than a cognitive affordance for an action, implying that it's already marked for deletion. However, because the check box is not checked, it's not entirely clear. Our suggestion was to relabel the box in the unchecked state to read **Check to Mark for Deletion**, making it a true cognitive affordance for action in this state. After checking, **Marked for Deletion** works fine.

Data value formats. Provide cognitive affordances to indicate formatting within data fields.

Support user needs to know how to enter data, such as in a form field, with a cognitive affordance or cue to help with format and kinds of values that are acceptable.

Data entry is a user work activity where the formatting of data values is an issue. Entry in the "wrong" format, meaning a format the user thinks is right but the system designers didn't anticipate, can lead to errors that the user must spend time to resolve or, worse, undetected data errors. It's relatively easy for designers to indicate expected data formats, with cognitive affordances associated with the field labels, with sample data values, or both.

Example: How Should I Enter the Date?

In Fig. 32-17, we show a dialogue box that appears in an application that is, despite the cryptic title **Task Series**, for scheduling events. In the **Duration** section, the **Effective Date** field doesn't indicate the expected format for data values. Although many systems are capable of accepting date values in almost any format, new or intermittent users may not know if this application is that smart. It

Fig. 32-17

*Missing cognitive affordance about **Effective Date** data field format (screen image courtesy of Tobias Frans-Jan Theebe).*

would have been easy for the designer to save users from hesitation and uncertainty by suggesting a format here.

Constrain the formats of data values to avoid data entry errors.

Sometimes rather than just show the format, it's more effective to constrain values to prevent erroneous entries.

An easy way to constrain the formatting of a date value, for example, is to use drop-down lists, specialized to hold values appropriate for the month, day, and year parts of the date field. Another approach that many users like is a "date picker," a calendar that pops up when the user clicks on the date field. A date can be entered into the field only by way of selection from this calendar.

A calendar with one month of dates at a time is perhaps the most practical. Side arrows allow the user to navigate to earlier or later months or years. Clicking on a date within the month on the calendar causes that date to be picked for the value to be used. By using a date-picker, you are constraining both the data entry method and the format the user must employ, effectively eliminating errors due to either allowing inappropriate values or formatting ambiguity.

Provide clearly marked exits.

Support user ability to exit dialogue sequences confidently by using clearly labeled exits. Include destination information to help users predict where the action will go upon leaving the current dialogue sequence. For example, in a dialogue box you might use **Return to XYZ After Saving** instead of **OK** and **Return to XYZ Without Saving** instead of **Cancel**.

To qualify this example, we have to say that the terms **OK** and **Cancel** are so well accepted and so thoroughly part of our current shared conventions that, even though the example shows potentially better wordings, the conventions now carry the same meaning at least to experienced users.

Provide clear "do it" mechanism.

Some kinds of choice-making objects, such as drop-down or pop-up menus, commit to the choice as soon as the user indicates the choice; others require a separate "commit to this choice" action. This inconsistency can be unsettling for some users who are unsure about whether their choices have "taken." Becker (2004) argues for a consistent use of a "Go" action, such as a click, to commit to choices, for example, choices made in a dialogue box or drop-down menu. And we caution to make its usage clear to avoid task completion slips where users think they have completed making the menu choice, for example, and move on without committing to it with the Go button.

32.6.3.3 Distinguishability of choices in cognitive affordances
Make choices cognitively distinguishable.

Support user ability to differentiate two or more possible choices or actions by distinguishable expressions of meaning in their cognitive affordances. If two similar cognitive affordances lead to different outcomes, careful design is needed so users can avoid errors by distinguishing the cases.

Often distinguishability is the key to correct user choices by the process of elimination; if you provide enough information to rule out the cases not wanted, users will be able to make the correct choice. Focus on differences of meaning in the wording of names and labels. Make larger differences graphically in similar icons.

Example: Tragic Airplane Crash

This is an unfortunate, but true, story that evinces the reality that human lives can be lost due to simple confusion over labeling of controls. This is a very serious usability case involving the October 31, 1999, EgyptAir Flight 990 airliner crash (Acohido, 1999) possibly as a result of poor usability in design. According to the news account, the pilot may have been confused by two sets of switches that were similar in appearance, labeled very similarly, as "**Cut out**" and "**Cut off**", and located relatively close to each other in the Boeing 767 cockpit design.

Exacerbating the situation, both switches are used infrequently, only under unusual flight conditions. This latter point is important because it means that the pilots would not have been experienced in using either one. Knowing pilots receive extensive training, designers assumed their users are experts. But because these particular controls are rarely used, most pilots are novices in their use, implying the need for more effective cognitive affordances than usual.

One conjecture is that one of the flight crew attempted to pull the plane out of an unexpected dive by setting the **Cut out** switches connected to the stabilizer trim, but instead accidentally set the **Cut off** switches, shutting off fuel to both engines. The black box flight recorder did confirm that the plane did go into a sudden dive, and that a pilot did flip the fuel system cutoff switches soon thereafter.

There seem to be two critical design issues, the first of which is the distinguishability of the labeling, especially under conditions of stress and infrequent use. To us, not knowledgeable in piloting large planes, the two labels seem so similar as to be virtually synonymous.

Making the labels more complete would have made them much more distinguishable. In particular, adding a noun to the verb of the labels would have made a huge difference: **Cut out trim** versus **Cut off fuel**. Putting the all-important noun first might have been an even better distinguisher: **Fuel off** and **Trim out**. Just this simple UX improvement might have averted the disaster.

The second design issue is the apparent physical proximity of the two controls, inviting the physical slip of grabbing the wrong one, despite knowing the difference. Surely stabilizer trim and fuel functions are completely unrelated. Regrouping by related functions—locating the **Fuel off** switch with other fuel-related functions and the **Trim out** switch with other stabilizer-related controls—might have helped the pilots distinguish them, preventing the catastrophic error.

Finally, we have to assume that safety (absolute error avoidance in this situation) was a top priority UX goal for this design. To meet this goal, the Fuel off switch could have been further protected from accidental operation by adding a mechanical feature that requires an additional conscious action by the pilot to operate this seldom-used but dangerous control. One possibility is a physical cover over the switch that has to be lifted before the switch can be flipped, a safety feature used in the design of missile launch switches, for example.

32.6.3.4 Consistency of cognitive affordances

Be consistent with cognitive affordances.
Use consistent wording in labels for menus, buttons, icons, fields.

Consistency is one of those concepts that everyone thinks they understand, but almost no one can define. Being consistent in wording has two sides: using the same terms for the same things and using different terms for different things.

Use similar names for similar kinds of things.
Don't use multiple synonyms for the same thing.

Example: Continue or Retry?

This example comes from the very old days of floppy disks, but could apply to external hard disks of today as well. It's a great example of using two different words for the same thing in the short space of the one little message dialogue box in Fig. 32-18.

Fig. 32-18

Inconsistent wording:
Continue *or* **Retry**? *(screen image courtesy of Tobias Frans-Jan Theebe).*

If, upon learning that the current disk is full, the user inserts a new disk and intends to continue copying files, for example, what should she click, **Retry** or **Cancel**? Hopefully she can find the right choice by the process of elimination, as **Cancel** will almost certainly terminate the operation. But **Retry** carries the connotation of starting over. Why not match the goal of continuing with a button labeled **Continue**?

Use the same term in a reference to an object as the name or label of the object.

If a cognitive affordance suggests an action on a specific object, such as **Click on Add Record**, the name or label on that object must be the same, in this case also **Add Record**.

Example: Press What?

From more modern days and a website for Virginia Tech employees, Fig. 32-19 is another clear example of how easy it is for this kind of design flaw to slip by designers, a type of flaw that is usually found by expert UX inspection.

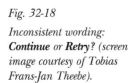

Fig. 32-19

Cannot click on **View Pay Stub Summary***.*

This is another example of inconsistency of wording. The cognitive affordance in the line above the **Pay Stub Year** selection menu says press **View Pay Stub Summary**, but the label on the button to be pressed says **Display**. Maybe this big a difference in what is supposed to be the same is due to having different people working on different parts of the design. In any case, we noticed that in a subsequent version, someone had found and fixed the problem, as seen in Fig. 32-20.

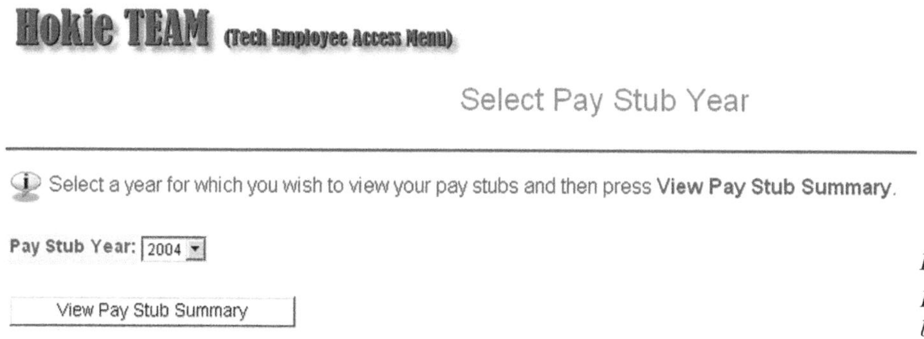

Hokie TEAM (Tech Employee Access Menu)

Select Pay Stub Year

_____

ⓘ Select a year for which you wish to view your pay stubs and then press **View Pay Stub Summary**.

Pay Stub Year: [2004 ▾]

[View Pay Stub Summary]

Fig. 32-20

Problem fixed with new button label.

In passing, we note an additional UX problem with each of these screens, the cognitive affordance **Select Pay Stub Year** above the line in the frame is redundant with **Select a year for which you wish to view your pay stubs** in the bottom section. We would recommend keeping the second one, as it's more informative and is grouped with the pull-down menu for year selection (which, in itself, might be sufficient without further instructions).

The first **Select Pay Stub Year** looks like some kind of title but is really kind of an orphan. The distance between this cognitive affordance and the user interface object to which it applies, plus the solid line, makes for a strong separation between two design elements that should be closely associated. Because it's unnecessary and separate from the year menu, it could be confusing.

Use different terms for different things, especially when the difference is subtle.

This is the flip side of the guideline that says to use the same terms for the same things. As we will see in the following example, terms such as **Add** can mean several different but closely related things. If you, the UX designer, don't distinguish the differences with appropriately precise terminology, it can lead to confusion for the user.

Example: The User Thought Files Were Already "Added"

When using Nero Express to burn CDs and DVDs for data transfer and backup, users put in a blank disc and choose the **Create a Data Disc** option and see the window shown in Fig. 32-21.

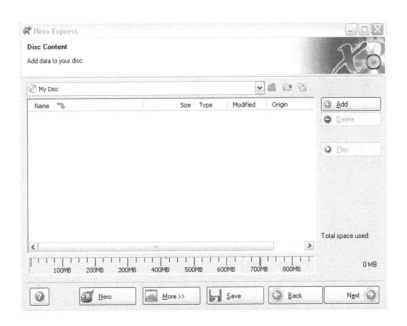

Fig. 32-21
*First Nero **Add** button.*

In the middle of this window is an empty space that looks like a file directory. Most users will figure out that this is for the list of the files and folders they want to put on the disc. At the top, where it will be seen only if the user looks around, it gives the cue: **Add data to your disc**. In the normal task path, there is really only one action that makes sense, which is clicking on the **Add** button at the top on the right-hand side.

This is taken by the user to be the way you add files and folders to this list. When users click on **Add**, they get the next window, shown in Fig. 32-22, overlapping the initial window.

This window also shows a directory space in the middle for browsing the files and folders and selecting those to be added to the list for the disc. The way that one commits the selected files to go on the list for the disc is to click on the **Add** button in this window. Here, the term **Add** really means to add the selected files to the disc list. In the first window, however, the term **Add** really meant proceed to file selection for the disc list, which is related but slightly different. Yes, the difference is subtle, but it's our job to be precise in wording.

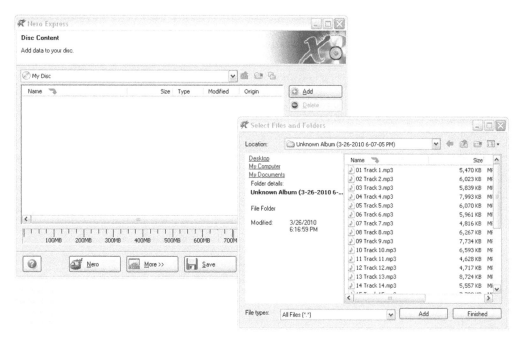

Fig. 32-22
*Another window and another **Add** button.*

Be consistent in the way that similar choices or parameter settings are made.

If a certain set of related parameters are all selected or set with one method, such as check boxes or radio buttons, then all parameters related to that set should be selected or set the same way.

Example: The Find **Dialogue Box in Microsoft Word**

Setting and clearing search parameters for the **Find** function are done with check boxes on the lower left-hand side (Fig. 32-23) and with pull-down menus at the bottom of the dialogue box for font, paragraph, and other format attributes and special characteristics. We have observed many users having trouble turning off the format attributes, which is because the "command" for that is different from all the others.

It's accomplished by clicking on the **No Formatting** button on the right-hand side at the bottom; see Fig. 32-23. Many users simply don't see that because nothing else uses a button to set or reset a parameter, so they are not looking for a button.

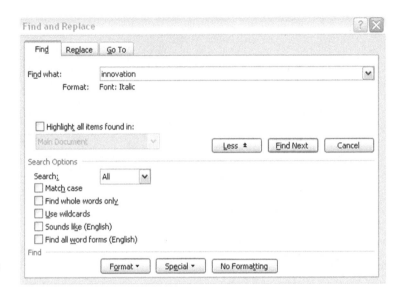

Fig. 32-23

*Format with a menu but **No Formatting** with a button.*

The following example is an instance of the same kind of inconsistency (not using the same kind of selection method for related parameters), only this example is from the world of food ordering.

Example: Circle Your Selections

In Fig. 32-24, you see an order slip for a sandwich at Au Bon Pain. Under **Create Your Own Sandwich** it says **Please circle all selections,** but the very next choice is between two check boxes for selecting the sandwich size. It's a minor thing that probably doesn't impact user performance, but, to a UX stickler, it stands out as an inconsistency in the design.

We wrap up this section on consistency of cognitive affordances with the following example about how many problems with consistency in terminology we found in an evaluation of one web-based application.

Example: Consistency Problems

In this example, we consider only problems relating to wording consistency from a lab-based UX evaluation of an academic web application for classroom support. We suspect this pervasiveness of inconsistency was due to having different people doing the design in different places and not having a project-wide custom style guide or not using one to document working terminology choices.

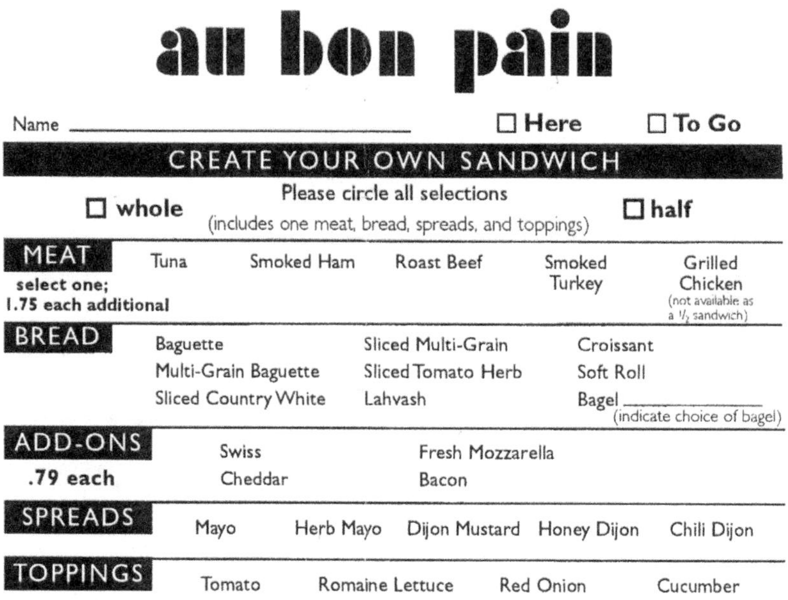

au bon pain

Name ____________ ☐ Here ☐ To Go

CREATE YOUR OWN SANDWICH

☐ whole — Please circle all selections (includes one meat, bread, spreads, and toppings) — ☐ half

MEAT select one; 1.75 each additional	Tuna	Smoked Ham	Roast Beef	Smoked Turkey	Grilled Chicken (not available as a 1/2 sandwich)
BREAD	Baguette Multi-Grain Baguette Sliced Country White	Sliced Multi-Grain Sliced Tomato Herb Lahvash	Croissant Soft Roll Bagel ______ (indicate choice of bagel)		
ADD-ONS .79 each	Swiss Cheddar	Fresh Mozzarella Bacon			
SPREADS	Mayo	Herb Mayo	Dijon Mustard	Honey Dijon	Chili Dijon
TOPPINGS	Tomato	Romaine Lettuce	Red Onion	Cucumber	

Fig. 32-24

***Circle all selections**, but size choice is by check boxes.*

In any case, when the design contains different terms for the same thing, it can confuse the user, especially the new user who is trying to conquer the system vocabulary. Here are some examples of our UX problem descriptions, "sanitized" to protect the guilty.

- The terms **Revise** and **Edit** were used interchangeably to denote an action to modify an information object within the application. For example, **Revise** is used as an action option for a selected object in the **Worksite Setup** page of **My Workspace**, whereas **Edit is** used inside the **Site Info** page of a given worksite.
- The terms "**worksite**" and "**site**" are used interchangeably for the same meaning. For example, many of the options in the menu bar of **My Workspace** use the term "**worksite**," whereas the **Membership** page uses "**site**," as in **My Current Sites**.
- The terms **Add** and **New** are used interchangeably, referring to the same concept. Under the **Manage Groups** option, there is a link for adding a group, called **New**. Most everywhere else, such as for adding an event to a schedule, the link for creating a new information object is labeled **Add**.
- The way that lists are used to present information is inconsistent:
  - In some lists, such as the list on the **Worksite Setup** page, check boxes are on the left-hand side, but for most other lists, such as the list on the **Group List** page, check boxes are on the right.
  - To edit some lists, the user must select a list item check box and then choose the **Revise** option in a menu bar (of links) at the top of the page and separated from the list. In other lists, each item has its own **Revise** link. For yet other lists there is a collection of links, one for each of the multiple ways the user can edit an item.

32.6.3.5 Controlling complexity of cognitive affordance content and meaning

Decompose complex instructions into simpler parts.

Cognitive affordances don't afford anything if they are too complex to understand or follow. Try decomposing long and complicated instructions into smaller, more meaningful, and more easily digested parts.

Example: Say What?

The cognitive affordance of Fig. 32-25 contains instructions that can bewilder even the most attentive user, especially someone in a wheelchair who needs to get out of there fast.

Fig. 32-25

Good luck in evacuating quickly.

Use layout and grouping of cognitive affordances to control content and meaning complexity.

Use appropriate layout and grouping by function of cognitive affordances to control content and meaning complexity.

Support user cognitive affordance content understanding through layout and spatial grouping to show relationships of task and function.

Group together objects and design elements associated with related tasks and functions.

Functions, user interface objects, and controls related to a given task or function should be grouped together spatially. The indication of relationship is strengthened by a graphical demarcation, such as a box around the group. Label the group with words that reflect the common functionality of the relationship. Grouping and labeling related data fields are especially important for data entry.

Don't group together objects and design elements that are not associated with related tasks and functions.

This guideline, the converse of the previous one, seems to be observed more often in the breach in real-world designs.

Example: Here Are Your Options

The Options dialogue box in Fig. 32-26, from an older version of Microsoft Word, illustrates a case where some controls are grouped incorrectly with some parameter settings.

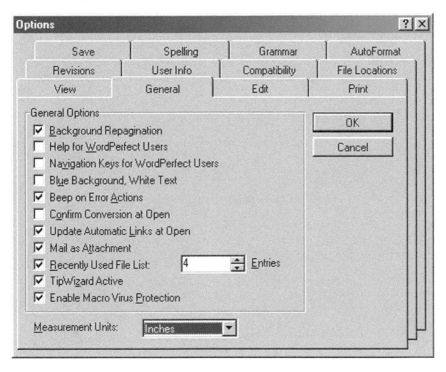

Fig. 32-26

OK *and* **Cancel** *controls on individual tab "card" (screen image courtesy of Tobias Frans-Jan Theebe).*

The metaphor in this design is that of a deck of tabbed index cards. The user has clicked on the **General** tab, which took the user to this **General** "card" where the user made a change in the options listed. While in the business of setting options, the user then wishes to go to another tab for more settings. The user hesitates, concerned that moving to another tab without saving the settings made in the current tab might cause them to be lost.

So, this user clicks on the **OK** to get closure for this tabbed card before moving on. To his surprise, the entire dialogue box disappears, and he must start over by selecting **Options** from the **Tools** menu at the top of the screen.

The surprise and extra work to recover were the price of the use of layout and grouping as an incorrect indication of the scope or range covered by the **OK** and **Cancel** buttons. Designers have made the buttons actually apply to the entire **Options** dialogue box, but they put the buttons on the currently open tabbed card, making them appear to apply just to the card or, in this case, just to the **General** category of options.

The **Options** dialogue box from a different version of Microsoft PowerPoint in Fig. 32-27 is a better design that places all the tabbed cards on a larger background and the **OK** and **Cancel** controls are on this background, showing clearly that the controls are grouped with the whole dialogue box and not with individual tabbed cards.

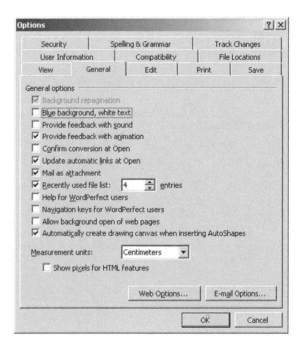

Fig. 32-27

OK *and* **Cancel** *controls on background underneath all the tab "cards" (screen image courtesy of Tobias Frans-Jan Theebe).*

Example: Where to Put the Search Button?

The original design of some parameters associated with a search function in a digital library are shown in Fig. 32-28. The **Search** button is located right next to the OR radio-button choice at the bottom. Perhaps it's associated with the **Combine fields with** feature?

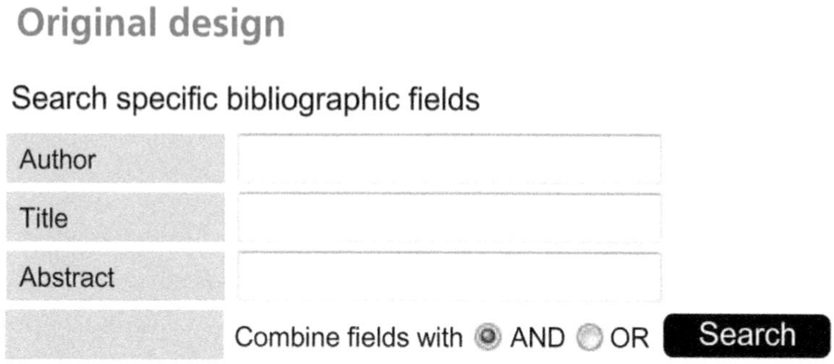

Original design

Search specific bibliographic fields

Author	
Title	
Abstract	
	Combine fields with ● AND ○ OR **Search**

Fig. 32-28
Uncertain association with **Search.**

No, it actually was intended to be associated with the entire search box, as shown in the "Suggested redesign" in Fig. 32-29.

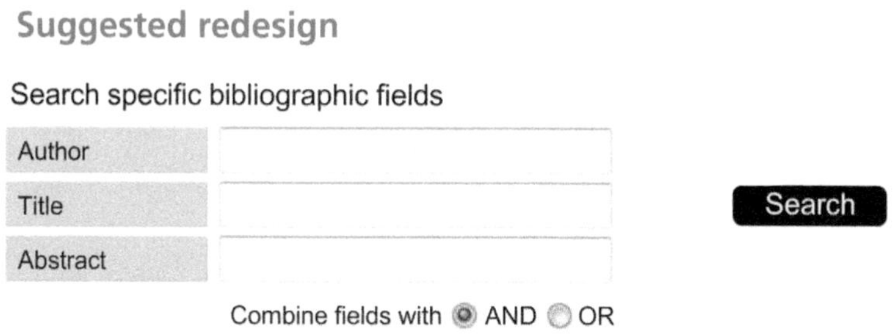

Suggested redesign

Search specific bibliographic fields

Author	
Title	
Abstract	

Search

Combine fields with ● AND ○ OR

Fig. 32-29
Problem fixed with better layout and grouping.

Example: Are We Going to Eindhoven or Catalonia?

Here is a noncomputer (sort of) example from the airlines. While waiting in Milan to board a flight to Eindhoven, passengers saw the display shown in Fig. 32-30. As the display suggests, the Eindhoven flight followed a flight to Catalonia (in Spain) from the same gate.

As the flight to Catalonia began boarding, confusion started brewing in the boarding area. Many people were unsure about which flight was boarding, as both flights were displayed on the board. The main source of trouble was due to the way parts of the text were grouped in the flight announcements

Fig. 32-30

A sketch of the airline departure board in Milan.

on the overhead board. The state information **Embarco** (departing) was closer to the Eindhoven listing than to that of Catalonia, as shown in Fig. 32-30. So **Embarco** seemed to be grouped with and applied to the Eindhoven flight.

Confusion was compounded by the fact that it was 9:30 AM; the Catalonia flight was boarding late enough so that boarding could have been mistaken for the one to Eindhoven. Further conspiring against the waiting passengers was the fact that there were no oral announcements of the boardings, although there was a public-address system. Many Eindhoven passengers were getting into the Catalonia boarding line. You could see them turning Eindhoven passengers away, but still there was no announcement to clear up the problem.

Sometime later, the flight state information **Embarco** changed to **Chiuso** (closed), as seen in Fig. 32-31.

Fig. 32-31

Oh, no, Chiuso.

Many of the remaining Eindhoven passengers immediately became agitated, seeing the **Chiuso** and thinking that the Eindhoven flight was closed before they had a chance to board. In the end, everything was fine, but the poor layout of the display on the flight announcement board caused stress among passengers and extra work for the airline gate attendants. Given that this situation can occur many times a day, involving many people every day, the cost of this poor UX must have been very high, even though the airline workers seemed to be oblivious as they contemplated their cappuccino breaks.

Example: Hot Wash, Anyone?

In another simple example, in Fig. 32-32, we depict a row of push-button controls once seen on a clothes-washing machine.

The choices of **Hot wash/cold rinse**, **Warm wash/cold rinse**, and **Cold wash/cold rinse** all represent similar semantics (wash and rinse temperatures settings) and, therefore, should be grouped together. They are also expressed in similar syntax and words, so it's consistent labeling. However, because all three choices include a cold rinse, why not just say that with a separate label and not include it in all the choices?

The real problem, though, is that the fourth button, labeled **Start,** represents completely different functionality and should not be grouped with the other push buttons. Why do you think the designers made such an obvious mistake in

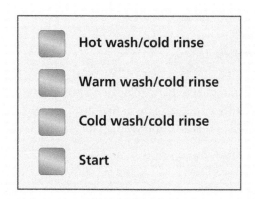

Fig. 32-32

Clothes-washing machine controls with one little inconsistency.

grouping by related functionality? We think it's because one single switch assembly is less expensive to buy and install than two separate assemblies. Here, cost won over usability.

Example: There Goes the Flight Attendant, Again

On an airplane flight once, we noticed a design flaw in the layout of the overhead controls for a pair of passengers in a two-seat configuration, a flaw that created problems for flight attendants and passengers. This control panel had push-button switches at the left and right for turning the left and right reading lights on and off.

The problem is that the flight attendant call switch was located just between the two light controls. It looked nice and symmetric, but its close proximity to the light controls made it a frequent target of unintended operation. On this flight, we saw flight attendants moving through the cabin frequently, resetting call buttons for numerous passengers.

In this design, switches for two related functions were separated by an unrelated one; the grouping of controls within the layout was not by function. Another reason calling for even further physical separation of the two kinds of switches is that light switches are used frequently, while the call switch is not.

32.6.3.6 Likely user choices and useful defaults

Sometimes it's possible to anticipate menu and button choices, choices of data values, and choices of task paths that users will most likely want or need to take. By providing direct access to those choices, and, in some cases, making them the defaults, we can help make the task more efficient for users.

Support user choices with likely and useful defaults.

Many user tasks require data entry into data fields in dialogue box and screens. Data entry is often a tedious and repetitive chore, and we should do everything we can to alleviate some of the dreary labor of this task by providing the most likely or most useful data values as defaults.

Example: What is the Date?

Many forms call for the current date in one of the fields. Using today's date as the default value for that field should be a no-brainer.

Example: Tragic Choice of Defaults

Here is a serious example of a case where the choice of default values resulted in dire consequences. This story was relayed by a participant in one of our UX short courses at a military installation. We cannot vouch for its verity but, even if it's apocryphal, it makes the point well.

A front-line spotter for missile strikes has a GPS unit on which he can calculate the exact location of an enemy facility on a map overlay. The GPS unit also serves as a radio through which he can send the enemy location back to the missile firing emplacement, which will send a missile strike with deadly accuracy.

He entered the coordinates of the enemy just before sending the message, but unfortunately, the GPS battery died before he could send the message. Because time was of the essence, he replaced the battery quickly and hit Send. The missile was fired and it hit and killed the spotter instead of the enemy.

When the old battery was removed, the system didn't retain the enemy coordinates and, when the new battery was installed, the system entered its own current GPS location as default values for the coordinates. Not having any useful alternatives, designers decided to use an easily obtained value, the local GPS coordinates of where the spotter was standing, figuring that the user would then change it.

In isolation from other important considerations, it was a bit like putting in today's date as the default for a date; it's conveniently available. But in this case, the result of that convenience was death by friendly fire. With a moment's thought, no one could imagine making the spotter's coordinates the default for aiming a missile. The problem was fixed immediately!

Provide the most likely or most useful default selections.

Among the most common violations of this guideline is the failure to select an item for a user when there is only one item from which to select, as illustrated in the next example.

Example: Only One Item to Select From

Here is a special case of applying this guideline where there is only one item from which to select. In this case, it was one item in a dialogue box list. When this user opened a directory in this dialogue box showing only one item, the **Select** button was grayed out because the user is required to select something from the list before the **Select** button becomes active. However, because there was only one item, the user assumed that the item would be selected by default.

When he clicked the grayed-out **Select** button, however, nothing happened. The user didn't realize that even though there is only one item in the list, the design requires selecting it before proceeding to click on the **Select** button. If no item is chosen, then the **Select** button doesn't give an error message nor does it prompt the user; it just sits there waiting for the user to do the "right thing." The difficulty could have been avoided by displaying the list of one item with that item already selected and highlighted, thus providing a useful default selection and allowing the **Select** button to be active from the start.

Offer most useful default cursor position.

It's a small thing in a design, but it can be so nice to have the cursor just where you need it when you arrive at a dialogue box or window in which you have to work. As a designer, you can save users the work and irritation of extra physical actions, such as an extra mouse click before typing, by providing appropriate default cursor location, for example, in a data field or text box, or within the user interface object where the user is most likely to work next.

Example: Please Set the Cursor for Me

Fig. 32-33 contains a dialogue box for planning events in a calendar system. Designers chose to highlight the frequency of occurrences of the event in terms of the number of weeks, in the **Weekly** section. This might be a little helpful to

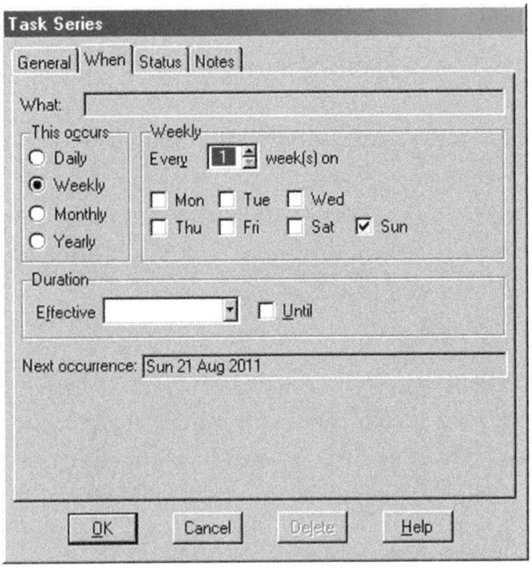

Fig. 32-33

Placement of default working location could be better (screen image courtesy of Tobias Frans-Jan Theebe).

users who will type a value into the "increment box" of this data field, but users are just as likely to use the up and down arrows of the increment box to set **Values**, in which case, the default highlighting doesn't help. Further evaluation will be necessary to confirm this, but it's possible that putting the default cursor in the **Effective Date** field at the bottom might be more useful.

32.6.3.7 Supporting human memory limitations in cognitive affordances

Earlier (Section 32.3) we elaborated on the concept of human memory limitations in UX design. In this section, we get to put this knowledge to work in specific UX design situations.

Relieve human short-term memory loads by maintaining task context visibly or audibly for the user.

Provide reminders to users of what they are doing and where they are within the task flow. Post important parts of the task context, parameters the user must keep track of within the task, so that the user doesn't have to commit them to memory.

Support human memory limits with recognition over recall.

For cases where choices, alternatives, or possible data entry values are known, designing to use recognition over recall means allowing the user to select an item from among choices rather than having to specify the choice strictly from memory. Selection among presented choices also makes for more precise communication about choices and data values, helping avoid errors from wording variations and typos.

One of the most important applications of this guideline is in the naming of files for an operation such as opening a file. This guideline says that we should allow users to select the desired file name from a directory listing rather than requiring the user to remember and type in the file name.

Example: What Do You Want, the Part Number?

To begin with, the cognitive affordance shown in Fig. 32-34 describing the desired user action is too vague and open-ended to get any kind of specific input from a user. What if the user doesn't know the exact model number and what kind of description is needed? This illustrates a case in which it would be better to use a set of hierarchical menus to narrow down the category of the product in mind and then offer a list in a pull-down menu to identify the exact item.

Enter the **model number and description of the product** you wish to purchase.

Fig. 32-34

What do you want, the part number?

Example: Help with Save As

In Fig. 32-35, we show a very early **Save As** dialogue box in a Microsoft Office application. At the top is the name of the current folder, and the user can navigate to any other folder in the usual way. But it doesn't show the names of files in the current folder.

This design precedes modern versions that show a list of existing files in this current folder, as shown in Fig. 32-36.

Fig. 32-35

*Early **Save As** dialogue box with no listing of files in current folder (screen image courtesy of Tobias Frans-Jan Theebe).*

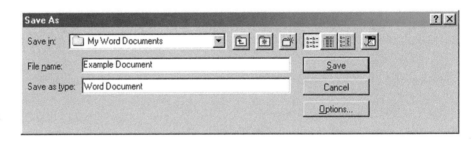

Fig. 32-36

Problem solved with listing of files in current folder.

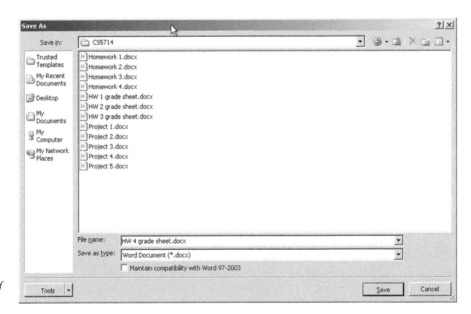

This list supports memory by showing the names of other, possibly similar, files in the folder. If the user is employing any kind of implicit file-naming convention, it will be evident, by example, in this list.

For example, if this folder is for letters to the IRS and files are named by date, such as "letter to IRS, 3-30-2018," the list serves as an effective reminder of this naming convention. Further, if the user is saving another letter to the IRS here, dated 4-2-2018, that can be done by clicking on the 3-30-2018 letter and getting that name in the **File name:** text box, and, with a few keystrokes, editing it to be the new name.

Avoid requirement to retype or copy from one place to another.

In some applications, moving from one subtask to another requires users to remember key data or other related information and bring it to the second subtask themselves. For example, suppose a user selects an item of some kind during a task and then wishes to go to a different part of the application and apply another function to which that item is an input. We have experienced applications that required us to remember the item ourselves and reenter it as we arrived at the new functionality.

Be suspicious of usage situations that require users to write something down in order to use it somewhere else in the application; this is a sign of an opportunity to support human memory better in the design. As an example, consider a user of a Calendar Management System who needs to reschedule an appointment. If the design forces the user to delete the old one and add the new one, the user has to remember details and reenter them. Such a design doesn't follow this guideline.

Support special human memory needs in audio UX design.

Voice menus, such as telephone menus, are more difficult to remember because there is no visual reminder of the choices as there is in a screen display. Therefore, we have to organize and state menu choices in a way to reduce human memory load.

For example, we can give the most likely or most frequently used choices first because the deeper the user goes into the list, the more previous choices there are to remember. As each new choice is articulated, the user must compare it with each of the previous choices to determine the most appropriate one. If the desired item comes early, the user gets cognitive closure and doesn't need to remember the rest of the items.

32.6.3.8 Cognitive directness in cognitive affordances

Cognitive directness is about avoiding mental transformations for the user. It's about what Norman (1990, p. 23) calls "natural mapping." A good example from the world of physical actions is a lever that goes up and down on a console but is used to steer something to the left or the right. Each time it's used, the user must rethink the connection, "Let us see; lever up means steer to the left."

A classic example of cognitive directness, or the lack thereof, in product design is in the arrangement of knobs that control the burners of a cook top. If the spatial layout of the knobs is a spatial map to the burner configuration, it's easy to see which knob controls which burner. It seems easy, but many designs over the years have violated this simple idea, and users have frequently had to reconstruct their own cognitive mapping.

Avoid cognitive indirectness.

Support user cognitive affordance content understanding by presenting choices and information in cognitively direct expressions rather than in some kind of encoding that requires the user to make a mental translation. The objective of this guideline is to help the user avoid an extra step of translation, resulting in less cognitive effort and fewer errors.

Example: Rotating a Graphical Object

For a user to rotate a two-dimensional graphical object, there are two directions: clockwise and counterclockwise. While **Rotate Left** and **Rotate Right** are not technically correct, they might be better understood by many than **Rotate CW** and **Rotate CCW**. A better solution might be to show small graphical icons, circles with an arc arrow over the top pointing in clockwise and counterclockwise directions.

Example: Up and Down in Dreamweaver

Macromedia Dreamweaver is an application used to set up simple web pages. It's easy to use in many ways, but the old version we discuss here contains an interesting and definitive example of cognitive indirectness in its design. In the right-hand side pane of the site files window in Fig. 32-37 are local files as they reside on the user's PC.

The left-hand side pane of Fig. 32-37 shows a list of essentially the same files as they reside on the remote machine, the website server. As users interact with Dreamweaver to edit and test webpages locally on their PCs, they upload them

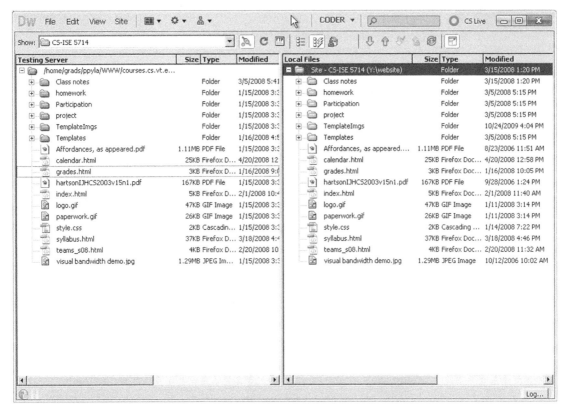

Fig. 32-37

*Dreamweaver up and down
arrows for uploading and
downloading.*

periodically to the server to make them part of the operational website.
Dreamweaver has a convenient built-in "ftp" function to implement this file
transfer. Uploading is accomplished by clicking on the up-arrow icon just above
the **Local** site label, and downloading uses the down arrow.

The problem comes in when users, weary from editing web pages, click on the
wrong arrow. The download arrow brings the remote copy of the just-edited
file into the PC. Because the ftp function replaces files with the same name as
new ones arriving without asking for confirmation, this feature is dangerous and
can be costly. Click on the wrong icon, and you can lose a lot of work (and we
have suffered from just that).

"Uploading" and "downloading" are system-centered, not usage-centered,
terms and have arbitrary meaning about the direction of data flow, at least to the
average nonsystems person. The up- and down-arrow icons do nothing to
mitigate this poor mapping of meaning. Because the sets of files are on the
left-hand side and right-hand side, not up and down, often users must stop and
think about whether they want to transfer data left or right on the screen and

then translate it into "up" or "down." The icons for transfer of data should reflect this directly; a left arrow and a right arrow would do nicely. Furthermore, given that the "upload" action is the more frequent operation, making the corresponding arrow (left in this example) larger provides a better cognitive (and physical affordance in terms of click target size) affordance.

Example: The Surprise Action of a Car Heater Control

In Fig. 32-38, you can see a photo of the heater control in a car. It looks extremely simple; just turn the knob.

However, to a new user, the interaction here could be surprising. The control looks as though you grab the knob and the whole thing turns, including the numbers on its face. However, in actuality, only the outside rim turns, moving the indicator across the numbers, as seen in the sequence of Fig. 32-39.

So, if the user's mental model of the device is that rotating the knob clockwise slows down the heater fan, thinking the decreasing numbers will pass the indicator mark, the user is in for a surprise. In fact, the clockwise rotation moves the indicator to higher numbers, thus speeding up the heater fan. It can take users a long time to get used to that kind of a cognitive transformation.

Fig. 32-38

How does this car heater fan control work? (Photo courtesy of Mara Guimarães da Silva).

Fig. 32-39

Now you can see clockwise rotation where the outer rim is what turns (Photos courtesy of Mara Guimarães da Silva).

32.6.3.9 Complete information in cognitive affordances

Be complete in your design of cognitive affordances; include enough information for users to determine correct action.

For each label, menu choice, and so on, the designer should ask "Is there enough information and are there enough words used to distinguish cases?"

Support the user's understanding of cognitive affordances by providing complete and sufficient expression of meaning, to disambiguate, make more precise, and clarify. The expression of a cognitive affordance should be complete enough to allow users to predict the consequences of actions on the corresponding object.

Prevent loss of productivity due to hesitation, pondering.

Completeness helps the user distinguish alternatives without having to stop and contemplate the differences. Complete expressions of cognitive affordance meaning help avoid errors and lost productivity due to error recovery.

Use enough words for unambiguous labels.

Some people think button labels, menu choices, and verbal prompts should be terse; no one wants to read a paragraph on a button label. However, reasonably long labels are not necessarily bad, and adding words can add precision. Often, a verb plus a noun are needed to tell the whole story. For example, for the label on a button controlling a step in a task to add a record in an application, consider using **Add Record** instead of just **Add**.

As another example of completeness in labeling, for the label on a knob controlling the speed of a machine, rather than **Adjust** or **Speed**, consider using **Adjust Speed** or maybe even **Clockwise to Increase Speed**, which includes information about how to make the adjustment.

Add supplementary information, if necessary.

If you cannot reasonably get all the necessary information in the label of a button or tab or link, for example, consider using a fly-over pop-up to supplement the label with more information.

Give enough information for users to make confident decisions.

Example: What Do You Mean "Revert?"

In Fig. 32-40 is a message from an old version of Microsoft Word that has given us pause more than once. We think we know what button we should click, but we are not entirely confident, and it seems as though it could have a significant effect on our file.

Fig. 32-40

What are the consequences of "reverting?"

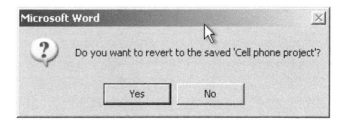

Give enough alternatives for user needs.

Few things are as frustrating to a user as a dialogue box or other UX object presenting choices that don't include the one alternative that user really needs.

32.6.3.10 User/usage centeredness in cognitive affordances

Employ usage-centered wording, the language of the user and the work context, in cognitive affordances.

We find that many of our students don't understand what it means to be user centered or usage centered in UX design. Mainly, it means to use the vocabulary and concepts of the user's work context rather than the vocabulary and context of the system. This difference between the language of the user's work domain and the language of the system is the essence of "translation" in the translation part of the Interaction Cycle.

As designers, we have to help users make that translation so they don't have to encode or convert their work domain vocabulary into the corresponding concepts in the system domain.

Example: What Is Your Phone?

As a modest but compelling example of user-centeredness in its simplest meaning, consider the difference between the terms "cell phone" and "mobile phone." The first term is system- and technology-centered because it refers to implementation technology (cellular networking). The second term is user-centered because it refers to how it is used (a usage capability).

Example: User-Centeredness versus Branding

In a town in South Carolina, we have seen a jewelry shop called *The Jeweler's Bench*. Not far from there is another called *Bling for You*. The first name in inwardly directed and jeweler-centered. The second is outwardly directed and customer-centered. How do these names fare with respect to branding? It depends on the image you wish to project. The first image is process-oriented and implies technical prowess and precision. The second is product-oriented and suggests beautiful things you can buy for yourself.

Example: A Mysterious Toaster

This example is about a toaster that we observed at a hotel brunch buffet, and it's right on target to illustrate user/usage centeredness. Users put bread on the input side of a conveyor belt going into the toaster system. Inside were overhead heating coils, and the bread came out the other end as toast.

The machine had a single control, a knob labeled **Speed** with additional labels for **Faster** (clockwise rotation of the knob) and **Slower** (counterclockwise rotation). A slower moving belt makes darker toast because the bread is under the heating coils longer; faster movement means lighter toast. Even though this concept is simple, there was a distinct language gulf and it led to a bit of confusion and discussion on the part of users we observed. The concept of speed somehow just didn't match their mental model of toast making. We even heard one person ask, "Why do we have a knob to control toaster speed? Why would anyone want to wait to make toast slowly when they could get it faster?" The knob had been labeled with the language of the system's physical control domain.

This is a good example of a design that fails to help the user with the translation from task or work domain language to system control language. Indeed, the knob did make the belt move faster or slower. But the user doesn't really care about the physics of the system domain; the user is living in the work domain of making toast. In that domain, the system control terms translate to **Lighter** and **Darker**, which would have been more effective as knob labels by helping bridge the gulf of execution from the system toward the user's task at hand.

32.6.3.11 Avoiding errors with cognitive affordances

The Japanese have a term, "poka-yoke," that means error proofing. It refers to a manufacturing technique to prevent parts of products from being made, assembled, or used incorrectly. Most physical safety interlocks are examples. For instance, interlocks in most automatic transmissions enforce a bit of safety by not allowing the driver to remove the key until the transmission is in park and not allowing shifting out of park unless the brake is depressed.

Find ways to anticipate and avoid user errors in your design.

Anticipating user errors in the workflow, of course, stems back to usage research, and concern for avoiding errors continues throughout requirements, design, and UX evaluation.

Help users avoid inappropriate and erroneous choices.

This guideline has three parts: one to disable the choices, the second to show the user that they are disabled, and the third to explain why they are disabled.

Disable buttons, menu choices to make inappropriate choices unavailable.

Help users avoid errors within the task flow by disabling choices in buttons, menus, and icons that are inappropriate at a given point in the interaction.

Gray out to make inappropriate choices appear unavailable.

As a corollary to the previous guideline, support user awareness of unavailable choices by making cognitive affordances for those choices *appear* unavailable, in addition to *being* unavailable. This is done by making some adjustment to the presentation of the corresponding cognitive affordance.

One way is to remove the presentation of that cognitive affordance, but this leads to an inconsistent overall display and leaves the user wondering where that cognitive affordance went. The conventional approach is to "gray out" the cognitive affordance in question, which is universally taken to mean the function denoted by the cognitive affordance still exists as part of the system but is currently unavailable or inappropriate.

But help users understand why a choice is unavailable.

If a system operation or function is not available or not appropriate, it's usually because the conditions for its use are not met. One of the most frustrating things for users, however, is to have a button or menu choice grayed out but no indication about *why* the corresponding function is unavailable, and what has to be done to get this button un-grayed and make the function available.

We suggest an approach that would be a break with traditional GUI object behavior but that could help avoid that source of user frustration. Clicking on or hovering over a grayed-out object could yield a pop up (e.g., a "tool tip") with this crucial explanation of why it's grayed out and what you must do to create the conditions to activate the function of that user interface object.

Example: When Am I Supposed to Click the Button?

In a document retrieval system, one of the user tasks is adding new keywords to existing documents, documents already entered into the system. Associated with this task is a text box for typing in a new keyword and a button labeled **Add Keyword**. The user was not sure whether to click on the **Add Keyword** button first to initiate that task or to type the new keyword and then click on **Add Keyword** to "put it away."

A user tried the former and nothing happened, no observable action and no feedback, so the user deduced that the proper sequence was to first type the keyword and then click the button. No harm was done except a little confusion and lost time. However, the same glitch is likely to happen again with other users and with this user at a later time.

The solution is to gray out the **Add Keyword** button to show when it doesn't apply, making it obvious that it's not active until a keyword is entered. Per our suggestion earlier, we could add an informative pop-up message that appears when someone clicks on the grayed-out button to the effect that the user must first type something into the new keyword text box before this button becomes active and allows the user to commit to adding that keyword.

32.6.3.12 Cognitive affordances for error recovery
Provide a clear way to undo and reverse actions.

As much as possible, provide ways for users to back out of error situations by "undo" actions. Although they are more difficult to implement, multiple levels of undo and selective undo among steps are more powerful for the user.

Offer constructive help for error recovery.

Users learn about errors through error messages as feedback, which is considered in the assessment part of the Interaction Cycle. Feedback occurs as part of the system response (Section 32.9.1). A system response designed to support error recovery will usually supplement the feedback with feed-forward, a cognitive affordance here in the translation part of the Interaction Cycle to help users know what actions or task steps to take for error recovery.

32.6.3.13 Cognitive affordances for modes

Modes are states in which actions have different meanings than the same actions in different states. The simplest example is a hypothetical email system. When in the mode of managing email files and directories, the command **Ctrl-S** means **Save**. However, when you are in the mode of composing an email message, **Ctrl-S** means **Send**. This design, which we have seen in the "old days," is an invitation to errors. Many a message has been sent prematurely out of the habit of doing a **Ctrl-S** periodically out of habit to be sure everything is saved.

The problem with most modes in UX design is the abrupt change of the meanings of user actions. It's often difficult for users to shift focus between modes, and when they forget to shift as they cross modal boundaries, the outcomes can be confusing and even damaging. It's a kind of bait and switch; you just get your users comfortable in doing something one way and then change the meaning of the actions they are using.

Modes within UX designs can also work strongly against experienced users, who move fast and habitually without thinking much about their actions. In a kind of "UX karate," they start leaning one way in one mode, and then their own usage momentum is used against them in the other mode.

Avoid confusing modalities.

If it's possible to avoid modes altogether, the best advice is to do so.

Example: Don't Be in a Bad Mode

Think about old school digital watches. Enough said.

Distinguish modes clearly.

If modes become necessary in your UX design, the next-best advice is to be sure that users are aware of each mode and avoid confusion across modes.

Not all modes are bad. The use of modes in design can represent a case for interpreting design guidelines, not just applying them blindly. The guideline to avoid modes is often good advice because modes tend to create confusion. But modes can also be used in designs in ways that are helpful and not at all confusing.

Example: Are You in a Good Mode?

An example of a good mode needed in a design comes from audio equalizer controls on the stereo in a particular car. As with most radio equalizers, there are choices of fixed equalizer settings, often called "presets," including audio styles such as voice, jazz, rock, classical, new age, and so on.

However, because there is no indication in the radio display of the current equalizer setting, you have to guess or have faith. If you push the Equalizer button to check the current setting, it changes the setting, and then you have to toggle back through all the values to recover the original setting. This is a nonmodal design because the Equalizer button means the same thing every time you push it. It's consistent; every button push yields the same result: toggling the setting.

It would be better to have a slightly moded design so that it starts in a "display mode," which means an initial button push causes it to display the current setting without changing the setting so that you can check the equalizer setting without disturbing the setting itself. If you do wish to change the setting, you push the same Equalizer button again within a certain short time period to change it to the "setting mode" in which button pushes will toggle the setting. Most such buttons behave in this good, moded way, except in this particular car.

32.6.4 Task Structure

In Fig. 32-41, we highlight the "task structure" portion of the translation part of the Interaction Cycle.

Support of task structure in this part of the Interaction Cycle means supporting user needs with the logical flow of tasks and task steps, including human memory support in the task structure; task design simplicity, flexibility, and efficiency; maintaining the locus of control with the user within a task; and offering natural direct manipulation interaction.

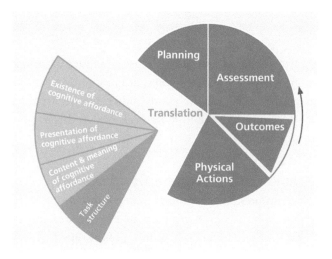

Fig. 32-41

The task structure part of translation.

32.6.4.1 Human working memory loads in task structure
Support human memory limitations in the design of task structure.

The most important way to support human memory limitations within the design of task structure is to provide task closure as soon and as often as possible, avoiding interruption and stacking of subtasks. This means "chunking" tasks into small sequences with closure after each part.

While it may seem tidy from the computer science point of view to use a "preorder" traversal of the hierarchical task structure, it can overload the user's working memory, requiring stacking of context each time the user goes to a deeper level and "popping" the stack, or remembering the stacked context, each time the user emerges up a level in the structure.

Interruption and stacking occur when the user must consider other tasks before completing the current one. Having to juggle several "balls" in the air, several tasks in a partial state of completion, adds an often-unnecessary load to human memory.

32.6.4.2 Design task structure for flexibility and efficiency
Support user with effective task structure and interaction control.

Support user needs for flexibility within the logical task flow by providing alternative ways to do tasks. Meet user needs for efficiency with shortcuts for frequently performed tasks and provide support for task thread continuity, supporting the most likely next step.

Provide alternative ways to perform tasks.

One of the most striking observations during task-based UX evaluation is the amazing variety of ways users approach task structure. Users take paths never imagined by the designers.

There are two ways designers can become attuned to this diversity of task paths. One is through careful attention to multiple ways of doing things in user research, and the other is to leverage observations of such user behavior in UX evaluation. Don't just discount observations of users gone "astray" as "incorrect" task performance; try to learn about valuable alternative paths.

Provide shortcuts.

No one wants to have to make too many mouse clicks or other user actions to complete a task, especially in complex task sequences (Wright, Lickorish, & Milroy, 1994). For efficiency within frequently performed tasks, experienced users especially need shortcuts, such as "hot key" (or "accelerator key") alternatives for other more complicated action combinations, such as selecting choices from pull-down menus.

Keyboard alternatives are particularly useful in tasks that otherwise require keyboard actions such as form filling or word processing; staying within the keyboard for these "commands" avoids having the physical "switching" actions required for moving between (for example) the keyboard and mouse, two physically different devices.

32.6.4.3 Grouping for task efficiency
Provide logical grouping in layout of objects.
Group together objects and functions related by task or user work activity.

Under the topic of layout and grouping to control content and meaning complexity, we grouped related things to make their meanings clear. Here, we advocate grouping objects and other things related to the same task or user work activity as a means of conveniently having the needed components for a task at hand. This kind of grouping can be accomplished spatially with screen or other device layout, or it can be manifest sequentially, as in a sequence of menu choices.

As Norman (2006) illustrates, in a taxonomic "hardware store" organization, hammers of all different kinds are all hanging together, and all different kinds of nails are organized in bins somewhere else. But a carpenter organizes his or her tools so that the hammer and nails are in proximity because the two are used together in work activities.

But avoid grouping of objects and functions if they need to be dealt with separately.

Grouping user interface objects such as buttons, menus, value settings, and so on, creates the impression that the group comprises a single focus for user action. If more is needed for that task goal, each requiring separate actions, don't group the objects tightly together, but make clear the separate objectives and the requirement for separate actions.

Example: Oops, I Forgot to Do the Rest of It

A dialogue box sketch from a paper prototype of a Ticket Kiosk System is shown in Fig. 32-42.

It contains two objectives and two corresponding objects for value settings by the user—proximity of the starting time of a movie and the distance of the movie theater from the kiosk. Most of the participants who used this dialogue box as part of a ticket-buying task made the first setting and clicked on Continue, not noticing the second component. The solution that worked was to separate the two value-setting operations into two dialogue boxes, forcing a separation of the focus and linearizing the two actions.

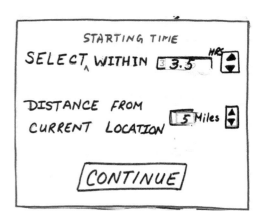

Fig. 32-42

An overloaded dialogue box in a paper prototype.

32.6.4.4 Task thread continuity: Anticipating the most likely next step or task path

Support task thread continuity by anticipating the most likely next task, step, or action.

Task thread continuity is a design goal relating to task flow in which the user can pursue a task thread of possibly many steps without an interruption or "discontinuity." It's accomplished in design by anticipating most likely and other possible next steps at any point in the task flow and providing, at hand, the necessary cognitive, physical, and functional affordances to continue the thread.

The likely next steps to support can include tasks or steps the user may wish to take but which are not necessarily part of what designers envisioned as the "main" task thread. Therefore, these various task directions might not be identified by pure task analysis, but are steps that a practitioner or designer might see in usage research while watching users perform the tasks in a real work activity context. Effective observation in UX evaluation also can reveal diversions, branching, and alternative task paths that users associate with the main thread.

Attention to task thread continuity is especially important when designing the contents of context menus, right-click menus associated with objects or steps in tasks. It's also important when designing message dialogue boxes that offer branching in the task path, which is when users need at hand other possibilities associated with the current task.

Example: If You Tell Them What They Should Do, Help Them Get There

Probably the most defining example of task thread continuity is seen in a message dialogue box that describes a problematic system state and suggests one or more possible courses of action as a remedy. But then the user is frustrated by a lack of any help in getting to these suggested new task paths.

Task thread continuity is easily supported by adding buttons that offer a direct way to follow each of the suggested actions. Suppose a dialogue box message tells a user that the page margins are too wide to fit on a printed page and suggests resetting page margins so that the document can be printed. It's enormously helpful if this guideline is followed by including a button that will take the user directly to the page margin setup screen.

Example: Seeing the Query With the Results

Designers of information retrieval systems sometimes see the task sequence of formulating a query, submitting it, and getting the results as closure on the task structure, and it often is. So, in some designs, the query screen is replaced with the results screen. However, for many users, this is not the end of the task thread.

Once the results are displayed, the next step is to assess the success of the retrieval. If the query is complex or much has happened since the query was submitted, the user will need to review the original query to determine whether the results were what was expected. The next step may be to modify the query and try again. So, this often-simple linear task can have a thread with larger scope. The design should support these likely alternative task paths by not *replacing* the query display with that of the results and by providing an option to modify the query from the results page.

Example: May We Help You Spend More Money?

Designers of successful online shopping sites such as Amazon.com have figured out how to make it convenient for shoppers by providing for likely next steps (seeing and then buying) in their shopping tasks. They support convenience in ordering with the ubiquitous **Buy It Now** or **Add to Cart** buttons. They also support product research. If a potential customer shows interest in a product, the site quickly displays links to reviews, other products, accessories that go with it, and alternative similar products that other customers have bought.

Example: What If I Want to Save It In a New Folder?

In early Microsoft Office applications, the **Save As** dialogue box didn't contain the icon for creating a new folder (the second icon to the left of **Tools** in the dialogue box in Fig. 32-43). Eventually, designers realized that, as part of the **Save As** task, users had to think about where to put the file, and, as part of that planning for organizing their file structures, they often needed to create new folders to modify or expand the current file structure.

Early users had to back out of the **Save As** task and go to Windows Explorer, navigate to the proper context, create the folder, and then return to the Office application and do the **Save As** all over again. By including the ability to create a new folder within the **Save As** dialogue box, this likely next step was accommodated directly.

In some cases, the most likely next step is so likely that task thread continuity is supported by adding a slight amount of automation and doing the step for the user. The following example is about a case in which this kind of help was needed.

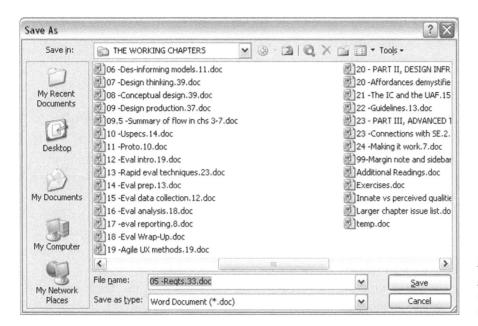

Fig. 32-43

*Addition of an icon to create a new file in the **Save As** dialogue box.*

Example: Resetting Over and Over

For frequent users of Word, the Outline view helps organize material within a document. You can use the Outline view to move quickly from where you are in the document to another specific location. In the Outline view, you get a choice of the number of levels of outline to be shown. It's common for users to want to keep this Outline view level setting at a high level, affording a view of the whole outline. So, for many users, the most likely-used setting would be that high setting. Many users rarely even choose anything else.

Regardless of any user's level preferences, if a user goes to the Outline view, it's because he or she wants to see and use the outline. But the default level setting in Word's Outline view is the only setting that really is not an outline. The default Word Outline view, **Show all levels**, is a useless mash-up of outline parts and nonoutline text. As a default, this setting is the least useful for anyone.

Every time users launch a Word document, they face that annoying Outline view setting. Even once you have shown your preference by setting the level, the system inevitably strays away from that setting during editing, forcing you to reset it frequently. Frequent users of Word will have made this setting thousands of times over the years. Why can't Word help users by saving the settings they use so consistently and have set so often?

Designers might argue that they cannot assume they know what level a user needs, so they follow the guideline to "give the user control." But why design a default that guarantees the user will have to change it instead of something that might be useful to at least some users some of the time? Why not detect the highest level present in the document and use that as a default? After all, the user did request to see the outline.

Example: Why Make Me Choose from Just One Thing?

Earlier, we described an example in which the user had to select an item from a dialogue box list of choices, even though there was only one item in the list. Our point there was that preselecting the item for the user made for a useful default.

The same idea applies here: When there is only one choice, the designer can support user efficiency through task thread continuity by assuming the most likely next action to be selecting that only choice and making the selection in advance for the user. An example of this comes from Microsoft Outlook.

When an Outlook user selects **Rules and Alerts** from the **Tools** menu and clicks on the **Run Rules Now** button, the **Run Rules Now** dialogue box appears. In cases where there is only one rule, it's highlighted in the display, making it *look* selected. However, be careful, that rule is not selected; the highlighting is a false affordance.

Look closely and you see that the checkbox to its left is unchecked, and *that* is the indication of what is selected. The result is the **Run Now** button is grayed out, causing some users to pause in confusion about why the rule cannot now be run. Most such users figure it out eventually, but lose time and patience in the confusion. This UX glitch can be avoided by preselecting this only choice as the default.

32.6.4.5 Not undoing user work

Make the most of user's work.
Don't make the user redo any work.
Don't require users to reenter data.

Don't you hate it when you fill out part of a form and go away to get more information or to attend temporarily to something else, and, when you come back, you return to an empty form? Or, when you encounter an error with the data in one field, the form comes back empty? This usually comes from lazy programming because it takes some buffering to retain your partial information. Don't do this disservice to your users.

Retain user state information.

Retention helps users keep track of state information, such as user preferences, that they set in the course of usage. It's exasperating to have to reset preferences and other state settings that don't persist across different work sessions.

Example: Hey, Remember What I Was Doing?

It would help users if Windows could be a little bit more helpful in keeping track of the focus of their work, especially keeping track of where they have been working within the directory structure. Too often, you have to reestablish your work context by searching through the whole file directory in a dialogue box to, say, open a file.

Then, later, if you wish to do a **Save As** with the file, you may have to search that whole file directory again from the top to place the new file near the original one. We are not asking for built-in artificial intelligence, but it would seem that if you are working on a file in a certain part of the directory structure and want to do a **Save As**, it's very likely that the file is related to the original, and, therefore, needs to be saved close to it in the file structure.

Fortunately, in Windows 10, the **Save As** function now does offer choices of recent files and folders to help solve this problem of keeping your place in the directory structure (Fig. 32-44).

32.6.4.6 Keeping users in control
Avoid the feeling of loss of control.

Sometimes, although users are still actually in control, interaction dialogue can make users feel as though the computer is taking control. Although designers may not give a second thought to language such as, "You need to answer your email," these words can project a bossy attitude to users. Something such as, "You have new email," or, "New email is ready for reading," conveys the same meaning but does so in a way that helps users feel that they are not being commanded to do something; they can respond whenever they find it convenient.

Avoid real loss of control.

More bothersome to users and more detrimental to productivity is a real loss of user control. You, the designer, may think you know what is best for the user, but

Fig. 32-44

Fig. 32-44

*Windows 10 **Save As** help
with recent working
locations in the directory.*

you would do best to avoid the temptation of being high-handed in matters of control within interaction. Few kinds of user experience more readily give rise to anger in users than a loss of control. It doesn't make them behave the way you think they should; it only forces them to take extra effort to work around your design.

One of the most maddening examples of loss of user control we have experienced comes from EndNote, an otherwise powerful and effective bibliographic support application for word processing. This problem has existed in every version of EndNote we have ever used. When EndNote is used as a plug-in to Microsoft Word, it can be scanning your document invisibly for actions to take with regard to your bibliographic citations.

If an action is deemed necessary, for example, to format an in-line citation, EndNote often arbitrarily takes control away from a user doing editing and moves the cursor to the location where the action is needed, often many pages away from the focus of attention of the user and usually without any indication of what happened. At that point, users are probably not interested in thinking about bibliographic citations, but are more concerned with their task at hand, such as editing. All of a sudden, control is jerked away, and the working context disappears. It takes extra cognitive energy and extra physical actions to get back to where the user was working. The worst part is that it can happen repeatedly, each time with an increasingly negative emotional user reaction. I have actually uninstalled EndNote for a time while working on the chapters of this book!

Always provide a way for the user to "bail out" of an ongoing operation.

Don't trap a user in an interaction. Always allow a way for users to escape if they decide not to proceed after getting part way into a task sequence. The usual way to design for this guideline is to include a **Cancel**, usually as a dialogue box button.

32.7 PHYSICAL ACTIONS

Fitts' law
An empirically-based theory expressed as a set of mathematical formulae that predict the time to make a cursor or other movement is proportional to $\log_2$ of distance moved and inversely proportional to $\log_2$ of target cross-section normal to the direction of movement (Section 30.3.2.5).

Physical actions guidelines support users in doing physical actions, including typing, clicking, dragging in a GUI, scrolling on a web page, speaking with a voice interface, walking in a virtual environment, moving one's hands in gestural interaction, and gazing with the eyes. This is the one part of the user's Interaction Cycle where there is essentially no cognitive component; the user already knows what to do and how to do it.

Issues here are limited to how well the design supports the physical actions of doing it, acting upon user interface objects to access all features, and functionality within the system. The two primary areas of design considerations are how well the design supports users in sensing the object(s) to be manipulated and how well the design supports users in doing the physical manipulation. As a simple example, it's about seeing a button and clicking on it.

Physical actions are the one place in the Interaction Cycle where physical affordances are relevant, where you will find issues about Fitts' law, manual dexterity, physical disabilities, awkwardness, and physical fatigue.

32.7.1 Sensing Objects of Physical Actions

In Fig. 32-45, we highlight the "sensing user interface object" part within the breakdown of the physical actions part of the Interaction Cycle.

32.7.1.1 Sensing objects to manipulate

The "Sensing user interface object" portion of the physical actions part is about designing to support user sensory (for example, visual, auditory, or tactile) needs in locating the appropriate physical affordance quickly in order to manipulate it. Sensing for physical actions is about presentation of physical affordances, and the associated design issues are similar to those of the presentation of cognitive affordances in other parts of the Interaction Cycle,

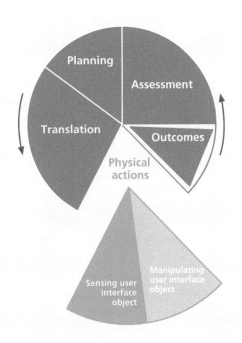

Fig. 32-45

Sensing the user interface (UI) object, within physical actions.

including visibility, noticeability, findability, distinguishability, discernibility, sensory disabilities, and presentation medium.

Support users making physical actions with effective sensory affordances for sensing physical affordances.

Make objects to be manipulated visible, discernable, legible, noticeable, and distinguishable. When possible, locate the focus of attention (the cursor, for example) near the objects to be manipulated.

32.7.1.2 Sensing objects during manipulation

Not only is it important to be able to sense objects statically to initiate physical actions, but users also need to be able to sense the cursor and the physical affordance object dynamically to keep track of them during manipulation. As an example, in dragging a graphical object, the user's dynamic sensory needs are supported by showing an outline of the graphical object, aiding its placement in a drawing application.

As another very simple example, if the cursor is the same color as the background, the cursor can disappear into the background while moving it, making it difficult to judge how far to move the mouse back to get it visible again.

32.7.2 Help User in Doing Physical Actions

In Fig. 32-46, we highlight the "manipulating user interface object" part within the breakdown of the physical actions part of the Interaction Cycle.

This part of the Interaction Cycle is about supporting user physical needs at the time of making physical actions; it's about making user interface object manipulation physically easy. It's especially about designing to make physical actions efficient for expert users.

Physicality

Referring to real direct physical interaction with real physical (hardware) devices like in the grasping and moving of knobs and levers (Section 30.3.2.4).

Support user with effective physical affordances for manipulating objects, help in doing actions.

Issues relevant to supporting physical actions include awkwardness and physical disabilities, manual dexterity and Fitts' law, plus haptics and physicality.

32.7.2.1 Awkwardness and physical disabilities

One of the easiest aspects of designing for physical actions is avoiding awkwardness. It's also one of the easiest areas in which to find existing problems in UX evaluation.

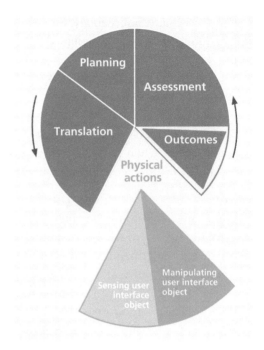

Fig. 32-46

Manipulating the user interface (UI) object within physical actions.

Avoid physical awkwardness.

Issues of physical awkwardness are often about time and energy expended in physical motions. The classic example of this issue is a user having to alternate constantly among multiple input devices such as between a keyboard and a mouse or between either device and a touchscreen.

This device switching involves constant "homing" actions that require time-consuming and effortful distraction of cognitive focus and visual attention. Keyboard combinations requiring multiple fingers on multiple keys can also be awkward user actions that hinder smooth and fast interaction.

Accommodate physical disabilities.

Not all human users have the same physical abilities—range of motion, fine motor control, vision, or hearing. Some users are innately limited; some have disabilities due to accidents. Although in-depth coverage of accessibility issues is beyond our scope, accommodation of user disabilities is an extremely important part of designing for the physical actions part of the Interaction Cycle.

32.7.2.2 Manual dexterity and Fitts' law

Design issues related to Fitts' law are about movement distances, mutual object proximities, and target object size. Performance is reckoned in terms of both time and errors. In a strict interpretation, an error would be clicking anywhere except on the correct object. A more practical interpretation would limit errors to clicking on incorrect objects that are near the correct object; this is the kind of error that can have a more negative effect on the interaction. This discussion leads to the following guidelines.

Design layout to support manual dexterity and Fitts' law.

Support targeted cursor movement by making selectable objects large enough.

The bottom line about sizes and cursor movement among targets is simple: small objects are harder to click on than large ones. Give your interaction objects enough size, both in cross-section for accuracy in the cursor movement direction and in their depth to support accurate termination of movement within the target object.

Group clickable objects related by task flow close together.

Avoid fatigue and slow movement times. Large movement distances require more time and can lead to more targeting errors. Short distances between related objects will result in shorter movement times and fewer errors.

But don't group objects too close, and don't include unrelated objects in the grouping.

Avoid erroneous selection that can be caused by close proximity of target objects to nontarget objects.

Example: Oops, I Missed the Icon

A software drawing application has a very large number of functions, most of which are accessible via small icons in a tool bar. Each function can also be invoked by another way (e.g., a menu choice), but our observations tell us that expert users like to use the tool bar icons.

But there are problems in using the icons because there are so many icons, they are small, and they are crowded together. This, combined with the fast actions of experienced users, leads to clicking on the wrong icon more often than users would like.

32.7.2.3 Constraining physical actions to avoid physical overshoot errors

Design physical movement to avoid physical overshoot.

Just as in the case of cursor movement, other kinds of physical actions can be at risk for overshoot, extending the movement beyond what was intended. This concept is best illustrated by the hair dryer switch example that follows.

Example: Blow Dry, Anyone?

Suppose you are using a hair dryer on the low setting, and you are ready to switch it off. To move the hair dryer switch takes a certain threshold pressure to overcome initial resistance. Once in motion, however, unless the user is adept at reducing this pressure instantly, the switch can move beyond the intended setting.

A strong detent at each switch position can help prevent the movement from overshooting, but it's still easy to push the switch too far, as the photo of a hair dryer switch in Fig. 32-47 illustrates. Starting in the **LOW** position and pushing the switch toward **OFF**, the switch configuration makes it easy to move accidentally beyond **OFF** over to the **HIGH** setting.

This physical overshoot is preventable with a switch design that goes directly from **HIGH** to **LOW** and then to **OFF** in a logical progression. Having the

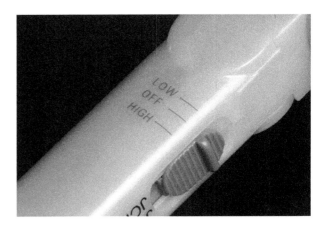

Fig. 32-47

A hair dryer control switch inviting physical overshoot.

OFF position at one end of the physical movement is a kind of physical constraint or boundary condition that allows you to push the switch to **OFF** firmly and quickly without a careful touch or worrying about overshooting.

Why do essentially all hair dryers have this UX flaw? It's probably easier to manufacture a switch with the neutral **OFF** position in the middle.

32.7.2.4 Haptics and physicality

Haptics is about the sense of touch and physical grasping, and physicality is about real physical interaction using real physical devices, such as real knobs and levels, instead of "virtual" interaction via "soft" devices.

Include physicality in your design when the alternatives are not as satisfying to the user.

Example: Beamer Without Knobs

The BMW iDrive idea seemed so good on paper. It was simplicity in itself. No panels cluttered with knobs and buttons. How cool and forward looking. Designers realized that drivers could do *anything* via a set of menus. But drivers soon realized that the controls for everything were buried in a maze of hierarchical menus. No longer could you reach out and tweak the heater fan speed without looking. Fortunately, physical knobs are now coming back in BMWs.

Example: Roger's New Microwave

Here is an old email from our friend, Roger Ehrich, only slightly edited:

> Hey Rex, since our microwave was about 25 years old, we worried about radiation leakage, so we reluctantly got a new one. The old one had a knob that you twisted to set the time, and a START button that, unlike in Windows, actually started the thing. The new one had a digital interface and Marion and I spent over 10 minutes trying to get it to even turn on, but we got nothing but an error message. I feel you should never get an error message from an appliance! Eventually we got it to turn on. The sequence was not complicated, but it will not tolerate any variation in user behavior. The problem is that the design is modal, some buttons being multi-functional and sequential. A casual user like me will forget and get it wrong again. Better for me to take my popcorn over to a neighbor who remembers what to do. Anyway, here's to the good old days and the timer knob.
>
> – Regards, Roger

Example: Great Physicality in Truck Radio and Heater Knobs

Fig. 32-48 is a photo of the radio and heater controls of a pickup truck.

Fig. 32-48

Great physicality in the radio volume control and heater control knobs.

The large and easily grasped outside ring of the volume control knob is a joy to use, and it's not doubled up with any other mode. Also note the heater control knobs below the radio. Again, the physicality of grabbing and adjusting these knobs gives great pleasure on a cold winter morning.

The only downside: no tuning knob.

32.8 OUTCOMES

In Fig. 32-49, we highlight the outcomes part of the Interaction Cycle.

The outcomes part of the Interaction Cycle is about usefulness for supporting users through complete and correct "backend" functionality, effective functional affordances. There are no other UX issues in outcomes, because outcomes are computations and state changes that are internal to the system, invisible to users.

Usefulness

A component of user experience based on utility, system functionality that gives users the ability to accomplish the goals of work (or play) through using the system or product (Section 1.4.3).

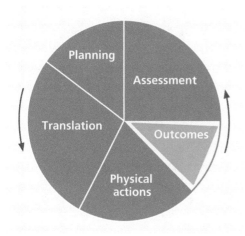

Fig. 32-49
The outcomes part of the
Interaction Cycle.

32.8.1 System Functionality

The outcomes part of the Interaction Cycle is mainly about nonuser-interface system functionality, which includes all issues about software bugs on the software engineering side and issues about completeness and correctness of the backend functional software.

Check your functionality for missing features.
Don't let your functionality grow into a Jack-of-all-trades, but master of none.

   If you try to do too many things in the functionality of your system, you may end up not doing anything well. Norman has warned us against general-purpose machines intended to do many different functions. He suggests, rather, "information appliances" (Norman, 1998), each intended for more specialized functions.

Check your functionality for nonuser-interface software bugs.

32.8.2 System Response Time

Slow system response can impact their perceived usage experience. Computer hardware performance, networking, and communications are usually to blame. The only thing we can do in the UX design to help is to communicate the status of user actions via effective feedback (Section 32.9.2).

32.8.3 Automation Issues

Automation, in the sense we are using the term here, means moving functions and control from the user to the internal system functionality. This can result in users not having what they need. When designers try to guess what users will need, they almost always end up getting it wrong. Design questions about automation and user control can be tricky.

Avoid loss of user control from too much automation.

The following examples show very small-scale cases of automation, taking control from the user. Small though they may be, they can still be frustrating to users who encounter them.

Example: Does the IRS Know About This?

The problem in this example no longer exists in Windows Explorer, but an early version of Windows Explorer would not let you name a new folder with all uppercase letters. In particular, suppose you needed a folder for tax documents and tried to name it "IRS." With that version of Windows, after you pressed **Enter**, the name would be changed to "Irs."

So, in slight confusion, you try again, but no deal. This had to be a deliberate "feature," probably made by a software person to protect users from what appeared to be a typographic error, but that ended up being a high-handed grasping of user control.

Example: The John Hancock Problem

Suppose a user named H. John Hancock is typing a business letter in an early version of Microsoft Word, intending to sign it at the end as:

H. John Hancock
Sr. Vice President

Instead he got (Fig. 32-50):

H. John Hancock
I. Sr. Vice President

Mr. Hancock, not being used to the technology of the 21st century, was confused about the "I", so he backed up and typed the name again, but, when he pressed **Enter** again, he got the same result. At first, he didn't know what was happening, why the "I" appeared, or how to finish the letter without getting the "I" there. At least for a few moments, the task was blocked, and Mr. Hancock was frustrated.

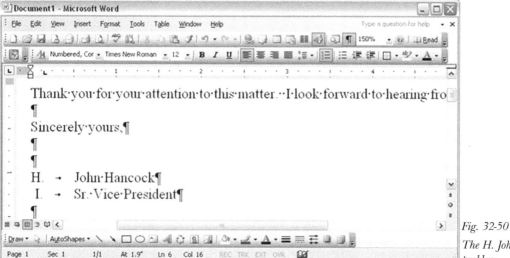

Fig. 32-50
The H. John Hancock
problem.

Being a somewhat experienced user of Word, his composition of text going back to some famous early American documents, he eventually determined that the cause of the problem was that the **Automatic Numbered List** option was turned on as a kind of mode. At least for this occasion and this user, the **Automatic Numbered List** option imposed too much automation and not enough user control, and the user had difficulty understanding what was happening.

There was, in fact, useful feedback indicating the user was in the Automatic Numbered List mode, but it was presented as a "status" message displayed at the top of the window (Fig. 32-51).

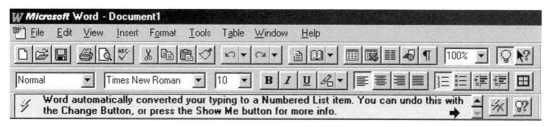

Fig. 32-51

If only Mr. Hancock had seen this (screen image courtesy of Tobias Frans-Jan Theebe).

However, Mr. Hancock didn't notice this feedback message because it violated the assessment guideline to "Locate feedback within the user's focus of attention, perhaps in a pop-up dialogue box but not in a message or status line at the top or bottom of the screen."

Help the user by automating where there is an obvious need.

In some cases, automation can be helpful. The following example is about one such case.

Example: Sorry, Off Route; You Lose!

No matter how good your GPS system is, as a human driver you can still make mistakes and drive off course, deviating from the route planned by the system. Today's GPS units are very good at helping the driver recover and get back on route. It recalculates a new route from the current position immediately and automatically, without missing a beat. Recovery is so smooth and easy that it hardly seems like an error.

Before this kind of GPS, in the early days of GPS map systems for travel navigation, there was another system developed by Microsoft, called Streets and Trips. It used a GPS antenna and receiver plugged into a USB port in a laptop. But, when the driver got off track, the screen displayed the error message Off Route! in a large bright red font.

Somehow you just had to know that you had to press one of the **F**, or function, keys to request recalculation of the route in order to recover. When you are busy contending with traffic and road signs, that is the time you would gladly have the system take control and share more of the responsibility. To be fair, this option probably was available in one of the preference settings or other menu choices, but the default behavior was not very usable, and this option was not easily discovered.

Designers of the Microsoft system may have decided to follow the design guideline to "keep the locus of control with the user." While user control is often the best thing, there are times when it's critical for the system to take charge and do what is needed. The work context of this UX problem includes:

- The user is busy with other tasks that cannot be automated.
- It's dangerous to distract the user/driver with additional workload.
- Getting off track can be stressful, detracting further from the focus.
- Having to intervene and tell the system to recalculate the route interferes with the user's most important task, that of driving.

This interpretation of the guideline means that, on one hand, the system doesn't insist on staying on the current route regardless of driver actions, but quietly allows the driver to make impromptu detours while the system continues to recalculate the route to help the driver eventually reach the destination.

32.9 ASSESSMENT

Assessment guidelines are to support users in understanding information displays of the results of outcomes and other feedback about outcomes such as error indications. Assessment, along with translation, is one of the places in the Interaction Cycle where cognitive affordances play a primary role.

32.9.1 System Response

A system response can contain:

- Feedback, information about course of interaction so far
- Information display, results of outcome computation
- Feed-forward, information about what to do next.

As an example, consider this message: "The value you entered for your phone number was not accepted by the system. Please try again using only numeric characters."

- The first sentence, "The value you entered for your phone number was not accepted by the system," is feedback (in the assessment part of the Interaction Cycle) about a slight problem in the course of interaction.
- The second sentence, "Please try again using only numeric characters," is feed-forward, a cognitive affordance for the translation part of the next iteration within the Interaction Cycle.

32.9.2 Assessment of System Feedback

Fig. 32-52 highlights the assessment part of the Interaction Cycle.

Feedback about errors and interaction problems is essential in supporting users in understanding the course of their interactions. Feedback is the only way users will know if an error has occurred and why. There is a strong parallel between assessment issues about cognitive affordances as feedback and translation issues about cognitive affordances as feed-forward, including existence of feedback when it's needed, sensing feedback through effective

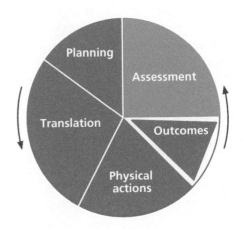

Fig. 32-52
The assessment part of the
Interaction Cycle.

presentation, and understanding feedback through effective representation of content and meaning.

32.9.3 Existence of Feedback

In Fig. 32-53 we highlight the "existence of feedback" portion of the assessment part of the Interaction Cycle.

The "existence of feedback" portion of the assessment part of the Interaction Cycle is about providing necessary feedback to support users' need to know whether the course of interaction is proceeding toward meeting their planning goals.

Provide feedback for all user actions.

For most systems and applications, the existence of feedback is essential for users; feedback keeps users on track. One notable exception is the Unix operating system, in which no news is good news. No feedback in Unix means no errors. For expert users, this tacit positive feedback is efficient and keeps out of the way of high-powered interaction. For most users of most other systems, however, no news is just no news.

Provide progress feedback on long operations.

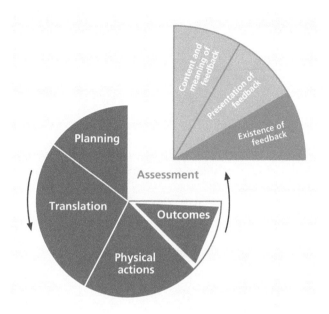

Fig. 32-53
Existence of feedback,
within assessment.

For a system operation requiring significant processing time, it's essential to inform the user when the system is still computing. Keep users aware of function or operation progress with some kind of feedback as a progress report, such as a percent-done indicator.

Example: Database System Not Helpful about Progress in Pack **Operation**

Consider the case of a user of a dbase-family database application who had been deleting lots of records in a large database. He knew that, in dbase applications, "deleted" records are really only marked for deletion and can still be undeleted until a **Pack** operation is performed, permanently removing all records marked for deletion.

At some point, he did the **Pack** operation, but it didn't seem to work. After waiting what seemed like a long time (several seconds), he pushed the **Escape** key to get back control of the computer, and things just got more confusing about the state of the system.

It turns out that the **Pack** operation was working, but there was no indication to the user of its progress. By pushing the **Escape** key while the system was still performing the **Pack** function, the user may have left things in an indeterminate state. If the system had let him know it was, in fact, still doing the requested **Pack** operation, he would have waited for it to complete.

Request confirmation as a kind of intervening feedback.

To prevent costly errors, it's wise to solicit user confirmation before proceeding with potentially destructive actions.

But don't overuse confirmation requests and annoy.

When the upcoming action is reversible or not potentially destructive, the annoyance of having to deal with a confirmation may outweigh any possible protection for the user.

32.9.4 Presentation of Feedback

Fig. 32-54 highlights the "presentation of feedback" portion of the assessment part of the Interaction Cycle.

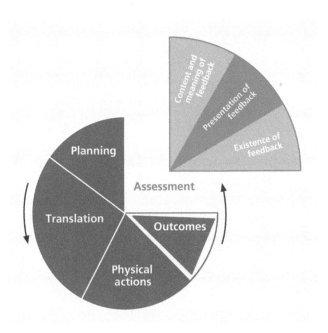

Fig. 32-54

Presentation of feedback, within assessment.

This portion of the assessment part of the Interaction Cycle is about supporting user sensing, such as seeing, hearing, or feeling, of feedback with effective design of feedback presentation and appearance. Presentation of feedback is about how feedback *appears* to users, not how it conveys meaning. Users must be able to sense (e.g., see or hear) feedback before it can be useful to them in usage.

Support user with effective sensory affordances in presentation of feedback.

32.9.4.1 Feedback visibility

Obviously, feedback cannot be effective if it cannot be seen or heard when it's needed.

Make feedback visible.

It's the designer's job to be sure each instance of feedback is visible when it's needed in the interaction.

32.9.4.2 Feedback noticeability

Make feedback noticeable.

When needed feedback exists and is visible, the next consideration is its noticeability or likelihood of being noticed or sensed. Just putting feedback on the screen is not enough, especially if the user doesn't necessarily know it exists or is not necessarily looking for it.

These design issues are largely about supporting awareness. Relevant feedback should come to users' attention without users seeking it. The primary design factor in this regard is location, putting feedback within the users' focus of attention. It's also about contrast, size, and layout complexity and their effect on separation of feedback from the background and from the clutter of other user interface objects.

Locate feedback within the user's focus of attention.

A pop-up dialogue box that appears directly within the user's focus of attention in the middle of the screen is much more noticeable than a message or status line at the top or bottom of the screen.

Make feedback large enough to notice.

32.9.4.3 Feedback legibility

Make text legible, readable.

Text legibility is about being discernable, not about its content being understandable. Font size, font type, color, and contrast are the primary relevant design factors.

32.9.4.4 Feedback presentation complexity

Control feedback presentation complexity with effective layout, organization, and grouping.

Support user needs to locate and be aware of feedback by controlling layout complexity of user interface objects. Screen clutter can obscure needed feedback.

32.9.4.5 Feedback timing

Support user needs to notice feedback with appropriate timing of appearance or display of feedback. Present feedback promptly and with adequate persistence, that is, avoid flashing the feedback briefly and removing it.

Help users detect error situations early.

Example: Don't Let Them Get Into Too Much Trouble

A local software company asked us to inspect one of their software tools. In this tool, users are restricted to certain subsets of functionality based on privileges, which, in turn, are based on various key work roles. A UX problem with a large impact on users arose when users were not aware of which parts of the functionality they were allowed to use.

As the result of a designer assumption that each user would know their privilege-based limitations, users were allowed to navigate deeply into the structure of tasks that they were not supposed to be performing. They could carry out all the steps of the corresponding transactions, but when they tried to "commit" the transaction at the end, they were told they didn't have the privileges to do that task and were blocked, and their time and effort were wasted. The moment when users try to save their work might be a convenient time for a program to check permissions, but it is better for users to realize much earlier when they are on a path to an error, thereby saving lost productivity.

32.9.4.6 Feedback presentation consistency

Maintain a consistent appearance across similar kinds of feedback.
Maintain a consistent location of feedback presentation on the screen to help users notice it quickly.

32.9.4.7 Feedback presentation medium

Consider appropriate alternatives for presenting feedback.

Use the most effective feedback presentation medium.
Consider audio as an alternative channel.

Audio can be more effective than visual media to get users' attention in cases of a heavy task load or heavy sensory work load. Audio is also an excellent alternative for vision-impaired users.

32.9.5 Content and Meaning of Feedback

In Fig. 32-55, we highlight the "content and meaning of feedback" portion of the assessment part of the Interaction Cycle.

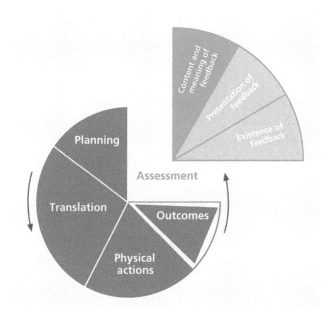

Fig. 32-55
Content/meaning of feedback, within assessment.

The content and meaning of feedback represent the knowledge that must be conveyed to users to be effective in helping them understand action outcomes and interaction progress. This understanding is conveyed through effective content and meaning in feedback, which is dependent on clarity, completeness, proper tone, usage centeredness, and consistency of feedback content.

Help users understand outcomes with effective content/meaning in feedback.

Support user ability to determine the outcomes of their actions through understanding and comprehension of feedback content and meaning.

32.9.5.1 Clarity of feedback

Design feedback for clarity.

Use precise wording and carefully chosen vocabulary to compose correct, complete, and sufficient expressions of content and meaning of feedback.

Support clear understanding of outcome (system state change) so users can assess effect of actions.
Give clear indication of error conditions.

Example: Unavailable?

Fig. 32-56 contains an error message that occurred during a **Save As** file operation in an early version of Microsoft Word. This is a classic example that has generated considerable discussion among our students. The UX problems and design issues extend well beyond just the content of the error message.

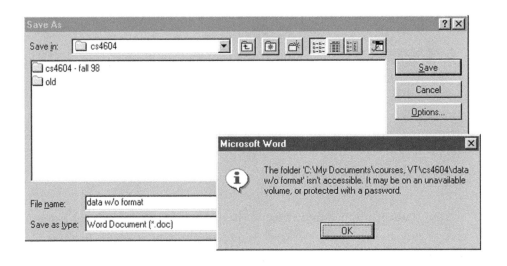

Fig. 32-56

A confusing and seemingly irrelevant error message.

In this **Save As** operation the user was attempting to save a file of unformatted data, calling it "data w/o format" for short. The resulting error message is confusing because it's about a folder not being accessible because of things like unavailable volumes or password protection. This seems about as unclear and unrelated to the task as it could be.

In fact, the only way to understand this message is to understand something more fundamental about the **Save As** dialogue box. The design of the **File Name:** text field is *overloaded*. The usual input entered here is a file name, which is by default associated with the folder name in the **Save in:** field at the top.

But some designer must have said, "That is fine for all the GUI cowards, but what about our legions of former DOS users, our heroic power users who want to enter the full command-style directory path name for the file?" So, the design was overloaded to accept full path names of files as well, but no clue was added to the labeling to reveal this option. Because path names contain the slash (/) as a dedicated delimiter, a slash within a file name cannot be parsed unambiguously, so it's not allowed.

In our class discussions of this example, it usually takes students a long time to realize that the design solution is to unload the overloading by the simple addition of a third text field at the bottom for **Full File Directory Path Name**. Slashes in file names still cannot be allowed because any file name can also appear in a path name, but at least now, when a slash does appear in a file name in the **File Name:** field, a simple message, "Slash is not allowed in file names," can be used to give a clear indication of the real error.

A more recent version of Word half-way solves the problem by adding to the original error message: "or the file name contains a \ or /".

32.9.5.2 Precise wording

Support user understanding of feedback content by precise expression of meaning through precise word choices. Don't allow wording of feedback to be treated as an unimportant part of UX design.

32.9.5.3 Completeness of feedback

Support user understanding of feedback by providing complete information through sufficient expression of meaning, to disambiguate, make more precise, and clarify. For each feedback message, the designer should ask "Is there enough information?" "Are there enough words used to distinguish cases?"

Be complete in your design of feedback; include enough information for users to fully understand outcomes and be either confident that their command worked or certain about why it didn't.

The expression of a cognitive affordance should be complete enough to allow users to fully understand the outcomes of their actions and the status of their course of interaction.

Prevent loss of productivity due to hesitation, pondering.

Having to ponder over the meaning of feedback can lead to lost productivity. Help your users move on to the next step quickly, even if it's error recovery.

Add supplementary information, if necessary.

Short feedback is not necessarily the most effective. If necessary, add additional information to make sure that your feedback information is complete and sufficient.

Give enough information for users to make confident decisions about the status of their course of interaction.
Help users understand what the real error is.
Give enough information about the possibilities or alternatives so users can make an informed response to a confirmation request.

Example: Quick, What to Do?

The exit message from the Microsoft Outlook email system in Fig. 32-57 is an example of not giving enough information for users to make confident decisions. This message is displayed when a user tries to exit the Outlook email system before all queued messages are sent.

When users first encountered this message, they were often unsure about how to respond because it didn't inform them of the consequences of either choice. What are the consequences of "exiting anyway?" If the user exits anyway, does it

Fig. 32-57

Not enough information in this feedback (and feed-forward) message.

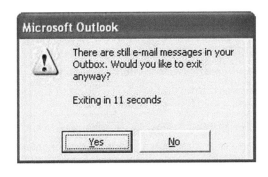

still send the outstanding messages, or do they get lost? One would hope that the system could go ahead and send the messages, regardless, but why, then, did it give this message? So, maybe the user will lose those messages. What made it worse was the fact that control would be snatched away in 11 seconds, and counting. How imperious!

Fig. 32-58 is an updated version of this same message, only this time, it gives a bit more information about the repercussions of exiting prematurely, but it still doesn't say if exiting will cause messages to be lost or just queued for later.

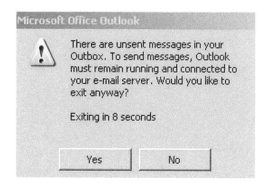

Fig. 32-58
This is better, but still could be more helpful.

32.9.5.4 Tone of feedback expression

When writing the content of a feedback message, it can be tempting to castigate the user for making a "stupid" mistake. As a professional UX designer, you must separate yourself from those feelings and put yourselves in the shoes of the user. You cannot know the conditions under which your error messages are received, but the occurrence of errors could well mean that the user is already in a stressful situation, so don't be guilty of adding to the user's distress with a caustic, sarcastic, or scornful tone.

Design feedback wording, especially error messages, for positive psychological impact.

Make the system take blame for errors.
Be positive, to encourage.
Provide helpful, informative error messages, not "cute" unhelpful messages.

32.9.5.5 Usage centeredness of feedback

Employ usage-centered wording, the language of the user and the work context, in displays, messages, and other feedback.

We mentioned that user centeredness is a design concept that often seems unclear to students and some practitioners. Because it's mainly about using the vocabulary and concepts of the user's work context rather than the technical vocabulary and context of the system, we should probably call it "work-context-centered" design.

In Fig. 32-59, we see a real email system feedback message received by one of us many years ago. It's clearly system centered, if anything, and not user or work context centered. Systems people will argue correctly that the technical information in this message is valuable to them in tracing the source of the problem.

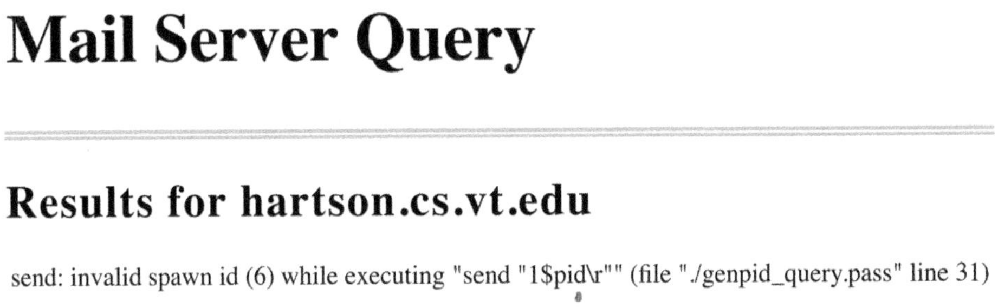

Mail Server Query

Results for hartson.cs.vt.edu

Fig. 32-59
Gobbledygook email message.

send: invalid spawn id (6) while executing "send "1$pid\r"" (file "./genpid_query.pass" line 31)

That is not the issue here; rather, it's a question of the message audience. This message is sent to users, not the systems people, and it's clearly an unacceptable message to users. Designers must seek ways to get the right message to the right audience. One solution is to give a nontechnical explanation here and add a button that says **Click here for a technical description of the problem for your systems representative.** Then, save this jargon for the systems people.

This message in the next example is similar in some ways, but is more interesting in other ways.

Example: Out of Paper, Again?

As an in-class exercise, we used to display the computer message in Fig. 32-60 and ask the students to comment on it.

Some students, usually ones who were not engineering majors, would react negatively from the start. After the usual comments pro and con, we would ask the class whether they thought it was usage centered. This usually caused some confusion and much disagreement. Then we ask a very specific question: Do you think this message is really about an *error*? In truth, the correct answer to this depends on your viewpoint, a reply we *never* got from a student.

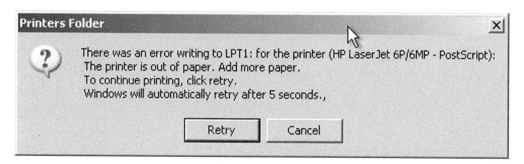

Fig. 32-60

Classic system-centered "error" message.

The system-centered answer is yes; technically an "error condition" arose in the operating system error-handling component when it got an interrupt from the printer, flagging a situation in which there is a need for action to fix a problem. The process used inside the operating system is carried out by what the software systems people call an error-handling routine. This answer is correct, but not absolute.

From a user-, usage-, or work-context-centered view, it's definitely and 100% *not an error.* If you use the printer enough, it will run out of paper, and you will have to replace the supply. So, running out of paper is part of the normal workflow, a natural occurrence that signals a point where the human has a responsibility within the overall collaborative human-system task flow. From this perspective, we told our students we had to conclude that this was not an acceptable message to send to a user; it was not usage centered.

We decided that this exercise was a definitive litmus test for determining whether students could think user centrically. Some of our undergraduate CS students never got it. They stubbornly stuck to their judgment that there was an error and that it was perfectly appropriate to send this message to a user.

32.9.5.6 Consistency of feedback

Be consistent with feedback.

In the context of feedback, the requirement for consistency is essentially the same as it was for the expression of cognitive affordances: choose one term for each concept and use it throughout the application.

Label outcome or destination screen or object consistently with starting point, or departure, and action.

This guideline is a special case of consistency that applies to a situation where a button or menu selection leads the user to a new screen or dialogue box, a common occurrence in interaction flow. This guideline requires that the name of the destination given in the departure button label or menu choice be the same as its name when you arrive at the new screen or dialogue box. The next example is typical of a common violation of this guideline.

Example: Am I in the Right Place?

In Fig. 32-61, we see an overlay of two partial windows within an old personal document system. In the bottom layer is a menu listing some possible operations within this document system. When you click on **Add New Entry**, you go to the window in the top layer, but the title of that window is not **Add New Entry**, it's

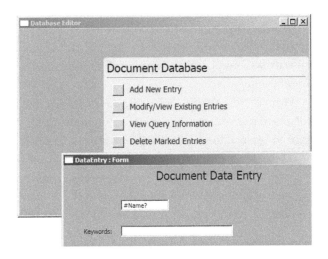

Fig. 32-61

Arrival label doesn't match departure label (screen image courtesy of Raphael Summers).

Document Data Entry. To a user, this *could* mean the same thing, but the words used at the point of departure were **Add New Entry**.

Finding different words, **Document Data Entry**, at the destination can be confusing and can raise doubts about the success of the user action. The explanation given us by the designer was that the destination window in the top layer is a destination shared by both the **Add New Entry** menu choice and the **Modify/View Existing Entries** menu choice. Because state variables are passed in the transition, the corresponding functionality is applied correctly, but the same window was used to do the processing.

Therefore, the designer had picked a name that sort of represented both menu choices. Our opinion was that the destination window name ended up representing neither choice well, and it takes only a little more effort to use two separate windows.

Example: Title of Destination Doesn't Match Simple Search Tab Label

In this example, consider the **Simple Search** tab, displayed at the top of most screens in this digital library application and shown in Fig. 32-62.

Simple Search	Advanced Search	Browse	Register	Submit to CoRR

Fig. 32-62

*The **Simple Search** tab at the top of a digital library application screen.*

That tab leads to a screen that is labeled **Search all bibliographic fields**, as shown in Fig. 32-63.

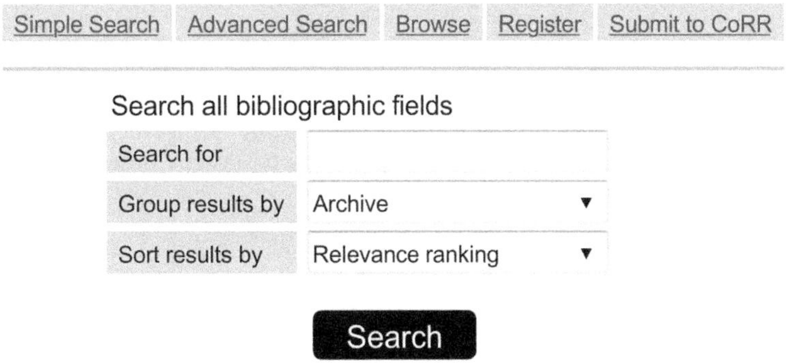

Simple Search	Advanced Search	Browse	Register	Submit to CoRR

Search all bibliographic fields

Search for	
Group results by	Archive ▾
Sort results by	Relevance ranking ▾

Search

Fig. 32-63

*However, it leads to **Search all bibliographic fields**, not a match.*

We had to conclude that the departure label on the **Simple Search** tab and the destination label, Search all bibliographic fields, don't match well enough because we observed users showing surprise upon arrival and not being sure about whether they had arrived at the right place. We suggested a slight change in the wording of the destination label for the **Simple Search** function to include the same name, **Simple Search**, used in the tab and not to sacrifice the additional information in the destination label, **Search all bibliographic fields**, as shown in Fig. 32-64.

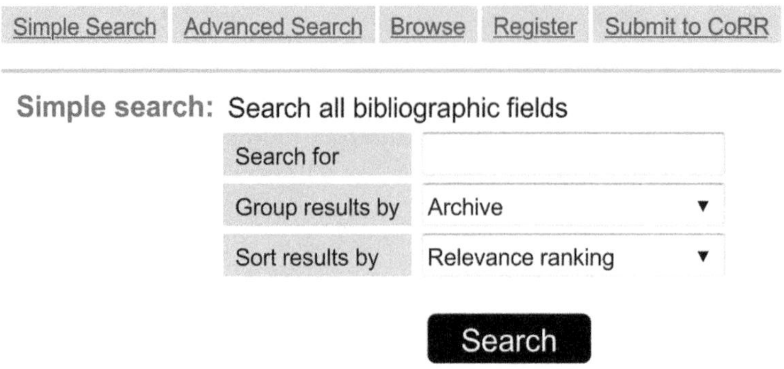

Simple search: Search all bibliographic fields

Search for	
Group results by	Archive ▼
Sort results by	Relevance ranking ▼

Search

Fig. 32-64

Problem fixed by adding **Simple Search:** *to the destination label.*

Fig. 32-65 shows an example of departure and arrival label matching in a network services tool I helped design for Network Infrastructure & Services at Virginia Tech.

Notice how the wording of the button label, **Add Announcement**, in the first screen matches the same wording in the title of the subsequent screen.

32.9.5.7 User control over feedback detail
Organize feedback for ease of understanding.

When a significant volume of feedback detail is available, it's best not to overwhelm the user by giving all the information at once. Rather, give the most important information upfront, establishing the nature of the situation, and provide controls affording the user a way to ask for more details, as needed.

Provide user control over amount and detail of feedback.
Give only most important information at first; more on demand.

32.9.6 Assessment of Information Displays
32.9.6.1 Information organization for presentation
Organize information displays for ease of understanding.

There are entire books available on the topics of information visualization and information display design, among which the work of Tufte (1983, 1990, 1997) is perhaps the most well-known. We don't attempt to duplicate that material here, but rather reference the interested reader to pursue these topics in detail from those sources. We can, however, offer a few simple

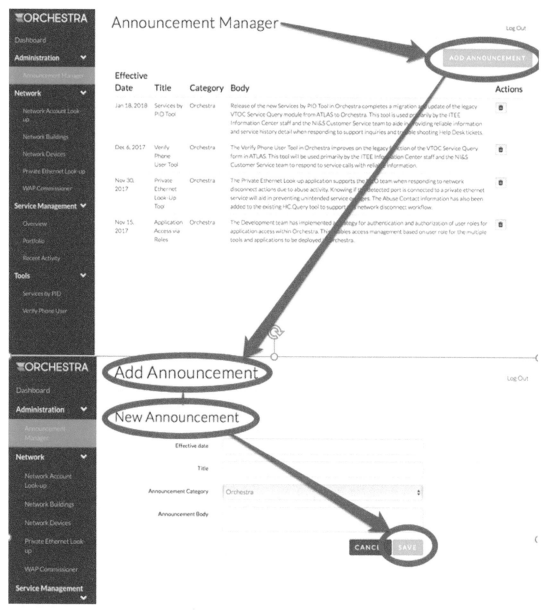

guidelines to help with the routine presentation of information in your displays of results.

Eliminate unnecessary words.
Group related information.
Control density of displays; use white space to set off.

Fig. 32-65

Matching departure and arrival labels in a network services tool. Thanks for permission to use this example to Joe Hutson and Mathew Mathai, Network Infrastructure and Services, Virginia Tech.

Columns are easier to read than wide rows.

This guideline is the reason that newspapers are printed in columns.

Use abstraction per Shneiderman's "mantra": Overview first; zoom and filter; details on demand.

Ben Shneiderman has a "mantra" for controlling complexity in information display design (Shneiderman & Plaisant, 2005, p. 583):

- Overview first.
- Zoom and filter.
- Details on demand.

Example: The Great Train Mystery

Train passengers in Europe will notice entering passengers competing for seats that face the direction of travel. At first, it might seem that this is simply about what people were used to in cars and busses. But some people we interviewed had stronger feelings about it, saying they really were uncomfortable traveling backward and could not enjoy the scenery nearly as much that way.

Believing people in both seats see the same things out the window, we wondered if it really mattered, so we did a little psychological experiment and compared our own user experiences from both sides. We began to think about the view in the train window as an information display.

In terms of bandwidth, though, it didn't seem to matter; the total amount of viewable information was the same. All passengers see the same things and they see each thing for the same amount of time. Then we recalled Ben Shneiderman's rules for controlling complexity in information display design (see earlier discussion).

Applying this guideline to the view from a train window, we realized that a passenger traveling forward is moving *toward* what is in the view. This traveler sees the overview in the distance first, selects aspects of interest, and, as the trains goes by, zooms in on those aspects for details.

In contrast, a passenger traveling backward sees the close-up details first, which then zoom out and fade into an overview in the distance. But this close-up view is not very useful because it arrives too soon without a point of focus. By the time the passenger identifies something of interest, the chance to zoom in on it has passed; it's already getting further away. The result can be an unsatisfying user experience.

32.9.6.2 Visual bandwidth for information display

One of the factors that limit the ability of users to perceive and process displayed information is visual bandwidth of the display medium. If we are talking about the usual computer display, we must use a display monitor with a very small space for all our information presentation. This is tiny in comparison to, say, a newspaper.

When folded open, a newspaper has many times the area, and many times the capacity to display information, of the average computer screen. And a reader/user can scan or browse a newspaper much more rapidly. Reading devices such as Amazon's Kindle and Apple's iPad are pretty good for reading and thumbing through single book pages, but they lack the visual bandwidth afforded for "fanning" through pages for perusal or scanning provided by a real paper book.

Designs that speed up scrolling and paging do help, but it's difficult to beat the browsing bandwidth of paper. A reader can put a finger in one page of a newspaper, scan the major stories on another page, and flash back effortlessly to the "book-marked" page for detailed reading.

Example: Visual Bandwidth

In our UX classes, we used to have an in-class demonstration to illustrate this concept. We started with sheets of paper covered with printed text. Then we gave students a set of cardboard pieces the same size as the paper but each with a smaller cutout through which they must read the text.

One had a narrow vertical cutout that the reader had to scan, or scroll, horizontally across the page. Another had a low horizontal cutout that the reader had to scan vertically up and down the page. A third one had a small square in the middle that limited visual bandwidth in both vertical and horizontal directions and required the user to scroll in both directions.

You can achieve the same effect on a computer screen by resizing the window and adjusting the width and height accordingly. For example, in Fig. 32-66, you can see limited horizontal visual bandwidth, requiring excessive horizontal scrolling to read. In Fig. 32-67, you can see limited vertical visual bandwidth, requiring excessive vertical scrolling to read. And in Fig. 32-68, you can see limited horizontal and vertical visual bandwidth, requiring excessive scrolling in both directions. It was easy for students to conclude that any visual bandwidth limitation, plus the necessary scrolling, was a palpable barrier to the task of reading information displays.

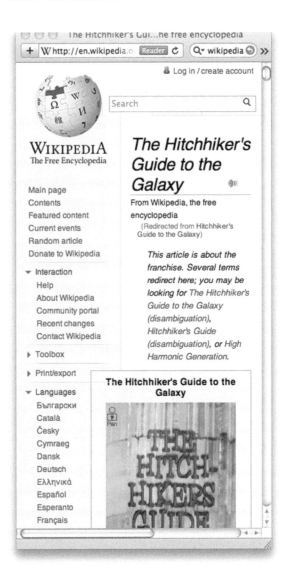

Fig. 32-66

Limited horizontal visual bandwidth.

32.10 OVERALL

This section concludes the litany of guidelines with a set of guidelines that apply globally and generally to an overall UX design rather than being associated with a specific part of the Interaction Cycle.

32.10.1 Overall Simplicity

As Norman (2007b) points out, most people think of simplicity in terms of a product that has all the features but operates with a single button. His point is that people genuinely want features and only say they want simplicity. At least for

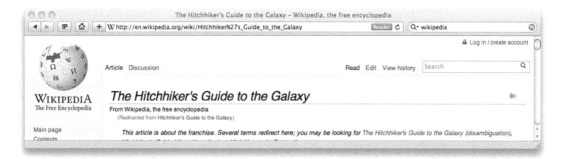

Fig. 32-67
Limited vertical visual bandwidth.

Fig. 32-68
Limited horizontal and vertical visual bandwidth.

consumer appliances, it's all about marketing, and marketing people know that features sell. And more features imply more controls.

Norman (2007b) says that even if a product design automates some features well enough so that fewer controls are necessary, people are willing to pay more for machines with more controls. Users don't want to give up control. Also, more controls give the *appearance* of more power, more functionality, and more features.

But in the computer you use to get things done at work, complexity can be a barrier to productivity. The desire is for full functionality without sacrificing UX.

Don't try to achieve the appearance of simplicity by just reducing usefulness.

A well-known web-search service provider seeking improved ease of use "simplified" their search page. Unfortunately, they did it without a real understanding of what simplicity means. They just reduced their functionality but did nothing to improve the usability of the remaining functionality. The result was a less useful search function, and the user was still left to figure out how to use it.

Organize complex systems to make the most frequent operations simple.

Some systems cannot be entirely simple, but you can still design to make some of the most frequently used operations or tasks as simple as possible. See Isaacson (2012) for an in-depth account of the role of simplicity in Steve Jobs' vision of design. Simplicity for the user often came from attention to the tiniest of details.

Honan (2013) tells us the simple way to simplicity in design: Have the courage to remove layers and features rather than adding them. "Simple doesn't just sell, it sticks. Simple made hits of the Nest thermostat, Fitbit, and TiVo. Simple brought Apple back from the dead. It's why you have Netflix."

Example: Oh, No, They Changed the Phone System!

Years ago, our university began using a special digital phone system. It had, and still has, an enormous amount of functionality. Everyone in the university was asked to attend a one-day workshop on how to use the new phone system. Most employees rebelled and refused to attend a workshop to learn how to use a telephone—something they had been using all their lives.

They were issued a 50-page user's guide entitled "Excerpts from the PhoneMail System User Guide." Fifty pages and still an excerpt; who is going to read that? The answer is that almost everyone had to read at least parts of it because the designer's approach was to make all functions equally difficult to do. The 10% of the functionality that people had to use every day was just as mysterious as the other 90% that most people would never need. Decades later, people still don't like that phone system, but they were captive users.

32.10.2 Overall Consistency

Historically, "be consistent" is one of the earliest UX design guidelines ever and probably the most often quoted. Things that work the same way in one place as they do in another just make logical sense.

But when HCI researchers have looked closely at the concept of consistency in UX design over the years, many have concluded that it's often difficult to pin it down in specific designs. Grudin (1989) shows that the concept is difficult to define (p. 1164) and hard to identify in a design, concluding that it's an issue without much real substance. The transfer effects that support ease of learning can conflict with ease of use (p. 1166). In the context of designing an ecology, consistency across devices is trumped by more important issues such as maintaining usage context as users cross device boundaries (Pyla, Tungare, & Pérez-Quiñones, 2006). And blind adherence without interpretation within usage context to the rule can lead to foolish or undesirable consistency, as shown in the next example.

Be consistent by doing similar things in similar ways.

Example: And What Country Shall We Send It To?

Suppose that the menu choices in all pull-down menus in an application are ordered alphabetically for fast searching. But one pull-down menu is in a form in which the user enters a mailing address. One of the fields in the form is for "country," and the pull-down list contains dozens of entries. Because the majority of customers for this website are expected to live in the United States, ease of use will be better in a design with "United States" at the top of the pull-down list instead of near the bottom of an alphabetical list, even though that is inconsistent with all the other pull-down menus in the application.

Use consistent layout/location for objects across screens.
Maintain custom style guides to support consistency.

32.10.2.1 Structural consistency

We think Reisner (1977) helped clarify the concept of consistency, in the context of database query languages, when she coined the term "structural consistency." In referring to the use of query languages, structural consistency simply required similar syntax (wording or user actions) to denote similar or related semantics. So, in our context, the expression of cognitive affordances for two similar functions should also be similar.

However, in some situations, consistency can work against distinguishability. For example, if a design contains two different kinds of delete functions, one of which is used routinely to delete objects within an application, but the other is dangerous because it applies to files and folders at a higher level, the need to distinguish these delete functions for safety may override this guideline for making them similar.

Use structurally similar names and labels for objects and functions that are structurally similar.

Example: Next and Previous

A simple example is seen in the common **Next** and **Previous** buttons that might appear, for example, for navigation among pictures in an online photo gallery. Although these two buttons are opposite in meaning, they both are a similar *kind* of thing; they are symmetric and structurally similar navigation controls. Therefore, they should be labeled in a similar way. For example, **Go Forward** and **Previous Picture** are not as symmetric and not as similar from a linguistic perspective.

32.10.2.2 Consistency is not absolute

Many design situations have more than one consistency issue, and sometimes, they trade off against each other. We have a good example to illustrate.

Example: May I Mix You a Screwdriver?

Consider the case of multi-blade screwdrivers that are handy for dealing with different sizes and types of screws. In particular, they each have both flat-head and Phillips-head driver bits, and each of these types comes in both small and large sizes.

Fig. 32-69 illustrates two of these so-called "4-in-1" screwdrivers. As part of a discussion of consistency, we bring screwdrivers like these to class for an in-class

Fig. 32-69
Multipurpose screwdrivers.

exercise with students. We begin by showing the class the screwdrivers and explain how the bits are interchangeable to get the needed combination of head type and size.

Next, we pick a volunteer to hold and study one of these tools and then speak to the class about consistency issues in its design. They pull it apart, as shown in Fig. 32-70.

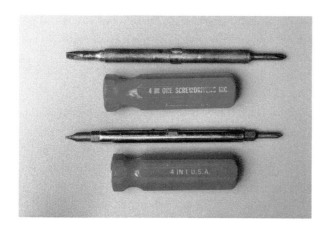

Fig. 32-70
Revealing the inner parts of the two screwdrivers.

The conclusion always is that it's a consistent design. We have another volunteer study the other screwdriver, always reaching the same conclusion. Then, we show the class that there are differences between the two designs, which become apparent when you compare the bits at the ends of each tool, as shown in Fig. 32-71.

One tool is consistent by head type, having both flat heads, large and small, on one insertable piece and both Phillips heads on the other piece. The other

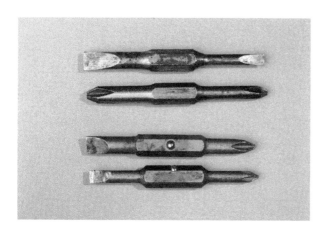

Fig. 32-71
The two sets of screwdriver bits.

tool is consistent by size, having both large heads on one insertable piece and both small heads on the other piece.

We now ask them if they still think each design is consistent, and they do. They are each consistent; they each have intra-product consistency. Neither is more consistent than the other, but each is consistent in a different way and are not consistent with each other.

Consistency in design is supposed to aid predictability, but, because there is more than one way to be consistent in this example, you still lack interproduct consistency, and you don't necessarily get predictability. Such is one difficulty of interpreting and applying this seemingly simple design guideline.

32.10.2.3 Consistency can work against innovation

Final caveat: While a style guide works in favor of consistency and reuse, remember that it also can be a barrier to inventiveness and innovation (Kantrovich, 2004). Being the same all the time is not necessarily cool! When the need arises to break with consistency for the sake of innovation, throw off the constraints and barriers and be creative.

32.10.3 Reducing Friction

A recent term for poor usability is "friction." One definition is: "In user experience, friction is defined as interactions that inhibit people from intuitively and painlessly achieving their goals within a digital interface.[4]" "Frictionless UX has now become the new standard." Part of the requirement is to capture the full user/customer journey on your usage research. Perhaps the most important aspect is to understand and design for the entire ecology, not just tasks and devices.

Example: Frictionless Apple

In one of his *Scientific American* TechnoFiles column, David Pogue gave a good example of low friction in an ecology (Pogue, 2012): "A few months back I was at the main Apple Store in New York City. I wanted to buy a case for my son's iPod Touch—but it was December 23. The crowds were so thick, I envied sardines.

Fortunately, I knew something that most of these people didn't: I could grab an item off the shelf, scan it with my iPhone and walk right out. Thanks to the free

---

[4]https://www.dtelepathy.com/blog/business/strategic-ux-the-art-of-reducing-friction

Apple Store app, I didn't have to wait in line or even find an employee. The purchase was instantly billed to my Apple account. I was in and out of there in two minutes."

32.10.4 Humor

Avoid poor attempts at humor.

Poor attempts at humor usually don't work. It's easy to do humor badly, and it can easily be misinterpreted by users. You may be sitting in your office feeling good and want to write a cute error message, but users receiving it may be tired and stressed, and the last thing they need is the irritation of a bad joke, especially if this is not the first time they were subjected to it.

32.10.5 Anthropomorphism

Simply put, anthropomorphism is the attribution of human characteristics to nonhuman objects. We do it every day; it's a form of humor. You say, "my car is sick today," or "my computer doesn't like me," and everyone understands what you mean. In UX design, however, the context is usually about getting work done, and anthropomorphism can be less appreciated. A case can be made for and against anthropomorphism. We start with the case against.

32.10.5.1 Avoiding anthropomorphism

Avoid the use of anthropomorphism in UX designs.

Shneiderman and Plaisant (2005, pp. 80, 484) say that a model of computers that leads one to believe they can think, know, or understand in ways that humans do is erroneous and dishonest. When the deception is revealed, it undermines trust.

Avoid using first-person speech in system dialogue.

"Sorry, but I cannot find the file you need" is less honest and no more informative than something such as "File not found" or "File doesn't exist." If attribution must be given to what it is that cannot find your file, you can reduce anthropomorphism by using the third person, referring to the software, as in "Windows is unable to find the application that created this file." This guideline urges us to especially eschew chatty and overly friendly use of first-person cuteness, as we see in the next example.

Example: Who Is There?

Fig. 32-72 contains a message from a database system after a search request had been submitted. Ignoring other obvious UX problems with this dialogue box and message, most users find this kind of use of first person as dishonest, demeaning, and unnecessary.

Fig. 32-72

Message tries to make computer seem like a person.

Avoid condescending offers to help.

Just when you think all hope is lost, then along comes Clippy or Bob, your personal office assistant or helpful agent. How intrusive and ingratiating! Most users dislike this kind of pandering and insinuating into your affairs, offering blandishments of hope when real help is preferred.

People expect other humans to be able to solve problems better than a machine. If your interaction dialogue portrays the machine as a human, users will expect more. When you cannot deliver, however, it's overpromising. The example that follows is ridiculous and cute, but it also makes our point.

Example: Come on, Clippy, You Can Do Better

Clearly the pop-up "help" in Fig. 32-73 is not a real example, but this kind of pop-up in general can be intrusive. In real usage situations, most users expect better.

32.10.5.2 The case in favor of anthropomorphism

On the affirmative side, Murano (2006) shows that, in some contexts, anthropomorphic feedback can be more effective than the equivalent nonanthropomorphic feedback. He also makes the case for why users sometimes prefer anthropomorphic feedback, based on subconscious social behavior of humans toward computers.

Fig. 32-73
Only too glad to help.

In his first study, Murano (2006) explored user reactions to language-learning software with speech input and output using speech recognition. Users were given anthropomorphic feedback in the form of dynamically loaded and software-activated video clips of a real language tutor giving feedback.

In this kind of software usage situation, where the objectives and interaction are very similar to what would be expected from a human language tutor, "the statistical results suggested the anthropomorphic feedback to be more effective. Users were able to self-correct their pronunciation errors more effectively with the anthropomorphic feedback. Furthermore, it was clear that users preferred the anthropomorphic feedback." The positive results are not surprising because this kind of application naturally uses human-computer interaction that is very close to natural human-to-human interaction.

In another study, Murano (2006) determined that, for direction-finding tasks, a map plus some guiding text was more effective than anthropomorphic feedback using video clips of a human giving directions verbally, with user preferences nearly evenly divided. The bottom line for Murano is that some application domains are more suited for anthropomorphic interaction than others.

Well-known studies by Reeves and Nass (1996) attempted to answer the question why anthropomorphic interaction might be better for some users in some kinds of applications. They concluded that people naturally tend to interact with a computer the same social way we interact with people, in cases where feedback is given as natural language speech (Nass, Steuer, & Tauber, 1994). People treat computers in a social manner if the output of computers treats them in a social manner. And, of course, the case in favor of anthropomorphism is strong for systems specifically designing to carry out conversations and otherwise behave as a living being, such as Apple's Siri and Amazon's Alexa.

While a social manner of interaction did seem to be effective and desired by users of tasks that have a human-to-human counterpart, including tasks such as natural language learning and tutoring in a teacher-student kind of interaction, it's unlikely that a mutually social style and anthropomorphic interaction would have a place in the thousands of other kinds of tasks that make up a large portion of real computer usage—installing a device driver software, creating a text document, updating a data spreadsheet,

The bottom line is to tread carefully with anthropomorphism: A computer is not human. Eventually, expectations will not be met. Especially for the use of computers to get things done in business and work environments, we expect users to tire quickly of anthropomorphic feedback, particularly if it soon becomes boring by a lack of variety over time.

32.10.6 Tone and Psychological Impact

Use a tone in dialogue that supports a positive psychological impact.
Avoid violent, negative, demeaning terms.
Avoid use of psychologically threatening terms, such as "illegal," "invalid," and "abort."
Avoid use of the term "hit"; instead use "press" or "click."

32.10.7 Use of Sound and Color

"Color is one of the most powerful tools in the designer's toolkit. You can use color to impact users' emotions, draw their attention, and put them in the right frame of mind to make a purchase. It's also one of the main factors in customers' perception of a brand," (Alvarez, 2014).

Avoid irritation with annoying sound and color in displays.

Glaring colors, blinking graphics, and harsh audio not only are annoying but can have a negative effect on user productivity and the user experience over the long-term.

Use color conservatively.

Don't count on color to convey much information in your designs. It's good advice to render your design in black and white first so that you know it works without reliance on color. That will rule out usability problems some users may have with color perception due to different forms of color blindness, for example.

Use pastels, not bright colors.

Bright colors seem attractive at first, but soon lead to distraction, visual fatigue, and distaste. Exception: Bright colors on websites are memorable (Alvarez, 2014).

Be aware of color conventions (e.g., avoid red, except for urgency).

Again, color conventions are beyond our scope. They are complicated and differ with international cultural conventions. One clear-cut convention in our Western culture is about the use of red. Beyond very limited use for emergency or urgent situations, red, especially blinking red, is alarming as well as irritating and distracting.

Complementary color schemes (e.g., red/green, blue/orange, purple/yellow) are energizing (Alvarez, 2014).
Red is associated with danger, hunger, speed. So a website for fast food would include both latter factors (Alvarez, 2014).

Shades of blue and green are calming (Alvarez, 2014).
Low color contrast can be aesthetic, but high color contrast is easier to read (Alvarez, 2014).

Example: Help, Am I at Sea?

Fig. 32-74 is a map of the Outer Banks in North Carolina. We have never been able to use this map easily because it violates deeply ingrained color conventions used in maps. Blue is almost always used to denote water in maps, while gray, brown, green, or something similar is used for land. In this map, however, a deep blue is used to represent land and because there is about as much land as sea in this map, users experience a cognitive disconnect that confuses and makes it difficult to get oriented.

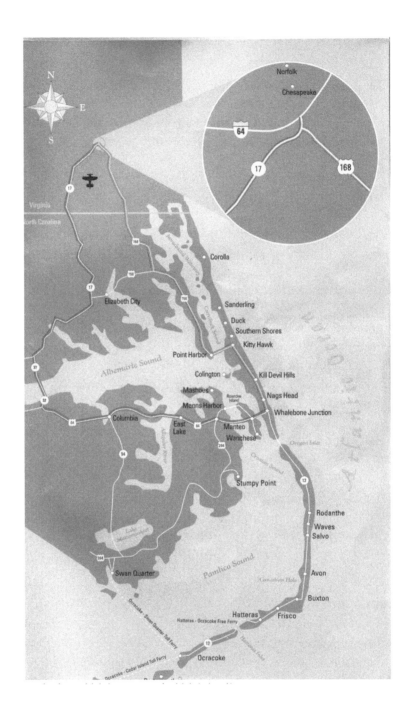

Fig. 32-74

Map of Outer Banks, but which is water and which is land?

Watch out for focusing problem with red and blue.

Chromostereopsis is the phenomenon humans face when viewing an image containing significant amounts of pure red and pure blue. Because red and blue are at opposite ends of the visual light spectrum and occur at different frequencies, they focus at slightly different depths within the eye and can appear to be at different distances from the eye. Adjacent red and blue in an image can cause the muscles used to focus the eye to oscillate, moving back and forth between the two colors, eventually leading to blurriness and fatigue.

Example: Roses Are Red; Violets Are Blue

In Fig. 32-75 we placed adjacent patches of blue and red. If the color reproduction in the book is good, some readers may experience chromostereopsis while viewing this figure.

Fig. 32-75

Chromostereopsis: humans focus at different depths in the eye for red and blue.

Get professional help with color in design.

The use of color in design is a complex topic that fills volumes of publications for research and practice, well beyond the scope of this book. Read more about it in some of these classic works (Albers, 1974; Christ, 1975; Nowell, Schulman, & Hix, 2002; Rice, 1991a, 1991b).

Bera (2016) points out the dangers of misusing color in UX designs. Too often color choices are left to software developers, who frequently select them indiscriminately. "Business dashboards that overuse or misuse colors cause cognitive overload for users who then take longer to make decisions." "Use of colors can needlessly attract viewers' attention, causing them to search for meaning that is not there." One possible solution might be to build smart color capabilities into UX designer and software developer tools (Webster, 2014).

Color and branding. Branding is about eliciting emotion in favor of a product or brand.

Beyond this kind of commercial or organizational constraint, there are too many considerations about the use of color in design to cover completely here. The use of color in visual design involves many complicated psychological factors, and color "standards" can be complicated and will differ by international cultural conventions. The topic deserves a book or a course all on its own.

32.10.8 Text Legibility

It's obvious that text cannot convey the intended content if it's illegible.

Make presentation of text legible.
Make font size large enough for all users.
Use good contrast with background.

Use both color and intensity to provide contrast.

Use mixed case for extensive text.
Avoid too many different fonts, sizes.
Use legible fonts.
Use color other than blue for text.

It's difficult for the human retina to focus on pure blue for reading.

Accommodate sensory disabilities and limitations.

Support visually challenged, color blind users.

32.10.9 User Preferences

Allow user settings, preference options to control presentational parameters.

Afford users control of sound levels, blinking, color, and so on. Vision-impaired users, especially, need preference settings or options to adjust the text size in application displays and possibly to hear an alternative audio version of the text.

32.10.10 Accommodation of User Differences

As we have said, a treatise on accessibility is outside our scope and is treated well in the literature. Nonetheless, all UX designers should be aware of the requirement to accommodate users with special needs.

Accommodate different levels of expertise/experience with preferences.

Most of us have seen this sign in our offices or on a bumper sticker: Lead, follow, or get out of the way. In UX design, we might modify that slightly to: Lead, follow, *and* get out of the way.

- Lead novice users with adequate cognitive affordances.
- Follow intermittent or intermediate users with lots of feedback to keep them on track.
- Get out of the way of expert users; keep cognitive affordances from interfering with their physical actions.

Constantine (1994b) has made the case to design for intermediate users, which he calls the most neglected user segment. He claims that there are more intermediate users than beginners or experts.

Don't let affordances for new users be performance barriers to experienced users.

Although cognitive affordances provide essential scaffolding for inexperienced users, expert users interested in pure productivity need effective physical affordances and few cognitive affordances.

32.10.11 Helpful Help
Be helpful with Help.

Don't send your users to Help in a handbasket. For those who share our warped sense of humor, we quote from the manual for Dirk Gently's (Adams, 1990, p. 101) electronic *I Ching* calculator as an example of perhaps not so helpful help. As the protagonist consults the calculator for help to a burning personal question,

> The little book of instructions suggested that he should simply concentrate "soulfully" on the question which was "besieging" him, write it down, ponder on it, enjoy the silence, and then once he had achieved inner harmony and tranquility,

he should push the red button. There wasn't a red button, but there was a blue button marked "Red" and this Dirk took to be the one.

Entertaining, yes; helpful, no. Note that it also makes reference at the end to an amusing little problem with cognitive affordance consistency.

32.11 CONCLUSIONS

Be cautious using guidelines.
Use careful thought and interpretation when using guidelines.
In application, guidelines can conflict and overlap.
Guidelines don't guarantee a quality user experience.
Using guidelines doesn't eliminate need for UX testing.
Design by guidelines, not by politics or personal opinion.

Background: Affordances, the Interaction Cycle, and UX Design Guidelines

33

Highlights

- A little background on affordances.
- Confusion over affordances in early HCI/UX.
- How functional affordances fit in with Gibson's ecological view of affordances.
- Examples of how cognitive affordances can be informed by shared conventions.
- Where did UX design guidelines come from?

33.1 THIS IS A REFERENCE CHAPTER

This chapter contains reference material relevant to the other chapters of Part 7. This chapter is not intended to be read through as a regular chapter, but each section is supposed to be read when a reference to it in the main chapters is encountered.

33.2 A LITTLE HISTORY OF THE CONCEPT OF AFFORDANCES

Who "invented" the concept of affordances? Of course, we all know it was Donald Norman (not really).

Donald Norman. Norman was the one who introduced the concept of affordances to HCI and UX, using the term in his 1988 book, *The Psychology of Everyday Things*, a book he later renamed *The Design of Everyday Things*. He was a psychologist and rightly saw that usage and usability were about psychology, but the real point of his book was design. In any case, Norman was not the first to use the term "affordance" itself.

J. J. Gibson. It's always risky to make a claim about who used a particular term first, but we think in this case it was J. J. Gibson, more than a decade earlier than when it emerged in HCI. In 1977, he wrote an article on the theory of affordances (Gibson, 1977), and followed up with a complete book on his ecological approach to visual perception (Gibson, 1979).

As an ecological psychologist, Gibson saw animal perception, especially human perception, tied closely to the setting—to the objects that constitute the environment of the animal and how they offer different capabilities to the animal. So, in this light, an affordance is something in a person's environment that helps them do what they need to while they are living their life.

One of the simplest examples he gave was to think about the hard surface of the ground. If it can support my weight, it affords my standing or sitting on that piece of ground. That was Gibson's notion of affordance.

Gaver. Beyond Gibson and Norman, Gaver (1991) had an influence on our thinking about affordances. Gaver (1991) saw affordances in design as a way of focusing on strengths and weaknesses of technologies with respect to the possibilities they offer to people who use them.

He extended the concepts by showing how complex actions can be described in terms of groups of affordances, sequential in time and/or nested in space, showing how affordances can be revealed over time, with successive user actions, for example, in the multiple actions of a hierarchical drop-down menu. Gaver (1991) defined his own terms somewhat differently from those of Norman or Gibson.

McGrenere and Ho. McGrenere and Ho (2000) were another important influence on our work, but they used yet a different terminology that they then compared to Gaver's vocabulary, demonstrating the need for a richer, more consistent, standard vocabulary. Now, the literature about affordances continues to grow. For example, it was featured prominently in CHI 2012, the annual conference in HCI and UX.

That McGrenere and Ho (2000) also needed to calibrate their terminology against Gaver's further demonstrates the difficulty of discussing these concepts without a structured understanding and a more consistent vocabulary.

In most of the related literature, design of cognitive affordances (whatever they are called in a given paper) is acknowledged to be about design for the cognitive part of usability, ease of use in the form of learnability for new and intermittent users (who need the most help in knowing how to do something). All authors who write about affordances give their own definitions of the concept, but there is scant mention beyond cognitive affordances to, for example, physical affordance design.

Physical affordance

A design feature that helps, aids, supports, facilitates, or enables user physical actions: clicking, touching, pointing, gesturing, and moving things (Section 30.3).

Sensory affordance is neglected even more in the literature. Most other authors include sensory affordance only implicitly and/or lumped in with cognitive affordance rather than featuring it as a separate explicit concept. Thus, when these authors talk about perceiving affordances, including Gaver's (1991) and McGrenere and Ho's (2000) phrase "perceptibility of an affordance," they are referring (in our terms) to a combination of sensing (e.g., seeing) and understanding physical affordances through sensory affordances and cognitive affordances.

Gaver refers to this same mix of affordances when he says, "People perceive the environment directly in terms of its potential for action." In contrast, our use of the term "sense" has a markedly narrower orientation toward discerning via sensory inputs such as seeing and hearing.

33.3 CONFUSION OVER AFFORDANCES IN EARLY HCI/UX

Norman rightly thought that this idea of affordance was useful in usability and interaction design. But the problem was that people were using the term very loosely in the HCI literature. The term "affordance" was becoming overused, misused, confused, and abused. As a result, the concept was not working well as part of our common ground to communicate efficiently and precisely.

Preamble to Norman's, 1999 article. And Norman, seeing this confusion, got upset and, in good Norman fashion, he decried this situation in his 1999 article, "I was lurking in the background of a CHI-Web discussion, when I lost all reason: I just couldn't take it anymore. 'I put an affordance here and an affordance there,' a participant would say, 'I wonder if that object affords clicking.' 'Affordances this, affordances that...' 'No!' I screamed, and out came this note," (Norman, 1999).

In hopes of clarifying the distinctions among types of affordances, Norman came up with terms like "real affordances" and "perceived affordances" and tried to tie them to the concepts of Gibson, with whom he had spent some time in discussion.

However, it seems that his attempt to clarify only muddied the waters. People still didn't get it and continued to use the term "affordance" with little shared understanding.

Hartson's taxonomy of affordances. So, I decided to try my hand at it and wrote a paper using terminology that I thought could help HCI and UX practitioners correctly identify and use the different kinds of affordances (Hartson, 2003).

I tried to connect affordances to human-centered interaction concepts, to the things we humans do as we interact with any kind of machine—our sensory actions, our cognitive actions, and our physical actions. I also thought it was important to show how you can think of interaction design in terms of the affordances that go with these different kinds of actions. So far, the ideas in this article have held up well over time, and they are the foundation for Chapter 30 on affordances.

33.4 EXAMPLES OF HOW COGNITIVE AFFORDANCES CAN BE INFORMED BY SHARED CULTURAL CONVENTIONS

Mailboxes as a symbolic cognitive affordance. One of your authors, Pardha Pyla, grew up in India, and when he would see early software computer systems that used an icon like this for a mail program, he would wonder, well, "What is that thing?" Most homes in India don't even have a mailbox, the postman knocks (twice?) on the door and delivers the mail directly to the occupant. Even when places did have an external mailbox, they didn't *look* like this. So, he had no context for sharing that convention.

Only when Pardha got to the United States did he see these things, and, upon close investigation, realize that these are mailboxes. Only later did he also discover it's a federal offense to investigate other people's mailboxes.

Exit Signs in the United States versus Europe. The pictures in Fig. 33-1 show two different kinds of exit signs.

The one on the left has shared meaning in the United States. It is bright red, signifying danger (although maybe an exit should represent safety in the face of danger, but never mind). It has arrows indicating the direction to go.

However, in Europe and some other parts of the world, they use something like the sign on the right-hand side of the figure. Its meaning seems fairly clear on

Fig. 33-1

Exit signs from two different cultures.

the surface of it, but in this country, a panicked person in a state of emergency might find it unfamiliar and possibly confusing.

Relying on the inherent characteristics of a Coke bottle. As we said in Section 30.2.1.4, a shared cultural understanding often conveys much of the meaning of cognitive affordances. In the absence of an applicable cultural convention, we are left to rely solely on deducing meaning from the inherent characteristics of an object.

What do you think of the very familiar shape of a Coke bottle? What are some affordances that you can think of that might go with it? Just by looking at it, what do you think you can do with it? Good physical affordance to grip it, the functional affordance to hold liquid to drink, possibly a nice aesthetic look as an emotional affordance. All of these are relative to our own experience in seeing, holding, and using these bottles for their intended purpose—a container for a refreshing drink.

In a graduate class of UX design students, we raised the question of how some of our most reliable cognitive affordances (e.g., how to operate a doorknob) might be perceived by people "from another planet," who did not have the same shared conventions. We handed out identical empty Coke bottles to several groups and asked them to look at the bottles, to hold and handle them, and to think about what kinds of uses the inherent affordances evoke. We wanted them to get down to Gibson's ecological level.

Students responded with the usual answers about affordances evinced by sight and touch. Visually, a Coke bottle has obvious affordances as a vessel to hold, for example, flowers, or it can serve as a rough volume-measuring device. The heft and sturdiness sensed when held in one's hand indicate affordances to serve as a paperweight, a plumb bob on a string, or even an oddly shaped rolling pin.

But what if you've never seen or heard of a Coke bottle before? Then how do you figure out what it is and what it is used for? That is the basis for the movie *The Gods Must Be Crazy.*

It opens with the pilot of a small plane flying over Southern Africa. He is drinking the last of a Coke, and he throws the empty bottle out the window. Down and down it floats.

As this puzzling artifact from another culture lands at the feet of a bushman in the deep Kalahari, the scene deals directly with affordances. This man is seeing a Coke bottle for the first time. Naturally, he takes it back to his village to show his friends. To the villagers, it is a strange and beautiful thing, but they are puzzled about what it could be used for (its functional affordances) and how to use it (the cognitive affordances).

Emotional affordance

A design feature that helps a user make an emotional connection resulting in emotional impact within the user experience (Section 30.6).

Its appearance triggers a curious exploration of the possibilities of this object within their own Kalahari culture. It is transparent, like water, but it was very hard. They wonder why the "gods" have sent this thing down to the earth, and what it might be used for.

This part of the movie makes the point about ecological affordances so well. Because the Kalahari Bushmen have never seen a Coke bottle (or any drink bottle) in their lives, there is no shared convention about its "meaning"—namely, what it is used for. They can rely only on its inherent characteristics as clues to deduce its possible uses, without influence from cultural conventions or practice. These characteristics are pure ecological cognitive affordances, the inherent, raw, Gibson-style affordances of an object in its environment.

Their ecological exploration led to interesting and sometimes amusing effects. One guy got his finger stuck in the top, and the children thought *that* was funny. By blowing over the opening, some discovered it could be an entertainment device with which they could make odd sounds and music. After much exploration they saw the smooth, hard, and curved surface was *perfect* for curing snake skins. Perhaps it could even be used as a weapon to attack one another.

Every day they discovered a new use for the thing sent by the gods. One obvious use was to transport water. Its efficacy in mashing soft roots and other vegetables and grinding grain made it a most useful labor-saving device. You can learn quite a bit about affordances by watching Kalahari Bushmen explore a newfound Coke bottle.

That these affordances became so apparent to the Bushmen, but might not be obvious to most people from an industrialized part of the world, indicates the impact of social experience and cultural conventions on influencing, and even prejudicing, one's perception of an object's affordances.

Gibson's ecological view of affordances

Perspective on affordances that says knowledge inherent in objects and devices can give us clues as to their operation. Gibson (1977) studied the relationship between a living being (e.g., a human) and its environment, in particular what the environment offers or affords being— for example, how a horizontal rigid surface affords support for a person for standing (Section 30.2.1.3).

33.5 HOW FUNCTIONAL AFFORDANCES FIT IN WITH GIBSON'S ECOLOGICAL VIEW

We bring Gibson's ecological view into UX design by describing a purpose for each instance of a user interaction, namely, the associated functional affordance. Putting the user's purpose into the picture harmonizes nicely with our interaction- and user-oriented view in which *an affordance helps or aids the user in doing something.*

McGrenere and Ho (2000) also refer to the concept of application usefulness, something they call "affordances in software," which are at the root of supporting a connection between the dual concepts of usability and usefulness (Landauer, 1995). In an external view, it is easy to see a system function as an affordance because it helps the user do something in the work domain.

This again demonstrates the need for a richer vocabulary, and conceptual framework, to take the discussion of affordances beyond user interfaces to the larger context of overall system design. We use the term *functional affordance* to denote this kind of higher level user enablement in the work domain.

Usefulness

A component of user experience based on utility, system functionality that gives users the ability to accomplish the goals of work (or play) through using the system or product (Section 1.4.3).

33.6 WHERE DID UX DESIGN GUIDELINES COME FROM?

We cannot talk about UX design guidelines without giving a profound acknowledgement to what is perhaps the mother (and father) of all guidelines publications, the book of 944 design guidelines for text-based user interfaces of bygone days that Smith and Mosier of Mitre Corporation developed for the U.S. Air Force (Mosier & Smith, 1986; Smith & Mosier, 1986).

We were already working in human-computer interaction (HCI) and read it with great interest when it came out. Almost a decade later, an electronic version became available (Iannella, 1995). Other early guidelines collections include Engel and Granda (1975), Brown (1988), and Boff and Lincoln (1988).

UX design guidelines appropriate to the technology of the day appeared throughout the history of HCI, including "the design of idiot-proof interactive programs" (Wasserman, 1973); ground rules for a "well-behaved" system (Kennedy, 1974); design guidelines for interactive systems (Pew & Rollins, 1975); usability maxims (Lund, 1997); and eight golden rules of interface design (Shneiderman, 1998). Every author and practitioner had a favorite set of design guidelines or maxims.

Eventually, of course, the attention of design guidelines followed the transition to graphical user interfaces (Nielsen, 1990; Nielsen et al., 1992). As GUIs evolved, many of the guidelines became platform specific, such as style guides for Microsoft Windows and Apple. Each has its own set of detailed requirements for compliance with the respective product lines.

As an example from the 1990s, an interactive product from Apple called Making it Macintosh (Alben, Faris, & Saddler, 1994; Apple Computer Inc, 1993) used computer animations to highlight the Macintosh user interface design principles, primarily to preserve the Macintosh look and feel. Many of the early style guides, such as OSF Motif (Open Software Foundation, 1990) and IBM's Common User Access (Berry, 1988), came built into software tools for enforcing that particular style.

The principles behind the guidelines came mainly from human psychology. Our friend Tom Hewett (1999) was probably the most steadfast HCI voice for understanding psychology as a foundation for UX design principles and guidelines. These principles first evolved into design guidelines in human factors engineering.

Some UX design guidelines, especially those coming from human factors, are supported with empirical data. Most guidelines, however, have earned their authority from a strong grounding in the practice and shared experience of the UX community—experience in design and evaluation, experience in analyzing and solving UX problems.

Based on the National Cancer Institute's Research-Based Web Design and Usability Guidelines project begun in March 2000, the U.S. Department of Health and Human Services has published a book containing an extensive set of UX design guidelines and associated reference material (U.S. Department of Health and Human Services, 2006). Each guideline has undergone extensive internal and external review with respect to tracking down its sources, estimating its relative importance in application, and determining the "strength of evidence," for example, strong research support versus weak research support, supporting the guideline.

As is the case in most domains, design guidelines finally opened the way for standards (Abernethy, 1993; Billingsley, 1993; Brown, 1993; Quesenbery, 2005; Strijland, 1993).

Parting Thoughts

Congratulations! You made it through the book. Thank you for hanging in there. If you get to apply this as a UX practitioner, good luck and don't forget these guiding principles:

Be goal-directed.
If it ain't broke, you can still fix it and make it fantastic.
Don't be dogmatic; use your common sense.
Envision usage in context.

The answer to most questions is "it depends."

It's about the people.
Everything should be evaluated in its own way.
Improvise, adapt, and overcome.
But first, plan, prepare, and anticipate.
Keep calm and carry on.
Failure is a good option, only we call it succeeding by learning early about what doesn't work.
The answer is 42.

References

ABC News Nightline (1999). *Deep Dive.*

Abernethy, C. N. (1993). Expanding jurisdictions and other facets of human-machine interface IT standards. *Standard View, 1*(1), 9–21. https://doi.org/10.1145/174683.174685.

Acohido, B. (1999). Did similar switches confuse pilots?—Controls' proximity another aspect of crash probe. In: *Seattle Times Investigative Reporter.* November 18, Retrieved from http://community.seattletimes.nwsource.com/archive/?date=19991118&slug=2996058.

Adams, D. (1990). *The long dark tea-time of the soul* (1st ed.). New York, NY: Pocket Books.

Adler, C. (2011). Ideas are overrated: startup guru Eric Ries' radical new theory. *Wired Magazine, 19*(09), 34.

Alben, L., Faris, J., & Saddler, H. (1994). Making it Macintosh: designing the message when the message is design. *interactions, 1*(1), 11–20. https://doi.org/10.1145/174800.174802.

Albers, J. (1974). *Interaction of color.* New Haven, CN: Yale University Press.

Alvarez, H. (2014). *A guide to color, UX, and conversion rates.* Retrieved from https://www.usertesting.com/blog/2014/12/02/color-ux-conversion-rates/.

Ann, E. (2009). What's design got to do with the world financial crisis? *interactions, 16*(3), 20–27.

Antle, A. N. (2009). Embodied child computer interaction: why embodiment matters. *interactions, 16*(2), 27–30.

Apple Computer Inc. (1993). *Making it Macintosh: The Macintosh human interface guidelines companion.* Reading, MA: Addison-Wesley.

Arnowitz, J. (2013). Taking the fast RIDE: designing while being agile. *interactions, 20*(4), 76–79. https://doi.org/10.1145/2486227.2486243.

Bangor, A., Kortum, P. T., & Miller, J. T. (2008). An empirical evaluation of the system usability scale. *International Journal of Human Computer Interaction, 24*(6), 574–594.

Barnard, P. (1993). The contributions of applied cognitive psychology to the study of human-computer interaction. In: R. M. Baecker, J. Grudin, B. Buxton, & S. Greenberg (Eds.), *Readings in human computer interaction: Toward the year 2000* (pp. 640–658). San Francisco, CA: Morgan Kaufmann.

Baskinger, M. (2008). Pencils before pixels: a primer in hand-generated sketching. *interactions, 15*(2), 28–36.

Baskinger, M., & Gross, M. (2010). Tangible interaction = Form + computing. *interactions, 17*(1), 6–11.

Bastien, J. M. C., & Scapin, D. L. (1995). Evaluating a user interface with ergonomic criteria. *International Journal of Human Computer Interaction, 7*(2), 105–121.

Baty, S. (2010). Solving complex problems through design. *interactions, 17*(5), 70–73.

Beale, R. (2007). Slanty design. *Communications of the ACM, 50*(1), 21–24. https://doi.org/10.1145/1188913.1188934.

Beck, K. (1999). Embracing change with extreme programming. *IEEE Computer, 32*(10), 70–77.

Beck, K. (2000). *Extreme programming explained: Embrace change*. Boston, MA: Addison-Wesley.

Beck, K., & Andres, C. (2004). *Extreme programming explained: Embrace change, 2nd edition (the XP series)* (2nd ed.). Boston, MA: Addison-Wesley.

Becker, K. (2004). Log on, tune in, drop down: (and click "go" too!). *interactions, 11*(5), 30–35. https://doi.org/10.1145/1015530.1015543.

Bell, T. E., & Thayer, T. A. (1976). Software requirements: are they really a problem? In: *Proceedings of the 2nd international conference on software engineering, San Francisco, California, USA.*

Benington, H. D. (1956). United States, navy mathematical computing advisory panel. In: *Symposium on advanced programming methods for digital computers.* Washington, DC: Office of Naval Research, Dept. of the Navy.

Benington, H. D. (1983). Production of large computer programs. *IEEE Annals of the History of Computing, 5*(4), 350–361. https://doi.org/10.1109/mahc.1983.10102.

Bennett, J. L. (1984). Managing to meet usability requirements: establishing and meeting software development goals. In: J. Bennett, D. Case, J. Sandelin, & M. Smith (Eds.), *Visual display terminals* (pp. 161–184). Englewood Cliffs, NJ: Prentice-Hall.

Bera, P. (2016). How colors in business dashboards affect users' decision making. *Communications of the ACM, 59*(4), 50–57.

Berry, R. E. (1988). Common user access—a consistent and usable human-computer interface for the SAA environments. *IBM Systems Journal, 27*(3), 281–300. https://doi.org/10.1147/sj.273.0281.

Beyer, H., & Holtzblatt, K. (1997). *Contextual design: A customer-centered approach to systems designs* (1st ed.). San Francisco, CA: Morgan Kaufmann.

Beyer, H., & Holtzblatt, K. (1998). *Contextual design: Defining customer-centered systems* (1st ed.). San Francisco, CA: Morgan-Kaufman.

Beyer, H., Holtzblatt, K., & Baker, L. (2004). An agile customer-centered method: rapid contextual design. In: *Extreme programming and agile methods (LNCS 3134)* (pp. 50–59). Calgary, Canada: Springer Berlin/Heidelberg.

Bias, R. G., & Mayhew, D. J. (2005). *Cost-justifying usability: An update for the internet age* (2nd ed.). San Francisco, CA: Morgan Kaufmann.

Billingsley, P. A. (1993). Reflections on ISO 9241: software usability may be more than the sum of its parts. *Standard View, 1*(1), 22–25. https://doi.org/10.1145/174683.174686.

Bittner, K., & Spence, I. (2003). *Use case modeling.* Boston, MA: Addison-Wesley.

Bjerknes, G., Ehn, P., & Kyng, M. (Eds.), (1987). *Computers and democracy: A Scandinavian challenge.* Aldershot, UK: Avebury.

Blythin, S., Rouncefield, M., & Hughes, J. A. (1997). Never mind the ethno' stuff, what does all this mean and what do we do now: ethnography in the commercial world. *interactions, 4*(3), 38–47. https://doi.org/10.1145/255392.255400.

Bødker, S. (1991). *Through the interface: A human activity approach to user interface design.* Hillsdale, NJ: Lawrence Erlbaum.

Bødker, S. (2015). Third-wave HCI, 10 years later—participation and sharing. *interactions, 22*(5), 24–31. https://doi.org/10.1145/2804405.

Bødker, S., & Buur, J. (2002). The design collaboratorium—a place for usability design. *ACM Transactions on Computer-Human Interaction, 9*(2), 152–169.

Bødker, S., Ehn, P., Kammersgaard, J., Kyng, M., & Sundblad, Y. (1987). A utopian experience. In: G. Bjerknes, P. Ehn, & M. Kyng (Eds.), *Computers and Democracy—A Scandinavian Challenge* (pp. 251–278). Aldershot, UK: Avebury.

Boehm, B. W. (1988). A spiral model of software development and enhancement. *IEEE Computer, 21*(5), 61–72.

Boff, K. R., & Lincoln, J. E. (1988). *Engineering data compendium: Human perception and performance*. Ohio: Wright-Patterson AFB, Harry G. Armstrong Aerospace Medical Research Laboratory. Retrieved from Dayton.

Bolchini, D., Pulido, D., & Faiola, A. (2009). "Paper in screen" prototyping: an agile technique to anticipate the mobile experience. *interactions, 16*(4), 29–33.

Boling, E., & Smith, K. M. (2012). The design case: rigorous design knowledge for design practice. *interactions, 19*(5), 48–53.

Borchers, J. (2001). *A pattern approach to interaction design*. New York, NY: Wiley.

Borman, L., & Janda, A. (1986). The CHI conferences: a bibliographic history. *SIGCHI Bulletin, 17*(3), 51.

Bradley, M. M., & Lang, P. J. (1994). Measuring emotion: the self-assessment manikin and the semantic differential. *Journal of Behavior Therapy and Experimental Psychiatry, 25*(1), 49–59.

Branscomb, L. M. (1981). The human side of computers. *IBM Systems Journal, 20*(2), 120–121.

Brooke, J. (1996). SUS: a quick and dirty usability scale. In: P. W. Jordan, B. Thomas, B. A. Weerdmeester, & I. L. McClleland (Eds.), *Usability evaluation in industry* (pp. 189–194). London, UK: Taylor & Francis.

Brown, C. M. (1988). *Human-computer interface design guidelines*. Norwood, NJ: Ablex Publishing.

Brown, L. (1993). Human-computer interaction and standardization. *Standard View, 1*(1), 3–8. https://doi.org/10.1145/174683.174684.

Brown, T. (2008). Design thinking. June, *Harvard Business Review*, 84–92.

Buchenau, M., & Suri, J. F. (2000). Experience prototyping. In: *Proceedings of the conference on designing interactive systems: Processes, practices, methods, and techniques (DIS)*.

Buxton, B. (1986). There's more to interaction than meets the eye: some issues in manual input. In: A. D. Norman & S. W. Draper (Eds.), *User centered system design: New perspectives on human-computer interaction* (pp. 319–337). Hillsdale, NJ: Lawrence Erlbaum.

Buxton, B. (2007a). Sketching and experience design. In: *Stanford university human-computer interaction seminar (CS 547)*. Retrieved from http://www.youtube.com/watch?v=xx1WveKV7aE.

Buxton, B. (2007b). *Sketching user experiences: Getting the design right and the right design*. San Francisco, CA: Morgan Kaufmann.

Buxton, B., Lamb, M. R., Sherman, D., & Smith, K. C. (1983). Towards a comprehensive user interface management system. *SIGGRAPH Computer Graphics, 17*(3), 35–42. https://doi.org/10.1145/964967.801130.

Buxton, B., & Sniderman, R. (1980). Iteration in the design of the human-computer interface. In: *Proceedings of the 13th annual meeting of the Human Factors Association of Canada*.

Capra, M. G. (2006). *Usability problem description and the evaluator effect in usability testing*. PhD Dissertation, Blacksburg: Virginia Tech.

Card, S. K., Moran, T. P., & Newell, A. (1980). The keystroke-level model for user performance time with interactive systems. *Communications of the ACM, 23*(7), 396–410. https://doi.org/10.1145/358886.358895.

Card, S. K., Moran, T. P., & Newell, A. (1983). *The psychology of human-computer interaction*. Hillsdale, NJ: Lawrence Erlbaum.

Carmel, E., Whitaker, R. D., & George, J. F. (1993). PD and joint application design: a transatlantic comparison. *Communications of the ACM, 36*(6), 40–48. https://doi.org/10.1145/153571.163265.

Carroll, J. M., Mack, R. L., & Kellogg, W. A. (1988). Interface metaphors and user interface design. In: M. Helander (Ed.), *Handbook of human-computer interaction* (pp. 67–85). Holland: Elsevier Science.

Carroll, J. M., & Olson, J. R. (1987). *Mental models in human-computer interaction: research issues about what the user of software knows.* Washington, DC: National Academy Press.

Carroll, J. M., Singley, M. K., & Rosson, M. B. (1992). Integrating theory development with design evaluation. *Behaviour & Information Technology, 11*(5), 247–255.

Carroll, J. M., & Thomas, J. C. (1982). Metaphor and the cognitive representation of computing systems. *IEEE Transactions on Systems, Man, and Cybernetics, 12*(2), 107–116.

Carroll, J. M., & Thomas, J. C. (1988). Fun. *SIGCHI Bulletin, 19*(3), 21–24.

Carter, P. (2007). Liberating usability testing. *interactions, 14*(2), 18–22. https://doi.org/10.1145/1229863.1229864.

Castillo, J. C., & Hartson, R. (2000). Critical Incident Data and Their Importance in Remote Usability Evaluation. In: *Proceedings of the Human Factors and Ergonomics Society annual meeting.*

Chin, J. P., Diehl, V. A., & Norman, K. L. (1988). Development of an instrument measuring user satisfaction of the human-computer interface. In: *Proceedings of the CHI conference on human factors in computing systems, Washington, DC, May 15–19.*

Christ, R. E. (1975). Review and analysis of color coding research for visual displays. *Human Factors, 17*(6), 542–570.

Churchill, E. F. (2009). Ps and Qs: on trusting your socks to find each other. *interactions, 16*(2), 32–36.

Churchill, E. F. (2010). Enticing engagement. *interactions, 17*(3), 82–87. https://doi.org/10.1145/1744161.1744180.

Clement, A., & Besselaar, P. V. d. (1993). A retrospective look at PD projects. *Communications of the ACM, 36*(6), 29–37. https://doi.org/10.1145/153571.163264.

Cockton, G., Lavery, D., & Woolrych, A. (2003a). Changing analysts' tunes: the surprising impact of a new instrument for usability inspection method assessment. In: *Proceedings of the international conference on human-computer interaction (HCI International).*

Cockton, G., & Woolrych, A. (2001). Understanding inspection methods: lessons from an assessment of heuristic evaluation. In: *Proceedings of the international conference on human-computer interaction (HCI International) and IHM 2001.*

Cockton, G., & Woolrych, A. (2002). Sale must end: should discount methods be cleared off HCI's shelves? *interactions, 9*(5), 13–18. https://doi.org/10.1145/566981.566990.

Cockton, G., Woolrych, A., Hall, L., & Hindmarch, H. (2003b). Changing analysts' tunes: the surprising impact of a new instrument for usability inspection method assessment? In: P. Johnson & P. Palanque (Eds.), *Vol. XVII. People and computers.* London: Springer-Verlag.

Constantine, L. L. (1994a). Essentially speaking. *Software Development, 2*(11), 95–96.

Constantine, L. L. (1994b). Interfaces for intermediates. *IEEE Software, 11*(4), 96–99.

Constantine, L. L. (1995). Essential modeling: use cases for user interfaces. *interactions, 2*(2), 34–46. https://doi.org/10.1145/205350.205356.

Constantine, L. L. (2002). Process agility and software usability: toward lightweight usage-centered design. *Information Age, 8*(2), 1–10.

Constantine, L. L., & Lockwood, L. A. D. (1999). *Software for use: A practical guide to the models and methods of usage-centered design.* Boston, MA: Addison Wesley Longman, Inc.

Constantine, L. L., & Lockwood, L. A. D. (2003). Card-based user and task modeling for agile usage-centered design. In: *Proceedings of the CHI conference on human factors in computing systems (tutorial).*

Cooper, A. (2004). *The inmates are running the asylum: Why high tech products drive us crazy and how to restore the sanity* (1st ed.). Indianapolis, IN: Sams-Pearson Education.

Cooper, A., Reimann, R., & Dubberly, H. (2003). *About Face 2.0: The essentials of interaction design.* New York, NY: John Wiley.

Cooper, G. (1998). *Research into cognitive load theory & instructional design at UNSW.* Retrieved from http://paedpsych.jku.at:4711/LEHRTEXTE/Cooper98.html.

Cordes, R. E. (2001). Task-selection bias: a case for user-defined tasks. *International Journal of Human Computer Interaction, 13*(4), 411–419.

Costabile, M. F., Ardito, C., & Lanzilotti, R. (2010). Enjoying cultural heritage thanks to mobile technology. *interactions, 17*(3), 30–33.

Cox, D., & Greenberg, S. (2000). Supporting collaborative interpretation in distributed Groupware. In: *Proceedings of the ACM conference on computer supported cooperative work, Philadelphia, Pennsylvania.*

Cross, N. (2001). Design cognition: results from protocol and other empirical studies of design activity. In: C. M. Eastman, W. M. McCracken, & W. C. Newstetter (Eds.), *Design knowing and learning: Cognition in design education* (pp. 79–103). Oxford, UK: Elsevier.

Cross, N. (2006). *Designerly ways of knowing.* London, UK: Springer.

Dearden, A. M., & Wright, P. C. (1997). Experiences using situated and non-situated techniques for studying work in context. In: *Proceedings of the INTERACT conference on human-computer interaction.*

del Galdo, E. M., Williges, R. C., Williges, B. H., & Wixon, D. R. (1986). An evaluation of critical incidents for software documentation design. In: *Proceedings of the Human Factors and Ergonomics Society annual meeting.*

Demarcating User eXperience Seminar (2010). Retrieved from Schloss Dagstuhl, Germany, http://www.dagstuhl.de/10373.

Department of Defense (1998). *Defense Systems Software Development (Vol. DOD-STD-2167A).*

Desmet, P. (2003). Measuring emotions: development and application of an instrument to measure emotional responses to products. In: M. A. Blythe, A. F. Monk, K. Overbeeke, & P. C. Wright (Eds.), *Funology: From usability to enjoyment* (pp. 111–123). Dordrecht, The Netherlands: Kluwer Academic.

Dick, W., & Carey, L. (1978). *The systematic design of instruction.* Glenview, IL: Scott, Foresman.

Donohue, J. (1989). *Fixing fallingwater's flaws* (pp. 99–101). Architecture.

Dormann, C. (2003). Affective experiences in the home: measuring emotion. In: *Proceedings of the conference on home oriented informatics and telematics, the networked home of the future (HOIT), Irvine, CA.*

Dorst, K. (2015). *Frame innovation: Create new thinking by design.* Cambridge MA: The MIT Press.

Dourish, P. (2001). *Where the action is: The foundations of embodied interaction.* Cambridge, MA: MIT Press.

Draper, S. W., & Barton, S. B. (1993). Learning by exploration, and affordance bugs. In: *Proceedings of the CHI conference on human factors in computing systems (INTERCHI Adjunct), New York, NY.*

Dray, S., & Siegel, D. (2004). Remote possibilities? International usability testing at a distance. *interactions, 11*(2), 10–17. https://doi.org/10.1145/971258.971264.

Dubberly, H. (2012). What can Steve Jobs and Jonathan Ive teach us about designing? *interactions, 19*(3), 82–85. https://doi.org/10.1145/2168931.2168948.

Dubberly, H., & Evenson, S. (2011). Design as learning—or "knowledge creation"—the SECI model. *interactions, 18*(1), 75–79. https://doi.org/10.1145/1897239.1897256.

Dubberly, H., & Pangaro, P. (2009). What is conversation, and how can we design for it? *interactions, 16*(4), 22–28.

Dumas, J. S., Molich, R., & Jeffries, R. (2004). Describing usability problems: are we sending the right message? *interactions, 11*(4), 24–29. https://doi.org/10.1145/1005261.1005274.

Dzida, W., Wiethoff, M., & Arnold, A. G. (1993). *ERGOGuide: The quality assurance guide to ergonomic software.* Joint internal technical report of GMD (Germany) and Delft University of Technology (The Netherlands).

Ehn, P. (1988). *Work-Oriented Design of Computer Artifacts* (1st ed.). Stockholm, Sweden: Arbetslivcentrum.

Ehn, P. (1990). *Work-oriented design of computer artifacts* (2nd ed.). Hillsdale, NJ: Lawrence Erlbaum.

Ekman, P., & Friesen, W. (1975). *Unmasking the face: A guide to recognizing emotions from facial clues.* Englewood Cliffs, NJ: Prentice Hall.

Engel, S. E., & Granda, R. E. (1975). *Guidelines for man/display interfaces (TR 00.2720).* Poughkeepsie, NY: IBM Corporation.

Fitts, P. M. (1954). The information capacity of the human motor system in controlling the amplitude of movement. *Journal of Experimental Psychology, 47*(6), 381–391. https://doi.org/10.1037/h0055392.

Fitts, P. M., & Jones, R. E. (1947). Psychological aspects of instrument display: analysis of factors contributing to 460 "pilot error" experiences in operating aircraft controls. In: H. W. Sinaiko (Ed.), *Reprinted in selected papers on human factors in the design and use of control systems (1961)* (pp. 332–358). New York, NY: Dover.

Flanagan, J. C. (1954). The critical incident technique. *Psychological Bulletin, 51*(4), 327–358.

Foley, J. D., & Van Dam, A. (1982). *Fundamentals of interactive computer graphics.* Reading, MA: Addison-Wesley Longman.

Foley, J. D., Van Dam, A., Feiner, S. K., & Hughes, J. F. (1990). *Computer graphics: Principles and practice* (2nd ed.). Boston, MA: Addison-Wesley Longman Publishing Co., Inc.

Foley, J. D., & Wallace, V. L. (1974). The art of natural graphic man-machine conversation. *ACM Computer Graphics, 8*(3), 87.

Forlizzi, J. (2005). Robotic products to assist the aging population. *interactions, 12*(2), 16–18.

Forlizzi, J. (2010). All look same?: a comparison of experience design and service design. *interactions, 17*(5), 60–62. https://doi.org/10.1145/1836216.1836232.

Frank, B. (2006). The science of segmentation. *interactions, 13*(3), 12–13. https://doi.org/10.1145/1125864.1125878.

Frishberg, N. (2006). Prototyping with junk. *interactions, 13*(1), 21–23.

Gajendar, U. (2012). Finding the sweet spot of design. *interactions, 19*(3), 10–11.

Gaver, W. W. (1991). Technology affordances. In: *Proceedings of the CHI conference on human factors in computing systems, New Orleans, Louisiana.*

Gellersen, H. (2005). Smart-Its: computers for artifacts in the physical world. *Communications of the ACM, 48*(3), 66.

Gershman, A., & Fano, A. (2005). Examples of commercial applications of ubiquitous computing. *Communications of the ACM, 48*(3), 71.

Gibson, J. J. (1977). The theory of affordances. In: R. Shaw & J. Bransford (Eds.), *Perceiving, acting, and knowing: Toward an ecological psychology* (pp. 67–82). Hillsdale, NJ: Lawrence Erlbaum.

Gibson, J. J. (1979). *The ecological approach to visual perception.* Boston, MA: Houghton Mifflin.

Giesecke, F. E., Mitchell, A., Hill, H. C., Spencer, I. L., Novak, J. T., Dygdon, J. E., et al. (2018). *Case study 1: The snake light*. The Companion Website for Giesecke on the Web. Retrieved from http://www.prenhall.com/giesecke/html/cases/snake.html.

Gilb, T. (1987). Design by objectives. *SIGSOFT Software Engineering Notes, 12*(2), 42–49.

Gillham, R. (2014). *The user experience of enterprise technology. Retrieved from* http://www.fool proof.co.uk/thinking/the-user-experience-of-enterprise-technology/.

Gladwell, M. (2007). *Blink: The power of thinking without thinking*. New York, NY: Little, Brown and Company.

Good, M. D. (1989). Seven experiences with contextual field research. *SIGCHI Bulletin, 20*(4), 25–32. https://doi.org/10.1145/67243.67246.

Good, M. D., Spine, T., Whiteside, J. A., & George, P. (1986). User derived impact analysis as a tool for usability engineering. In: *Proceedings of the CHI conference on human factors in computing systems, New York, NY, April 13–17*.

Good, M. D., Whiteside, J. A., Wixon, D. R., & Jones, S. J. (1984). Building a user-derived interface. *Communications of the ACM, 27*(10), 1032–1043. https://doi.org/10.1145/358274.358284.

Gothelf, J., & Seiden, J. (2016). *Lean UX: Designing great products with agile teams* (2nd ed.). Sebastopol, CA: O'Reilly Media.

Graves, M. (2012). Architecture and the Lost Art of Drawing. *The New York Times*, Retrieved from http://www.nytimes.com/2012/09/02/opinion/sunday/architecture-and-the-lost-art-of-drawing.html.

Gray, W. D., & Salzman, M. C. (1998). Damaged merchandise? A review of experiments that compare usability evaluation methods. *Human Computer Interaction, 13*(3), 203–261.

Greenbaum, J. M., & Kyng, M. (Eds.), (1991). *Design at Work: Cooperative design of computer systems*. Hillsdale, NJ: Lawrence Erlbaum.

Grudin, J. (1989). The case against user interface consistency. *Communications of the ACM, 32*(10), 1164–1173. https://doi.org/10.1145/67933.67934.

Grudin, J. (2006). The GUI shock: computer graphics and human-computer interaction. *interactions. 13*(2), 46ff. https://doi.org/10.1145/1116715.1116751.

Hackman, G., & Biers, D. (1992). Team usability testing: are two heads better than one. In: *Proceedings of the Human Factors and Ergonomics Society annual meeting*.

Hafner, K. (2007). Inside apple stores, a certain aura enchants the faithful. *The New York Times*. December 27. Retrieved from http://www.nytimes.com/2007/12/27/business/27apple.html?ei=5124&en=6b1c27bc8cec74b5&ex=1356584400&partner=permalink&exprod=permalink&pagewanted=all.

Hammond, N., Gardiner, M. M., & Christie, B. (1987). The role of cognitive psychology in user-interface design. In: M. M. Gardiner & B. Christie (Eds.), *Applying cognitive psychology to user-interface design* (pp. 13–52): Wiley.

Hamner, E., Lotter, M., Nourbakhsh, I., & Shelly, S. (2005). Case study: up close and personal from Mars. *interactions, 12*(2), 30–36.

Hansen, W. (1971). User engineering principles for interactive systems. In: *Proceedings of the fall joint computer conference, Montvale, NJ*.

Harrison, S., Back, M., & Tatar, D. (2006). "It's Just a Method!": a pedagogical experiment in interdisciplinary design. In: *Proceedings of the 6th conference on designing interactive systems, University Park, PA, USA*.

Harrison, S., & Tatar, D. (2011). On methods. *interactions, 18*(2), 10–11. https://doi.org/10.1145/1925820.1925823.

Harrison, S., Tatar, D., & Sengers, P. (2007). The three paradigms of HCI. In: *Proceedings of the Alt.chi, CHI conference on human factors in computing systems, San Jose, CA*.

Hartson, R. (2003). Cognitive, physical, sensory, and functional affordances in interaction design. *Behaviour & Information Technology, 22*(5), 315–338.

Hartson, R., Andre, T. S., & Williges, R. C. (2003). Criteria for evaluating usability evaluation methods. *International Journal of Human Computer Interaction, 15*(1), 145–181.

Hartson, R., & Castillo, J. C. (1998). Remote evaluation for post-deployment usability improvement. In: *Proceedings of the Conference on Advanced Visual Interfaces (AVI), L'Aquila, Italy*.

Hartson, R., & Smith, E. C. (1991). Rapid prototyping in human-computer interface development. *Interacting with Computers, 3*(1), 51–91.

Hassenzahl, M. (2012). Everything can be beautiful. *interactions, 19*(4), 60–65. https://doi.org/10.1145/2212877.2212892.

Hassenzahl, M., Beu, A., & Burmester, M. (2001). Engineering joy. *IEEE Software, 18*(1), 70–76.

Hassenzahl, M., Burmester, M., & Koller, F. (2003). AttrakDiff: Ein Fragebogen zur Messung wahrgenommener hedonischer und pragmatischer Qualität (AttrakDif: a questionnaire for the measurement of perceived hedonic and pragmatic quality). In: *Proceedings of the Mensch & Computer 2003: Interaktion in Bewegung, Stuttgart*.

Hassenzahl, M., Platz, A., Burmester, M., & Lehner, K. (2000). Hedonic and ergonomic quality aspects determine a software's appeal. In: *Proceedings of the CHI conference on human factors in computing systems, The Hague, The Netherlands*.

Hassenzahl, M., & Roto, V. (2007). Being and doing: a perspective on user experience and its measurement. *Interfaces, 72*, 10–12.

Hassenzahl, M., Schöbel, M., & Trautmann, T. (2008). How motivational orientation influences the evaluation and choice of hedonic and pragmatic interactive products: the role of regulatory focus. *Interacting with Computers, 20*, 473–479.

Hazzan, O., & Kramer, J. (2016). Assessing abstraction skills. *Communications of the ACM, 59*(12), 43–45. https://doi.org/10.1145/2926712.

Heller, F., & Borchers, J. (2012). Physical prototyping of an on-outlet power-consumption display. *interactions, 19*(1), 14–17. https://doi.org/10.1145/2065327.2065332.

Hertzum, M., & Jacobsen, N. E. (2003). The evaluator effect: a chilling fact about usability evaluation methods. *International Journal of Human Computer Interaction, 15*(1), 183–204.

Hewett, T. T. (1999). Cognitive factors in design: basic phenomena in human memory and problem solving. In: *Proceedings of the CHI conference on human factors in computing systems (extended abstracts)*.

Hinckley, K., Pausch, R., Goble, J. C., & Kassell, N. F. (1994). A survey of design issues in spatial input. In: *Proceedings of the ACM Symposium on User Interface Software and Technology, Marina del Rey, California*.

Hix, D., & Hartson, R. (1993). *Developing user interfaces: Ensuring usability through product & process*. New York, NY: John Wiley.

Holtzblatt, K. (1999). Introduction to special section on contextual design. *interactions, 6*(1), 30–31. https://doi.org/10.1145/291224.291226.

Holtzblatt, K. (2011). What makes things cool?: intentional design for innovation. *interactions, 18*(6), 40–47. https://doi.org/10.1145/2029976.2029988.

Holtzblatt, K., Wendell, J. B., & Wood, S. (2004). *Rapid contextual design: A how-to guide to key techniques for user-centered design*. San Francisco: Morgan Kaufmann.

Honan, M. (2013). The simple complex. *Wired Magazine, 21*(2), 44.

Hornbæk, K., & Frøkjær, E. (2005). Comparing usability problems and redesign proposals as input to practical systems development. In: *Proceedings of the CHI conference on human factors in computing systems, Portland, Oregon, USA*.

Houben, S., Marquardt, N., Vermeulen, J., Klokmose, C., Schöning, J., Reiterer, H., et al. (2017). Opportunities and challenges for cross-device interactions in the wild. *interactions, 24*(5), 58–63.

Howarth, D. (2002). *Custom cupholder a shoe-in* (p. 10). Roundel, BMW Car Club Publication.

Hudson, J. M., & Viswanadha, K. (2009). Can "wow" be a design goal? *interactions, 16*(1), 58–61. https://doi.org/10.1145/1456202.1456217.

Hudson, W. (2001). How many users does it take to change a Web site? *SIGCHI Bulletin*, 6. https://doi.org/10.1145/967222.967230.

Hughes, J., King, V., Rodden, T., & Andersen, H. (1994). Moving out from the control room: ethnography in system design. In: *Proceedings of the ACM conference on computer supported cooperative work, Chapel Hill, North Carolina.*

Hughes, J., King, V., Rodden, T., & Andersen, H. (1995). The role of ethnography in interactive systems design. *interactions, 2*(2), 56–65. https://doi.org/10.1145/205350.205358.

Human Factor Research Group. (1996). WAMMI Questionnaire. Retrieved from http://www.ucc.ie/hfrg/questionnaires/wammi/index.html.

Human Factor Research Group. (2010). Human Factors Research Group. Retrieved from http://www.ucc.ie/hfrg/.

Hutchins, E. L., Hollan, J. D., & Norman, D. A. (1986). Direct manipulation interfaces. In: D. A. Norman & S. W. Draper (Eds.), *User centered system design: New perspectives on human-computer interaction* (pp. 87–125). Hillsdale, NJ: Lawrence Erlbaum.

Iannella, R. (1995). HyperSAM: a management tool for large user interface guideline sets. *SIGCHI Bulletin, 27*(2), 42–45. https://doi.org/10.1145/202511.202522.

Isaacson, W. (2012). Keep it simple. September, *Smithsonian Magazine, 41–49,* 90–92.

Ishii, H., & Ullmer, B. (1997). Tangible bits: towards seamless interfaces between people, bits and atoms. In: *Proceedings of the CHI conference on human factors in computing systems, Atlanta, Georgia.*

ISO 9241-11 (1997). *Ergonomic requirements for office work with visual display terminals (VDTs) Part 11: Guidance on usability.*

Jacob, R. J. K. (1993). Eye movement-based human-computer interaction techniques: toward non-command interfaces. In: R. Hartson & D. Hix (Eds.), Vol. 4. *Advances in human-computer interaction* (pp. 151–190). Norwood, NJ: Ablex Publishing Corporation.

Johnson, J. (2000). Textual bloopers: an excerpt from GUI bloopers. *interactions, 7*(5), 28–48. https://doi.org/10.1145/345242.345255.

Johnson, J., & Henderson, A. (2002). Conceptual models: begin by designing what to design. *interactions, 9*(1), 25–32. https://doi.org/10.1145/503355.503366.

Jokela, T. (2004). When good things happen to bad products: where are the benefits of usability in the consumer appliance market? *interactions, 11*(6), 28–35. https://doi.org/10.1145/1029036.1029050.

Jones, B. D., Winegarden, C. R., & Rogers, W. A. (2009). Supporting healthy aging with new technologies. *interactions, 16*(4), 48–51.

Judge, T. K., Pyla, P. S., McCrickard, S., & Harrison, S. (2008). Affinity diagramming in multiple display environments. In: *Proceedings of the CSCW 2008 workshop on beyond the laboratory: Supporting authentic collaboration with multiple displays, San Diego, CA.*

Kane, D. (2003). Finding a place for discount usability engineering in agile development: throwing down the gauntlet. In: *Proceedings of the conference on agile development.*

Kantrovich, L. (2004). To innovate or not to innovate. *interactions, 11*(1), 24–31. https://doi.org/10.1145/962342.962354.

Kapoor, A., Picard, R. W., & Ivanov, Y. (2004). Probabilistic combination of multiple modalities to detect interest. In: *Proceedings of the international conference on pattern recognition (ICPR)*.

Karat, C. -M., Campbell, R., & Fiegel, T. (1992). Comparison of empirical testing and walk-through methods in user interface evaluation. In: *Proceedings of the CHI conference on human factors in computing systems, New York, NY, May 3–7*.

Karn, K. S., Perry, T. J., & Krolczyk, M. J. (1997). Testing for power usability: a CHI 97 workshop. *SIGCHI Bulletin, 29*(4), 63–67.

Kaur, K., Maiden, N., & Sutcliffe, A. (1999). Interacting with virtual environments: an evaluation of a model of interaction. *Interacting with Computers, 11*(4), 403–426.

Kawakita, J. (1982). *The original KJ method*. Tokio: Kawakita Research Institute.

Kennedy, S. (1989). Using video in the BNR usability lab. *SIGCHI Bulletin, 21*(2), 92–95. https://doi.org/10.1145/70609.70624.

Kennedy, T. C. S. (1974). The design of interactive procedures for man-machine communication. *International Journal of Man-Machine Studies, 6*, 309–334.

Kensing, F., & Munk-Madsen, A. (1993). PD: structure in the toolbox. *Communications of the ACM, 36*(6), 78–85.

Kern, D., & Pfleging, B. (2013). Supporting interaction through haptic feedback in automotive user interfaces. *interactions, 20*(2), 16–21.

Kieras, D. E., & Polson, P. G. (1985). An approach to the formal analysis of user complexity. *International Journal of Man-Machine Studies, 22*, 365–394.

Kim, J., & Moon, J. Y. (1998). Designing towards emotional usability in customer interfaces—trustworthiness of cyber-banking system interfaces. *Interacting with Computers, 10*(1), 1–29.

Kim, J. H., Gunn, D. V., Schuh, E., Phillips, B. C., Pagulayan, R. j., & Wixon, D. (2008). Tracking real-time user experience (TRUE): a comprehensive instrumentation for complex systems. In: *Proceedings of the CHI conference on human factors in computing systems, Florence, Italy*.

Knemeyer, D. (2015). Design thinking and UX: two sides of the same coin. *interactions, 22*(5), 66–68. https://doi.org/10.1145/2802679.

Koenemann-Belliveau, J., Carroll, J. M., Rosson, M. B., & Singley, M. K. (1994). Comparative usability evaluation: critical incidents and critical threads. In: *Proceedings of the CHI conference on human factors in computing systems, Boston, Massachusetts*.

Kolko, J. (2015a). Design thinking comes of age. September 2015, *Harvard Business Review*, 66–71.

Kolko, J. (2015b). Moving on from requirements. *interactions, 22*(6), 22–23. https://doi.org/10.1145/2824754.

Krippendorff, K. (2006). *The semantic turn: A new foundation for design*. Boca Raton, FL: CRC Press.

Krueger, R. A., & Casey, M. A. (2008). *Focus groups: A practical guide for applied research* (4th ed.). Thousand Oaks, CA: Sage Publications.

Kugler, L. (2015). Touching the virtual. *Communications of the ACM, 58*(8), 16–18.

Kuniavsky, M. (2003). *Observing the user experience: A practitioner's guide to user research*. San Francisco, CA: Morgan Kaufmann.

Kyng, M. (1994). Scandinavian design: users in product development. In: *Proceedings of the CHI conference on human factors in computing systems*.

Lafrenière, D. (1996). CUTA: a simple, practical, low-cost approach to task analysis. *interactions, 3*(5), 35–39. https://doi.org/10.1145/234757.234761.

Landauer, T. K. (1995). *The trouble with computers: Usefulness, usability, and productivity.* Cambridge, MA: The MIT Press.

Landry, S. (2016). Instant gratification requires total control. *Wired Magazine, 24*(5), 56.

Lantz, A., & Gulliksen, J. (2003). Editorial: design versus design: a Nordic perspective. *International Journal of Human Computer Interaction, 15*(1), 1–4.

Lathan, C., Brisben, A., & Safos, C. (2005). CosmoBot levels the playing field for disabled children. *interactions, 12*(2), 14–16.

Lavery, D., & Cockton, G. (1997). Representing predicted and actual usability problems. In: *Proceedings of the international workshop on representations in interactive software development, London.*

Lavie, T., & Tractinsky, N. (2004). Assessing dimensions of perceived visual aesthetics of web sites. *International Journal of Human-Computer Studies, 60,* 269–298.

LeCompte, M. D., & Preissle, J. (1993). *Ethnography and qualitative design in educational research* (2nd ed.). San Diego: Academic Press.

Lewis, C. (1982). *Using the 'thinking-aloud' method in cognitive interface design.* (Research Report RC 9265). Yorktown Heights, NY: IBM Thomas J. Watson Research Center.

Lewis, C., Polson, P. G., Wharton, C., & Rieman, J. (1990). Testing a walkthrough methodology for theory-based design of walk-up-and-use interfaces. In: *Proceedings of the CHI conference on human factors in computing systems, Seattle, WA.*

Lewis, J. R. (1994). Sample sizes for usability studies: additional considerations. *The Journal of the Human Factors and Ergonomics Society, 36,* 368–378.

Lewis, J. R. (1995). IBM computer usability satisfaction questionnaires: psychometric evaluation and instructions for use. *International Journal of Human Computer Interaction, 7,* 57–78.

Lewis, J. R. (2002). Psychometric evaluation of the PSSUQ using data from five years of usability studies. *International Journal of Human Computer Interaction, 14,* 463–488.

Lewis, R. O. (1992). *Independent verification and validation: A life cycle engineering process for quality software.* New York, NY: John Wiley & Sons, Inc.

Lewis, S., Mateas, M., Palmiter, S., & Lynch, G. (1996). Ethnographic data for product development: a collaborative process. *interactions, 3*(6), 52–69. https://doi.org/10.1145/242485.242505.

Likert, R. (1932). A technique for the measurement of attitudes. *Archives of Psychology, 140,* 55.

Löwgren, J. (2004). Animated use sketches: as design representations. *interactions, 11*(6), 23–27.

Lubow, A. (2009). The triumph of Frank Lloyd Wright. June, *Smithsonian Magazine,* 52–61.

Lund, A. M. (1997). Expert ratings of usability maxims. *Ergonomics in Design, 5*(3), 15–20.

Lund, A. M. (2001). Measuring usability with the USE questionnaire. *Usability & User Experience (the STC Usability SIG Newsletter), 8*(2).

Lund, A. M. (2004). *Measuring usability with the USE questionnaire.* Retrieved from http://www.stcsig.org/usability/newsletter/0110_measuring_with_use.html.

MacKenzie, I. S. (1992). Fitts' law as a research and design tool in human-computer interaction. *Human Computer Interaction, 7,* 91–139.

Macleod, M., Bowden, R., Bevan, N., & Curson, I. (1997). The MUSiC performance measurement method. *Behaviour & Information Technology, 16*(4), 279–293.

Mantei, M. M., & Teorey, T. J. (1988). Cost/benefit analysis for incorporating human factors in the software lifecycle. *Communications of the ACM, 31*(4), 428–439. https://doi.org/10.1145/42404.42408.

Markopoulos, P., Ruyter, B. d., Privender, S., & Breemen, A. v. (2005). Case study: bringing social intelligence into home dialogue systems. *interactions, 12*(4), 37–44. https://doi.org/10.1145/1070960.1070984.

Marsh, G. P. (1864). *Man and nature: Or, physical geography as modified by human action.* New York, NY: Charles Scribner.

Martin, B., & Hanington, B. M. (2012). *Universal methods of design: 100 ways to research complex problems, develop innovative ideas, and design effective solutions.* Beverly, MA: Rockport Publishers.

Mason, J. G. (1968). How to be of two minds. *Nation's Business,* (October), 94–97.

Mayhew, D. J. (1999). *The usability engineering lifecycle: A practitioner's handbook for user interface design* (1st ed.). San Francisco, CA: Morgan Kaufmann.

McCullough, M. (2004). *Digital ground: Architecture, pervasive computing, and environmental knowing.* Cambridge, MA: MIT Press.

McGrenere, J., & Ho, W. (2000). Affordances: clarifying and evolving a concept. In: *Proceedings of the graphics interface.*

McInerney, P., & Maurer, F. (2005). UCD in agile projects: dream team or odd couple? *interactions, 12*(6), 19–23. https://doi.org/10.1145/1096554.1096556.

Meads, J. (2010). *Personal communication with Rex Hartson.* June.

Medlock, M. C., Wixon, D., McGee, M., & Welsh, D. (2005). The rapid iterative test and evaluation method: better products in less time. In: R. G. Bias & D. J. Mayhew (Eds.), *Cost justifying usability: An update for an internet age* (pp. 489–517). San Francisco, CA: Morgan Kaufmann.

Medlock, M. C., Wixon, D., Terrano, M., Romero, R., & Fulton, B. (2002). Using the RITE method to improve products: a definition and a case study. In: *Proceedings of the UPA international conference, Orlando, FL.*

Memmel, T., Gundelsweiler, F., & Reiterer, H. (2007). Agile human-centered software engineering. In: *Proceedings of the British HCI Group annual conference on people and computers, University of Lancaster, United Kingdom.*

Miller, G. A. (1956). The magical number seven, plus or minus two: some limits on our capacity for processing information. *Psychological Review, 63*(2), 81–97. https://doi.org/10.1037/h0043158.

Miller, L. (2010). *Case study of customer input for a successful product.* Retrieved from http://www.agileproductdesign.com/useful_papers/miller_customer_input_in_agile_projects.pdf.

Miller, L., & Sy, D. (2009). Agile user experience SIG. In: *Proceedings of the CHI conference on human factors in computing systems, Boston, April 4–9.*

Moggridge, B. (2007). *Designing interactions.* Cambridge, MA: MIT Press.

Molich, R., Bevan, N., Butler, S., Curson, I., Kindlund, E., & Kirakowski, J. (1998). Comparative evaluation of usability tests. In: *Proceedings of the UPA international conference, Washington, DC, June.*

Molich, R., & Dumas, J. S. (2008). Comparative usability evaluation (CUE-4). *Behaviour & Information Technology, 27*(3), 263–282.

Molich, R., & Nielsen, J. (1990). Improving a human-computer dialogue. *Communications of the ACM, 33*(3), 338–348. https://doi.org/10.1145/77481.77486.

Molich, R., Thomsen, A. D., Karyukina, B., Schmidt, L., Ede, M., van Oel, W., et al. (1999). Comparative evaluation of usability tests. In: *Proceedings of the CHI conference on human factors in computing systems (extended abstracts), Pittsburgh, Pennsylvania.*

Moore, N. C. (2017). How to disrupt: lessons from Tony Fadell. *The Michigan Engineering, Spring, 2017,* 56–63.

Moran, T. P. (1981a). The command language grammar: a representation for the user interface of interactive computer systems. *International Journal of Man-Machine Studies, 15*(1), 3–50.

Moran, T. P. (1981b). Guest editor's introduction: an applied psychology of the user. *ACM Computing Surveys, 13*(1), 1–11. https://doi.org/10.1145/356835.356836.

Morville, P., & Rosenfeld, L. (2006). *Information architecture for the World Wide Web* (3rd ed.). Sebastopol, CA: O'Reilly Media, Inc.

Mosier, J. N., & Smith, S. L. (1986). Application of guidelines for designing user interface software. *Behaviour & Information Technology, 5*(1), 39–46.

Muller, M. J. (1991). PICTIVE—an exploration in participatory design. In: *Proceedings of the CHI conference on human factors in computing systems, New Orleans, Louisiana.*

Muller, M. J. (1992). Retrospective on a year of participatory design using the PICTIVE technique. In: *Proceedings of the CHI conference on human factors in computing systems, Monterey, California.*

Muller, M. J. (2003). Participatory design: the third space in HCI. In: J. A. Jacko & A. Sears (Eds.), *The human-computer interaction handbook: Fundamentals, evolving technologies and emerging applications* (pp. 1051–1058). Mahwah, NJ: Lawrence Erlbaum.

Muller, M. J., & Kuhn, S. (1993). Participatory design. *Communications of the ACM, 36*(4), 24–28.

Muller, M. J., Matheson, L., Page, C., & Gallup, R. (1998). Participatory heuristic evaluation. *interactions, 5*(5), 13–18. https://doi.org/10.1145/285213.285219.

Muller, M. J., Wildman, D. M., & White, E. A. (1993a). 'Equal opportunity' PD using PICTIVE. *Communications of the ACM, 36*(6), 64. https://doi.org/10.1145/153571.214818.

Muller, M. J., Wildman, D. M., & White, E. A. (1993b). Participatory design. *Communications of the ACM, 36*(6), 26–27.

Mumford, E. (1981). Participative systems design: structure and method. *Systems, Objectives, Solutions, 1*(1), 5–19.

Murano, P. (2006). Why anthropomorphic user interface feedback can be effective and preferred by users. In: C. -S. Chen, J. Filipe, I. Seruca, & J. Cordeiro (Eds.), Vol. 7. *Enterprise information systems* (pp. 241–248). Dordrecht, The Netherlands: Springer.

Murphy, R. R. (2005). Humans, robots, rubble, and research. *interactions, 12*(2), 37–39.

Myers, B. A. (1989). User-interface tools: introduction and survey. *IEEE Software, 6*(1), 15–23.

Myers, B. A. (1992). *State of the art in user interface software tools.* Retrieved from http://citeseerx.ist.psu.edu/viewdoc/download?doi=10.1.1.70.5148&rep=rep1&type=pdf.

Myers, B. A. (1993). State of the art in user interface software tools. In: R. Hartson & D. Hix (Eds.), *Vol. 4. Advances in human-computer interaction.* Norwood, NJ: Ablex.

Myers, B. A. (1995). State of the art in user interface software tools. In: R. M. Baecker, J. Grudin, W. A. S. Buxton, & S. Greenberg (Eds.), *Readings in human-computer interaction: Toward the Year 2000* (pp. 323–343). San Francisco: Morgan-Kaufmann Publishers, Inc.

Myers, B. A., Hudson, S. E., & Pausch, R. (2000). Past, present, and future of user interface software tools. *ACM Transactions on Computer-Human Interaction, 7*(1), 3–28.

Myers, I. B., McCaulley, M. H., Quenk, N. L., & Hammer, A. L. (1998). *MBTI manual (a guide to the development and use of the Myers Briggs type indicator)* (3rd ed.). Palo Alto, CA: Consulting Psychologists Press.

Nass, C., Steuer, J., & Tauber, E. R. (1994). In: *Computers are social actors. Paper presented at the the CHI conference on human factors in computing systems, Boston, Massachusetts.*

Nayak, N. P., Mrazek, D., & Smith, D. R. (1995). Analyzing and communicating usability data: now that you have the data what do you do? a CHI'94 workshop. *SIGCHI Bulletin*, *27*(1), 22–30. https://doi.org/10.1145/202642.202649.

Newman, W. M. (1968). A system for interactive graphical programming. In: *Proceedings of the spring joint computer conference, Atlantic City, New Jersey.*

Newman, W. M. (1998). On simulation, measurement, and piecewise usability evaluation. G. M. Olson & T. P. Moran (Eds.), Vol. 13, Issue 3, *Commentary #10 on "damaged merchandise", Human-Computer Interaction* (pp. 316–323).

Nielsen, J. (1989). Usability engineering at a discount. In: *Proceedings of the international conference on human-computer interaction (HCI International), Boston, Massachusetts.*

Nielsen, J. (1990). Traditional dialogue design applied to modern user interfaces. *Communications of the ACM*, *33*(10), 109–118. https://doi.org/10.1145/84537.84559.

Nielsen, J. (1992). Finding usability problems through heuristic evaluation. In: *Proceedings of the CHI conference on human factors in computing systems, Monterey, California.*

Nielsen, J. (1993). *Usability engineering.* Chestnut Hill, MA: Academic Press Professional.

Nielsen, J. (1994). Enhancing the explanatory power of usability heuristics. In: *Proceedings of the CHI conference on human factors in computing systems, Boston, Massachusetts.*

Nielsen, J., Bush, R. M., Dayton, T., Mond, N. E., Muller, M. J., & Root, R. W. (1992). Teaching experienced developers to design graphical user interfaces. In: *Proceedings of the CHI conference on human factors in computing systems, Monterey, California.*

Nielsen, J., & Landauer, T. K. (1993). A mathematical model of the finding of usability problems. In: *Proceedings of the INTERACT conference on human-computer interaction and chi conference on human factors in computing systems (INTERCHI), Amsterdam, The Netherlands.*

Nielsen, J., & Molich, R. (1990). Heuristic evaluation of user interfaces. In: *Proceedings of the CHI conference on human factors in computing systems, Seattle, Washington.*

Nilsson, P., & Ottersten, I. (1998). Interaction design: leaving the engineering perspective behind. In: L. E. Wood (Ed.), *User interface design: Bridging the gap from user requirements to design* (pp. 131–152). Boca Raton, FL: CRC Press.

Norman, D. A. (1986). Cognitive engineering. In: D. A. Norman & S. W. Draper (Eds.), *User centered system design: New perspectives on human-computer interaction* (pp. 31–61). Hillsdale, NJ: Lawrence Erlbaum.

Norman, D. A. (1990). *The design of everyday things.* New York, NY: Basic Books.

Norman, D. A. (1998). *The invisible computer—Why good products can fail, the personal computer is so complex, and information appliances are the solution.* Cambridge, MA: MIT Press.

Norman, D. A. (1999). Affordance, conventions, and design. *interactions*, *6*(3), 38–43. https://doi.org/10.1145/301153.301168.

Norman, D. A. (2002). Emotion and design: attractive things work better. *interactions*, *9*(4), 36–42.

Norman, D. A. (2004). *Emotional design: Why we love (or hate) everyday things* (1st ed.). New York, NY: Basic Books.

Norman, D. A. (2005). Human-centered design considered harmful. *interactions*, *12*(4), 14–19. https://doi.org/10.1145/1070960.1070976.

Norman, D. A. (2006). Logic versus usage: the case for activity-centered design. *interactions*, *13*(6), 45–63. https://doi.org/10.1145/1167948.1167978.

Norman, D. A. (2007a). The next UI breakthrough, part 2: physicality. *interactions*, *14*(4), 46–47. https://doi.org/10.1145/1273961.1273986.

Norman, D. A. (2007b). Simplicity is highly overrated. *interactions*, *14*(2), 40–41. https://doi.org/10.1145/1229863.1229885.

Norman, D. A. (2008). Simplicity is not the answer. *interactions, 15*(5), 45–46.

Norman, D. A. (2009). Systems thinking: a product is more than a product. *interactions, 16*(5), 52–54.

Norman, D. A., & Draper, S. W. (1986). *User centered system design; new perspectives on human-computer interaction.* L. Erlbaum Associates Inc.

Nowell, L., Schulman, R., & Hix, D. (2002). Graphical encoding for information visualization: an empirical study. In: *Proceedings of the IEEE symposium on information visualization (INFOVIS).*

O'Conner, P. T., & Kellerman, S. (2013). Write and wrong. *Smithsonian, 43*(109), 24.

Object Management Group (2010). *UML.* Retrieved from http://www.uml.org/.

Obrist, M., Velasco, C., Vi, C., Ranasinghe, N., Israr, A., Cheok, A., et al. (2016). Sensing the future of HCI: touch, taste, and smell user interfaces. *interactions, 23*(5), 40–49.

Olsen, D. R., Jr. (1983). Automatic generation of interactive systems. *Computer Graphics, 17*(1), 53–57.

O'Malley, C., Draper, S., & Riley, M. (1984). Constructive interaction: a method for studying human-computer-human interaction. In: *Proceedings of the INTERACT conference on human-computer interaction, London, UK, September 4–7.*

Open Software Foundation (1990). *OSF/motif style guide: Revision 1.0.* Upper Saddle River, NJ: Prentice-Hall, Inc.

Palen, L., & Salzman, M. (2002). Beyond the handset: designing for wireless communications usability. *ACM Transactions on Computer-Human Interaction, 9*(2), 125–151. https://doi.org/10.1145/513665.513669.

Patel, N. S., & Hughes, D. E. (2012). Revolutionizing human-computer interfaces: the auditory perspective. *interactions, 19*(1), 34–37.

Patton, J. (2002). Hitting the target: adding interaction design to agile software development. In: *Proceedings of the OOPSLA 2002 Practitioners Reports, Seattle, Washington.*

Patton, J. (2008). *Twelve emerging best practices for adding UX work to Agile development, 6/27/2008.* Retrieved from http://agileproductdesign.com/blog/emerging_best_agile_ux_practice.html.

Patton, J. (2014). *User story mapping: Discover the whole story, build the right product.* Sebastopol, CA: O'Reilly Media.

Paulk, M. C., Curtis, B., Chrissis, M. B., & Weber, C. (1993). *Capability maturity model for software, Version 1.1 (CMU/SEI-93-TR-24).* Pittsburgh, PA: Carnegie Mellon University.

Pering, C. (2002). Interaction design prototyping of communicator devices: towards meeting the hardware-software challenge. *interactions, 9*(6), 36–46.

Petersen, M. G., Madsen, K. H., & Kjaer, A. (2002). The usability of everyday technology: emerging and fading opportunities. *ACM Transactions on Computer-Human Interaction, 9*(2), 74–105. https://doi.org/10.1145/513665.513667.

Pew, R. N., & Rollins, A. M. (1975). *Dialog specification procedure (5129 (Revised Ed)).* Cambridge, MA: Bolt Beranek and Newman.

Pinker, S. (2014). *The sense of style: The thinking person's guide to writing in the 21st century.* New York, NY: Penguin Books.

Pogue, D. (2011). *Appeal of iPad 2 is a matter of emotions.* Retrieved from http://www.nytimes.com/2011/03/10/technology/personaltech/10pogue.html?_r=2&hpw.

Pogue, D. (2012). Technology's friction problem. April, *Scientific American, 28.*

Porter, L. H. (1895). *Cycling for health and pleasure. An indispensable guide to the successful use of the wheel.* New York, NY: Dodd, Mead and Company.

Potosnak, K. (1988). Getting the most out of design guidelines. *IEEE Software, 5*(1), 85–86.

Pressman, R. (2009). *Software engineering: A practitioner's approach* (7th ed.). New York, NY: McGraw-Hill.

Pyla, P. S., Tungare, M., Holman, J., & Pérez-Quiñones, M. A. (2009). Continuous UIs for seamless task migration in MPUIs: Bridging task-disconnects. *Ambient, Ubiquitous and Intelligent Interaction: Lecture Notes in Computer Science, 5612*(Pt III), 77–85.

Pyla, P. S., Tungare, M., & Pérez-Quiñones, M. A. (2006). Multiple user interfaces: why consistency is not everything, and seamless task migration is key. In: *Proceedings of the CHI 06 workshop on the many faces of consistency in cross-platform design, Montréal, Québec, Canada.*

Quesenbery, W. (2005). Usability standards: connecting practice around the world. In: *Proceedings of the IEEE International Professional Communication Conference (IPCC), 10–13 July 2005.*

Radoll, P. (2009). Reconstructing Australian aboriginal governance by systems design. *interactions, 16*(3), 46–49.

Reeves, B., & Nass, C. I. (1996). *The media equation: How people treat computers, television, and new media like real people and places.* Stanford, CA: CSLI Publications.

Reisner, P. (1977). Use of psychological experimentation as an aid to development of a query language. *IEEE Transactions on Software Engineering, SE-3*(3), 218–229.

Resmini, A., & Rosati, L. (2011). *Pervasive information architecture: Designing cross-channel user experiences.* Burlington, MA: Morgan Kaufmann.

Rhee, Y., & Lee, J. (2009). A model of mobile community: designing user interfaces to support group interaction. *interactions, 16*(6), 46–51.

Rice, J. F. (1991a). Display color coding: 10 rules of thumb. *IEEE Software, 8*(1), 86.

Rice, J. F. (1991b). Ten rules for color coding. *Information Display, 7*(3), 12–14.

Ries, E. (2011). *The lean startup: How today's entrepreneurs use continuous innovation to create radically successful businesses.* New York, NY: Crown Publishing Group of Random House.

Rising, L., & Janoff, N. S. (2000). The scrum software development process for small teams. *IEEE Software, 17*(4), 26–32.

Rogers, Y., & Bellotti, V. (1997). Grounding blue-sky research: how can ethnography help? *interactions, 4*(3), 58–63. https://doi.org/10.1145/255392.255404.

Rosenblum, L. D. (2013). A confederacy of senses. *Scientific American, 308*(1), 72–75.

Rosson, M. B., & Carroll, J. M. (2002). *Usability engineering: Scenario-based development of human-computer interaction.* San Francisco: Morgan Kaufman.

Roto, V., Law, E. L. -C., Vermeeren, A. P. O. S., & Hoonhout, J. (2011). *User experience white paper: Bringing clarity to the concept of user experience.* Retrieved from http://www.allaboutux.org/files/UX-WhitePaper.pdf.

Royce, W. W. (1970). Managing the development of large scale software systems. In: *Proceedings of the IEEE Western Electronic Show and Convention (WESCON) technical papers. Reprinted in proceedings of the ninth international conference on software engineering, Pittsburgh, 1989, August 25–28,* (pp. 328–338). Los Angeles, CA: ACM Press.

Russell, D. M., Streitz, N. A., & Winograd, T. (2005). Building disappearing computers. *Communications of the ACM, 48*(3), 42–48.

Savio, N. (2010). Solving the world's problems through design. *interactions, 17*(3), 52–54.

Schleicher, D., Jones, P., & Kachur, O. (2010). Bodystorming as embodied designing. *interactions, 17*(6), 47–51. https://doi.org/10.1145/1865245.1865256.

Schleifer, A. (2008). *Yahoo! design pattern library.* June 4, UX Magazine.

Scholtz, J. (2005). Have robots, need interaction with humans! *interactions, 12*(2), 12–14.

Schrepp, M., Held, T., & Laugwitz, B. (2006). The influence of hedonic quality on the attractiveness of user interfaces of business management software. *Interacting with Computers, 18*(5), 1055–1069.

Scriven, M. (1967). The methodology of evaluation. In: R. Tyler, R. Gagne, & M. Scriven (Eds.), *Perspectives of curriculum evaluation* (pp. 39–83). Chicago: Rand McNally.

Sears, A. (1997). Heuristic walkthroughs: finding the problems without the noise. *International Journal of Human Computer Interaction, 9*(3), 213–234.

Sellen, A., Eardley, R., Izadi, S., & Harper, R. (2006). The whereabouts clock: early testing of a situated awareness device. In: *Proceedings of the CHI conference on human factors in computing systems (extended abstracts)*.

Shattuck, L. W., & Woods, D. D. (1994). The critical incident technique: 40 years later. In: *Proceedings of the Human Factors and Ergonomics Society annual meeting*.

Shih, Y. -H., & Liu, M. (2007). The importance of emotional usability. *Journal of Educational Technology Usability, 36*(2), 203–218.

Shneiderman, B. (1983). Direct manipulation: a step beyond programming languages. *IEEE Computer, 16*(8), 57–69.

Shneiderman, B. (1998). *Designing the user interface: Strategies for effective human-computer interaction* (3rd ed.). Menlo Park, CA: Addison Wesley.

Shneiderman, B., & Plaisant, C. (2005). *Designing the user interface: Strategies for effective human-computer interaction* (4th ed.). Reading, MA: Addison-Wesley.

Sidner, C., & Lee, C. (2005). Robots as laboratory hosts. *interactions, 12*(2), 24–26.

Siegel, D. A. (2012). The role of enticing design in usability. *interactions, 19*(4), 82–85. https://doi.org/10.1145/2212877.2212895.

Simon, H. A. (1974). How big is a chunk? *Science, 183*(4124), 482–488.

Simonsen, J., & Kensing, F. (1997). Using ethnography in contextural design. *Communications of the ACM, 40*(7), 82–88. https://doi.org/10.1145/256175.256190.

Slivka, E. (2009). *Apple job offer 'unboxing' pictures posted* (p. 2). MacRumors. 10/05/2009. Retrieved from http://www.macrumors.com/2009/10/05/apple-job-offer-unboxing-pictures-posted/.

Smith, D. C., Irby, C., Kimball, R., Verplank, B., & Harslem, E. (1989). Designing the star user interface (1982). In: *Perspectives on the computer revolution* (pp. 261–283). Norwood, NJ: Ablex Publishing.

Smith, S. L., & Mosier, J. N. (1986). *Guidelines for designing user interface software (MTR-10090)*. Bedford, MA: Mitre Corporation.

Soon, W. (2013). *Design tips from Don Norman!* Retrieved from http://vorkspace.com/blog/index.php/hacking-don-norman/.

Souza, F. d., & Bevan, N. (1990). The use of guidelines in menu interface design: evaluation of a draft standard. In: *Proceedings of the INTERACT conference on human-computer interaction*.

Spool, J., & Schroeder, W. (2001). Testing web sites: five users is nowhere near enough. In: *Proceedings of the CHI conference on human factors in computing systems (extended abstracts), Seattle, Washington*.

Stake, R. (2004). *Standards-based and responsive evaluation*. Thousand Oaks, CA: Sage Publications.

Steve, J. (2000). *Apple's one-dollar-a-year man.* January 24th, 2000, Fortune.

Stock, W. G., & Stock, M. (2015). *Handbook of information science*. Berlin, Germany: K G Saur Verlag Gmbh & Co.

Strijland, P. (1993). Human interface standards: can we do better? *Standard View, 1*(1), 26–30. https://doi.org/10.1145/174683.174777.

Suchman, L. A. (1987). *Plans and situated actions: The problem of human-machine communication.* New York, NY: Cambridge University Press.

Sutherland, I. E. (1963). *Sketchpad: A man-machine graphical communication system* (PhD Dissertation). Cambridge, MA: MIT.

Sutherland, I. E. (1964). *Sketchpad: A man-machine graphical communication system.* Cambridge, UK: University of Cambridge.

Sweller, J. (1988). Cognitive load during problem solving: effects on learning. *Cognitive Science, 12,* 257–285.

Sweller, J. (1994). Cognitive load theory, learning difficulty, and instructional design. *Learning and Instruction, 4*(4), 295–312.

Taylor, F. W. (1911). *The principles of scientific management.* New York, NY, USA and London, UK: Harper & Brothers.

Theofanos, M., & Quesenbery, W. (2005). Towards the design of effective formative test reports. *Journal of Usability Studies, 1*(1), 27–45.

Theofanos, M., Quesenbery, W., Snyder, C., Dayton, D., & Lewis, J. (2005). Reporting on formative testing—a UPA 2005 workshop report. In: *Proceedings of the UPA international conference, Montreal, Quebec, June 27–July 1.*

Thomas, J. C., & Kellogg, W. A. (1989). Minimizing ecological gaps in interface design. *IEEE Software, 6*(1), 78–86.

Thomas, P., & Macredie, R. D. (2002). Introduction to the new usability. *ACM Transactions on Computer-Human Interaction, 9*(2), 69–73. https://doi.org/10.1145/513665.513666.

Thompson, C. (2010). The emotional gadget. *Wired Magazine, 18*(11), 66.

Thompson, C., & Vandenbroucke, B. (2015). Good vibrations: tech that talks through your skin. *Wired Magazine, 23*(1), 26.

Tidwell, J. (2011). *Designing interfaces: Patterns for effective interaction design* (2nd ed.). Sebastopol, CA: O'Reilly Media, Inc.

Tohidi, M., Buxton, B., Baecker, R. M., & Sellen, A. (2006). User sketches: a quick, inexpensive, and effective way to elicit more reflective user feedback. In: *Proceedings of the Nordic conference on human-computer interaction, Oslo, Norway.*

Truss, L. (2003). *Eats, shoots & leaves: The zero tolerance approach to punctuation.* United Kingdom: Profile Books.

Tufte, E. R. (1983). *The visual display of quantitative data.* Cheshire, Connecticut: Graphics Press.

Tufte, E. R. (1990). *Envisioning information.* Cheshire, Connecticut: Graphics Press.

Tufte, E. R. (1997). *Visual explanations: Images and quantities, evidence and narrative.* Cheshire, Connecticut: Graphics Press.

Tullis, T. S. (1990). High-fidelity prototyping throughout the design process. In: *Proceedings of the human factors and ergonomics society annual meeting, Santa Monica, CA.*

Tullis, T. S., & Albert, B. (2008). *Measuring the user experience.* Burlington, MA: Morgan Kaufmann.

Tullis, T. S., & Stetson, J. N. (2004). A comparison of questionnaires for assessing website usability. In: *Proceedings of the UPA international conference.*

Tungare, M., Pyla, P. S., Glina, V., Bafna, P., Balli, U., Zheng, W., et al. (2006). Embodied data objects: tangible interfaces to information appliances. In: *Proceedings of the 44th ACM southeast conference (ACMSE).*

U.S. Department of Health and Human Services (2006). *Research-based web design & usability guidelines.* .

Usability Net (2006). *Questionnaire resources.* Retrieved from http://www.usabilitynet.org/tools/r_questionnaire.htm.

Veer, G. C. v. d., & Melguizo, M. d. C. P. (2003). Mental models. In: *The human-computer interaction handbook* (pp. 52–80). Mahwah, NJ: Lawrence Erlbaum Associates Inc.

Vermeeren, A. P. O. S., van Kesteren, I. E. H., & Bekker, M. M. (2003). Managing the evaluator effect in user testing. In: *Proceedings of the INTERACT conference on human-computer interaction, Zurich, Switzerland.*

Vertelney, L. (1989). Using video to prototype user interfaces. *SIGCHI Bulletin, 21*(2), 57–61.

Virzi, R. A. (1990). Streamlining the design process: running fewer subjects. In: *Proceedings of the human factors and ergonomics society annual meeting.*

Virzi, R. A. (1992). Refining the test phase of usability evaluation: how many subjects is enough? *The Journal of the Human Factors and Ergonomics Society, 34*(4), 457–468.

Wasserman, A. I. (1973). The design of 'idiot-proof' interactive programs. In: *Proceedings of the national computer conference.*

Wasserman, A. I., & Shewmake, D. T. (1982a). Rapid prototyping of interactive information systems. *ACM SIGSOFT Software Engineering Notes: Special Issue on Rapid Prototyping, 7*(5), 171–180.

Wasserman, A. I., & Shewmake, D. T. (1982b). Rapid prototyping of interactive information systems. In: *Proceedings of the workshop on rapid prototyping, Columbia, Maryland.*

Webster, M. (2014). Integrating color usability components into design tools. *Communications of the ACM, 21*(3), 56–61.

Weiser, M. (1991). The computer for the 21st century. September, *Scientific American, 265,* 94–100.

Welie, M. v., & Hallvard, T. (2000). Interaction patterns in user interfaces. In: *Proceedings of the 7th pattern languages of programs conference, Monticello, Illinois.*

Westerman, S., Gardner, P. H., & Sutherland, E. J. (2006). *HUMAINE D9g, taxonomy of affective systems usability testing (Workpackage 9 deliverable).* Retrieved from https://pdfs.semanticscholar.org/5270/0d8282b807fb1dfd4fa0f7af454ee4a89447.pdf.

Whiteside, J. A., Bennett, J., & Holtzblatt, K. (1988). Usability engineering: our experience and evolution. In: M. Helander (Ed.), *Handbook of human-computer interaction* (pp. 791–817). Amsterdam, The Netherlands: Elsevier Science.

Whiteside, J. A., & Wixon, D. (1985). Developmental theory as a framework for studying human-computer interaction. In: R. Hartson (Ed.), Vol. 1. *Advances in human-computer interaction* (pp. 29–48). Norwood, NJ: Ablex Publishing.

Whiteside, J. A., & Wixon, D. (1987). Improving human-computer interaction—a quest for cognitive science. In: *Interfacing thought: Cognitive aspects of human-computer interaction* (pp. 353–365). Cambridge, MA: MIT Press.

Wickens, C. D., & Hollands, J. G. (2000). *Engineering psychology and human performance* (3rd ed.). Upper Saddle River, NJ: Prentice-Hall Inc.

Wildman, D. (1995). Getting the most from paired-user testing. *interactions, 2*(3), 21–27. https://doi.org/10.1145/208666.208675.

Williges, R. C. (1982). Applying the human information processing approach to human/computer interactions. In: W. C. Howell & E. A. Fleishman (Eds.), Vol. 2. *Information processing and decision making* (pp. 83–119). Hillsdale, NJ: Lawrence Erlbaum.

Williges, R. C. (1984). Evaluating human-computer software interfaces. In: *Proceedings of the international conference on occupational ergonomics, Toronto, May.*

Wilson, C. (2011). *Perspective-based inspection (Method 10 in 100 user experience design and evaluation methods for your toolkit).* March. Retrieved from http://dux.typepad.com/dux/2011/03/.

Winchester, W. W., III (2009). Catalyzing a perfect storm: mobile phone-based HIV-prevention behavioral interventions. *interactions, 16*(6), 5–12.

Wixon, D. (1995). Qualitative research methods in design and development. *interactions, 2*(4), 19–26. https://doi.org/10.1145/225362.225365.

Wixon, D. (2003). Evaluating usability methods: why the current literature fails the practitioner. *interactions, 10*(4), 28–34. https://doi.org/10.1145/838830.838870.

Wixon, D., Holtzblatt, K., & Knox, S. (1990). Contextual design: an emergent view of system design. In: *Proceedings of the CHI conference on human factors in computing systems, Seattle, Washington.*

Wixon, D., & Ramey, J. (Eds.), (1996). *Field methods casebook for software design.* New York, NY: John Wiley.

Wood, L. E. (Ed.), (1998). *User interface design: Bridging the gap from user requirements to design.* Boca Raton, FL: CRC Press.

Wright, P., Lickorish, A., & Milroy, R. (1994). Remembering while mousing: the cognitive costs of mouse clicks. *SIGCHI Bulletin, 26*(1), 41–45. https://doi.org/10.1145/181526.181534.

Wright, P. K. (2005). Rapid prototyping in consumer product design. *Communications of the ACM, 48*(6), 36–41.

Ye, S. X., & Qiu, R. G. (2003). Global identification code scheme for promptly retrieving the pertinent information of a worldwide uniquely identifiable object. In: *Proceedings of the international conference on control and automation (ICCA).*

Young, R. M., Green, T. R. G., & Simon, T. (1989). Programmable user models for predictive evaluation of interface designs. In: *Proceedings of the CHI conference on human factors in computing systems.*

Young, R. R. (2001). *Effective requirements practices.* Boston, MA: Addison-Wesley Professional.

Zhang, P. (2009). Theorizing the relationship between affect and aesthetics in the ICT design and use context. In: *Proceedings of the international conference on information resources management, Dubai, United Arab Emirates.*

Zhang, P., & Li, N. (2005). The importance of affective quality. *Communications of the ACM, 48*(9), 105–110.

Zhang, Z., Basili, V., & Shneiderman, B. (1999). Perspective-based usability inspection: an empirical validation of efficacy. *Empirical Software Engineering, 4*(1), 43–69. https://doi.org/10.1023/a:1009803214692.

Zieniewicz, M. J., Johnson, D. C., Wong, D. C., & Flatt, J. D. (2002). The evolution of army wearable computers. *IEEE Pervasive Computing, 1*(4), 30–40.

Index

Note: Page numbers followed by *f* indicate figures, *t* indicate tables, *b* indicate boxes and *np* indicate footnotes.